MW01235409

A NEXTEXT ANTHOLOGY

Major World
DRAMAS

nextext

Printed in the United States of America.

ISBN 0-618-10724-X

1 2 3 4 5 6 7 — QKT — 06 05 04 03 02 01

Major World Dramas

Throughout the anthology, vocabulary words appear in boldface type and are footnoted. Specialized or technical words and phrases appear in lightface type and are footnoted.

Reading a Play

Drama is a type of literature that is primarily written to be performed for an audience. When reading a play, it is important to keep certain features of drama in mind. Some of these features relate to drama as literature; others reflect its character as a performance.

Types of Drama

The two main types of drama are tragedy and comedy. A <u>tragedy</u> is a play in which the main character experiences disaster, but faces this downfall in such a way as to attain heroic stature. Although it has what is conventionally called a "sad ending," tragedy's purpose is not to express gloom, but rather to inspire exaltation at the greatness human beings can attain even in defeat.

Comedy differs from tragedy both in the events it presents and the mood it is intended to inspire. In its purest form, <u>comedy</u> closes with a peaceful resolution of the main conflict. A romantic comedy, for example, typically ends with a marriage or the expectation of one. The mood of a comedy is generally much lighter and often there is a significant element of humor. It is also important to recognize that many dramas include both tragic and comic elements.

Comedy itself is further divided into high and low forms. In <u>high comedy</u>, the humor arises from subtle characterization, social satire, and sophisticated wit. <u>Low comedy</u> emphasizes absurd dialogue, bawdy jokes, visual gags, and physical humor. Many plays include elements of both high and low comedy. In Shakespeare's comedies, for example, the main characters provide the high comedy, and the clowns provide the low comedy.

Typical forms of high comedy are romantic comedy and satiric comedy. In <u>romantic comedy</u> the main characters are lovers, and the plot tends to follow the pattern of "boy gets girl, boy loses girl, boy gets girl again." <u>Satiric comedy</u> uses humor to ridicule foolish ideas or customs with the purpose of improving society. One common form of satiric comedy is the <u>comedy of manners</u>, which satirizes the vices and follies of the upper classes. A typical form of low comedy is <u>farce</u>, which relies on exaggeration, absurdity, and slapstick.

In between tragedy and comedy is a third type of play, sometimes referred to as "<u>straight drama</u>" (or simply "drama"). Such plays deal with serious subjects, but do not end in disaster. This type of play developed as a result of the realistic movement in literature at the end of the 1800s. Many modern plays fall into this category.

Elements of Drama

As in fiction, the plot in a drama grows out of conflicts between opposing forces. There are two main types of conflict. An external conflict pits a character against nature or fate, society, or another character; an internal conflict is between opposing forces within a character. The elements of plot in drama—exposition, rising action, climax, falling action, and resolution—parallel those in fiction. The conflict intensifies, reaches a peak, and is eventually resolved.

Many of the same types of characters that populate fiction are also found in drama. The protagonist is the central character of the play and often undergoes radical changes as the action progresses. The antagonist is the character who opposes the main character. Some plays also include a foil, a minor character whose traits contrast sharply with those of the protagonist.

In drama the playwright develops the story line through the characters' actions and dialogue. Dialogue, or conversations between characters, is the essence of drama. Nearly everything of consequence in a play—from details of plot to revelations of character—is presented through dialogue. Other speech devices used by dramatists include the monologue, a long speech spoken by a single character to himself or herself, or to the audience; the soliloquy, a monologue in which a character speaks his or her private thoughts aloud and appears to be unaware of the audience; and the aside, a short speech or comment delivered by a character to the audience, but unheard by the other characters who are present.

Conventions of Drama

A play lists the cast of characters in the beginning, before the action starts. Dramatic plots have been subdivided in various ways. The most familiar structure is the modern arrangement of acts and scenes. An act is a major division of a play. Renaissance dramas were generally divided into five acts; modern plays typically contain three. An act may be subdivided into scenes, with each scene establishing a different time or place. In Greek drama there was no division into acts, but choral dances helped indicate divisions between scenes.

A dramatist's instructions for performing a play are called stage directions. Usually set in italics, stage directions are located at the beginning of a play and throughout the text. Stage directions provide information about characters and setting of the play and suggest the use of costumes, scenery, props, lighting, and sound effects. Stage directions indicate the entrances and exits of characters (thus indicating who is on stage during a particular scene). Stage directions also indicate how characters act, move, speak, and react to other characters' words and actions. Full stage directions are a relatively modern convention of drama. Earlier playwrights, such as Shakespeare, used few stage directions. In translations of ancient Greek dramas, the stage directions are provided by the translator.

Part One

Greek Drama

From Myth to Stage

*In the first great period of Western theater, Athenian playwrights of
the 5th century B.C. created powerful dramas presenting the stories
of the gods and heroes of Greek mythology.*

Oedipus the King SOPHOCLES

Medea EURIPIDES

◀ In this modern production of *Oedipus*, actors wear the masks that
were used in ancient Greek theater.

Sophocles ▶

Oedipus the King

BY SOPHOCLES

Greek drama had its origins in religious rituals associated with annual festivals honoring the god Dionysus. These rituals, which included choral singing and dancing, eventually developed into rudimentary dramas dealing with episodes from the lives of various gods and heroes. Between 500 and 400 B.C., Greek drama reached its high point with the works of a series of Athenian playwrights, Aeschylus, Sophocles, and Euripides. These dramatists used narratives drawn from myths and heroic legends, which they shaped to reflect contemporary issues. For the Greeks, attending the theater was an important civic responsibility that helped them confront current political or religious problems.

Greek Stagecraft

Greek theater was performed in large, circular, open-air auditoriums that could seat thousands of spectators. Greek theaters did not have a raised stage but instead used a central performance area known as the orchestra. Because of the great size of these theater spaces, the performers—all males—had to depend for theatrical effect on big, simple, physical gestures and the power of poetry. There was no scenery, but the actors wore elaborate costumes and stylized masks. These masks identified their characters and probably helped amplify the performers' voices. The great Greek tragic dramatists were innovators. The earliest Greek dramas had involved only a single actor and a chorus. Aeschylus (525–456 B.C.) added a second actor, allowing for more realistic action and dialogue. Sophocles (496–406 B.C.) added a third, permitting still more dramatically complex scenes.

The Function of the Chorus

The performers playing the main characters in a Greek play interacted with the chorus, an essential feature of Greek theater. In general, the performers in the chorus represent the people of the community in which the events of the drama occur. As the play unfolds, they react to and comment on the action. The chorus serves as a reminder of the social and political functions of Greek drama. In his plays, Sophocles also uses the chorus as an emotional link between episodes, reinforcing the content of the preceding scene and preparing the audience for what is to follow.

The Ideal Dramatist

The plays of Sophocles were very popular with his contemporaries, winning many victories in the dramatic competitions that were a central part of Greek theater. His works were regarded as models of dramatic composition and poetic beauty. In his Poetics, the Greek philosopher Aristotle bases his analysis of tragic drama on Sophocles' Oedipus the King. Oedipus is the archetype of the tragic hero, "a man who is not eminently good and just, yet whose misfortune is brought about not by vice and depravity, but by some error or frailty." Aristotle also stresses what became known as the "dramatic unities" of time, place, and action: a play was to present only one principal action occupying only one day and showing only what could be observed by a spectator sitting in one place. Another convention of Greek drama was that violence never happens onstage, but is instead reported to the audience.

The Story of Oedipus

Oedipus was the son of Laius, king of Thebes, and his wife, Jocasta. Before Oedipus was born, it was prophesied that he was destined to kill his father and marry his mother. To prevent this, Jocasta ordered a servant to abandon the infant on Mount Cithaeron to die. Instead, the servant gave Oedipus to a shepherd from the neighboring kingdom of Corinth, and its king and queen, who were childless, adopted the infant. When he grew up, Oedipus learned of the sinister prophecy about his destiny and attempted to avoid it by fleeing Corinth. At a crossroads, Oedipus refused to give way to a wealthy traveler and his servants. A quarrel followed, and Oedipus killed the man and all but one of those with him. Continuing on his way, he arrived at Thebes, which was haunted by a monster, the Sphinx, who killed everyone who could not answer her riddle: "What walks on four legs in the morning, two at noon, and three in the evening." Oedipus correctly answered "Man"—who crawls on all fours as an infant, walks on two legs unassisted in middle life, and needs a cane in old age. When her riddle was answered, the Sphinx destroyed herself. The overjoyed people of Thebes—whose king had recently been killed—offered the king's crown and widowed queen to Oedipus, who accepted both. Oedipus ruled Thebes well, and he and Jocasta had several children. But shortly before the action of the play begins, the city was devastated by a plague. Oedipus sent his brother-in-law, Creon, to the shrine of Apollo at Delphi, to ask the god what must be done to save Thebes.

CHARACTERS

Oedipus, king of Thebes
Priest of Zeus, king of the gods
Creon, brother of Jocasta
Chorus of Theban citizens and their leader
Tiresias, a blind prophet
Jocasta, the queen, wife of Oedipus
Messenger from Corinth

Shepherd
Messenger from inside the palace
Antigone, Ismene, daughters of Oedipus and Jocasta
Guards
Attendants
Priests of Thebes

TIME AND SCENE: The royal house of Thebes. Double doors dominate the façade: a stone altar stands at the center of the stage.

Many years have passed since Oedipus solved the riddle of the Sphinx and ascended the throne of Thebes, and now a plague has struck the city. A procession of priests enters; suppliants,[1] broken and **despondent**,[2] *they carry branches wound in wool[3] and lay them on the altar.*

The doors open. Guards assemble. Oedipus comes forward, majestic but for a telltale limp,[4] and slowly views the condition of his people.

> **Oedipus.** Oh my children, the new blood of ancient Thebes,
> why are you here? Huddling at my altar,
> praying before me, your branches wound in wool.
> Our city reeks with the smoke of burning incense,
> 5   rings with cries for the Healer[5] and wailing for the dead.
> I thought it wrong, my children, to hear the truth
> from others, messengers. Here I am myself—
> you all know me, the world knows my fame:
> I am Oedipus. [*Helping a* Priest *to his feet.*]
>   Speak up, old man. Your years,
> 10   your dignity—you should speak for the others.
> Why here and kneeling, what preys upon you so?
> Some sudden fear? some strong desire?
> You can trust me; I am ready to help,
> I'll do anything. I would be blind to misery
> 15   not to pity my people kneeling at my feet.
>
> **Priest.** Oh Oedipus, king of the land, our greatest power!
> You see us before you, men of all ages
> clinging to your altars. Here are boys,
> still too weak to fly from the nest,
> 20   and here the old, bowed down with the years,
> the holy ones—a priest of Zeus myself—and here
> the picked, unmarried men, the young hope of Thebes.
> And all the rest, your great family gathers now,
> branches wreathed, massing in the squares,

---

[1] *suppliants*—humble petitioners.

[2] **despondent**—depressed from loss of hope.

[3] *branches wound in wool*—symbolic objects carried by those seeking divine help.

[4] *telltale limp*—When Oedipus was born, his ankles were pinned together before he was given to the servant to be abandoned in the wilderness. It was from this injury that he derived his name, Oedipus, which means "swollen foot."

[5] Healer—the god Apollo.

25	kneeling before the two temples of queen Athena[6]
	or the river-shrine where the embers glow and die
	and Apollo sees the future in the ashes.[7] Our city—
	look around you, see with your own eyes—
	our ship pitches wildly, cannot lift her head
30	from the depths, the red waves of death . . .
	Thebes is dying. A **blight**[8] on the fresh crops
	and the rich pastures, cattle sicken and die,
	and the women die in labor, children stillborn,
	and the plague, the fiery god of fever hurls down
35	on the city, his lightning slashing through us—
	raging plague in all its vengeance, devastating
	the house of Cadmus![9] And Black Death luxuriates
	in the raw, wailing miseries of Thebes.
	Now we pray to you. You cannot equal the gods,
40	your children know that, bending at your altar.
	But we do rate you first of men,
	both in the common crises of our lives
	and face-to-face encounters with the gods.
	You freed us from the Sphinx; you came to Thebes
45	and cut us loose from the bloody tribute we had paid
	that harsh, brutal singer. We taught you nothing,
	no skill, no extra knowledge, still you triumphed.
	A god was with you, so they say, and we believe it—
	you lifted up our lives. So now again,
50	Oedipus, king, we bend to you, your power—
	we **implore**[10] you, all of us on our knees:
	find us strength, rescue! Perhaps you've heard
	the voice of a god or something from other men,
	Oedipus . . . what do you know?[11]
55	The man of experience—you see it every day—
	his plans will work in a crisis, his first of all.

---

[6] Athena—daughter of Zeus and goddess of wisdom.

[7] river-shrine . . . ashes—site near Thebes where priests of Apollo foretold the future from the appearance of the ashes produced by the burning of sacrificial offerings.

[8] **blight**—disease.

[9] Cadmus—legendary founder of Thebes.

[10] **implore**—beg.

[11] what do you know?—In the original Greek, this question (oistha pou) is an ironic pun on the name Oedipus. The irony is that this all-knowing hero is even ignorant of his own identity.

Act now—we beg you, best of men, raise up our city!
Act, defend yourself, your former glory!
Your country calls you savior now
60   for your zeal, your action years ago.
Never let us remember of your reign:
you helped us stand, only to fall once more.
Oh raise up our city, set us on our feet.
The omens were good that day you brought us joy—
65   be the same man today!
Rule our land, you know you have the power,
but rule a land of the living, not a wasteland.
Ship and towered city are nothing, stripped of men
alive within it, living all as one.

Oedipus.   My children,
70   I pity you. I see—how could I fail to see
what longings bring you here? Well I know
you are sick to death, all of you,
but sick as you are, not one is sick as I.
Your pain strikes each of you alone, each
75   in the confines of himself, no other. But my spirit
grieves for the city, for myself and all of you.
I wasn't asleep, dreaming. You haven't wakened me—
I've wept through the nights, you must know that,
groping, laboring over many paths of thought.
80   After a painful search I found one cure:
I acted at once, I sent Creon,
my wife's own brother, to Delphi—
Apollo the Prophet's oracle[12]—to learn
what I might do or say to save our city.
85   Today's the day. When I count the days gone by
it torments me . . . what is he doing?
Strange, he's late, he's gone too long.
But once he returns, then, then I'll be a traitor
if I do not do all the god makes clear.
90   **Priest.** Timely words. The men over there
are signaling—Creon's just arriving.

---

[12] oracle—shrine where priests delivered a god's answer to questions posed by worshippers.

Oedipus [*sighting* Creon, *then turning, to the altar*]. Lord Apollo,
let him come with a lucky word of rescue,
shining like his eyes!

Priest. Welcome news, I think—he's crowned, look,
95   and the laurel wreath[13] is bright with berries.

Oedipus. We'll soon see. He's close enough to hear—

[*Enter* Creon *from the side; his face is shaded with a wreath.*]

Creon, prince, my kinsman, what do you bring us?
What message from the god?

Creon.   Good news.
I tell you even the hardest things to bear,
100   if they should turn out well, all would be well.

Oedipus. Of course, but what were the god's *words*? There's no hope
and nothing to fear in what you've said so far.

Creon. If you want my report in the presence of these people . . .

[*Pointing to the priests while drawing* Oedipus *toward the palace.*]

I'm ready now, or we might go inside.

Oedipus.   Speak out,
105   speak to us all. I grieve for these, my people,
far more than I fear for my own life.

Creon.   Very well,
I will tell you what I heard from the god.
Apollo commands us—he was quite clear—
"Drive the corruption[14] from the land,
110   don't harbor it any longer, past all cure,
don't nurse it in your soil—root it out!"

Oedipus. How can we cleanse ourselves—what rites?
What's the source of the trouble?

Creon. Banish the man, or pay back blood with blood.
115   Murder sets the plague-storm on the city.

Oedipus.   Whose murder?
Whose fate does Apollo bring to light?

Creon.   Our leader,
my lord, was once a man named Laius,
before you came and put us straight on course.

---

[13] laurel wreath—leaves of an evergreen tree sacred to Apollo. The laurel wreath was a symbol of victory.

[14] corruption—The Greeks believed that the blood of a murdered person polluted not only those responsible but the entire community.

Oedipus.   I know—
    or so I've heard. I never saw the man myself.

120 **Creon.** Well, he was killed, and Apollo commands us now—
    he could not be more clear,
    "Pay the killers back—whoever is responsible."

Oedipus. Where on earth are they? Where to find it now,
    the trail of the ancient guilt so hard to trace?

125 **Creon.** "Here in Thebes," he said.
    Whatever is sought for can be caught, you know,
    whatever is neglected slips away.

Oedipus.   But where,
    in the palace, the fields or foreign soil,
    where did Laius meet his bloody death?

130 **Creon.** He went to consult an oracle, Apollo said,
    and he set out and never came home again.

Oedipus. No messenger, no fellow-traveler saw what happened?
    Someone to cross-examine?

Creon.   No,
    they were all killed but one. He escaped,
135   terrified, he could tell us nothing clearly,
    nothing of what he saw—just one thing.

Oedipus.   What's that?
    One thing could hold the key to it all,
    a small beginning give us grounds for hope.

Creon. He said thieves attacked them—a whole band,
140   not single-handed, cut King Laius down.

Oedipus.   A thief,
    so daring, wild, he'd kill a king? Impossible,
    unless conspirators paid him off in Thebes.

Creon. We suspected as much. But with Laius dead
    no leader appeared to help us in our troubles.

145 **Oedipus.** Trouble? Your *king* was murdered—royal blood!
    What stopped you from tracking down the killer
    then and there?

Creon.   The singing, riddling Sphinx.
    She . . . persuaded us to let the mystery go
    and concentrate on what lay at our feet.

Oedipus.   No,
150   I'll start again—I'll bring it all to light myself!

Apollo is right, and so are you, Creon,
to turn our attention back to the murdered man.
Now you have *me* to fight for you, you'll see:
I am the land's avenger by all rights
155   and Apollo's champion too.
But not to assist some distant kinsman, no,
for my own sake I'll rid us of this corruption.
Whoever killed the king may decide to kill me too,
with the same violent hand—by avenging Laius
160   I defend myself. [*To the priests.*] Quickly, my children.
Up from the steps, take up your branches now. [*To the guards.*]
One of you summon the city here before us,
tell them I'll do everything. God help us,
we will see our triumph—or our fall.

[Oedipus *and* Creon *enter the palace, followed by the guards.*]

165 **Priest.** Rise, my sons. The kindness we came for
Oedipus volunteers himself.
Apollo has sent his word, his oracle—
Come down, Apollo, save us, stop the plague.

[*The priests rise, remove their branches and exit to the side. Enter a* Chorus, *the
citizens of Thebes, who have not heard the news that* Creon *brings. They march
around the altar, chanting.*]

Chorus.   Zeus!
Great welcome voice of Zeus, what do you bring?
170   What word from the gold vaults of Delphi
comes to brilliant Thebes? I'm racked with terror—
                      terror shakes my heart
and I cry your wild cries, Apollo, Healer of Delos[15]
I worship you in dread . . . what now, what is your price?
175   Some new sacrifice? some ancient rite from the past
come round again each spring?—
                what will you bring to birth?
Tell me, child of golden Hope
        warm voice that never dies!
180   You are the first I call, daughter of Zeus
deathless Athena—I call your sister Artemis,
heart of the market place enthroned in glory,[16]

---

[15] Delos—island birthplace of Apollo.

[16] Artemis . . . enthroned in glory—Artemis, twin sister of Apollo and goddess of the moon and the hunt, had a shrine in the market.

guardian of our earth—
I call Apollo, Archer astride the thunderheads of heaven—
185   O triple shield against death, shine before me now!
If ever, once in the past, you stopped some ruin
launched against our walls
you hurled the flame of pain
far, far from Thebes—you gods
190   come now, come down once more!

No, no
the miseries numberless, grief on grief, no end—
too much to bear, we are all dying
O my people . . .
Thebes like a great army dying
195   and there is no sword of thought to save us, no
and the fruits of our famous earth, they will not ripen
no and the women cannot scream their pangs to birth—
screams for the Healer, children dead in the womb
and life on life goes down
200   you can watch them go
like seabirds winging west, outracing the day's fire
down the horizon, irresistibly
streaking on to the shores of Evening
Death
so many deaths, numberless deaths on deaths, no end—
205   Thebes is dying, look, her children
stripped of pity . . .
generations strewn on the ground
unburied, unwept, the dead spreading death
and the young wives and gray-haired mothers with them
210   cling to the altars, trailing in from all over the city—
Thebes, city of death, one long **cortege**[17]
and the suffering rises
wails for mercy rise
and the wild hymn for the Healer blazes out
215   clashing with our sobs our cries of mourning—
O golden daughter of god,[18] send rescue

---

[17] **cortege**—funeral procession.
[18] golden daughter of god—Athena.

radiant as the kindness in your eyes!
Drive him back!—the fever, the god of death
        that raging god of war[19]

220   not armored in bronze, not shielded now, he burns me,
battle cries in the **onslaught**[20] burning on—
O rout him from our borders!
Sail him, blast him out to the Sea-queen's chamber[21]
        the black Atlantic gulfs

225   or the northern harbor, death to all
where the Thracian surf[22] comes crashing.
Now what the night spares he comes by day and kills—
the god of death.
        O lord of the stormcloud,
you who twirl the lightning, Zeus, Father,

230   thunder Death to nothing!
Apollo, lord of the light, I beg you—
        whip your longbow's golden cord
showering arrows on our enemies—shafts of power
champions strong before us rushing on!

235   Artemis, Huntress,
torches flaring over the eastern ridges—
        ride Death down in pain!
God of the headdress gleaming gold, I cry to you—
your name and ours are one, Dionysus[23]—

240   come with your face aflame with wine
        your raving women's cries[24]
      your army on the march! Come with the lightning
come with torches blazing, eyes ablaze with glory!
Burn that god of death that all gods hate!

[Oedipus *enters from the palace to address the* Chorus, *as if addressing the entire city of Thebes.*]

245   **Oedipus.** You pray to the gods? Let me grant your prayers.
Come, listen to me—do what the plague demands:

---

[19] god of war—Ares.

[20] **onslaught**—attack.

[21] Sea-queen's chamber—the undersea dwelling of Amphitrite, the wife of the god Poseidon, ruler of the sea.

[22] Thracian surf—Ares was often associated with Thrace, a wild region north of Greece.

[23] your name . . . Dionysus—The wine god Dionysus was the son of Zeus and Semele, a woman of Thebes.

[24] your raving women's cries—The wine-induced frenzies of the female worshippers of Dionysus (also referred to in the following line as "your army on the march") were accompanied by wild shouting. See illustration on page 107.

you'll find relief and lift your head from the depths.
I will speak out now as a stranger to the story,
a stranger to the crime. If I'd been present then,
250   there would have been no mystery, no long hunt
without a clue in hand. So now, counted
a native Theban years after the murder,
to all of Thebes I make this proclamation:
if any one of you knows who murdered Laius,
255   the son of Labdacus, I order him to reveal
the whole truth to me. Nothing to fear,
even if he must denounce himself,
let him speak up
and so escape the brunt of the charge—
260   he will suffer no unbearable punishment,
nothing worse than exile, totally unharmed.

[Oedipus *pauses, waiting for a reply.*]

Next, if anyone knows the murderer is a stranger,
a man from alien soil, come, speak up.
I will give him a handsome reward, and lay up
265   gratitude in my heart for him besides.

[*Silence again, no reply.*]

But if you keep silent, if anyone panicking,
trying to shield himself or friend or kin,
rejects my offer, then hear what I will do.
I order you, every citizen of the state
270   where I hold throne and power: banish this man—
whoever he may be—never shelter him, never
speak a word to him, never make him partner
to your prayers, your victims burned to the gods.
Never let the holy water[25] touch his hands,
275   Drive him out, each of you, from every home.
He is the plague, the heart of our corruption,
as Apollo's oracle has revealed to me
just now. So I honor my obligations:
I fight for the god and for the murdered man.
280   Now my curse on the murderer. Whoever he is,
a lone man unknown in his crime

---

[25] holy water—used in the Greek rite of purification.

or one among many, let that man drag out
his life in agony, step by painful step—
I curse myself as well . . . if by any chance
285   he proves to be an intimate of our house,
here at my hearth, with my full knowledge,
may the curse I just called down on him strike me!
These are your orders: perform them to the last.
I command you, for my sake, for Apollo's, for this country
290   blasted root and branch by the angry heavens.
Even if god had never urged you on to act,
how could you leave the crime uncleansed so long?
A man so noble—your king, brought down in blood—
you should have searched. But I am the king now,
295   I hold the throne that he held then, possess his bed
and a wife who shares our seed . . . why, our seed
might be the same, children born of the same mother
might have created blood-bonds between us
if his hope of offspring hadn't met disaster—
300   but fate swooped at his head and cut him short.
So I will fight for him as if he were my father,
stop at nothing, search the world
to lay my hands on the man who shed his blood,
the son of Labdacus descended of Polydorus,
305   Cadmus of old and Agenor, founder of the line:
their power and mine are one. Oh dear gods,
my curse on those who disobey these orders!
Let no crops grow out of the earth for them—
shrivel their women, kill their sons,
310   burn them to nothing in this plague
that hits us now, or something even worse.
But you, loyal men of Thebes who approve my actions,
may our champion, Justice, may all the gods
be with us, fight beside us to the end!
315 **Leader.** In the grip of your curse, my king, I swear
I'm not the murderer, cannot point him out.
As for the search, Apollo pressed it on us—
he should name the killer.

Oedipus.   Quite right,
            but to force the gods to act against their will—
320   no man has the power.
      Leader.   Then if I might mention
            the next best thing . . .
      Oedipus.   The third best too—
            don't hold back, say it.
      Leader.   I still believe . . .
            Lord Tiresias sees with the eyes of Lord Apollo.
            Anyone searching for the truth, my king,
325   might learn it from the prophet, clear as day.
      Oedipus. I've not been slow with that. On Creon's cue
            I sent the escorts, twice, within the hour.
            I'm surprised he isn't here.
      Leader.   We need him—
            without him we have nothing but old, useless rumors.
330   **Oedipus.** Which rumors? I'll search out every word.
      Leader. Laius was killed, they say, by certain travelers.
      Oedipus. I know—but no one can find the murderer.
      Leader. If the man has a trace of fear in him
            he won't stay silent long,
335   not with your curses ringing in his ears.
      Oedipus. He didn't flinch at murder,
            he'll never flinch at words.
            [*Enter* Tiresias, *the blind prophet, led by a boy with escorts in attendance. He
            remains at a distance.*]
      Leader. Here is the one who will convict him, look,
            they bring him on at last, the **seer**,[26] the man of god.
340   The truth lives inside him, him alone.
      Oedipus.   O Tiresias,
            master of all the mysteries of our life,
            all you teach and all you dare not tell,
            signs in the heavens, signs that walk the earth!
            Blind as you are, you can feel all the more
345   what sickness haunts our city. You, my lord,
            are the one shield, the one savior we can find.
            We asked Apollo—perhaps the messengers

---

[26] **seer**—prophet, person skilled in reading omens.

haven't told you—he sent his answer back:
"Relief from the plague can only come one way.
350   Uncover the murderers of Laius,
put them to death or drive them into exile."
So I beg you, grudge us nothing now, no voice,
no message plucked from the birds, the embers
or the other mantic[27] ways within your grasp.
355   Rescue yourself, your city, rescue me—
rescue everything infected by the dead.
We are in your hands. For a man to help others
with all his gifts and native strength:
that is the noblest work.

Tiresias.   How terrible—to see the truth
360   when the truth is only pain to him who sees!
I knew it well, but I put it from my mind,
else I never would have come.

Oedipus. What's this? Why so grim, so dire?

Tiresias. Just send me home. You bear your burdens,
365   I'll bear mine. It's better that way,
please believe me.

Oedipus.   Strange response—unlawful,
unfriendly too to the state that bred and raised you;
you're withholding the word of god.

Tiresias.   I fail to see
that your own words are so well-timed.
370   I'd rather not have the same thing said of me . . .

Oedipus. For the love of god, don't turn away,
not if you know something. We beg you,
all of us on our knees.

Tiresias.   None of you knows—
and I will never reveal my dreadful secrets,
375   not to say your own.

Oedipus. What? You know and you won't tell?
You're bent on betraying us, destroying Thebes?

Tiresias. I'd rather not cause pain for you or me.
So why this . . . useless interrogation?
380   You'll get nothing from me.

---

[27] mantic—prophetic.

Oedipus.   Nothing! You,
    you scum of the earth, you'd enrage a heart of stone!
    You won't talk? Nothing moves you?
    Out with it, once and for all!

Tiresias. You criticize my temper . . . unaware
385   of the one *you* live with, you **revile**[28] me.

Oedipus. Who could restrain his anger hearing you?
    What outrage—you spurn the city!

Tiresias. What will come will come.
    Even if I shroud it all in silence.

390 **Oedipus.** What will come? You're bound to *tell* me that.

Tiresias. I'll say no more. Do as you like, build your anger
    to whatever pitch you please, rage your worst—

Oedipus. Oh I'll let loose, I have such fury in me—
    now I see it all. You helped hatch the plot,
395   you did the work, yes, short of killing him
    with your own hands—and given eyes I'd say
    you did the killing single-handed!

Tiresias.   Is that so!
    I charge you, then, submit to that decree
    You just laid down: from this day onward
400   speak to no one, not these citizens, not myself.
    You are the curse, the corruption of the land!

Oedipus. You, shameless—
    aren't you **appalled**[29] to start up such a story?
    You think you can get away with this?

Tiresias.   I have already.
405   The truth with all its power lives inside me.

Oedipus. Who primed you for this? Not your prophet's trade.

Tiresias. You did, you forced me, twisted it out of me.

Oedipus. What? Say it again—I'll understand it better.

Tiresias. Didn't you understand, just now?
410   Or are you tempting me to talk?

Oedipus. No, I can't say I grasped your meaning.
    Out with it, again!

Tiresias. I say you are the murderer you hunt.

Oedipus. That obscenity, twice—by god, you'll pay.

---

[28] **revile**—abuse.
[29] **appalled**—horrified.

415   **Tiresias.** Shall I say more, so you can really rage?

Oedipus. Much as you want. Your words are nothing—
    futile.[30]

Tiresias. You cannot imagine . . . I tell you,
    you and your loved ones live together in **infamy**,[31]
    you cannot see how far you've gone in guilt.

420   **Oedipus.** You think you can keep this up and never suffer?

Tiresias. Indeed, if the truth has any power.

Oedipus.   It does
    but not for you, old man. You've lost your power,
    stone-blind, stone-deaf—senses, eyes blind as stone!

Tiresias. I pity you, flinging at me the very insults

425   each man here will fling at you so soon.

Oedipus.   Blind,
    lost in the night, endless night that nursed you!
    You can't hurt me or anyone else who sees the light—
    you can never touch me.

Tiresias.   True, it is not your fate
    to fall at my hands. Apollo is quite enough,

430   and he will take some pains to work this out.

Oedipus. Creon! Is this conspiracy his or yours?

Tiresias. Creon is not your downfall, no, you are your own.

Oedipus.   O power—
    wealth and empire, skill outstripping skill
    in the heady rivalries of life,

435   what envy lurks inside you! Just for this,
    the crown the city gave me—I never sought it,
    they laid it in my hands—for this alone, Creon,
    the soul of trust, my loyal friend from the start
    steals against me . . . so hungry to overthrow me

440   he sets this wizard on me, this scheming quack,[32]
    this fortune-teller peddling lies, eyes peeled
    for his own profit—seer blind in his craft!
    Come here, you pious fraud. Tell me,
    when did you ever prove yourself a prophet?

---

[30] **futile**—useless.

[31] **infamy**—evil.

[32] quack—fake doctor.

445	When the Sphinx, that chanting Fury[33] kept her deathwatch
	here,
	why silent then, not a word to set our people free?
	There was a riddle, not for some passer-by to solve—
	it cried out for a prophet. Where were you?
	Did you rise to the crisis? Not a word,
450	you and your birds,[34] your gods—nothing.
	No, but I came by, Oedipus the ignorant,
	I stopped the Sphinx! With no help from the birds,
	the flight of my own intelligence hit the mark.
	And this is the man you'd try to overthrow?
455	You think you'll stand by Creon when he's king?
	You and the great mastermind—
	you'll pay in tears, I promise you, for this,
	this witch-hunt. If you didn't look so **senile**[35]
	the lash would teach you what your scheming means!

Leader. I'd suggest his words were spoken in anger,
460   Oedipus . . . yours too, and it isn't what we need.
The best solution to the oracle, the riddle
posed by god—we should look for that.

Tiresias. You are the king no doubt, but in one respect,
465   at least, I am your equal: the right to reply.
I claim that privilege too.
I am not your slave. I serve Apollo.
I don't need Creon to speak for me in public.
So, you mock my blindness? Let me tell you this.
470   You with your precious eyes,
you're blind to the corruption of your life,
to the house you live in, those you live with—
who *are* your parents? Do you know? All unknowing
you are the scourge of your own flesh and blood,
475   the dead below the earth and the living here above,
and the double lash of your mother and your father's curse
will whip you from this land one day, their footfall[36]
treading you down in terror, darkness shrouding

---

[33] Fury—Oedipus compares the Sphinx to one of the goddesses who punished crimes against blood relatives with madness.

[34] birds—The Greeks believed that the flight patterns of birds foretold the future.

[35] **senile**—weak from age.

[36] footfall—step.

your eyes that now can see the light! Soon, soon
480   you'll scream aloud—what haven won't **reverberate?**[37]
What rock of Cithaeron won't scream back in echo?
That day you learn the truth about your marriage,
the wedding-march that sang you into your halls,
the lusty voyage home to the fatal harbor!
485   And a crowd of other horrors you'd never dream
will level you with yourself and all your children.
There. Now smear us with insults—Creon, myself
and every word I've said. No man will ever
be rooted from the earth as brutally as you.

490   **Oedipus.** Enough! Such filth from him? Insufferable—
what, still alive? Get out—
faster, back where you came from—vanish!

Tiresias. I'd never have come if you hadn't called me here.

Oedipus. If I thought you'd blurt out such absurdities,
495   you'd have died waiting before I'd had you summoned.

Tiresias. Absurd, am I? To you, not to your parents:
the ones who bore you found me sane enough.

Oedipus. Parents—who? Wait . . . who is my father?

Tiresias. This day will bring your birth and your destruction.

500   **Oedipus.** Riddles—all you can say are riddles, murk and darkness.

Tiresias. Ah, but aren't you the best man alive at solving riddles?

Oedipus. Mock me for that, go on, and you'll reveal my greatness.

Tiresias. Your great good fortune, true, it was your ruin.

Oedipus. Not if I saved the city—what do I care?

505   **Tiresias.** Well then, I'll be going. [*To his attendant.*] Take me home, boy.

Oedipus. Yes, take him away. You're a nuisance here.
Out of the way, the irritation's gone.

[*Turning his back on* Tiresias, *moving toward the palace.*]

Tiresias.   I will go,
once I have said what I came here to say.
I'll never shrink from the anger in your eyes—
510   you can't destroy me. Listen to me closely:
the man you've sought so long, proclaiming,
cursing up and down, the murderer of Laius—
he is here. A stranger,
you may think, who lives among you,

---

[37] **reverberate**—echo.

515   he soon will be revealed a native Theban

but he will take no joy in the revelation.

Blind who now has eyes, beggar who now is rich,

he will grope his way toward a foreign soil,

a stick tapping before him step by step.

[Oedipus *enters the palace.*]

520   Revealed at last, brother and father both

to the children he embraces, to his mother

son and husband both—he sowed the loins

his father sowed, he spilled his father's blood!

Go in and reflect on that, solve that.

525   And if you find I've lied

from this day onward call the prophet blind.

[Tiresias *and the boy exit to the side.*]

Chorus.   Who—

who is the man the voice of god denounces

resounding out of the rocky **gorge**[38] of Delphi?

     The horror too dark to tell,

530   whose ruthless bloody hands have done the work?

His time has come to fly

     to outrace the stallions of the storm

           his feet a streak of speed—

Cased in armor, Apollo son of the Father

535   lunges on him, lightning-bolts afire!

And the grim unerring Furies

          closing for the kill.

                     Look,

the word of god has just come blazing

flashing off Parnassus' snowy heights![39]

540   That man who left no trace—

after him, hunt him down with all our strength!

Now under bristling timber

     up through rocks and caves he stalks

          like the wild mountain bull—

545   cut off from men, each step an agony, frenzied, racing blind

but he cannot outrace the dread voices of Delphi

---

[38] **gorge**—deep ravine.

[39] Parnassus' snowy heights—Mount Parnassus was associated with Apollo.

ringing out of the heart of Earth,[40]

the dark wings beating around him shrieking doom

the doom that never dies, the terror—

550   The skilled prophet scans the birds and shatters me with terror!

I can't accept him, can't deny him, don't know what to say,

I'm lost, and the wings of dark foreboding beating—

I cannot see what's come, what's still to come . . .

and what could breed a blood feud between

555   Laius' house and the son of Polybus?[41]

I know of nothing, not in the past and not now,

no charge to bring against our king, no cause

to attack his fame that rings throughout Thebes—

not without proof—not for the ghost of Laius,

560   not to avenge a murder gone without a trace.

Zeus and Apollo know, they know, the great masters

of all the dark and depth of human life.

But whether a mere man can know the truth,

whether a seer can fathom more than I

565   there is no test, no certain proof

though matching skill for skill

a man can outstrip a rival. No, not till I see

these charges proved will I side with his accusers.

We saw him then, when the she-hawk[42] swept against him,

570   saw with our own eyes his skill, his brilliant triumph—

there was the test—he was the joy of Thebes!

Never will I convict my king, never in my heart.

[*Enter* Creon *from the side.*]

Creon. My fellow-citizens, I hear King Oedipus

levels terrible charges at me. I had to come.

575   I resent it deeply. If, in the present crisis,

he thinks he suffers any abuse from me,

anything I've done or said that offers him

the slightest injury, why, I've no desire

to linger out this life, my reputation a shambles.

580   The damage I'd face from such an accusation

is nothing simple. No, there's nothing worse:

---

[40] the heart of Earth—Delphi was believed to mark the center of the earth.

[41] Polybus—king of Corinth and adoptive father of Oedipus.

[42] she-hawk—the Sphinx.

          branded a traitor in the city, a traitor
          to all of you and my good friends.

Leader.   True,
          but a slur might have been forced out of him,
585   by anger perhaps, not any firm conviction.

Creon. The charge was made in public, wasn't it?
          I put the prophet up to spreading lies?

Leader. Such things were said . . .
          I don't know with what intent, if any.

590 **Creon.** Was his glance steady, his mind right
          when the charge was brought against me?

Leader. I really couldn't say. I never look
          to judge the ones in power. [*The doors open.* Oedipus *enters.*]
          Wait, here's Oedipus now.

Oedipus.   You—here? You have the gall[43]
595   to show your face before the palace gates?
          You, plotting to kill me, kill the king—
          I see it all, the **marauding**[44] thief himself
          scheming to steal my crown and power! Tell me,
          in god's name, what did you take me for,
600   coward or fool, when you spun out your plot?
          Your treachery—you think I'd never detect it
          creeping against me in the dark? Or sensing it,
          not defend myself? Aren't you the fool,
          You and your high adventure. Lacking numbers,
605   powerful friends, out for the big game of empire—
          You need riches, armies to bring that quarry down!

Creon. Are you quite finished? It's your turn to listen
          for just as long as you've . . . instructed me.
          Hear me out, then judge me on the facts.

610 **Oedipus.** You've a wicked way with words, Creon,
          but I'll be slow to learn—from you.
          I find you a menace, a great burden to me.

Creon. Just one thing, hear me out in this.

Oedipus.   Just one thing,
          don't tell *me* you're not the enemy, the traitor.

---

[43] **gall**—disrespect.
[44] **marauding**—raiding in search of plunder.

615 **Creon.** Look, if you think crude, mindless stubbornness
        such a gift, you've lost your sense of balance.
  Oedipus. If you think you can abuse a kinsman,
        then escape the penalty, you're insane.
  Creon. Fair enough, I grant you. But this injury
620   you say I've done you, what is it?
  Oedipus. Did you **induce**[45] me, yes or no,
        to send for that **sanctimonious**[46] prophet?
  Creon. I did. And I'd do the same again.
  Oedipus. All right then, tell me, how long is it now
625   since Laius . . .
  Creon.   Laius—what did *he* do?
  Oedipus.   Vanished,
        swept from sight, murdered in his tracks.
  Creon. The count of the years would run you far back . . .
  Oedipus. And that far back, was the prophet at his trade?
  Creon. Skilled as he is today, and just as honored.
630 **Oedipus.** Did he ever refer to me then, at that time?
  Creon.   No,
        never, at least, when I was in his presence.
  Oedipus. But you did investigate the murder, didn't you?
  Creon. We did our best, of course, discovered nothing.
  Oedipus. But the great seer never accused me then—why not?
635 **Creon.** I don't know. And when I don't, *I* keep quiet.
  Oedipus. You do know this, you'd tell it too—
        if you had a shred of decency.
  Creon.   What?
If I know, I won't hold back.
  Oedipus.   Simply this:
        if the two of you had never put heads together,
640   we would never have heard about *my* killing Laius.
  Creon. If that's what he says . . . well, you know best.
        But now I have a right to learn from you
        as you just learned from me.
  Oedipus.   Learn your fill,
        you never will convict me of the murder.
645 **Creon.** Tell me, you're married to my sister, aren't you?

---

[45] **induce**—persuade.
[46] **sanctimonious**—making a show of holiness.

Oedipus. A genuine discovery—there's no denying that.

Creon. And you rule the land with her, with equal power?

Oedipus. She receives from me whatever she desires.

Creon. And I am the third, all of us are equals?

650   **Oedipus.** Yes, and it's there you show your stripes—
you betray a kinsman.

Creon.   Not at all.
Not if you see things calmly, rationally,
as I do. Look at it this way first:
who in his right mind would rather rule

655   and live in anxiety than sleep in peace?
Particularly if he enjoys the same authority.
Not I, I'm not the man to yearn for kingship,
not with a king's power in my hands. Who would?
No one with any sense of self-control.

660   Now, as it is, you offer me all I need,
not a fear in the world. But if I wore the crown . . .
there'd be many painful duties to perform,
hardly to my taste. How could kingship
please me more than influence, power

665   without a qualm? I'm not that **deluded**[47] yet,
to reach for anything but privilege outright,
profit free and clear.
Now all men sing my praises, all salute me,
now all who request your favors curry[48] mine.

670   I'm their best hope: success rests in me.
Why give up that, I ask you, and borrow trouble?
A man of sense, someone who sees things clearly
would never resort to treason.
No, I've no lust for conspiracy in me,

675   nor could I ever suffer one who does.
Do you want proof? Go to Delphi yourself,
examine the oracle and see if I've reported
the message word-for-word. This too:
if you detect that I and the clairvoyant[49]

680   have plotted anything in common, arrest me,

---

[47] **deluded**—deceived.

[48] curry—seek by flattery.

[49] clairvoyant—prophet, that is, Tiresias.

execute me. Not on the strength of one vote,
two in this case, mine as well as yours.
But don't convict me on sheer unverified surmise.[50]
How wrong it is to take the good for bad,
685 purely at random, or take the bad for good.
But reject a friend, a kinsman? I would as soon
tear out the life within us, priceless life itself.
You'll learn this well, without fail, in time.
Time alone can bring the just man to light;
690 the criminal you can spot in one short day.

Leader.   Good advice,
my lord, for anyone who wants to avoid disaster.
Those who jump to conclusions may be wrong.

Oedipus. When my enemy moves against me quickly,
plots in secret, I move quickly too, I must,
695 I plot and pay him back. Relax my guard a moment,
waiting his next move—he wins his objective,
I lose mine.

Creon.   What do you want?
You want me banished?

Oedipus.   No, I want you dead.

Creon. Just to show how ugly a grudge can . . .

Oedipus.   So,
700 still stubborn? you don't think I'm serious?

Creon. I think you're insane.

Oedipus.   Quite sane—in my behalf.

Creon. Not just as much in mine?

Oedipus.   You—my mortal enemy?

Creon. What if you're wholly wrong?

Oedipus.   No matter—I must rule.

Creon. Not if you rule unjustly.

Oedipus.   Hear him, Thebes, my city!

705 **Creon.** My city too, not yours alone!

Leader. Please, my lords. [*Enter* Jocasta *from the palace.*]
                    Look, Jocasta's coming,
and just in time too. With her help
you must put this fighting of yours to rest.

---

[50] unverified surmise—unproved guesswork.

Jocasta. Have you no sense? Poor misguided men,
710   such shouting—why this public outburst?
        Aren't you ashamed, with the land so sick,
        to stir up private quarrels? [*To* Oedipus.]
        Into the palace now. And Creon, you go home.
        Why make such a furor over nothing?

715 **Creon.** My sister, it's dreadful . . . Oedipus, your husband,
        he's bent on a choice of punishments for me,
        banishment from the fatherland or death.

Oedipus. Precisely. I caught him in the act, Jocasta,
        plotting, about to stab me in the back.

720 **Creon.** Never—curse me, let me die and be damned
        if I've done you any wrong you charge me with.

Jocasta. Oh god, believe it, Oedipus,
        honor the solemn oath he swears to heaven.
        Do it for me, for the sake of all your people.

[*The* Chorus *begins to chant.*]

725 **Chorus.** Believe it, be sensible
           give way, my king, I beg you!

Oedipus. What do you want from me, **concessions**?[51]

Chorus. Respect him—he's been no fool in the past
        and now he's strong with the oath he swears to god.

730 **Oedipus.** You know what you're asking?

Chorus.   I do.

Oedipus.   Then out with it!

Chorus. The man's your friend your kin, he's under oath—
        don't cast him out, disgraced
        branded with guilt on the strength of hearsay only.

Oedipus. Know full well, if that's what you want
735   you want me dead or banished from the land.

Chorus.   Never—
        no, by the blazing Sun, first god of the heavens!
          Stripped of the gods, stripped of loved ones,
        let me die by inches[52] if that ever crossed my mind.
        But the heart inside me sickens, dies as the land dies
740   and now on top of the old griefs you pile this,
        your fury—both of you!

---

[51] **concessions**—acknowledgements, often reluctant, of the truth or rightness of something.

[52] by inches—slowly.

Oedipus.   Then let him go,
   even if it does lead to my ruin, my death
   or my disgrace, driven from Thebes for life.
   It's you, not him I pity—your words move me.
745   He, wherever he goes, my hate goes with him.
Creon. Look at you, sullen in yielding, brutal in your rage—
   you'll go too far. It's perfect justice:
   natures like yours are hardest on themselves.
Oedipus. Then leave me alone—get out!
Creon.   I'm going.
750   You're wrong, so wrong. These men know I'm right.
[*Exit to the side. The* Chorus *turns to* Jocasta.]
Chorus. Why do you hesitate, my lady
   why not help him in?
Jocasta. Tell me what's happened first.
Chorus. Loose, ignorant talk started dark suspicions
755   and a sense of injustice cut deeply too.
Jocasta. On both sides?
Chorus.   Oh yes.
Jocasta.   What did they say?
Chorus. Enough, please, enough! The land's so racked already
   or so it seems to me . . .
   End the trouble here, just where they left it.
760   **Oedipus.** You see what comes of your good intentions now?
   And all because you tried to blunt my anger.
Chorus.   My king,
   I've said it once, I'll say it time and again—
   I'd be insane, you know it,
   senseless, ever to turn my back on you.
765   You who set our beloved land—storm-tossed, shattered—
   straight on course. Now again, good helmsman,
   steer us through the storm!
[*The* Chorus *draws away, leaving* Oedipus *and* Jocasta *side by side.*]
Jocasta.   For the love of god,
   Oedipus, tell me too, what is it?
   Why this rage? You're so unbending.
770   **Oedipus.** I will tell you. I respect you, Jocasta,
   much more than these men here . . . [*Glancing at the* Chorus.]
   Creon's to blame. Creon schemes against me.

Jocasta. Tell me clearly, how did the quarrel start?

Oedipus. He says I murdered Laius—I am guilty.

775 **Jocasta.** How does he know? Some secret knowledge
or simply hearsay?

Oedipus.   Oh, he sent his prophet in
to do his dirty work. You know Creon,
Creon keeps his own lips clean.

Jocasta.   A prophet?
Well then, free yourself of every charge!

780 Listen to me and learn some peace of mind:
no skill in the world,
nothing human can penetrate the future.
Here is proof, quick and to the point.
An oracle came to Laius one fine day

785 (I won't say from Apollo himself
but his underlings, his priests) and it said
that doom would strike him down at the hands of a son,
our son, to be born of our own flesh and blood. But Laius,
so the report goes at least, was killed by strangers,

790 thieves, at a place where three roads meet . . . my son—
he wasn't three days old and the boy's father
fastened his ankles, had a henchman fling him away
on a barren, trackless mountain. There, you see?
Apollo brought neither thing to pass. My baby

795 no more murdered his father than Laius suffered—
his wildest fear—death at his own son's hands.
That's how the seers and their revelations
mapped out the future. Brush them from your mind.
Whatever the god needs and seeks

800 he'll bring to light himself, with ease.

Oedipus.   Strange,
hearing you just now . . . my mind wandered,
my thoughts racing back and forth.

Jocasta. What do you mean? Why so anxious, startled?

Oedipus. I thought I heard you say that Laius

805 was cut down at a place where three roads meet.

Jocasta. That was the story. It hasn't died out yet.

Oedipus. Where did this thing happen? Be precise.

Jocasta. A place called Phocis, where two branching roads,
      one from Daulia, one from Delphi,
810   come together—a crossroads.
Oedipus. When? How long ago?
Jocasta. The heralds no sooner reported Laius dead
      than you appeared and they hailed you king of Thebes.
Oedipus. My god, my god—what have you planned to do to me?
815 **Jocasta.** What, Oedipus? What haunts you so?
Oedipus.   Not yet.
      Laius—how did he look? Describe him.
      Had he reached his prime?
Jocasta.   He was swarthy,
      and the gray had just begun to streak his temples,
      and his build . . . wasn't far from yours.
Oedipus.   Oh no no,
820   I think I've just called down a dreadful curse
      upon myself—I simply didn't know!
Jocasta. What are you saying? I shudder to look at you.
Oedipus. I have a terrible fear the blind seer can see.
      I'll know in a moment. One thing more—
Jocasta.   Anything,
825   afraid as I am—ask, I'll answer, all I can.
Oedipus. Did he go with a light or heavy escort,
      several men-at-arms, like a lord, a king?
Jocasta. There were five in the party, a herald among them,
      and a single wagon carrying Laius.
Oedipus.   Ai—
830   now I can see it all, clear as day.
      Who told you all this at the time, Jocasta?
Jocasta. A servant who reached home, the lone survivor.
Oedipus. So, could he still be in the palace—even now?
Jocasta. No indeed. Soon as he returned from the scene
835   and saw you on the throne with Laius dead and gone,
      he knelt and clutched my hand, pleading with me
      to send him into the hinterlands, to pasture,
      far as possible, out of sight of Thebes.
      I sent him away. Slave though he was,
840   he'd earned that favor—and much more.
Oedipus. Can we bring him back, quickly?

Jocasta. Easily. Why do you want him so?

Oedipus.   I'm afraid,
  Jocasta, I have said too much already.
  That man—I've got to see him.

Jocasta.   Then he'll come.
845   But even I have a right, I'd like to think,
  to know what's torturing you, my lord.

Oedipus. And so you shall—I can hold nothing back from you,
  now I've reached this pitch of dark foreboding.
  Who means more to me than you? Tell me,
850   whom would I turn toward but you
  as I go through all this?
  My father was Polybus, king of Corinth.
  My mother, a Dorian, Merope. And I was held
  the prince of the realm among the people there,
855   till something struck me out of nowhere,
  something strange . . . worth remarking perhaps,
  hardly worth the anxiety I gave it.
  Some man at a banquet who had drunk too much
  shouted out—he was far gone, mind you—
860   that I am not my father's son. Fighting words!
  I barely restrained myself that day
  but early the next I went to mother and father,
  questioned them closely, and they were enraged
  at the accusation and the fool who let it fly.
865   So as for my parents I was satisfied,
  but still this thing kept gnawing at me,
  the slander spread—I had to make my move. And so,
  unknown to mother and father I set out for Delphi,
  and the god Apollo spurned me, sent me away
870   denied the facts I came for,
  but first he flashed before my eyes a future
  great with pain, terror, disaster—I can hear him cry,
  "You are fated to couple with your mother, you will bring
  a breed of children into the light no man can bear to see—
875   you will kill your father, the one who gave you life!"
  I heard all that and ran. I abandoned Corinth,
  from that day on I gauged its landfall[53] only

---

[53] gauged its landfall—calculated its location.

by the stars, running, always running
toward some place where I would never see
880 the shame of all those oracles come true.
And as I fled I reached that very spot
where the great king, you say, met his death.
Now, Jocasta, I will tell you all.
Making my way toward this triple crossroad
885 I began to see a herald, then a brace[54] of colts
drawing a wagon, and mounted on the bench . . . a man,
just as you've described him, coming face-to-face,
and the one in the lead and the old man himself
were about to thrust me off the road—brute force—
890 and the one shouldering me aside, the driver,
I strike him in anger!—and the old man, watching me
coming up along his wheels—he brings down
his prod,[55] two prongs straight at my head!
I paid him back with interest!
895 Short work, by god—with one blow of the staff
in this right hand I knock him out of his high seat,
roll him out of the wagon, sprawling headlong—
I killed them all—every mother's son!
Oh, but if there is any blood-tie
900 between Laius and this stranger . . .
what man alive more miserable than I?
More hated by the gods? *I* am the man
no alien, no citizen welcomes to his house,
law forbids it—not a word to me in public,
905 driven out of every hearth and home.
And all these curses I—no one but I
brought down these piling curses on myself!
And you, his wife, I've touched your body with these,
the hands that killed your husband cover you with blood.
910 Wasn't I born for torment? Look me in the eyes!
I am **abomination**[56]—heart and soul!
I must be exiled, and even in exile

---

[54] brace—pair.
[55] prod—goad.
[56] **abomination**—cause of abhorrence or disgust.

never see my parents, never set foot
on native earth again. Else I'm doomed

915 to couple with my mother and cut my father down . . .
Polybus who reared me, gave me life. But why, why?
Wouldn't a man of judgment say—and wouldn't he be right—
some savage power has brought this down upon my head?
On no, not that, you pure and awesome gods,

920 never let me see that day! Let me slip
from the world of men, vanish without a trace
before I see myself stained with such corruption,
stained to the heart.

Leader. My lord you fill our hearts with fear.

925 But at least until you question the witness,
do take hope.

Oedipus. Exactly. He is my last hope—
I'm waiting for the shepherd. He is crucial.

Jocasta. And once he appears, what then? Why so urgent?

Oedipus. I'll tell you. If it turns out that his story

930 matches yours, I've escaped the worst.

Jocasta. What did I say? What struck you so?

Oedipus. You said *thieves*—
he told you a whole band of them murdered Laius.
So, if he still holds to the same number,
I cannot be the killer. One can't equal many.

935 But if he refers to one man, one alone,
clearly the scales come down on me:
I am guilty.

Jocasta. Impossible. Trust me,
I told you precisely what he said,
and he can't retract it now;

940 the whole city heard it, not just I.
And even if he should vary his first report
by one man more or less, still, my lord,
he could never make the murder of Laius
truly fit the prophecy. Apollo was **explicit:**[57]

945 my son was doomed to kill my husband . . . my son,

---

[57] **explicit**—clear.

poor defenseless thing, he never had a chance
to kill his father. They destroyed him first.
So much for prophecy. It's neither here nor there.
From this day on, I wouldn't look right or left.

950 **Oedipus.** True, true. Still, that shepherd,
someone fetch him—now!

Jocasta. I'll send at once. But do let's go inside.
I'd never displease you, least of all in this.

[Oedipus *and* Jocasta *enter the palace.*]

Chorus. Destiny guide me always
955 Destiny find me filled with reverence
pure in word and deed.
Great laws tower above us, reared on high
born for the brilliant vault of heaven—
Olympian[58] Sky their only father,
960 nothing mortal, no man gave them birth,
their memory deathless, never lost in sleep:
within them lives a mighty god, the god does not grow old.
Pride breeds the tyrant
violent pride, gorging, crammed to bursting
965 with all that is overripe and rich with ruin—
clawing up to the heights, headlong pride
crashes down the abyss—sheer doom!
No footing helps, all foothold lost and gone.
But the healthy strife that makes the city strong—
970 I pray that god will never end that wrestling:
god, my champion, I will never let you go.
But if any man comes striding, high and mighty
in all he says and does,
no fear of justice, no reverence
975 for the temples of the gods—
let a rough doom tear him down,
repay his pride, breakneck, ruinous pride!
If he cannot reap his profits fairly
cannot restrain himself from outrage—
980 mad, laying hands on the holy things untouchable!

---

[58] Olympian—heavenly. Olympus was the world of the Greek gods.

Can such a man, so desperate, still boast
he can save his life from the flashing bolts of god?
If all such violence goes with honor now
why join the sacred dance?

985   Never again will I go reverent to Delphi,
the inviolate[59] heart of Earth
or Apollo's ancient oracle at Abae
or Olympia[60] of the fires—
unless these prophecies all come true

990   for all mankind to point toward in wonder.
King of kings, if you deserve your titles
Zeus, remember, never forget!
You and your deathless, everlasting reign.
They are dying, the old oracles sent to Laius,

995   now our masters strike them off the rolls.
Nowhere Apollo's golden glory now—
the gods, the gods go down.

[*Enter* Jocasta *from the palace, carrying a suppliant's branch wound in wool.*]

Jocasta. Lords of the realm, it occurred to me,
just now, to visit the temples of the gods,

1000   so I have my branch in hand and incense too.
Oedipus is beside himself. Racked with anguish,
no longer a man of sense, he won't admit
the latest prophecies are hollow as the old—
he's at the mercy of every passing voice

1005   if the voice tells of terror.
I urge him gently, nothing seems to help;
so I turn to you, Apollo, you are nearest.

[*Placing her branch on the altar, while an old herdsman enters from the side, not
the one just summoned by the King, but an unexpected* Messenger *from Corinth.*]

I come with prayers and offerings . . . I beg you,
cleanse us, set us free of **defilement!**[61]

1010   Look at us, passengers in the grip of fear,
watching the pilot of the vessel go to pieces.

---

[59] inviolate—unprofaned, pure.

[60] Abae . . . Olympia—shrines of Apollo and Zeus, respectively.

[61] **defilement**—filth, pollution.

Messenger [*approaching* Jocasta *and the* Chorus].
  Strangers, please, I wonder if you could lead us
  to the palace of the king . . . I think it's Oedipus.
  Better, the man himself—you know where he is?

1015 **Leader.** This is his palace, stranger. He's inside.
  But here is his queen, his wife and mother
  of his children.

Messenger.   Blessings on you, noble queen,
  queen of Oedipus crowned with all your family—
  blessings on you always!

1020 **Jocasta.** And the same to you, stranger, you deserve it . . .
  such a greeting. But what have you come for?
  Have you brought us news?

Messenger.   Wonderful news—
  for the house, my lady, for your husband too.

Jocasta. Really, what? Who sent you?

Messenger.   Corinth.

1025 I'll give you the message in a moment.
  You'll be glad of it—how could you help it?—
  though it costs a little sorrow in the bargain.

Jocasta. What can it be, with such a double edge?

Messenger. The people there, they want to make your Oedipus

1030 king of Corinth, so they're saying now.

Jocasta. Why? Isn't old Polybus still in power?

Messenger. No more. Death has got him in the tomb.

Jocasta. What are you saying? Polybus, dead?—dead?

Messenger.   If not,
  if I'm not telling the truth, strike me dead too.

1035 **Jocasta** [*to a servant*]. Quickly, go to your master, tell him this!
  You prophecies of the gods, where are you now?
  This is the man that Oedipus feared for years,
  he fled him, not to kill him—and now he's dead,
  quite by chance, a normal, natural death,

1040 not murdered by his son.

Oedipus [*emerging from the palace*]. Dearest,
  what now? Why call me from the palace?

Jocasta [*bringing the* Messenger *closer*]. Listen to *him*, see for yourself
   what all
  those awful prophecies of god have come to.

Oedipus. And who is he? What can he have for me?

1045 **Jocasta.** He's from Corinth, he's come to tell you
your father is no more—Polybus—he's dead!

Oedipus [*wheeling on the* Messenger]. What? Let me have it from your lips.

Messenger. Well, if that's what you want first, then here it is:
make no mistake. Polybus is dead and gone.

1050 **Oedipus.** How—murder? sickness?—what? what killed him?

Messenger. A light tip of the scales can put old bones to rest.

Oedipus. Sickness then—poor man, it wore him down.

Messenger.   That,
and the long count of years he'd measured out.

Oedipus.   So!
Jocasta, why, why look to the Prophet's hearth,

1055 the fires of the future? Why scan the birds
that scream above our heads? They winged me on
to the murder of my father, did they? That was my doom?
Well look, he's dead and buried, hidden under the earth,
and here I am in Thebes, I never put hand to sword—

1060 unless some longing for me wasted him away,
then in a sense you'd say I caused his death.
But now, all those prophecies I feared—Polybus
packs them off to sleep with him in hell![62]
They're nothing, worthless.

Jocasta.   There.

1065 Didn't I tell you from the start?

Oedipus. So you did. I was lost in fear.

Jocasta. No more, sweep it from your mind forever.

Oedipus. But my mother's bed, surely I must fear—

Jocasta.   Fear?
What should a man fear? It's all chance,

1070 chance rules our lives. Not a man on earth
can see a day ahead, groping through the dark.
Better to live at random, best we can.
And as for this marriage with your mother—
have no fear. Many a man before you,

1075 in his dreams, has shared his mother's bed.
Take such things for shadows, nothing at all—

---

[62] hell—In Greek belief, the world of the dead was not in general a place of punishment.

Live, Oedipus,
as if there's no tomorrow!

Oedipus. Brave words
and you'd persuade me if mother weren't alive.
1080   But mother lives, so for all your reassurances
I live in fear, I must.

Jocasta. But your father's death,
that, at least, is a great blessing, joy to the eyes!

Oedipus. Great, I know . . . but I fear *her*—she's still alive.

Messenger. Wait, who is this woman, makes you so afraid?

1085   **Oedipus.** Merope, old man. The wife of Polybus.

Messenger. The queen? What's there to fear in her?

Oedipus. A dreadful prophecy, stranger, sent by the gods.

Messenger. Tell me, could you? Unless it's forbidden
other ears to hear.

Oedipus. Not at all.
1090   Apollo told me once—it is my fate—
I must make love with my own mother,
shed my father's blood with my own hands.
So for years I've given Corinth a wide berth,
and it's been my good fortune too. But still,
1095   to see one's parents and look into their eyes
is the greatest joy I know.

Messenger. You're afraid of that?
That kept you out of Corinth?

Oedipus. My *father*, old man—
so I wouldn't kill my father.

Messenger. So that's it.
Well then, seeing I came with such good will, my king,
1100   why don't I rid you of that old worry now?

Oedipus. What a rich reward you'd have for that.

Messenger. What do you think I came for, majesty?
So you'd come home and I'd be better off.

Oedipus. Never, I will never go near my parents.

1105   **Messenger.** My boy, it's clear, you don't know what you're doing.

Oedipus. What do you mean, old man? For god's sake, explain.

Messenger. If you ran from *them,* always dodging home . . .

Oedipus. Always, terrified Apollo's oracle might come true—

Messenger. And you'd be covered with guilt, from both your parents.

1110 **Oedipus.** That's right, old man, that fear is always with me.

Messenger. Don't you know? You've really nothing to fear.

Oedipus. But why? If I'm their son—Merope, Polybus?

Messenger. Polybus was nothing to you, that's why, not in blood.

Oedipus. What are you saying—Polybus was not my father?

1115 **Messenger.** No more than I am. He and I are equals.

Oedipus. My father—
how can my father equal nothing? You're nothing to me!

Messenger. Neither was he, no more your father than I am.

Oedipus. Then why did he call me his son?

Messenger. You were a gift,
years ago—know for a fact he took you

1120 from my hands.

Oedipus. No, from another's hands?
Then how could he love me so? He loved me, deeply . . .

Messenger. True, and his early years without a child
made him love you all the more.

Oedipus. And you, did you . . .
buy me? find me by accident?

Messenger. I stumbled on you,

1125 down the woody flanks of Mount Cithaeron.

Oedipus. So close,
what were you doing here, just passing through?

Messenger. Watching over my flocks, grazing them on the slopes.

Oedipus. A herdsman, were you? A **vagabond**,[63] scraping for wages?

Messenger. Your savior too, my son, in your worst hour.

Oedipus. Oh—

1130 when you picked me up, was I in pain? What exactly?

Messenger. Your ankles . . . they tell the story. Look at them.

Oedipus. Why remind me of that, that old affliction?

Messenger. Your ankles were pinned together; I set you free.

Oedipus. That dreadful mark—I've had it from the cradle.

1135 **Messenger.** And you got your name, from that misfortune too,
the name's still with you.

Oedipus. Dear god, who did it?—
mother? father? Tell me.

---

[63] **vagabond**—wanderer.

Messenger.   I don't know.
  The one who gave you to me, he'd know more.

Oedipus. What? You took me from someone else?
  You didn't find me yourself?

1140 **Messenger.**   No sir,
  another shepherd passed you on to me.

Oedipus. Who? Do you know? Describe him.

Messenger. He called himself a servant of . . .
  if I remember rightly—Laius. [Jocasta *turns sharply.*]

1145 **Oedipus.** The king of the land who ruled here long ago?

Messenger. That's the one. That herdsman was his man.

Oedipus. Is he still alive? Can I see him?

Messenger. They'd know best, the people of these parts.

[Oedipus *and the* Messenger *turn to the* Chorus.]

Oedipus. Does anyone know that herdsman,

1150 the one he mentioned? Anyone seen him
  in the fields, in town? Out with it!
  The time has come to reveal this once for all.

Leader. I think he's the very shepherd you wanted to see,
  a moment ago. But the queen, Jocasta,

1155 she's the one to say.

Oedipus.   Jocasta,
  you remember the man we just sent for?
  Is *that* the one he means?

Jocasta.   That man . . .
  why ask? Old shepherd, talk, empty nonsense,
  don't give it another thought, don't even think—

1160 **Oedipus.** What—give up now, with a clue like this?
  Fail to solve the mystery of my birth?
  Not for all the world!

Jocasta.   Stop—in the name of god,
  if you love your own life, call off this search!
  My suffering is enough.

Oedipus.   Courage!

1165 Even if my mother turns out to be a slave,
  and I a slave, three generations back,
  you would not seem common.

Jocasta.   Oh no,
  listen to me, I beg you, don't do this.

Oedipus. Listen to you? No more. I must know it all,

1170   see the truth at last.

Jocasta.   No, please—

for your sake—I want the best for you!

Oedipus. Your best is more than I can bear.

Jocasta.   You're doomed—

may you never fathom who you are!

Oedipus [*to a servant*]. Hurry, fetch me the herdsman, now!

1175   Leave her to glory in her royal birth.

Jocasta. Aieeeeee—man of agony—

that is the only name I have for you,

that, no other—ever, ever, ever!

[*Flinging through the palace doors. A long, tense silence follows.*]

Leader. Where's she gone, Oedipus?

1180   Rushing off, such wild grief . . .

I'm afraid that from this silence

something monstrous may come bursting forth.

Oedipus. Let it burst! Whatever will, whatever must!

I must know my birth, no matter how common

1185   it may be—must see my origins face-to-face.

She perhaps, she with her woman's pride

may well be **mortified**[64] by my birth,

but I, I count myself the son of Chance,

the great goddess, giver of all good things—

1190   I'll never see myself disgraced. She is my mother!

And the moons have marked me out, my blood-brothers,

one moon on the wane,[65] the next moon great with power.

That is my blood, my nature—I will never betray it,

never fail to search and learn my birth!

1195 **Chorus.** Yes—if I am a true prophet

if I can grasp the truth,

by the boundless skies of Olympus,

at the full moon of tomorrow, Mount Cithaeron

you will know how Oedipus glories in you—

1200   You, his birthplace, nurse, his mountain-mother!

And we will sing you, dancing out your praise—

---

[64] **mortified**—humiliated.

[65] on the wane—growing smaller.

you lift our monarch's heart!
Apollo, Apollo, god of the wild cry
may our dancing please you! Oedipus—

1205   son, dear child, who bore you?
Who of the nymphs[66] who seem to live forever
mated with Pan,[67] the mountain-striding Father?
Who was your mother? who, some bride of Apollo
the god who loves the pastures spreading toward the sun?

1210   Or was it Hermes,[68] king of the lightning ridges?
Or Dionysus, lord of frenzy, lord of the barren peaks—
did he seize you in his hands, dearest of all his lucky finds?—
found by the nymphs, their warm eyes dancing, gift
to the lord who loves them dancing out his joy!

[Oedipus *strains to see a figure coming from the distance. Attended by palace guards, an old* Shepherd *enters slowly, reluctant to approach the* King.]

1215 **Oedipus.** I never met the man, my friends . . . still,
if I had to guess, I'd say that's the shepherd,
the very one we've looked for all along.
Brothers in old age, two of a kind,
he and our guest here. At any rate

1220 the ones who bring him in are my own men,
I recognize them. [*Turning to the* Leader.] But you know more than I,
you should, you've seen the man before.

Leader. I know him, definitely. One of Laius' men,
a trusty shepherd, if there ever was one.

1225 **Oedipus.** You, I ask you first, stranger,
you from Corinth—is this the one you mean?

Messenger. You're looking at him. He's your man.

Oedipus [*to the* Shepherd]. You, old man, come over here—
look at me. Answer all my questions.

1230 Did you ever serve King Laius?

Shepherd.   So I did . . .
a slave, not bought on the block[69] though,
born and reared in the palace.

Oedipus. Your duties, your kind of work?

---

[66] nymphs—minor nature goddesses who inhabit forests and mountains.

[67] Pan—god of the fields and woods, patron of shepherds.

[68] Hermes—messenger of the gods, patron of travelers.

[69] block—auction block in a slave market.

Shepherd. Herding the flocks, the better part of my life.

1235 **Oedipus.** Where, mostly? Where did you do your grazing?

Shepherd. Well, Cithaeron sometimes, or the foothills round about.

Oedipus. This man—you know him? ever see him there?

Shepherd [confused, glancing from the Messenger to the King]. Doing
   what?—what man do you mean?

Oedipus [pointing to the Messenger]. This one here—ever
      have dealings with him?

1240 **Shepherd.** Not so I could say, but give me a chance,
   my memory's bad . . .

Messenger. No wonder he doesn't know me, master.
   But let me refresh his memory for him.
   I'm sure he recalls old times we had

1245 on the slopes of Mount Cithaeron:
   he and I, grazing our flocks, he with two
   and I with one—we both struck up together,
   three whole seasons, six months at a stretch
   from spring to the rising of Arcturus[70] in the fall,

1250 then with winter coming on I'd drive my herds
   to my own pens, and back he'd go with his
   to Laius' folds. [To the Shepherd.] Now that's how it was,
   wasn't it—yes or no?

Shepherd.   Yes, I suppose . . .
   it's all so long ago.

Messenger.   Come, tell me,

1255 you gave me a child back then, a boy, remember?
   A little fellow to rear, my very own.

Shepherd. What? Why rake up that again?

Messenger. Look, here he is, my fine old friend—
   the same man who was just a baby then.

1260 **Shepherd.** Damn you, shut your mouth—quiet!

Oedipus. Don't lash out at him, old man—
   you need lashing more than he does.

Shepherd.   Why,
   master, majesty—what have I done wrong?

Oedipus. You won't answer his question about the boy.

1265 **Shepherd.** He's talking nonsense, wasting his breath.

---

[70] Arcturus—very bright star in the constellation Boötes; to the Greeks, its rising signaled the end of summer.

Oedipus. So, you won't talk willingly—
then you'll talk with pain. [*The guards seize the* Shepherd.]

Shepherd. No, dear god, don't torture an old man!

Oedipus. Twist his arms back, quickly!

Shepherd.   God help us, why?—
1270   what more do you need to know?

Oedipus. Did you give him that child? He's asking.

Shepherd. I did . . . I wish to god I'd died that day.

Oedipus. You've got your wish if you don't tell the truth.

Shepherd. The more I tell, the worse the death I'll die.

1275   **Oedipus.** Our friend here wants to stretch things out, does he?
[*Motioning to his men for torture.*]

Shepherd. No, no, I gave it to him—I just said so.

Oedipus. Where did you get it? Your house? Someone else's?

Shepherd. It wasn't mine, no, I got it from . . . someone.

Oedipus. Which one of them? [*Looking at the citizens.*]
Whose house?

Shepherd.   No—
1280   god's sake, master, no more questions!

Oedipus. You're a dead man if I have to ask again.

Shepherd. Then—the child came from the house . . .
of Laius.

Oedipus. A slave? or born of his own blood?

Shepherd.   Oh no,
I'm right at the edge, the horrible truth—I've got to say it!

1285   **Oedipus.** And I'm at the edge of hearing horrors, yes, but I must hear!

Shepherd. All right! His son, they said it was—his son!
But the one inside, your wife,
she'd tell it best.

Oedipus. My wife—
1290   *she* gave it to you?

Shepherd. Yes, yes, my king.

Oedipus. Why, what for?

Shepherd. To kill it.

Oedipus. Her own child,
1295   how could she?

Shepherd. She was afraid—
frightening prophecies.

Oedipus. What?

Shepherd.   They said—
he'd kill his parents.

1300   **Oedipus.** But you gave him to this old man—why?

Shepherd. I pitied the little baby, master,
hoped he'd take him off to his own country,
far away, but he saved him for this, this fate.
If you are the man he says you are, believe me,

1305   you were born for pain.

Oedipus.   O god—
all come true, all burst to light!
O light—now let me look my last on you!
I stand revealed at last—
cursed in my birth, cursed in marriage

1310   cursed in the lives I cut down with these hands!

[*Rushing through the doors with a great cry. The Corinthian* Messenger, *the*
Shepherd *and attendants exit slowly to the side.*]

Chorus. O the generations of men
the dying generations—adding the total
of all your lives I find they come to nothing . . .
                does there exist, is there a man on earth

1315   who seizes more joy than just a dream, a vision?
And the vision no sooner dawns than dies
blazing into **oblivion**.⁷¹
You are my great example, you, your life,
your destiny, Oedipus, man of misery—

1320   I count no man blest. You outranged⁷² all men!
            Bending your bow to the breaking-point
you captured priceless glory, O dear god,
and the Sphinx came crashing down,
                the virgin, claws hooked

1325   like a bird of omen singing, shrieking death—
like a fortress reared in the face of death
you rose and saved our land.
From that day on we called you king
we crowned you with honors, Oedipus, towering over all—

---

⁷¹ **oblivion**—forgetfulness.

⁷² outranged—surpassed.

1330 mighty king of the seven gates of Thebes.
    But now to hear your story—is there a man more agonized?
    More wed to pain and frenzy? Not a man on earth,
    the joy of your life ground down to nothing
    O Oedipus, name for the ages—
1335   one and the same wide harbor served you
          son and father both
    son and father came to rest in the same bridal chamber.
    How, how could the furrows your father plowed
    bear you, your agony, harrowing on
1340 in silence O so long? But now for all your power
    Time, all-seeing Time has dragged you to the light,
    judged your marriage monstrous from the start—
    the son and the father tangling, both one—
    O child of Laius, would to god
1345   I'd never seen you, never never!
      Now I weep like a man who wails the dead
    and the dirge[73] comes pouring forth with all my heart!
    I tell you the truth, you gave me life
    my breath leapt up in you
1350 and now you bring down night upon my eyes.
    [*Enter a* Messenger *from the palace.*]
    Messenger. Men of Thebes, always the first in honor,
    what horrors you will hear, what you will see,
    what a heavy weight of sorrow you will shoulder . . .
    if you are true to your birth, if you still have
1355 some feeling for the royal house of Thebes.
    I tell you neither the waters of the Danube
    nor the Nile[74] can wash this palace clean.
    Such things it hides, it soon will bring to light—
    terrible things, and none done blindly now,
1360 all done with a will. The pains
    we inflict upon ourselves hurt most of all.
    Leader. God knows we have pains enough already.
    What can you add to them?
    Messenger. The queen is dead.

---

[73] dirge—song for the dead.

[74] Danube nor the Nile—great rivers. Sophocles actually alluded to the Danube and the Rion, both rivers that flow into the Black Sea.

Leader.   Poor lady—how?

1365 **Messenger.** By her own hand. But you are spared the worst,
           you never had to watch . . . I saw it all,
           and with all the memory that's in me
           you will learn what that poor woman suffered.
           Once she'd broken in through the gates,
1370   dashing past us, frantic, whipped to fury,
           ripping her hair out with both hands—
           straight to her rooms she rushed, flinging herself
           across the bridal-bed, doors slamming behind her—
           once inside, she wailed for Laius, dead so long,
1375   remembering how she bore his child long ago,
           the life that rose up to destroy him, leaving
           its mother to mother living creatures
           with the very son she'd borne.
           Oh how she wept, mourning the marriage-bed
1380   where she let loose that double brood—monsters—
           husband by her husband, children by her child. And then—
           but how she died is more than I can say. Suddenly
           Oedipus burst in, screaming, he stunned us so
           we couldn't watch her agony to the end,
1385   our eyes were fixed on him. Circling
           like a maddened beast, stalking, here, there,
           crying out to us—Give him a sword! His wife,
           no wife, his mother, where can he find the mother earth
           that cropped two crops at once, himself and all his children?
1390   He was raging—one of the dark powers pointing the way,
           none of us mortals crowding around him, no,
           with a great shattering cry—someone, something leading him on—
           he hurled at the twin doors and bending the bolts back
           out of their sockets, crashed through the chamber.
1395   And there we saw the woman hanging by the neck,
           cradled high in a woven noose, spinning,
           swinging back and forth. And when he saw her,
           giving a low, wrenching sob that broke our hearts,
           slipping the halter[75] from her throat, he eased her down,
1400   in a slow embrace he laid her down, poor thing . . .

---

[75] halter—rope with a noose used for execution by hanging.

then, what came next, what horror we beheld!
He rips off her brooches, the long gold pins
holding her robes—and lifting them high,
looking straight up into the point,
1405   he digs them down the sockets of his eyes, crying, "You,
you'll see no more the pain I suffered, all the pain I caused!
Too long you looked on the ones you never should have seen,
blind to the ones you longed to see, to know! Blind
from this hour on! Blind in the darkness—blind!"
1410   His voice like a dirge, rising, over and over
raising the pins, raking them down his eyes,
And at each stroke blood spurts from the roots,
splashing his beard, a swirl of it, nerves and clots—
black hail of blood pulsing, gushing down.
1415   These are the griefs that burst upon them both,
coupling[76] man and woman. The joy they had so lately,
the fortune of their old ancestral house
was deep joy indeed. Now, in this one day,
wailing, madness and doom, death, disgrace,
1420   all the griefs in the world that you can name,
all are theirs forever.

Leader.   Oh poor man, the misery—
has he any rest from pain now? [*A voice within, in torment.*]

Messenger.   He's shouting,
"Loose the bolts, someone, show me to all of Thebes!
My father's murderer, my mother's—"
1425   No, I can't repeat it, it's unholy.
Now he'll tear himself from his native earth,
not linger, curse the house with his own curse.
But he needs strength, and a guide to lead him on.
This is sickness more than he can bear. [*The palace doors open.*]
                                              Look,
1430   he'll show you himself. The great doors are opening—
You are about to see a sight, a horror
even his mortal enemy would pity.

[*Enter* Oedipus, *blinded, led by a boy. He stands at the palace step as if surveying his people once again.*]

---

76 coupling—uniting in grief (as well as sexually).

Chorus.   O the terror—
the suffering, for all the world to see,
the worst terror that ever met my eyes.
1435   What madness swept over you? What god,
what dark power leapt beyond all bounds,
beyond belief, to crush your wretched life?—
godforsaken, cursed by the gods!
I pity you but I can't bear to look.
1440   I've much to ask, so much to learn,
so much fascinates my eyes,
but you . . . I shudder at the sight.

Oedipus.   Oh, Ohhh—
the agony! I am agony—
where am I going? where on earth?
1445   where does all this agony hurl me?
where's my voice?—
             winging, swept away on a dark tide—
My destiny, my dark power, what a leap you made!

Chorus. To the depths of terror, too dark to hear, to see.

1450   **Oedipus.** Dark, horror of darkness
my darkness, drowning, swirling around me
crashing wave on wave—unspeakable, irresistible
           headwind, fatal harbor! Oh again,
the misery, all at once, over and over
1455   the stabbing daggers, stab of memory
raking me insane.

Chorus.   No wonder you suffer
twice over, the pain of your wounds,
the lasting grief of pain.

Oedipus.   Dear friend, still here?
Standing by me, still with a care for me,
1460   the blind man? Such compassion,
           loyal to the last. Oh it's you,
I know you're here, dark as it is
I'd know you anywhere, your voice—
it's yours, clearly yours.

Chorus.   Dreadful, what you've done . . .
1465   how could you bear it, gouging out your eyes?
What superhuman power drove you on?

Oedipus. Apollo, friends, Apollo—
he ordained my agonies—these, my pains on pains!
But the hand that struck my eyes was mine,
1470   mine alone—no one else—
I did it all myself!
What good were eyes to me?
Nothing I could see could bring me joy.

Chorus. No, no, exactly as you say.

Oedipus.   What can I ever see?
1475   What love, what call of the heart
can touch my ears with joy? Nothing, friends.
Take me away, far, far from Thebes,
quickly, cast me away, my friends—
this great murderous ruin, this man cursed to heaven,
1480   the man the deathless gods hate most of all!

Chorus. Pitiful, you suffer so, you understand so much . . .
I wish you'd never known.

Oedipus.   Die, die—
whoever he was that day in the wilds
who cut my ankles free of the ruthless pins,
1485   he pulled me clear of death, he saved my life
for this, this kindness—
Curse him, kill him!
If I'd died then, I'd never have dragged myself,
my loved ones through such hell.

1490 **Chorus.** Oh if only . . . would to god.

Oedipus.   I'd never have come to this,
my father's murderer—never been branded
mother's husband, all men see me now! Now,
loathed by the gods, son of the mother I defiled
coupling in my father's bed, spawning lives in the loins[77]
1495   that spawned my wretched life. What grief can crown this grief?
It's mine alone, my destiny—I am Oedipus!

Chorus. How can I say you've chosen for the best?
Better to die than be alive and blind.

Oedipus. What I did was best—don't lecture me,
1500   no more advice. I, with *my* eyes,

---

[77] loins—sexual organs.

how could I look my father in the eyes
when I go down to death? Or mother, so abused . . .
I've done such things to the two of them,
crimes too huge for hanging. Worse yet,
1505   the sight of my children, born as they were born,
how could I long to look into their eyes?
No, not with these eyes of mine, never.
Not this city either, her high towers,
the sacred glittering images of her gods—
1510   I am misery! I, her best son, reared
as no other son of Thebes was ever reared,
I've stripped myself, I gave the command myself.
All men must cast away the great blasphemer,
the curse now brought to light by the gods,
1515   the son of Laius—I, my father's son!
Now I've exposed my guilt, horrendous guilt,
could I train a level glance on you, my countrymen?
Impossible! No, if I could just block off my ears,
the springs of hearing, I would stop at nothing—
1520   I'd wall up my **loathsome**[78] body like a prison,
blind to the sound of life, not just the sight.
Oblivion—what a blessing . . .
for the mind to dwell a world away from pain.
O Cithaeron, why did you give me shelter?
1525   Why didn't you take me, crush my life out on the spot?
I'd never have revealed my birth to all mankind.
O Polybus, Corinth, the old house of my fathers,
so I believed—what a handsome prince you raised—
under the skin, what sickness to the core.
1530   Look at me! Born of outrage, outrage to the core.
O triple roads—it all comes back, the secret,
dark ravine, and the oaks closing in
where the three roads join . . .
You drank my father's blood, my own blood
1535   spilled by my own hands—you still remember me?
What things you saw me do? Then I came here
and did them all once more! Marriages! O marriage,

---

[78] **loathsome**—disgusting.

you gave me birth, and once you brought me into the world
you brought my sperm rising back, springing to light
1540   fathers, brothers, sons—one murderous breed—
brides, wives, mothers. The blackest things
a man can do, I have done them all! No more—
it's wrong to name what's wrong to do. Quickly,
for the love of god, hide me somewhere,
1545   kill me, hurl me into the sea
where you can never look on me again.

[*Beckoning to the* Chorus *as they shrink away.*]

                                 Closer,

it's all right. Touch the man of sorrow.
Do. Don't be afraid. My troubles are mine
and I am the only man alive who can sustain them.

[*Enter* Creon *from the palace, attended by palace guards.*]

1550 **Leader.** Put your requests to Creon. Here he is,
just when we need him. He'll have a plan, he'll act.
Now that he's the sole defense of the country
in your place.

Oedipus.   Oh no, what can I say to him?
How can I ever hope to win his trust?
1555   I wronged him so, just now, in every way.
You must see that—I was so wrong, so wrong.

Creon. I haven't come to mock you, Oedipus,
or to criticize your former failings. [*Turning to the guards.*]
                              You there,
have you lost all respect for human feeling?
1560   At least revere the Sun, the holy fire
that keeps us all alive. Never expose a thing
of guilt and holy dread so great it appalls
the earth, the rain from heaven, the light of day!
Get him into the halls—quickly as you can.
1565   Piety demands no less. Kindred alone
should see a kinsman's shame. This is obscene.

Oedipus. Please, in god's name . . . you wipe my fears away,
coming so generously to me, the worst of men.
Do one thing more, for your sake, not mine.
1570 **Creon.** What do you want? Why so **insistent**?[79]

---

[79] **insistent**—demanding.

Oedipus. Drive me out of the land at once, far from sight,
where I can never hear a human voice.

Creon. I'd have done that already, I promise you.
First I wanted the god to clarify my duties.

1575 **Oedipus.** The god? His command was clear, every word:
death for the father-killer, the curse—
he said destroy me!

Creon. So he did. Still, in such a crisis
it's better to ask precisely what to do. So miserable—

1580 **Oedipus.** You would consult the god about a man like me?

Creon. By all means. And this time, I assume,
even you will obey the god's decrees.

Oedipus.   I will.
I will. And you, I command you—I beg you . . .
the woman inside, bury her as you see fit.

1585 It's the only decent thing,
to give your own the last rites. As for me,
never condemn the city of my fathers
to house my body, not while I'm alive, no,
let me live on the mountains, on Cithaeron,

1590 my favorite haunt, I have made it famous.
Mother and father marked out that rock
to be my everlasting tomb—buried alive.
Let me die there, where they tried to kill me.
Oh but this I know: no sickness can destroy me,

1595 nothing can. I would never have been saved
from death—I have been saved
for something great and terrible, something strange.
Well let my destiny come and take me on its way!
About my children, Creon, the boys at least,

1600 don't burden yourself. They're men;
wherever they go, they'll find the means to live.
But my two daughters, my poor helpless girls,
clustering at our table, never without me
hovering near them . . . whatever I touched,

1605 they always had their share. Take care of them,
I beg you. Wait, better—permit me, would you?
Just to touch them with my hands and take
our fill of tears. Please . . . my king.

Grant it, with all your noble heart.
1610   If I could hold them, just once, I'd think
I had them with me, like the early days
when I could see their eyes.

[Antigone *and* Ismene, *two small children, are led in from the palace by a nurse.*]

                 What's that?
O god! Do I really hear you sobbing?—
my two children. Creon, you've pitied me?
1615   Sent me my darling girls, my own flesh and blood!
Am I right?

Creon.   Yes, it's my doing.
I know the joy they gave you all these years,
the joy you must feel now.

Oedipus.   Bless you, Creon!
May god watch over you for this kindness,
1620   better than he ever guarded me. Children, where are you?
Here, come quickly—

[*Groping for* Antigone *and* Ismene, *who approach their father cautiously, then embrace him.*]

                 Come to these hands of mine,
your brother's hands, your own father's hands
that served his once bright eyes so well—
that made them blind. Seeing nothing, children,
1625   knowing nothing, I became your father,
I fathered you in the soil that gave me life.
How I weep for you—I cannot see you now . . .
just thinking of all your days to come, the bitterness,
the life that rough mankind will thrust upon you.
1630   Where are the public gatherings you can join,
the banquets of the clans? Home you'll come,
in tears, cut off from the sight of it all,
the brilliant rites unfinished.
And when you reach perfection, ripe for marriage,
1635   who will he be, my dear ones? Risking all
to shoulder the curse that weighs down my parents,
yes and you too—that wounds us all together.
What more misery could you want?
Your father killed his father, sowed his mother,
1640   one, one and the selfsame womb sprang you—

he cropped the very roots of his existence.
Such disgrace, and you must bear it all!
Who will marry you then? Not a man on earth.
Your doom is clear: you'll wither away to nothing,
1645   single, without a child. [*Turning to* Creon.]

                        Oh Creon,
you are the only father they have now . . .
we who brought them into the world
are gone, both gone at a stroke—
Don't let them go begging, abandoned,
1650   women without men. Your own flesh and blood!
Never bring them down to the level of my pains.
Pity them. Look at them, so young, so vulnerable,
shorn of everything—you're their only hope.
Promise me, noble Creon, touch my hand.

[*Reaching toward* Creon, *who draws back.*]

1655   You, little ones, if you were old enough
to understand, there is much I'd tell you.
Now, as it is, I'd have you say a prayer.
Pray for life, my children,
live where you are free to grow and season.
1660   Pray god you find a better life than mine,
the father who begot you.

Creon.   Enough.
You've wept enough. Into the palace now.

Oedipus. I must, but I find it very hard.

Creon. Time is the great healer, you will see.

1665 **Oedipus.** I am going—you know on what condition?

Creon. Tell me. I'm listening.

Oedipus. Drive me out of Thebes, in exile.

Creon. Not I. Only the gods can give you that.

Oedipus. Surely the gods hate me so much—

1670 **Creon.** You'll get your wish at once.

Oedipus.   You consent?

Creon. I try to say what I mean; it's my habit.

Oedipus. Then take me away. It's time.

Creon. Come along, let go of the children.

Oedipus. No—

don't take them away from me, not now! No no no!

[*Clutching his daughters as the guards wrench them loose and take them through the palace doors.*]

1675 **Creon.** Still the king, the master of all things?

No more: here your power ends.

None of your power follows you through life.

[*Exit Oedipus and Creon to the palace. The Chorus comes forward to address the audience directly.*]

Chorus. People of Thebes, my countrymen, look on Oedipus.

He solved the famous riddle with his brilliance,

1680 he rose to power, a man beyond all power.

Who could behold his greatness without envy?

Now what a black sea of terror has overwhelmed him.

Now as we keep our watch and wait the final day,

count no man happy till he dies, free of pain at last.

[*Exit in procession.*]

UNDERSTANDING THE PLAY

Lines 1–572

1. What message does Creon bring back from the oracle of Delphi?

2. What function is served by the Chorus in lines 167–244? lines 526–572?

3. In his speech beginning at line 245, how does Oedipus propose to identify Laius's killer?

4. Why won't Tiresias at first reveal what he knows? What causes him to change his mind?

5. What is your impression of Oedipus at this point in the play?

Lines 573–997

1. In his speech beginning in line 651, how does Creon argue that he has not conspired against Oedipus?

2. What role does the Chorus take in the quarrel between Oedipus and Creon?

3. How does Jocasta attempt to quiet Oedipus's fears? How does he react?

4. Why does Oedipus feel that the account of the surviving member of Laius's party is crucial?

5. What attitude toward prophecy is expressed by the Chorus in lines 985–990?

Lines 998–1214

1. Why are Oedipus and Jocasta relieved by the news of the death of Polybus?

2. What information brought by the Messenger shocks Oedipus?

3. At what point does Jocasta become convinced of Oedipus's real identity?

4. In lines 1183–1194, what does Oedipus seem to believe about his parentage?

5. How does the Chorus respond to Oedipus at this point?

Lines 1215–1684

1. Why is the Shepherd unwilling to talk? What compels him?

2. Why did Oedipus choose to blind himself rather than commit suicide?

3. What future does Oedipus anticipate for his daughters?

4. How does Creon respond to Oedipus's request for exile?

5. At the play's end, what moral does the Chorus see in the story of Oedipus?

ANALYZING THE PLAY

1. The conflict in a play is the struggle between opposing forces that gives movement to the dramatic plot. What is the fundamental conflict in *Oedipus the King*?

2. The climax—or crisis—in the plot is the turning point in the struggle when one of the contending forces gets the upper hand. In *Oedipus the King,* where does this turning point occur?

3. According to Aristotle, a tragic hero is one whose fall is brought about "not by vice and depravity, but by some error or frailty." What faults in his character cause Oedipus's fall?

4. What attitude toward religious belief is reflected in this play?

Euripides ▶

Medea

BY EURIPIDES

Greek theater was rooted in religious ritual and was a vital forum for exploring important political and social problems. (For general background on Greek drama, see the introduction for Oedipus the King, page 2.) Between 500 and 400 B.C., Greek drama reached its height in the works of three Athenian playwrights, Aeschylus, Sophocles, and Euripides.

An Unorthodox Dramatist

Euripides (480–406 B.C.), the youngest of the three, differed sharply from his older contemporaries in his life and career. In addition to their work as dramatists, Aeschylus and Sophocles were both active in Athenian public life; according to tradition, Euripides was morose, a loner. The two older playwrights were also much more successful professionally than Euripides, winning many more victories in the dramatic competitions that were a central part of theater in Athens. Euripides' plays were far less popular with his contemporaries. His real fame as a dramatist did not begin until after his death. Euripides' unpopularity in his own time was partly because of his unorthodox views. He was skeptical about Greek religion and critical of Athenian society. Aeschylus and Sophocles examined how large questions of religion and morality affected the community. Euripides was far more interested in the emotions and their effect on individual character. He also concerned himself with those marginalized by Greek society, such as women, outsiders (like the foreigner Medea), and victims (like the Trojan women).

Jason and Medea

The background of Euripides' Medea is the story of Jason. He was the son of the rightful king of Iolcus in northern Greece, but his uncle Pelias had seized the throne. Pelias sent Jason on what he intended would be a fatal quest for the Golden Fleece. Jason and his companions sailed on board the ship Argo to the distant land of Colchis in search of this great treasure. After many adventures, they reached their goal. There Jason met Medea, daughter of the king of Colchis. Medea fell in love with Jason and, because she was skilled in witchcraft, was able to help him perform the various tasks her father required before he would give up the Golden Fleece. When the king still declined to surrender his treasure, she helped Jason steal it and fled with him on the Argo, taking her brother along. When her father pursued them, Medea murdered and dismembered her brother, throwing the pieces of his corpse into the sea to force her father to stop and gather up his son's body.

When Jason and Medea reached Iolcus, she helped him revenge himself on his usurping uncle. She told Pelias's daughters they could rejuvenate their father by dismembering his body and boiling it in a pot with magical herbs. Persuaded by a magical demonstration Medea provided, they killed their father, cut him up, and boiled the pieces. Outraged by this deed, the people of Iolcus exiled Jason and Medea, who went to Corinth, where they settled and raised two sons. When the play opens, Jason has decided to marry the daughter of Creon, king of Corinth.

CHARACTERS

Medea, princess of Colchis and wife of Jason
Jason, son of Aeson, king of Iolcus
Two **children** of Medea and Jason
Creon, king of Corinth
Aegeus, king of Athens

Nurse to Medea
Tutor to Medea's children
Messenger
Chorus of Corinthian Women

SCENE: In front of Medea's house in Corinth. Enter from the house Medea's Nurse.

Nurse. How I wish the *Argo* never had reached the land
Of Colchis, skimming through the blue Symplegades,[1]
Nor ever had fallen in the glades of Pelion[2]
The smitten fir-tree to furnish oars for the hands
5 Of heroes who in Pelias' name attempted
The Golden Fleece! For then my mistress Medea
Would not have sailed for the towers of the land of Iolcus,
Her heart on fire with passionate love for Jason;
Nor would she have persuaded the daughters of Pelias
10 To kill their father, and now be living here
In Corinth with her husband and children. She gave
Pleasure to the people of her land of exile,
And she herself helped Jason in every way.
This is indeed the greatest salvation of all—
15 For the wife not to stand apart from the husband.
But now there's hatred everywhere, Love is diseased.
For, deserting his own children and my mistress,
Jason has taken a royal wife to his bed,
The daughter of the ruler of this land, Creon.
20 And poor Medea is slighted, and cries aloud on the

---

[1] Symplegades—the "clashing rocks," one of the obstacles faced by the *Argo* on its voyage to Colchis. Located at the entrance of the Black Sea, on whose shores Colchis lay, the Symplegades were two rocks that periodically crashed together, making passage between them difficult.

[2] Pelion—mountain in Greece whose trees provided wood to build the *Argo*.

Vows they made to each other, the right hands clasped
In eternal promise. She calls upon the gods to witness
What sort of return Jason has made to her love.
She lies without food and gives herself up to suffering,
25   Wasting away every moment of the day in tears.
So it has gone since she knew herself slighted by him.
Not stirring an eye, not moving her face from the ground,
No more than either a rock or surging sea water
She listens when she is given friendly advice.
30   Except that sometimes she twists back her white neck and
Moans to herself, calling out on her father's name,
And her land, and her home betrayed when she came away with
A man who now is determined to dishonor her.
Poor creature, she has discovered by her sufferings
35   What it means to one not to have lost one's own country.
She has turned from the children and does not like to see them.
I am afraid she may think of some dreadful thing,
For her heart is violent. She will never put up with
The treatment she is getting. I know and fear her
40   Lest she may sharpen a sword and thrust to the heart,
Stealing into the palace where the bed is made,
Or even kill the king and the new-wedded groom,
And thus bring a greater misfortune on herself.
She's a strange woman. I know it won't be easy
45   To make an enemy of her and come off best.
But here the children come. They have finished playing.
They have no thought at all of their mother's trouble.
Indeed it is not usual for the young to grieve.

[*Enter from the right the slave who is the* Tutor *to* Medea's *two small children.
The* children *follow him.*]

Tutor. You old retainer of my mistress' household,
50   Why are you standing here all alone in front of the
Gates and moaning to yourself over your misfortune?
Medea could not wish you to leave her alone.

Nurse. Old man, and guardian of the children of Jason,
If one is a good servant, it's a terrible thing
55   When one's master's luck is out; it goes to one's heart.
So I myself have got into such a state of grief

That a longing stole over me to come outside here
And tell the earth and air of my mistress' sorrows.

Tutor. Has the poor lady not yet given up her crying?

60 **Nurse.** Given up? She's at the start, not halfway through her tears.

Tutor. Poor fool—if I may call my mistress such a name—
How ignorant she is of trouble more to come.

Nurse. What do you mean, old man? You needn't fear to speak.

Tutor. Nothing. I take back the words which I used just now.

65 **Nurse.** Don't, by your beard, hide this from me, your fellow-servant.
If need be, I'll keep quiet about what you tell me.

Tutor. I heard a person saying, while I myself seemed
Not to be paying attention, when I was at the place
Where the old draught-players[3] sit, by the holy fountain,

70 That Creon, ruler of the land, intends to drive
These children and their mother in exile from Corinth.
But whether what he said is really true or not
I do not know. I pray that it may not be true.

Nurse. And will Jason put up with it that his children

75 Should suffer so, though he's no friend to their mother?

Tutor. Old ties give place to new ones. As for Jason, he
No longer has a feeling for this house of ours.

Nurse. It's black indeed for us, when we add new to old
Sorrows before even the present sky has cleared.

80 **Tutor.** But you be silent, and keep all this to yourself.
It is not the right time to tell our mistress of it.

Nurse. Do you hear, children, what a father he is to you?
I wish he were dead—but no, he is still my master.
Yet certainly he has proved unkind to his dear ones.

85 **Tutor.** What's strange in that? Have you only just discovered
That everyone loves himself more than his neighbor?
Some have good reason, others get something out of it.
So Jason neglects his children for the new bride.

Nurse. Go indoors, children. That will be the best thing.

90 And you, keep them to themselves as much as possible.
Don't bring them near their mother in her angry mood.
For I've seen her already blazing her eyes at them
As though she meant some mischief and I am sure that

---

[3] draught-players—players of a board game like checkers.

She'll not stop raging until she has struck at someone.
95   May it be an enemy and not a friend she hurts!

[Medea *is heard inside the house.*]

Medea. Ah, wretch! Ah, lost in my sufferings,
I wish, I wish I might die.

Nurse. What did I say, dear children? Your mother
Frets her heart and frets it to anger.
100   Run away quickly into the house,
And keep well out of her sight.
Don't go anywhere near, but be careful
of the wildness and bitter nature
Of that proud mind.
105   Go now! Run quickly indoors.
It is clear that she soon will put lightning
In that cloud of her cries that is rising
With a passion increasing. O, what will she do,
Proud-hearted and not to be checked on her course,
110   A soul bitten into with wrong?

[*The* Tutor *takes the children into the house.*]

Medea. Ah, I have suffered
What should be wept for bitterly. I hate you,
Children of a hateful mother. I curse you
And your father. Let the whole house crash.

115 **Nurse.** Ah, I pity you, you poor creature.
How can your children share in their father's
Wickedness? Why do you hate them? Oh children,
How much I fear that something may happen!
Great people's tempers are terrible, always
120   Having their own way, seldom checked,
Dangerous they shift from mood to mood.
How much better to have been accustomed
To live on equal terms with one's neighbors.
I would like to be safe and grow old in a
125   Humble way. What is moderate sounds best,
Also in practice *is* best for everyone.
Greatness brings no profit to people.
God indeed, when in anger, brings
Greater ruin to great men's houses.

[*Enter, on the right, a* Chorus *of Corinthian women. They have come to inquire about Medea and to attempt to console her.*]

130 **Chorus.** I heard the voice, I heard the cry
      Of Colchis' wretched daughter.
      Tell me, mother, is she not yet
      At rest? Within the double gates
      Of the court I heard her cry. I am sorry
135   For the sorrow of this home. O, say, what has happened?

Nurse. There is no home. It's over and done with.
      Her husband holds fast to his royal wedding,
      While she, my mistress, cries out her eyes
      There in her room, and takes no warmth from
140   Any word of any friend.

Medea. Oh, I wish
      That lightning from heaven would split my head open.
      Oh, what use have I now for life?
      I would find my release in death
145   And leave hateful existence behind me.

Chorus. O God and Earth and Heaven!
      Did you hear what a cry was that
      Which the sad wife sings?
      Poor foolish one, why should you long
150   For that appalling rest?
      The final end of death comes fast.
      No need to pray for that.
      Suppose your man gives honor
      To another woman's bed.
155   It often happens. Don't be hurt.
      God will be your friend in this.
      You must not waste away
      Grieving too much for him who shared your bed.

Medea. Great Themis, lady Artemis,[4] behold
160   The things I suffer, though I made him promise,
      My hateful husband. I pray that I may see him,
      Him and his bride and all their palace shattered
      For the wrong they dare to do me without cause.

---

[4] Themis . . . Artemis—Themis was an earth goddess associated with the moral order of nature; the Nurse later calls her "the goddess of Promises." Artemis, the goddess who protected wild beasts, was sometimes linked with Themis.

Oh, my father! Oh, my country! In what dishonor
165   I left you, killing my own brother for it.

Nurse. Do you hear what she says, and how she cries
On Themis, the goddess of Promises, and on Zeus,
Whom we believe to be the Keeper of Oaths?
Of this I am sure, that no small thing
170   Will appease my mistress' anger.

Chorus. Will she come into our presence?
Will she listen when we are speaking
To the words we say?
I wish she might relax her rage
175   And temper of her heart.
My willingness to help will never
Be wanting to my friends.
But go inside and bring her
Out of the house to us,
180   And speak kindly to her: hurry,
Before she wrongs her own.
This passion of hers moves to something great.

Nurse. I will, but I doubt if I'll manage
To win my mistress over.
185   But still I'll attempt it to please you.
Such a look she will flash on her servants
If any comes near with a message,
Like a lioness guarding her cubs.
It is right, I think, to consider
190   Both stupid and lacking in foresight
Those poets of old who wrote songs
For revels and dinners and banquets,
Pleasant sounds for men living at ease;
But none of them all has discovered
195   How to put to an end with their singing
Or musical instruments grief,
Bitter grief, from which death and disaster
Cheat the hopes of a house. Yet how good
If music could cure men of this! But why raise
200   To no purpose the voice at a banquet? For *there* is
Already abundance of pleasure for men
With a joy of its own.

[*The* Nurse *goes into the house.*]

Chorus. I heard a shriek that is laden with sorrow.
    Shrilling out her hard grief she cries out
205   Upon him who betrayed both her bed and her marriage.
    Wronged, she calls on the gods,
    On the justice of Zeus, the oath sworn,
    Which brought her away
    To the opposite shore of the Greeks
210   Through the gloomy salt straits to the gateway
    Of the salty unlimited sea.

[Medea, *attended by servants, comes out of the house.*]

Medea. Women of Corinth, I have come outside to you
    Lest you should be indignant with me; for I know
    That many people are overproud, some when alone,
215   And others when in company. And those who live
    Quietly, as I do, get a bad reputation.
    For a just judgment is not evident in the eyes
    When a man at first sight hates another, before
    Learning his character, being in no way injured;
220   And a foreigner especially must adapt himself.
    I'd not approve of even a fellow-countryman
    Who by pride and want of manners offends his neighbors.
    But on me this thing has fallen so unexpectedly,
    It has broken my heart. I am finished. I let go
225   All my life's joy. My friends, I only want to die.
    It was everything to me to think well of one man,
    And he, my own husband, has turned out wholly vile.
    Of all things which are living and can form a judgment
    We women are the most unfortunate creatures.
230   Firstly, with an excess of wealth it is required
    For us to buy a husband and take for our bodies
    A master; for not to take one is even worse.
    And now the question is serious whether we take
    A good or bad one; for there is no easy escape
235   For a woman, nor can she say no to her marriage.
    She arrives among new modes of behavior and manners,
    And needs prophetic power, unless she has learned at home,
    How best to manage him who shares the bed with her.
    And if we work out all this well and carefully,

240 And the husband lives with us and lightly bears his yoke,[5]
Then life is enviable. If not, I'd rather die.
A man, when he's tired of the company in his home,
Goes out of the house and puts an end to his boredom
And turns to a friend or companion of his own age.
245 But we are forced to keep our eyes on one alone.
What they say of us is that we have a peaceful time
Living at home, while they do the fighting in war.
How wrong they are! I would very much rather stand
Three times in the front of battle than bear one child.
250 Yet what applies to me does not apply to you.
You have a country. Your family home is here.
You enjoy life and the company of your friends.
But I am deserted, a refugee, thought nothing of
By my husband—something he won in a foreign land.
255 I have no mother or brother, nor any relation
With whom I can take refuge in this sea of woe.
This much then is the service I would beg from you:
If I can find the means or devise any scheme
To pay my husband back for what he has done to me—
260 Him and his father-in-law and the girl who married him—
Just to keep silent. For in other ways a woman
Is full of fear, defenseless, dreads the sight of cold
Steel; but, when once she is wronged in the matter of love,
No other soul can hold so many thoughts of blood.
265 **Chorus.** This I will promise. You are in the right, Medea,
In paying your husband back. I am not surprised at you
For being sad.
But look! I see our King Creon
Approaching. He will tell us of some new plan.
[*Enter, from the right,* Creon, *with attendants.*]
270 **Creon.** You, with that angry look, so set against your husband,
Medea, I order you to leave my territories
An exile, and take along with you your two children,
And not to waste time doing it. It is my decree,
And I will see it done. I will not return home
275 Until you are cast from the boundaries of my land.

---

[5] yoke—link or tie, as in a cooperative relationship such as marriage.

Medea. Oh, this is the end for me. I am utterly lost.
Now I am in the full force of the storm of hate
And have no harbor from ruin to reach easily.
Yet still, in spite of it all, I'll ask the question:
280   What is your reason, Creon, for banishing me?

Creon. I am afraid of you—why should I **dissemble**[6] it?—
Afraid that you may injure my daughter mortally.
Many things accumulate to support my feeling.
You are a clever woman, **versed**[7] in evil arts,
285   And are angry at having lost your husband's love.
I hear that you are threatening, so they tell me,
To do something against my daughter and Jason
And me, too. I shall take my precautions first.
I tell you, I prefer to earn your hatred now
290   Than to be soft-hearted and afterward regret it.

Medea. This is not the first time, Creon. Often previously
Through being considered clever I have suffered much.
A person of sense ought never to have his children
Brought up to be more clever than the average.
295   For, apart from cleverness bringing them no profit,
It will make them objects of envy and ill-will.
If you put new ideas before the eyes of fools
They'll think you foolish and worthless into the bargain;
And if you are thought superior to those who have
300   Some reputation for learning, you will become hated.
I have some knowledge myself of how this happens;
For being clever, I find that some will envy me,
Others object to me. Yet all my cleverness
Is not so much.
                  Well, then, are you frightened, Creon,
305   That I should harm you? There is no need. It is not
My way to **transgress**[8] the authority of a king.
How have you injured me? You gave your daughter away
To the man you wanted. Oh, certainly I hate
My husband, but you, I think, have acted wisely;

---

[6] **dissemble**—disguise.

[7] **versed**—skilled.

[8] **transgress**—act in violation of.

310	Nor do I grudge it you that your affairs go well.
	May the marriage be a lucky one! Only let me
	Live in this land. For even though I have been wronged,
	I will not raise my voice, but submit to my betters.
	Creon. What you say sounds gentle enough. Still in my heart
315	I greatly dread that you are plotting some evil,
	And therefore I trust you even less than before.
	A sharp-tempered woman, or, for that matter, a man,
	Is easier to deal with than the clever type
	Who holds her tongue. No. You must go. No need for more
320	Speeches. The thing is fixed. By no manner of means
	Shall you, an enemy of mine, stay in my country.
	Medea. I beg you. By your knees,[9] by your new-wedded girl.
	Creon. Your words are wasted. You will never persuade me.
	Medea. Will you drive me out, and give no heed to my prayers?
325	**Creon.** I will, for I love my family more than you.
	Medea. O my country! How bitterly now I remember you!
	Creon. I love my country too—next after my children.
	Medea. Oh what an evil to men is passionate love!
	Creon. That would depend on the luck that goes along with it.
330	**Medea.** O God, do not forget who is the cause of this!
	Creon. Go. It is no use. Spare me the pain of forcing you.
	Medea. I'm spared no pain. I lack no pain to be spared me.
	Creon. Then you'll be removed by force by one of my men.
	Medea. No, Creon, not that! But do listen, I beg you.
335	**Creon.** Woman, you seem to want to create a disturbance.
	Medea. I *will* go into exile. *This* is not what I beg for.
	Creon. Why then this violence and clinging to my hand?
	Medea. Allow me to remain here just for this one day,
	So I may consider where to live in my exile,
340	And look for support for my children, since their father
	Chooses to make no kind of provision for them.
	Have pity on them! You have children of your own.
	It is natural for you to look kindly on them.
	For myself I do not mind if I go into exile.
345	It is the children being in trouble that I mind.

---

[9] knees—In ancient Greece the custom was to clasp the knees of someone from whom a favor was begged.

Creon. There is nothing tyrannical about my nature,
And by showing mercy I have often been the loser.
Even now I know that I am making a mistake.
All the same you shall have your will. But this I tell you,

350   That if the light of heaven tomorrow shall see you,
You and your children in the confines of my land,
You die. This word I have spoken is firmly fixed.
But now, if you must stay, stay for this day alone.
For in it you can do none of the things I fear.

[*Exit* Creon *with his attendants.*]

355   **Chorus.** Oh, unfortunate one! Oh, cruel!
Where will you turn? Who will help you?
What house or what land to preserve you
From ill can you find?
Medea, a god has thrown suffering

360   Upon you in waves of despair.

     Medea. Things have gone badly every way. No doubt of that
But not these things this far, and don't imagine so.
There are still trials to come for the new-wedded pair,
And for their relations pain that will mean something.

365   Do you think that I would ever have fawned on[10] that man
Unless I had some end to gain or profit in it?
I would not even have spoken or touched him with my hands.
But he has got to such a pitch of foolishness
That, though he could have made nothing of all my plans

370   By exiling me, he has given me this one day
To stay here, and in this I will make dead bodies
Of three of my enemies—father, the girl, and my husband.
I have many ways of death which I might suit to them,
And do not know, friends, which one to take in hand;

375   Whether to set fire underneath their bridal mansion,
Or sharpen a sword and thrust it to the heart,
Stealing into the palace where the bed is made.
There is just one obstacle to this. If I am caught
Breaking into the house and scheming against it,

380   I shall die, and give my enemies cause for laughter.

---

[10] fawned on—tried to win affection by flattery and shows of affection.

It is best to go by the straight road, the one in which
I am most skilled, and make away with them by poison.
So be it then.
And now suppose them dead. What town will receive me?
385   What friend will offer me a refuge in his land,
Or the guaranty[11] of his house and save my own life?
There is none. So I must wait a little time yet,
And if some sure defense should then appear for me,
In craft and silence I will set about this murder.
390   But if my fate should drive me on without help,
Even though death is certain, I will take the sword
Myself and kill, and steadfastly advance to crime.
It shall not be—I swear it by her, my mistress,
Whom most I honor and have chosen as partner,
395   Hecate,[12] who dwells in the recesses of my hearth—
That any man shall be glad to have injured me.
Bitter I will make their marriage for them and mournful,
Bitter the alliance and the driving me out of the land.
Ah, come, Medea, in your plotting and scheming
400   Leave nothing untried of all those things which you know.
Go forward to the dreadful act. The test has come
For resolution. You see how you are treated. Never
Shall you be mocked by Jason's Corinthian wedding,
Whose father was noble, whose grandfather Helius.[13]
405   You have the skill. What is more, you were born a woman,
And women, though most helpless in doing good deeds,
Are of every evil the cleverest of contrivers.

Chorus. Flow backward to your sources, sacred rivers,
And let the world's great order be reversed.
410   It is the thoughts of *men* that are deceitful,
Their pledges that are loose.
Story shall now turn my condition to a fair one,
Women are paid their due.
No more shall evil-sounding fame be theirs.

---

[11] guaranty—security.

[12] Hecate—goddess who was a patron of witches.

[13] Helius—sun god.

415	Cease now, you muses of the ancient singers,
	To tell the tale of my unfaithfulness;
	For not on us did Phoebus,[14] lord of music,
	Bestow the lyre's divine
	Power, for otherwise I should have sung an answer
420	To the other sex. Long time
	Has much to tell of us, and much of them.

You sailed away from your father's home,
With a heart on fire you passed
The double rocks of the sea.

425 And now in a foreign country
You have lost your rest in a widowed bed,
And are driven forth, a refugee
In dishonor from the land.

Good faith has gone, and no more remains

430 In great Greece a sense of shame.
It has flown away to the sky.
No father's house for a haven
Is at hand for you now, and another queen
Of your bed has dispossessed you and

435 Is mistress of your home.

[*Enter* Jason, *with attendants.*]

Jason. This is not the first occasion that I have noticed
How hopeless it is to deal with a stubborn temper.
For, with reasonable submission to our ruler's will,
You might have lived in this land and kept your home.

440 As it is you are going to be exiled for your loose speaking.
Not that I mind myself. You are free to continue
Telling everyone that Jason is a worthless man.
But as to your talk about the king, consider
Yourself most lucky that exile is your punishment.

445 I, for my part, have always tried to calm down
The anger of the king, and wished you to remain.
But you will not give up your folly, continually
Speaking ill of him, and so you are going to be banished.

---

[14] Phoebus—the god Apollo, patron of artists. His symbol was the lyre, an ancient stringed instrument.

All the same, and in spite of your conduct, I'll not desert

450 My friends, but have come to make some provision for you,
So that you and the children may not be penniless
Or in need of anything in exile. Certainly
Exile brings many troubles with it. And even
If you hate me, I cannot think badly of you.

455 **Medea.** O coward in every way—that is what I call you,
With bitterest reproach for your lack of manliness,
You have come, you, my worst enemy, have come to me!
It is not an example of overconfidence
Or of boldness thus to look your friends in the face,

460 Friends you have injured—no it is the worst of all
Human diseases, shamelessness. But you did well
To come, for I can speak ill of you and lighten
My heart, and you will suffer while you are listening.
And first I will begin from what happened first.

465 I saved your life, and every Greek knows I saved it,
Who was a shipmate of yours aboard the *Argo*,
When you were sent to control the bulls that breathed fire[15]
And yoke them, and when you would sow that deadly field.
Also that snake,[16] who encircled with his many folds

470 The Golden Fleece and guarded it and never slept,
I killed, and so gave you the safety of the light.
And I myself betrayed my father and my home,
And came with you to Pelias' land of Iolcus.
And then, showing more willingness to help than wisdom,

475 I killed him, Pelias, with a most dreadful death
At his own daughters' hands, and took away your fear.
This is how I behaved to you, you wretched man,
And you forsook me, took another bride to bed,
Though you had children; for if that had not been,

480 You would have had an excuse for another wedding.
Faith in your word has gone. Indeed, I cannot tell
Whether you think the gods whose names you swore by then
Have ceased to rule and that new standards are set up,
Since you must know you have broken your word to me.

---

[15] bulls that breathed fire—The first labor demanded by the king of Colchis was that Jason yoke two fire-breathing bulls. Medea helped him by covering his body with a magical ointment that protected him from the bulls' fiery breath.

[16] snake—The Golden Fleece was guarded by a snake that never slept until Medea drugged it.

485   O my right hand, and the knees which you often clasped

In **supplication**,[17] how senselessly I am treated

By this bad man, and how my hopes have missed their mark!

Come, I will share my thoughts as though you were a friend—

You! Can I think that you would ever treat me well?

490   But I will do it, and these questions will make you

Appear the baser. Where am I to go? To my father's?

Him I betrayed and his land when I came with you.

To Pelias' wretched daughters? What a fine welcome

They would prepare for me who murdered their father!

495   For this is my position—hated by my friends

At home, I have, in kindness to you, made enemies

Of others whom there was no need to have injured.

And how happy among Greek women you have made me

On your side for all this! A distinguished husband

500   I have—for breaking promises. When in misery

I am cast out of the land and go into exile,

Quite without friends and all alone with my children,

That will be a fine shame for the new-wedded groom,

For his children to wander as beggars and she who saved him.

505   O God, you have given to mortals a sure method

Of telling the gold that is pure from the counterfeit;

Why is there no mark engraved upon men's bodies,

By which we could know the true ones from the false ones?

Chorus. It is a strange form of anger, difficult to cure,

510   When two friends turn upon each other in hatred.

Jason. As for me, it seems I must be no bad speaker.

But, like a man who has a good grip of the tiller,[18]

Reef up his sail,[19] and so run away from under

This mouthing tempest, woman, of your bitter tongue.

515   Since you insist on building up your kindness to me,

My view is that Cypris[20] was alone responsible

Of men and gods for the preserving of my life.

You are clever enough—but really I need not enter

Into the story of how it was love's inescapable

---

[17] **supplication**—humble request.

[18] tiller—rudder by which a ship is steered.

[19] Reef up his sail—roll up the sail (done during a storm).

[20] Cypris—Aphrodite, goddess of love (born of seafoam near the island of Cyprus).

520	Power that compelled you to keep my person safe.
	On this I will not go into too much detail.
	In so far as you helped me, you did well enough.
	But on this question of saving me, I can prove
	You have certainly got from me more than you gave.
525	Firstly, instead of living among barbarians,
	You inhabit a Greek land and understand our ways,
	How to live by law instead of the sweet will of force.
	And all the Greeks considered you a clever woman.
	You were honored for it; while, if you were living at
530	The ends of the earth, nobody would have heard of you.
	For my part, rather than stores of gold in my house
	Or power to sing even sweeter songs than Orpheus,²¹
	I'd choose the fate that made me a distinguished man.
	There is my reply to your story of my labors.
535	Remember it was you who started the argument.
	Next for your attack on my wedding with the princess:
	Here I will prove that, first, it was a clever move,
	Secondly, a wise one, and, finally, that I made it
	In your best interests and the children's. Please keep calm.
540	When I arrived here from the land of Iolcus,
	Involved, as I was, in every kind of difficulty,
	What luckier chance could I have come across than this,
	An exile to marry the daughter of the king?
	It was not—the point that seems to upset you—that I
545	Grew tired of your bed and felt the need of a new bride;
	Nor with any wish to outdo your number of children.
	We have enough already. I am quite content.
	But—this was the main reason—that we might live well,
	And not be short of anything. I know that all
550	A man's friends leave him stone-cold if he becomes poor.
	Also that I might bring my children up worthily
	Of my position, and, by producing more of them
	To be brothers of yours, we would draw the families
	Together and all be happy. You need no children.
555	And it pays me to do good to those I have now
	By having others. Do you think this a bad plan?

---

²¹ Orpheus—magical singer who had been one of Jason's companions on the *Argo*.

You wouldn't if the love question hadn't upset you.
But you women have got into such a state of mind
That, if your life at night is good, you think you have
560   Everything; but, if in that quarter things go wrong,
You will consider your best and truest interests
Most hateful. It would have been better far for men
To have got their children in some other way, and women
Not to have existed. Then life would have been good.

565   **Chorus.** Jason, though you have made this speech of yours look well,
Still I think, even though others do not agree,
You have betrayed your wife and are acting badly.

Medea. Surely in many ways I hold different views
From others, for I think that the **plausible**[22] speaker
570   Who is a villain deserves the greatest punishment.
Confident in his tongue's power to adorn evil,
He stops at nothing. Yet he is not really wise.
As in your case. There is no need to put on the airs
Of a clever speaker, for one word will lay you flat.
575   If you were not a coward, you would not have married
Behind my back, but discussed it with me first.

Jason. And you, no doubt, would have furthered the proposal,
If I had told you of it, you who even now
Are incapable of controlling your bitter temper.

580   **Medea.** It was not that. No, you thought it was not respectable
As you got on in years to have a foreign wife.

Jason. Make sure of this: it was not because of a woman
I made the royal alliance in which I now live,
But, as I said before, I wished to preserve you
585   And breed a royal progeny[23] to be brothers
To the children I have now, a sure defense to us.

Medea. Let me have no happy fortune that brings pain with it,
Or prosperity which is upsetting to the mind!

Jason. Change your ideas of what you want, and show more sense.
590   Do not consider painful what is good for you,
Nor, when you are lucky, think yourself unfortunate.

---

[22] **plausible**—believable, convincing.

[23] **progeny**—children.

Medea. You can insult me. You have somewhere to turn to.
　　　　But I shall go from this land into exile, friendless.
Jason. It was what you chose yourself. Don't blame others for it.
595　　**Medea.** And how did I choose it? Did I betray my husband?
Jason. You called down wicked curses on the king's family.
Medea. A curse, that is what I am become to your house too.
Jason. I do not propose to go into all the rest of it;
　　　　But, if you wish for the children or for yourself
600　　In exile to have some of my money to help you,
　　　　Say so, for I am prepared to give with open hand,
　　　　Or to provide you with introductions to my friends
　　　　Who will treat you well. You are a fool if you do not
　　　　Accept this. Cease your anger and you will profit.
605　　**Medea.** I shall never accept the favors of friends of yours,
　　　　Nor take a thing from you, so you need not offer it.
　　　　There is no benefit in the gifts of a bad man.
Jason. Then, in any case, I call the gods to witness that
　　　　I wish to help you and the children in every way,
610　　But you refuse what is good for you. **Obstinately**²⁴
　　　　You push away your friends. You are sure to suffer for it.
Medea. Go! No doubt you hanker for your virginal bride,
　　　　And are guilty of lingering too long out of her house.
　　　　Enjoy your wedding. But perhaps—with the help of God—
615　　You will make the kind of marriage that you will regret.
[Jason *goes out with his attendants.*]
Chorus. When love is in excess
　　　　It brings a man no honor
　　　　Nor any worthiness.
　　　　But if in moderation Cypris comes,
620　　There is no other power at all so gracious.
　　　　O goddess, never on me let loose the unerring ²⁵
　　　　Shaft of your bow in the poison of desire.

　　　　Let my heart be wise.
　　　　It is the gods' best gift.
625　　On me let mighty Cypris

---

²⁴ **Obstinately**—stubbornly.
²⁵ unerring—unfailing, certain to hit its target.

Inflict no wordy wars or restless anger
To urge my passion to a different love.
But with **discernment**[26] may she guide women's weddings,
Honoring most what is peaceful in the bed.

630   O country and home,
Never, never may I be without you,
Living the hopeless life,
Hard to pass through and painful,
Most pitiable of all.

635   Let death first lay me low and death
Free me from this daylight.
There is no sorrow above
The loss of a native land.

I have seen it myself,
640   Do not tell of a secondhand story.
Neither city nor friend
Pitied you when you suffered
The worst of sufferings.
O let him die ungraced whose heart
645   Will not reward his friends,
Who cannot open an honest mind
No friend will he be of mine.

[*Enter* Aegeus, *king of Athens, an old friend of* Medea.]

Aegeus. Medea, greeting! This is the best introduction
Of which men know for conversation between friends.

650 **Medea.** Greeting to you too, Aegeus, son of King Pandion.
Where have you come from to visit this country's soil?

Aegeus. I have just left the ancient oracle of Phoebus.[27]

Medea. And why did you go to earth's prophetic center?[28]

Aegeus. I went to inquire how children might be born to me.

655 **Medea.** Is it so? Your life still up to this point is childless?

Aegeus. Yes. By the fate of some power we have no children.

Medea. Have you a wife, or is there none to share your bed?

---

[26] **discernment**—good judgment.

[27] ancient oracle of Phoebus—Delphi, the most sacred spot in the Greek world, site of a shrine to the god Phoebus Apollo where a priestess delivered the god's answers to questions brought by pilgrims.

[28] earth's prophetic center—Delphi was believed to be the center of the world.

Aegeus. There is. Yes, I am joined to my wife in marriage.

Medea. And what did Phoebus say to you about children?

660 **Aegeus.** Words too wise for a mere man to guess their meaning.

Medea. It is proper for me to be told the god's reply?

Aegeus. It is. For sure what is needed is cleverness.

Medea. Then what was his message? Tell me, if I may hear.

Aegeus. I am not to loosen the hanging foot of the wine-skin[29] . . .

665 **Medea.** Until you have done something, or reached some country?

Aegeus. Until I return again to my hearth and house.

Medea. And for what purpose have you journeyed to this land?

Aegeus. There is a man called Pittheus, king of Troezen.

Medea. A son of Pelops, they say, a most righteous man.

670 **Aegeus.** With him I wish to discuss the reply of the god.

Medea. Yes. He is wise and experienced in such matters.

Aegeus. And to me also the dearest of all my spear-friends.[30]

Medea. Well, I hope you have good luck, and achieve your will.

Aegeus. But why this downcast eye of yours, and this pale cheek?

675 **Medea.** O Aegeus, my husband has been the worst of all to me.

Aegeus. What do you mean? Say clearly what has caused this grief.

Medea. Jason wrongs me, though I have never injured him.

Aegeus. What has he done? Tell me about it in clearer words.

Medea. He has taken a wife to his house, **supplanting**[31] me.

680 **Aegeus.** Surely he would not dare to do a thing like that.

Medea. Be sure he has. Once dear, I now am slighted by him.

Aegeus. Did he fall in love? Or is he tired of your love?

Medea. He was greatly in love, this traitor to his friends.

Aegeus. Then let him go, if, as you say, he is so bad.

685 **Medea.** A passionate love—for an alliance with the king.

Aegeus. And who gave him his wife? Tell me the rest of it.

Medea. It was Creon, he who rules this land of Corinth.

Aegeus. Indeed, Medea, your grief was understandable.

Medea. I am ruined. And there is more to come: I am banished.

690 **Aegeus.** Banished? By whom? Here you tell me of a new wrong.

Medea. Creon drives me an exile from the land of Corinth.

Aegeus. Does Jason consent? I cannot approve of this.

---

[29] hanging foot of the wine-skin—opening in a bag made from the skin of an animal that is used for holding wine.

[30] spear-friends—companions in arms, fellow-soldiers.

[31] **supplanting**—replacing.

Medea. He pretends not to, but he will put up with it.
Ah, Aegeus, I beg and beseech you, by your beard
695 And by your knees I am making myself your suppliant,
Have pity on me, have pity on your poor friend,
And do not let me go into exile desolate,
But receive me in your land and at your very hearth.
So may your love, with God's help, lead to the bearing
700 Of children, and so may you yourself die happy.
You do not know what a chance you have come on here.
I will end your childlessness, and I will make you able
To beget children. The drugs I know can do this.

Aegeus. For many reasons, woman, I am anxious to do
705 This favor for you. First, for the sake of the gods,
And then for the birth of children which you promise,
For in that respect I am entirely at my wits' end.
But this is my position: if you reach my land,
I, being in my rights, will try to befriend you.
710 But this much I must warn you of beforehand:
I shall not agree to take you out of this country;
But if you by yourself can reach my house, then you
Shall stay there safely. To none will I give you up
But from this land you must make your escape yourself,
715 For I do not wish to incur blame from my friends.

Medea. It shall be so. But, if I might have a pledge from you
For this, then I would have from you all I desire.

Aegeus. Do you not trust me? What is it rankles[32] with you?

Medea. I trust you, yes. But the house of Pelias hates me,
720 And so does Creon. If you are bound by this oath,
When they try to drag me from your land, you will not
Abandon me; but if our pact is only words,
With no oath to the gods, you will be lightly armed,
Unable to resist their summons. I am weak,
725 While they have wealth to help them and a royal house.

Aegeus. You show much foresight for such negotiations.
Well, if you will have it so, I will not refuse.
For, both on my side this will be the safest way

---

[32] rankles—festers.

> To have some excuse to put forward to your enemies,
> 730   And for you it is more certain. You may name the gods.
> **Medea.** Swear by the plain of Earth, and Helius, father
>   of my father, and name together all the gods. . .
> **Aegeus.** That I will act or not act in what way? Speak.
> **Medea.** That you yourself will never cast me from your land,
> 735   Nor, if any of my enemies should demand me,
>   Will you, in your life, willingly hand me over.
> **Aegeus.** I swear by the Earth, by the holy light of Helius
>   By all the gods, I will abide by this you say.
> **Medea.** Enough. And, if you fail, what shall happen to you?
> 740 **Aegeus.** What comes to those who have no regard for heaven.
> **Medea.** Go on your way. Farewell. For I am satisfied.
>   And I will reach your city as soon as I can,
>   Having done the deed I have to do and gained my end.
> [Aegeus *goes out.*]
> **Chorus.** May Hermes,[33] god of travelers,
> 745   Escort you, Aegeus, to your home!
>   And may you have the things you wish
>   So eagerly; for you
>   Appear to me to be a generous man.
> **Medea.** God, and God's daughter, justice, and light of Helius!
> 750   Now, friends, has come the time of my triumph over
>   My enemies, and now my foot is on the road.
>   Now I am confident they will pay the penalty.
>   For this man, Aegeus, has been like a harbor to me
>   In all my plans just where I was most distressed.
> 755   To him I can fasten the cable[34] of my safety
>   When I have reached the town and fortress of Pallas.[35]
>   And now I shall tell to you the whole of my plan.
>   Listen to these words that are not spoken idly.
>   I shall send one of my servants to find Jason
> 760   And request him to come once more into my sight.
>   And when he comes, the words I'll say will be soft ones.
>   I'll say that I agree with him, that I approve

---

[33] Hermes—swift messenger of the Greek gods and a patron of travelers.

[34] cable—ship's anchor rope.

[35] town and fortress of Pallas—Athens, whose patron was the goddess Pallas Athena.

The royal wedding he has made, betraying me.
I'll say it was profitable, an excellent idea.

765 But I shall beg that my children may remain here:
Not that I would leave in a country that hates me
Children of mine to feel their enemies' insults,
But that by a trick I may kill the king's daughter.
For I will send the children with gifts in their hands

770 To carry to the bride, so as not to be banished—
A finely woven dress and a golden diadem.[36]
And if she takes them and wears them upon her skin
She and all who touch the girl will die in agony;
Such poison will I lay upon the gifts I send.

775 But there, however, I must leave that account paid.
I weep to think of what a deed I have to do
Next after that; for I shall kill my own children.
My children, there is none who can give them safety.
And when I have ruined the whole of Jason's house,

780 I shall leave the land and flee from the murder of my
Dear children, and I shall have done a dreadful deed.
For it is not bearable to be mocked by enemies.
So it must happen. What profit have I in life?
I have no land, no home, no refuge from my pain.

785 My mistake was made the time I left behind me
My father's house, and trusted the words of a Greek,
Who, with heaven's help, will pay me the price for that.
For those children he had from me he will never
See alive again, nor will he on his new bride

790 Beget another child, for she is to be forced
To die a most terrible death by these my poisons.
Let no one think me a weak one, feeble-spirited,
A stay-at-home, but rather just the opposite,
One who can hurt my enemies and help my friends;

795 For the lives of such persons are most remembered.
Chorus. Since you have shared the knowledge of your plan with us,
I both wish to help you and support the normal
Ways of mankind, and tell you not to do this thing.

---

[36] diadem—crown.

Medea. I can do no other thing. It is understandable

800   For you to speak thus. You have not suffered as I have.

Chorus. But can you have the heart to kill your flesh and blood?

Medea. Yes, for this is the best way to wound my husband.

Chorus. And you, too. Of women you will be most unhappy.

Medea. So it must be. No compromise is possible.

[*She turns to the* Nurse.]

805   Go, you, at once, and tell Jason to come to me.

       You I employ on all affairs of greatest trust.

       Say nothing of these decisions which I have made,

       If you love your mistress, if you were born a woman.

Chorus. From of old the children of Erechtheus[37] are

810   Splendid, the sons of blessed gods. They dwell

       In Athens' holy and unconquered land,

       Where famous Wisdom[38] feeds them and they pass gaily

       Always through that most brilliant air where once, they say,

       That golden Harmony gave birth to the nine

815   Pure Muses of Pieria.[39]

       And beside the sweet flow of Cephisus' stream,[40]

       Where Cypris sailed, they say, to draw the water,

       And mild soft breezes breathed along her path,

       And on her hair were flung the sweet-smelling garlands

820   Of flowers of roses by the Lovers, the companions

       Of Wisdom, her escort, the helpers of men

       In every kind of excellence.

       How then can these holy rivers

       Or this holy land love you,

825   Or the city find you a home,

       You, who will kill your children,

       You, not pure with the rest?

       O think of the blow at your children

       And think of the blood that you shed.

---

[37] Erechtheus—early king of Athens.

[38] Wisdom—Athena, goddess of wisdom.

[39] Muses of Pieria—The Muses were nine goddesses who inspired artists and scholars. Their birthplace was Pieria, a region in northern Greece.

[40] Cephisus' stream—river near Athens.

830   O, over and over I beg you,
        By your knees I beg you do not
        Be the murderess of your babes!

        O where will you find the courage
        Or the skill of hand and heart,
835   When you set yourself to attempt
        A deed so dreadful to do?
        How, when you look upon them,
        Can you tearlessly hold the decision
        For murder? You will not be able,
840   When your children fall down and implore you,
        You will not be able to dip
        Steadfast your hand in their blood.

[*Enter* Jason *with attendants.*]

Jason. I have come at your request. Indeed, although you are
        Bitter against me, this you shall have: I will listen
845   To what new thing you want, woman, to get from me.

Medea. Jason, I beg you to be forgiving toward me
        For what I said. It is natural for you to bear with
        My temper, since we have had much love together.
        I have talked with myself about this and I have
850   **Reproached**[41] myself. "Fool" I said, "why am I so mad?
        Why am I set against those who have planned wisely?
        Why make myself an enemy of the authorities
        And of my husband, who does the best thing for me
        By marrying royalty and having children who
855   Will be as brothers to my own? What is wrong with me?
        Let me give up anger, for the gods are kind to me.
        Have I not children, and do I not know that we
        In exile from our country must be short of friends?"
        When I considered this I saw that I had shown
860   Great lack of sense, and that my anger was foolish.
        Now I agree with you. I think that you are wise
        In having this other wife as well as me, and I
        Was mad. I should have helped you in these plans of yours,
        Have joined in the wedding, stood by the marriage bed,

---

[41] **Reproached**—blamed, rebuked.

865 Have taken pleasure in attendance on your bride.
But we women are what we are—perhaps a little
Worthless; and you men must not be like us in this,
Nor be foolish in return when we are foolish.
Now, I give in, and admit that then I was wrong.
870 I have come to a better understanding now.

[*She turns toward the house.*]

Children, come here, my children, come outdoors to us!
Welcome your father with me, and say goodbye to him,
And with your mother, who just now was his enemy,
Join again in making friends with him who loves us.

[*Enter the* children, *attended by the* Tutor.]

875 We have made peace, and all our anger is over.
Take hold of his right hand—O God, I am thinking
Of something which may happen in the secret future.
O children, will you just so, after a long life,
Hold out your loving arms at the grave? O children,
880 How ready to cry I am, how full of foreboding![42]
I am ending at last this quarrel with your father,
And look my soft eyes have suddenly filled with tears.

Chorus. And the pale tears have started also in my eyes.
O may the trouble not grow worse than now it is!

885 **Jason.** I approve of what you say. And I cannot blame you
Even for what you said before. It is natural
For a woman to be wild with her husband when he
Goes in for secret love. But now your mind has turned
To better reasoning. In the end you have come to
890 The right decision, like the clever woman you are.
And of you, children, your father is taking care.
He has made, with God's help, ample provision for you.
For I think that a time will come when you will be
The leading people in Corinth with your brothers.
895 You must grow up. As to the future, your father
And those of the gods who love him will deal with that.
I want to see you, when you have become young men,
Healthy and strong, better men than my enemies.
Medea, why are your eyes all wet with pale tears?

---

[42] foreboding—sense of impending evil.

900   Why is your cheek so white and turned away from me?

Are not these words of mine pleasing for you to hear?

Medea. It is nothing. I was thinking about these children.

Jason. You must be cheerful. I shall look after them well.

Medea. I will be. It is not that I distrust your words,

905   But a woman is a frail thing, prone to crying.

Jason. But why then should you grieve so much for these children?

Medea. I am their mother. When you prayed that they might live

I felt unhappy to think that these things will be.

But come, I have said something of the things I meant

910   To say to you, and now I will tell you the rest.

Since it is the king's will to banish me from here—

And for me, too, I know that this is the best thing,

Not to be in your way by living here or in

The king's way, since they think me ill-disposed to them—

915   I then am going into exile from this land;

But do you, so that you may have the care of them,

Beg Creon that the children may not be banished.

Jason. I doubt if I'll succeed, but still I'll attempt it.

Medea. Then you must tell your wife to beg from her father

920   That the children may be **reprieved**[43] from banishment.

Jason. I will, and with her I shall certainly succeed.

Medea. If she is like the rest of us women, you will.

And I, too, will take a hand with you in this business,

For I will send her some gifts which are far fairer,

925   I am sure of it, than those which now are in fashion,

A finely woven dress and a golden diadem,

And the children shall present them. Quick, let one of you

Servants bring here to me that beautiful dress.

[*One of her attendants goes into the house.*]

She will be happy not in one way, but in a hundred,

930   Having so fine a man as you to share her bed,

And with this beautiful dress which Helius of old,

My father's father, bestowed on his descendants.

[*Enter attendant carrying the poisoned dress and diadem.*]

There, children, take these wedding presents in your hands.

---

[43] **reprieved**—spared.

Take them to the royal princess, the happy bride,
935   And give them to her. She will not think little of them.
Jason. No, don't be foolish, and empty your hands of these.
      Do you think the palace is short of dresses to wear?
      Do you think there is no gold there? Keep them, don't give them
      Away. If my wife considers me of any value,
940   She will think more of me than money, I am sure of it.
Medea. No, let me have my way. They say the gods themselves
      Are moved by gifts, and gold does more with men than words.
      Hers is the luck, her fortune that which god blesses;
      She is young and a princess; but for my children's reprieve
945   I would give my very life, and not gold only.
      Go children, go together to that rich palace,
      Be suppliants to the new wife of your father,
      My lady, beg her not to let you be banished.
      And give her the dress—for this is of great importance,
950   That she should take the gift into her hand from yours.
      Go, quick as you can. And bring your mother good news
      By your success of those things which she longs to gain.
[Jason *goes out with his attendants, followed by the* Tutor *and the* children
carrying the poisoned gifts.]
Chorus. Now there is no hope left for the children's lives.
      Now there is none. They are walking already to murder.
955   The bride, poor bride, will accept the curse of the gold,
      Will accept the bright diadem.
      Around her yellow hair she will set that dress
      Of death with her own hands.

      The grace and the perfume and glow of the golden robe
960   Will charm her to put them upon her and wear the wreath,
      And now her wedding will be with the dead below,
      Into such a trap she will fall,
      Poor thing, into such a fate of death and never
      Escape from under that curse.

965   You, too, O wretched bridegroom, making your match with kings,
      You do not see that you bring
      Destruction on your children and on her,

Your wife, a fearful death.
Poor soul, what a fall is yours!

970 In your grief, too, I weep, mother of little children,
You who will murder your own,
In vengeance for the loss of married love
Which Jason has betrayed
As he lives with another wife.

[*Enter the* Tutor *with the* children.]

975 **Tutor.** Mistress, I tell you that these children are reprieved,
And the royal bride has been pleased to take in her hands
Your gifts. In that quarter the children are secure.
But come,
Why do you stand confused when you are fortunate?

980 Why have you turned round with your cheek away from me?
Are not these words of mine pleasing for you to hear?

Medea. Oh! I am lost!

Tutor. That word is not in harmony with my tidings.

Medea. I am lost, I am lost!

Tutor. Am I in ignorance in telling you

985 Of some disaster, and not the good news I thought?

Medea. You have told what you have told. I do not blame you.

Tutor. Why then this downcast eye, and this weeping of tears?

Medea. Oh, I am forced to weep, old man. The gods and I,
I in a kind of madness, have contrived all this.

990 **Tutor.** Courage! You, too, will be brought home by your children.

Medea. Ah, before that happens I shall bring others home.

Tutor. Others before you have been parted from their children.
Mortals must bear in resignation their ill luck.

Medea. That is what I shall do. But go inside the house,

995 And do for the children your usual daily work.

[*The* Tutor *goes into the house.* Medea *turns to her* children.]

O children, O my children, you have a city,
You have a home, and you can leave me behind you,
And without your mother you may live there forever.
But I am going in exile to another land

1000 Before I have seen you happy and taken pleasure in you,
Before I have dressed your brides and made your marriage beds
And held up the torch at the ceremony of wedding.

Oh, what a wretch I am in this my self-willed thought!
What was the purpose, children, for which I reared you?
1005 For all my travail[44] and wearing myself away?
They were sterile, those pains I had in the bearing of you.
Oh surely once the hopes in you I had, poor me,
Were high ones: you would look after me in old age,
And when I died would deck me well with your own hands;
1010 A thing which all would have done. Oh but now it is gone,
That lovely thought. For, once I am left without you,
Sad will be the life I'll lead and sorrowful for me.
And you will never see your mother again with
Your dear eyes, gone to another mode of living.
1015 Why, children, do you look upon me with your eyes?
Why do you smile so sweetly that last smile of all?
Oh, Oh, what can I do? My spirit has gone from me,
Friends, when I saw that bright look in the children's eyes.
I cannot bear to do it. I renounce my plans
1020 I had before. I'll take my children away from
This land. Why should I hurt their father with the pain
They feel, and suffer twice as much of pain myself?
No, no, I will not do it. I renounce my plans.
Ah, what is wrong with me? Do I want to let go
1025 My enemies unhurt and be laughed at for it?
I must face this thing. Oh, but what a weak woman
Even to admit to my mind these soft arguments.
Children, go into the house. And he whom law forbids
To stand in attendance at my sacrifices,
1030 Let him see to it. I shall not mar my handiwork.
Oh! Oh!
Do not, O my heart, you must not do these things!
Poor heart, let them go, have pity upon the children.
If they live with you in Athens they will cheer you.
1035 No! By Hell's avenging Furies[45] it shall not be—
This shall never be, that I should suffer my children
To be the prey of my enemies' **insolence**.[46]

---

[44] travail—pain, especially that of childbirth.

[45] Furies—several goddesses who punished crimes against blood relatives.

[46] **insolence**—rudeness, disrespect.

Every way is it fixed. The bride will not escape.
No, the diadem is now upon her head, and she,
1040   The royal princess, is dying in the dress, I know it.
But—for it is the most dreadful of roads for me
To tread, and them I shall send on a more dreadful still—
I wish to speak to the children.

[*She calls the* children *to her.*]

Come, children, give
Me your hands, give your mother your hands to kiss them.
1045   Oh the dear hands, and O how dear are these lips to me,
And the generous eyes and the bearing of my children!
I wish you happiness, but not here in this world.
What is here your father took. Oh how good to hold you!
How delicate the skin, how sweet the breath of children!
1050   Go, go! I am no longer able, no longer
To look upon you. I am overcome by sorrow.

[*The* children *go into the house.*]

I know indeed what evil I intend to do,
But stronger than all my afterthoughts is my fury,
Fury that brings upon mortals the greatest evils.

[*She goes out to the right, toward the royal palace.*]

1055   **Chorus.** Often before
I have gone through more subtle reasons,
And have come upon questionings greater
Than a woman should strive to search out.
But we too have a goddess to help us
1060   And accompany us into wisdom.
Not all of us. Still you will find
Among many women a few,
And our sex is not without learning.
This I say, that those who have never
1065   Had children, who know nothing of it,
In happiness have the advantage
Over those who are parents.
The childless, who never discover
Whether children turn out as a good thing
1070   Or as something to cause pain, are spared
Many troubles in lacking this knowledge.
And those who have in their homes

The sweet presence of children, I see that their lives
Are all wasted away by their worries.
1075   First they must think how to bring them up well and
How to leave them something to live on.
And then after this whether all their toil
Is for those who will turn out good or bad,
Is still an unanswered question.
1080   And of one more trouble, the last of all,
That is common to mortals I tell.
For suppose you have found them enough for their living,
Suppose that the children have grown into youth
And have turned out good, still, if God so wills it,
1085   Death will away with your children's bodies,
And carry them off into Hades.[47]
What is our profit, then, that for the sake of
Children the gods should pile upon mortals
After all else
1090   This most terrible grief of all?

[*Enter* Medea, *from the spectators' right.*]

Medea. Friends, I can tell you that for long I have waited
For the event. I stare toward the place from where
The news will come. And now, see one of Jason's servants
Is on his way here, and that labored breath of his
1095   Shows he has tidings for us, and evil tidings.

[*Enter, also from the right, the* Messenger.]

Messenger. Medea, you who have done such a dreadful thing,
So outrageous, run for your life, take what you can,
A ship to bear you hence or chariot on land.

Medea. And what is the reason deserves such flight as this?

1100 **Messenger.** She is dead, only just now, the royal princess,
And Creon dead, too, her father, by your poisons.

Medea. The finest words you have spoken. Now and hereafter
I shall count you among my benefactors and friends.

Messenger. What! Are you right in the mind? Are you not mad,
1105   Woman? The house of the king is outraged by you.
Do you enjoy it? Not afraid of such doings?

---

[47] Hades—the world of the dead.

Medea. To what you say I on my side have something too
    To say in answer. Do not be in a hurry, friend,
    But speak. How did they die? You will delight me twice
1110   As much again if you say they died in agony.
Messenger. When those two children, born of you, had entered in,
    Their father with them, and passed into the bride's house,
    We were pleased, we slaves who were distressed by your wrongs.
    All through the house we were talking of but one thing,
1115   How you and your husband had made up your quarrel.
    Some kissed the children's hands and some their yellow hair,
    And I myself was so full of my joy that I
    Followed the children into the women's quarters.
    Our mistress, whom we honor now instead of you,
1120   Before she noticed that your two children were there,
    Was keeping her eye fixed eagerly on Jason.
    Afterwards, however, she covered up her eyes,
    Her cheek paled, and she turned herself away from him,
    So disgusted was she at the children's coming there.
1125   But your husband tried to end the girl's bad temper,
    And said "You must not look unkindly on your friends.
    Cease to be angry. Turn your head to me again.
    Have as your friends the same ones as your husband has.
    And take these gifts, and beg your father to reprieve
1130   These children from their exile. Do it for my sake."
    She, when she saw the dress, could not restrain herself.
    She agreed with all her husband said, and before
    He and the children had gone far from the palace,
    She took the gorgeous robe and dressed herself in it,
1135   And put the golden crown around her curly locks,
    And arranged the set of the hair in a shining mirror,
    And smiled at the lifeless image of herself in it.
    Then she rose from her chair and walked about the room,
    With her gleaming feet stepping most soft and delicate,
1140   All overjoyed with the present. Often and often
    She would stretch her foot out straight and look along it.
    But after that it was a fearful thing to see.
    The color of her face changed, and she staggered back,
    She ran, and her legs trembled, and she only just
1145   Managed to reach a chair without falling flat down.

An aged woman servant who, I take it, thought
This was some seizure of Pan[48] or another god,
Cried out "God bless us," but that was before she saw
The white foam breaking through her lips and her rolling
1150 The pupils of her eyes and her face all bloodless.
Then she raised a different cry from that "God bless us,"
A huge shriek, and the women ran, one to the king,
One to the newly wedded husband to tell him
What had happened to his bride; and with frequent sound
1155 The whole of the palace rang as they went running.
One walking quickly round the course of a race-track
Would now have turned the bend and be close to the goal,
When she, poor girl, opened her shut and speechless eye,
And with a terrible groan she came to herself.
1160 For a twofold pain was moving up against her.
The wreath of gold that was resting around her head
Let forth a fearful stream of all-devouring fire,
And the finely woven dress your children gave to her,
Was fastening on the unhappy girl's fine flesh.
1165 She leapt up from the chair, and all on fire she ran,
Shaking her hair now this way and now that, trying
To hurl the diadem away; but fixedly
The gold preserved its grip, and, when she shook her hair,
Then more and twice as fiercely the fire blazed out.
1170 Till, beaten by her fate, she fell down to the ground,
Hard to be recognized except by a parent.
Neither the setting of her eyes was plain to see,
Nor the shapeliness of her face. From the top of
Her head there oozed out blood and fire mixed together.
1175 Like the drops on pine-bark, so the flesh from her bones
Dropped away, torn by the hidden fang of the poison.
It was a fearful sight; and terror held us all
From touching the corpse. We had learned from what had happened.
But her wretched father, knowing nothing of the event,
1180 Came suddenly to the house, and fell upon the corpse,
And at once cried out and folded his arms about her,
And kissed her and spoke to her, saying, "O my poor child,

---

[48] Pan—god to whose influence the Greeks attributed sudden, unreasoning attacks of fear ("panics").

What heavenly power has so shamefully destroyed you?
And who has set me here like an ancient sepulcher,[49]
1185   Deprived of you? O let me die with you, my child!"
And when he had made an end of his wailing and crying,
Then the old man wished to raise himself to his feet;
But, as the ivy clings to the twigs of the laurel,
So he stuck to the fine dress, and he struggled fearfully.
1190   For he was trying to lift himself to his knee,
And she was pulling him down, and when he tugged hard
He would be ripping his aged flesh from his bones.
At last his life was quenched, and the unhappy man
Gave up the ghost, no longer could hold up his head.
1195   There they lie close, the daughter and the old father,
Dead bodies, an event he prayed for in his tears.
As for your interests, I will say nothing of them,
For you will find your own escape from punishment.
Our human life I think and have thought a shadow,
1200   And I do not fear to say that those who are held
Wise among men and who search the reasons of things
Are those who bring the most sorrow on themselves.
For of mortals there is no one who is happy.
If wealth flows in upon one, one may be perhaps
1205   Luckier than one's neighbor, but still not happy.
[*Exit.*]

Chorus. Heaven, it seems, on this day has fastened many
Evils on Jason, and Jason has deserved them.
Poor girl, the daughter of Creon, how I pity you
And your misfortunes, you who have gone quite away
1210   To the house of Hades because of marrying Jason.

Medea. Women, my task is fixed: as quickly as I may
To kill my children, and start away from this land,
And not, by wasting time, to suffer my children
To be slain by another hand less kindly to them.
1215   Force every way will have it they must die, and since
This must be so, then I, their mother, shall kill them.
Oh, arm yourself in steel, my heart! Do not hang back
From doing this fearful and necessary wrong.

---

[49] sepulcher—tomb.

Oh, come, my hand, poor wretched hand, and take the sword,
1220   Take it, step forward to this bitter starting point,
And do not be a coward, do not think of them,
How sweet they are, and how you are their mother. Just for
This one short day be forgetful of your children,
Afterward weep; for even though you will kill them,
1225   They were very dear—Oh, I am an unhappy woman!

[*With a cry she rushes into the house.*]

Chorus. O Earth, and the far shining
Ray of the Sun, look down, look down upon
This poor lost woman, look, before she raises
The hand of murder against her flesh and blood.
1230   Yours was the golden birth from which
She sprang, and now I fear divine
Blood may be shed by men.
O heavenly light, hold back her hand,
Check her, and drive from out the house
1235   The bloody Fury raised by fiends of Hell.

Vain waste, your care of children;
Was it in vain you bore the babes you loved,
After you passed the inhospitable strait[50]
Between the dark blue rocks, Symplegades?
1240   O wretched one, how has it come,
This heavy anger on your heart,
This cruel bloody mind?
For God from mortals asks a stern
Price for the stain of kindred blood
1245   In like disaster falling on their homes.

[*A cry from one of the children is heard.*]

Chorus. Do you hear the cry, do you hear the children's cry?
O you hard heart, O woman fated for evil!

One of the children [*from within*]. What can I do and how escape my
    mother's hands?

Another child [*from within*]. O my dear brother, I cannot tell. We are lost.

1250   **Chorus.** Shall I enter the house? Oh, surely I should
Defend the children from murder.

---

[50] inhospitable strait—unfriendly channel.

A child [*from within*]. O help us, in God's name, for now we need your help.
    Now, now we are close to it. We are trapped by the sword.
Chorus. O your heart must have been made of rock or steel,

1255   You who can kill
    With your own hand the fruit of your own womb.
    Of one alone I have heard, one woman alone
    Of those of old who laid her hands on her children,
    Ino, sent mad by heaven when the wife of Zeus[51]

1260   Drove her out from her home and made her wander;
    And because of the wicked shedding of blood
    Of her own children she threw
    Herself, poor wretch, into the sea and stepped away
    Over the sea-cliff to die with her two children.

1265   What horror more can be? O women's love,
    So full of trouble,
    How many evils have you caused already!
[*Enter* Jason, *with attendants.*]
Jason. You women, standing close in front of this dwelling,
    Is she, Medea, she who did this dreadful deed,

1270   Still in the house, or has she run away in flight?
    For she will have to hide herself beneath the earth,
    Or raise herself on wings into the height of air,
    If she wishes to escape the royal vengeance.
    Does she imagine that, having killed our rulers,

1275   She will herself escape uninjured from this house?
    But I am thinking not so much of her as for
    The children—her the king's friends will make to suffer
    For what she did. So I have come to save the lives
    Of my boys, in case the royal house should harm them

1280   While taking vengeance for their mother's wicked deed.
Chorus. O Jason, if you but knew how deeply you are
    Involved in sorrow, you would not have spoken so.
Jason. What is it? That she is planning to kill me also?
Chorus. Your children are dead, and by their own mother's hand.

1285 **Jason.** What! That is it? O woman, you have destroyed me!
Chorus. You must make up your mind your children are no more.
Jason. Where did she kill them? Was it here or in the house?

---

[51] Ino . . . wife of Zeus—Hera, the jealous wife of Zeus, resented Ino because she had nursed Dionysus, Zeus's son by Semele. Hera revenged herself by driving Ino mad.

Chorus. Open the gates and there you will see them murdered.

Jason. Quick as you can unlock the doors, men, and undo
1290   The fastenings and let me see this double evil,
       My children dead and her—Oh her I will repay.

[*His attendants rush to the door.* Medea *appears above the house in a chariot drawn by dragons. She has the dead bodies of the children with her.*]

Medea. Why do you batter these gates and try to unbar them,
       Seeking the corpses and for me who did the deed?
       You may cease your trouble, and, if you have need of me,
1295   Speak, if you wish. You will never touch me with your hand,
       Such a chariot has Helius, my father's father,
       Given me to defend me from my enemies.

Jason. You hateful thing, you woman most utterly loathed
       By the gods and me and by all the race of mankind,
1300   You who have had the heart to raise a sword against
       Your children, you, their mother, and left me childless—
       You have done this, and do you still look at the sun
       And at the earth, after these most fearful doings?
       I wish you dead. Now I see it plain, though at that time
1305   I did not, when I took you from your foreign home
       And brought you to a Greek house, you, an evil thing,
       A traitress to your father and your native land.
       The gods hurled the avenging curse of yours on me.
       For your own brother you slew at your own hearthside,
1310   And then came aboard that beautiful ship, the *Argo*.
       And that was your beginning. When you were married
       To me, your husband, and had borne children to me,
       For the sake of pleasure in the bed you killed them.
       There is no Greek woman who would have dared such deeds,
1315   Out of all those whom I passed over and chose you
       To marry instead, a bitter destructive match,
       A monster, not a woman, having a nature
       Wilder than that of Scylla[52] in the Tuscan sea.
       Ah! no, not if I had ten thousand words of shame
1320   Could I sting you. You are naturally so brazen.
       Go, worker in evil, stained with your children's blood.
       For me remains to cry aloud upon my fate,

---

[52] Scylla—she-monster who devoured strangers.

Who will get no pleasure from my newly wedded love,
And the boys whom I begot and brought up, never

1325   Shall I speak to them alive. Oh, my life is over!

Medea. Long would be the answer which I might have made to
These words of yours, if Zeus the father did not know
How I have treated you and what you did to me.
No, it was not to be that you should scorn my love,

1330   And pleasantly live your life through, laughing at me;
Nor would the princess, nor he who offered the match,
Creon, drive me away without paying for it.
So now you may call me a monster, if you wish,
A Scylla housed in the caves of the Tuscan sea.

1335   I too, as I had to, have taken hold of your heart.

Jason. You feel the pain yourself. You share in my sorrow.

Medea. Yes, and my grief is gain when you cannot mock it.

Jason. O children, what a wicked mother she was to you!

Medea. They died from a disease they caught from their father.

1340   **Jason.** I tell you it was not my hand that destroyed them.

Medea. But it was your **insolence**,[53] and your virgin wedding.

Jason. And just for the sake of that you chose to kill them.

Medea. Is love so small a pain, do you think, for a woman?

Jason. For a wise one, certainly. But you are wholly evil.

1345   **Medea.** The children are dead. I say this to make you suffer.

Jason. The children, I think, will bring down curses on you.

Medea. The gods know who was the author of this sorrow.

Jason. Yes, the gods know indeed, they know your loathsome heart.

Medea. Hate me. But I tire of your barking bitterness.

1350   **Jason.** And I of yours. It is easier to leave you.

Medea. How then? What shall I do? I long to leave you too.

Jason. Give me the bodies to bury and to mourn them.

Medea. No, that I will not. I will bury them myself,
Bearing them to Hera's temple on the **promontory**;[54]

1355   So that no enemy may evilly treat them
By tearing up their grave. In this land of Corinth
I shall establish a holy feast and sacrifice

---

[53] **insolence**—arrogance.

[54] **promontory**—high ridge of land or rock jutting out in a body of water; headland.

Each year for ever to atone for the blood guilt.
And I myself go to the land of Erechtheus

1360   To dwell in Aegeus' house, the son of Pandion.
While you, as is right, will die without distinction,
Struck on the head by a piece of the *Argo*'s timber,[55]
And you will have seen the bitter end of my love.

Jason. May a Fury for the children's sake destroy you,

1365   And justice, Requitor[56] of blood.

Medea. What heavenly power lends an ear
To a breaker of oaths, a deceiver?

Jason. Oh, I hate you, murderess of children.

Medea. Go to your palace. Bury your bride.

1370 **Jason.** I go, with two children to mourn for.

Medea. Not yet do you feel it. Wait for the future.

Jason. Oh, children I loved!

Medea.   I loved them, you did not.

Jason. You loved them, and killed them.

Medea.   To make you feel pain.

Jason. Oh, wretch that I am, how I long

1375   To kiss the dear lips of my children!

Medea. Now you would speak to them, now you would kiss them.
Then you rejected them.

Jason.   Let me, I beg you,
Touch my boys' delicate flesh.

Medea. I will not. Your words are all wasted.

1380 **Jason.** O God, do you hear it, this persecution,
These my sufferings from this hateful
Woman, this monster, murderess of children?
Still what I can do that I will do:
I will lament and cry upon heaven,

1385   Calling the gods to bear me witness
How you have killed my boys and prevent me from
Touching their bodies or giving them burial.
I wish I had never begot them to see them
Afterward slaughtered by you.

---

[55] the *Argo*'s timber—One story says Jason was killed when some of the rotten wood of the *Argo* fell on him.

[56] Requitor—revenger.

1390   **Chorus.** Zeus in Olympus is the overseer
         Of many doings. Many things the gods
         Achieve beyond our judgment. What we thought
         Is not confirmed and what we thought not god
         Contrives. And so it happens in this story. [*Curtain.*]

UNDERSTANDING THE PLAY

Lines 1–435

1. What is the dramatic purpose of the Nurse's opening speech?

2. How does the Chorus first react to Medea's sufferings?

3. How does Medea view her situation as a foreigner in Corinth?

4. How does she view her situation as a wife and mother?

5. Why does Creon order Medea to leave his country?

6. What opinion of women does Medea express in lines 405–407?

Lines 436–647

1. According to Jason, why is Medea going to be exiled?

2. What accusations does Medea make against Jason?

3. Why does Jason feel that Medea had helped him in the past?

4. What reasons does he give for marrying Creon's daughter?

5. In his defense of himself, what type of person does Jason reveal himself to be?

Lines 648–842

1. Why did Aegeus go to the Delphic oracle?

2. What is Medea's mood after she secures Aegeus's pledge to help?

3. How is Medea going to revenge herself on Creon's daughter?

4. Why does Medea intend to kill her children?

5. In lines 809–829, why does the Chorus celebrate the holiness of Athens?

Lines 843–974

1. How does Medea's manner toward Jason change at this point?

2. Why does her manner change?

3. How does Jason respond to this change in her manner?

4. In lines 891–898, Jason speaks to his sons. How does Medea react to this?

5. What is Jason's reaction to Medea's proposal to send gifts to Creon's daughter?

Lines 975–1394

1. After sending off her children with the poisoned gifts for the princess, why does Medea at first decide to renounce her plan to kill them?

2. Why does she return to her original plan?

3. In lines 1055–1090, why do you think the Chorus argue that the childless are happier than those who are parents?

4. Why do you think Euripides includes this detailed account of the deaths of the princess and her father?

5. What does Jason attribute to Medea's foreignness?

ANALYZING THE PLAY

1. According to Aristotle, a tragic hero's fall should arouse pity and fear in the audience. In what way is this true in *Medea*?

2. The climax—or crisis—in the plot is the turning point in the struggle when one of the contending forces gets the upper hand. In *Medea*, where does this turning point occur?

3. How does Euripides present Jason in the play?

4. What attitude do you think Euripides had toward women?

5. At the play's end, Jason cries out, "Oh, children I loved!" Medea replies, "I loved them, you did not." What does she mean?

On Social Plays

BY ARTHUR MILLER

In his play A View from the Bridge, *American dramatist Arthur Miller (1915–   ) presented a contemporary story of a doomed family in the manner of a Greek tragedy. In the following excerpt from his preface to this work, Miller discusses how puzzled the ancient Greeks would be by the categorizing of some modern dramas as "social plays."*

A Greek living in the classical period would be bewildered by the dichotomy[1] implied in the very term "social play." Especially for the Greek, a drama created for public performance had to be "social." A play to him was by definition a dramatic consideration of the way men ought to live. But in this day of extreme individualism even that phrase must be further defined. When we say "how men ought to live," we are likely to be thinking of psychological therapy, of ridding ourselves individually of neurotic compulsions and destructive inner tendencies, of "learning how to love" and thereby gaining "happiness."

It need hardly be said that the Greek dramatist had more than a passing interest in psychology and character on the stage. But for him these were means to a larger end, and the end was what we isolate today as social. That is, the relations of man as a social animal, rather than his definition as a separated entity, was the dramatic goal. Why this should have come to be is a large historical question which others are more competent to explain, as several already have. For our purposes it will be sufficient to indicate one element in the life of classical Greece that differs so radically from anything existing in the modern world as to throw a bright light on certain of our attitudes which we take for granted and toward which we therefore are without a proper perspective.

The Greek citizen of that time thought of himself as belonging not to a "nation" or a "state" but to a *polis*.[2] The poleis were small units, apparently deriving from an earlier tribal social organization, whose

---

[1] dichotomy—division into two usually contradictory parts.
[2] *polis*—(plural *poleis*) city-state of ancient Greece.

members probably knew one another personally because they were relatively few in number and occupied a small territory. In war or peace the whole people made the vital decisions, there being no profession of politics as we know it; any man could be elected magistrate, judge, even a general in the armed forces. It was an amateur world compared to our stratified and specialized one, a world in which everyone knew enough about almost any profession to practice it, because most things were simple to know. The thing of importance for us is that these people were *engaged*, they could not imagine the good life excepting as it brought each person into close contact with civic matters. . . . The people had a special sense of pride in the polis and thought that it in itself distinguished them from the barbarians outside who lived under tyrannies.

The preoccupation of the Greek drama with ultimate law, with the Grand Design, so to speak, was therefore an expression of a basic assumption of the people, who could not yet conceive, luckily, that any man could long prosper unless his polis prospered. The individual was at one with his society; his conflicts with it were, in our terms, like family conflicts the opposing sides of which nevertheless shared a mutuality of feeling and responsibility. Thus the drama written for them, while for us it appears wholly religious, was religious for them in a more than mystical way. Religion is the only way we have any more of expressing our genuinely social feelings and concerns, for in our bones we as a

people do not otherwise believe in our oneness with a larger group. But the religiousness of the Greek drama of the classical time was more worldly; it expressed a social concern, to be sure, but it did so on the part of a people already unified on earth rather than the drive of a single individual toward personal salvation. The great gap we feel between religious or "high" emotion and the emotions of daily life was not present in their mass affairs. The religious expression was not many degrees higher for them than many other social expressions, of which their drama is the most complete example.

It is necessary to add that as the polis withered under the impact of war and historical change, as commerce grew and a differentiation of interest separated man from man, the Greek drama found it more and more difficult to stand as a kind of universal mass statement or prayer. Nevertheless, to the end the Greek drama clearly conceived its right function as something far wider than a purely private examination of individuality for the sake of the examination or for art's sake. In every dramatic hero there is the idea of the Greek people, their fate, their will, and their destiny.

QUESTIONS TO CONSIDER

1. Why does Miller argue all Greek drama was "social"?

2. How was the Greeks' religious sense reflected in their drama?

Medea at Pescara

BY JAN KOTT

In the following essay, drama critic Jan Kott (1914–   ) reflects on a performance of Euripides's Medea *that he saw performed in the town of Pescara, a town in central Italy near the Adriatic Sea.*

The amphitheater in Pescara is a new one, but it is situated outside the town, and there is nothing in its immediate vicinity. Only the sea is near. The night I was there, a cold wind was blowing from the sea, while hot air still came from the mountains. The stage area consisted of large stone steps. On top of them stood the Doric portico[1] of Medea's house, with a huge closed door. Above the portico the moon was shining, quite low, cut in half. It was covered by clouds in the second half of the performance, almost immediately after Medea said she would murder her children and her rival.

Sometimes natural scenery gives unexpected effects, as when all of sudden the sky or birds start playing their part. Once I saw *Hamlet* performed in the courtyard of Elsinore Castle.[2] During the first great soliloquy some gulls flew just above Hamlet's head, and a couple of them suddenly squatted at his feet.

In the enclosed theater there is no room for the Chorus, even when the designer extends the forestage halfway through the front rows. The entry of the Chorus is artificial. One does not know whether to keep it there, or to let it come on and off the stage every time. In every performance of Greek tragedies that I had seen, the Chorus had always been a disguised ballet. But the Chorus in Sophocles and Euripides is not a ballet interlude, or an intellectual commentary. It is not external or added on to the tragedy; it does not need any justification. The Chorus is simply the people. Fourteen young women stopped on the stone steps. They had entered the way peasant women do, like the girls in Pescocostanzo when they assemble in the evening by the fountain in the town square. All day long they had pored over the tombolo, heavy bags

---

[1] Doric portico—porch with a roof supported by Doric columns.

[2] Elsinore Castle—seacoast fortress in Denmark that is the setting of Shakespeare's *Hamlet*.

stuffed with hay and sawdust, onto which a newly begun lace is pinned. Lace is made by the **arduous**[3] and patient manipulation of small wooden bobbins with threads. These bobbins are called *fazzoletti* here. The same kind of lace is made in the same way in Poland, from Zywiec to Zawoja, in all the hungry mountain villages under Babia and Barania Góra.

I do not know what impression *Medea* makes in the marble amphitheater of Greece. Perhaps it seems monumental and remote. Here in Pescara, from the very first scene, Medea and the Chorus of young women seemed to belong to the soil, the landscape. Medea was in buskins,[4] I suppose because the part was played by a tiny actress. She was an ordinary Medea, humanly unhappy and humanly **vindictive;**[5] she was like those peasant women, stiff, and erect under the fifty-pound loads on their heads, tired but still full of dignity. There was something about her too, of that night, when the sea blew cold wind alternately with the stifling hot wind from the Maiella ridge.

The action of Euripides' *Medea* lasts from the early morning until late in the night. But here the real time and the time of performance were the same. A few hours of such a night were enough to accomplish mad deeds that would seem impossible in the daytime. Daylight would disperse madness like the mists that drowned Pescocostanzo in the mornings.

Not only time was condensed. The unity of place seemed just as natural, there was nothing of contrived poetics about it. . . . To me, the unity of place in an indoor

theater always seemed artificial. Here, however, everything is close at hand. In the *Medea* at Pescara, night was really night, stone steps were stone steps, the nearby sea was a nearby sea. It was the same with *Hamlet* at Elsinore, which suddenly revealed itself through architecture. *Hamlet* proved itself in Elsinore, not only because Shakespeare placed the action there, but also perhaps because the performance began at dusk; in its second half, the beam from its lighthouse placed in a tower of Elsinore Castle swept the scaffolding erected in the courtyard with its light, in yellow and red in turn. Hamlet's father's ghost appeared on real battlements and his voice reached the audience from there.

Medea does not address the gods. They do not exist for her, just as the world does not exist, as her children do not exist. For her, they are Jason's children. More than that, they are Jason himself. She kills them not only to revenge herself on him but because she cannot kill Jason; she kills Jason in them. But actually even Jason does not exist for Medea. Only she exists; she and her defeat. She cannot even for a moment talk or think about anything else. She is locked within herself with her misfortune as if inside an egg. Medea's mad monomania is undoubtedly a Euripidean discovery. Monomania singles Medea out, separates and cuts her off from the real world. Through her monomania Medea is alone. Heroes of tragedy have to be alone.

---

[3] **arduous**—difficult.

[4] buskins—thick-soled laced half-boots worn by actors of Greek and Roman tragedies.

[5] **vindictive**—revengeful.

But the Chorus of women is of this world. They have come from the village, from the small harbor which is also a village. They have come to **commiserate**[6] with Medea. She has been deserted by her husband; now they want to take her sons away. In its first odes the Chorus complains of the injustice of the human lot and says that bitter is the life of a girl who remains unmarried, and bitter the life of a woman who marries. The women are on Medea's side and will remain so to the end. But gradually they become more and more terrified, not only by Medea's designs but by the ordeal sent her by the gods. The women's gestures become more and more liturgical. They fall on their knees, begin to beg for mercy and pity, but not for themselves. They beg the god for mercy who takes revenge on Medea, Jason, Creon; who takes vengeance on children for parents' misdeeds, and on grandchildren for those of their grandparents.

It suddenly seemed to me that the women, who went to the top of the stairs to the shut door of Medea's house, began to recite the litany to the Virgin, or to the Heart of Jesus. They were praying, and their prayers was one long moan.

---

[6] **commiserate**—express pity for.

QUESTIONS TO CONSIDER

1. How did the Chorus function in the production of *Medea* at Pescara?

2. How does Kott see the dramatic unities of time and place function in this performance?

On Stage

Ancient Theater

Theater has its roots in ancient and worldwide traditions of ritual, dance, and storytelling. The religious rites through which early human beings sought to get in contact with gods and secure divine protection for their communities evolved into the first plays. The expressive and imitative movements of dance eventually acquired a dramatic quality and became acting. Oral traditions of storytelling preserved a people's essential myths and tales, providing a repository of plots for the dramatists to come. All these traditions came together in the theater of the ancient Greeks.

▲

Perhaps as early as 2500 B.C., a ritual in dramatic form presenting the myth of the Egyptian god Osiris (shown on the right in this illustration from a copy of the *Book of the Dead*) began to be performed annually in Egypt.

▲

The masks and costumes worn by dancers at an initiation ritual among the Bopende people of Central Africa express the performers' transformation into something outside themselves—an essential part of theater.

A Bison dance among the Mandan people of the Great Plains displays the elements of pantomime and rhythmic movement that are significant aspects of theatrical performance.

▲
Greek theater had its earliest origins in the ecstatic dances of the female worshippers of the Greek god Dionysus.

◄ The essentially religious character of ancient Greek drama is indicated by the presence of this elaborate ceremonial seat of honor for the priest of Dionysus at the theater in Athens.

▲
Greek theater was performed in large, circular, open-air auditoriums, such as the Theater of Dionysus at Athens (shown here in a reconstruction), that could seat thousands of spectators.

This sculpture of an ancient Greek tragic mask shows the typical open mouth and domelike upper portion. ▶

This Roman wall painting shows a tragic actor resting after a performance, his hair still tousled by the mask he has just removed. ▶

This Roman mosaic shows tragic and comic masks. The actual masks were made of cloth or wood and fit over the entire head.
▼

▲
An actor costumed as Hercules and holding a tragic mask is shown in this detail
from an ancient vase painting.

▲
Masked actors playing Jocasta, Oedipus, and Creon are shown in a scene from the 1957 film version of *Oedipus* directed by Tyrone Guthrie.

Oedipus and Jocasta wear masklike makeup in this production of *Oedipus.* ▶

◀ This poster of French actress Sarah
Bernhardt costumed as Medea for a
1898 production emphasizes the horror
of Medea's act.

▲
Australian-born actress Judith Anderson created a
powerful interpretation of Medea in 1947 in a version
of Euripides's play by American poet Robinson Jeffers.

Medea's anguish is conveyed by the actress playing her in a
1948 production at the Edinburgh Festival in Scotland. ▶

Part Two

Renaissance and Neoclassical Drama

Inventing the Human

Moving away from the religious drama of the Middle Ages, Renaissance playwrights used their new freedom to explore the potentialities of the human personality.

A Midsummer Night's Dream
WILLIAM SHAKESPEARE

Othello, the Moor of Venice
WILLIAM SHAKESPEARE

The Misanthrope MOLIÈRE

◀ This painting from 1670 shows actors at the Théâtre Royal in Paris, including several *commedia dell'arte* performers and Molière (far left).

William Shakespeare ▶

A Midsummer Night's Dream

BY WILLIAM SHAKESPEARE

The English drama of Shakespeare and his contemporaries that developed during the later 1500s drew on a number of sources. One source was the popular religious drama of the Middle Ages. These included mystery plays based on episodes from the Bible; miracle (or saint) plays, which presented the lives of saints; and morality plays, in which the characters are personifications of abstract qualities such as knowledge, beauty, strength, and so on. Another influence was the masque, the lavish dramatic spectacle that was a feature of entertainments at the English court in the late 1500s and early 1600s. A third source was classical drama, though largely the plays of the Roman dramatists rather than Greek ones. Imitations of classical drama were studied and produced by university students, and some of these "university wits" began writing their own plays for London theater companies. The most important was Christopher Marlowe (1564–1593), whose blank verse dramas were a great influence on Shakespeare.

Elizabethan Theater

Beginning in the late 1570s, a number of permanent theaters were built in London and its suburbs. The most famous of these playhouses, Shakespeare's Globe Theater, was an eight-sided structure open to the sky (an adaptation of the inn yards where companies of touring players had previously given their performances). The main acting area was a thrust stage extending into a yard ("the Pit") that provided standing room for spectators who couldn't afford seats in the surrounding galleries. Both male and female roles were played by men. There was no scenery. Costumes were elaborate, but contemporary; no attempt was made to suggest the look of a historical period.

A Man of the Theater

William Shakespeare (1564–1616) was born into a moderately well-to-do family in the country town of Stratford-on-Avon. He received a good education at the local grammar school, married young, had three children, and sometime between 1585 and 1592 went to London and embarked on a career in the theater. Shakespeare participated in all phases of the theater of his time— serving as an actor, manager, and playwright for a London theater company. Shakespeare never bothered to publish his plays during his lifetime—he wrote to be performed. The First Folio of 1623, the first substantially complete edition of his works, was collected only after his death. His plays include a broad variety of theatrical forms, including comedies, tragedies, and histories (a cycle of plays based on the lives of English kings).

The Course of True Love

A Midsummer Night's Dream is one of Shakespeare's early comedies. A tragedy ends with the downfall of its main character. Shakespeare's romantic comedies reverse this pattern, ending with a marriage (or promise of marriage). Like tragedy, comedy has conflict, but in comedy this conflict is generally expressed in witty dialogue rather than physical violence. In A Midsummer Night's Dream, the chief conflict involves two pairs of young lovers. During the course of a nightlong wandering in a forest, a misapplied magic charm scrambles the affections of these young people. As one them ruefully observes, "The course of true love never did run smooth."

A Complex Plot

The misadventures of the young lovers form only one of four interconnected plots in A Midsummer Night's Dream. Another plot deals with the wedding of Theseus, Duke of Athens, and his bride, the Amazon queen Hippolyta. This forms the frame narrative of the play. A third plot involves a quarrel between Oberon and Titania, the king and queen of the Fairies, who inhabit the forest where much of the action of A Midsummer Night's Dream takes place. Finally, a comic subplot deals with a group of local men who are performing an absurd "lamentable comedy" as part of the entertainment for the wedding of Theseus and Hippolyta. Shakespeare skillfully weaves all four of these plots into a pattern that joyfully expresses the wonder and folly of love.

CHARACTERS

Theseus, Duke of Athens

Hippolyta, Queen of the Amazons, betrothed to Theseus

Philostrate, Master of the Revels[1]

Egeus, father of Hermia

Hermia, daughter of Egeus, in love with Lysander

Lysander, in love with Hermia

Demetrius, in love with Hermia and favored by Egeus

Helena, in love with Demetrius

Oberon, King of the Fairies

Titania, Queen of the Fairies

Puck, or Robin Goodfellow

Peaseblossom, fairy attending Titania

Cobweb, fairy attending Titania

Mote, fairy attending Titania

Mustardseed, fairy attending Titania

Other **Fairies** attending

Peter Quince, a carpenter, representing Prologue

Nick Bottom, a weaver, representing Pyramus

Francis Flute, a bellows mender, representing Thisbe

Tom Snout, a tinker,[2] representing Wall

Snug, a joiner,[3] representing Lion

Robin Starveling, a tailor, representing Moonshine

[1] Master . . . Revels—officer of a royal household in charge of court entertainment.

[2] tinker—mender of metal household utensils, such as kettles and pots.

[3] joiner—cabinetmaker.

SCENE: Athens, and a wood near it.

Act One, Scene One

[*Enter* Theseus, Hippolyta, *(and* Philostrate*), with others.*]

Theseus. Now, fair Hippolyta, our **nuptial**[4] hour
    Draws on apace.[5] Four happy days bring in
    Another moon; but, O, methinks, how slow
    This old moon wanes! She lingers my desires,

5   Like to a stepdame or a dowager[6]
    Long withering out a young man's revenue.

Hippolyta. Four days will quickly steep themselves in night;
    Four nights will quickly dream away the time;
    And then the moon, like to a silver bow

10   New bent in heaven, shall behold the night
    Of our solemnities.

Theseus.   Go, Philostrate,
    Stir up the Athenian youth to merriments.
    Awake the **pert and nimble**[7] spirit of mirth.
    Turn melancholy forth to funerals;

15   The pale companion is not for our pomp.[8]
    [*Exit* Philostrate.] Hippolyta, I wooed thee with my sword
    And won thy love doing thee injuries;
    But I will wed thee in another key,
    With pomp, with triumph, and with reveling.
    [*Enter* Egeus *and his daughter* Hermia, *and* Lysander, *and* Demetrius.]

20 **Egeus.** Happy be Theseus, our renownèd duke!

Theseus. Thanks, good Egeus. What's the news with thee?

Egeus. Full of vexation come I, with complaint
    Against my child, my daughter Hermia.
    Stand forth, Demetrius.—My noble lord,

25   This man hath my consent to marry her.—
    Stand forth, Lysander.—And, my gracious Duke,
    This man hath bewitched the bosom of my child.
    Thou, thou Lysander, thou hast given her rhymes

---

[4] **nuptial**—of or relating to marriage or the wedding ceremony.

[5] apace—swiftly.

[6] stepdame . . . dowager—a widow (whose right of inheritance from her dead husband is eating into her son's estate).

[7] **pert and nimble**—high-spirited and quick in movement.

[8] pomp—ceremonial magnificence.

And interchanged love tokens with my child.

30 Thou hast by moonlight at her window sung

With feigning voice verses of feigning[9] love,

And stol'n the impression of her fantasy[10]

With bracelets of thy hair, rings, gauds, conceits,[11]

Knacks, trifles, nosegays, sweetmeats—messengers

35 Of strong prevailment in unhardened youth.

With cunning hast thou filched my daughter's heart,

Turned her obedience, which is due to me,

To stubborn harshness. And, my gracious Duke,

Be it so[12] she will not here before Your Grace

40 Consent to marry with Demetrius,

I beg the ancient privilege of Athens:

As she is mine, I may dispose of her,

Which shall be either to this gentleman

Or to her death, according to our law

45 Immediately provided in that case.

Theseus. What say you, Hermia? Be advised, fair maid.

To you your father should be as a god—

One that composed your beauties, yea, and one

To whom you are but as a form in wax

50 By him imprinted, and within his power

To leave the figure or disfigure it.

Demetrius is a worthy gentleman.

Hermia. So is Lysander.

Theseus. In himself he is;

But in this kind,[13] wanting your father's voice,

55 The other must be held the worthier.

Hermia. I would my father looked but with my eyes.

Theseus. Rather your eyes must with his judgment look.

Hermia. I do **entreat**[14] Your Grace to pardon me.

I know not by what power I am made bold,

---

[9] feigning . . . feigning—false . . . desirous.

[10] And . . . fantasy—and made her fall in love with you (imprinting your image on her imagination) by stealthy and dishonest means.

[11] gauds, conceits—toys, fanciful trifles.

[12] Be it so—if.

[13] kind—respect.

[14] **entreat**—make an earnest request of.

60   Nor how it may concern[15] my modesty
     In such a presence here to plead my thoughts;
     But I beseech Your Grace that I may know
     The worst that may befall me in this case
     If I refuse to wed Demetrius.

65   **Theseus.** Either to die the death[16] or to **abjure**[17]
     Forever the society of men.
     Therefore, fair Hermia, question your desires,
     Know of your youth, examine well your blood,[18]
     Whether, if you yield not to your father's choice,

70   You can endure the livery[19] of a nun,
     For aye to be in shady cloister mewed,[20]
     To live a barren sister all your life,
     Chanting faint hymns to the cold fruitless moon.
     Thrice blessèd they that master so their blood

75   To undergo such maiden pilgrimage;
     But earthlier happy[21] is the rose distilled[22]
     Than that which, withering on the virgin thorn,
     Grows, lives, and dies in single blessedness.

     Hermia. So will I grow, so live, so die, my lord,

80   Ere I will yield my virgin patent[23] up
     Unto his lordship, whose unwishèd yoke[24]
     My soul consents not to give sovereignty.

     Theseus. Take time to pause, and by the next new moon—
     The sealing day betwixt my love and me

85   For everlasting bond of fellowship—
     Upon that day either prepare to die
     For disobedience to your father's will,
     Or else to wed Demetrius, as he would,

---

[15] concern—befit.

[16] die the death—be executed by legal process.

[17] **abjure**—renounce under oath.

[18] blood—passions.

[19] livery—habit, costume.

[20] aye . . . mewed—ever to be shut in a quiet convent.

[21] earthlier happy—happier as respects this world.

[22] distilled—made into perfume.

[23] patent—privilege.

[24] yoke—bond.

Or on Diana's altar[25] to protest[26]

90 For aye **austerity**[27] and single life.

Demetrius. Relent, sweet Hermia, and, Lysander, yield

Thy crazèd title to my certain right.

Lysander. You have her father's love, Demetrius;

Let me have Hermia's. Do you marry him.

95 **Egeus.** Scornful Lysander! True, he hath my love,

And what is mine my love shall render him.

And she is mine, and all my right of her

I do estate unto[28] Demetrius.

Lysander. I am, my lord, as well derived as he,

100 As well possessed;[29] my love is more than his;

My fortunes every way as fairly ranked,

If not with vantage,[30] as Demetrius';

And, which is more than all these boasts can be,

I am beloved of beauteous Hermia.

105 Why should not I then prosecute my right?

Demetrius, I'll avouch it to his head,[31]

Made love to Nedar's daughter, Helena,

And won her soul; and she, sweet lady, dotes,

Devoutly dotes, dotes in idolatry

110 Upon this spotted and inconstant[32] man.

Theseus. I must confess that I have heard so much,

And with Demetrius thought to have spoke thereof;

But, being overfull of self-affairs,

My mind did lose it. But, Demetrius, come,

115 And come, Egeus, you shall go with me;

I have some private schooling[33] for you both.

For you, fair Hermia, look you arm yourself

To fit your fancies to your father's will,

Or else the law of Athens yields you up—

---

[25] Diana's altar—Diana was the virgin goddess of the moon.

[26] protest—vow.

[27] **austerity**—severe self-discipline.

[28] estate unto—settle or bestow upon.

[29] as well derived . . . possessed—as well born and as well endowed with wealth.

[30] vantage—superiority.

[31] avouch . . . head—swear it to his face.

[32] spotted and inconstant—morally stained and unfaithful.

[33] schooling—advice.

120	Which by no means we may extenuate[34]—
	To death or to a vow of single life.
	Come, my Hippolyta. What cheer, my love?
	Demetrius and Egeus, go along.
	I must employ you in some business
125	Against our nuptial, and confer with you
	Of something nearly that[35] concerns yourselves.

Egeus. With duty and desire we follow you.

[*Exeunt all but* Lysander *and* Hermia.]

Lysander. How now, my love, why is your cheek so pale?
How chance the roses there do fade so fast?

130 **Hermia.** Belike[36] for want of rain, which I could well
Beteem[37] them from the tempest of my eyes.

Lysander. Ay me! For aught that I could ever read,
Could ever hear by tale or history,
The course of true love never did run smooth;

135 But either it was different in blood[38]—

Hermia. O cross! Too high to be enthralled[39] to low.

Lysander. Or else misgrafted in respect of years—

Hermia. O spite! Too old to be engaged to young.

Lysander. Or else it stood upon the choice of friends

140 **Hermia.** O hell, to choose love by another's eyes!

Lysander. Or if there were a sympathy in choice,
War, death, or sickness did lay siege to it,
Making it momentany[40] as a sound,
Swift as a shadow, short as any dream,

145 Brief as the lightning in the collied[41] night
That in a spleen[42] unfolds both heaven and earth,
And ere a man hath power to say "Behold!"
The jaws of darkness do devour it up.
So quick bright things come to confusion.

---

[34] extenuate—relax.

[35] nearly that—that closely.

[36] Belike—very likely.

[37] Beteem—grant, afford.

[38] blood—hereditary station, social rank.

[39] enthralled—enslaved.

[40] momentany—lasting but a moment.

[41] collied—blackened (as with coal dust), darkened.

[42] in a spleen—in a swift impulse, in a violent flash.

Hermia. If then true lovers have been ever crossed,
It stands as an **edict**[43] in destiny.
Then let us teach our trial patience,
Because it is a customary cross,
As due to love as thoughts, and dreams, and sighs,
Wishes, and tears, poor fancy's followers.

Lysander. A good persuasion. Therefore, hear me, Hermia:
I have a widow aunt, a dowager
Of great revenue, and she hath no child.
From Athens is her house remote seven leagues;[44]
And she respects me as her only son.
There, gentle Hermia, may I marry thee,
And to that place the sharp Athenian law
Cannot pursue us. If thou lovest me, then,
Steal forth thy father's house tomorrow night;
And in the wood, a league without[45] the town,
Where I did meet thee once with Helena
To do observance to a morn of May,[46]
There will I stay for thee.

Hermia.   My good Lysander!
I swear to thee, by Cupid's strongest bow,
By his best arrow with the golden head,[47]
By the simplicity[48] of Venus' doves,[49]
By that which knitteth souls and prospers loves,
And by that fire which burned the Carthage queen
When the false Trojan[50] under sail was seen,
By all the vows that ever men have broke,
In number more than ever women spoke,
In that same place thou hast appointed me
Tomorrow truly will I meet with thee.

---

[43] **edict**—decree.

[44] seven leagues—21 miles (a league equals three miles).

[45] without—outside.

[46] do . . . May—perform the ceremonies of May Day (May 1, which is traditionally the beginning of spring).

[47] Cupid's . . . golden head—Cupid is the god of love. His sharp gold-pointed arrows were supposed to induce love; his blunt arrows tipped with lead to cause aversion.

[48] simplicity—innocence.

[49] Venus' doves—Cupid's mother Venus is the goddess of love. Her chariot is supposed to be drawn by doves.

[50] Carthage queen . . . false Trojan—Dido, Queen of Carthage, burned herself to death on a funeral pyre after having been deserted by the Trojan hero Aeneas.

Lysander. Keep promise, love. Look, here comes Helena.

[*Enter Helena.*]

180 **Hermia.** God speed, fair[51] Helena! Whither away?

Helena. Call you me fair? That "fair" again unsay.
　　　Demetrius loves your fair.[52] O happy fair!
　　　Your eyes are lodestars,[53] and your tongue's sweet air
　　　More tunable than lark to shepherd's ear
185　　When wheat is green, when hawthorn buds appear.
　　　Sickness is catching. O, were favor[54] so,
　　　Yours would I catch, fair Hermia ere I go;
　　　My ear should catch your voice, my eye your eye,
　　　My tongue should catch your tongue's sweet melody.
190　　Were the world mine, Demetrius being bated,[55]
　　　The rest I'd give to be to you translated.[56]
　　　O, teach me how you look and with what art
　　　You sway the motion of Demetrius' heart.

Hermia. I frown upon him, yet he loves me still.

195 **Helena.** O, that your frowns would teach my smiles such skill!

Hermia. I give him curses, yet he gives me love.

Helena. O, that my prayers could such affection move!

Hermia. The more I hate, the more he follows me.

Helena. The more I love, the more he hateth me.

200 **Hermia.** His folly, Helena, is no fault of mine.

Helena. None, but your beauty. Would that fault were mine!

Hermia. Take comfort. He no more shall see my face.
　　　Lysander and myself will fly this place.
　　　Before the time I did Lysander see
205　　Seemed Athens as a paradise to me.
　　　O, then, what graces in my love do dwell,
　　　That he hath turned a heaven unto a hell?

Lysander. Helen, to you our minds we will unfold.
　　　Tomorrow night, when Phoebe[57] doth behold

---

[51] fair—fair-complexioned (generally regarded by the Elizabethans as more beautiful than a dark complexion).

[52] your fair—your beauty (even though Hermia is dark-complexioned).

[53] lodestars—guiding stars.

[54] favor—looks, appearance.

[55] bated—excepted.

[56] translated—transformed.

[57] Phoebe—Diana, the moon.

210   Her silver **visage**[58] in the watery glass,[59]

Decking with liquid pearl the bladed grass,

A time that lovers' flights doth still[60] conceal,

Through Athens' gates have we devised to steal.

Hermia. And in the wood, where often you and I

215   Upon faint primrose beds were wont[61] to lie,

Emptying our bosoms of their counsel[62] sweet,

There my Lysander and myself shall meet,

And thence from Athens turn away our eyes

To seek new friends and stranger companies.[63]

220   Farewell, sweet playfellow. Pray thou for us,

And good luck grant thee thy Demetrius!

Keep word, Lysander. We must starve our sight

From lovers' food till morrow deep midnight.

Lysander. I will, my Hermia. [*Exit* Hermia.] Helena, adieu.

225   As you on him, Demetrius dote on you! [*Exit* Lysander.]

Helena. How happy some o'er other some can be!

Through Athens I am thought as fair as she.

But what of that? Demetrius thinks not so;

He will not know what all but he do know.

230   And as he errs, doting on Hermia's eyes,

So I, admiring of his qualities.

Things base and vile, holding no quantity,[64]

Love can transpose to form and dignity.

Love looks not with the eyes, but with the mind,

235   And therefore is winged Cupid painted blind.

Nor hath Love's mind of any judgment taste;

Wings and no eyes figure unheedy haste.

And therefore is Love said to be a child,

Because in choice he is so oft beguiled.[65]

240   As waggish boys in game themselves forswear,

---

[58] **visage**—face.

[59] glass—mirror.

[60] still—always.

[61] wont—accustomed.

[62] counsel—secret thought.

[63] stranger companies—company of strangers.

[64] holding no quantity—unsubstantial, unshapely.

[65] beguiled—self-deceived, making unaccountable choices.

So the boy Love is **perjured**[66] everywhere.
For ere Demetrius looked on Hermia's eyne,[67]
He hailed down oaths that he was only mine;
And when this hail some heat from Hermia felt,
245 So he dissolved, and showers of oaths did melt.
I will go tell him of fair Hermia's flight.
Then to the wood will he tomorrow night
Pursue her; and for this intelligence[68]
If I have thanks, it is a dear expense.[69]
250 But herein mean I to enrich my pain,
To have his sight thither and back again. [*Exit.*]

Act One, Scene Two

[*Enter* Quince *the carpenter, and* Snug *the joiner, and* Bottom *the weaver, and* Flute *the bellows mender, and* Snout *the tinker, and* Starveling *the tailor.*]

Quince. Is all our company here?

Bottom. You were best to call them generally,[70] man by man, according to the scrip.[71]

Quince. Here is the scroll of every man's name which is thought fit,
5 through all Athens, to play in our interlude[72] before the Duke and the Duchess on his wedding day at night.

Bottom. First, good Peter Quince, say what the play treats on, then read the names of the actors, and so grow to a point.

Quince. Marry,[73] our play is "The most lamentable comedy and most
10 cruel death of Pyramus and Thisbe."[74]

Bottom. A very good piece of work, I assure you, and a merry. Now, good Peter Quince, call forth your actors by the scroll. Masters, spread yourselves.

Quince. Answer as I call you. Nick Bottom, the weaver.

---

[66] **perjured**—guilty of perjury, testifying falsely under oath.

[67] eyne—eyes (old form of plural).

[68] intelligence—information.

[69] dear expense—trouble worth taking.

[70] generally—blunder for "individually."

[71] scrip—scrap; error for "script."

[72] interlude—play.

[73] Marry—originally, by the Virgin Mary; a mild oath.

[74] Pyramus and Thisbe—tragic lovers in a classical myth retold by the Roman poet Ovid in his *Metamorphoses*.

15   **Bottom.** Ready. Name what part I am for, and proceed.

Quince. You, Nick Bottom, are set down for Pyramus.

Bottom. What is Pyramus? A lover or a tyrant?

Quince. A lover, that kills himself most gallant for love.

Bottom. That will ask some tears in the true performing of it. If I do it,
20   let the audience look to their eyes. I will move storms; I will condole
in some measure.[75] To the rest—yet my chief humor[76] is for a tyrant. I
could play Ercles[77] rarely, or a part to tear a cat in, to make all split.[78]

"The raging rocks
And shivering shocks
25   Shall break the locks
Of prison gates;
And Phibbus' car[79]
Shall shine from far
And make and mar
30   The foolish Fates."

This was lofty! Now name the rest of the players. This is
Ercles' vein, a tyrant's vein. A lover is more condoling.

Quince. Francis Flute, the bellows mender.

Flute. Here, Peter Quince.

35   **Quince.** Flute, you must take Thisbe on you.

Flute. What is Thisbe? A wandering knight?

Quince. It is the lady that Pyramus must love.

Flute. Nay, faith, let not me play a woman. I have a
beard coming.

40   **Quince.** That's all one.[80] You shall play it in a mask, and you may
speak as small[81] as you will.

Bottom. An[82] I may hide my face, let me play Thisbe too. I'll speak in a
monstrous little voice: "Thisbe, Thisbe!" "Ah, Pyramus, my lover
dear! Thy Thisbe dear, and lady dear!"

45   **Quince.** No, no, you must play Pyramus, and Flute, you Thisbe.

---

[75] condole . . . measure—arouse pity to a great degree.

[76] humor—disposition of my character; inclination.

[77] Ercles—the classical hero Hercules, presented in Roman drama as a raging character.

[78] to tear . . . split—to rant, to cause a stir (to bring down the house).

[79] Phibbus' car—the chariot of Phoebus, the sun god.

[80] That's all one—it makes no difference.

[81] small—high-pitched.

[82] An—if.

Bottom. Well, proceed.

Quince. Robin Starveling, the tailor.

Starveling. Here, Peter Quince.

Quince. Robin Starveling, you must play Thisbe's mother. Tom Snout,
50   the tinker.

Snout. Here, Peter Quince.

Quince. You, Pyramus' father; myself, Thisbe's father; Snug, the joiner,
you, the lion's part; and I hope here is a play fitted.

Snug. Have you the lion's part written? Pray you, if it be, give it me, for I
55   am slow of study.

Quince. You may do it **extempore**,[83] for it is nothing but roaring.

Bottom. Let me play the lion too. I will roar that I will do any man's
heart good to hear me. I will roar that I will make the Duke say, "Let
him roar again, let him roar again."

60 **Quince.** An you should do it too terribly, you would fright the Duchess
and the ladies, that they would shriek; and that were enough to hang
us all.

All. That would hang us, every mother's son.

Bottom. I grant you, friends, if you should fright the ladies out of their
65   wits, they would have no more discretion[84] but to hang us; but I will
aggravate[85] my voice so that I will roar you as gently as any sucking
dove; I will roar you an 'twere any nightingale.

Quince. You can play no part but Pyramus; for Pyramus is a sweet-faced
man, a proper[86] man as one shall see in a summer's day, a most lovely
70   gentlemanlike man. Therefore you must needs play Pyramus.

Bottom. Well, I will undertake it. What beard were I best to play it in?

Quince. My, what you will.

Bottom. I will discharge it in either your straw-color beard, your
orange-tawny beard, your purple-in-grain[87] beard, or your French-
75   crown-color[88] beard, your perfect yellow.

Quince. Some of your French crowns[89] have no hair at all, and then you
will play barefaced. But, masters, here are your parts. [*He distributes*

---

[83] **extempore**—unrehearsed; ad-libbed.

[84] no more discretion—no other choice.

[85] aggravate—blunder for "moderate."

[86] proper—handsome.

[87] purple-in-grain—dyed a very deep red.

[88] French-crown-color—color of a French crown, a gold coin.

[89] crowns—heads bald from syphilis, the "French disease."

parts.] And I am to entreat you, request you, and desire you to con[90]
them by tomorrow night, and meet me in the palace wood, a mile
80 without the town, by moonlight. There will we rehearse; for if we
meet in the city, we shall be dogged with company, and our devices
known. In the meantime I will draw a bill[91] of properties, such as our
play wants.[92] I pray you, fail me not.
Bottom. We will meet, and there we may rehearse most obscenely[93] and
85 courageously. Take pains, be perfect.[94] Adieu.
Quince. At the Duke's oak we meet.
Bottom. Enough. Hold, or cut bowstrings.[95] [*Exeunt.*]

Act Two, Scene One

[*Enter a* Fairy *at one door, and* Robin Goodfellow, Puck, *at another.*]
Puck. How now, spirit, whither wander you?
Fairy. Over hill, over dale,
Thorough[1] bush, thorough brier,
Over park, over pale,[2]
5 Thorough flood, thorough fire,
I do wander everywhere,
Swifter than the moon's sphere;[3]
And I serve the Fairy Queen,
To dew her orbs[4] upon the green.
10 The cowslips tall her pensioners[5] be.
In their gold coats spots you see;
Those be rubies, fairy favors;
In those freckles live their savors.
I must go seek some dewdrops here

---

[90] con—learn by heart.

[91] draw a bill—make a list.

[92] wants—needs.

[93] obscenely—blunder for whatever Bottom means to say.

[94] perfect—letter-perfect in memorizing your parts.

[95] Hold . . . bowstrings—An archer's expression, not definitely explained, but probably meaning here, "Keep your promises or give up the play."

[1] Thorough—through.

[2] pale—enclosure.

[3] sphere—orbit.

[4] orbs—circles, fairy rings (circular bands of grass, darker than the surrounding area, caused by fungi enriching the soil).

[5] cowslips . . . pensioners—flowers be her retainers, member of her royal bodyguard.

15	And hang a pearl in every cowslip's ear.
	Farewell, thou lob[6] of spirits; I'll be gone.
	Our Queen and all her elves come here anon.[7]
	Puck. The King doth keep his revels here tonight.
	Take heed the Queen come not within his sight.
20	For Oberon is passing fell and wrath,[8]
	Because that she as her attendant hath
	A lovely boy, stolen from an Indian king;
	She never had so sweet a changeling.[9]
	And jealous Oberon would have the child
25	Knight of his train,[10] to trace[11] the forests wild.
	But she perforce[12] withholds the lovèd boy,
	Crowns him with flowers, and makes him all her joy.
	And now they never meet in grove or green,
	By fountain clear, or spangled starlight sheen,
30	But they do square,[13] that all their elves for fear
	Creep into acorn cups and hide them there.
	Fairy. Either I mistake your shape and making quite,
	Or else you are that shrewd and knavish sprite[14]
	Called Robin Goodfellow. Are not you he
35	That frights the maidens of the villagery,
	Skim milk,[15] and sometimes labor in the quern,[16]
	And bootless[17] make the breathless huswife churn,
	And sometimes make the drink to bear no barm,[18]
	Mislead night wanderers, laughing at their harm?
40	Those that "Hobgoblin" call you, and "Sweet Puck,"

[6] lob—country bumpkin.

[7] anon—at once.

[8] passing . . . wrath—exceedingly fierce and angry.

[9] changeling—child exchanged for another by the fairies.

[10] train—retinue, band of followers.

[11] trace—range through.

[12] perforce—forcibly.

[13] square—quarrel.

[14] shrewd . . . sprite—mischievous and rascally spirit.

[15] Skim milk—steal cream.

[16] quern—hand mill (where Puck presumably hampers the grinding of the corn).

[17] bootless—in vain (Puck prevents the cream from turning into butter).

[18] barm—head on the ale. (Puck prevents the barm or yeast from fermenting).

You do their work, and they shall have good luck.
Are you not he?

Puck.   Thou speakest aright;
I am that merry wanderer of the night.
I jest to Oberon and make him smile

45 When I a fat and bean-fed horse beguile,
Neighing in likeness of a filly foal;
And sometimes lurk I in a gossip's[19] bowl
In very likeness of a roasted crab,[20]
And when she drinks, against her lips I bob

50 And on her withered dewlap[21] pour the ale.
The wisest aunt, telling the saddest[22] tale,
Sometimes for three-foot stool mistaketh me;
Then slip I from her bum, down topples she,
And "Tailor"[23] cries, and falls into a cough;

55 And then the whole choir hold their hips and laugh,
And waxen[24] in their mirth, and neeze,[25] and swear
A merrier hour was never wasted there.
But, room, fairy! Here comes Oberon.

Fairy. And here my mistress. Would that he were gone!
[*Enter* Oberon *the* King of Fairies *at one door, with his train, and* Titania *the*
Queen *at another, with hers.*]

60 **Oberon.** Ill met by moonlight, proud Titania.

Titania. What, jealous Oberon? Fairies, skip hence.
I have forsworn his bed and company.

Oberon. Tarry, rash wanton.[26] Am not I thy lord?

Titania. Then I must be thy lady; but I know

65 When thou hast stolen away from Fairyland
And in the shape of Corin[27] sat all day,

---

[19] gossip's—old woman's.

[20] crab—crab apple.

[21] dewlap—loose skin on the neck.

[22] saddest—most serious.

[23] Tailor—possibly because she ends up sitting cross-legged on the floor, looking like a tailor, or else referring to the *tail*, (or buttocks).

[24] waxen—increase.

[25] neeze—sneeze.

[26] wanton—headstrong creature.

[27] Corin—with Phillida (line 68), conventional names of pastoral lovers.

Playing on pipes of corn[28] and versing love
To amorous Phillida. Why art thou here
Come from the farthest step of India,
70   But that, forsooth,[29] the bouncing Amazon,
Your buskined[30] mistress and your warrior love,
To Theseus must be wedded, and you come
To give their bed joy and prosperity.
Oberon. How canst thou thus for shame, Titania,
75   Glance at my credit with Hippolyta,
Knowing I know thy love to Theseus?
Didst not thou lead him through the glimmering night
From Perigenia, whom he ravished?
And make him with fair Aegles break his faith,
80   With Ariadne and Antiopa?
Titania. These are the forgeries of jealousy;
And never, since the middle summer's spring,[31]
Met we on hill, in dale, forest, or mead,[32]
By paved fountain or by rushy brook,
85   Or in the beached margent[33] of the sea,
To dance our ringlets[34] to the whistling wind,
But with thy brawls thou hast disturbed our sport.
Therefore[35] the winds, piping to us in vain,
As in revenge, have sucked up from the sea
90   Contagious[36] fogs which, falling in the land,
Hath every pelting river made so proud
That they have overborne their continents.[37]
The ox hath therefore stretched his yoke[38] in vain,
The plowman lost his sweat, and the green corn
95   Hath rotted ere his youth attained a beard;

---

[28] pipes of corn—panpipes (primitive wind instrument) made from oat stalks.

[29] forsooth—indeed.

[30] buskined—wearing half-boots called *buskins*.

[31] middle summer's spring—beginning of midsummer.

[32] mead—meadow.

[33] margent—margin, edge, border.

[34] ringlets—dances in a ring.

[35] Therefore—because of our quarrel.

[36] Contagious—noxious.

[37] pelting . . . continents—paltry rivers filled so full that they have overflowed their banks.

[38] stretched his yoke—pulled at his yoke in plowing.

The fold[39] stands empty in the drownèd field,
And crows are fatted with the murrain[40] flock;
The nine-men's morris[41] is filled up with mud,
And the quaint mazes in the wanton green
100   For lack of tread are undistinguishable.
The human mortals want their winter[42] here;
No night is now with hymn or carol blessed.
Therefore the moon, the governess of floods,
Pale in her anger, washes[43] all the air,
105   That rheumatic diseases[44] do abound.
And thorough this distemperature we see
The seasons alter: hoary-headed frosts
Fall in the fresh lap of the crimson rose,
And on old Hiems'[45] thin and icy crown
110   An odorous chaplet of sweet summer buds
Is, as in mockery, set. The spring, the summer,
The childing[46] autumn, angry winter, change
Their wonted liveries, and the mazèd[47] world
By their increase now knows not which is which.
115   And this same **progeny**[48] of evils comes
From our debate, from our **dissension**.[49]
We are their parents and original.
Oberon. Do you amend it, then. It lies in you.
Why should Titania cross her Oberon?
120   I do but beg a little changeling boy
To be my henchman.[50]
Titania.   Set your heart at rest.
The fairy land buys not the child of me.

---

[39] fold—pen for sheep or cattle.

[40] murrain—having died of the plague.

[41] nine-men's morris—portion of the village green marked out in a square for a game played with nine pebbles or pegs.

[42] winter—regular winter season; or proper observances of winter, such as the *hymn* or *carol* in the next line.

[43] washes—saturates with moisture.

[44] rheumatic diseases—colds, flu, and other respiratory infections.

[45] Hiems'—the winter god's.

[46] childing—fruitful.

[47] mazèd—bewildered.

[48] **progeny**—offspring or descendants considered as a group.

[49] **dissension**—difference of opinion.

[50] henchman—attendant, page.

His mother was a vot'ress of my order,[51]
And in the spicèd Indian air by night
125 Full often hath she gossiped by my side
And sat with me on Neptune's yellow sands,
Marking th' embarkèd traders on the flood,[52]
When we have laughed to see the sails conceive
And grow big-bellied with the wanton wind;
130 Which she, with pretty and with swimming[53] gait,
Following—her womb then rich with my young squire—
Would imitate, and sail upon the land
To fetch me trifles, and return again
As from a voyage, rich with merchandise.
135 But she, being mortal, of that boy did die;
And for her sake do I rear up her boy,
And for her sake I will not part with him.

Oberon. How long within this wood intend you stay?

Titania. Perchance till after Theseus' wedding day.
140 If you will patiently dance in our round
And see our moonlight revels, go with us;
If not, shun me, and I will spare your haunts.

Oberon. Give me that boy, and I will go with thee.

Titania. Not for thy fairy kingdom. Fairies, away!
145 We shall **chide**[54] downright, if I longer stay.

[*Exeunt* Titania *with her train.*]

Oberon. Well, go thy way. Thou shalt not from this grove
Till I torment thee for this injury.
My gentle Puck, come hither. Thou rememb'rest
Since once I sat upon a promontory,
150 And heard a mermaid on a dolphin's back
Uttering such dulcet[55] and harmonious breath
That the rude sea grew civil at her song,
And certain stars shot madly from their spheres
To hear the sea-maid's music?

Puck.   I remember.

---

[51] was . . . order—had taken a vow to serve me.

[52] traders . . . flood—merchant ships on the flood tide.

[53] swimming—smooth, gliding.

[54] **chide**—scold.

[55] dulcet—sweet.

155 **Oberon.** That very time I saw, but thou couldst not,
Flying between the cold moon and the earth
Cupid, all armed. A certain[56] aim he took
At a fair vestal throned by the west,[57]
And loosed his love shaft smartly from his bow
160 As it should pierce a hundred thousand hearts;
But I might see young Cupid's fiery shaft
Quenched in the chaste beams of the watery moon,
And the imperial votress passèd on,
In maiden meditation, fancy-free.
165 Yet marked I where the bolt of Cupid fell:
It fell upon a little western flower,
Before milk-white, now purple with love's wound,
And maidens call it love-in-idleness.[58]
Fetch me that flower; the herb I showed thee once.
170 The juice of it on sleeping eyelids laid
Will make or man or woman madly dote
Upon the next live creature that it sees.
Fetch me this herb, and be thou here again
Ere the **leviathan**[59] can swim a league.
175 **Puck.** I'll put a girdle round about the earth
In forty minutes. [*Exit.*]
Oberon. Having once this juice,
I'll watch Titania when she is asleep
And drop the liquor of it in her eyes.
The next thing then she waking looks upon,
180 Be it on lion, bear, or wolf, or bull,
On meddling monkey, or on busy ape,
She shall pursue it with the soul of love.
And ere I take this charm from off her sight,
As I can take it with another herb,
185 I'll make her render up her page to me.
But who comes here? I am invisible,
And I will overhear their conference.

---

[56] certain—sure.

[57] vestal . . . west—complimentary allusion to Elizabeth I, "Virgin Queen" of England. The vestal virgins were a powerful order of priestesses of the goddess Vesta in ancient Rome.

[58] love-in-idleness—pansy, heartsease.

[59] **leviathan**—sea monster, whale.

[*Enter* Demetrius, Helena *following him.*]

Demetrius. I love thee not; therefore pursue me not.
Where is Lysander and fair Hermia?

190 The one I'll slay; the other slayeth me.
Thou toldst me they were stol'n unto this wood;
And here am I, and wood[60] within this wood
Because I cannot meet my Hermia.
Hence, get thee gone, and follow me no more.

195 **Helena.** You draw me, you hardhearted adamant![61]
But yet you draw not iron, for my heart
Is true as steel. Leave you your power to draw,
And I shall have no power to follow you.

Demetrius. Do I entice[62] you? Do I speak you fair?

200 Or rather do I not in plainest truth
Tell you I do not nor I cannot love you?

Helena. And even for that do I love you the more.
I am your spaniel; and, Demetrius,
The more you beat me I will fawn on you.

205 Use me but as your spaniel, spurn me, strike me,
Neglect me, lose me; only give me leave,
Unworthy as I am, to follow you.
What worser place can I beg in your love—
And yet a place of high respect with me—

210 Than to be used as you use your dog?

Demetrius. Tempt not too much the hatred of my spirit,
For I am sick when I do look on thee.

Helena. And I am sick when I look not on you.

Demetrius. You do impeach[63] your modesty too much

215 To leave the city and commit yourself
Into the hands of one that loves you not,
To trust the opportunity of night
And the ill counsel of a desert place
With the rich worth of your virginity.

---

[60] wood—mad, frantic (with word play on *wood,* "forest").

[61] adamant—lodestone, magnet (with a pun on *hardhearted,* since adamant was also thought to be the hardest of all stones and was confused with the diamond).

[62] **entice**—lure.

[63] impeach—call into question.

220	**Helena.** Your virtue is my privilege.[64] For that
	It is not night when I do see your face,
	Therefore I think I am not in the night;
	Nor doth this wood lack worlds of company,
	For you, in my respect, are all the world.
225	Then how can it be said I am alone
	When all the world is here to look on me?
	Demetrius. I'll run from thee and hide me in the brakes,[65]
	And leave thee to the mercy of wild beasts.
	Helena. The wildest hath not such a heart as you.
230	Run when you will. The story shall be changed:
	Apollo flies and Daphne holds the chase,[66]
	The dove pursues the griffin,[67] the mild hind[68]
	Makes speed to catch the tiger—bootless speed,
	When cowardice pursues and valor flies!
235	**Demetrius.** I will not stay thy questions. Let me go!
	Or if thou follow me, do not believe
	But I shall do thee mischief in the wood.
	Helena. Ay, in the temple, in the town, the field,
	You do me mischief. Fie, Demetrius!
240	Your wrongs do set a scandal on my sex.[69]
	We cannot fight for love, as men may do;
	We should be wooed and were not made to woo.
	[*Exit* Demetrius.]
	I'll follow thee and make a heaven of hell,
	To die upon the hand I love so well. [*Exit.*]
245	**Oberon.** Fare thee well, nymph. Ere he do leave this grove
	Thou shalt fly him, and he shall seek thy love.
	[*Enter* Puck.]
	Hast thou the flower there? Welcome, wanderer.
	Puck. Ay, there it is. [*He offers the flower.*]

---

[64] privilege—safeguard, warrant.

[65] brakes—thickets.

[66] Apollo . . . chase—In the ancient myth, Daphne fled from the god Apollo and was saved from his pursuit by being transformed into a laurel tree; here it is the female who *holds the chase*, or pursues, instead of the male.

[67] griffin—fabulous monster with the head and wings of an eagle and the body of a lion.

[68] hind—female deer.

[69] Your . . . sex—the wrongs that you do me cause me to act in a manner that disgraces my sex.

Oberon. I pray thee, give it me.

I know a bank where the wild thyme blows,

250 Where oxlips and the nodding violet grows,

Quite overcanopied with luscious woodbine,

With sweet muskroses and with eglantine.

There sleeps Titania sometime of the night,

Lulled in these flowers with dances and delight;

255 And there the snake throws[70] her enameled skin,

Weed[71] wide enough to wrap a fairy in.

And with the juice of this I'll streak her eyes

And make her full of hateful fantasies.

Take thou some of it, and seek through this grove.

[He gives some love juice.]

260 A sweet Athenian lady is in love

With a disdainful youth. Anoint his eyes,

But do it when the next thing he **espies**[72]

May be the lady. Thou shalt know the man

By the Athenian garments he hath on.

265 Effect it with some care, that he may prove

More fond on her than she upon her love;

And look thou meet me ere the first cock crow.

Puck. Fear not, my lord, your servant shall do so.

[Exeunt separately.]

Act Two, Scene Two

[Enter Titania, Queen of Fairies, *with her train.]*

Titania. Come, now a roundel[73] and a fairy song;

Then, for the third part of a minute, hence—

Some to kill cankers[74] in the muskrose buds,

Some war with reremice[75] for their leathern wings

5 To make my small elves coats, and some keep back

---

[70] throws—sloughs off, sheds.

[71] Weed—garment.

[72] **espies**—sees.

[73] roundel—dance in a ring.

[74] cankers—cankerworms (caterpillars or grubs).

[75] reremice—bats.

The **clamorous**[76] owl, that nightly hoots and wonders
At our quaint spirits. Sing me now asleep.
Then to your offices, and let me rest.
[Fairies *sing.*]
First Fairy. You spotted snakes with double[77] tongue,
10   Thorny hedgehogs, be not seen;
          Newts and blindworms,[78] do no wrong;
          Come not near our Fairy Queen.
Chorus [*dancing*]. Philomel,[79] with melody
          Sing in our sweet lullaby;
15   Lulla, lulla, lullaby, lulla, lulla, lullaby.
          Never harm
          Nor spell nor charm
          Come our lovely lady nigh.
          So good night, with lullaby.
20 **First Fairy.** Weaving spiders, come not here;
          Hence, you long-legged spinners, hence!
          Beetles black, approach not near;
          Worm nor snail, do no offense.
Chorus [*dancing*]. Philomel, with melody
25   Sing in our sweet lullaby;
          Lulla, lulla, lullaby, lulla, lulla, lullaby.
          Never harm
          Nor spell nor charm
          Come our lovely lady nigh.
30   So good night, with lullaby.
[Titania *sleeps.*]
Second Fairy. Hence, away! Now all is well.
          One aloof stand sentinel.[80]
[*Exeunt* Fairies, *leaving one sentinel.*]
[*Enter* Oberon *and squeezes the flower on* Titania's *eyelids.*]
Oberon. What thou seest when thou dost wake,
          Do it for thy true love take;

---

[76] **clamorous**—noisy.

[77] double—forked.

[78] Newts and blindworms—water lizards and small snakes with tiny eyes (both considered poisonous).

[79] Philomel—the nightingale. According to Ovid's *Metamorphoses*, Philomela, daughter of King Pandion, was transformed into a nightingale after she had been raped by her sister Procne's husband, Tereus.

[80] sentinel—Presumably Oberon is able to outwit or intimidate this guard.

35   Love and **languish**[81] for his sake.
            Be it ounce,[82] or cat, or bear,
            Pard,[83] or boar with bristled hair,
            In thy eye that shall appear
            When thou wakst, it is thy dear.
40   Wake when some vile thing is near. [*Exit.*]
        [*Enter* Lysander *and* Hermia.]
        Lysander. Fair love, you faint with wandering in the wood;
                    And to speak truth, I have forgot our way.
                We'll rest us, Hermia, if you think it good,
                    And tarry for the comfort of the day.
45   **Hermia.** Be it so, Lysander. Find you out a bed,
            For I upon this bank will rest my head.
        Lysander. One turf shall serve as pillow for us both;
            One heart, one bed, two bosoms, and one troth.[84]
        Hermia. Nay, good Lysander, for my sake, my dear,
50   Lie further off yet. Do not lie so near.
        Lysander. O, take the sense, sweet, of my innocence![85]
            Love takes the meaning in love's conference.[86]
            I mean that my heart unto yours is knit,
            So that but one heart we can make of it;
55   Two bosoms interchainèd with an oath—
            So then two bosoms and a single troth.
            Then by your side no bed-room me deny,
            For lying so, Hermia, I do not lie.[87]
        Hermia. Lysander riddles very prettily.
60   Now much beshrew[88] my manners and my pride
            If Hermia meant to say Lysander lied.
            But, gentle friend, for love and courtesy
            Lie further off, in human[89] modesty.

---

[81] **languish**—become downcast; pine.

[82] ounce—lynx.

[83] Pard—leopard.

[84] troth—trothplight, promise to marry.

[85] take . . . innocence—interpret my intention as innocent.

[86] Love . . . conference—when lovers confer, love teaches each lover to interpret the other's meaning lovingly.

[87] lie—tell a falsehood (with a riddling pun on *lie*, "recline").

[88] beshrew—curse (but mildly meant).

[89] human—courteous.

Such separation as may well be said

65　Becomes a virtuous bachelor and a maid,

So far be distant; and, good night, sweet friend.

Thy love ne'er alter till thy sweet life end!

Lysander. Amen, amen, to that fair prayer, say I,

And then end life when I end loyalty!

70　Here is my bed. Sleep give thee all his rest!

Hermia. With half that wish the wisher's eyes be pressed!

[*They sleep, separated by a short distance.*]

[*Enter* Puck.]

Puck. Through the forest have I gone,

But Athenian found I none

On whose eyes I might approve[90]

75　This flower's force in stirring love.

Night and silence—Who is here?

Weeds of Athens he doth wear.

This is he, my master said,

Despisèd the Athenian maid;

80　And here the maiden, sleeping sound,

On the **dank**[91] and dirty ground.

Pretty soul, she durst not lie

Near this lack-love, this kill-courtesy.

Churl,[92] upon thy eyes I throw

85　All the power this charm doth owe.[93]

[*He applies the love juice.*]

When thou wak'st, let love forbid

Sleep his seat on thy eyelid.

So awake when I am gone,

For I must now to Oberon. [*Exit.*]

[*Enter* Demetrius *and* Helena, *running.*]

90　**Helena.** Stay, though thou kill me, sweet Demetrius!

Demetrius. I charge thee, hence, and do not haunt me thus.

Helena. O, wilt thou darkling[94] leave me? Do not so.

Demetrius. Stay, on thy peril! I alone will go. [*Exit.*]

---

[90] approve—test.

[91] **dank**—disagreeably damp.

[92] Churl—rude, boorish person.

[93] owe—possess.

[94] darkling—in the dark.

Helena. O, I am out of breath in this fond chase!

95 The more my prayer, the lesser is my grace.[95]

Happy is Hermia, wheresoe'er she lies,

For she hath blessèd and attractive eyes.

How came her eyes so bright? Not with salt tears;

If so, my eyes are oftener washed than hers.

100 No, no, I am as ugly as a bear,

For beasts that meet me run away for fear.

Therefore no marvel though Demetrius

Do, as a monster, fly my presence thus.[96]

What wicked and dissembling glass[97] of mine

105 Made me compare with Hermia's sphery eyne?[98]

But who is here? Lysander, on the ground?

Dead, or asleep? I see no blood, no wound.

Lysander, if you live, good Sir, awake.

Lysander [*awaking*]. And run through fire I will for thy sweet sake.

110 Transparent[99] Helena! Nature shows art,

That through thy bosom makes me see thy heart.

Where is Demetrius? O, how fit a word

Is that vile name to perish on my sword!

Helena. Do not say so, Lysander; say not so.

115 What though he love your Hermia? Lord, what though?

Yet Hermia still loves you. Then be content.

Lysander. Content with Hermia? No! I do repent

The tedious minutes I with her have spent.

Not Hermia but Helena I love.

120 Who will not change a raven for a dove?

The will[100] of man is by his reason swayed,

And reason says you are the worthier maid.

Things growing are not ripe until their season;

So I, being young, till now ripe not to reason.

125 And, touching now the point[101] of human skill,

---

[95] my grace—the favor I obtain.

[96] no marvel . . . thus—no wonder that Demetrius flies from me as from a monster.

[97] dissembling glass—false mirror.

[98] compare . . . eyne—vie with Hermia's eyes as bright as stars in their spheres.

[99] Transparent—radiant; able to be seen through, lacking deceit.

[100] will—desire.

[101] point—summit.

Reason becomes the marshal to my will
And leads me to your eyes, where I o'erlook[102]
Love's stories written in love's richest book.

Helena. Wherefore was I to this keen mockery born?
130   When at your hands did I deserve this scorn?
Is 't not enough, is 't not enough, young man,
That I did never—no, nor never can—
Deserve a sweet look from Demetrius' eye,
But you must flout my insufficiency?[103]
135   Good troth, you do me wrong, good sooth,[104] you do,
In such disdainful manner me to woo.
But fare you well. Perforce I must confess
I thought you lord of more true gentleness.
O, that a lady, of one man refused,
140   Should of another therefore be abused! [*Exit.*]

Lysander. She sees not Hermia. Hermia, sleep thou there,
And never mayst thou come Lysander near!
For as a **surfeit**[105] of the sweetest things
The deepest loathing to the stomach brings,
145   Or as the heresies that men do leave
Are hated most of those they did deceive,
So thou, my surfeit and my heresy,
Of all be hated, but the most of me!
And, all my powers, address your love and might
150   To honor Helen and to be her knight! [*Exit.*]

Hermia [*awaking*]. Help me, Lysander, help me! Do thy best
To pluck this crawling serpent from my breast!
Ay me, for pity! What a dream was here!
Lysander, look how I do quake with fear.
155   Methought a serpent ate my heart away,
And you sat smiling at his cruel prey.
Lysander! What, removed? Lysander! Lord!
What, out of hearing? Gone? No sound, no word?
Alack, where are you? Speak, an if you hear;
160   Speak, of all loves! I swoon almost with fear.

---

[102] o'erlook—read.

[103] flout my insufficiency—scorn my failing.

[104] Good troth, good sooth—indeed, truly.

[105] **surfeit**—excess.

No? Then I well perceive you are not nigh.
Either death, or you, I'll find immediately.
[*Exit. The sleeping* Titania *remains.*]

Act Three, Scene One

[*Enter the clowns*[1] Quince, Snug, Bottom, Flute, Snout, *and* Starveling.]
Bottom. Are we all met?
Quince. Pat,[2] pat; and here's a marvelous convenient place for our rehearsal.
  This green plot shall be our stage, this hawthorn brake our tiring-
  house,[3] and we will do it in action as we will do it before the Duke.
5 **Bottom.** Peter Quince?
Quince. What sayest thou, bully[4] Bottom?
Bottom. There are things in this comedy of Pyramus and Thisbe that
  will never please. First, Pyramus must draw a sword to kill himself,
  which the ladies cannot abide. How answer you that?
10 **Snout.** By 'r lakin,[5] a parlous[6] fear.
Starveling. I believe we must leave the killing out, when all is done.
Bottom. Not a whit. I have a device to make all well. Write me a prologue, and let the prologue seem to say, we will do no harm with our
  swords, and that Pyramus is not killed indeed; and for the more
15 better assurance, tell them that I, Pyramus, am not Pyramus but
  Bottom the weaver. This will put them out of fear.
Quince. Well, we will have such a prologue, and it shall be written in
  eight and six.
Bottom. No, make it two more: let it be written in eight and eight.
20 **Snout.** Will not the ladies be afeard of the lion?
Starveling. I fear it, I promise you.
Bottom. Masters, you ought to consider with yourself, to bring in—God
  shield us!—a lion among ladies is a most dreadful thing. For there is
  not a more fearful wildfowl than your lion living, and we ought to
25 look to 't.
Snout. Therefore another prologue must tell he is not a lion.

---

[1] clowns—rustics.

[2] Pat—on the dot, punctually.

[3] tiring-house—attiring-house, hence backstage.

[4] bully—worthy, jolly, fine fellow.

[5] By 'r lakin—by our ladykin, the Virgin Mary.

[6] parlous—perilous, alarming.

Bottom. Nay, you must name his name, and half his face must be seen through the lion's neck, and he himself must speak through, saying thus or to the same defect:[7] "Ladies," or "Fair ladies, I would wish

30 you," or "I would request you," or "I would entreat you, not to fear, not to tremble; my life for yours.[8] If you think I come hither as a lion, it were pity of my life. No, I am no such thing; I am a man as other men are." And there indeed let him name his name, and tell them plainly he is Snug the joiner.

35 **Quince.** Well, it shall be so. But there is two hard things: that is, to bring the moonlight into a chamber; for, you know, Pyramus and Thisbe meet by moonlight.

Snout. Doth the moon shine that night we play our play?

Bottom. A calendar, a calendar! Look in the almanac. Find out moon-
40 shine, find out moonshine.

[*They consult an almanac.*]

Quince. Yes, it doth shine that night.

Bottom. Why then may you leave a casement of the great chamber window where we play open, and the moon may shine in at the casement.

Quince. Ay; or else one must come in with a bush of thorns[9] and a
45 lantern and say he comes to disfigure, or to present, the person of Moonshine. Then there is another thing—we must have a wall in the great chamber; for Pyramus and Thisbe, says the story, did talk through the chink of a wall.

Snout. You can never bring in a wall. What say you, Bottom?

50 **Bottom.** Some man or other must present Wall. And let him have some plaster, or some loam, or some roughcast[10]about him, to signify wall; or let him hold his fingers thus, and through that cranny shall Pyramus and Thisbe whisper.

Quince. If that maybe, then all is well. Come, sit down, every mother's
55 son, and rehearse your parts. Pyramus, you begin. When you have spoken your speech, enter into that brake, and so everyone according to his cue.[11]

[*Enter Puck.*]

---

[7] defect—blunder for "effect."

[8] my life for yours—I pledge my life to make your lives safe.

[9] bush of thorns—bundle of thornbush fagots (part of the equipment of the man in the moon, according to the popular notions of the time, along with his lantern and his dog).

[10] loam . . . roughcast—materials used in masonry.

[11] cue—final line in a speech that signals an actor to begin the next speech.

Puck [*aside*]. What hempen homespuns[12] have we swaggering here
　　So near the cradle of the Fairy Queen?
60　　What, a play toward?[13] I'll be an auditor,
　　An actor, too, perhaps, if I see cause.
Quince. Speak, Pyramus. Thisbe, stand forth.
Bottom [*as Pyramus*]. "Thisbe, the flowers of odious savors sweet—"
Quince. Odors, odors.
65　**Bottom.** "—Odors savors sweet;
　　So hath thy breath, my dearest Thisbe dear.
　　But hark, a voice! Stay thou but here awhile,
　　And by and by I will to thee appear." [*Exit*.]
Puck. A stranger Pyramus than e'er played here. [*Exit*.]
70　**Flute.** Must I speak now?
Quince. Ay, marry, must you; for you must understand he goes but to
　　see a noise that he heard, and is to come again.
Flute [*as Thisbe*]. "Most radiant Pyramus, most lily-white of hue,
　　Of color like the red rose on triumphant brier,
75　　Most brisky juvenal[14] and eke[15] most lovely Jew,[16]
　　　As true as truest horse that yet would never tire.
　　I'll meet thee, Pyramus, at Ninny's tomb."
Quince. "Ninus' tomb," man. Why, you must not
　　speak that yet. That you answer to Pyramus. You speak all
80　　your part[17] at once, cues and all. Pyramus, enter. Your cue is past;
　　it is "never tire."
Flute. O— "As true as truest horse, that yet would never tire."
[*Enter* Puck, *and* Bottom *as Pyramus with the ass head*.]
Bottom. "If I were fair, Thisbe, I were only thine."
Quince. O, monstrous! O, strange! We are haunted.
85　　Pray, masters! Fly, masters! Help!
[*Exeunt* Quince, Snug, Flute, Snout, *and* Starveling.]
Puck. I'll follow you, I'll lead you about a round,
　　Thorough bog, thorough bush, thorough brake, thorough brier.

---

[12] hempen homespuns—rustics dressed in clothes woven of coarse, homespun fabric made from hemp.

[13] toward—about to take place.

[14] brisky juvenal—lively youth.

[15] eke—also.

[16] Jew—absurd repetition of the first syllable of *juvenal* and an indication of how desperately Quince searches
for his rhymes.

[17] part—An actor's *part* was a script consisting only of his speeches and their cues.

Sometimes a horse I'll be, sometimes a hound,
        A hog, a headless bear, sometimes a fire;[18]
90   And neigh, and bark, and grunt, and roar, and burn,
        Like horse, hound, hog, bear, fire, at every turn. [*Exit*.]

Bottom. Why do they run away? This is a knavery of them to make
        me afeard.

[*Enter* Snout.]

Snout. O Bottom, thou art changed! What do I see on thee?

95   **Bottom.** What do you see? You see an ass head of your own, do you?

[*Exit* Snout.]

[*Enter* Quince.]

Quince. Bless thee, Bottom, bless thee! Thou art translated. [*Exit*.]

Bottom. I see their knavery. This is to make an ass of me, to fright me, if
        they could. But I will not stir from this place, do what they can. I will
        walk up and down here, and will sing, that they shall hear I am not
100   afraid. [*He sings*.]
        The ouzel cock so black of hue,
            With orange-tawny bill,
        The throstle with his note so true,
            The wren with little quill—

105   **Titania** [*awaking*]. What angel wakes me from my flowery bed?

Bottom [*sings*]. The finch, the sparrow, and the lark,
            The plainsong cuckoo gray,
        Whose note full many a man cloth mark,
            And dares not answer nay[19]—

110   For indeed, who would set his wit to[20] so foolish a bird? Who
        would give a bird the lie,[21] though he cry "cuckoo" never so?[22]

Titania. I pray thee, gentle mortal, sing again.
        Mine ear is much enamored of thy note;
        So is mine eye enthrallèd to thy shape;
115   And thy fair virtue's force perforce doth move me
        On the first view to say, to swear, I love thee.

---

[18] fire—will-o'-the-wisp, a phosphorescent light that hovers and flits over swampy ground at night, possibly from spontaneous combustion of gases emitted by rotting organic matter.

[19] note . . . nay—Bottom's song plays on the association between the sound of the cuckoo's call and the word *cuckold*, meaning a man whose wife is unfaithful to him.

[20] set his wit to—employ his intelligence to answer.

[21] give . . . lie—call the bird a liar.

[22] never so—ever so much.

Bottom. Methinks, mistress, you should have little reason for that. And yet, to say the truth, reason and love keep little company together nowadays—the more the pity that some honest neighbors will not make them friends. Nay, I can gleek[23] upon occasion.

Titania. Thou art as wise as thou art beautiful.

Bottom. Not so, neither. But if I had wit enough to get out of this wood, I have enough to serve mine own turn.

Titania. Out of this wood do not desire to go.

    Thou shalt remain here, whether thou wilt or no.

    I am a spirit of no common rate.

    The summer still doth tend upon my state,[24]

    And I do love thee. Therefore, go with me.

    I'll give thee fairies to attend on thee,

    And they shall fetch thee jewels from the deep,

    And sing while thou on pressèd flowers dost sleep.

    And I will purge thy mortal grossness[25] so

    That thou shalt like an airy spirit go.

    Peaseblossom, Cobweb, Mote,[26] and Mustardseed!

[*Enter four Fairies:* Peaseblossom, Cobweb, Mote, *and* Mustardseed.]

Peaseblossom. Ready.

Cobweb. And I.

Mote.   And I.

Mustardseed.   And I.

All.   Where shall we go?

Titania. Be kind and courteous to this gentleman.

    Hop in his walks and **gambol**[27] in his eyes;[28]

    Feed him with apricots and dewberries,

    With purple grapes, green figs, and mulberries;

    The honey bags steal from the humble-bees,

    And for night tapers crop their waxen thighs

    And light them at the fiery glowworms' eyes,

    To have my love to bed and to arise;

    And pluck the wings from painted butterflies

120

125

130

135

140

145

---

[23] gleek—jest.

[24] still . . . state—always waits upon me as part of my royal routine.

[25] mortal grossness—materiality, the physical body of a mortal being.

[26] Mote—speck. The two words *moth* and *mote* were pronounced alike, and both meanings may be present.

[27] **gambol**—leap about playfully; frolic.

[28] in his eyes—in his sight, in front of him.

To fan the moonbeams from his sleeping eyes.
Nod to him, elves, and do him courtesies.

Peaseblossom. Hail, mortal!

Cobweb. Hail!

150 **Mote.** Hail!

Mustardseed. Hail!

Bottom. I cry your worships mercy, heartily. I beseech your worship's name.

Cobweb. Cobweb.

155 **Bottom.** I shall desire you of more acquaintance, good Master Cobweb. If I cut my finger, I shall make bold with you.[29]—Your name, honest gentleman?

Peaseblossom. Peaseblossom.

Bottom. I pray you, commend me to Mistress Squash, your mother, and
160 to Master Peascod,[30] your father. Good Master Peaseblossom, I shall desire you of more acquaintance too.—Your name, I beseech you, Sir?

Mustardseed. Mustardseed.

Bottom. Good Master Mustardseed, I know your patience[31] well. That same cowardly, giantlike ox-beef hath devoured many a gentleman of
165 your house. I promise you, your kindred hath made my eyes water ere now. I desire you of more acquaintance, good Master Mustardseed.

Titania. Come wait upon him; lead him to my bower.
The moon methinks looks with a watery eye;
170 And when she weeps,[32] weeps every little flower,
Lamenting some enforcèd chastity.
Tie up my lover's tongue;[33] bring him silently.
[*Exeunt.*]

Act Three, Scene Two

[*Enter* Oberon, King of Fairies.]

Oberon. I wonder if Titania be awaked;
Then, what it was that next came in her eye,

---

[29] If . . . you—Cobwebs were used to stop bleeding.

[30] Squash . . . Peascod—unripe and ripe pea pod, respectively.

[31] your patience—what you have endured. (Mustard is eaten with beef.)

[32] she weeps—she causes dew.

[33] Tie . . . tongue—Presumably Bottom is braying like an ass.

Which she must dote on in extremity.

[*Enter* Puck.]

Here comes my messenger. How now, mad spirit?

5 What night-rule[34] now about this haunted grove?

Puck. My mistress with a monster is in love.

Near to her close[35] and consecrated bower,

While she was in her dull and sleeping hour,

A crew of patches, rude mechanicals,[36]

10 That work for bread upon Athenian stalls,

Were met together to rehearse a play

Intended for great Theseus' nuptial day.

The shallowest thickskin of that barren sort,[37]

Who Pyramus presented, in their sport

15 Forsook his scene and entered in a brake.

When I did him at this advantage take,

An ass's noll[38] I fixèd on his head.

Anon his Thisbe must be answered

And forth my mimic comes. When they him spy,

20 As wild geese that the creeping fowler eye,

Or russet-pated choughs,[39] many in sort,

Rising and cawing at the gun's report,

Sever[40] themselves and madly sweep the sky,

So, at his sight, away his fellows fly;

25 And, at our stamp, here o'er and o'er one falls;

He "Murder!" cries and help from Athens calls.

Their sense thus weak, lost with their fears thus strong,

Made senseless things begin to do them wrong,

For briers and thorns at their apparel snatch;

30 Some, sleeves—some, hats; from yielders all things catch.[41]

I led them on in this distracted fear

And left sweet Pyramus translated there,

---

[34] night-rule—diversion or misrule for the night.

[35] close—secret, private.

[36] patches, rude mechanicals—fools, ignorant artisans.

[37] shallowest . . . sort—dullest oaf of that stupid company.

[38] noll—head.

[39] choughs—jackdaws, birds similar to crows.

[40] Sever—scatter.

[41] from . . . catch—everything preys on those who yield to fear.

When in that moment, so it came to pass,

Titania waked and straightway loved an ass.

35   **Oberon.** This falls out better than I could devise.

But hast thou yet latched[42] the Athenian's eyes

With the love juice, as I did bid thee do?

   Puck. I took him sleeping—that is finished too—

And the Athenian woman by his side,

40   That, when he waked, of force she must be eyed.

[*Enter* Demetrius *and* Hermia.]

   Oberon. Stand close. This is the same Athenian.

   Puck. This is the woman, but not this the man.

[*They stand aside.*]

   Demetrius. O, why **rebuke**[43] you him that loves you so?

Lay breath so bitter on your bitter foe.

45   **Hermia.** Now I but chide; but I should use thee worse,

For thou, I fear, hast given me cause to curse.

If thou hast slain Lysander in his sleep,

Being o'er shoes[44] in blood, plunge in the deep,

And kill me too.

50   The sun was not so true unto the day

As he to me. Would he have stolen away

From sleeping Hermia? I'll believe as soon

This whole earth may be bored,[45] and that the moon

May through the center creep, and so displease

55   Her brother's[46] noontide with th' Antipodes.[47]

It cannot be but thou hast murdered him;

So should a murderer look, so dead,[48] so grim.

   Demetrius. So should the murdered look, and so should I,

Pierced through the heart with your stern cruelty.

60   Yet you, the murderer, look as bright, as dear

As yonder Venus in her glimmering sphere.

---

[42] latched—fastened, snared.

[43] **rebuke**—criticize sharply.

[44] Being o'er shoes—having waded in so far.

[45] whole . . . bored—solid world may have a hole through it.

[46] Her brother's—the sun's.

[47] th' Antipodes—the people on the opposite side of the earth (where the moon is imagined bringing night to noontime).

[48] dead—deadly, or deathly pale.

Hermia. What's this to my Lysander? Where is he?

Ah, good Demetrius, wilt thou give him me?

Demetrius. I had rather give his carcass to my hounds.

65   **Hermia.** Out, dog! Out, cur! Thou driv'st me past the bounds

Of maiden's patience. Hast thou slain him, then?

Henceforth be never numbered among men.

O, once tell true, tell true, even for my sake:

Durst thou have looked upon him being awake?

70   And hast thou killed him sleeping? O brave touch![49]

Could not a worm,[50] an adder, do so much?

An adder did it; for with doubler tongue

Than thine, thou serpent, never adder stung.

Demetrius. You spend your passion on a misprised mood.[51]

75   I am not guilty of Lysander's blood,

Nor is he dead, for aught that I can tell.

Hermia. I pray thee, tell me then that he is well.

Demetrius. And if I could, what should I get therefor?

Hermia. A privilege never to see me more.

80   And from thy hated presence part I so.

See me no more, whether he be dead or no. [*Exit.*]

Demetrius. There is no following her in this fierce vein.

Here therefore for a while I will remain.

So sorrow's heaviness doth heavier grow

85   For debt that bankrupt[52] sleep doth sorrow owe,

Which now in some slight measure it will pay,

If for his tender here I make some stay.[53]

[*He lies down and sleeps.*]

Oberon. What hast thou done? Thou hast mistaken quite

And laid the love juice on some true love's sight.

90   Of thy misprision[54] must perforce ensue

Some true love turned, and not a false turned true.

---

[49] brave touch!—fine stroke! (said ironically).

[50] worm—serpent.

[51] misprised mood—anger based on misconception.

[52] bankrupt—Demetrius is saying that his sleepiness adds to the wearines caused by sorrow.

[53] Which . . . stay—to a small extent, I will be able to "payback" and hence find some relief from sorrow, if I pause here awhile (*make some stay*) while sleep "tenders" or offers itself by way of paying the dept owed to sorrow.

[54] misprision—mistake.

Puck. Then fate o'errules, that, one man holding troth,[55]
        A million fad, confounding oath on oath.[56]

Oberon. About the wood go swifter than the wind,
95   And Helena of Athens look thou find.
        All fancy-sick she is and pale of cheer[57]
        With sighs of love, that cost the fresh blood[58] dear.
        By some illusion see thou bring her here.
        I'll charm his eyes against she do appear.

100 **Puck.** I go, I go, look how I go,
        Swifter than arrow from the Tartar's bow.[59] [*Exit.*]

Oberon [*applying love juice to Demetrius' eyes*].
        Flower of this purple dye,
        Hit with Cupid's archery,
        Sink in apple[60] of his eye.
105   When his love he doth espy,
        Let her shine as gloriously
        As the Venus of the sky.
        When thou wak'st if she be by,
        Beg of her for remedy.

[*Enter Puck.*]

110 **Puck.** Captain of our fairy band,
        Helena is here at hand,
        And the youth, mistook by me,
        Pleading for a lover's fee.[61]
        Shall we their fond pageant see?
115   Lord, what fools these mortals be!

Oberon. Stand aside. The noise they make
        Will cause Demetrius to awake.

Puck.   Then will two at once woo one;
        That must needs be sport alone.[62]

---

[55] that . . . troth—for each man keeping true faith in love.

[56] confounding . . . oath—breaking oath after oath.

[57] cheer—face.

[58] sighs . . . blood—allusion to the physiological theory that each sigh cost the heart a drop of blood.

[59] Tartar's bow—The Tartars were central Asian peoples famed for their skill with the bow.

[60] apple—pupil.

[61] fee—privilege, reward.

[62] alone—unequaled.

120	And those things do best please me
	That befall **preposterously**.[63] [*They stand aside.*]

[*Enter* Lysander *and* Helena.]

Lysander. Why should you think that I should woo in scorn?
　　　　　Scorn and **derision**[64] never come in tears.
　　　Look when I vow, I weep; and vows so born,
125　　　　In their nativity all truth appears.
　　　How can these things in me seem scorn to you,
　　　　Bearing the badge of faith to prove them true?

Helena. You do advance your cunning more and more.
　　　　　When truth kills truth,[65] O, devilish-holy fray!
130　　　These vows are Hermia's. Will you give her o'er?
　　　　　Weigh oath with oath, and you will nothing weigh.
　　　Your vows to her and me, put in two scales,
　　　Will even weigh, and both as light as tales.[66]

Lysander. I had no judgment when to her I swore.

135 **Helena.** Nor none, in my mind, now you give her o'er.

Lysander. Demetrius loves her, and he loves not you.

Demetrius [*awaking*]. O Helen, goddess, nymph, perfect, divine!
　　　To what, my love, shall I compare thine eyne?
　　　Crystal is muddy. O, how ripe in show
140　　Thy lips, those kissing cherries, tempting grow!
　　　That pure congealèd white, high Taurus'[67] snow,
　　　Fanned with the eastern wind, turns to a crow
　　　When thou hold'st up thy hand. O, let me kiss
　　　This princess of pure white, this seal of bliss!

145 **Helena.** O spite! O hell! I see you all are bent
　　　To set against me for your merriment.
　　　If you were civil and knew courtesy,
　　　You would not do me thus much injury.
　　　Can you not hate me, as I know you do,
150　　But you must join in souls to mock me too?
　　　If you were men, as men you are in show,
　　　You would not use a gentle lady so—

---

[63] **preposterously**—absurdly.

[64] **derision**—ridicule.

[65] truth kills truth—one of Lysander's vows must invalidate the other.

[66] tales—lies.

[67] Taurus'—lofty mountain range in Asia Minor.

To vow, and swear, and superpraise my parts,[68]
When I am sure you hate me with your hearts.

155   You both are rivals, and love Hermia,
And now both rivals to mock Helena.
A trim[69] exploit, a manly enterprise,
To conjure tears up in a poor maid's eyes
With your derision! None of noble sort

160   Would so offend a virgin and extort
A poor soul's patience, all to make you sport.

Lysander. You are unkind, Demetrius. Be not so.
For you love Hermia; this you know I know.
And here, with all good will, with all my heart,

165   In Hermia's love I yield you up my part;
And yours of Helena to me bequeath,
Whom I do love, and will do till my death.

Helena. Never did mockers waste more idle breath.

Demetrius. Lysander, keep thy Hermia;

170   I will none.[70] If e'er I loved her, all that love is gone.
My heart to her but as guestwise **sojourned**, [71]
And now to Helen is it home returned,
There to remain.

Lysander.   Helen, it is not so.

Demetrius. **Disparage**[72] not the faith thou dost not know,

175   Lest, to thy peril, thou aby[73] it dear.
Look where thy love comes; yonder is thy dear.

[*Enter* Hermia.]

Hermia. Dark night, that from the eye his function takes,
The ear more quick of apprehension makes;
Wherein it doth impair the seeing sense,

180   It pays the hearing double **recompense**.[74]
Thou art not by mine eye, Lysander, found;

---

[68] superpraise my parts—overpraise my qualities.

[69] trim—pretty, fine (said ironically).

[70] will none—want no part of her.

[71] **sojourned**—visited.

[72] **Disparage**—speak of in a slighting way; belittle.

[73] aby—pay for.

[74] **recompense**—amends made, as for a loss.

Mine ear, I thank it, brought me to thy sound.
But why unkindly didst thou leave me so?

Lysander. Why should he stay, whom love doth press to go?

185   **Hermia.** What love could press Lysander from my side?

Lysander. Lysander's love, that would not let him bide
Fair Helena, who more engilds[75] the night
Than all yon fiery oes[76] and eyes of light.
Why seek'st thou me? Could not this make thee know
190   The hate I bear thee made me leave thee so?

Hermia. You speak not as you think. It cannot be.

Helena. Lo, she is one of this confederacy!
Now I perceive they have conjoined all three
To fashion this false sport, in spite of me.
195   Injurious Hermia, most ungrateful maid!
Have you conspired, have you with these contrived
To bait[77] me with this foul derision?
Is all the counsel that we two have shared—
The sisters' vows, the hours that we have spent
200   When we have chid the hasty-footed time
For parting us—O, is all forgot?
All schooldays' friendship, childhood innocence?
We, Hermia, like two artificial[78] gods
Have with our needles created both one flower,
205   Both on one sampler,[79] sitting on one cushion,
Both warbling of one song, both in one key,
As if our hands, our sides, voices, and minds
Had been incorporate.[80] So we grew together,
Like to a double cherry, seeming parted,
210   But yet an union in partition,
Two lovely berries molded on one stem;
So, with two seeming bodies but one heart,
Two of the first, like coats in heraldry,

---

[75] engilds—gilds, brightens with a golden light.

[76] oes—spangles (here, stars).

[77] bait—torment, as one sets on dogs to bait a bear.

[78] artificial—skilled in art or creation.

[79] sampler—piece of needlework.

[80] incorporate—of one body.

Due but to one and crownèd with one crest.[81]

215 And will you rend our ancient love asunder,
To join with men in scorning your poor friend?
It is not friendly, 'tis not maidenly.
Our sex, as well as I, may chide you for it,
Though I alone do feel the injury.

220 **Hermia.** I am amazèd at your passionate words.
I scorn you not. It seems that you scorn me.

Helena. Have you not set Lysander, as in scorn,
To follow me and praise my eyes and face?
And made your other love, Demetrius,

225 Who even but now did spurn me with his foot,
To call me goddess, nymph, divine, and rare,
Precious, **celestial**?[82] Wherefore speaks he this
To her he hates? And wherefore doth Lysander
Deny your love, so rich within his soul,

230 And tender me, forsooth, affection,
But by your setting on, by your consent?
What though I be not so in grace as you,
So hung upon with love, so fortunate,
But miserable most, to love unloved?

235 This you should pity rather than despise.

Hermia. I understand not what you mean by this.

Helena. Ay, do! Persever,[83] counterfeit sad looks,
Make mouths upon me when I turn my back,
Wink each at other, hold the sweet jest up.

240 This sport, well carried, shall be chronicled.
If you have any pity, grace, or manners,
You would not make me such an argument.[84]
But fare ye well. 'Tis partly my own fault,
Which death, or absence, soon shall remedy.

245 **Lysander.** Stay, gentle Helena; hear my excuse,
My love, my life, my soul, fair Helena!

Helena. O excellent!

---

[81] Two . . . crest—we have two separate bodies, just as a coat of arms in heraldry can be represented twice on a shield but surmounted by a single crest.

[82] **celestial**—heavenly.

[83] Persever—persevere, persist.

[84] argument—subject of a jest.

Hermia [*to* Lysander]. Sweet, do not scorn her so.

Demetrius [*to* Lysander]. If she cannot entreat, I can compel.

Lysander. Thou canst compel no more than she entreat.

250   Thy threats have no more strength than her weak prayers.

        Helen, I love thee, by my life, I do!

        I swear by that which I will lose for thee,

        To prove him false that says I love thee not.

Demetrius [*to* Helena]. I say I love thee more than he can do.

255   **Lysander.** If thou say so, withdraw, and prove it too.[85]

Demetrius. Quick, come!

Hermia.   Lysander, whereto tends all this?

Lysander. Away, you Ethiope![86]

        [*He tries to break away from* Hermia.]

Demetrius.   No, no; he'll

        Seem to break loose; take on as[87] you would follow,

        But yet come not. You are a tame man. Go!

260   **Lysander** [*to* Hermia]. Hang off,[88] thou cat, thou burr! Vile thing, let loose,

        Or I will shake thee from me like a serpent!

Hermia. Why are you grown so rude? What change is this,

        Sweet love?

Lysander.   Thy love? Out, tawny Tartar, out!

        Out, loathèd med'cine! O hated potion, hence!

265   **Hermia.** Do you not jest?

Helena.   Yes, sooth, and so do you.

Lysander. Demetrius, I will keep my word with thee.

Demetrius. I would I had your bond, for I perceive

        A weak bond[89] holds you. I'll not trust your word.

Lysander. What, should I hurt her, strike her, kill her dead?

270   Although I hate her, I'll not harm her so.

Hermia. What, can you do me greater harm than hate?

        Hate me? Wherefore? O me, what news, my love?

        Am not I Hermia? Are not you Lysander?

---

[85] withdraw . . . too—withdraw with me and prove your claim in a duel. (The two gentlemen are armed.)

[86] Ethiope—Ethiopian, African (referring to Hermia's relatively dark hair and complexion; see also *tawny Tartar* six lines later).

[87] take on as—act as if, make a fuss as if.

[88] Hang off—let go.

[89] weak bond—Hermia's arm (with a pun on *bond*, "oath," in the previous line).

I am as fair now as I was erewhile.[90]

275 Since night you loved me; yet since night you left me.

Why, then you left me—O the gods forbid!—

In earnest, shall I say?

Lysander.   Ay, by my life!

And never did desire to see thee more.

Therefore be out of hope, of question, of doubt;

280 Be certain, nothing truer. 'Tis no jest

That I do hate thee and love Helena.

Hermia [*to* Helena]. O me! You juggler! You cankerblossom!

You thief of love! What, have you come by night

And stol'n my love's heart from him?

Helena.   Fine, i' faith!

285 Have you no modesty, no maiden shame,

No touch of bashfulness? What, will you tear

Impatient answers from my gentle tongue?

Fie, fie! You counterfeit, you puppet,[91] you!

Hermia. "Puppet"? Why, so! Ay, that way goes the game.

290 Now I perceive that she hath made compare

Between our statures; she hath urged her height,

And with her personage, her tall personage,

Her height, forsooth, she hath prevailed with him.

And are you grown so high in his esteem

295 Because I am so dwarfish and so low?

How low am I, thou painted maypole? Speak!

How low am I? I am not yet so low

But that my nails can reach unto thine eyes.

[*She flails at* Helena *but is restrained.*]

Helena. I pray you, though you mock me, gentlemen,

300 Let her not hurt me. I was never curst;[92]

I have no gift at all in shrewishness;

I am a right maid for my cowardice.

Let her not strike me. You perhaps may think,

Because she is something lower than myself,

305 That I can match her.

Hermia.   Lower? Hark, again!

---

[90] erewhile—just now.

[91] puppet—dwarfish woman (in reference to Hermia's smaller stature).

[92] curst—shrewish.

Helena. Good Hermia, do not be so bitter with me.
   I evermore did love you, Hermia,
   Did ever keep your counsels, never wronged you,
   Save that, in love unto Demetrius

310   I told him of your stealth unto this wood.
   He followed you; for love I followed him.
   But he hath chid me hence and threatened me
   To strike me, spurn me, nay, to kill me too.
   And now, so you will let me quiet go,

315   To Athens will I bear my folly back
   And follow you no further. Let me go.
   You see how simple and how fond I am.

Hermia. Why, get you gone. Who is 't that hinders you?

Helena. A foolish heart, that I leave here behind.

320 **Hermia.** What, with Lysander?

Helena.   With Demetrius.

Lysander. Be not afraid; she shall not harm thee, Helena.

Demetrius. No, Sir, she shall not, though you take her part.

Helena. O, when she is angry, she is keen[93] and shrewd.
   She was a vixen when she went to school;

325   And though she be but little, she is fierce.

Hermia. "Little" again? Nothing but "low" and "little"?
   Why will you suffer her to flout me thus?
   Let me come to her.

Lysander.   Get you gone, you dwarf!
   You minimus,[94] of hindering knotgrass[95] made!

330   You bead, you acorn!

Demetrius.   You are too officious
   In her behalf that scorns your services.
   Let her alone. Speak not of Helena;
   Take not her part. For, if thou dost intend[96]
   Never so little show of love to her,

335   Thou shalt aby it.

Lysander.   Now she holds me not.

---

[93] keen—fierce.

[94] minimus—tiny creature.

[95] knotgrass—weed, an infusion of which was thought to stunt the growth.

[96] intend—give sign of.

Now follow, if thou dar'st to try whose right,
Of thine or mine, is most in Helena. [*Exit.*]
Demetrius. Follow? Nay, I'll go with thee, cheek by jowl.[97]
[*Exit, following* Lysander.]
Hermia. You, mistress, all this coil is 'long of you.[98]
340   Nay, go not back.
Helena.   I will not trust you, I,
Nor longer stay in your curst company.
Your hands than mine are quicker for a fray;
My legs are longer, though, to run away. [*Exit.*]
Hermia. I am amazed and know not what to say. [*Exit.*]
[Oberon *and* Puck *come forward.*]
345   **Oberon.** This is thy negligence. Still thou mistak'st,
Or else committ'st thy knaveries willfully.
Puck. Believe me, king of shadows, I mistook.
Did not you tell me I should know the man
By the Athenian garments he had on?
350   And so far blameless proves my enterprise
That I have 'nointed an Athenian's eyes;
And so far am I glad it so did sort,
As this their jangling I esteem a sport.
Oberon. Thou seest these lovers seek a place to fight.
355   Hie[99] therefore, Robin, overcast the night;
The starry welkin[100] cover thou anon
With drooping fog as black as Acheron,[101]
And lead these **testy**[102] rivals so astray
As one come not within another's way.
360   Like to Lysander sometimes frame thy tongue,
Then stir Demetrius up with bitter wrong;
And sometimes rail thou like Demetrius.
And from each other look thou lead them thus,
Till o'er their brows death-counterfeiting sleep
365   With leaden legs and batty wings doth creep.

---

[97] cheek by jowl—side by side.

[98] coil . . . you—turmoil is on account of you.

[99] Hie—hasten.

[100] welkin—sky.

[101] Acheron—river of Hades (here representing Hades itself).

[102] **testy**—angry.

Then crush this herb into Lysander's eye, [*giving herb*]
Whose liquor hath this virtuous property,
To take from thence all error with his might
And make his eyeballs roll with wonted sight.
370   When they next wake, all this derision
Shall seem a dream and fruitless vision,
And back to Athens shall the lovers wend
With league whose date[103] till death shall never end.
Whiles I in this affair do thee employ,
375   I'll to my queen and beg her Indian boy;
And then I will her charmèd eye release
From monster's view, and all things shall be peace.
    Puck. My fairy lord, this must be done with haste,
For night's swift dragons cut the clouds full fast,
380   And yonder shines Aurora's harbinger,[104]
At whose approach ghosts, wand'ring here and there,
Troop home to churchyards. Damnèd spirits all,
That in crossways and floods have burial,[105]
Already to their wormy beds are gone.
385   For fear lest day should look their shames upon,
They willfully themselves exile from light
And must for aye consort with black-browed night.
    Oberon. But we are spirits of another sort.
I with the Morning's love[106] have oft made sport,
390   And, like a forester, the groves may tread
Even till the eastern gate, all fiery red,
Opening on Neptune with fair blessèd beams,
Turns into yellow gold his salt green streams.
But notwithstanding, haste, make no delay.
395   We may effect this business yet ere day. [*Exit.*]
    Puck. Up and down, up and down,
I will lead them up and down.
I am feared in field and town.

---

[103] league whose date—friendship whose term of existence.

[104] Aurora's harbinger—morning star, precursor of Aurora, goddess of dawn.

[105] crossways . . . burial—Those who committed suicide were buried at crossways, with a stake driven through them; those who intentionally or accidentally drowned (in *floods* or deep water) would be condemned to wander disconsolately for lack of burial rites.

[106] Morning's love—Cephalus, a beautiful youth beloved of Aurora; or perhaps the goddess of dawn herself.

Goblin, lead them up and down.

400 Here comes one.

[*Enter* Lysander.]

Lysander. Where art thou, proud Demetrius? Speak thou now.

Puck [*mimicking* Demetrius]. Here, villain, drawn and ready.
   Where art thou?

Lysander. I will be with thee straight.

Puck.   Follow me, then,
  To plainer ground.

[Lysander *wanders about, following the voice.*]

[*Enter* Demetrius.]

Demetrius.   Lysander! Speak again!

405 Thou runaway, thou coward, art thou fled?
  Speak! In some bush? Where dost thou hide thy head?

Puck [*mimicking* Lysander]. Thou coward, art thou bragging to the stars,
  Telling the bushes that thou look'st for wars,
  And wilt not come? Come, recreant;[107] come, thou child,

410 I'll whip thee with a rod. He is defiled
  That draws a sword on thee.

Demetrius.   Yea, art thou there?

Puck. Follow my voice. We'll try no manhood here.

  [*Exeunt.*]

  [Lysander *returns.*]

Lysander. He goes before me and still dares me on.
  When I come where he calls, then he is gone.

415 The villain is much lighter-heeled than I.
  I followed fast, but faster he did fly,
  That fallen am I in dark uneven way,
  And here will rest me. [*He lies down.*] Come, thou gentle day!
  For if but once thou show me thy gray light,

420 I'll find Demetrius and revenge this spite. [*He sleeps.*]

  [*Enter* Puck *and* Demetrius.]

Puck. Ho, ho, ho! Coward, why com'st thou not?

Demetrius. Abide me, if thou dar'st; for well I wot
  Thou runn'st before me, shifting every place,
  And dar'st not stand nor look me in the face.

425 Where art thou now?

---

[107] recreant—cowardly wretch.

Puck.   Come hither. I am here.

Demetrius. Nay, then, thou mock'st me. Thou shalt buy this dear,
    If ever I thy face by daylight see.
    Now go thy way. Faintness constraineth me
    To measure out my length on this cold bed.
430   By day's approach look to be visited.
    [*He lies down and sleeps.*]
    [*Enter* Helena.]

Helena. O weary night, O long and tedious night,
    Abate thy hours! Shine comforts from the east,
    That I may back to Athens by daylight
    From these that my poor company detest;
435   And sleep, that sometimes shuts up sorrow's eye,
    Steal me awhile from mine own company.
    [*She lies down and sleeps.*]

Puck. Yet but three? Come one more;
    Two of both kinds makes up four.
    Here she comes, curst and sad.
440   Cupid is a knavish lad,
    Thus to make poor females mad.
    [*Enter* Hermia.]

Hermia. Never so weary, never so in woe,
    Bedabbled with the dew and torn with briers,
    I can no further crawl, no further go;
445   My legs can keep no pace with my desires.
    Here will I rest me till the break of day.
    Heavens shield Lysander, if they mean a fray!
    [*She lies down and sleeps.*]

Puck. On the ground
    Sleep sound.
450   I'll apply
    To your eye,
    Gentle lover, remedy.
    [*He squeezes the juice on* Lysander's *eyes.*]
    When thou wak'st,
    Thou tak'st
455   True delight
    In the sight
    Of thy former lady's eye;

And the country proverb known,
That every man should take his own,
460   In your waking shall be shown:
     Jack shall have Jill;
     Naught shall go ill;
The man shall have his mare again, and all shall be well.
[*Exit. The four sleeping lovers remain.*]

Act Four, Scene One

[*Enter* Titania, Bottom, *and* Fairies; *and* Oberon, *behind them.*]

Titania. Come, sit thee down upon this flowery bed,
   While I thy amiable[1] cheeks do coy,[2]
   And stick muskroses in thy sleek smooth head,
   And kiss thy fair large ears, my gentle joy.
[*They recline.*]

5 **Bottom.** Where's Peaseblossom?

Peaseblossom. Ready.

Bottom. Scratch my head, Peaseblossom. Where's Monsieur Cobweb?

Cobweb. Ready.

Bottom. Monsieur Cobweb, good monsieur, get you your weapons in
10   your hand, and kill me a red-hipped humble-bee on the top of a this-
    tle; and, good monsieur, bring me the honey bag. Do not fret yourself
    too much in the action, monsieur; and, good monsieur, have a care
    the honey bag break not. I would be loath to have you overflown with
    a honey bag, signor. [*Exit* Cobweb.] Where's Monsieur Mustardseed?

15 **Mustardseed.** Ready.

Bottom. Give me your neaf,[3] Monsieur Mustardseed.
   Pray you, leave your courtesy,[4] good monsieur.

Mustardseed. What's your will?

Bottom. Nothing, good monsieur, but to help Cavalery[5] Cobweb to
20   scratch. I must to the barber's, monsieur, for methinks I am marvelous
    hairy about the face; and I am such a tender ass, if my hair do but
    tickle me I must scratch.

---

[1] amiable—lovely.

[2] coy—caress.

[3] neaf—fist.

[4] leave your courtesy—stop bowing or put on your hat.

[5] Cavalery—cavalier (form of address for a gentleman).

Titania. What, wilt thou hear some music, my sweet love?

Bottom. I have a reasonable good ear in music. Let's have the tongs and
25   the bones.[6]

[*Music: tongs, rural music.*]

Titania. Or say, sweet love, what thou desirest to eat.

Bottom. Truly, a peck of **provender.**[7] I could munch your good dry oats.
     Methinks I have a great desire to a bottle[8] of hay. Good hay, sweet
     hay, hath no fellow.[9]

30 **Titania.** I have a venturous[10] fairy that shall seek
     The squirrel's hoard, and fetch thee new nuts.

Bottom. I had rather have a handful or two of dried peas. But, I pray
     you, let none of your people stir me. I have an exposition of sleep
     come upon me.

35 **Titania.** Sleep thou, and I will wind thee in my arms.
     Fairies, begone, and be all ways away.

[*Exeunt* Fairies.]

     So doth the woodbine the sweet honeysuckle
     Gently entwist; the female ivy so
     Enrings the barky fingers of the elm.

40   O, how I love thee! How I dote on thee!

[*They sleep.*]

[*Enter* Puck.]

Oberon [*coming forward*]. Welcome, good Robin. Seest thou this sweet sight?
     Her dotage[11] now I do begin to pity.
     For, meeting her of late behind the wood
     Seeking sweet favors for this hateful fool,

45   I did **upbraid**[12] her and fall out with her.
     For she his hairy temples then had rounded
     With coronet of fresh and fragrant flowers;
     And that same dew, which sometime on the buds
     Was wont to swell like round and orient pearls,

---

[6] tongs . . . bones—instruments for rustic music. The tongs were played like a triangle, whereas the bones were held
between the fingers and used as clappers.

[7] **provender**—dry food, such as hay, used as feed for livestock.

[8] bottle—bundle.

[9] fellow—equal.

[10] venturous—daring.

[11] dotage—foolish affection.

[12] **upbraid**—scold.

50	Stood now within the pretty flowerets' eyes
	Like tears that did their own disgrace bewail.
	When I had at my pleasure taunted her,
	And she in mild terms begged my patience,
	I then did ask of her her changeling child,
55	Which straight she gave me, and her fairy sent
	To bear him to my bower in Fairyland.
	And, now I have the boy, I will undo
	This hateful imperfection of her eyes.
	And, gentle Puck, take this transformèd scalp
60	From off the head of this Athenian swain,[13]
	That he, awaking when the other do,
	May all to Athens back again repair,[14]
	And think no more of this night's accidents
	But as the fierce vexation of a dream.
65	But first I will release the Fairy Queen.

[*He squeezes an herb on her eyes.*]

    Be as thou wast wont to be;

    See as thou wast wont to see.

    Dian's bud o'er Cupid's flower

    Hath such force and blessèd power.

70   Now, my Titania, wake you, my sweet queen.

Titania [*awaking*]. My Oberon! What visions have I seen!
    Methought I was enamored of an ass.

Oberon. There lies your love.

Titania. How came these things to pass?

75   O, how mine eyes do loathe his visage now!

Oberon. Silence awhile. Robin, take off this head.
    Titania, music call, and strike more dead
    Than common sleep of all these five the sense.

Titania. Music, ho! Music, such as charmeth sleep! [*Music.*]

80 **Puck** [*removing the ass head*]. Now, when thou wak'st, with thine own
fool's eyes peep.

Oberon. Sound, music! Come, my queen, take hands with me,
    And rock the ground whereon these sleepers be.
    [*They dance.*]

---

[13] swain—country lad.

[14] repair—return.

Now thou and I are new in **amity**,[15]
And will tomorrow midnight solemnly

85 Dance in Duke Theseus' house triumphantly,
And bless it to all fair prosperity.
There shall the pairs of faithful lovers be
Wedded, with Theseus, all in jollity.

Puck. Fairy King, attend, and mark:

90 I do hear the morning lark.

Oberon. Then, my queen, in silence sad,
Trip we after night's shade.
We the globe can compass soon,
Swifter than the wandering moon.

95 **Titania.** Come, my lord, and in our flight
Tell me how it came this night
That I sleeping here was found
With these mortals on the ground.

[*Exeunt* Oberon, Titania, *and* Puck.]
[*Wind horn within.*]
[*Enter* Theseus *and all his train;* Hippolyta, Egeus.]

Theseus. Go, one of you, find out the forester,

100 For now our observation is performed;
And since we have the vaward[16] of the day,
My love shall hear the music of my hounds.
Uncouple[17] in the western valley; let them go.
Dispatch, I say, and find the forester.
[*Exit an* Attendant.]

105 We will, fair queen, up to the mountain's top
And mark the musical confusion
Of hounds and echo in conjunction.

Hippolyta. I was with Hercules and Cadmus[18] once
When in a wood of Crete they bayed[19] the bear

110 With hounds of Sparta. Never did I hear
Such gallant chiding; for, besides the groves,
The skies, the fountains, every region near

---

[15] **amity**—friendship.

[16] vaward—vanguard, earliest part.

[17] Uncouple—set free for the hunt.

[18] Cadmus—mythical founder of the ancient Greek city of Thebes. This story about him is unknown.

[19] bayed—brought to bay, cornered.

Seemed all one mutual cry. I never heard
So musical a discord, such sweet thunder.

115 **Theseus.** My hounds are bred out of the Spartan kind,
So flewed,[20] so sanded;[21] and their heads are hung
With ears that sweep away the morning dew;
Crook-kneed, and dewlapped[22] like Thessalian bulls;
Slow in pursuit, but matched in mouth like bells,
120 Each under each.[23] A cry[24] more tunable
Was never holloed to nor cheered with horn
In Crete, in Sparta, nor in Thessaly.
Judge when you hear. [*He sees the sleepers.*] But soft![25]
    What nymphs are these?

Egeus. My lord, this is my daughter here asleep,
125 And this Lysander, this Demetrius is;
This Helena, old Nedar's Helena.
I wonder of their being here together.

Theseus. No doubt they rose up early to observe
The rite of May, and hearing our intent,
130 Came here in grace of our solemnity[26]
But speak, Egeus. Is not this the day
That Hermia should give answer of her choice?

Egeus. It is, my lord.

Theseus. Go bid the huntsmen wake them with their horns.
[*Exit an* Attendant.]
[*Shout within. Wind horns. They all start up.*]
135 Good morrow, friends. Saint Valentine is past.
Begin these woodbirds but to couple now?[27]

Lysander. Pardon, my lord. [*They kneel.*]

Theseus.   I pray you all, stand up.
[*They stand.*]
I know you two are rival enemies;

---

[20] So flewed—similarly having large chaps, or fleshy covering of the jaw.

[21] sanded—of sandy color.

[22] dewlapped—having pendulous folds of skin under the neck.

[23] matched . . . each—harmoniously matched in their cries like a set of bells, from treble down to bass.

[24] cry—pack of hounds.

[25] soft—gently, wait a minute.

[26] in . . . solemnity—in honor of our wedding ceremony.

[27] Saint Valentine . . . now—Birds were supposed to choose their mates on Saint Valentine's Day.

How comes this gentle concord in the world,

140 That hatred is so far from jealousy[28]

To sleep by hate and fear no **enmity**?[29]

Lysander. My lord, I shall reply amazedly,

Half sleep, half waking; but as yet, I swear,

I cannot truly say how I came here.

145 But, as I think—for truly would I speak,

And now I do bethink me, so it is

I came with Hermia hither. Our intent

Was to be gone from Athens, where we might,

Without the peril of the Athenian law—

150 **Egeus.** Enough, enough, my lord; you have enough.

I beg the law, the law, upon his head.

They would have stol'n away; they would, Demetrius,

Thereby to have defeated[30] you and me,

You of your wife and me of my consent,

155 Of my consent that she should be your wife.

Demetrius. My lord, fair Helen told me of their stealth,

Of this their purpose hither to this wood, I

And I in fury hither followed them,

Fair Helena in fancy[31] following me.

160 But, my good lord, I wot not by what power—

But by some power it is—my love to Hermia,

Melted as the snow, seems to me now

As the remembrance of an idle gaud

Which in my childhood I did dote upon;

165 And all the faith, the virtue of my heart,

The object and the pleasure of mine eye,

Is only Helena. To her, my lord,

Was I betrothed ere I saw Hermia,

But like a sickness did I loathe this food;

170 But, as in health, come to my natural taste,

Now I do wish it, love it, long for it,

And will forevermore be true to it.

---

[28] jealousy—suspicion.

[29] **enmity**—hatred.

[30] defeated—defrauded.

[31] in fancy—driven by love.

Theseus. Fair lovers, you are fortunately met.
    Of this discourse we more will hear anon.
175   Egeus, I will overbear[32] your will;
    For in the temple, by and by, with us
    These couples shall eternally be knit.
    And, for the morning now is something worn,[33]
    Our purposed hunting shall be set aside.
180   Away with us to Athens. Three and three,
    We'll hold a feast in great solemnity.
    Come, Hippolyta.
    [*Exeunt* Theseus, Hippolyta, Egeus, *and train.*]

Demetrius. These things seem small and undistinguishable,
    Like far-off mountains turnèd into clouds.
185 **Hermia.** Methinks I see these things with parted[34] eye,
    When everything seems double.

Helena.   So methinks;
    And I have found Demetrius like a jewel,
    Mine own, and not mine own.[35]

Demetrius.   Are you sure
    That we are awake? It seems to me
190   That yet we sleep, we dream. Do not you think
    The Duke was here, and bid us follow him?

Hermia. Yea, and my father.

Helena.   And Hippolyta.

Lysander. And he did bid us follow to the temple.

Demetrius. Why, then, we are awake. Let's follow him,
195   And by the way let us recount our dreams.
    [*Exeunt the lovers.*]

Bottom [*awaking*]. When my cue comes, call me, and I will answer. My
    next is "Most fair Pyramus." Heigh-ho! Peter Quince! Flute, the bellows
    mender! Snout, the tinker! Starveling! God's[36] my life, stolen hence
    and left me asleep! I have had a most rare vision. I have had a dream,
200   past the wit of man to say what dream it was. Man is but an ass if he

---

[32] overbear—prevail over.

[33] something worn—somewhat passed, it's getting late in the morning.

[34] parted—improperly focused.

[35] like . . . mine own—like a jewel that one finds by chance and therefore possesses but cannot certainly consider one's own property.

[36] God's—may God save.

go about[37] to **expound**[38] this dream. Methought I was—there is no man can tell what. Methought I was—and methought I had—but man is but a patched[39] fool if he will offer to say what methought I had. The eye of man hath not heard, the ear of man hath not seen, man's hand is not able to taste, his tongue to conceive, nor his heart to report,[40] what my dream was. I will get Peter Quince to write a ballad of this dream. It shall be called "Bottom's Dream," because it hath no bottom;[41] and I will sing it in the latter end of a play, before the Duke. Peradventure, to make it the more gracious, I shall sing it at her death. [*Exit.*]

205

210

Act Four, Scene Two

[*Enter* Quince, Flute, Snout, *and* Starveling.]

Quince. Have you sent to Bottom's house? Is he come home yet?

Starveling. He cannot be heard of. Out of doubt he is transported.[42]

Flute. If he come not, then the play is marred. It goes not forward. Doth it?

5 **Quince.** It is not possible. You have not a man in all Athens able to discharge[43] Pyramus but he.

Flute. No, he hath simply the best wit of any handicraft man in Athens.

Quince. Yea, and the best person[44] too, and he is a very paramour[45] for a sweet voice.

10 **Flute.** You must say "paragon." A paramour is, God bless us, a thing of naught.[46]

[*Enter* Snug *the joiner.*]

Snug. Masters, the Duke is coming from the temple, and there is two or three lords and ladies more married. If our sport had gone forward, we had all been made men.[47]

---

[37] go about—attempt.

[38] **expound**—explain, interpret.

[39] patched—wearing motley, the dress of various colors that was the uniform of the professional fool.

[40] The eye . . . report—Bottom garbles the phrases of I Corinthians 2:9.

[41] hath no bottom—is unfathomable.

[42] transported—carried off by fairies.

[43] discharge—perform.

[44] person—appearance.

[45] paramour—lover; blunder for *paragon*, "ideal."

[46] thing of naught—shameful thing.

[47] we . . . men—we would have had our fortunes made.

15 **Flute.** O sweet bully Bottom! Thus hath he lost sixpence a day[48] during his life; he could not have scaped sixpence a day. An the Duke had not given him sixpence a day for playing Pyramus, I'll be hanged. He would have deserved it. Sixpence a day in Pyramus, or nothing.

[*Enter* Bottom.]

Bottom. Where are these lads? Where are these hearts?[49]

20 **Quince.** Bottom! O most courageous day! O most happy hour!

Bottom. Masters, I am to discourse wonders.[50] But ask me not what, for if I tell you, I am no true Athenian. I will tell you everything, right as it fell out.

Quince. Let us hear, sweet Bottom.

25 **Bottom.** Not a word of me. And that I will tell you is that the Duke hath dined. Get your apparel together, good strings[51] to your beards, new ribbons to your pumps;[52] meet presently at the palace; every man look o'er his part; for the short and the long is, our play is preferred.[53] In any case, let Thisbe have clean linen; and let not him

30 that plays the lion pare his nails, for they shall hang out for the lion's claws. And, most dear actors, eat no onions nor garlic, for we are to utter sweet breath; and I do not doubt but to hear them say it is a sweet comedy. No more words. Away! Go, away! [*Exeunt.*]

Act Five, Scene One

[*Enter* Theseus, Hippolyta, *and* Philostrate, *lords, and attendants.*]

Hippolyta. 'Tis strange, my Theseus, that these lovers speak of.

Theseus. More strange than true. I never may believe
These antique fables nor these fairy toys.[1]
Lovers and madmen have such seething brains,
5   Such shaping fantasies,[2] that **apprehend**[3]
More than cool reason ever **comprehends**.[4]

---

[48] sixpence a day—as a royal pension.

[49] hearts—good fellows.

[50] am . . . wonders—have wonders to relate.

[51] strings—to attach the beards.

[52] pumps—light shoes or slippers.

[53] preferred—selected for consideration.

[1] fairy toys—trifling stories about fairies.

[2] fantasies—imaginations.

[3] **apprehend**—conceive.

[4] **comprehends**—understands.

The lunatic, the lover, and the poet
Are of imagination all compact.[5]
One sees more devils than vast hell can hold;
10   That is the madman. The lover, all as frantic,
Sees Helen's beauty in a brow of Egypt.[6]
The poet's eye, in a fine frenzy rolling,
Doth glance from heaven to earth, from earth to heaven;
And as imagination bodies forth
15   The forms of things unknown, the poet's pen
Turns them to shapes and gives to airy nothing
A local habitation and a name.
Such tricks hath strong imagination
That, if it would but apprehend some joy,
20   It comprehends some bringer of that joy;
Or in the night, imagining some fear,
How easy is a bush supposed a bear!
Hippolyta. But all the story of the night told over,
And all their minds transfigured so together,
25   More witnesseth than fancy's images[7]
And grows to something of great constancy;[8]
But, howsoever, strange and admirable.
[*Enter lovers:* Lysander, Demetrius, Hermia, *and* Helena.]
Theseus. Here come the lovers, full of joy and mirth.
Joy, gentle friends! Joy and fresh days of love
30   Accompany your hearts!
Lysander.   More than to us
Wait in your royal walks, your board, your bed!
Theseus. Come now, what masques,[9] what dances shall we have,
To wear away this long age of three hours
Between our after-supper and bedtime?
35   Where is our usual manager of mirth?
What revels are in hand? Is there no play
To ease the anguish of a torturing hour?
Call Philostrate.

---

[5] compact—formed, composed.

[6] Helen's . . . Egypt—beauty of Helen of Troy in the face of a gypsy.

[7] More . . . images—testifies to something more substantial than mere imaginings.

[8] constancy—certainty.

[9] masques—elaborate courtly entertainments.

Philostrate.   Here, mighty Theseus.

Theseus. Say, what abridgment[10] have you for this evening?

40   What masque? What music? How shall we beguile

The lazy time, if not with some delight?

Philostrate [*giving him a paper*].

There is a brief[11] how many sports are ripe.

Make choice of which Your Highness will see first.

Theseus [*reads*]. "The battle with the Centaurs,[12] to be sung

45   By an Athenian eunuch[13] to the harp"?

We'll none of that. That have I told my love,

In glory of my kinsman Hercules.

[*He reads.*] "The riot of the tipsy Bacchanals,

Tearing the Thracian singer in their rage"?[14]

50   That is an old device; and it was played

When I from Thebes came last a conqueror.

[*He reads.*] "The thrice three Muses[15] mourning for the death

Of Learning, late deceased in beggary"?

That is some satire, keen and critical,

55   Not sorting with a nuptial ceremony.

[*He reads.*] "A **tedious**[16] brief scene of young Pyramus

And his love Thisbe; very tragical mirth"?

Merry and tragical? Tedious and brief?

That is, hot ice and wondrous strange snow.

60   How shall we find the concord of this discord?

Philostrate. A play there is, my lord, some ten words[17] long,

Which is as brief as I have known a play;

But by ten words, my lord, it is too long,

Which makes it tedious. For in all the play

65   There is not one word apt, one player fitted.

---

[10] abridgment—pastime (to abridge or shorten the evening).

[11] brief—short written statement, summary.

[12] battle . . . Centaurs—The centaur was a creature with the head and torso of a human being and the body and legs of a horse. This probably refers to the battle of the Centaurs and the Lapithae, when the Centaurs attempted to carry off Hippodamia, bride of Theseus's friend Pirothous.

[13] eunuch—male singer castrated before puberty so as to retain a high voice.

[14] The riot . . . rage—This was the story of the death of Orpheus, the marvelous singer who was torn limb from limb by wine-maddened Bacchanals, female worshippers of the god Dionysus.

[15] Muses—nine goddesses who are patrons of the arts and learning.

[16] **tedious**—tiresome by reason of length, slowness, or dullness; boring.

[17] words—speeches.

And tragical, my noble lord, it is,
For Pyramus therein doth kill himself.
Which, when I saw rehearsed, I must confess,
Made mine eyes water; but more merry tears
70   The passion of loud laughter never shed.

Theseus. What are they that do play it?

Philostrate. Hardhanded men that work in Athens here,
Which never labored in their minds till now,
And now have toiled their unbreathed[18] memories
75   With this same play, against your nuptial.

Theseus. And we will hear it.

Philostrate.   No, my noble lord,
It is not for you. I have heard it over,
And it is nothing, nothing in the world;
Unless you can find sport in their intents,
80   Extremely stretched and conned with cruel pain
To do you service.

Theseus.   I will hear that play;
For never anything can be amiss
When simpleness and duty tender it.
Go, bring them in; and take your places, ladies.
[Philostrate *goes to summon the players.*]

85 **Hippolyta.** I love not to see wretchedness o'ercharged,[19]
And duty in his service perishing.

Theseus. Why, gentle sweet, you shall see no such thing.

Hippolyta. He says they can do nothing in this kind.

Theseus. The kinder we, to give them thanks for nothing.
90   Our sport shall be to take what they mistake;
And what poor duty cannot do, noble respect
Takes it in might, not merit.
Where I have come, great clerks[20] have purposed
To greet me with premeditated welcomes;
95   Where I have seen them shiver and look pale,
Make periods in the midst of sentences,
Throttle their practiced accent in their fears,
And in conclusion dumbly have broke off,

---

[18] unbreathed—unexercised.

[19] wretchedness o'ercharged—social or intellectual inferiors overburdened.

[20] clerks—learned men.

Not paying me a welcome. Trust me, sweet,
100 Out of this silence yet I picked a welcome;
And in the modesty of fearful duty
I read as much as from the rattling tongue
Of saucy and **audacious**[21] eloquence.
Love, therefore, and tongue-tied simplicity
105 In least speak most to my capacity.
[Philostrate *returns.*]

Philostrate. So please Your Grace, the Prologue is addressed.

Theseus. Let him approach. [*A flourish of trumpets.*]
[*Enter the* Prologue (Quince).]

Prologue. If we offend, it is with our good will.
That you should think, we come not to offend,
110 But with good will. To show our simple skill,
That is the true beginning of our end.
Consider, then, we come but in despite.
We do not come, as minding to content you,
Our true intent is. All for your delight
115 We are not here. That you should here repent you,
The actors are at hand; and, by their show,
You shall know all that you are like to know.

Theseus. This fellow doth not stand upon points.

Lysander. He hath rid his prologue like a rough colt;[22] he knows not
120 the stop. A good moral, my lord: it is not enough to speak, but to
speak true.

Hippolyta. Indeed, he hath played on his prologue like a child on a
recorder:[23] a sound, but not in government.

Theseus. His speech was like a tangled chain: nothing impaired, but
125 all disordered. Who is next?
[*Enter* Pyramus (Bottom), *and* Thisbe (Flute), *and* Wall (Snout), *and*
Moonshine (Starveling), *and* Lion (Snug).]

Prologue. Gentles, perchance you wonder at this show;
But wonder on, till truth make all things plain
This man is Pyramus, if you would know;
This beauteous lady Thisbe is, certain.
130 This man with time and roughcast cloth present

---

[21] **audacious**—fearless, bold.

[22] rid . . . colt—ridden his prologue like an unbroken horse.

[23] recorder—wind instrument like a flute.

Wall, that vile wall which did these lovers **sunder**;[24]
And through Wall's chink, poor souls, they are content
　　To whisper. At the which let no man wonder.
This man, with lantern, dog, and bush of thorn,
135　　　Presenteth Moonshine; for, if you will know,
By moonshine did these lovers think no scorn
　　To meet at Ninus' tomb, there, there to woo.
This grisly beast, which Lion hight[25] by name,
The trusty Thisbe coming first by night
140　Did scare away, or rather did affright;
And as she fled, her mantle she did fall,[26]
　　　Which Lion vile with bloody mouth did stain.
Anon comes Pyramus, sweet youth and tall,
　　And finds his trusty Thisbe's mantle slain;
145　　Whereat, with blade, with bloody, blameful blade,
　　　He bravely broached[27] his boiling bloody breast.
And Thisbe, tarrying in mulberry shade,
　　　His dagger drew, and died. For all the rest,
Let Lion, Moonshine, Wall, and lovers twain[28]
150　At large[29] discourse, while here they do remain.
　　[*Exeunt* Lion, Thisbe, *and* Moonshine.]

Theseus. I wonder if the lion be to speak.

Demetrius. No wonder, my lord. One lion may, when many asses do.

Wall. In this same interlude it doth befall
That I, one Snout by name, present a wall;
155　And such a wall as I would have you think
That had in it a crannied hole or chink,
Through which the lovers, Pyramus and Thisbe,
Did whisper often, very secretly.
This loam, this roughcast, and this stone doth show
160　That I am that same wall; the truth is so.

---

[24] **sunder**—divide; separate.

[25] hight—is called.

[26] her mantle . . . fall—she dropped her cloak.

[27] broached—stabbed.

[28] twain—two.

[29] At large—in full, at length.

And this the cranny is, right and sinister,[30]
Through which the fearful lovers are to whisper.

Theseus. Would you desire lime and hair to speak better?

Demetrius. It is the wittiest partition[31] that ever I heard discourse,
165   my lord.

[Pyramus *comes forward.*]

Theseus. Pyramus draws near the wall. Silence!

Pyramus. O grim-looked night! O night with hue so black!
     O night, which ever art when day is not!
O night, O night! Alack, alack, alack,
170   I fear my Thisbe's promise is forgot.
And thou, O wall, O sweet, O lovely wall,
     That stand'st between her father's ground and mine,
Thou wall, O wall, O sweet and lovely wall,
     Show me thy chink, to blink through with mine eyne.

[Wall *makes a chink with his fingers.*]

175   Thanks, courteous wall. Jove shield thee well for this.
     But what see I? No Thisbe do I see.
O wicked wall, through whom I see no bliss!
     Cursed be thy stones for thus deceiving me!

Theseus. The wall, methinks, being sensible,[32] should curse again.

180 **Pyramus.** No, in truth, Sir, he should not. "Deceiving me" is Thisbe's
     cue: she is to enter now, and I am to spy her through the wall. You
     shall see, it will fall pat as I told you. Yonder she comes.

[*Enter* Thisbe.]

Thisbe. O wall, full often hast thou heard my moans
     For parting my fair Pyramus and me.
185   My cherry lips have often kissed thy stones,
     Thy stones with lime and hair knit up in thee.

Pyramus. I see a voice. Now will I to the chink,
     To spy an I can hear my Thisbe's face.
     Thisbe!

Thisbe.   My love! Thou art my love, I think.

190 **Pyramus.** Think what thou wilt, I am thy lover's grace,
     And like Limander am I trusty still.

---

[30] right and sinister—the right side of it and the left; or running from the right to left, horizontally.

[31] partition—wall, with pun on *partition* meaning "section of a learned treatise or discourse."

[32] sensible—capable of feeling.

Thisbe. And I like Helen,[33] till the Fates me kill.

Pyramus. Not Shafalus to Procrus[34] was so true.

Thisbe. As Shafalus to Procrus, I to you.

195 **Pyramus.** O, kiss me through the hole of this vile wall!

Thisbe. I kiss the wall's hole, not your lips at all.

Pyramus. Wilt thou at Ninny's tomb meet me straightway?

Thisbe. 'Tide[35] life, 'tide death, I come without delay.

[*Exeunt* Pyramus *and* Thisbe.]

Wall. Thus have I, Wall, my part dischargèd so;

200 And, being done, thus Wall away doth go. [*Exit.*]

Theseus. Now is the mural down between the two neighbors.

Demetrius. No remedy, my lord, when walls are so willful to hear without warning.

Hippolyta. This is the silliest stuff that ever I heard.

205 **Theseus.** The best in this kind are but shadows; and the worst are no worse, if imagination amend them.

Hippolyta. It must be your imagination then, and not theirs.

Theseus. If we imagine no worse of them than they of themselves, they may pass for excellent men. Here come two noble beasts in,

210 a man and a lion.

[*Enter* Lion *and* Moonshine.]

Lion. You, ladies, you, whose gentle hearts do fear
   The smallest monstrous mouse that creeps on floor,
May now perchance both quake and tremble here,
   When lion rough in wildest rage doth roar.

215 Then know that I, as Snug the joiner, am
A lion fell, nor else no lion's dam;[36]
For, if I should as lion come in strife
Into this place, 'twere pity on my life.

Theseus. A very gentle beast, and of a good conscience.

220 **Demetrius.** The very best at a beast, my lord, that e'er I saw.

Lysander. This lion is a very fox for his valor.

Theseus. True; and a goose for his discretion.

Demetrius. Not so, my lord, for his valor cannot carry his discretion, and the fox carries the goose.

---

[33] Limander . . . Helen—blunders for Leander and Hero, legendary lovers.

[34] Shafalus . . . Procrus—blunders for Cephalus and Procrus, also famous lovers.

[35] 'Tide—betide, come.

[36] lion fell . . . lion's dam—fierce lion, lion's mother.

225 **Theseus.** His discretion, I am sure, cannot carry his valor; for the
goose carries not the fox. It is well. Leave it to his discretion, and
let us listen to the moon.

Moon. This lanthorn[37] doth the hornèd moon present—

Demetrius. He should have worn the horns on his head.

230 **Theseus.** He is no crescent,[38] and his horns are invisible within the
circumference.

Moon. This lanthorn doth the hornèd moon present;
Myself the man i' the moon do seem to be.

Theseus. This is the greatest error of all the rest. The man should be
235 put into the lanthorn. How is it else the man i' the moon?

Demetrius. He dares not come there for the candle, for you see it is
already in snuff.[39]

Hippolyta. I am aweary of this moon. Would he would change!

Theseus. It appears, by his small light of discretion, that he is in the
240 wane; but yet, in courtesy, in all reason, we must stay the time.

Lysander. Proceed, Moon.

Moon. All that I have to say is to tell you that the lanthorn is the
moon, I, the man i' the moon, this thornbush my thornbush, and
this dog my dog.

245 **Demetrius.** Why, all these should be in the lanthorn, for all these are
in the moon. But silence! Here comes Thisbe.
[*Enter* Thisbe.]

Thisbe. This is old Ninny's tomb. Where is my love?

Lion [*roaring*]. O!

Demetrius. Well roared, Lion.
[Thisbe *runs off, dropping her mantle.*]

250 **Theseus.** Well run, Thisbe.

Hippolyta. Well shone, Moon. Truly, the moon shines with a good
grace.
[*The* Lion *worries*[40] Thisbe's *mantle.*]

Theseus. Well moused,[41] Lion.
[*Enter* Pyramus; *exit* Lion.]

---

[37] lanthorn—lantern. This original spelling, *lanthorn*, may suggest a play on the horn of which lanterns were made and also on the invisible horns that the cuckold (a man whose wife was unfaithful) wore on his forehead.

[38] crescent—waxing moon.

[39] in snuff—both "offended" and "in need of snuffing or trimming."

[40] worries—seizes with the teeth and shakes or tugs at repeatedly.

[41] moused—shaken, torn, bitten.

Demetrius. And then came Pyramus.

Lysander. And so the lion vanished.

255 **Pyramus.** Sweet Moon, I thank thee for thy sunny beams;

I thank thee, Moon, for shining now so bright;

For, by thy gracious, golden, glittering gleams,

I trust to take of truest Thisbe sight.

But stay, O spite!

260 But mark, poor knight,

What dreadful dole is here?

Eyes, do you see?

How can it be?

O dainty duck! O dear!

265 Thy mantle good,

What, stained with blood?

Approach, ye Furies[42] fell!

O Fates,[43] come, come,

Cut thread and thrum;[44]

270 Quail, crush, conclude, and quell![45]

Theseus. This passion, and the death of a dear friend, would go near to make a man look sad.

Hippolyta. Beshrew my heart, but I pity the man.

Pyramus. O, wherefore, Nature, didst thou lions frame?[46]

275 Since lion vile hath here deflowered my dear,

Which is—no, no, which was—the fairest dame

That lived, that loved, that liked, that looked with cheer.

Come, tears, confound,

Out, sword, and wound

280 The pap[47] of Pyramus;

Ay, that left pap,

Where heart doth hop. [*He stabs himself.*]

Thus die I, thus, thus, thus.

Now am I dead,

285 Now am I fled;

---

[42] Furies—avenging goddesses of Greek myth.

[43] Fates—three goddesses of Greek myth who spun, measured, and severed the thread of human life.

[44] thread and thrum—everything, the good and bad alike; literally, the warp in weaving and the loose end of the warp.

[45] quell—kill, destroy.

[46] frame—create.

[47] pap—breast.

My soul is in the sky.

    Tongue, lose thy light;

    Moon, take thy flight. [*Exit* Moonshine.]

Now die, die, die, die, die. [Pyramus *dies*.]

290 **Demetrius.** No die, but an ace,[48] for him; for he is but one.

Lysander. Less than an ace, man; for he is dead, he is nothing.

Theseus. With the help of a surgeon he might yet recover, and yet prove
    an ass.

Hippolyta. How chance Moonshine is gone before Thisbe comes back
295   and finds her lover?

Theseus. She will find him by starlight.

    [*Enter* Thisbe.]

    Here she comes; and her passion ends the play.

Hippolyta. Methinks she should not use a long one for such a Pyramus.
    I hope she will be brief.

300 **Demetrius.** A mote will turn the balance, which Pyramus, which Thisbe,
    is the better: he for a man, God warrant us; she for a woman, God
    bless us.

Lysander. She hath spied him already with those sweet eyes.

Demetrius. And thus she means, videlicet:[49]

305 **Thisbe.** Asleep, my love?

    What, dead, my dove?

    O Pyramus, arise!

    Speak, speak. Quite dumb?

    Dead, dead? A tomb

310 Must cover thy sweet eyes.

    These lily lips,

    This cherry nose,

These yellow cowslip cheeks,

    Are gone, are gone!

315   Lovers, make moan.

His eyes were green as leeks.

    O Sisters Three,[50]

    Come, come to me,

With hands as pale as milk;

---

[48] ace—on the side of the die featuring the single spot. The pun is on *die* as a singular of *dice*. Bottom's performance is not worth a whole *die* but rather one single face of it, a small portion.

[49] videlicet—to wit, namely.

[50] Sisters Three—the Fates.

320	Lay them in gore,
	Since you have shore[51]
	With shears his thread of silk.
	Tongue, not a word.
	Come, trusty sword,
325	Come, blade, my breast imbrue![52]
	[*She stabs herself.*]
	And farewell, friends.
	Thus Thisbe ends.
	Adieu, adieu, adieu. [*She dies.*]

Theseus. Moonshine and Lion are left to bury the dead.

330 **Demetrius.** Ay, and Wall too.

Bottom [*starting up, as* Flute *does also*]. No, I assure you, the wall is down that parted their fathers. Will it please you to see the epilogue, or to hear a Bergomask dance[53] between two of our company?
[*The other players enter.*]

Theseus. No epilogue, I pray you; for your play needs no excuse. Never
335 excuse; for when the players are all dead, there need none to be blamed. Marry, if he that writ it had played Pyramus and hanged himself in Thisbe's garter, it would have been a fine tragedy; and so it is, truly, and very notably discharged. But, come, your Bergomask. Let your epilogue alone. [*A dance.*]

340	The iron tongue[54] of midnight hath told twelve.
	Lovers, to bed, 'tis almost fairy time.
	I fear we shall outsleep the coming morn
	As much as we this night have overwatched.
	This palpable-gross[55] play hath well beguiled
345	The heavy gait of night. Sweet friends, to bed.
	A fortnight[56] hold we this solemnity,
	In nightly revels and new jollity. [*Exeunt.*]
	[*Enter* Puck, *carrying a broom.*]

Puck. Now the hungry lion roars,
　　　　And the wolf behowls the moon,

---

[51] shore—shorn, cut.

[52] imbrue—stain with blood.

[53] Bergomask dance—rustic dance named from Bergamo, a province in the state of Venice.

[54] iron tongue—a bell.

[55] palpable-gross—palpably gross, obviously crude.

[56] fortnight—two weeks.

350   Whilst the heavy plowman snores,
            All with weary task fordone.
        Now the wasted brands[57] do glow,
            Whilst the screech owl, screeching loud,
        Puts the wretch that lies in woe
355   In remembrance of a shroud.
        Now it is the time of night
            That the graves, all gaping wide,
        Every one lets forth his sprite,
            In the church-way paths to glide.
360   And we fairies, that do run
            By the triple Hecate's[58] team.
        From the presence of the sun,
            Following darkness like a dream,
        Now are frolic. Not a mouse
365   Shall disturb this hallowed house.
        I am sent with broom before,
        To sweep the dust behind the door.

[*Enter* Oberon *and* Titania, *King and Queen of Fairies, with all their train.*]

Oberon. Through the house give glimmering light,
            By the dead and drowsy fire;
370   Every elf and fairy sprite
            Hop as light as bird from brier;
        And this ditty, after me,
        Sing, and dance it trippingly.

Titania. First, rehearse your song by rote,
375   To each word a warbling note.
        Hand in hand, with fairy grace,
        Will we sing, and bless this place.

[*Song and dance.*]

Oberon. Now, until the break of day,
        Through this house each fairy stray.
380   To the best bride-bed will we,
        Which by us shall blessèd be;
        And the issue there create[59]

---

[57] wasted brands—burned out logs.

[58] triple Hecate's—The goddess Hecate ruled in three capacities: as Luna or Cynthia in heaven, as Diana on earth, and as Proserpina in hell.

[59] issue there create—children conceived there.

Ever shall be fortunate.
So shall all the couples three
385 Ever true in loving be;
And the blots of Nature's hand
Shall not in their issue stand;
Never mole, harelip, nor scar,
Nor mark prodigious,[60] such as are
390 Despisèd in nativity,
Shall upon their children be.
With, this field dew consecrate,
Every fairy take his gait,[61]
And each several chamber bless,
395 Through this palace, with sweet peace;
And the owner of it blest
Ever shall in safety rest.
Trip away; make no stay;
Meet me all by break of day.

[*Exeunt* Oberon, Titania, *and train.*]

Puck [*to the audience*].
400 If we shadows have offended,
Think but this, and all is mended,
That you have but slumbered here
While these visions did appear.
And this weak and idle theme
405 No more yielding but a dream:
Gentles, do not reprehend.
If you pardon, we will mend.
And, as I am an honest Puck,
If we have unearnèd luck
410 Now to scape the serpent's tongue,[62]
We will make amends ere long;
Else the Puck a liar call.
So, good night unto you all
Give your hands,[63] if we be friends,
415 And Robin shall restore amends [*Exit*].

---

[60] prodigious—monstrous, unnatural.

[61] take his gait—go his way.

[62] serpent's tongue—hissing.

[63] Give . . . hands—applaud.

UNDERSTANDING THE PLAY

Act One

1. In Scene One, what is the conflict between Hermia and her father?

2. According to Athenian law, what choices does Hermia have?

3. What is Helena's attitude toward Hermia?

4. In Scene Two, what kind of personality does Bottom reveal?

5. What attitude does Shakespeare seem to express toward Bottom and his friends?

Act Two

1. In Scene One, what kind of a creature is Puck?

2. What is the source of the conflict between Titania and Oberon?

3. What effect has their disagreement had on the world around them?

4. In Scene Two, Helena and Demetrius are both suffering from frustrated love. How does each respond? What do these responses reveal about their characters?

5. In lines 121–128, what is ironic about Lysander's arguments that reason now guides him to love Helena?

Act Three

1. In Scene One, how effective are Bottom and his friends in preparing for their performance?

2. What does Bottom's response to Titania's expression of love reveal about him?

3. In Scene Two, why is Helena particularly distressed when she believes Hermia has joined with the men in mocking her?

4. What quality does the argument between the two women assume?

5. What elements contribute to the humor of Scene Two?

Act Four

1. In Scene One, to what extent does Bottom seem aware of his transformation?

2. What prompts Oberon to remove the spell on Titania?

3. On awakening, how do Titania and Bottom differ in their reactions to the experience they have shared?

4. What do the lovers' different responses on awakening convey about them?

5. In Scene Two, what do the responses of Bottom's friends to his disappearance and his return suggest about their feelings for him?

Act Five

1. Why does Theseus see a similarity between madness, love, and poetry?

2. Why do Theseus and Hipployta disagree about whether Bottom and his friends should put on their play?

3. What does the play performed by Bottom and his friends convey about their understanding of the theater?

4. How do the courtiers respond to the play? What do their responses convey about them?

5. What dramatic functions are served by the reappearance of the fairies at the end of the play?

ANALYZING THE PLAY

1. What different groups of characters are presented in *A Midsummer Night's Dream?*

2. The conflict in a play is the struggle between opposing forces that gives movement to the dramatic plot. What are the fundamental conflicts in *A Midsummer Night's Dream?*

3. What dramatic functions are served by Bottom and his friends?

4. The mood of a literary work is the general atmosphere or prevailing emotional quality. How would you describe the mood of *A Midsummer Night's Dream?* What elements contribute to this mood?

5. In what different ways does the play present the relationship between love and reason?

William Shakespeare ▶

Othello, the Moor of Venice

BY WILLIAM SHAKESPEARE

(For general background on Elizabethan theater and Shakespeare's career, see the introduction for A Midsummer Night's Dream, *page 116.)*

Shakespearean Tragedy

Elizabethan tragedy had two basic sources. The first was a medieval tradition of "the fall of princes" and "the wheel of fortune." This tradition was embodied in moral tales of the great who are brought down, either through their own sinful pride or the turn of fortune's wheel. One element of this medieval tradition that appears in the work of Elizabethan dramatists—including Shakespeare—is the introduction of comic scenes into tragedies.

The second and more important source of Elizabethan tragedy was classical drama. The Elizabethans were not familiar with the works of Greek tragic playwrights such as Sophocles and Euripides; nor were they particularly influenced by Aristotle's ideas of the dramatic unities of time, place, and action (see page 2). Instead, their knowledge of classical tragedy came from the plays of the Roman dramatist Seneca. From Seneca, the Elizabethan dramatists derived a number of elements, including a five-act structure, plots based on revenge, the introduction of ghosts to serve as messengers of doom, long grandiloquent speeches, and an emphasis on blood and horror. These characteristics were particularly evident in the works of Thomas Kyd and Christopher Marlowe, the popular dramatists whom the young Shakespeare imitated.

Othello, Desdemona, and Iago

Compared to Shakespeare's other great tragedies, such as Hamlet, Macbeth, *and* King Lear, Othello *is very dramatically unified, dealing with a single action taking place over a small space of time and concentrating on three principal characters—Othello, Desdemona, and Iago. Othello is a Moor, a North African, definitely a black man, and for the Elizabethan English, a very exotic figure. He is a brave and skillful general who serves the city-state of Venice, a great power in the Mediterranean region during the Renaissance. It may be Othello's exotic presence that has attracted Desdemona, the gentle, beautiful daughter of one of the wealthy rulers of Venice. One of Othello's military aides is Iago, who shares with a few other Shakespearean villains a seeming delight in doing evil for its own sake.*

CHARACTERS

Othello, the Moor[1]
Brabantio, a senator, father to Desdemona
Cassio, an honorable lieutenant to Othello
Iago, Othello's ancient,[2] a villain
Roderigo, a gulled[3] gentleman
Duke of Venice
Senators of Venice
Montano, Governor of Cyprus
Gentlemen of Cyprus
Lodovico and **Gratiano,** kinsmen to
 Brabantio, two noble Venetians

Sailors
Clown
Desdemona, daughter to Brabantio and wife
 to Othello
Emilia, wife to Iago
Bianca, a courtesan[4] and mistress to Cassio
A Messenger
A Herald
A Musician
Servants, Attendants, Officers, Senators,
Musicians, Gentlemen

SCENE: Venice; a seaport in Cyprus.

Act One, Scene One

[*Enter* Roderigo *and* Iago.]

Roderigo. Tush, never tell me! I take it much unkindly
 That thou, Iago, who hast had my purse
 As if the strings were thine, shouldst know of this.[5]

Iago. 'Sblood,[6] but you'll not hear me.
5   If ever I did dream of such a matter,
 Abhor[7] me.

Roderigo. Thou toldst me thou didst hold him in thy hate.

Iago. Despise me
 If I do not. Three great ones of the city,
10   In personal suit to make me his lieutenant,
 Off-capped to him;[8] and by the faith of man,
 I know my price, I am worth no worse a place.
 But he, as loving his own pride and purposes,
 Evades them with a bombast circumstance

---

[1] Moor—North African.
[2] ancient—standard-bearer, ensign.
[3] gulled—deceived.
[4] courtesan—prostitute.
[5] this—that is, Desdemona's elopement.
[6] 'Sblood—by His (Christ's) blood.
[7] **Abhor**—hate.
[8] him—Othello.

15	Horribly stuffed with epithets of war,[9]
	And, in conclusion,
	Nonsuits[10] my mediators. For, "Certes,"[11] says he,
	"I have already chose my officer."
	And what was he?
20	Forsooth, a great arithmetician,[12]
	One Michael Cassio, a Florentine,
	A fellow almost damned in a fair wife,
	That never set a squadron in the field
	Nor the division of a battle knows
25	More than a spinster—unless the bookish theoric,
	Wherein the togaed consuls [13] can propose
	As masterly as he. Mere prattle without practice
	Is all his soldiership. But he, sir, had th' election;
	And I, of whom his[14] eyes had seen the proof
30	At Rhodes, at Cyprus, and on other grounds
	Christened and heathen, must be beleed and calmed
	By debitor and creditor. This countercaster,[15]
	He, in good time, must his lieutenant be,
	And I—God bless the mark!—his Moorship's ancient.
35	**Roderigo.** By heaven, I rather would have been his hangman.
	Iago. Why, there's no remedy. 'Tis the curse of service;
	Preferment goes by letter and affection,
	And not by old gradation,[16] where each second
	Stood heir to th' first. Now, Sir, be judge yourself
40	Whether I in any just term am affined[17]
	To love the Moor.
	Roderigo. I would not follow him then.
	Iago. Sir, content you.
	I follow him to serve my turn upon him.
45	We cannot all be masters, nor all masters

---

[9] bombast circumstance . . . epithets of war—wordy evasion (*bombast* is cotton padding) full of military expressions.

[10] Nonsuits—rejects the petition of.

[11] Certes—certainly.

[12] arithmetician—that is, a man whose military knowledge is merely theoretical, based on books of tactics.

[13] togaed consuls—counselors or senators in togas (robes worn by adult males in ancient Rome).

[14] his—Othello's.

[15] countercaster—bookkeeper, one who casts, or tallies, with counters, or metal disks. A contempuous reference to Cassio.

[16] by letter . . . gradation—by personal influence and by favoritism, not by seniority.

[17] affined—bound.

Cannot be truly followed. You shall mark
Many a duteous and knee-crooking knave
That, doting on his own **obsequious**[18] bondage,
Wears out his time, much like his master's ass,
For naught but provender, and when he's old, cashiered.
Whip me such honest knaves. Others there are
Who, trimmed in forms and visages of duty,
Keep yet their hearts attending on themselves,
And, throwing but shows of service on their lords,
Do well thrive by them, and when they have lined their coats,
Do themselves homage. These fellows have some soul,
And such a one do I profess myself. For, sir,
It is as sure as you are Roderigo,
Were I the Moor I would not be Iago.[19]
In following him, I follow but myself—
Heaven is my judge, not I for love and duty,
But seeming so for my peculiar[20] end.
For when my outward action doth demonstrate
The native act and figure of my heart
In compliment extern,[21] 'tis not long after
But I will wear my heart upon my sleeve
For daws to peck at. I am not what I am.

Roderigo. What a full fortune does the thick-lips owe,[22]
If he can carry 't thus!

Iago.   Call up her father.
Rouse him, make after him, poison his delight,
Proclaim him in the streets; incense her kinsmen,
And, though he in a fertile climate dwell,
Plague him with flies. Though that his joy be joy,
Yet throw such changes of vexation on 't
As it may lose some color.

Roderigo. Here is her father's house. I'll call aloud.

---

[18] **obsequious**—servile.

[19] Were . . . Iago—that is, if I were able to assume command, I certainly would not choose to remain a subordinate, or I would keep a suspicious eye on a flattering subordinate.

[20] peculiar—particular, personal.

[21] native act and figure . . . in compliment extern—innate workings and intention of my heart in outward show.

[22] owe—own.

Iago. Do, with like timorous[23] accent and dire yell

As when, by night and negligence, the fire

Is spied in populous cities.

80 **Roderigo.** What ho, Brabantio! Signor Brabantio, ho!

Iago. Awake! What ho, Brabantio! Thieves, thieves, thieves!

Look to your house, your daughter, and your bags!

Thieves, thieves!

[Brabantio *enters above at a window.*[24]]

Brabantio. What is the reason of this terrible summons?

85 What is the matter there?

Roderigo. Signor, is all your family within?

Iago. Are your doors locked?

Brabantio. Why, wherefore ask you this?

Iago. Zounds,[25] sir, you're robbed. For shame, put on your gown!

Your heart is burst; you have lost half your soul.

90 Even now, now, very now, an old black ram

Is tupping[26] your white ewe. Arise, arise!

Awake the snorting citizens with the bell,

Or else the devil will make a grandsire of you.

Arise, I say!

Brabantio. What, have you lost your wits?

95 **Roderigo.** Most reverend signor, do you know my voice?

Brabantio. Not I. What are you?

Roderigo. My name is Roderigo.

Brabantio. The worser welcome.

I have charged thee not to haunt about my doors.

100 In honest plainness thou hast heard me say

My daughter is not for thee; and now, in madness,

Being full of supper and distempering drafts,[27]

Upon malicious bravery dost thou come

To start[28] my quiet.

105 **Roderigo.** Sir, sir, sir—

---

[23] timorous—frightening.

[24] *at a window*—This stage direction probably calls for an appearance on the small upper stage above and to the rear of the main platform stage. The upper stage was modeled on the projecting upper story of an Elizabethan house.

[25] Zounds—by His (Christ's) wounds.

[26] tupping—covering, copulating with (said of sheep).

[27] distempering draughts—intoxicating drinks.

[28] start—startle, disrupt.

Brabantio. But thou must needs be sure
My spirits and my place[29] have in their power
To make this bitter to thee.

Roderigo. Patience, good sir.

Brabantio. What tell'st thou me of robbing? This is Venice;
My house is not a grange.[30]

Roderigo. Most grave Brabantio,

110   In simple and pure soul I come to you.

Iago. Zounds, sir, you are one of those that will not serve God if the devil
bid you. Because we come to do you service and you think we are
ruffians, you'll have your daughter covered with a Barbary[31] horse;
you'll have your nephews neigh to you; you'll have coursers for

115   cousins and jennets for germans.[32]

Brabantio. What profane wretch art thou?

Iago. I am one, sir, that comes to tell you your daughter and the Moor are
now making the beast with two backs.

Brabantio. Thou art a villain.

Iago. You are—a senator.

120   **Brabantio.** This thou shalt answer. I know thee, Roderigo.

Roderigo. Sir, I will answer anything. But I beseech you,
If 't be your pleasure and most wise consent—
As partly I find it is—that your fair daughter,
At this odd-even[33] and dull watch o' the night,

125   Transported with no worse nor better guard
But with a knave of common hire, a gondolier,
To the gross clasps of a lascivious Moor—
If this be known to you and your allowance
We then have done you bold and saucy wrongs.

130   But if you know not this, my manners tell me
We have your wrong rebuke. Do not believe
That, from the sense of all civility,
I thus would play and trifle with your reverence.
Your daughter, if you have not given her leave,

---

[29] My spirits and my place—my temperment and my authority of office.

[30] grange—isolated country house.

[31] Barbary—from northern Africa (and hence associated with Othello).

[32] nephews neigh . . . coursers for cousins . . . jennets for germans—grandsons who whinny, powerful horses for kinsmen, and small Spanish horses for blood relations.

[33] odd-even—between one day and the next, that is, about midnight.

135   I say again, hath made a gross revolt,
      Tying her duty, beauty, wit, and fortunes
      In an extravagant[34] and wheeling stranger
      Of here and everywhere. Straight satisfy yourself.
      If she be in her chamber or your house,
140   Let loose on me the justice of the state
      For thus deluding you.

Brabantio. Strike on the tinder, ho!
      Give me a taper! Call up all my people!
      This accident is not unlike my dream.
145   Belief of it oppresses me already.
      Light, I say, light! [*Exit above.*]

Iago.   Farewell, for I must leave you.
      It seems not meet nor wholesome to my place
      To be producted[35]—as, if I stay, I shall—
      Against the Moor. For I do know the state,
150   However this may gall him with some check,[36]
      Cannot with safety cast[37] him, for he's embarked
      With such loud reason to the Cyprus wars,
      Which even now stands in act,[38] that, for their souls,
      Another of his fathom[39] they have none
155   To lead their business; in which regard,
      Though I do hate him as I do hell pains,
      Yet for necessity of present life
      I must show out a flag and sign of love,
      Which is indeed but sign. That you shall surely find him,
160   Lead to the Sagittary[40] the raisèd search,
      And there will I be with him. So farewell. [*Exit.*]

[*Enter below* Brabantio *in his nightgown with servants and torches.*]

Brabantio. It is too true an evil. Gone she is;
      And what's to come of my despisèd time
      Is naught but bitterness. Now, Roderigo,

---

[34] extravagant—wandering far from home.

[35] producted—produced (as a witness).

[36] check—rebuke.

[37] cast—dismiss.

[38] stands in act—are going on.

[39] fathom—ability; that is, depth of experience.

[40] Sagittary—an inn or house where Othello and Desdemona are staying, named for its sign of Sagittarius, or Centaur.

165	Where didst thou see her?—O unhappy girl!—
	With the Moor, sayst thou?—Who would be a father!—
	How didst thou know 'twas she?—O, she deceives me
	Past thought!—What said she to you?—Get more tapers.
	Raise all my kindred.—Are they married, think you?

Roderigo. Truly, I think they are.

Brabantio. O heaven! How got she out? O treason of the blood!
Fathers, from hence trust not your daughters' minds
By what you see them act. Is there not charms
By which the property of youth and maidhood
May be abused? Have you not read, Roderigo,
Of some such thing?

Roderigo.   Yes, sir, I have indeed.

Brabantio. Call up my brother.—O, would you had had her!—
Some one way, some another.—Do you know
Where we may apprehend her and the Moor?

Roderigo. I think I can discover him, if you please
To get good guard and go along with me.

Brabantio. Pray you, lead on. At every house I'll call;
I may command at most.—Get weapons, ho!
And raise some special officers of night.—
On, good Roderigo. I will deserve your pains.[41]

[*Exeunt.*]

Act One, Scene Two

[*Enter* Othello, Iago, *attendants with torches.*]

Iago. Though in the trade of war I have slain men,
Yet do I hold it very stuff o' the conscience
To do no contrived murder. I lack **iniquity**[42]
Sometimes to do me service. Nine or ten times
I had thought t' have yerked him[43] here under the ribs.

Othello. 'Tis better as it is.

Iago.   Nay, but he prated,
And spoke such scurvy and provoking terms
Against your honor

---

[41] deserve your pains—show gratitude for the trouble you've taken.

[42] **iniquity**—evil.

[43] yerked him—stabbed Rodrigo.

That, with the little godliness I have,

10   I did full hard forbear him. But, I pray you, sir,

Are you fast married? Be assured of this,

That the magnifico[44] is much beloved,

And hath in his effect a voice potential

As double as the Duke's.[45] He will divorce you,

15   Or put upon you what restraint or grievance

The law, with all his might to enforce it on,

Will give him cable.[46]

Othello.   Let him do his spite.

My services which I have done the seigniory[47]

Shall out-tongue his complaints. 'Tis yet to know[48]—

20   Which, when I know that boasting is an honor,

I shall **promulgate**[49]—I fetch my life and being

From men of royal siege,[50] and my demerits[51]

May speak unbonneted to as proud a fortune

As this that I have readied. For know, Iago,

25   But that I love the gentle Desdemona

I would not my unhousèd[52] free condition

Put into **circumscription**[53] and confine

For the sea's worth. But look, what lights come yond?

[*Enter* Cassio *and certain officers with torches.*]

Iago. Those are the raisèd father and his friends.

30   You were best go in.

Othello.   Not I. I must be found.

My parts, my title, and my perfect soul[54]

Shall manifest me rightly. Is it they?

Iago. By Janus,[55] I think no.

---

[44] magnifico—Venetian nobleman; that is, Brabantio.

[45] hath in his effect . . . double as the Duke's—has at his command an influence as powerful as the Duke's.

[46] cable—scope.

[47] seigniory—rulers of Venice.

[48] yet to know—not yet widely known.

[49] **promulgate**—make known publicly.

[50] siege—rank (literally, a seat used by a person of distinction).

[51] demerits—deserts.

[52] unhousèd—unconfined, undomesticated.

[53] **circumscription**—restriction.

[54] My parts . . . soul—my natural gifts, my position of reputation, and my unflawed conscience.

[55] Janus—two-faced Roman god of beginnings.

Othello. The servants of the Duke? And my lieutenant?

35 The goodness of the night upon you, friends!
    What is the news?

Cassio.   The Duke does greet you, General,
    And he requires your haste-post-haste appearance
    Even on the instant.

Othello.   What is the matter, think you?

Cassio. Something from Cyprus, as I may divine.

40 It is a business of some heat. The galleys
    Have sent a dozen sequent[56] messengers
    This very night at one another's heels,
    And many of the consuls, raised and met,
    Are at the Duke's already. You have been hotly called for;

45 When, being not at your lodging to be found,
    The Senate hath sent about three several quests
    To search you out.

Othello.   'Tis well I am found by you.
    I will but spend a word here in the house
    And go with you. [*Exit.*]

Cassio.   Ancient, what makes he here?

50 **Iago.** Faith, he tonight hath boarded a land carrack.[57]
    If it prove lawful prize, he's made forever.

Cassio. I do not understand.

Iago.   He's married.

Cassio.   To who?

[*Enter* Othello.]

Iago. Marry,[58] to—Come, Captain, will you go?

Othello. Have with you.[59]

55 **Cassio.** Here comes another troop to seek for you.

[*Enter* Brabantio, Roderigo, *with officers and torches.*]

Iago. It is Brabantio, General, be advised.
    He comes to bad intent.

Othello.   Holla! Stand there!

Roderigo. Signor, it is the Moor.

---

[56] sequent—successive.

[57] boarded a…carrack—gone aboard and seized (with sexual suggestion) a large merchant ship.

[58] Marry—an oath, originally, "by the Virgin Mary"; here used with wordplay on *married.*

[59] Have with you—let's go.

Brabantio. Down with him, thief!

[They draw on both sides.]

Iago. You, Roderigo! Come, sir, I am for you.

60   **Othello.** Keep up your bright swords, for the dew will rust them.

     Good signor, you shall more command with years

     Than with your weapons.

Brabantio. O thou foul thief, where hast thou stowed my daughter?

     Damned as thou art, thou hast enchanted her!

65   For I'll refer me to all things of sense,

     If she in chains of magic were not bound

     Whether a maid so tender, fair, and happy,

     So opposite to marriage that she shunned

     The wealthy curlèd darlings of our nation,

70   Would ever have, t' incur a general mock,

     Run from her guardage to the sooty bosom

     Of such a thing as thou—to fear, not to delight.

     Judge me the world if 'tis not gross in sense

     That thou hast practiced[60] on her with foul charms,

75   Abused her delicate youth with drugs or minerals

     That weakens motion.[61] I'll have 't disputed on;

     'Tis probable and **palpable**[62] to thinking.

     I therefore apprehend and do attach[63] thee

     For an abuser of the world, a practicer

80   Of arts inhibited and out of warrant.[64]—

     Lay hold upon him! If he do resist,

     Subdue him at his peril.

Othello.   Hold your hands,

     Both you of my inclining and the rest.

     Were it my cue to fight, I should have known it

85   Without a prompter.—Whither will you that I go

     To answer this your charge?

Brabantio. To prison, till fit time

---

[60] practiced—used tricks.

[61] weakens motion—impair the vital faculties.

[62] **palpable**—obvious.

[63] attach—arrest.

[64] Arts . . . warrant—arts prohibited and illegal (that is, black magic).

Of law and course of direct session
Call thee to answer.

Othello.   What if I do obey?

90   How may the Duke be therewith satisfied,
Whose messengers are here about my side
Upon some present business of the state
To bring me to him?

Officer.   'Tis true, most worthy signor.
The Duke's in council, and your noble self,

95   I am sure, is sent for.

Brabantio.   How? The Duke in council?
In this time of the night? Bring him away.
Mine's not an idle cause. The Duke himself,
Or any of my brothers of the state,
Cannot but feel this wrong as 'twere their own;

100   For if such actions may have passage free,
Bondslaves and pagans shall our statesmen be.

[*Exeunt.*]

Act One, Scene Three

[*Enter* Duke *and* Senators *and sit at a table, with lights, and* Officers. *The* Duke *and* Senators *are reading dispatches.*]

Duke. There is no composition[65] in these news
That gives them credit.

First Senator. Indeed, they are disproportioned.
My letters say a hundred and seven galleys.

5   **Duke.** And mine, a hundred forty.

Second Senator.   And mine, two hundred.
But though they jump not on a just account[66]—
As in these cases, where the aim[67] reports
'Tis oft with difference—yet do they all confirm
A Turkish fleet, and bearing up to Cyprus.

10   **Duke.** Nay, it is possible enough to judgment.
I do not so secure me in the error

---

[65] composition—consistency.

[66] jump . . . just account—do not agree on an exact number.

[67] aim—conjecture.

But the main article I do approve
In fearful sense.[68]

Sailor [*within*].   What ho, what ho, what ho!

[*Enter* Sailor.]

Officer. A messenger from the galleys.

15 **Duke.** Now, what's the business?

Sailor. The Turkish preparation makes for Rhodes.
So was I bid report here to the state
By Signor Angelo.

Duke. How say you by this change?

First Senator.   This cannot be

20 By no assay of reason. 'Tis a pageant
To keep us in false gaze.[69] When we consider
Th' importancy of Cyprus to the Turk,
And let ourselves again but understand
That, as it more concerns the Turk than Rhodes,

25 So may he with more facile question bear it,[70]
For that it stands not in such warlike brace,[71]
But altogether lacks th' abilities
That Rhodes is dressed in—if we make thought of this,
We must not think the Turk is so unskillful

30 To leave that latest which concerns him first,
Neglecting an attempt of ease and gain
To wake and wage a danger profitless.

Duke. Nay, in all confidence, he's not for Rhodes.

Officer. Here is more news.

[*Enter a* Messenger.]

35 **Messenger.** The Ottomites,[72] reverend and gracious,
Steering with due course toward the isle of Rhodes,
Have there injointed them with an after fleet.[73]

First Senator. Ay, so I thought. How many, as you guess?

Messenger. Of thirty sail; and now they do restem,

40 Their backward course, bearing with frank appearance

---

[68] I do . . . sense—I do not take such (false) comfort in the discrepancies that I fail to perceive the main point; that is, that the Turkish fleet is threatening.

[69] pageant . . . false gaze—mere show to keep us looking the wrong way.

[70] So may he . . . bear it—so also the Turk may more easily capture Cyprus.

[71] brace—state of defense.

[72] Ottomites—Turks (from Ottoman Empire).

[73] injointed . . . fleet—joined themselves with a second fleet.

Their purposes toward Cyprus. Signor Montano,
Your trusty and most valiant servitor,
With his free duty[74] recommends[75] you thus,
And prays you to believe him.

45 **Duke.** 'Tis certain then for Cyprus.
Marcus Luccicos, is not he in town?

First Senator. He's now in Florence.

Duke. Write from us to him, post-post-haste. Dispatch.

First Senator. Here comes Brabantio and the valiant Moor.

[*Enter* Brabantio, Othello, Cassio, Iago, Roderigo, *and officers.*]

50 **Duke.** Valiant Othello, we must straight employ you
Against the general enemy Ottoman.
[*To* Brabantio] I did not see you; welcome, gentle signor.
We lacked your counsel and your help tonight.

Brabantio. So did I yours. Good Your Grace, pardon me;
55 Neither my place nor aught I heard of business
Hath raised me from my bed, nor doth the general care
Take hold on me, for my particular grief
Is of so floodgate[76] and o'erbearing nature
That it engluts and swallows other sorrows
60 And it is still itself.

Duke. Why, what's the matter?

Brabantio. My daughter!, my daughter!

Duke and Senators. Dead?

Brabantio. Ay, to me.
She is abused, stol'n from me, and corrupted
By spells and medicines bought of mountebanks;[77]
For nature so preposterously to err,
65 Being not deficient, blind, or lame of sense,
Sans[78] witchcraft could not.

Duke. Whoe'er he be that in this foul proceeding
Hath thus beguiled your daughter of herself,
And you of her, the bloody book of law
70 You shall yourself read in the bitter letter

---

[74] free duty—freely given and loyal service.

[75] recommends—reports to.

[76] floodgate—overwhelming (as when floodgates are opened).

[77] mountebanks—quack doctors.

[78] Sans—without.

After your own sense—yea, though our proper son
Stood in your action.[79]

Brabantio.   Humbly I thank Your Grace.
Here is the man, this Moor, whom now it seems
Your special **mandate**[80] for the state affairs
75   Hath hither brought.

All.   We are very sorry for 't.

Duke [*to* Othello]. What, in your own part, can you say to this?

Brabantio. Nothing, but this is so.

Othello. Most potent, grave, and reverend signors,
My very noble and approved good masters:
80   That I have ta'en away this old man's daughter,
It is most true; true, I have married her.
The very head and front of my offending
Hath this extent, no more. Rude[81] am I in my speech,
And little blessed with the soft phrase of peace;
85   For since these arms of mine had seven years' pith,[82]
Till now some nine moons wasted,[83] they have used
Their dearest action in the tented field;
And little of this great world can I speak
More than pertains to feats of broils and battle,
90   And therefore little shall I grace my cause
In speaking for myself. Yet, by your gracious patience,
I will a round unvarnished tale deliver
Of my whole course of love—what drugs, what charms,
What conjuration, and what mighty magic,
95   For such proceeding I am charged withal,
I won his daughter.

Brabantio.   A maiden never bold;
Of spirit so still and quiet that her motion
Blushed at herself;[84] and she, in spite of nature,
Of years, of country, credit, everything,
100   To fall in love with what she feared to look on!

---

[79] our proper son . . . action—my own son were under your accusation.

[80] **mandate**—command.

[81] Rude—unpolished.

[82] seven years' pith—seven-year-old strength; since he was seven.

[83] nine moons wasted—nine months ago.

[84] Of spirit . . . herself—so modest that she could blush even when alone.

It is a judgment maimed and most imperfect
That will confess perfection so could err
Against all rules of nature, and must be driven
To find out practices of cunning hell
105   Why this should be. I therefore vouch again
That with some mixtures powerful o'er the blood,
Or with some dram conjured to this effect,
He wrought upon her.

Duke.   To vouch this is no proof,
Without more wider and more **overt**[85] test
110   Than these thin habits and poor likelihoods
Of modern seeming[86] do prefer against him.

First Senator. But Othello, speak.
Did you by indirect and forcèd courses
Subdue and poison this young maid's affections?
115   Or came it by request and such fair question
As soul to soul affordeth?

Othello.   I do beseech you,
Send for the lady to the Sagittary
And let her speak of me before her father.
If you do find me foul in her report,
120   The trust, the office I do hold of you
Not only take away, but let your sentence
Even fall upon my life.

Duke.   Fetch Desdemona hither.

Othello. Ancient, conduct them. You best know the place.
[*Exeunt* Iago *and attendants.*]
And, till she come, as truly as to heaven
125   I do confess the vices of my blood,
So justly to your grave ears I'll present
How I did thrive in this fair lady's love,
And she in mine.

Duke. Say it, Othello.

130 **Othello.** Her father loved me, oft invited me,
Still[87] questioned me the story of my life
From year to year—the battles, sieges, fortunes

---

[85] **overt**—open and observable.

[86] habits . . . modern seeming—clothing (that is, appearances) and weak inferences based on trivialities.

[87] Still—continually.

That I have passed.
I ran it through, even from my boyish days
135 To th' very moment that he bade me tell it,
Wherein I spoke of most disastrous chances,
Of moving accidents by flood and field,
Of hairbreadth scapes i' th' imminent deadly breach,[88]
Of being taken by the insolent foe
140 And sold to slavery, of my redemption thence,
And portance[89] in my travels' history,
Wherein of antres vast and deserts idle,[90]
Rough quarries, rocks, and hills whose heads touch heaven,
It was my hint to speak—such was my process—
145 And of the Cannibals that each other eat,
The Anthropophagi,[91] and men whose heads
Do grow beneath their shoulders. These things to hear
Would Desdemona seriously incline;
But still the house affairs would draw her thence,
150 Which ever as she could with haste dispatch
She'd come again, and with a greedy ear
Devour up my discourse. Which I, observing,
Took once a pliant[92] hour, and found good means
To draw from her a prayer of earnest heart
155 That I would all my pilgrimage dilate,[93]
Whereof by parcels she had something heard,
But not intentively.[94] I did consent,
And often did beguile her of her tears,
When I did speak of some distressful stroke
160 That my youth suffered. My story being done,
She gave me for my pains a world of sighs.
She swore, in faith, 'twas strange, 'twas passing[95] strange,
'Twas pitiful, 'twas wondrous pitiful.

---

[88] imminent deadly breach—death-threatening gap made in a fortification.

[89] portance—conduct.

[90] antres vast and deserts idle—huge caves and barren wastes.

[91] Anthropophagi—man-eaters.

[92] pliant—opportune.

[93] dilate—relate in detail.

[94] intentively—with full attention, continuously.

[95] passing—exceedingly.

She wished she had not heard it, yet she wished

165 That heaven had made her such a man. She thanked me,

And bade me, if I had a friend that loved her,

I should but teach him how to tell my story,

And that would woo her. Upon this hint I spake.

She loved me for the dangers I had passed,

170 And I loved her that she did pity them.

This only is the witchcraft I have used.

Here comes the lady. Let her witness it.

[*Enter* Desdemona, Iago, *and attendants.*]

Duke. I think this tale would win my daughter too.

Good Brabantio,

175 Take up this mangled matter at the best.[96]

Men do their broken weapons rather use

Than their bare hands.

Brabantio.   I pray you, hear her speak.

If she confess that she was half the wooer,

Destruction on my head if my bad blame

180 Light on the man!—Come hither, gentle mistress.

Do you perceive in all this noble company

Where most you owe obedience?

Desdemona.   My noble Father,

I do perceive here a divided duty.

To you I am bound for life and education;

185 My life and education both do learn me

How to respect you. You are the lord of duty;

I am hitherto your daughter. But here's my husband,

And so much duty as my mother showed

To you, preferring you before her father,

190 So much I challenge[97] that I may profess

Due to the Moor my lord.

Brabantio. God be with you! I have done.

Please it Your Grace, on to the state affairs.

I had rather to adopt a child than get it.

195 Come hither, Moor. [*He joins the hands of* Othello *and* Desdemona.]

I here do give thee that with all my heart

---

[96] Take up . . . the best—make the best of a bad bargain.

[97] challenge—claim.

Which, but thou hast already, with all my heart
I would keep from thee.—For your sake, jewel,
I am glad at soul I have no other child,

200   For thy escape would teach me tyranny,
To hang clogs[98] on them.—I have done, my lord.

Duke. Let me speak like yourself,[99] and lay a sentence[100]
Which, as a grece or step, may help these lovers
Into your favor.

205   When remedies are past, the griefs are ended
By seeing the worst, which late on hopes depended.[101]
To mourn a mischief that is past and gone
Is the next[102] way to draw new mischief on.
What cannot be preserved when fortune takes,

210   Patience her injury a mockery makes.
The robbed that smiles steals something from the thief;
He robs himself that spends a bootless grief.[103]

Brabantio. So let the Turk of Cyprus us beguile,
We lose it not, so long as we can smile.

215   He bears the sentence well that nothing bears
But the free comfort which from thence he hears,
But he bears both the sentence and the sorrow
That, to pay grief, must of poor patience borrow.
These sentences, to sugar or to gall,

220   Being strong on both sides, are **equivocal**.[104]
But words are words. I never yet did hear
That the bruised heart was piercèd through the ear.[105]
I humbly beseech you, proceed to th' affairs of state.

Duke. The Turk with a most mighty preparation makes for Cyprus.

225   Othello, the fortitude[106] of the place is best known to you; and
though we have there a substitute of most allowed sufficiency,[107]

---

[98] clogs—blocks of wood fastened to the legs of criminals or convicts to inhibit escape.

[99] speak like yourself—that is, as you would in your proper temper.

[100] lay a sentence—apply a maxim.

[101] which late on hopes depended—which griefs are sustained until recently by hopeful anticipation.

[102] next—nearest.

[103] spends a bootless grief—indulges in unavailing grief.

[104] **equivocal**—double-meaning.

[105] piercèd . . . ear—surgically lanced and curèd by mere words of advice.

[106] fortitude—military strength.

[107] substitute of most allowed sufficiency—deputy of highly acknowledged capacity.

yet opinion, a sovereign mistress of effects, throws a more safer
voice on you.[108] You must therefore be content to slubber[109]
the gloss of your new fortunes with this more stubborn and
230 boisterous[110] expedition.

Othello. The tyrant custom, most grave senators,
Hath made the flinty and steel couch of war
My thrice-driven[111] bed of down. I do agnize[112]
A natural and prompt **alacrity**[113]
235 I find in hardness, and do undertake
These present wars against the Ottomites.
Most humbly therefore bending to your state,
I crave fit disposition for my wife,
Due reference of place and exhibition,[114]
240 With such accommodation and besort
As levels with her breeding.[115]

Duke. Why, at her father's.

Brabantio. I will not have it so.

Othello. Nor I.

Desdemona. Nor I. I would not there reside,
To put my father in impatient thoughts
245 By being in his eye. Most gracious Duke,
To my unfolding lend your prosperous ear,[116]
And let me find a charter[117] in your voice,
T' assist my simpleness.

Duke. What would you, Desdemona?

250 **Desdemona.** That I did love the Moor to live with him,
My downright violence and storm of fortunes
May trumpet to the world. My heart's subdued

---

[108] opinion . . . on you—general opinion, an important determiner of affairs, chooses you as the best man.

[109] slubber—soil, sully.

[110] stubborn and boisterous—rough and violent.

[111] thrice-driven—thrice sifted, softest.

[112] agnize—know in myself; acknowledge.

[113] **alacrity**—eagerness.

[114] Due reference...exhibition—provision of appropriate place to live and allowance of money.

[115] accommodation . . . breeding—provision and attendance that suit her social position or upbringing.

[116] my unfolding...ear—my proposal lend your favorable attention.

[117] charter—privilege, authorization.

Even to the very quality of my lord.[118]
I saw Othello's visage in his mind,

255 And to his honors and his valiant parts
Did I my soul and fortunes consecrate.
So that, dear lords, if I be left behind
A moth of peace, and he go to the war,
The rites[119] for why I love him are bereft me,

260 And I a heavy interim shall support
By his dear absence. Let me go with him.
Othello. Let her have your voice.[120]
Vouch with me, heaven, I therefor beg it not
To please the palate of my appetite,

265 Nor to comply with heat[121]—the young affects[122]
In me defunct—and proper satisfaction,
But to be free and bounteous to her mind.
And heaven defend your good souls that you think
I will your serious and great business scant

270 When she is with me. No, when light-winged toys
Of feathered Cupid seel[123] with wanton dullness
My speculative and officed instruments,[124]
That my disports corrupt and taint my business,
Let huswives make a skillet of my helm,

275 And all indign[125] and base adversities
Make head against my estimation![126]
Duke. Be it as you shall privately determine,
Either for her stay or going. Th' affair cries haste,
And speed must answer it.
A Senator. You must away tonight.

280 **Desdemona.** Tonight, my lord?
Duke. This night.
Othello. With all my heart.

---

[118] My heart's … lord—I have become one in nature with my husband (and therefore want to go to war with him like a soldier).

[119] rites—both rites of love and of war (with a suggestion, too, of "rights," sharing).

[120] voice—consent.

[121] heat—sexual passion.

[122] young affects—passions of youth, desires.

[123] seel—make blind.

[124] speculative and officed instruments—eyes and other faculties used in the performance of duty.

[125] indign—unworthy, shameful.

[126] Make head … estimation—raise an army (attack) my reputation.

Duke. At nine i' the morning here we'll meet again.
　　Othello, leave some officer behind,
　　And he shall our commission bring to you,
　　With such things else of quality and respect
285　As doth import you.   ·
Othello.   So please Your Grace, my ancient;
　　A man he is of honesty and trust.
　　To his conveyance I assign my wife,
　　With what else needful Your Good Grace shall think
　　To be sent after me.
Duke.   Let it be so.
290　Good night to everyone. [*To* Brabantio.] And, noble signor,
　　If virtue no delighted[127] beauty lack,
　　Your son-in-law is far more fair than black.
First Senator. Adieu, brave Moor. Use Desdemona well.
Brabantio. Look to her, Moor, if thou hast eyes to see.
295　She has deceived her father, and may thee.
　　[*Exeunt* Duke, Brabantio, Cassio, Senators, *and officers.*]
Othello. My life upon her faith! Honest Iago,
　　My Desdemona must I leave to thee.
　　I prithee, let thy wife attend on her,
　　And bring them after in the best advantage.[128]
300　Come, Desdemona. I have but an hour
　　Of love, of worldly matters and direction,
　　To spend with thee. We must obey the time.
　　[*Exit with* Desdemona.]
Roderigo. Iago—
Iago. What sayst thou, noble heart?
305　**Roderigo.** What will I do, think'st thou?
Iago. Why, go to bed and sleep.
Roderigo. I will incontinently[129] drown myself.
Iago. If thou dost, I shall never love thee after. Why, thou silly gentleman?
Roderigo. It is silliness to live when to live is torment; and then have
310　we a prescription to die when death is our physician.
Iago. O villainous! I have looked upon the world for four times seven
　　years, and, since I could distinguish betwixt a benefit and an injury,

---

[127] delighted—capable of delighting.
[128] in the best advantage—at the most favorable opportunity.
[129] incontinently—immediately, without self-restraint.

I never found a man that knew how to love himself. Ere I would say
I would drown myself for the love of a guinea hen, I would change
315   my humanity with a baboon.

Roderigo. What should I do? I confess it is my shame to be so fond, but
it is not in my virtue[130] to amend it.

Iago. Virtue? A fig! 'Tis in ourselves that we are thus or thus. Our bodies
are our gardens, to the which our wills are gardeners; so that if we
320   will plant nettles or sow lettuce, set hyssop and weed up thyme, supply it with one gender of herbs or distract it with[131] many, either to
have it sterile with idleness or manured with industry—why, the
power and corrigible authority[132] of this lies in our wills. If the
beam[133] of our lives had not one scale of reason to poise another of
325   sensuality, the blood and baseness of our natures would conduct us
to most **preposterous**[134] conclusions. But we have reason to cool our
raging motions, our carnal stings, our unbitted[135] lusts, whereof I
take this that you call love to be a sect or scion.[136]

Roderigo. It cannot be.

330 **Iago.** It is merely a lust of the blood and a permission of the will. Come,
be a man. Drown thyself? Drown cats and blind puppies. I have pro-
fessed me thy friend, and I confess me knit to thy deserving with
cables of perdurable toughness. I could never better stead[137] thee
than now. Put money in thy purse. Follow thou the wars; defeat thy
335   favor with an usurped beard.[138] I say, put money in thy purse. It cannot be long that Desdemona should continue her love to the Moor—put
money in thy purse—nor he his to her. It was a violent commencement
in her, and thou shalt see an answerable sequestration[139]—put but
money in thy purse. These Moors are changeable in their wills—fill
340   thy purse with money. The food that to him now is as luscious as

---

[130] virtue—strength, nature.

[131] distract it with—divide it among.

[132] corrigible authority—power to correct.

[133] beam—balance.

[134] **preposterous**—absurd.

[135] unbitted—unbridled, uncontrolled.

[136] sect or scion—cutting or offshoot.

[137] stead—assist.

[138] defeat . . . beard—disguise your face with an assumed beard. (The suggestion is that Roderigo is not man enough to
have a beard of his own.)

[139] answerable sequestration—corresponding separation or estrangement.

locusts[140] shall be to him shortly as bitter as coloquintida.[141] She must change for youth; when she is sated with his body, she will find the error of her choice. She must have change, she must. Therefore put money in thy purse. If thou wilt needs damn thyself, do it a more delicate way than drowning. Make all the money thou canst. If sanctimony[142] and a frail vow betwixt an erring[143] barbarian and a supersubtle Venetian be not too hard for my wits and all the tribe of hell, thou shalt enjoy her. Therefore make money. A pox of drowning thyself! It is clean out of the way. Seek thou rather to be hanged in compassing[144] thy joy than to be drowned and go without her.

Roderigo. Wilt thou be fast to my hopes if I depend on the issue?

Iago. Thou art sure of me. Go, make money. I have told thee often, and I retell thee again and again, I hate the Moor. My cause is hearted;[145] thine hath no less reason. Let us be conjunctive[146] in our revenge against him. If thou canst cuckold[147] him, thou dost thyself a pleasure, me a sport. There are many events in the womb of time which will be delivered. Traverse, go, provide thy money. We will have more of this tomorrow. Adieu.

Roderigo. Where shall we meet i' the morning?

Iago. At my lodging.

Roderigo. I'll be with thee betimes.[148] [*He starts to leave.*]

Iago. Go to, farewell.—Do you hear, Roderigo?

Roderigo. What say you?

Iago. No more of drowning, do you hear?

Roderigo. I am changed.

Iago. Go to, farewell. Put money enough in your purse.

Roderigo. I'll sell all my land. [*Exit.*]

Iago. Thus do I ever make my fool my purse;
For I mine own gained knowledge should profane
If I would time expend with such a snipe[149]

---

[140] locusts—fruits of the carob tree or perhaps honeysuckle.

[141] coloquintada—colocynth or bitter apple, a purgative.

[142] sanctimony—sacred ceremony, marriage.

[143] erring—wandering.

[144] compassing—encompassing, embracing.

[145] hearted—fixed in the heart, heartfelt.

[146] conjunctive—united.

[147] cuckold—cause his wife to be unfaithful.

[148] betimes—early.

[149] snipe—woodcock, that is, fool.

But for my sport and profit. I hate the Moor;
And it is thought abroad that twixt my sheets
He's done my office. I know not if 't be true;
But I, for mere suspicion in that kind,

375   Will do as if for surety.[150] He holds me well;
The better shall my purpose work on him.
Cassio's a proper[151] man. Let me see now:
To get his place and to plume up my will[152]
In double knavery—How, how?—Let's see:

380   After some time, to abuse Othello's ear
That he[153] is too familiar with his wife.
He hath a person and a smooth dispose[154]
To be suspected, framed[155] to make women false.
The Moor is of a free and open nature,

385   That thinks men honest that but seem to be so,
And will as tenderly[156] be led 'by the nose
As asses are.
I have 't. It is engendered. Hell and night
Must bring this monstrous birth to the world's light.
[*Exit.*]

Act Two, Scene One

[*Enter* Montano *and two* Gentlemen.]

Montano. What from the cape can you discern at sea?

First Gentleman. Nothing at all. It is a high-wrought flood.
I cannot, twixt the heaven and the main,
Descry a sail.

5   **Montano.** Methinks the wind hath spoke aloud at land;
A fuller blast ne'er shook our battlements.
If it hath ruffianed so upon the sea,

---

[150] do . . . surety—act as if on certain knowledge.

[151] proper—handsome.

[152] plume up my will—gratify my ego.

[153] he—Cassio.

[154] dispose—disposition.

[155] framed—designed.

[156] tenderly—readily.

What ribs of oak, when mountains[1] melt on them,
Can hold the mortise?[2] What shall we hear of this?

10 **Second Gentleman.** A segregation[3] of the Turkish fleet.
For do but stand upon the foaming shore,
The chidden billow seems to pelt the clouds;
The wind-shaked surge, with high and monstrous mane,[4]
Seems to cast water on the burning Bear
15 And quench the guards of th' ever-fixèd pole.[5]
I never did like molestation view
On the enchafèd flood.

Montano. If that the Turkish fleet
Be not ensheltered and embayed, they are drowned;
20 It is impossible to bear it out.

[*Enter a* Third Gentleman.]

Third Gentleman. News, lads! Our wars are done.
The desperate tempest hath so banged the Turks
That their designment halts. A noble ship of Venice
Hath seen a grievous wreck and sufferance[6]
25 On most part of their fleet.

Montano. How? Is this true?

Third Gentleman. The ship is here put in,
A Veronesa;[7] Michael Cassio,
Lieutenant to the warlike Moor Othello,
30 Is come on shore; the Moor himself at sea,
And is in full commission here for Cyprus.

Montano. I am glad on 't. 'Tis a worthy governor.

Third Gentleman. But this same Cassio, though he speak of comfort
Touching the Turkish loss, yet he looks sadly
35 And prays the Moor be safe, for they were parted
With foul and violent tempest.

Montano.   Pray heaven he be,
For I have served him, and the man commands

---

[1] mountains—that is, of water.

[2] hold the mortise—hold their joints together. (A *mortise* is a socket hollowed out in fitting timbers.)

[3] segregation—dispersal.

[4] monstrous mane—the surf is like the mane of a wild beast.

[5] burning Bear . . . pole—the constellation Ursa Minor, or the Little Bear, includes and thus *guards* the Pole Star.

[6] wreck and sufferance—shipwreck and disaster.

[7] Veronesa—(ship) from the Italian city of Verona.

Like a full soldier. Let's to the seaside, ho!
As well to see the vessel that's come in
40   As to throw out our eyes for brave Othello,
Even till we make the main and th' aerial blue
An indistinct regard.[8]

Third Gentleman.   Come, let's do so,
For every minute is expectancy
Of more arrivance.[9]

[*Enter* Cassio.]

45   **Cassio.** Thanks, you the valiant of this warlike isle,
That so approve the Moor! O, let the heavens
Give him defense against the elements,
For I have lost him on a dangerous sea.

Montano. Is he well shipped?

50   **Cassio.** His bark is stoutly timbered, and his pilot
Of very expert and approved allowance;[10]
Therefore my hopes, not surfeited to death,[11]
Stand in bold cure.[12]

[*A cry within:* "A sail, a sail, a sail!"]

Cassio. What noise?

55   **A Gentleman.** The town is empty. On the brow o' the sea
Stand ranks of people, and they cry "A sail!"

Cassio. My hopes do shape him for the governor.

[*A shot within.*]

Second Gentleman. They do discharge their shot of courtesy;
Our friends at least.

Cassio.   I pray you, sir, go forth,
60   And give us truth who 'tis that is arrived.

Second Gentleman. I shall. [*Exit.*]

Montano. But, good Lieutenant, is your general wived?

Cassio. Most fortunately. He hath achieved a maid
That paragons description and wild fame,[13]

---

[8] the main . . . regard—sea and sky are indistinguishable in our view.

[9] arrivance—arrival.

[10] approved allowance—tested reputation.

[11] surfeited to death—overextended, worn thin through repeated application or delayed fulfillment.

[12] in bold cure—in strong hopes of fulfillment.

[13] paragons . . . wild fame—surpasses extravagant report.

65   One that excels the quirks[14] of blazoning[15] pens,
        And in th' essential vesture of creation
        Does tire the enginer.[16]
        [*Enter* Second Gentleman.]
                                        How now? Who has put in?
Second Gentleman. 'Tis one Iago, ancient to the General.
Cassio. He's had most favorable and happy speed.
70   Tempests themselves, high seas, and howling winds,
        The guttered[17] rocks and congregated sands—
        Traitors ensteeped[18] to clog the guiltless keel—
        As having sense of beauty, do omit
        Their mortal natures, letting go safely by
75   The divine Desdemona.
Montano.   What is she?
Cassio. She that I spake of, our great captain's captain,
        Left in the conduct of the bold Iago,
        Whose footing[19] here anticipates our thoughts
        A sennight's[20] speed. Great Jove, Othello guard,
80   And swell his sail with thine own powerful breath,
        That he may bless this bay with his tall ship,
        Make love's quick pants in Desdemona's arms,
        Give renewed fire to our extinct spirits,
        And bring all Cyprus comfort!
        [*Enter* Desdemona, Iago, Roderigo, *and* Emilia.]
                                        O, behold,
85   The riches of the ship is come on shore!
        You men of Cyprus, let her have your knees.
        [*The gentlemen make curtsy to* Desdemona.]
        Hail to thee, lady! And the grace of heaven
        Before, behind thee, and on every hand
        Enwheel thee round!

---

[14] quirks—witty phrases.

[15] blazoning—praising.

[16] in th' essential . . . enginer—in her real, God-given beauty, (Desdemona) defeats any attempt to praise her.

[17] guttered—jagged.

[18] ensteeped—lying underwater.

[19] footing—landing.

[20] sennight's—week's.

Desdemona.   I thank you, valiant Cassio.

90   What tidings can you tell me of my lord?

Cassio. He is not yet arrived, nor know I aught

But that he's well and will be shortly here.

Desdemona. O, but I fear—How lost you company?

Cassio. The great contention of the sea and skies

95   Parted our fellowship.

[*Within:* "A sail, a sail!" *A shot.*]

But hark. A sail!

Second Gentleman. They give their greeting to the citadel.

This likewise is a friend.

Cassio.   See for the news.

[*Exit* Second Gentleman.]

Good Ancient, you are welcome. [*Kissing* Emilia.] Welcome,
       mistress.

Let it not gall your patience, good Iago,

100   That I extend[21] my manners; 'tis my breeding

That gives me this bold show of courtesy.

Iago. Sir, would she give you so much of her lips

As of her tongue she oft bestows on me,

You would have enough.

105 **Desdemona.** Alas, she has no speech![22]

Iago. In faith, too much.

I find it still,[23] when I have list to sleep.

Marry, before your ladyship, I grant,

She puts her tongue a little in her heart

110   And chides with thinking.

Emilia.   You have little cause to say so.

Iago. Come on, come on. You are pictures out of doors,[24]

Bells in your parlors, wildcats in your kitchens,

Saints[25] in your injuries, devils being offended,

Players in your huswifery,[26] and huswives in your beds.[27]

---

[21] extend—give scope to.

[22] she has no speech—she's not a chatterbox.

[23] still—always.

[24] pictures out of doors—silent and well-behaved in public.

[25] Saints—martyrs.

[26] Players . . . huswifery—idlers in your housekeeping.

[27] huswives . . . beds—thrifty in dispensing sexual favors.

115	**Desdemona.** O, fie upon thee, slanderer!
	Iago. Nay, it is true, or else I am a Turk.
	You rise to play, and go to bed to work.
	Emilia. You shall not write my praise.
	Iago. No, let me not.
	Desdemona. What wouldst write of me, if thou shouldst praise me?
120	**Iago.** O gentle lady, do not put me to 't,
	For I am nothing if not critical.
	Desdemona. Come on, essay.[28]—There's one gone to the harbor?
	Iago. Ay, madam.
	Desdemona. I am not merry, but I do beguile
125	The thing I am by seeming otherwise.
	Come, how wouldst thou praise me?
	Iago. I am about it, but indeed my invention
	Comes from my pate as birdlime does from frieze—
	It plucks out brains and all.[29] But my Muse labors,
130	And thus she is delivered:[30]
	If she be fair[31] and wise, fairness and wit,
	The one's for use, the other useth it.
	Desdemona. Well praised! How if she be black[32] and witty?
	Iago. If she be black, and thereto have a wit,
135	She'll find a white that shall her blackness fit.
	Desdemona. Worse and worse.
	Emilia. How if fair and foolish?
	Iago. She never yet was foolish that was fair,
	For even her folly helped her to an heir.
	Desdemona. These are old fond[33] **paradoxes**[34] to make fools laugh i'
140	th' alehouse. What miserable praise hast thou for her that's foul
	and foolish?
	Iago. There's none so foul and foolish thereunto,
	But does foul pranks which fair and wise ones do.

---

[28] essay—try.

[29] invention . . . brains and all—Iago protests that for him thinking is as painful as removing birdlime (sticky substance used to catch small birds) from frieze (a coarse woolen cloth).

[30] labors . . . delivered—Iago puns on two senses of *labor:* "exert oneself" and "deliver a child."

[31] fair—blonde, beautiful.

[32] black—dark-complexioned, brunette.

[33] fond—foolish.

[34] **paradoxes**—seemingly contradictory statements that may nonetheless be true.

Desdemona. O heavy ignorance! Thou praisest the worst best. But
what praise couldst thou bestow on a deserving woman indeed,
one that, in the authority of her merit, did justly put on the
vouch[35] of very malice itself?

Iago. She that was ever fair, and never proud,
Had tongue at will, and yet was never loud,
Never lacked gold and yet went never gay,[36]
Fled from her wish, and yet said, "Now I may,"
She that being angered, her revenge being nigh,
Bade her wrong stay and her displeasure fly,
She that in wisdom never was so frail
To change the cod's head for the salmon's tail,[37]
She that could think and ne'er disclose her mind,
See suitors following and not look behind,
She was a wight,[38] if ever such wight were—

Desdemona. To do what?

Iago. To suckle fools and chronicle small beer.[39]

Desdemona. O most lame and impotent conclusion! Do not learn of
him, Emilia, though he be thy husband. How say you, Cassio? Is
he not a most profane and liberal[40] counselor?

Cassio. He speaks home, madam. You may relish him more in the
soldier than in the scholar.

[Cassio *and* Desdemona *stand together, conversing intimately.*]

Iago [*aside*]. He takes her by the palm. Ay, well said, whisper. With
as little a web as this will I ensnare as great a fly as Cassio. Ay,
smile upon her, do; I will gyve[41] thee in thine own courtship. You
say true; 'tis so, indeed. If such tricks as these strip you out of your
lieutenantry, it had been better you had not kissed your three fingers
so oft, which now again you are most apt to play the sir[42] in. Very
good; well kissed! An excellent courtesy! 'Tis so, indeed. Yet again

---

[35] put on the vouch—compel the approval.

[36] gay—extravagantly clothed.

[37] cod's head . . . salmon's tail—lackluster husband for sexy lover.

[38] wight—being.

[39] suckle fools . . . small beer—breastfeed babies and keep petty household accounts.

[40] liberal—licentious, free-spoken.

[41] gyve—fetter, shackle.

[42] play the sir—act the fine gentleman.

your fingers to your lips? Would they were clyster pipes[43] for
your sake! [*Trumpet within.*] The Moor! I know his trumpet.

175 **Cassio.** 'Tis truly so.

Desdemona. Let's meet him and receive him.

Cassio. Lo, where he comes!

[*Enter* Othello *and attendants.*]

Othello. O my fair warrior!

Desdemona.   My dear Othello!

Othello. It gives me wonder great as my content
180   To see you here before me. O my soul's joy,
          If after every tempest come such calms,
          May the winds blow till they have wakened death,
          And let the laboring bark climb hills of seas
          Olympus-high,[44] and duck again as low
185   As hell's from heaven! If it were now to die,
          'Twere now to be most happy, for I fear
          My soul hath her content so absolute
          That not another comfort like to this
          Succeeds in unknown fate.

Desdemona.   The heavens forbid
190   But that our loves and comforts should increase
          Even as our days do grow!

Othello. Amen to that, sweet powers!
          I cannot speak enough of this content.
          It stops me here; it is too much of joy.
195   And this, and this, the greatest discords be
[*They kiss.*]
          That e'er our hearts shall make!

Iago [*aside*]. O, you are well tuned now!
          But I'll set down the pegs[45] that make this music,
          As honest as I am.

200 **Othello.** Come, let us to the castle.
          News, friends! Our wars are done, the Turks are drowned.
          How does my old acquaintance of this isle?—

---

[43] clyster pipes—tubes used for enemas and douches.

[44] Olympus-high—lofty as the mountain where the Greek gods dwelt; heaven-high.

[45] set down the pegs—loosen the strings on (and therefore untune) a musical instrument.

Honey, you shall be well desired[46] in Cyprus;
I have found great love amongst them. O my sweet,
205   I prattle out of fashion, and I dote
In mine own comforts.—I prithee, good Iago,
Go to the bay and disembark my coffers.[47]
Bring thou the master to the citadel;
He is a good one, and his worthiness
210   Does challenge much respect.—Come, Desdemona.—
Once more, well met at Cyprus!
[*Exeunt* Othello *and* Desdemona *and all but* Iago *and* Roderigo.]
Iago [*to an attendant*]. Do thou meet me presently at the harbor. [*To*
Roderigo.] Come hither. If thou be'st valiant—as, they say, base
men[48] being in love have then a nobility in their natures more than
215   is native to them—list me. The Lieutenant tonight watches on the
court of guard. First, I must tell thee this: Desdemona is directly in
love with him.

Roderigo. With him? Why, 'tis not possible.

Iago. Lay thy finger thus, and let thy soul be instructed. Mark me with
220   what violence she first loved the Moor, but for bragging and telling
her fantastical lies. To love him still for prating? Let not thy discreet
heart think it. Her eye must be fed; and what delight shall she have
to look on the devil? When the blood is made dull with the act of
sport,[49] there should be, again to inflame it and to give satiety a
225   fresh appetite, loveliness in favor,[50] sympathy in years,[51] manners,
and beauties—all which the Moor is defective in. Now, for want of
these required conveniences, her delicate tenderness will find itself
abused, begin to heave the gorge,[52] disrelish and abhor the Moor.
Very nature will instruct her in it and compel her to some second
230   choice. Now, sir, this granted—as it is a most pregnant[53] and
unforced position—who stands so **eminent**[54] in the degree of

---

[46] desired—welcomed.

[47] coffers—chests, baggage.

[48] base men—even lowly born men.

[49] act of sport—sex.

[50] favor—appearance.

[51] sympathy in years—similarity in age.

[52] heave the gorge—experience nausea.

[53] pregnant—evident.

[54] **eminent**—exalted.

this fortune as Cassio does? A knave very voluble,[55] no further
conscionable than in putting on the mere form of civil and humane
seeming for the better compassing of his salt[56] and most hidden loose
affection. Why, none, why, none. A slipper[57] and subtle knave, a finder
out of occasions, that has an eye can stamp and counterfeit advan-
tages, though true advantage never present itself; a devilish knave.
Besides, the knave is handsome, young, and hath all those requisites
in him that folly and green minds look after. A pestilent complete
knave, and the woman hath found him already.

235

240

Roderigo. I cannot believe that in her. She's full of most blessed condition.

Iago. Blessed fig's end! The wine she drinks is made of grapes. If she
had been blessed, she would never have loved the Moor. Blessed
pudding! Didst thou not see her paddle with the palm of his hand?
Didst not mark that?

245

Roderigo. Yes, that I did; but that was but courtesy.

Iago. Lechery, by this hand. An index[58] and obscure prologue to the history of lust and foul thoughts. They met so near with their lips that
their breaths embraced together. Villainous thoughts, Roderigo! When
these mutualities so marshal the way, hard at hand comes the master
and main exercise, th' incorporate conclusion. Pish! But, sir, be you
ruled by me. I have brought you from Venice. Watch you tonight; for
the command, I'll lay 't upon you. Cassio knows you not. I'll not be
far from you. Do you find some occasion to anger Cassio, either by
speaking too loud, or tainting[59] his discipline, or from what other
course you please, which the time shall more favorably minister.

250

255

Roderigo. Well.

Iago. Sir, he's rash and very sudden in choler,[60] and haply may strike at
you. Provoke him that he may, for even out of that will I cause these
of Cyprus to mutiny,[61] whose qualification shall come into no true
taste again[62] but by the displanting of Cassio. So shall you have a

260

---

[55] voluble—facile, glib.

[56] salt—licentiousness.

[57] slipper—slippery.

[58] index—table of contents.

[59] tainting—disparaging.

[60] choler—wrath.

[61] mutiny—riot.

[62] qualification . . . taste again—appeasement will not be gained. (Wine was "qualified" by adding water.)

shorter journey to your desires by the means I shall then have to prefer them, and the **impediment**[63] most profitably removed, without the which there were no expectation of our prosperity.

265 **Roderigo.** I will do this, if you can bring it to any opportunity.

Iago. I warrant thee. Meet me by and by at the citadel.

I must fetch his necessaries ashore. Farewell.

Roderigo. Adieu. [*Exit.*]

Iago. That Cassio loves her, I do well believe 't,

270   That she loves him, 'tis apt and of great credit.[64]

The Moor, howbeit that I endure him not,

Is of a constant, loving, noble nature,

And I dare think he'll prove to Desdemona

A most dear husband. Now, I do love her too,

275   Not out of absolute lust—though peradventure

I stand accountant[65] for as great a sin—

But partly led to diet my revenge

For that I do suspect the lusty Moor

Hath leaped into my seat, the thought whereof

280   Doth, like a poisonous mineral, gnaw my innards;

And nothing can or shall content my soul

Till I am evened with him, wife for wife,

Or failing so, yet that I put the Moor

At least into a jealousy so strong

285   That judgment cannot cure. Which thing to do,

If this poor trash[66] of Venice, whom I trace[67]

For his quick hunting, stand the putting on,

I'll have our Michael Cassio on the hip,[68]

Abuse him to the Moor in the rank garb—

290   For I fear Cassio with my nightcap too—

Make the Moor thank me, love me, and reward me

For making him **egregiously**[69] an ass

---

[63] **impediment**—obstacle.

[64] apt and of great credit—probable and of great credibility.

[65] accountant—accountable.

[66] trash—that is, Roderigo.

[67] trace—follow, like a hunting dog.

[68] on the hip—at my mercy, where I can throw him (a wrestling term).

[69] **egregiously**—conspicuously badly.

And practicing upon his peace and quiet
Even to madness. 'Tis here, but yet confused.
295   Knavery's plain face is never seen till used. [*Exit.*]

Act Two, Scene Two

[*Enter* Othello's Herald *with a proclamation.*]

Herald. It is Othello's pleasure, our noble and valiant general, that, upon
certain tidings now arrived, importing the mere perdition[70] of the
Turkish fleet, every man put himself into triumph: some to dance,
some to make bonfires, each man to what sport and revels his addic-
5   tion leads him. For, besides these beneficial news, it is the celebration
of his **nuptial**.[71] So much was his pleasure should be proclaimed. All
offices are open, and there is full liberty of feasting from this present
hour of five till the bell have told eleven. Heaven bless the isle of
Cyprus and our noble general Othello!

[*Exit.*]

Act Two, Scene Three

[*Enter* Othello, Desdemona, Cassio, *and attendants.*]

Othello. Good Michael, look you to the guard tonight.
Let's teach ourselves that honorable stop
Not to outsport discretion.[72]

Cassio. Iago hath direction what to do,
5   But notwithstanding, with my personal eye
Will I look to 't.

Othello.   Iago is most honest.
Michael, good night. Tomorrow with your earliest
Let me have speech with you. [*To* Desdemona.] Come, my dear love,
The purchase made, the fruits are to ensue;
10   That profit's yet to come 'tween me and you.—
Good night.

[*Exit* Othello, *with* Desdemona *and attendants.*]

[*Enter* Iago.]

---

[70] mere perdition—complete destruction.

[71] **nuptial**—wedding ceremony.

[72] outsport discretion—celebrate beyond the bounds of good judgment.

Cassio. Welcome, Iago. We must to the watch.

Iago. Not this hour, Lieutenant, 'tis not yet ten o' the clock. Our general cast[73] us thus early for the love of his Desdemona; who[74] let us not

15 therefore blame. He hath not yet made wanton the night with her, and she is sport for Jove.

Cassio. She's a most exquisite lady.

Iago. And, I'll warrant her, full of game.

Cassio. Indeed, she's a most fresh and delicate creature.

20 **Iago.** What an eye she has! Methinks it sounds a parley[75] to provocation.

Cassio. An inviting eye, and yet methinks right modest.

Iago. And when she speaks, is it not an alarum to love?

Cassio. She is indeed perfection.

Iago. Well, happiness to their sheets! Come, Lieutenant, I have a stoup[76]

25 of wine, and here without are a brace of Cyprus gallants that would fain have a measure to the health of black Othello.

Cassio. Not tonight, good Iago. I have very poor and unhappy brains for drinking. I could well wish courtesy would invent some other custom of entertainment.

30 **Iago.** O, they are our friends. But one cup! I'll drink for you.

Cassio. I have drunk but one cup tonight, and that was craftily qualified too, and behold what innovation it makes here.[77] I am unfortunate in the infirmity and dare not task my weakness with any more.

Iago. What, man? 'Tis a night of revels. The gallants desire it.

35 **Cassio.** Where are they?

Iago. Here at the door. I pray you, call them in.

Cassio. I'll do 't, but it dislikes me. [*Exit.*]

Iago. If I can fasten but one cup upon him,
With that which he hath drunk tonight already,

40 He'll be as full of quarrel and offense
As my young mistress' dog. Now, my sick fool Roderigo,
Whom love hath turned almost the wrong side out,
To Desdemona hath tonight caroused
Potations pottle-deep;[78] and he's to watch.

---

[73] cast—dismissed.

[74] who—that is, Othello.

[75] sounds a parley—calls a conference, issues an invitation.

[76] stoup—measure of liquor, two quarts.

[77] innovation . . . here—disturbance it makes in my head.

[78] Potations pottle-deep—drinks to the bottom of the tankard.

45	Three lads of Cyprus—noble swelling spirits,
	That hold their honors in a wary distance,[79]
	The very elements of this warlike isle—
	Have I tonight flustered with flowing cups,
	And they watch too. Now, 'mongst this flock of drunkards
50	Am I to put our Cassio in some action
	That may offend the isle.—But here they come.

[*Enter* Cassio, Montano, *and* Gentlemen; *servants following with wine.*]

If consequence do but approve my dream,
My boat sails freely both with wind and stream.

Cassio. 'Fore God, they have given me a rouse[80] already.

55 **Montano.** Good faith, a little one; not past a pint, as I am a soldier.

Iago. Some wine, ho!

[*He sings.*] "And let me the cannikin clink, clink,
    And let me the cannikin clink.
    A soldier's a man,
60   O, man's life's but a span;
    Why, then, let a soldier drink."
    Some wine, boys!

Cassio. 'Fore God, an excellent song.

Iago. I learned it in England, where indeed they are most potent in pot-
65 ting. Your Dane, your German, and your swag-bellied Hollander—
drink, ho!—are nothing to your English.

Cassio. Is your Englishman so exquisite in his drinking?

Iago. Why, he drinks you, with facility, your Dane dead drunk; he sweats
not to overthrow your Almain;[81] he gives your Hollander a vomit ere
70 the next pottle can be filled.

Cassio. To the health of our general!

Montano. I am for it, Lieutenant, and I'll do you justice.

Iago. O sweet England! [*He sings.*]
    "King Stephen was and-a worthy peer,
75   His breeches cost him but a crown;
    He held them sixpence all too dear,
    With that he called the tailor lown.[82]

---

[79] hold . . . distance—that is, are extremely sensitive of their honor.

[80] rouse—full draft of liquor.

[81] Almain—German.

[82] lown—lout, rascal.

He was a wight of high renown,
And thou art but of low degree.
80 'Tis pride that pulls the country down;
Then take thy auld cloak about thee."
Some wine, ho!

Cassio. 'Fore God, this is a more exquisite song than the other.

Iago. Will you hear 't again?

85 **Cassio.** No, for I hold him to be unworthy of his place that does
those things. Well, God's above all; and there be souls must be
saved, and there be souls must not be saved.

Iago. It's true, good Lieutenant.

Cassio. For mine own part—no offense to the General, nor any man
90 of quality—I hope to be saved.

Iago. And so do I too, Lieutenant.

Cassio. Ay, but, by your leave, not before me; the lieutenant is to be
saved before the ancient. Let's have no more of this; let's to our
affairs.—God forgive us our sins!—Gentlemen, let's look to our
95 business. Do not think, gentlemen, I am drunk. This is my
ancient, this is my right hand, and this is my left. I am not drunk
now. I can stand well enough, and speak well enough.

Gentlemen. Excellent well.

Cassio. Why, very well then; you must not think then that I am
100 drunk. [*Exit.*]

Montano. To th' platform, masters. Come, let's set the watch.
[*Exeunt* Gentlemen.]

Iago. You see this fellow that is gone before.
He's a soldier fit to stand by Caesar
And give direction; and do but see his vice.
105 'Tis to his virtue a just equinox,[83]
The one as long as th' other. 'Tis pity of him.
I fear the trust Othello puts him in,
On some odd time of his infirmity,
Will shake this island.

Montano.   But is he often thus?

110 **Iago.** 'Tis evermore the prologue to his sleep.
He'll watch the horologe a double set,[84]
If drink rock not his cradle.

---

[83] just equinox—exact counterpart. (*Eqinox* is an equal length of days and nights.)
[84] watch . . . set—stay awake twice around the clock or *horologe.*

Montano.   It were well

The General were put in mind of it.

Perhaps he sees it not, or his good nature

115   Prizes the virtue that appears in Cassio

And looks not on his evils. Is not this true?

[*Enter* Roderigo.]

Iago [*aside to him*]. How now, Roderigo?

I pray you, after the Lieutenant; go.

[*Exit* Roderigo.]

Montano. And 'tis great pity that the noble Moor

120   Should hazard such a place as his own second

With one of an engraffed[85] infirmity.

It were an honest action to say so

To the Moor.

Iago.   Not I, for this fair island.

I do love Cassio well and would do much

125   To cure him of this evil. [*Cry within:* "Help! Help!"]

But, hark! What noise?

[*Enter* Cassio, *pursuing* Roderigo.]

Cassio. Zounds, you rogue! You rascal!

Montano. What's the matter, Lieutenant?

Cassio. A knave teach me my duty? I'll beat the knave into a

twiggen[86] bottle.

130   **Roderigo.** Beat me?

Cassio. Dost thou prate, rogue? [*He strikes* Roderigo.]

Montano. Nay, good Lieutenant. [*Restraining him.*] I pray you, sir,

hold your hand.

Cassio. Let me go, sir, or I'll knock you o'er the mazard.[87]

135   **Montano.** Come, come, you're drunk.

Cassio. Drunk? [*They fight.*]

Iago [*aside to* Roderigo]. Away, I say. Go out and cry a mutiny.

[*Exit* Roderigo.]

Nay, good Lieutenant—God's will, gentlemen—

Help, ho!—Lieutenant—sir—Montano—sir—

140   Help masters!—Here's a goodly watch indeed!

---

[85] engraffed—engrafted, habitual.

[86] twiggen—wicker-covered. (Casssio vows to assail Roderigo until his skin resembles the wicker-work or until he has driven Roderigo through the holes in wicker-work.)

[87] mazard—that is, head (literally, a drinking vessel).

[*A bell rings.*]

        Who's that which rings the bell?—Diablo, ho!

        The town will rise. God's will, Lieutenant, hold!

        You'll be ashamed forever.

[*Enter* Othello *and attendants with weapons.*]

Othello. What is the matter here?

Montano.   Zounds, I bleed still.

145   I am hurt to th' death. He dies! [*He thrusts at* Cassio.]

Othello.   Hold, for your lives!

Iago. Hold, ho! Lieutenant—sir—Montano—gentlemen—

        Have you forgot all sense of place and duty?

        Hold! The General speaks to you. Hold, for shame!

Othello. Why, how now, ho! From whence ariseth this?

150   Are we turned Turks, and to ourselves do that

        Which heaven hath forbid the Ottomites?[88]

        For Christian shame, put by this barbarous brawl!

        He that stirs next to carve for his own rage

        Holds his soul light;[89] he dies upon his motion.

155   Silence that dreadful bell. It frights the isle

        From her propriety. What is the matter, masters?

        Honest Iago, that looks dead with grieving,

        Speak. Who began this? On thy love, I charge thee.

Iago. I do not know. Friends all but now, even now,

160   In quarter[90] and in terms like bride and groom

        Devesting them for bed; and then, but now—

        As if some planet had unwitted men—

        Swords out, and tilting one at others' breasts

        In opposition bloody. I cannot speak

165   Any beginning to this peevish odds;[91]

        And would in action glorious I had lost

        Those legs that brought me to a part of it!

Othello. How comes it, Michael, you are thus forgot?

Cassio. I pray you, pardon me. I cannot speak.

---

[88] to ourselves . . . Ottomites—inflict on ourselves the harm that heaven has prevented the Turks from doing (by destroying their fleet).

[89] Holds . . . light—places little value on his life.

[90] In quarter—in friendly conduct, within bounds.

[91] peevish odds—childish quarrel.

170   **Othello.** Worthy Montano, you were wont be civil;

                The gravity and stillness of your youth

                The world hath noted, and your name is great

                In mouths of wisest censure. What's the matter

                That you unlace[92] your reputation thus

175   And spend your rich opinion[93] for the name

                Of a night-brawler? Give me answer to it.

        Montano. Worthy Othello, I am hurt to danger.

                Your officer, Iago, can inform you—

                While I spare speech, which something now offends[94] me—

180   Of all that I do know; nor know I aught

                By me that's said or done amiss this night,

                Unless self-charity be sometimes a vice,

                And to defend ourselves it be a sin

                When violence assails us.

        Othello.   Now, by heaven,

185   My blood begins my safer guides to rule,

                And passion, having my best judgment collied,[95]

                Essays to lead the way. Zounds, if I stir,

                Or do but lift this arm, the best of you

                Shall sink in my rebuke. Give me to know

190   How this foul rout began, who set it on;

                And he that is approved in this offense,

                Though he had twinned with me, both at a birth,

                Shall lose me. What? In a town of war

                Yet wild, the people's hearts brim full of fear,

195   To manage[96] private and domestic quarrel?

                In night, and on the court and guard of safety?

                'Tis monstrous. Iago, who began 't?

        Montano [*to* Iago]. If partially affined, or leagued in office,[97]

                Thou dost deliver more or less than truth,

200   Thou art no soldier.

---

[92] unlace—undo, lay open (as one might loosen the strings of a purse).

[93] opinion—reputation.

[94] offends—pains.

[95] collied—darkened.

[96] manage—undertake.

[97] partially . . . office—made partial by some personal relationship or in league as fellow officers.

Iago.　　　　　　　　　　Touch me not so near.

　　I had rather have this tongue cut from my mouth

　　Than it should do offense to Michael Cassio;

　　Yet, I persuade myself, to speak the truth

　　Shall nothing wrong him. Thus it is, General.

205　　Montano and myself being in speech,

　　There comes a fellow crying out for help,

　　And Cassio following him with determined sword

　　To execute upon him. Sir, this gentleman

[*indicating* Montano]

　　Steps in to Cassio and entreats his pause.

210　　Myself the crying fellow did pursue,

　　Lest by his clamor—as it so fell out—

　　The town might fall in fright. He, swift of foot,

　　Outran my purpose, and I returned, the rather

　　For that I heard the clink and fall of swords

215　　And Cassio high in oath, which till tonight

　　I ne'er might say before. When I came back—

　　For this was brief—I found them close together

　　At blow and thrust, even as again they were

　　When you yourself did part them.

220　　More of this matter cannot I report.

　　But men are men; the best sometimes forget.

　　Though Cassio did some little wrong to him,

　　As men in rage strike those that wish them best,

　　Yet surely Cassio, I believe, received

225　　From him that fled some strange indignity,

　　Which patience could not pass.[98]

Othello.　　　　　　　　　　I know, Iago,

　　Thy honesty and love doth mince[99] this matter,

　　Making it light to Cassio. Cassio, I love thee,

　　But never more be officer of mine.

[*Enter* Desdemona *attended.*]

230　　Look if my gentle love be not raised up.

　　I'll make thee an example.

Desdemona. What is the matter, dear?

---

[98] pass—pass over, overlook.

[99] mince—lessen out of politeness.

Othello. All's well now, sweeting;
Come away to bed. [*To* Montano.] Sir, for your hurts,
Myself will be your surgeon.—Lead him off.
[Montano *is led off.*]

235 Iago, look with care about the town
And silence those whom this vile brawl distracted.
Come, Desdemona. 'Tis the soldiers' life
To have their balmy slumbers waked with strife.
[*Exit with all but* Iago *and* Cassio.]

Iago. What, are you hurt, Lieutenant?

240 **Cassio.** Ay, past all surgery.

Iago. Marry, God forbid!

Cassio. Reputation, reputation, reputation! O, I have lost my reputation!
I have lost the immortal part of myself, and what remains is bestial.
My reputation, Iago, my reputation!

245 **Iago.** As I am an honest man, I thought you had received some bodily
wound; there is more sense in that than in reputation. Reputation is
an idle and most false imposition,[100] oft got without merit and lost
without deserving. You have lost no reputation at all, unless you
repute yourself such a loser. What, man, there are more ways to

250 recover the General again. You are but now cast in his mood[101]—a
punishment more in policy[102] than in malice, even so as one would
beat his offenseless dog to affright an imperious lion. Sue to him
again and he's yours.

Cassio. I will rather sue to be despised than to deceive so good a com-

255 mander with so slight, so drunken, and so indiscreet an officer.
Drunk? And speak parrot? And squabble? Swagger? Swear? And discourse fustian[103] with one's own shadow? O thou invisible spirit of
wine, if thou hast no name to be known by, let us call thee devil!

Iago. What was he that you followed with your sword? What had he

260 done to you?

Cassio. I know not.

Iago. Is 't possible?

---

[100] false imposition—thing artificially imposed and of no real value.

[101] cast in his mood—dismissed in a moment of anger.

[102] in policy—done for expediency's sake and as a public gesture.

[103] speak parrot . . . discourse fustian—Both expressions mean to talk nonsense, rant. (*Fustian* was a coarse cotton cloth used for padding.)

Cassio. I remember a mass of things, but nothing distinctly; a quarrel, but nothing wherefore. O God, that men should put an enemy in their mouths to steal away their brains! That we should, with joy, pleasance, revel, and applause transform ourselves into beasts!

Iago. Why, but you are now well enough. How came you thus recovered?

Cassio. It hath pleased the devil drunkenness to give place to the devil wrath. One unperfectness shows me another, to make me frankly despise myself.

Iago. Come, you are too severe a moraler. As the time, the place, and the condition of this country stands, I could heartily wish this had not befallen; but since it is as it is, mend it for your own good.

Cassio. I will ask him for my place again; he shall tell me I am a drunkard. Had I as many mouths as Hydra,[104] such an answer would stop them all. To be now a sensible man, by and by a fool, and presently a beast! O, strange! Every inordinate cup is unblessed, and the ingredient is a devil.

Iago. Come, come, good wine is a good familiar creature, if it be well used. Exclaim no more against it. And, good Lieutenant, I think you think I love you.

Cassio. I have well approved it, sir. I drunk!

Iago. You or any man living may be drunk at a time, man. I'll tell you what you shall do. Our general's wife is now the general—I may say so in this respect, for that he hath devoted and given up himself to the contemplation, mark, and denotement of her parts[105] and graces. Confess yourself freely to her; **importune**[106] her help to put you in your place again. She is of so free, so kind, so apt, so blessed a disposition, she holds it a vice in her goodness not to do more than she is requested. This broken joint between you and her husband entreat her to splinter;[107] and, my fortunes against any lay[108] worth naming, this crack of your love shall grow stronger than it was before.

Cassio. You advise me well.

Iago. I protest, in the sincerity of love and honest kindness.

---

[104] Hydra—the Lernaean Hydra, a monster with many heads and the ability to grow two heads when one was cut off, slain by Hercules as the second of his twelve labors.

[105] mark . . . parts—both *mark* and *denotement* mean "observation." *Parts* means "qualities."

[106] **importune**—plead.

[107] splinter—bind with splints.

[108] lay—stake, wager.

295 **Cassio.** I think it freely; and betimes in the morning I will beseech the virtuous Desdemona to undertake for me. I am desperate of my fortunes if they check[109] me here.

Iago. You are in the right. Good night, Lieutenant. I must to the watch.

Cassio. Good night, honest Iago. [*Exit* Cassio.]

300 **Iago.** And what's he then that says I play the villain,
When this advice is free[110] I give, and honest,
Probal[111] to thinking, and indeed the course
To win the Moor again? For 'tis most easy
Th' inclining[112] Desdemona to subdue

305 In any honest suit; she's framed as fruitful[113]
As the free elements.[114] And then for her
To win the Moor—were 't to renounce his baptism,
All seals and symbols of redeemèd sin—
His soul is so enfettered to her love

310 That she may make, unmake, do what she list,
Even as her appetite[115] shall play the god
With his weak function.[116] How am I then a villain,
To counsel Cassio to this parallel course
Directly to his good? Divinity of hell!

315 When devils will the blackest sins put on,[117]
They do suggest at first with heavenly shows,[118]
As I do now. For whiles this honest fool
Plies Desdemona to repair his fortune,
And she for him pleads strongly to the Moor,

320 I'll pour this pestilence into his ear,
That she repeals him[119] for her body's lust;
And by how much she strives to do him good,

---

[109] check—repulse.

[110] free—free from guile; freely given.

[111] Probal—probable, reasonable.

[112] inclining—favorably disposed.

[113] framed as fruitful—created as generous.

[114] free elements—that is, earth, air, fire, and water, unrestrained and spontaneous.

[115] her appetite—her desire, or perhaps, his desire for her.

[116] function—exercise of faculties (weakened by fondness for her).

[117] put on—further; instigate.

[118] heavenly shows—virtous appearances.

[119] repeals him—attempts to get Cassio restored.

She shall undo her credit with the Moor.
So will I turn her virtue into pitch,
325 And out of her own goodness make the net
That shall enmesh them all.

[*Enter* Roderigo.]

How now, Roderigo?

Roderigo. I do follow here in the chase, not like a hound that hunts, but
one that fills up the cry.[120] My money is almost spent; I have been
tonight exceedingly well cudgeled; and I think the issue will be I shall
330 have so much[121] experience for my pains, and so, with no money at
all and a little more wit, return again to Venice.

Iago. How poor are they that have not patience!
What wound did ever heal but by degrees?
Thou knowst we work by wit, and not by witchcraft,
335 And wit depends on dilatory[122] time.
Does 't not go well? Cassio hath beaten thee,
And thou, by that small hurt, hast cashiered Cassio.
Though other things grow fair against the sun,
Yet fruits that blossom first will first be ripe.
340 Content thyself awhile. By the Mass, 'tis morning!
Pleasure and action make the hours seem short.
Retire thee; go where thou art billeted.
Away, I say! Thou shalt know more hereafter.
Nay, get thee gone. [*Exit* Roderigo.]
345 Two things are to be done.
My wife must move[123] for Cassio to her mistress;
I'll set her on;
Myself the while to draw the Moor apart
And bring him jump[124] when he may Cassio find
350 Soliciting his wife. Ay, that's the way.
Dull not device by coldness and delay.

[*Exit.*]

---

[120] fills up the cry—merely takes part as one of the pack.

[121] so much—just so much and no more.

[122] dilatory—slow, tending to delay.

[123] move—plead.

[124] jump—precisely.

Act Three, Scene One

[*Enter* Cassio *and* Musicians.]

Cassio. Masters, play here—I will content your pains[1]—
    Something that's brief, and bid "Good morrow, General." [*They play.*]

[*Enter* Clown.]

Clown. Why, masters, have your instruments been in Naples, that they
    speak i' the nose[2] thus?

5   **A Musician.** How, sir, how?

Clown. Are these, I pray you, wind instruments?

A Musician. Ay, marry, are they, sir.

Clown. O, thereby hangs a tail.

A Musician. Whereby hangs a tale, sir?

10   **Clown.** Marry, sir, by many a wind instrument that I know. But, masters,
    here's money for you. [*He gives money.*] And the General so likes
    your music that he desires you, for love's sake, to make no more
    noise with it.

A Musician. Well, sir, we will not.

15   **Clown.** If you have any music that may not be heard, to 't again; but, as
    they say, to hear music the General does not greatly care.

A Musician. We have none such, sir.

Clown. Then put up your pipes in your bag, for I'll away. Go, vanish
    into air, away! [*Exeunt* Musicians.]

20   **Cassio.** Dost thou hear, mine honest friend?

Clown. No, I hear not your honest friend; I hear you.

Cassio. Prithee, keep up thy quillets.[3] There's a poor piece of gold for
    thee. [*He gives money.*] If the gentlewoman that attends the General's
    wife be stirring, tell her there's one Cassio entreats her a little favor

25   of speech. Wilt thou do this?

Clown. She is stirring, sir. If she will stir hither, I shall seem to notify
    unto her.

Cassio. Do, good my friend. [*Exit* Clown.]

[*Enter* Iago.]

                    In happy time, Iago.

Iago. You have not been abed, then?

---

[1] content your pains—reward your efforts.

[2] speak . . . nose—sound nasal; sound like one whose nose has been attacked by syphilis. (Naples was popularly supposed to have a high incidence of venereal disease.)

[3] quillets—quibbles, puns.

30   **Cassio.** Why, no. The day had broke
      Before we parted. I have made bold, Iago,
      To send in to your wife. My suit to her
      Is that she will to virtuous Desdemona
      Procure me some access.

35   **Iago.** I'll send her to you presently;
      And I'll devise a means to draw the Moor
      Out of the way, that your converse and business
      May be more free.
      Cassio. I humbly thank you for 't. [*Exit* Iago.]
                                      I never knew

40   A Florentine[4] more kind and honest.
  [*Enter* Emilia.]
      Emilia. Good morrow, good Lieutenant. I am sorry
      For your displeasure;[5] but all will sure be well.
      The General and his wife are talking of it,
      And she speaks for you stoutly. The Moor replies

45   That he you hurt is of great fame in Cyprus
      And great affinity,[6] and that in wholesome wisdom
      He might not but refuse you; but he protests he loves you
      And needs no other suitor but his likings
      To take the safest occasion by the front

50   To bring you in again.
      Cassio.   Yet I beseech you,
      If you think fit, or that it may be done,
      Give me advantage of some brief discourse
      With Desdemon alone.
      Emilia.   Pray you, come in.
      I will bestow you where you shall have time

55   To speak your bosom[7] freely.
      Cassio. I am much bound to you.
  [*Exeunt.*]

---

[4] Florentine—that is, even a fellow Florentine. (Iago is a Venetian; Cassio is a Florentine.)

[5] displeasure—fall from favor.

[6] affinity—kindred, family connection.

[7] bosom—innermost thoughts.

Act Three, Scene Two

[*Enter* Othello, Iago, *and* Gentlemen.]

Othello [*giving letters*]. These letters give, Iago, to the pilot,
    And by him do my duties to the Senate.
    That done, I will be walking on the works;
    Repair[8] there to me.

Iago.   Well, my good lord, I'll do 't.

5   **Othello.** This fortification, gentlemen, shall we see 't?

Gentlemen. We'll wait upon your lordship.

[*Exeunt.*]

Act Three, Scene Three

[*Enter* Desdemona, Cassio, *and* Emilia.]

Desdemona. Be thou assured, good Cassio, I will do
    All my abilities in thy behalf.

Emilia. Good madam, do. I warrant it grieves my husband
    As if the cause were his.

5   **Desdemona.** O, that's an honest fellow. Do not doubt, Cassio,
    But I will have my lord and you again
    As friendly as you were.

Cassio.   Bounteous madam,
    Whatever shall become of Michael Cassio,
    He's never anything but your true servant.

10 **Desdemona.** I know 't. I thank you. You do love my lord;
    You have known him long, and be you well assured
    He shall in strangeness stand no farther off
    Than in a politic distance.[9]

Cassio.   Ay, but, lady,
    That policy may either last so long,

15   Or feed upon such nice and waterish diet,[10]
    Or breed itself so out of circumstance,[11]
    That, I being absent and my place supplied,[12]
    My general will forget my love and service.

---

[8] Repair—return, come.

[9] strangeness . . . distance—remain aloof no longer than required by wise policy.

[10] Or . . . diet—or sustain itself at length upon such trivial and meager technicalities.

[11] breed . . . circumstance—continually renews itself so out of chance events, or yield so few chances for my being pardoned.

[12] supplied—filled by another person.

Desdemona. Do not doubt[13] that. Before Emilia here

20   I give thee warrant of thy place. Assure thee,

    If I do vow a friendship I'll perform it

    To the last article. My lord shall never rest.

    I'll watch him tame[14] and talk him out of patience;

    His bed shall seem a school, his board a shrift;[15]

25   I'll intermingle everything he does

    With Cassio's suit. Therefore be merry, Cassio,

    For thy solicitor shall rather die

    Than give thy cause away.

[*Enter* Othello *and* Iago *at a distance.*]

Emilia. Madam, here comes my lord.

30 **Cassio.** Madam, I'll take my leave.

Desdemona. Why, stay, and hear me speak.

Cassio. Madam, not now. I am very ill at ease,

    Unfit for mine own purposes.

Desdemona. Well, do your discretion. [*Exit* Cassio.]

35 **Iago.** Ha? I like not that.

Othello. What dost thou say?

Iago. Nothing, my lord; or if—I know not what.

Othello. Was not that Cassio parted from my wife?

Iago. Cassio, my lord? No, sure, I cannot think it,

40   That he would steal away so guiltylike,

    Seeing you coming.

Othello. I do believe 'twas he.

Desdemona. How now, my lord?

    I have been talking with a suitor here,

45   A man that **languishes**[16] in your displeasure.

Othello. Who is 't you mean?

Desdemona. Why, your lieutenant, Cassio. Good my lord,

    If I have any grace or power to move you,

    His present reconciliation take;[17]

50   For if he be not one that truly loves you,

    That errs in ignorance and not in cunning,

---

[13] doubt—fear.

[14] watch him tame—tame him by keeping him from sleeping (a term from falconry).

[15] board a shrift—dining table (seem) a confessional.

[16] **languishes**—becomes feeble.

[17] His . . . take—let him be reconciled to you right away.

I have no judgment in an honest face.
I prithee, call him back.

Othello. Went he hence now?

55   **Desdemona.** Yes, faith, so humbled
That he hath left part of his grief with me
To suffer with him. Good love, call him back.

Othello. Not now, sweet Desdemon. Some other time.

Desdemona. But shall 't be shortly?

60   **Othello.** The sooner, sweet, for you.

Desdemona. Shall 't be tonight at supper?

Othello. No, not tonight.

Desdemona. Tomorrow dinner, then?

Othello. I shall not dine at home.

65   I meet the captains at the citadel.

Desdemona. Why, then, tomorrow night, or Tuesday morn,
On Tuesday noon, or night, on Wednesday morn.
I prithee, name the time, but let it not
Exceed three days. In faith, he's penitent;

70   And yet his trespass, in our common reason—
Save that, they say, the wars must make example
Out of her best—is not almost a fault
T' incur a private check.[18] When shall he come?
Tell me, Othello I wonder in my soul

75   What you would ask me that I should deny,
Or stand so mammering on.[19] What? Michael Cassio,
That came a-wooing with you, and so many a time,
When I have spoke of you dispraisingly,
Hath ta'en your part—to have so much to do

80   To bring him in! By 'r Lady, I could do much—

Othello. Prithee, no more. Let him come when he will;
I will deny thee nothing.

Desdemona. Why, this is not a boon.
'Tis as I should entreat you wear your gloves,

85   Or feed on nourishing dishes, or keep you warm,
Or sue to you to do a peculiar profit[20]
To your own person. Nay, when I have a suit

---

[18] not . . . check—scarcely required a private rebuke (much less public disgrace).

[19] mammering on—wavering about.

[20] peculiar profit—particular, personal good.

Wherein I mean to touch your love indeed,
It shall be full of poise[21] and difficult weight,
90   And fearful to be granted.

Othello. I will deny thee nothing.
Whereon, I do beseech thee, grant me this,
To leave me but a little to myself.

Desdemona. Shall I deny you? No. Farewell, my lord.

95   **Othello.** Farewell, my Desdemona. I'll come to thee straight.[22]

Desdemona. Emilia, come.—Be as your fancies teach you;
Whate'er you be, I am obedient. [*Exit with* Emilia.]

Othello. Excellent wretch! Perdition catch my soul
But I do love thee! And when I love thee not,
100   Chaos is come again.

Iago. My noble lord—

Othello. What dost thou say, Iago?

Iago. Did Michael Cassio, when you wooed my lady,
Know of your love?

105   **Othello.** He did, from first to last. Why dost thou ask?

Iago. But for a satisfaction of my thought;
No further harm.

Othello.   Why of thy thought, Iago?

Iago. I did not think he had been acquainted with her.

Othello. O, yes, and went between us very oft.

110   **Iago.** Indeed?

Othello. Indeed? Ay, indeed. Discern'st thou aught in that?
Is he not honest?

Iago. Honest, my lord?

Othello. Honest. Ay, honest.

115   **Iago.** My lord, for aught I know.

Othello. What dost thou think?

Iago. Think, my lord?

Othello. "Think, my lord?" By heaven, thou echo'st me,
As if there were some monster in thy thought
120   Too hideous to be shown. Thou dost mean something.
I heard thee say even now, thou lik'st not that,
When Cassio left my wife. What didst not like?

---

[21] poise—weight, heaviness; or equipoise, delicate balance involving a hard choice.
[22] straight—at once.

And when I told thee he was of my counsel[23]
In my whole course of wooing, thou criedst "Indeed?"
125 And didst contract and purse thy brow together
As if thou then hadst shut up in thy brain
Some horrible conceit.[24] If thou dost love me,
Show me thy thought.

Iago. My lord, you know I love you.

130 **Othello.** I think thou dost;
And, for I know thou'rt full of love and honesty,
And weigh'st thy words before thou giv'st them breath,
Therefore these stops[25] of thine fright me the more;
For such things in a false disloyal knave
135 Are tricks of custom,[26] but in a man that's just
They're close dilations,[27] working from the heart
That passion cannot rule.

Iago. For Michael Cassio,
I dare be sworn I think that he is honest.

Othello. I think so too.

Iago. Men should be what they seem;
140 Or those that be not, would they might seem none!

Othello. Certain, men should be what they seem.

Iago. Why, then, I think Cassio's an honest man.

Othello. Nay, yet there's more in this.
I prithee, speak to me as to thy thinkings,
145 As thou dost **ruminate**,[28] and give thy worst of thoughts
The worst of words.

Iago. Good my lord, pardon me.
Though I am bound to every act of duty,
I am not bound to that all slaves are free to.
Utter my thoughts? Why, say they are vile and false,
150 As where's that palace whereinto foul things
Sometimes intrude not? Who has that breast so pure
But some uncleanly apprehensions

---

[23] of my counsel—in my confidence.

[24] conceit—fancy, notion.

[25] stops—pauses.

[26] of custom—customary.

[27] close dilations—expressions of secret or involuntary thoughts.

[28] **ruminate**—turn a matter over and over in the mind.

Keep leets and law days,[29] and in sessions sit
With meditations lawful?

155 **Othello.** Thou dost conspire against thy friend, Iago,
If thou but think'st him wronged and mak'st his ear
A stranger to thy thoughts.

Iago.   I do beseech you,
Though I perchance am vicious in my guess—
As I confess it is my nature's plague
160 To spy into abuses, and oft my jealousy
Shapes faults that are not—that your wisdom then,
From one that so imperfectly conceits,
Would take no notice, nor build yourself a trouble
Out of his scattering and unsure observance.
165 It were not for your quiet nor your good,
Nor for my manhood, honesty, and wisdom,
To let you know my thoughts.

Othello.   What dost thou mean?

Iago. Good name in man and woman, dear my lord,
Is the immediate jewel of their souls.
170 Who steals my purse steals trash; 'tis something, nothing;
'Twas mine, 'tis his, and has been slave to thousands;
But he that filches from me my good name
Robs me of that which not enriches him
And makes me poor indeed.

175 **Othello.** By heaven, I'll know thy thoughts.

Iago. You cannot, if my heart were in your hand,
Nor shall not, whilst 'tis in my custody.

Othello. Ha?

Iago. O, beware, my lord, of jealousy.
180 It is the green-eyed monster which doth mock
The meat it feeds on. That cuckold[30] lives in bliss
Who, certain of his fate, loves not his wronger;
But O, what damnèd minutes tells[31] he o'er
Who dotes, yet doubts, suspects, yet fondly[32] loves!

185 **Othello.** O misery!

---

[29] Keep leets and law days—that is, hold court. (*Leets* are a kind of local court; *law days* are court sessions.)
[30] cuckold—husband whose wife is unfaithful.
[31] tells—counts.
[32] fondly—foolishly.

Iago. Poor and content is rich, and rich enough,
　　　　But riches fineless[33] is as poor as winter
　　　　To him that ever fears he shall be poor.
　　　　Good God, the souls of all my tribe defend
190　　From jealousy!
Othello. Why, why is this?
　　　　Think'st thou I'd make a life of jealousy,
　　　　To follow still the changes of the moon
　　　　With fresh suspicions?[34] No! To be once in doubt
195　　Is once to be resolved. Exchange me for a goat
　　　　When I shall turn the business of my soul
　　　　To such exsufflicate and blown surmises,[35]
　　　　Matching thy inference. 'Tis not to make me jealous
　　　　To say my wife is fair, feeds well, loves company,
200　　Is free of speech, sings, plays, and dances well;
　　　　Where virtue is, these are more virtuous.
　　　　Nor from mine own weak merits will I draw
　　　　The smallest fear or doubt of her revolt,
　　　　For she had eyes, and chose me. No, Iago,
205　　I'll see before I doubt; when I doubt, prove;
　　　　And on the proof, there is no more but this—
　　　　Away at once with love or jealousy.
Iago. I am glad of this, for now I shall have reason
　　　　To show the love and duty that I bear you
210　　With franker spirit. Therefore, as I am bound,
　　　　Receive it from me. I speak not yet of proof.
　　　　Look to your wife; observe her well with Cassio.
　　　　Wear your eyes thus, not jealous nor secure.
　　　　I would not have your free and noble nature,
215　　Out of self-bounty,[36] be abused. Look to 't.
　　　　I know our country disposition well;
　　　　In Venice they do let God see the pranks
　　　　They dare not show their husbands; their best conscience
　　　　Is not to leave 't undone, but keep 't unknown.
220　**Othello.** Dost thou say so?

---

[33] fineless—boundless.

[34] To follow . . . suspicions—to be constantly imagining new causes for suspicion, changing incessantly like the moon.

[35] exsufflicate . . . surmises—inflated and disgusting guesses.

[36] self-bounty—inherent or natural goodness and generosity.

Iago. She did deceive her father, marrying you;
　　　　And when she seemed to shake and fear your looks,
　　　　She loved them most.

Othello.　　　　　　　　And so she did.

Iago.　　　　　　　　　　　　Why, go to, then!
　　　　She that, so young, could give out such a seeming,
225　　To seel her father's eyes up close as oak,[37]
　　　　He thought 'twas witchcraft! But I am much to blame.
　　　　I humbly do beseech you of your pardon
　　　　For too much loving you.

Othello. I am bound to thee forever.

230　**Iago.** I see this hath a little dashed your spirits.

Othello. Not a jot, not a jot.

Iago.　　　　　　　　　I' faith, I fear it has.
　　　　I hope you will consider what is spoke
　　　　Comes from my love. But I do see you're moved.
　　　　I am to pray you not to strain[38] my speech
235　　To grosser issues nor to larger reach[39]
　　　　Than to suspicion.

Othello. I will not.

Iago. Should you do so, my lord,
　　　　My speech should fall into such vile success
240　　Which my thoughts aimed not. Cassio's my worthy friend.
　　　　My lord, I see you're moved.

Othello.　　　　　　　　No, not much moved.
　　　　I do not think but Desdemona's honest.

Iago. Long live she so! And long live you to think so!

Othello. And yet, how nature erring from itself—

245　**Iago.** Ay, there's the point! As—to be bold with you—
　　　　Not to affect many proposèd matches
　　　　Of her own clime, complexion, and degree,[40]
　　　　Whereto we see in all things nature tends—
　　　　Foh! One may smell in such a will most rank,
250　　Foul disproportion, thoughts unnatural.

---

[37] oak—a close-grained wood.

[38] strain—enlarge the meaning.

[39] reach—meaning, scope.

[40] clime . . . degree—country, color, and social position.

But pardon me. I do not in position[41]
Distinctly speak of her, though I may fear
Her will, recoiling to her better judgment,
May fall to match you with her country forms[42]
255   And happily repent.[43]
Othello.   Farewell, farewell!
If more thou dost perceive, let me know more.
Set on thy wife to observe. Leave me, Iago.
Iago [*going*]. My lord, I take my leave.
Othello. Why did I marry? This honest creature doubtless
260   Sees and knows more, much more, than he unfolds.
Iago [*returning*]. My Lord, I would I might entreat your honor
To scan this thing no farther. Leave it to time.
Although 'tis fit that Cassio have his place—
For, sure, he fills it up with great ability—
265   Yet, if you please to hold him off awhile,
You shall by that perceive him and his means.
Note if your lady strain his entertainment[44]
With any strong or **vehement**[45] importunity;
Much will be seen in that. In the meantime,
270   Let me be thought too busy in my fears—
As worthy cause I have to fear I am—
And hold her free, I do beseech your honor.
Othello. Fear not my government.[46]
Iago. I once more take my leave. [*Exit.*]
275   **Othello.** This fellow's of exceeding honesty,
And knows all qualities,[47] with a learnèd spirit,
Of human dealings. If I do prove her haggard,[48]
Though that her jesses[49] were my dear heartstrings,
I'd whistle her off and let her down the wind[50]

---

[41] position—argument, proposition.

[42] fall . . . forms—undertake to compare you with Venetian forms of happiness.

[43] happily repent—by chance repent (her marriage).

[44] strain his entertainment—urge his reinstatement.

[45] **vehement**—forceful.

[46] government—self-control, conduct.

[47] qualities—natures, types of people.

[48] haggard—wild (like a wild female hawk).

[49] jesses—straps fastened around the legs of a trained hawk.

[50] I'd . . . wind—that is, I'd let her go forever. (To release a hawk downwind was to invite it not to return.)

280	To prey at fortune.[51] Haply, for[52] I am black
	And have not those soft parts of conversation
	That chamberers have,[53] or for I am declined
	Into the vale of years—yet that's not much—
	She's gone. I am abused, and my relief
285	Must be to loathe her. O curse of marriage,
	That we can call these delicate creatures ours
	And not their appetites! I had rather be a toad
	And live upon the vapor of a dungeon
	Than keep a corner in the thing I love
290	For others' uses. Yet, 'tis the plague of great ones;
	Prerogatived are they less than the base.[54]
	'Tis destiny unshunnable, like death.
	Even then this forkèd[55] plague is fated to us
	When we do quicken.[56] Look where she comes.

[*Enter* Desdemona *and* Emilia.]

295	If she be false, O, then heaven mocks itself!
	I'll not believe 't.

Desdemona.　　　How now, my dear Othello?
　　Your dinner, and the generous islanders
　　By you invited, do attend your presence.

Othello. I am to blame.

Desdemona.　　　Why do you speak so faintly?

300　Are you not well?

Othello. I have a pain upon my forehead here.[57]

Desdemona. Faith, that's with watching. 'Twill away again.

[*She offers her handkerchief.*]

　　Let me but bind it hard, within this hour
　　It will be well.

Othello.　　　Your napkin[58] is too little.

305　Let it alone. Come, I'll go in with you.

---

[51] prey at fortune—fend for herself in the wild.

[52] Haply, for—perhaps, because.

[53] soft parts . . . chamberers have—pleasing graces of social behavior courtiers have.

[54] Prerogatived . . . base—privileged (to have honest wives) less than low-born men. (Othello asserts that socially prominent men are especially prone to the unavoidable destiny of being cuckolded and to the public shame that goes with it.)

[55] forkèd—an allusion to the imaginary horns that were the symbol of the cuckold.

[56] quicken—receive life.

[57] here—Othello gestures toward his imaginary horns.

[58] napkin—handkerchief.

[*He puts the handkerchief from him, and it drops.*]

Desdemona. I am very sorry that you are not well.

[*Exit with* Othello.]

Emilia [*picking up the handkerchief*]. I am glad I have found this napkin.
This was her first remembrance from the Moor.
My wayward husband hath a hundred times

310   Wooed me to steal it, but she so loves the token—
For he conjured her she should ever keep it—
That she reserves it evermore about her
To kiss and talk to. I'll have the work ta'en out,[59]
And give 't Iago. What he will do with it

315   Heaven knows, not I;
I nothing but to please his fantasy.[60]

[*Enter* Iago.]

Iago. How now? What do you here alone?

Emilia. Do not you chide. I have a thing for you.

Iago. You have a thing for me? It is a common thing—

320 **Emilia.** Ha?

Iago. To have a foolish wife.

Emilia. O, is that all? What will you give me now
For that same handkerchief?

Iago. What handkerchief?

325 **Emilia.** What handkerchief?
Why, that the Moor first gave to Desdemona;
That which so often you did bid me steal.

Iago. Hast stolen it from her?

Emilia. No, faith. She let it drop by negligence,

330   And to th' advantage I, being here, took 't up.
Look, here 'tis.

Iago.   A good wench! Give it me.

Emilia. What will you do with 't, that you have been so earnest
To have me filch it?

Iago [*snatching it*].   Why, what is that to you?

Emilia. If it be not for some purpose of import,

335   Give 't me again. Poor lady, she'll run mad
When she shall lack it.

---

[59] work ta'en out—design of the embroidery copied.

[60] I nothing . . . fantasy—I wish nothing but to please his whim.

Iago. Be not acknown on 't.[61]
I have use for it. Go, leave me. [*Exit* Emilia.]
I will in Cassio's lodging lose this napkin
And let him find it. Trifles light as air

340 Are to the jealous confirmations strong
As proofs of Holy Writ. This may do something.
The Moor already changes with my poison.
Dangerous conceits are in their natures poisons,
Which at the first are scarce found to distaste,[62]

345 But with a little act upon the blood
Burn like the mines of sulfur.

[*Enter* Othello.]
I did say so.
Look where he comes! Not poppy nor mandragora[63]
Nor all the drowsy syrups of the world
Shall ever medicine thee to that sweet sleep

350 Which thou owedst yesterday.

Othello. Ha, ha, false to me?

Iago. Why, how now, General? No more of that.

Othello. Avaunt! Begone! Thou hast set me on the rack.
I swear 'tis better to be much abused
Than but to know 't a little.

Iago. How now, my lord?

355 **Othello.** What sense had I of her stolen hours of lust?
I saw 't not, thought it not, it harmed not me.
I slept the next night well, fed well, was free and merry;
I found not Cassio's kisses on her lips.
He that is robbed, not wanting what is stolen,

360 Let him not know 't and he's not robbed at all.

Iago. I am sorry to hear this.

Othello. I had been happy if the general camp,
Pioners[64] and all, had tasted her sweet body,
So I had nothing known. O, now, forever

365 Farewell the tranquil mind! Farewell content!
Farewell the plumed troops and the big wars

---

[61] Be not . . . on 't—do not confess knowledge of it.

[62] distaste—be distasteful.

[63] poppy nor mandragora—sleep-inducing drugs.

[64] Pioners—diggers of mines, the lowest grade of soldiers.

That makes ambition virtue! O, farewell!
Farewell the neighing steed and the shrill trump,
The spirit-stirring drum, th' ear-piercing fife,
370 The royal banner, and all quality,
Pride, pomp, and circumstance[65] of glorious war!
O, you mortal engines,[66] whose rude throats
And immortal Jove's dread clamors[67] counterfeit,
Farewell! Othello's occupation's gone.

375 **Iago.** Is 't possible, my lord?

Othello. Villain, be sure thou prove my love a whore!
Be sure of it. Give me the ocular proof,
Or, by the worth of mine eternal soul,
Thou hadst been better have been born a dog
380 Than answer my waked wrath!

Iago.   Is 't come to this?

Othello. Make me to see 't, or at the least so prove it
That the probation[68] bear no hinge nor loop
To hang a doubt on, or woe upon thy life!

Iago. My noble lord—

385 **Othello.** If thou dost slander her and torture me,
Never pray more; abandon all remorse;
On horror's head horrors accumulate;
Do deeds to make heaven weep, all earth amazed;
For nothing canst thou to damnation add
390 Greater than that.

Iago.   O grace! O heaven forgive me!
Are you a man? Have you a soul or sense?
God b' wi' you; take mine office. O wretched fool,
That lov'st to make thine honesty a vice!
O monstrous world! Take note, take note, O world,
395 To be direct and honest is not safe.
I thank you for this profit, and from hence
I'll love no friend, sith,[69] love breeds such offense.

Othello. Nay, stay. Thou shouldst be honest.

---

[65] circumstance—pageantry.

[66] mortal engines—cannon.

[67] Jove's dread clamors—thunder.

[68] probation—proof.

[69] sith—since.

Iago. I should be wise, for honesty's a fool
400   And loses that it works for.

Othello.   By the world,
     I think my wife be honest and think she is not;
     I think that thou art just and think thou art not.
     I'll have some proof. My name, that was as fresh
     As Dian's[70] visage, is now begrimed and black
405   As mine own face. If there be cords, or knives,
     Poison, or fire, or suffocating streams,
     I'll not endure it. Would I were satisfied!

Iago. I see, sir, you are eaten up with passion.
     I do repent me that I put it to you.
410   You would be satisfied?

Othello.   Would? Nay, and I will.

Iago. And may; but how? How satisfied, my lord?
     Would you, the supervisor,[71] grossly gape on?
     Behold her topped?

Othello.   Death and damnation! O!

Iago. It were a tedious difficulty, I think,
415   To bring them to that prospect. Damn them then,[72]
     If ever mortal eyes do see them bolster[73]
     More than their own. What then? How then?
     What shall I say? Where's satisfaction?
     It is impossible you should see this,
420   Were they as prime[74] as goats, as hot as monkeys,
     As salt as wolves in pride,[75] and fools as gross
     As ignorance made drunk. But yet I say,
     If imputation and strong circumstances
     Which lead directly to the door of truth
425   Will give you satisfaction, you might have 't.

Othello. Give me a living reason she's disloyal.

Iago. I do not like the office.
     But sith I am entered in this cause so far,

---

[70] Dian's—Diana's. Diana was the Roman goddess of the moon and of chastity.

[71] supervisor—onlooker.

[72] Damn them then—that is, they would have to be really incorrigible.

[73] bolster—go to bed together, share a bolster.

[74] prime—lustful.

[75] salt . . . pride—wanton as wolves in heat.

pricked to 't by foolish honesty and love,
430   I will go on. I lay with Cassio lately,
And being troubled with a raging tooth
I could not sleep. There are a kind of men
So loose of soul that in their sleeps will mutter
Their affairs. One of this kind is Cassio.
435   In sleep I heard him say, "Sweet Desdemona,
Let us be wary, let us hide our loves!"
And then, sir, would he grip and wring my hand,
Cry "O sweet creature!", then kiss me hard,
As if he plucked up kisses by the roots
440   That grew upon my lips; then laid his leg
Over my thigh, and sighed, and kissed, and then
Cried, "Cursed fate that gave thee to the Moor!"

Othello. O monstrous! Monstrous!

Iago.   Nay, this was but his dream.

Othello. But this denoted a foregone conclusion.[76]
445   'Tis a shrewd doubt,[77] though it be but a dream.

Iago. And this may help to thicken other proofs
That do demonstrate thinly.

Othello.   I'll tear her all to pieces.

Iago. Nay, but be wise. Yet we see nothing done;
She may be honest yet. Tell me but this:
450   Have you not sometimes seen a handkerchief
Spotted with strawberries in your wife's hand?

Othello. I gave her such a one. 'Twas my first gift.

Iago. I know not that; but such a handkerchief—
I am sure it was your wife's did I today
455   See Cassio wipe his beard with.

Othello.   If it be that—

Iago. If it be that, or any that was hers,
It speaks against her with the other proofs.

Othello. O, that the slave[78] had forty thousand lives!
One is too poor, too weak for my revenge.
460   Now do I see 'tis true. Look here, Iago,
All my fond love thus do I blow to heaven.

---

[76] foregone conclusion—concluded experience or action.

[77] shrewd doubt—suspicious circumstance.

[78] slave—that is, Cassio.

'Tis gone.
Arise, black vengeance, from the hollow hell!
Yield up, O love, thy crown and hearted[79] throne
465 To tyrannous hate! Swell, bosom, with thy freight[80]
For 'tis of aspics'[81] tongues!
Iago. Yet be content.[82]
Othello. O, blood, blood, blood!
Iago. Patience, I say. Your mind perhaps may change.
470 **Othello.** Never, Iago. Like to the Pontic Sea,
Whose icy current and compulsive course
Ne'er feels retiring ebb, but keeps due on
To the Propontic and the Hellespont,[83]
Even so my bloody thoughts with violent pace
475 Shall ne'er look back, ne'er ebb to humble love
Till that a capable[84] and wide revenge
Swallow them up. Now, by yond marble heaven,
[*Kneeling*] In the due reverence of a sacred vow
I here engage my words.
Iago.   Do not rise yet.
480 [*He kneels.*] Witness, you ever-burning lights above,
Your elements that clip[85] us round about,
Witness that here Iago doth give up
The execution[86] of his wit, hands, heart,
To wronged Othello's service. Let him command,
485 And to obey shall be in me remorse,[87]
What bloody business ever.[88] [*They rise.*]
Othello.   I greet thy love,
Not with vain thanks, but with acceptance bounteous,

---

[79] hearted—fixed in the heart.

[80] freight—burden.

[81] aspics'—venomous serpents'.

[82] content—calm.

[83] Pontic Sea . . . Hellespont—A strong and constant current flows from the Black (or Pontic) Sea through the Sea of Marmora (or Propontic) and the Dardanelles (or Hellespont) into the Aegean Sea, where the water level is lower.

[84] capable—comprehensive.

[85] clip—encompass.

[86] execution—exercise, action.

[87] remorse—pity (for Othello's wrongs).

[88] ever—soever.

And will upon the instant put thee to 't.[89]

Within these three days let me hear thee say

490   That Cassio's not alive.

Iago.   My friend is dead;

'Tis done at your request. But let her live.

Othello. Damn her, lewd minx![90] O, damn her, damn her!

Come, go with me apart. I will withdraw

To furnish me with some swift means of death

495   For the fair devil. Now art thou my lieutenant.

Iago. I am your own forever.

[*Exeunt.*]

Act Three, Scene Four

[*Enter* Desdemona, Emilia, *and* Clown.]

Desdemona. Do you know, sirrah,[91] where Lieutenant Cassio lies?[92]

Clown. I dare not say he lies anywhere.

Desdemona. Why, man?

Clown. He's a soldier, and for me to say a soldier lies, 'tis stabbing.

5   **Desdemona.** Go to. Where lodges he?

Clown. To tell you where he lodges is to tell you where I lie.

Desdemona. Can anything be made of this?

Clown. I know not where he lodges and for me to devise a lodging and
say he lies here, or he lies there, were to lie in mine own throat.[93]

10   **Desdemona.** Can you inquire him out, and be edified by report?

Clown. I will catechize the world for him; that is, make questions, and
by them answer.

Desdemona. Seek him, bid him come hither. Tell him I have moved[94]
my lord on his behalf and hope all will be well.

15   **Clown.** To do this is within the compass of man's wit, and therefore I
will attempt the doing it. [*Exit* Clown.]

Desdemona. Where should I lose that handkerchief, Emilia?

Emilia. I know not, madam.

---

[89] to 't—to the proof.

[90] minx—wanton woman.

[91] sirrah—form of address to an inferior.

[92] lies—lodges.

[93] lie in mine own throat—lie egregiously and deliberately; use the windpipe to speak a lie.

[94] moved—petitioned.

Desdemona. Believe me, I had rather have lost my purse

20   Full of crusadoes;[95] and but my noble Moor

Is true of mind and made of no such baseness

As jealous creatures are, it were enough

To put him to ill thinking.

Emilia.   Is he not jealous?

Desdemona. Who, he? I think the sun where he was born

25   Drew all such humors[96] from him.

Emilia.   Look where he comes.

[*Enter* Othello.]

Desdemona. I will not leave him now till Cassio

Be called to him.—How is 't with you, my lord?

Othello. Well, my good lady. [*Aside.*] O, hardness to dissemble!—

How do you, Desdemona?

Desdemona.   Well, my good lord.

30   **Othello.** Give me your hand. [*She gives her hand.*] This hand is moist,

my lady.

Desdemona. It yet hath felt no age nor known no sorrow.

Othello. This argues fruitfulness and liberal[97] heart.

Hot, hot, and moist. This hand of yours requires

35   A sequester[98] from liberty, fasting and prayer,

Much castigation,[99] exercise devout;

For here's a young and sweating devil here

That commonly rebels. 'Tis a good hand,

A frank one.

Desdemona.   You may indeed say so,

40   For 'twas that hand that gave away my heart.

Othello. A liberal hand. The hearts of old gave hands,

But our new heraldry is hands, not hearts.[100]

Desdemona. I cannot speak of this. Come now, your promise.

Othello. What promise, chuck?[101]

45   **Desdemona.** I have sent to bid Cassio come speak with you.

---

[95] crusadoes—Portugese gold coins.

[96] humors—refers to the four bodily fluids thought to determine temperament.

[97] liberal—generous and sexually free.

[98] sequester—separation, sequestration.

[99] castigation—corrective discipline.

[100] But ... hearts—that is, in our decadent times the joining of hands is no longer a badge of (heraldry) to signify the giving of hearts.

[101] chuck—a term of endearment.

Othello. I have a salt and sorry rheum[102] offends me;
    Lend me thy handkerchief.

Desdemona. Here, my lord. [*She offers a handkerchief.*]

Othello. That which I gave you.

Desdemona.   I have it not about me.

50   **Othello.** Not?

Desdemona. No, faith, my lord.

Othello. That's a fault. That handkerchief
    Did an Egyptian to my mother give.
    She was a charmer,[103] and could almost read
55   The thoughts of people. She told her, while she kept it
    'Twould make her amiable[104] and subdue my father
    Entirely to her love, but if she lost it
    Or made a gift of it, my father's eye
    Should hold her loathèd and his spirits should hunt
60   After new fancies. She, dying, gave it me,
    And bid me, when my fate would have me wived,
    To give it her. I did so; and take heed on 't;
    Make it a darling like your precious eye.
    To lose 't or give it away were such perdition
65   As nothing else could match.

Desdemona.   Is 't possible?

Othello. 'Tis true. There's magic in the web[105] of it.
    A **sibyl**,[106] that had numbered in the world
    The sun to course two hundred compasses,
    In her prophetic fury[107] sewed the work;
70   The worms were hallowed that did breed the silk,
    And it was dyed in mummy[108] which the skillful
    Conserved of maidens' hearts.

Desdemona.   I' faith, Is 't true?

Othello. Most veritable. Therefore look to 't well.

Desdemona. Then would to God that I had never seen 't!

---

[102] salt . . . rheum—distressful head cold or watering of the eyes.

[103] charmer—sorceress.

[104] amiable—desirable.

[105] web—fabric, weaving.

[106] **sibyl**—prophetess.

[107] prophetic fury—frenzy of prophetic inspiration.

[108] mummy—medicinal or magical preparation made from mummified bodies.

75 **Othello.** Ha? Wherefore?

Desdemona. Why do you speak so startingly and rash?

Othello. Is 't lost? Is 't gone? Speak, is 't out o' the way?

Desdemona. Heaven bless us!

Othello. Say you?

80 **Desdemona.** It is not lost, but what an if[109] it were?

Othello. How?

Desdemona. I say it is not lost.

Othello.   Fetch 't, let me see 't.

Desdemona. Why, so I can, sir, but I will not now.
    This is a trick to put me from my suit.

85   Pray you, let Cassio be received again.

Othello. Fetch me the handkerchief! My mind misgives.

Desdemona. Come, come,
    You'll never meet a more sufficient[110] man.

Othello. The handkerchief!

Desdemona.   I pray, talk me of Cassio.

90 **Othello.** The handkerchief!

Desdemona.   A man that all his time
    Hath founded his good fortunes on your love,
    Shared dangers with you—

Othello. The handkerchief!

Desdemona. I' faith, you are to blame.

95 **Othello.** Zounds! [*Exit* Othello.]

Emilia. Is not this man jealous?

Desdemona. I ne'er saw this before.
    Sure, there's some wonder in this handkerchief.
    I am most unhappy in the loss of it.

100 **Emilia.** 'Tis not a year or two shows us a man.
    They are all but stomachs, and we all but food;
    They eat us hungerly, and when they are full
    They belch us.

[*Enter* Iago *and* Cassio.]
              Look you, Cassio and my husband.

Iago [*to* Cassio]. There is no other way; 'tis she must do 't.

105   And, lo, the happiness![111] Go and importune her.

---

[109] an if—if.

[110] sufficient—able, complete.

[111] the happiness—behold, in happy time, fortunately met.

Desdemona. How now, good Cassio? What's the news with you?

Cassio. Madam, my former suit. I do beseech you
    That by your virtuous means I may again
    Exist and be a member of his love

110   Whom I, with all the office of my heart,
    Entirely honor. I would not be delayed.
    If my offense be of such mortal kind
    That nor my service past, nor present sorrows,
    Nor purposed merit in futurity

115   Can ransom me into his love again,
    But to know so must be my benefit;[112]
    So shall I clothe me in a forced content,
    And shut myself up in some other course,
    To fortune's alms.

Desdemona.   Alas, thrice-gentle Cassio,

120   My advocation is not now in tune.
    My lord is not my lord; nor should I know him,
    Were he in favor[113] as in humor altered.
    So help me every spirit sanctified
    As I have spoken for you all my best

125   And stood within the blank[114] of his displeasure
    For my free speech! You must awhile be patient.
    What I can do I will, and more I will
    Than for myself I dare. Let that suffice you.

Iago. Is my lord angry?

Emilia.   He went hence but now,

130   And certainly in strange unquietness.

Iago. Can he be angry? I have seen the cannon
    When it hath blown his ranks into the air,
    And like the devil from his very arm
    Puffed his own brother—and is he angry?

135   Something of moment[115] then. I will go meet him.
    There's matter in 't indeed, if he be angry.

---

[112] But . . . benefit—merely to know that my case is hopeless will have to content me (and will be better than uncertainty).

[113] favor—appearance.

[114] within the blank—within point-blank range. (The *blank* is the center of the target.)

[115] of moment—of immediate importance, momentous.

Desdemona. I prithee, do so. [*Exit* Iago.]

Something, sure, of state,[116]

Either from Venice, or some unhatched practice[117]

Made demonstrable here in Cyprus to him,

140   Hath puddled[118] his clear spirit; and in such cases

Men's natures wrangle with inferior things,

Though great ones are their object. 'Tis even so;

For let our finger ache, and it indues[119]

Our other, healthful members even to a sense

145   Of pain. Nay, we must think men are not gods,

Nor of them look for such observancy

As fits the bridal. Beshrew me much, Emilia,

I was, unhandsome warrior as I am,

Arraigning[120] his unkindness with my soul;

150   But now I find I had suborned the witness,

And he's indicted falsely.

Emilia.   Pray heaven it be

State matters, as you think, and no conception

Nor no jealous toy[121] concerning you.

Desdemona. Alas the day! I never gave him cause.

155   **Emilia.** But jealous souls will not be answered so;

They are not ever jealous for the cause,

But jealous for they're jealous. It is a monster

Begot upon itself, born on itself.

Desdemona. Heaven keep that monster from Othello's mind!

160   **Emilia.** Lady, amen.

Desdemona. I will go seek him. Cassio, walk hereabout.

If I do find him fit,[122] I'll move your suit

And seek to effect it to my uttermost.

Cassio. I humbly thank your ladyship.

[*Exit* Desdemona *with* Emilia.]

[*Enter* Bianca.]

---

[116] of state—concerning state affairs.

[117] unhatched practice—as yet unexecuted or undiscovered plot.

[118] puddled—muddied.

[119] indues—brings to the same condition.

[120] **Arraigning**—calling (an accused person) before a court to answer a charge.

[121] toy—fancy.

[122] fit—approachable.

165   **Bianca.** Save you, friend Cassio!

Cassio.   What make you from home?

How is 't with you, my most fair Bianca?

I' faith, sweet love, I was coming to your house.

Bianca. And I was going to your lodging, Cassio.

What, keep a week away? Seven days and nights?

170   Eightscore-eight hours? And lovers' absent hours

More tedious than the dial[123] eightscore times?

O weary reckoning!

Cassio.   Pardon me, Bianca.

I have this while with leaden thoughts been pressed;

But I shall, in a more continuate[124] time,

175   Strike off this score of absence. Sweet Bianca,

[*giving her* Desdemona's *handkerchief*]

Take me this work out.

Bianca.   O Cassio, whence came this?

This is some token from a newer friend.[125]

To the felt absence now I feel a cause.

Is 't come to this? Well, well.

Cassio.   Go to, woman!

180   Throw your vile guesses in the devil's teeth,

From whence you have them. You are jealous now

That this is from some mistress, some remembrance.

No, by my faith, Bianca.

Bianca.   Why, whose is it?

Cassio. I know not, neither. I found it in my chamber.

185   I like the work well. Ere it be demanded—

As like enough it will—I would have it copied.

Take it and do 't, and leave me for this time.

Bianca. Leave you? Wherefore?

Cassio. I do attend here on the General,

190   And think it no addition,[126] nor my wish,

To have him see me womaned.

Bianca. Why, I pray you?

Cassio. Not that I love you not.

---

[123] dial—complete revolution of the clock.

[124] continuate—uninterrupted.

[125] friend—mistress.

[126] addition—that is, addition to my reputation.

Bianca. But that you do not love me.
195   I pray you, bring me on the way a little,
           And say if I shall see you soon at night.
Cassio. 'Tis but a little way that I can bring you,
           For I attend here; but I'll see you soon.
Bianca. 'Tis very good. I must be circumstanced.[127]
[*Exeunt omnes.*]

Act Four, Scene One

[*Enter* Othello *and* Iago.]
Iago. Will you think so?
Othello.   Think so, Iago?
Iago.   What,
           To kiss in private?
Othello.   An unauthorized kiss!
Iago. Or to be naked with her friend in bed
           An hour or more, not meaning any harm?
5   **Othello.** Naked in bed, Iago, and not mean harm?
           It is hypocrisy against the devil.
           They that mean virtuously and yet do so,
           The devil their virtue tempts, and they tempt heaven.
Iago. If they do nothing, 'tis a venial[1] slip.
10   But if I give my wife a handkerchief—
Othello. What then?
Iago. Why then, 'tis hers, my lord, and being hers,
           She may, I think, bestow 't on any man.
Othello. She is protectress of her honor too.
15   May she give that?
Iago. Her honor is an **essence**[2] that's not seen;
           They have it very oft that have it not.
           But, for the handkerchief—
Othello. By heaven, I would most gladly have forgot it.
20   Thou saidst—O, it comes o'er my memory

---

[127] circumstanced—be governed by circumstance, yield to your conditions.

[1] venial—pardonable.

[2] **essence**—crucial element.

As doth the raven o'er the infectious house,[3]
Boding to all—he had my handkerchief.

Iago. Ay, what of that?

Othello.   That's not so good now.

Iago.   What
If I had said I had seen him do you wrong?
25   Or heard him say—as knaves be such abroad,
Who having, by their own importunate suit,
Or voluntary dotage[4] of some mistress,
Convincèd or supplied[5] them, cannot choose
But they must blab—

Othello.   Hath he said anything?

30   **Iago.** He hath, my lord; but, be you well assured,
No more than he'll unswear.

Othello.   What hath he said?

Iago. Faith, that he did—I know not what he did.

Othello. What? What?

Iago. Lie—

Othello. With her?

Iago.   With her, on her; what you will.

35   **Othello.** Lie with her? Lie on her? We say "lie on her" when they belie
her. Lie with her? Zounds, that's fulsome.[6]—Handkerchief—confession—handkerchief!—To confess and be hanged for his labor—first to
be hanged and then to confess.[7]—I tremble at it. Nature would not
invest herself in such shadowing passion without some instruction.
40   It is not words that shakes me thus. Pish! Noses, ears, and lips.—Is 't
possible?—Confess—handkerchief!—O devil!

[*Falls in a trance.*]

Iago. Work on,
My medicine, work! Thus **credulous**[8] fools are caught,
And many worthy and chaste dames even thus,

---

[3] raven . . . house—allusion to the belief that the raven hovered over a house of sickness or infection, such as one visited by the plague.

[4] voluntary dotage—willing infatuation.

[5] Convincèd or supplied—seduced or sexually gratified.

[6] fulsome—foul.

[7] first . . . confess—Othello reverses the proverbial "confess and be hanged"; Cassio is to be given no time to confess before he dies.

[8] **credulous**—convinced too easily; gullible.

45   All guiltless, meet reproach.—What, ho! My lord!
      My lord, I say! Othello!
      [*Enter* Cassio.]
                                    How now, Cassio?
      Cassio. What's the matter?
      Iago. My lord is fall'n into an epilepsy.[9]
      This is his second fit. He had one yesterday.
50   **Cassio.** Rub him about the temples.
      Iago.   No, forbear.
      The lethargy[10] must have his quiet course.
      If not, he foams at mouth, and by and by
      Breaks out to savage madness. Look, he stirs.
      Do you withdraw yourself a little while.
55   He will recover straight. When he is gone,
      I would on great occasion speak with you.
      [*Exit* Cassio.]
      How is it, General? Have you not hurt your head?
      Othello. Dost thou mock me?
      Iago.   I mock you not, by heaven.
      Would you would bear your fortune like a man!
60   **Othello.** A hornèd man's a monster and a beast.
      Iago. There's many a beast then in a populous city,
      And many a civil[11] monster.
      Othello. Did he confess it?
      Iago. Good sir, be a man.
65   Think every bearded fellow that's but yoked
      May draw with you. There's millions now alive
      That nightly lie in those unproper beds
      Which they dare swear peculiar.[12] Your case is better.
      O, 'tis the spite of hell, the fiend's arch-mock,
70   To lip a wanton in a secure couch
      And to suppose her chaste! No, let me know,
      And knowing what I am, I know what she shall be.
      Othello. O, thou art wise. 'Tis certain.

---

[9] fall'n . . . epilepsy—having a seizure.

[10] lethargy—coma.

[11] civil—dwelling in a city.

[12] unproper . . . peculiar—beds not exclusively their own that they believe are private.

Iago. Stand you awhile apart;

75   Confine yourself but in a patient list.
Whilst you were here o'erwhelmed with your grief—
A passion most unsuiting such a man—
Cassio came hither. I shifted him away,
And laid good 'scuse upon your ecstasy,[13]

80   Bade him anon return and here speak with me,
The which he promised. Do but encave[14] yourself
And mark the fleers,[15] the gibes, and notable scorns
That dwell in every region of his face;
For I will make him tell the tale anew,

85   Where, how, how oft, how long ago, and when
He hath and is again to cope[16] your wife.
I say, but mark his gesture. Marry, patience!
Or I shall say you're all-in-all in spleen,[17]
And nothing of a man.

Othello.   Dost thou hear, Iago?

90   I will be found most cunning in my patience;
But—dost thou hear?—most bloody.

Iago.   That's not amiss;
But yet keep time in all. Will you withdraw?

[Othello *stands apart.*]

    Now will I question Cassio of Bianca,
A huswife that by selling her desires

95   Buys herself bread and clothes. It is a creature
That dotes on Cassio—as 'tis the strumpet's plague
To beguile many and be beguiled by one.
He, when he hears of her, cannot restrain
From the excess of laughter. Here he comes.

[*Enter* Cassio.]

100   As he shall smile, Othello shall go mad;
And his unbookish jealousy must conster
Poor Cassio's smiles, gestures, and light behaviors
Quite in the wrong.—How do you now, Lieutenant?

---

[13] ecstasy—trance.

[14] encave—conceal.

[15] fleers—sneers.

[16] cope—encounter, have sex with.

[17] all-in-all in spleen—utterly governed by passionate impulses.

Cassio. The worser that you give me the addition[18]

105   Whose want even kills me.

Iago. Ply Desdemona well and you are sure on 't.
[*Speaking lower.*] Now, if this suit lay in Bianca's power,
How quickly should you speed!

Cassio [*laughing*]. Alas, poor caitiff![19]

110   **Othello** [*aside*]. Look how he laughs already!

Iago. I never knew a woman love man so.

Cassio. Alas, poor rogue! I think, i' faith, she loves me.

Othello. Now he denies it faintly, and laughs it out.

Iago. Do you hear, Cassio?

Othello.   Now he importunes him

115   To tell it o'er. Go to! Well said, well said.

Iago. She gives it out that you shall marry her.
Do you intend it?

Cassio. Ha, ha, ha!

Othello. Do you triumph, Roman?[20] Do you triumph?

120   **Cassio.** I marry her? What? A customer?[21] Prithee, bear some charity
to my wit; do not think it so unwholesome. Ha, ha, ha!

Othello. So, so, so, so! They laugh that win.

Iago. Faith, the cry goes that you shall marry her.

Cassio. Prithee, say true.

125   **Iago.** I am a very villain else.

Othello. Have you scored me? Well.

Cassio. This is the monkey's own giving out. She is persuaded I will
marry her out of her own love and flattery, not out of my promise.

Othello. Iago beckons me. Now he begins the story.

130   **Cassio.** She was here even now; she haunts me in every place. I was
the other day talking on the seabank with certain Venetians, and
thither comes the bauble,[22] and, by this hand, she falls me thus
about my neck—
[*He embraces* Iago.]

Othello. Crying, "O dear Cassio!" as it were; his gesture imports it.

---

[18] addition—title.

[19] caitiff—wretch.

[20] Roman—The Romans were noted for their *triumphs* or triumphal processions.

[21] customer—prostitute.

[22] bauble—plaything.

135 **Cassio.** So hangs and lolls and weeps upon me, so shakes and pulls me. Ha, ha, ha!

Othello. Now he tells how she plucked him to my chamber. O, I see that nose of yours, but not that dog I shall throw it to.

Cassio. Well, I must leave her company.

140 **Iago.** Before me,[23] look where she comes.

[*Enter* Bianca *with* Othello's *handkerchief.*]

Cassio. 'Tis such another fitchew![24] Marry, a perfumed one.—What do you mean by this haunting of me?

Bianca. Let the devil and his dam haunt you! What did you mean by that same handkerchief you gave me even now? I was a fine fool to

145 take it. I must take out the work? A likely piece of work, that you should find it in your chamber and know not who left it there! This is some minx's token, and I must take out the work? There; give it your hobbyhorse.[25] [*She gives him the handkerchief.*] Wheresoever you had it, I'll take out no work on 't.

150 **Cassio.** How now, my sweet Bianca? How now? How now?

Othello. By heaven, that should be my handkerchief!

Bianca. If you'll come to supper tonight, you may; if you will not, come when you are next prepared for.[26] [*Exit.*]

Iago. After her, after her.

155 **Cassio.** Faith, I must. She'll rail in the streets else.

Iago. Will you sup there?

Cassio. Faith, I intend so.

Iago. Well, I may chance to see you, for I would very fain speak with you.

Cassio. Prithee, come. Will you?

160 **Iago.** Go to. Say no more. [*Exit* Cassio.]

Othello [*advancing*]. How shall I murder him, Iago?

Iago. Did you perceive how he laughed at his vice?

Othello. O, Iago!

Iago. And did you see the handkerchief?

165 **Othello.** Was that mine?

Iago. Yours, by this hand. And to see how he prizes the foolish woman your wife! She gave it him, and he hath given it his whore.

---

[23] Before me—on my soul.

[24] 'Tis . . . fitchew—What a polecat she is! Just like all the others. (Polecats were often compared with prostitutes because of their rank smell and presumed lechery.)

[25] hobbyhorse—prostitute.

[26] when . . . for—when I'm ready for you (that is, never).

Othello. I would have him nine years a-killing. A fine woman! A fair woman! A sweet woman!

170 **Iago.** Nay, you must forget that.

Othello. Ay, let her rot and perish, and be damned tonight, for she shall not live. No, my heart is turned to stone; I strike it, and it hurts my hand. O, the world hath not a sweeter creature! She might lie by an emperor's side and command him tasks.

175 **Iago.** Nay, that's not your way.

Othello. Hang her! I do but say what she is. So delicate with her needle! An admirable musician! O, she will sing the savageness out of a bear. Of so high and plenteous wit and invention!

Iago. She's the worse for all this.

180 **Othello.** O, a thousand, a thousand times! And then, of so gentle a condition!

Iago. Ay, too gentle.

Othello. Nay, that's certain. But yet the pity of it, Iago! O, Iago, the pity of it, Iago!

185 **Iago.** If you are so fond over her iniquity, give her patent to offend, for if it touch not you it comes near nobody.

Othello. I will chop her into messes.²⁷ Cuckold me?

Iago. O, 'tis foul in her.

Othello. With mine officer?

190 **Iago.** That's fouler.

Othello. Get me some poison, Iago, this night. I'll not **expostulate**²⁸ with her, lest her body and beauty unprovide my mind again. This night, Iago.

Iago. Do it not with poison. Strangle her in her bed, even the bed she

195 hath contaminated.

Othello. Good good! The justice of it pleases. Very good.

Iago. And for Cassio, let me be his undertaker. You shall hear more by midnight.

Othello. Excellent good. [*A trumpet within.*] What trumpet is that same?

200 **Iago.** I warrant, something from Venice.

[*Enter* Lodovico, Desdemona, *and attendants.*]

'Tis Lodovico. This comes from the Duke.

See, your wife's with him.

Lodovico. God save you, worthy General!

---

²⁷ messes—portions of meat.
²⁸ expostulate—reason with.

Othello.   With all my heart, sir

Lodovico [*giving him a letter*]. The Duke and the senators of Venice
    greet you.

205   **Othello.** I kiss the instrument of their pleasures.

[*He opens the letter, and reads.*]

Desdemona. And what's the news, good cousin Lodovico?

Iago. I am very glad to see you, signor.
    Welcome to Cyprus.

Lodovico. I thank you. How does Lieutenant Cassio?

210   **Iago.** Lives, sir.

Desdemona. Cousin, there's fall'n between him and my lord
    An unkind breach; but you shall make all well.

Othello. Are you sure of that?

Desdemona. My lord?

215   **Othello** [*reads*]. "This fail you not to do, as you will—"

Lodovico. He did not call; he's busy in the paper.
    Is there division twixt my lord and Cassio?

Desdemona. A most unhappy one. I would do much
    T' atone them, for the love I bear to Cassio.

220   **Othello.** Fire and brimstone!

Desdemona. My lord?

Othello. Are you wise?

Desdemona. What, is he angry?

Lodovico.   Maybe the letter moved him;
    For, as I think, they do command him home,

225   Deputing Cassio in his government.

Desdemona. By my troth, I am glad on 't.

Othello. Indeed?

Desdemona. My lord?

Othello. I am glad to see you mad.[29]

230   **Desdemona.** Why, sweet Othello—

Othello [*striking her*]. Devil!

Desdemona. I have not deserved this.

Lodovico. My lord, this would not be believed in Venice,
    Though I should swear I saw 't. 'Tis very much.[30]

235   Make her amends; she weeps.

---

[29] I am...mad—that is, I am glad to see you are insane enough to rejoice in Cassio's promotion.

[30] very much—too much, outrageous.

Othello.   O devil, devil!
    If that the earth could teem with woman's tears,
    Each drop she falls would prove a crocodile.[31]
    Out of my sight!
Desdemona.   I will not stay to offend you. [*Going.*]
Lodovico. Truly, an obedient lady.
    I do beseech your lordship, call her back.
Othello. Mistress!
Desdemona [*returning*]. My lord?
Othello. What would you with her, sir?
Lodovico. Who, I, my lord?
Othello. Ay, you did wish that I would make her turn.
    Sir, she can turn, and turn, and yet go on
    And turn again;[32] and she can weep, sir, weep;
    And she's obedient, as you say, obedient,
    Very obedient.—Proceed you in your tears.—
    Concerning this, sir—O well-painted passion!—
    I am commanded home.—Get you away;
    I'll send for you anon.—Sir, I obey the mandate
    And will return to Venice.—Hence avaunt!
[*Exit Desdemona.*]
    Cassio shall have my place. And, sir, tonight
    I do entreat that we may sup together.
    You are welcome, sir, to Cyprus.—Goats and monkeys!
[*Exit.*]
Lodovico. Is this the noble Moor whom our full Senate
    Call all in all sufficient? Is this the nature
    Whom passion could not shake? Whose solid virtue
    The shot of accident nor dart of chance
    Could neither graze nor pierce?
Iago.   He is much changed.
Lodovico. Are his wits safe? Is he not light of brain?
Iago. He's that he is. I may not breathe my censure
    What he might be. If what he might he is not,
    I would to heaven he were![33]

---

[31] crocodile—Crocodiles were supposed to weep hypocritical tears for their victims.

[32] turn again—Othello implies that Desdemona is pliant and will do a turn for any man.

[33] I may ... were—that is, I dare not venture an opinion as to whether he's of unsound mind, as you suggest, but, if he isn't, then it might be better to wish he were in fact insane, since only that could excuse his wild behavior.

Lodovico.   What, strike his wife?

Iago. Faith, that was not so well; yet would I knew
    That stroke would prove the worst!

Lodovico.   Is it his use?[34]
    Or did the letters work upon his blood
    And new-create his fault?

Iago.   Alas, alas!
270   It is not honesty in me to speak
    What I have seen and known. You shall observe him,
    And his own courses will denote[35] him so
    That I may save my speech. Do but go after,
    And mark how he continues.

275   **Lodovico.** I am sorry that I am deceived in him.
[Exeunt.]

Act Four, Scene Two

[Enter Othello *and* Emilia.]

Othello. You have seen nothing then?

Emilia. Nor ever heard, nor ever did suspect.

Othello. Yes, you have seen Cassio and she together.

Emilia. But then I saw no harm, and then I heard
5   Each syllable that breath made up between them.

Othello. What, did they never whisper?

Emilia. Never, my lord.

Othello. Nor send you out o' the way?

Emilia. Never.

10   **Othello.** To fetch her fan, her gloves, her mask, nor nothing?

Emilia. Never, my lord.

Othello. That's strange.

Emilia. I durst, my lord, to wager she is honest,
    Lay down my soul at stake. If you think other,
15   Remove your thought; it doth abuse your bosom.
    If any wretch have put this in your head,
    Let heaven requite it with the serpent's curse![36]

---

[34] use—custom.

[35] courses will denote—actions will reveal.

[36] the serpent's curse—the curse pronounced by God on the serpent for deceiving Eve, just as some man has done to Othello and Desdemona. (See Genesis 3:14.)

For if she be not honest, chaste, and true,

There's no man happy; the purest of their wives

20 Is foul as slander.

Othello.   Bid her come hither. Go.

[*Exit* Emilia.]

She says enough; yet she's a simple bawd

That cannot say as much.[37] This is a subtle whore,

A closet lock and key of villainous secrets.

And yet she'll kneel and pray; I have seen her do 't.

[*Enter* Desdemona *and* Emilia.]

25 **Desdemona.** My lord, what is your will?

Othello. Pray you, chuck, come hither.

Desdemona. What is your pleasure?

Othello.   Let me see your eyes.

Look in my face.

Desdemona.   What horrible fancy's this?

Othello [*to* Emilia]. Some of your function,[38] mistress.

30 Leave procreants[39] alone and shut the door;

Cough or cry "hem" if anybody come.

Your mystery,[40] your mystery! Nay, dispatch.

[*Exit* Emilia.]

Desdemona [*kneeling*]. Upon my knees, what doth your speech import?

I understand a fury in your words,

35 But not the words.

Othello. Why, what art thou?

Desdemona.   Your wife, my lord, your true

And loyal wife.

Othello.   Come, swear it, damn thyself,

Lest, being like one of heaven, the devils themselves

Should fear to seize thee. Therefore be double damned:

40 Swear thou art honest.

Desdemona.   Heaven doth truly know it.

Othello. Heaven truly knows that thou art false as hell.

Desdemona. To whom, my lord? With whom? How am I false?

---

[37] she's . . . much—that is, any bawd (a procuress or go-between) who couldn't make up a story as plausible as Emilia's would have to be pretty stupid.

[38] Some . . . function—that is, practice your chosen profession, that of bawd (by guarding the door).

[39] procreants—mating couples.

[40] mystery—trade, occupation.

Othello [*weeping*]. Ah, Desdemon! Away, away, away!

Desdemona. Alas the heavy day! Why do you weep?

45   Am I the motive of these tears, my lord?
If haply you my father do suspect
An instrument of this your calling back,
Lay not your blame on me. If you have lost him,
I have lost him too.

Othello.   Had it pleased heaven

50   To try me with affliction, had they[41] rained
All kinds of sores and shames on my bare head,
Steeped me in poverty to the very lips,
Given to captivity me and my utmost hopes,
I should have found in some place of my soul

55   A drop of patience. But, alas, to make me
A fixèd figure for the time of scorn[42]
To point his slow and moving finger[43] at!
Yet could I bear that too, well, very well.
But there where I have garnered[44] up my heart,

60   Where either I must live or bear no life,
The fountain from the which my current runs
Or else dries up—to be discarded thence!
Or keep it as a cistern for foul toads
To knot and gender in! Turn thy complexion there,[45]

65   Patience, thou young and rose-lipped cherubin—
Ay there look grim as hell![46]

Desdemona. I hope my noble lord esteems me honest.

Othello. O, ay, as summer flies are in the shambles[47]
That quicken even with blowing. O thou weed,

70   Who art so lovely fair and smell'st so sweet
That the sense aches at thee, would thou hadst ne'er been born!

Desdemona. Alas, what ignorant sin have I committed?

---

[41] they—that is, heavenly powers.

[42] time of scorn—scornful world.

[43] slow and moving finger—that is, hour hand of the clock, moving so slowly it seems hardly to move at all. (Othello pictures himself as being eternally pointed at by the scornful world as the numbers on a clock are pointed at by the hour hand.)

[44] garnered—stored.

[45] Turn . . . there—change your color, grow pale, at such a sight.

[46] Patience . . . hell—Even Patience, that rose-lipped cherub, will look grim and pale at this spectacle.

[47] shambles—slaughterhouse.

Othello. Was this fair paper, this most goodly book,
Made to write "whore" upon? What committed?

75 Committed? O thou public commoner![48]
I should make very forges of my cheeks,
That would to cinders burn up modesty,
Did I but speak thy deeds. What committed?
Heaven stops the nose at it and the moon winks;

80 The bawdy wind, that kisses all it meets,
Is hushed within the hollow mine of earth
And will not hear 't. What committed?
Impudent strumpet!

Desdemona.   By heaven, you do me wrong.

Othello. Are not you a strumpet?

85 **Desdemona.** No, as I am a Christian.
If to preserve this vessel for my lord
From any other foul unlawful touch
Be not to be a strumpet, I am none.

Othello. What, not a whore?

90 **Desdemona.** No, as I shall be saved.

Othello. Is 't possible?

Desdemona. O, heaven forgive us!

Othello.   I cry you mercy, then.
I took you for that cunning whore of Venice
That married with Othello. [*Calling out.*] You, mistress,

95 That have the office opposite to Saint Peter
And keep the gate of hell!

[*Enter* Emilia.]

                              You, you, ay, you!
We have done our course.[49] There's money for your pains.

[*He gives money.*]

I pray you, turn the key and keep our counsel. [*Exit.*]

Emilia. Alas, what does this gentleman conceive?

100 How do you, madam? How do you, my good lady?

Desdemona. Faith, half asleep.

Emilia. Good madam, what's the matter with my lord?

Desdemona. With who?

---

[48] commoner—prostitute.

[49] course—business (with an indecent suggestion at "trick," turn at sex).

Emilia. Why, with my lord, madam.

105 **Desdemona.** Who is thy lord?

Emilia. He that is yours, sweet lady.

Desdemona. I have none. Do not talk to me, Emilia.

I cannot weep, nor answers have I none

But what should go by water.[50] Prithee, tonight

Lay on my bed my wedding sheets, remember;

110 And call thy husband hither.

Emilia. Here's a change indeed! [*Exit.*]

Desdemona. 'Tis meet I should be used so, very meet.

How have I been behaved, that he might stick

The small'st opinion on my least misuse?

[*Enter* Iago *and* Emilia.]

115 **Iago.** What is your pleasure, madam? How is 't with you?

Desdemona. I cannot tell. Those that do teach young babes

Do it with gentle means and easy tasks.

He might have chid me so, for, in good faith,

I am a child to chiding.

120 **Iago.** What is the matter, lady?

Emilia. Alas, Iago, my lord hath so bewhored her,

Thrown such despite and heavy terms upon her,

That true hearts cannot bear it.

Desdemona. Am I that name, Iago?

125 **Iago.** What name, fair lady?

Desdemona. Such as she said my lord did say I was.

Emilia. He called her whore. A beggar in his drink

Could not have laid such terms upon his callet.[51]

Iago. Why did he so?

130 **Desdemona** [*weeping*]. I do not know. I am sure I am none such.

Iago. Do not weep, do not weep. Alas the day!

Emilia. Hath she forsook so many noble matches,

Her father and her country and her friends,

To be called whore? Would it not make one weep?

135 **Desdemona.** It is my wretched fortune.

Iago. Beshrew[52] him for 't!

How comes this trick upon him?

---

[50] go by water—be expressed by tears.

[51] callet—whore.

[52] Beshrew—curse.

Desdemona.   Nay, heaven doth know.

Emilia. I will be hanged if some eternal villain,
　　　Some busy and insinuating[53] rogue,
　　　Some cogging,[54] cozening[55] slave, to get some office,
140　　Have not devised this slander. I will be hanged else.

Iago. Fie, there is no such man. It is impossible.

Desdemona. If any such there be, heaven pardon him!

Emilia. A halter[56] pardon him! And hell gnaw his bones!
　　　Why should he call her whore? Who keeps her company?
145　　What place? What time? What form? What likelihood?
　　　The Moor's abused by some most villainous knave,
　　　Some base notorious knave, some scurvy fellow.
　　　O, heaven, that such companions thou'dst unfold,
　　　And put in every honest hand a whip
150　　To lash the rascals naked through the world
　　　Even from the east to th' west!

Iago.   Speak within door.

Emilia. O, fie upon them! Some such squire he was
　　　That turned your wit the seamy side without
　　　And made you to suspect me with the Moor.

155 **Iago.** You are a fool. Go to.

Desdemona.   Alas, Iago,
　　　What shall I do to win my lord again?
　　　Good friend, go to him; for, by this light of heaven,
　　　I know not how I lost him. Here I kneel. [*She kneels.*]
　　　If e'er my will did trespass 'gainst his love,
160　　Either in discourse of thought or actual deed,
　　　Or that mine eyes, mine ears, or any sense
　　　Delighted them in any other form;
　　　Or that I do not yet, and ever did,
　　　And ever will—though he do shake me off
165　　To beggarly divorcement—love him dearly,
　　　Comfort forswear me! Unkindness may do much,
　　　And his unkindness may defeat my life,
　　　But never taint my love. I cannot say "whore."

---

[53] insinuating—ingratiating, fawning, wheedling.

[54] cogging—cheating.

[55] cozening—defrauding.

[56] halter—hangman's noose.

It does abhor me now I speak the word;
170 To do the act that might the addition earn
Not the world's mass of vanity could make me.

[*She rises.*]

Iago. I pray you, be content. 'Tis but his humor.[57]
The business of the state does him offense,
And he does chide with you.

175 **Desdemona.** If 'twere no other—

Iago. It is but so, I warrant. [*Trumpets within.*]
Hark, how these instruments summon you to supper!
The messengers of Venice stays the meat.[58]
Go in, and weep not. All things shall be well.

[*Exeunt* Desdemona *and* Emilia.]

[*Enter* Roderigo.]

180 How now, Roderigo?

Roderigo. I do not find that thou deal'st justly with me.

Iago. What in the contrary?

Roderigo. Every day thou daff'st me with some device,[59] Iago, and
rather, as it seems to me now, keep'st from me all conveniency
185 than suppliest me with the least advantage of hope. I will indeed
no longer endure it, nor am I yet persuaded to put up[60] in peace
what already I have foolishly suffered.

Iago. Will you hear me, Roderigo?

Roderigo. Faith, I have heard too much, for your words and perfor-
190 mances are no kin together.

Iago. You charge me most unjustly.

Roderigo. With naught but truth. I have wasted myself out of my
means. The jewels you have had from me to deliver[61] Desdemona
would half have corrupted a votarist.[62] You have told me she hath
195 received them and returned me expectations and comforts of sudden respect and acquaintance, but I find none.

Iago. Well, go to, very well.

---

[57] humor—mood.

[58] stays the meat—are waiting to dine.

[59] daff'st me . . . device—put me off with some excuse, trick.

[60] put up—submit to, tolerate.

[61] deliver—deliver to.

[62] votarist—nun.

Roderigo. "Very well"! "Go to"! I cannot go to, man, nor 'tis not very well. By this hand, I think it is scurvy, and begin to find myself fopped[63] in it.

Iago. Very well.

Roderigo. I tell you 'tis not very well. I will make myself known to Desdemona. If she will return me my jewels, I will give over my suit and repent my unlawful solicitation; if not, assure yourself I will seek satisfaction of you.

Iago. You have said now?

Roderigo. Ay, and said nothing but what I protest intendment of doing.

Iago. Why, now I see there's mettle in thee, and even from this instant do build on thee a better opinion than ever before. Give me thy hand, Roderigo. Thou hast taken against me a most just exception; but yet I protest I have dealt most directly in thy affair.

Roderigo. It hath not appeared.

Iago. I grant indeed it hath not appeared, and your suspicion is not without wit and judgment. But, Roderigo, if thou hast that in thee indeed which I have greater reason to believe now than ever—I mean purpose, courage, and valor—this night show it. If thou the next night following enjoy not Desdemona, take me from this world with treachery and devise engines for[64] my life.

Roderigo. Well, what is it? Is it within reason and compass?

Iago. Sir, there is especial commission come from Venice to depute Cassio in Othello's place.

Roderigo. Is that true? Why, then Othello and Desdemona return again to Venice.

Iago. O, no; he goes into Mauritania[65] and takes away with him the fair Desdemona, unless his abode be lingered here by some accident; wherein none can be so determinate[66] as the removing of Cassio.

Roderigo. How do you mean, removing of him?

Iago. Why, by making him uncapable of Othello's place—knocking out his brains.

Roderigo. And that you would have me to do?

Iago. Ay, if you dare do yourself a profit and a right. He sups tonight with a harlotry, and thither will I go to him. He knows not yet of his

---

[63] fopped—fooled.

[64] engines for—plots against.

[65] Mauritania—country in northwest Africa.

[66] determinate—conclusive.

honorable fortune. If you will watch his going thence, which I will fashion to fall out between twelve and one, you may take him at your pleasure. I will be near to second your attempt, and he shall fall between us. Come, stand not amazed at it, but go along with me. I will show you such a necessity in his death that you shall think yourself bound to put it on him. It is now high suppertime, and the night grows to waste. About it.

Roderigo. I will hear further reason for this.

Iago. And you shall be satisfied.

[*Exeunt.*]

Act Four, Scene Three

[*Enter* Othello, Lodovico, Desdemona, Emilia, *and attendants.*]

Lodovico. I do beseech you, sir, trouble yourself no further.

Othello. O, pardon me; 'twill do me good to walk.

Lodovico. Madam, good night. I humbly thank your ladyship.

Desdemona. Your honor is most welcome.

Othello.   Will you walk, sir?

O, Desdemona!

Desdemona. My lord?

Othello. Get you to bed on th' instant. I will be returned forthwith. Dismiss your attendant there. Look 't be done.

Desdemona. I will, my lord.

[*Exit* Othello *with* Lodovico *and attendants.*]

Emilia. How goes it now? He looks gentler than he did.

Desdemona. He says he will return incontinent,⁶⁷
And hath commanded me to go to bed,
And bid me to dismiss you.

Emilia. Dismiss me?

Desdemona. It was his bidding. Therefore, good Emilia,
Give me my nightly wearing, and adieu.
We must not now displease him.

Emilia. I would you had never seen him!

Desdemona. So would not I. My love doth so approve him
That even his stubbornness, his checks, his frowns—
Prithee, unpin me—have grace and favor in them.

---

⁶⁷ incontinent—immediately.

[Emilia *prepares* Desdemona *for bed.*]

Emilia. I have laid those sheets you bade me on the bed.

Desdemona. All's one. Good faith, how foolish are our minds!
If I do die before thee, prithee shroud me
25 In one of these same sheets.

Emilia.   Come, come, you talk.[68]

Desdemona. My mother had a maid called Barbary.
She was in love, and he she loved proved mad[69]
And did forsake her. She had a song of "Willow."
An old thing 'twas, but it expressed her fortune,
30 And she died singing it. That song tonight
Will not go from my mind; I have much to do
But to go hang my head all at one side
And sing it like poor Barbary. Prithee, dispatch.

Emilia. Shall I go fetch your nightgown?

35 **Desdemona.** No, unpin me here.
This Lodovico is a proper man.

Emilia. A very handsome man.

Desdemona. He speaks well.

Emilia. I know a lady in Venice would have walked barefoot to Palestine
40 for a touch of his nether lip.

Desdemona [*singing*].
    "The poor soul sat sighing by a sycamore tree,
        Sing all a green willow;[70]
    Her hand on her bosom, her head on her knee,
        Sing willow, willow, willow.
45 The fresh streams ran by her and murmured her moans;
        Sing willow, willow, willow;
    Her salt tears fell from her, and softened the stones—"
Lay by these.
[*Singing.*] "Sing willow, willow, willow—"
50 Prithee, hie thee. He'll come anon.[71]
[*Singing.*] "Sing all a green willow must be my garland.
    Let nobody blame him; his scorn I approve—"
Nay, that's not next.—Hark! Who is 't that knocks?

---

[68] talk—that is, prattle, speak foolishly.

[69] mad—wild, faithless.

[70] willow—the willow was a conventional emblem of disappointed love.

[71] anon—right away.

Emilia. It's the wind.

Desdemona [*Singing*].

55   "I called my love false love; but what said he then?
            Sing willow, willow, willow;
        If I court more women, you'll couch with more men."
    So, get thee gone. Good night. Mine eyes do itch;
    Doth that bode weeping?

Emilia.   'Tis neither here nor there.

60 **Desdemona.** I have heard it said so. O, these men, these men!
    Dost thou in conscience think—tell me, Emilia—
    That there be women do abuse their husbands
    In such gross kind?

Emilia.   There be some such, no question.

Desdemona. Wouldst thou do such a deed for all the world?

65 **Emilia.** Why, would not you?

Desdemona.   No, by this heavenly light!

Emilia. Nor I neither by this heavenly light;
    I might do 't as well i' the dark.

Desdemona. Wouldst thou do such a deed for all the world?

Emilia. The world's a huge thing. It is a great price

70   For a small vice.

Desdemona. Good troth, I think thou wouldst not.

Emilia. By my troth, I think I should, and undo 't when I had done.
    Marry, I would not do such a thing for a joint ring, nor for measures
    of lawn, nor for gowns, petticoats, nor caps, nor any petty exhibi-

75   tion.[72] But for all the whole world! Uds[73] pity, who would not make
    her husband a cuckold to make him a monarch? I should venture
    purgatory for 't.

Desdemona. Beshrew me if I would do such a wrong
    For the whole world.

80 **Emilia.** Why, the wrong is but a wrong i' the world, and having the
    world for your labor, 'tis a wrong in your own world, and you might
    quickly make it right.

Desdemona. I do not think there is any such woman.

Emilia. Yes, a dozen, and as many

---

[72] exhibition—gift.

[73] Uds—God's.

To th' vantage[74] as would store[75] the world they played for.

But I do think it is their husbands' faults

If wives do fall. Say that they slack their duties

And pour our treasures into foreign laps,

Or else break out in peevish jealousies,

90   Throwing restraint upon us? Or say they strike us,

Or scant our former having in despite?

Why, we have galls, and though we have some grace,

Yet have we some revenge. Let husbands know

Their wives have sense like them. They see, and smell,

95   And have their palates both for sweet and sour,

As husbands have. What is it that they do

When they change us for others? Is it sport?[76]

I think it is. And doth affection[77] breed it?

I think it doth. Is 't frailty that thus errs?

100   It is so, too. And have not we affections,

Desires for sport, and frailty, as men have?

Then let them use us well; else let them know,

The ills we do, their ills instruct us so.

Desdemona. Good night, good night. God me such uses send

105   Not to pick bad from bad, but by bad mend![78]

[*Exeunt.*]

Act Five, Scene One

[*Enter* Iago *and* Roderigo.]

Iago. Here stand behind this bulk.[1] Straight will he come.

Wear thy good rapier bare, and put it home.

Quick, quick! Fear nothing. I'll be at thy elbow.

It makes us or it mars us. Think on that,

5   And fix most firm thy resolution.

Roderigo. Be near at hand. I may miscarry in 't.

Iago. Here, at thy hand. Be bold, and take thy stand.

---

[74] To th' vantage—in addition, to boot.

[75] store—populate.

[76] sport—sexual pastime.

[77] affection—passion.

[78] Not . . . mend—that is, not to learn bad conduct from others' badness (as Emilia has suggested women learn from men), but to mend my ways by perceiving what badness is; making spiritual benefit out of evil and adversity.

[1] bulk—framework projecting from the front of a shop.

[Iago *stands aside.* Roderigo *conceals himself.*]

Roderigo. I have no great devotion to the deed;

And yet he hath given me satisfying reasons.

10   'Tis but a man gone. Forth, my sword! He dies.

[*He draws.*]

Iago. I have rubbed this young quat almost to the sense,[2]

And he grows angry. Now, whether he kill Cassio

Or Cassio him, or each do kill the other,

Every way makes my gain. Live Roderigo,[3]

15   He calls me to a restitution large

Of gold and jewels that I bobbed[4] from him

As gifts to Desdemona.

It must not be. If Cassio do remain,

He hath a daily beauty in his life

20   That makes me ugly; and besides, the Moor

May unfold me to him; there stand I in much peril.

No, he must die. Be 't so. I hear him coming.

[*Enter* Cassio.]

Roderigo [*coming forth*]. I know his gait, 'tis he.—Villain, thou diest!

[*He attacks* Cassio.]

Cassio. That thrust had been mine enemy indeed,

25   But that my coat[5] is better than thou know'st

I will make proof of thine.

[*He draws, and wounds* Roderigo.]

Roderigo.   O, I am slain! [*He falls.*]

[Iago, *from behind, wounds* Cassio *in the leg, and exit.*]

Cassio. I am maimed forever. Help, ho! Murder! Murder!

[*Enter* Othello.]

Othello. The voice of Cassio! Iago keeps his word.

Roderigo. O, villain that I am!

30   **Othello.** It is even so.

Cassio. O, help, ho! Light! A surgeon!

Othello. 'Tis he. O brave Iago, honest and just,

That hast such noble sense of thy friend's wrong!

---

[2] quat . . . sense—pimple nearly raw.

[3] Live Roderigo—if Roderigo lives.

[4] bobbed—swindled.

[5] coat—possibly a garment of chain mail under the outer clothing, or simply a tougher coat than Roderigo expected.

<blockquote>
Thou teachest me. Minion,[6] your dear lies dead,
</blockquote>

35 And your unblest fate hies.[7] Strumpet, I come.

Forth of[8] my heart those charms, thine eyes, are blotted;

Thy bed, lust-stained, shall with lust's blood be spotted.

[*Exit* Othello.]

[*Enter* Lodovico *and* Gratiano.]

Cassio. What ho! No watch? No passage?[9] Murder! Murder!

Gratiano. 'Tis some mischance. The voice is very direful.

40 **Cassio.** O, help!

Lodovico. Hark!

Roderigo. O wretched villain!

Lodovico. Two or three groan. 'Tis heavy night;

These may be counterfeits. Let's think 't unsafe

45 To come in to the cry without more help.

[*They remain near the entrance.*]

Roderigo. Nobody come? Then shall I bleed to death.

[*Enter* Iago *in his shirtsleeves, with a light.*]

Lodovico. Hark!

Gratiano. Here's one comes in his shirt, with light and weapons.

Iago. Who's there? Whose noise is this that cries on murder?

50 **Lodovico.** We do not know.

Iago.   Did not you hear a cry?

Cassio. Here, here! For heaven's sake, help me!

Iago.   What's the matter?

[*He moves toward* Cassio.]

Gratiano [*to* Lodovico]. This is Othello's ancient, as I take it.

Lodovico [*to* Gratiano]. The same indeed, a very valiant fellow.

Iago [*to* Cassio]. What are you here that cry so grievously?

55 **Cassio.** Iago? O, I am spoiled,[10] undone by villains!

Give me some help.

Iago. O me, Lieutenant! What villains have done this?

Cassio. I think that one of them is hereabout,

And cannot make away.

Iago.   O treacherous villains!

---

[6] Minion—hussy (that is, Desdemona).

[7] hies—hastens on.

[8] Forth of—from out.

[9] passage—people passing by.

[10] spoiled—ruined, done for.

60   [*To* Lodovico *and* Gratiano.] What are you there? Come in, and give some
        help. [*They advance.*]

Roderigo. O, help me there!

Cassio. That's one of them.

Iago.   O murderous slave! O villain!

[*He stabs* Roderigo.]

Roderigo. O damned Iago! O inhuman dog!

Iago. Kill men i' the dark?—Where be these bloody thieves?—

65   How silent is this town!—Ho! Murder, murder!—

[*To* Lodovico *and* Gratiano.] What may you be? Are you of good or evil?

Lodovico. As you shall prove us, praise[11] us.

Iago. Signor Lodovico?

Lodovico. He, sir.

70 **Iago.** I cry you mercy. Here's Cassio hurt by villains.

Gratiano. Cassio?

Iago. How is 't, brother?

Cassio. My leg is cut in two.

Iago. Marry, heaven forbid!

75   Light, gentlemen! I'll bind it with my shirt.

[*He hands them the light, and tends to* Cassio's *wound.*]

[*Enter* Bianca.]

Bianca. What is the matter, ho? Who is 't that cried?

Iago. Who is 't that cried?

Bianca.   O my dear Cassio!

    My sweet Cassio! O Cassio, Cassio, Cassio!

Iago. O notable strumpet! Cassio, may you suspect

80   Who they should be that have thus mangled you?

Cassio. No.

Gratiano. I am sorry to find you thus. I have been to seek you.

Iago. Lend me a garter. [*He applies a tourniquet.*] So.— O, for a chair,[12]

    To bear him easily hence!

85 **Bianca.** Alas, he faints! O Cassio, Cassio, Cassio!

Iago. Gentlemen all, I do suspect this trash

    To be a party in this injury.—

    Patience awhile, good Cassio.—Come come;

    Lend me a light. [*He shines the light on* Roderigo.] Know we this face

        or no?

---

[11] praise—appraise.

[12] chair—litter.

90   Alas, my friend and my dear countryman
       Roderigo! No.—Yes, sure.—O heaven! Roderigo!

Gratiano. What, of Venice?

Iago. Even he, sir. Did you know him?

Gratiano. Know him? Ay.

95 **Iago.** Signor Gratiano? I cry your gentle pardon.
       These bloody accidents must excuse my manners
       That so neglected you.

Gratiano.   I am glad to see you.

Iago. How do you, Cassio? O, a chair, a chair!

Gratiano. Roderigo!

100 **Iago.** He, he, 'tis he. [*A litter is brought in.*] O, that's well said; the chair.
       Some good man bear him carefully from hence;
       I'll fetch the General's surgeon. [*To* Bianca.] For you, mistress,
       Save you your labor.—He that lies slain here, Cassio,
       Was my dear friend. What malice was between you?

105 **Cassio.** None in the world, nor do I know the man.

Iago [*to* Bianca]. What, look you pale?— O, bear him out o' th' air.[13]

[Cassio *and* Roderigo *are borne off.*]
       Stay you, good gentlemen.—Look you pale, mistress?—
       Do you perceive the gastness[14] of her eye?
       Nay, if you stare,[15] we shall hear more anon.—

110   Behold her well; I pray you, look upon her.
       Do you see, gentlemen? Nay, guiltiness
       Will speak, though tongues were out of use.

[*Enter* Emilia.]

Emilia. 'Las, what's the matter? What's the matter, husband?

Iago. Cassio hath here been set on in the dark

115   By Roderigo and fellows that are scaped.
       He's almost slain, and Roderigo dead.

Emilia. Alas, good gentleman! Alas, good Cassio!

Iago. This is the fruits of whoring. Prithee, Emilia,
       Go know[16] of Cassio where he supped tonight.

120   [*To* Bianca.] What, do you shake at that?

Bianca. He supped at my house, but I therefore shake not.

---

[13] bear . . . air—fresh air was thought to be dangerous for a wound.

[14] gastness—terror.

[15] stare—Iago pretends to interpret Bianca's wild looks as an involuntary confession of guilt.

[16] know—learn.

Iago. O, did he so? I charge you go with me.

Emilia. O, fie upon thee, strumpet!

Bianca. I am no strumpet, but of life as honest

125   As you that thus abuse me.

Emilia. As I? Faugh! Fie upon thee!

Iago. Kind gentlemen, let's go see poor Cassio dressed.[17]—

Come, mistress, you must tell 's another tale.

Emilia, run you to the citadel

130   And tell my lord and lady what hath happed.—

Will you go on afore? [*Aside.*] This is the night

That either makes me or fordoes[18] me quite.

[*Exeunt.*]

Act Five, Scene Two

[*Enter* Othello *with a light, and* Desdemona *in her bed.*]

Othello. It is the cause, it is the cause, my soul.

Let me not name it to you, you chaste stars!

It is the cause. Yet I'll not shed her blood,

Nor scar that whiter skin of hers than snow,

5   And smooth as monumental[19] alabaster.

Yet she must die, else she'll betray more men.

Put out the light, and then put out the light.

If I quench thee, thou flaming minister,

I can again thy former light restore,

10   Should I repent me;[20] but once put out thy light,

Thou cunning'st pattern of excelling nature,

I know not where is that Promethean heat[21]

That can thy light relume.[22] When I have plucked thy rose,

I cannot give it vital growth again;

15   It needs must wither. I'll smell thee on the tree.

[*He kisses her.*]

---

[17] Cassio dressed—Cassio's wounds dressed.

[18] fordoes—undoes, ruins.

[19] monumental—used in making tombs and funeral monuments.

[20] repent me—change my mind.

[21] Promethean heat—divine fire (an allusion to the theft of fire from heaven by Prometheus).

[22] relume—rekindle.

O balmy breath, that dost almost persuade
Justice to break her sword! One more, one more.
Be thus when thou art dead, and I will kill thee,
And love thee after. One more, and that's the last.

[*He kisses her.*]

20 So sweet was ne'er so fatal. I must weep,
But they are cruel tears. This sorrow's heavenly;
It strikes where it doth love. She wakes.

Desdemona. Who's there? Othello?

Othello. Ay, Desdemona.

25 **Desdemona.** Will you come to bed, my lord?

Othello. Have you prayed tonight, Desdemona?

Desdemona. Ay, my lord.

Othello. If you bethink yourself of any crime
Unreconciled as yet to heaven and grace,
30 Solicit for it straight.

Desdemona. Alack, my lord, what may you mean by that?

Othello. Well, do it, and be brief. I will walk by.
I would not kill thy unprepared spirit.
No, heaven forfend! I would not kill thy soul.

35 **Desdemona.** Talk you of killing?

Othello.   Ay, I do.

Desdemona.   Then heaven
Have mercy on me!

Othello.   Amen, with all my heart!

Desdemona. If you say so, I hope you will not kill me.

Othello. Humh!

Desdemona. And yet I fear you; for you're fatal then
40 When your eyes roll so. Why I should fear I know not,
Since guiltiness I know not; but yet I feel I fear.

Othello. Think on thy sins.

Desdemona.   They are loves I bear to you.[23]

Othello. Ay, and for that thou diest.

Desdemona. That death's unnatural that kills for loving.
45 Alas, why gnaw you so your nether lip?
Some bloody passion shakes your very frame.

---

[23] They are . . . you—that is, if I sinned, it was in loving you more than any father or more than God.

These are portents;[24] but yet I hope, I hope,
They do not point on me.

Othello. Peace, and be still!

50   **Desdemona.** I will so. What's the matter?

Othello. That handkerchief which I so loved and gave thee
Thou gav'st to Cassio.

Desdemona.   No, by my life and soul!
Send for the man and ask him.

Othello. Sweet soul, take heed, take heed of **perjury**.[25]

55   Thou art on thy deathbed.

Desdemona. Ay, but not yet to die.

Othello.   Yes, presently.
Therefore confess thee freely of thy sin;
For to deny each article with oath
Cannot remove nor choke the strong conception

60   That I do groan withal. Thou art to die.

Desdemona. Then Lord have mercy on me!

Othello.   I say, amen.

Desdemona. And have you mercy too! I never did
Offend you in my life; never loved Cassio
But with such general warranty[26] of heaven

65   As I might love. I never gave him token.

Othello. By heaven, I saw my handkerchief in 's hand.
O perjured woman! Thou dost stone [27] my heart,
And makes me call what I intend to do
A murder, which I thought a sacrifice.

70   I saw the handkerchief.

Desdemona.   He found it, then.
I never gave it him. Send for him hither;
Let him confess a truth.

Othello.   He hath confessed.

Desdemona. What, my lord?

Othello. That he hath used thee.

Desdemona.   How? Unlawfully?

Othello.   Ay.

---

[24] portents—omens.

[25] **perjury**—lying under oath.

[26] warranty—sanction.

[27] stone—turn to stone, harden.

Desdemona. He will not say so.

Othello.   No, his mouth is stopped;
    Honest Iago hath ta'en order for 't.

Desdemona. O, my fear interprets. What, is he dead?

Othello. Had all his hairs been lives, my great revenge
    Had stomach for them all.

Desdemona. Alas, he is betrayed and I undone! [*She weeps.*]

Othello. Out, strumpet! Weep'st thou for him to my face?

Desdemona. O, banish me, my lord, but kill me not!

Othello. Down, strumpet!

Desdemona. Kill me tomorrow; let me live tonight!

Othello. Nay, if you strive—

Desdemona. But half an hour!

Othello.   Being done, there is no pause.

Desdemona. But while I say one prayer!

Othello.   It is too late. [*Smothers her.*]

Emilia [*at the door*]. My lord, my lord! What, ho! My lord, my lord!

Othello. What noise is this? Not dead? Not yet quite dead?
    I that am cruel am yet merciful;
    I would not have thee linger in thy pain.
    [*He dispatches her.*]
        So, so.

Emilia [*within*]. What, ho! My lord, my lord!

Othello.   Who's there?

Emilia [*within*]. O, good my lord, I would speak a word with you!

Othello. Yes, 'tis Emilia.—By and by.— She's dead.
    'Tis like she comes to speak of Cassio's death.—
    The noise was here. Ha! No more moving?
    Still as the grave. Shall she come in? Were 't good?—
    I think she stirs again. No. What's best to do?
    If she come in, she'll sure speak to my wife.
    My wife! My wife! What wife? I have no wife.
    O, insupportable! O heavy hour!
    Methinks it should be now a huge eclipse
    Of sun and moon, and that th' affrighted globe
    Should yawn[28] at alteration.[29]

---

[28] yawn—gape in amazement; that is, move in an earthquake. (According to Pliny, earthquakes often happen during eclipses.)

[29] at alteration—at these cataclysmic events in nature, well suited to express the horror of Desdemona's death.

Emilia [*within*].   I do beseech you

105   That I may speak with you, O, good my lord!

Othello. I had forgot thee. O, come in, Emilia.—

     Soft,[30] by and by. Let me the curtains draw.—

[*He closes the bed-curtains and opens the door.*]

     Where art thou?

[*Enter Emilia.*]

               What's the matter with thee now?

Emilia. O, my good lord, yonder's foul murders done!

110 **Othello.** What, now?

Emilia. But now, my lord.

Othello. It is the very error of the moon;

     She comes more nearer earth than she was wont,

     And makes men mad.

115 **Emilia.** Cassio, my lord, hath killed a young Venetian

     Called Roderigo.

Othello.   Roderigo killed?

     And Cassio killed?

Emilia.   No, Cassio is not killed.

Othello. Not Cassio killed? Then murder's out of tune,

     And sweet revenge grows harsh.

120 **Desdemona.** O, falsely, falsely murdered!

Emilia. O Lord, what cry is that?

Othello. That? What?

Emilia. Out and alas, that was my lady's voice.

[*She opens the bed-curtains.*]

     Help, help, ho, help! O lady, speak again!

125   Sweet Desdemona! O sweet mistress, speak!

Desdemona. A guiltless death I die.

Emilia. O, who hath done this deed?

Desdemona. Nobody; I myself. Farewell.

     Commend me to my kind lord. O, farewell! [*She dies.*]

130 **Othello.** Why, how should she be murdered?

Emilia.   Alas, who knows?

Othello. You heard her say herself it was not I.

Emilia. She said so. I must needs report the truth.

---

[30] Soft—wait a minute.

Othello. She's like a liar gone to burning hell!

'Twas I that killed her.

Emilia. O, the more angel she,

135 And you the blacker devil!

Othello. She turned to folly,[31] and she was a whore.

Emilia. Thou dost belie her, and thou art a devil.

Othello. She was false as water.

Emilia. Thou art rash as fire to say

140 That she was false. O, she was heavenly true!

Othello. Cassio, did top her. Ask thy husband else.[32]

O, I were damned beneath all depth in hell

But that I did proceed upon just grounds

To this extremity. Thy husband knew it all.

145 **Emilia.** My husband?

Othello. Thy husband.

Emilia. That she was false to wedlock?

Othello. Ay, with Cassio. Nay, had she been true,

If heaven would make me such another world

150 Of one entire and perfect chrysolite,[33]

I'd not have sold her for it.

Emilia. My husband?

Othello. Ay, 'twas he that told me on her first.

An honest man he is, and hates the slime

155 That sticks on filthy deeds.

Emilia. My husband?

Othello. What needs this iterance,[34] woman? I say thy husband.

Emilia. O mistress, villainy hath made mocks with love!

My husband say she was false?

Othello. He, woman;

160 I say thy husband. Dost understand the word?

My friend, thy husband, honest, honest Iago.

Emilia. If he say so, may his **pernicious**[35] soul

Rot half a grain a day! He lies to th' heart.

She was too fond of her most filthy bargain.[36]

---

[31] folly—that is, wantonness, sensual sin.

[32] else—that is, if you don't believe me.

[33] chrysolite—precious topaz.

[34] iterance—iteration, repetition.

[35] **pernicious**—harmful, deadly.

[36] filthy bargain—that is, Othello.

165   **Othello.** Ha? [*He draws.*]
    Emilia. Do thy worst!
        This deed of thine is no more worthy heaven
        Than thou wast worthy her.
    Othello.   Peace, you were best.[37]
    Emilia. Thou hast not half that power to do me harm
170   As I have to be hurt. O gull! O dolt!
        As ignorant as dirt! Thou hast done a deed—
        I care not for thy sword; I'll make thee known,
        Though I lost twenty lives.—Help! Help, ho, help!
        The Moor hath killed my mistress! Murder, murder!
    [*Enter* Montano, Gratiano, *and* Iago.]
175   **Montano.** What is the matter? How now, General?
    Emilia. O, are you come, Iago? You have done well,
        That men must lay their murders on your neck.
    Gratiano. What is the matter?
    Emilia [*to* Iago]. Disprove this villain, if thou be'st a man.
180   He says thou toldst him that his wife was false.
        I know thou didst not; thou'rt not such a villain.
        Speak, for my heart is full.
    Iago. I told him what I thought, and told no more
        Than what he found himself was apt and true.
185   **Emilia.** But did you ever tell him she was false?
    Iago. I did.
    Emilia. You told a lie, an odious, damnèd lie!
        Upon my soul, a lie, a wicked lie.
        She false with Cassio? Did you say with Cassio?
190   **Iago.** With Cassio, mistress. Go to, charm[38] your tongue.
    Emilia. I will not charm my tongue; I am bound to speak.
        My mistress here lies murdered in her bed—
    All. O heavens forfend!
    Emilia. And your reports have set the murder on.
195   **Othello.** Nay, stare not, masters. It is true indeed.
    Gratiano. 'Tis a strange truth.
    Montano. O monstrous act!
    Emilia.   Villainy, villainy, villainy!
        I think upon 't—I think I smell 't! O villainy!

---

[37] you were best—it would be best for you.
[38] charm—keep silent (as though by a magic spell).

I thought so then—I'll kill myself for grief—

200   O villainy, villainy!

Iago. What, are you mad? I charge you, get you home.

Emilia. Good gentlemen, let me have leave to speak.

      'Tis proper I obey him, but not now.

      Perchance, Iago, I will ne'er go home.

205   **Othello.** O! O! O! [Othello *falls on the bed.*]

Emilia.   Nay, lay thee down and roar,

      For thou hast killed the sweetest innocent

      That e'er did lift up eye.[39]

Othello [*rising*].   O, she was foul!

      I scarce did know you, uncle. There lies your niece,

      Whose breath indeed these hands have newly stopped.

210   I know this act shows horrible and grim.

Gratiano. Poor Desdemon! I am glad thy father's dead.

      Thy match was mortal to him, and pure grief

      Shore his old thread in twain.[40] Did he live now,

      This sight would make him do a desperate turn,

215   Yea, curse his better angel from his side,

      And fall to reprobance.[41]

Othello. 'Tis pitiful. But yet Iago knows

      That she with Cassio hath the act of shame

      A thousand times committed. Cassio confessed it;

220   And she did gratify his amorous works

      With that recognizance[42] and pledge of love

      Which I first gave her. I saw it in his hand;

      It was a handkerchief, an antique token

      My father gave my mother.

225   **Emilia.** O God! O heavenly God!

Iago. Zounds, hold your peace.

Emilia.   'Twill out, 'twill out! I peace?

      No, I will speak as liberal as the north.[43]

      Let heaven and men and devils, let them all,

      All, all, cry shame against me, yet I'll speak.

---

[39] lift up eye—lift her eyes to heaven.

[40] Shore . . . twain—sheared the thread of his old age in two (as Atropos, one of the three fates, was thought to do).

[41] reprobance—damnation, that is, suicide.

[42] recognizance—token.

[43] liberal . . . north—freely as the north wind (blows).

230 **Iago.** Be wise, and get you home.

 Emilia.   I will not.

 [Iago *threatens* Emilia.]

 Gratiano.   Fie,

   Your sword upon a woman?

 Emilia. O thou dull Moor! That handkerchief thou speak'st of

   I found by fortune and did give my husband;

   For often, with a solemn earnestness,

235   More than indeed belonged to such a trifle,

   He begged of me to steal 't.

 Iago.   Villainous whore!

 Emilia. She give it Cassio? No, alas! I found it,

   And I did give 't my husband.

 Iago.   Filth, thou liest!

 Emilia. By heaven, I do not, I do not, gentlemen.

240   O murderous coxcomb![44] What should such a fool

   Do with so good a wife?

 Othello. Are there no stones[45] in heaven

   But what serves for the thunder?—Precious[46] villain!

 [*He runs at* Iago; Montano *disarms* Othello. Iago, *from behind, stabs* Emilia.]

 Gratiano. The woman falls! Sure he hath killed his wife.

245 **Emilia.** Ay, ay. O, lay me by my mistress' side.

 [*Exit* Iago.]

 Gratiano. He's gone, but his wife's killed.

 Montano. 'Tis a notorious villain. Take you this weapon,

   Which I have here recovered from the Moor.

   Come, guard the door without. Let him not pass,

250   But kill him rather. I'll after that same villain,

   For 'tis a damnèd slave.

 [*Exit with all but* Othello *and* Emilia, *who has been laid by* Desdemona's *side.*]

 Othello. I am not valiant neither,

   But every puny whipster[47] gets my sword.

   But why should honor outlive honesty?

255   Let it go all.

---

[44] coxcomb—fool (that is, Othello).

[45] stones—bolts, such as those used for thunderbolts.

[46] Precious—complete, utter.

[47] whipster—contemptible fellow (one who is always ready to whip out his sword).

Emilia. What did thy song bode, lady?
Hark, canst thou hear me? I will play the swan,
And die in music. [*She sings.*] "Willow, willow, willow."
Moor, she was chaste. She loved thee, cruel Moor.
So come my soul to bliss as I speak true.
260 So speaking as I think, alas, I die. [*She dies.*]
Othello. I have another weapon in this chamber;
It was a sword of Spain, the ice-brook's temper[48]—
O, here it is. [*He finds a sword.*] Uncle, I must come forth.
Gratiano [*within*]. If thou attempt it, it will cost thee dear.
265 Thou hast no weapon, and perforce must suffer.
Othello. Look in upon me then and speak with me,
Or, naked[49] as I am, I will assault thee.
[*Enter Gratiano.*]
Gratiano. What is the matter?
Othello.   Behold, I have a weapon;
A better never did itself sustain
270 Upon a soldier's thigh. I have seen the day
That, with this little arm and this good sword,
I have made my way through more impediments
Than twenty times your stop.[50] But O, vain boast!
Who can control his fate? 'Tis not so now.
275 Be not afraid, though you do see me weaponed;
Here is my journey's end, here is my butt[51]
And very seamark[52] of my utmost sail.
[Gratiano *steps back.*]
Do you go back dismayed? 'Tis a lost fear;
Man but a rush[53] against Othello's breast
280 And he retires. Where should Othello go?
[*He turns to* Desdemona.]
Now, how dost thou look now? O ill-starred wench!
Pale as thy smock! When we shall meet at compt,[54]
This look of thine will hurl my soul from heaven,

---

[48] ice-brook's temper—tempered in ice-cold water.
[49] naked—unarmed.
[50] stop—power (to stop).
[51] butt—goal, limit (an archery term).
[52] seamark—beacon (marking his destination or limit).
[53] Man . . . rush—wield no more than a reed.
[54] compt—account, judgment day.

And fiends will snatch at it. Cold, cold, my girl?

285 Even like thy chastity. O cursèd, cursèd slave![55]

Whip me, ye devils,

From the possession of this heavenly sight!

Blow me about in winds! Roast me in sulfur!

Wash me in steep-down gulfs of liquid fire!

290 O Desdemon! Dead, Desdemon! Dead! O! O!

[*Enter* Lodovico, Cassio *carried in a litter,* Montano, *and* Iago (*prisoner*), *with officers.*]

Lodovico. Where is this rash and most unfortunate man?

Othello. That's he that was Othello. Here I am.

Lodovico. Where is that viper? Bring the villain forth.

[Iago *is led forward.*]

Othello. I look down towards his feet;[56] but that's a fable.

295 If that thou be'st a devil, I cannot kill thee.

[*He wounds* Iago.]

Lodovico. Wrench his sword from him. [Othello *is disarmed.*]

Iago.   I bleed, sir, but not killed.

Othello. I am not sorry neither. I'd have thee live,

For in my sense 'tis happiness to die.

Lodovico. O thou Othello, that was once so good,

300 Fall'n in the practice[57] of a cursèd slave,

What shall be said to thee?

Othello.   Why, anything.

An honorable murderer, if you will,

For naught I did in hate, but all in honor.

Lodovico. This wretch hath part confessed his villainy.

305 Did you and he consent[58] in Cassio's death?

Othello. Ay.

Cassio. Dear General, I never gave you cause.

Othello. I do believe it, and I ask your pardon.

Will you, I pray, demand that demi-devil

310 Why he hath thus ensnared my soul and body?

Iago. Demand me nothing. What you know, you know.

From this time forth I never will speak word.

---

[55] slave—that is, Othello himself.

[56] towards his feet—that is, to see if they are cloven, as the devil's feet are fabled to be.

[57] in the practice—through the plotting, into the snare.

[58] consent—agree.

Lodovico. What, not to pray?

Gratiano. Torments will ope your lips.[59]

315   **Othello.** Well, thou dost best.

Lodovico. Sir, you shall understand what hath befall'n,
    Which, as I think, you know not. Here is a letter
    Found in the pocket of the slain Roderigo;
    And here another. [*He produces letters.*] The one of them imports
320   The death of Cassio, to be undertook
    By Roderigo.

Othello. O villain!

Cassio.   Most heathenish and most gross!

Lodovico [*showing another paper*]. Now here's another discontented[60] paper
    Found in his pocket too. And this, it seems,
325   Roderigo meant t' have sent this damnèd villain;
    But that belike Iago in the interim
    Came in and satisfied him.

Othello. O thou pernicious caitiff!—
    How came you, Cassio, by that handkerchief
330   That was my wife's?

Cassio.   I found it in my chamber;
    And he himself confessed but even now
    That there he dropped it for a special purpose
    Which wrought to his desire.

Othello.   O fool, fool, fool!

Cassio. There is besides in Roderigo's letter
335   How he upbraids[61] Iago, that he made him
    Brave[62] me upon the watch, whereon it came
    That I was cast; and even but now he spake,
    After long seeming dead, Iago hurt him,
    Iago set him on.

340   **Lodovico** [*to Othello*]. You must forsake this room and go with us.
    Your power and your command is taken off,
    And Cassio rules in Cyprus. For this slave,
    If there be any cunning cruelty
    that can torment him much and hold him long,

---

[59] Torments . . . lips—torture will force you to confess.

[60] discontented—full of discontent.

[61] upbraids—reproaches.

[62] Brave—defy.

345 It shall be his. You shall close prisoner rest[63]
Till that the nature of your fault be known
To the Venetian state.—Come, bring away.

Othello. Soft you; a word or two before you go.
I have done the state some service, and they know 't.
350 No more of that. I pray you, in your letters,
When you shall these unlucky[64] deeds relate,
Speak of me as I am; nothing **extenuate,**[65]
Nor set down aught in malice. Then must you speak
Of one that loved not wisely but too well;
355 Of one not easily jealous but, being wrought,[66]
Perplexed[67] in the extreme; of one whose hand,
Like the base Indian,[68] threw a pearl away
Richer than all his tribe; of one whose subdued[69] eyes,
Albeit[70] unusèd to the melting mood,
360 Drops tears as fast as the Arabian trees
Their medicinable gum.[71] Set you down this;
And say besides that in Aleppo once,
Where a **malignant**[72] and a turbaned Turk
Beat a Venetian and traduced[73] the state,
365 I took by th' throat the circumcisèd dog
And smote him, thus. [*He stabs himself.*]

Lodovico. O bloody period![74]

Gratiano. All that is spoke is marred.

Othello. I kissed thee ere I killed thee. No way but this,
Killing myself, to die upon a kiss.
[*He kisses* Desdemona *and dies.*]

---

[63] rest—remain.

[64] unlucky—unfortunate.

[65] **extenuate**—lessen.

[66] wrought—worked upon, worked into a frenzy.

[67] Perplexed—distraught.

[68] Indian—that is, an ignorant savage who cannot recognize the value of a precious jewel.

[69] subdued—that is, overcome by grief.

[70] Albeit—although.

[71] gum—that is, myrrh.

[72] **malignant**—showing great ill-will.

[73] traduced—slandered.

[74] period—termination, conclusion.

370   **Cassio.** This did I fear, but thought he had no weapon;

        For he was great of heart.

        Lodovico [*to* Iago]. O Spartan dog,[75]

        More fell[76] than anguish, hunger, or the sea!

        Look on the tragic loading of this bed.

375   This is thy work. The object poisons sight;

        Let it be hid. Gratiano, keep[77] the house,

    [*The bed-curtains are drawn.*]

        And seize upon the fortunes of the Moor,

        For they succeed on you. [*To* Cassio.] To you, Lord Governor,

        Remains the censure of this hellish villain,

380   The time, the place, the torture. O, enforce it!

        Myself will straight aboard, and to the state

        This heavy act with heavy heart relate.

    [*Exeunt.*]

---

[75] Spartan dog—Spartan dogs were noted for their savagery and silence.

[76] fell—cruel.

[77] keep—remain in.

UNDERSTANDING THE PLAY

Act One

1. In Scene One, what reason does Iago give Roderigo to explain his hatred for Othello?

2. In Scene Two, how does Brabantio feel that Othello has won Desdemona's love?

3. In Scene Three, how does Othello say that he won Desdemona's love?

4. Why does Desdemona feel she should be allowed to accompany Othello to Cyprus? Why does he agree?

5. How does Iago advise Roderigo?

Act Two

1. When Scene One opens, how has the military situation in Cyprus changed?

2. Under Desdemona's questioning, what attitudes does Iago reveal toward women?

3. In Scene Three, how does Iago arrange to bring Cassio into discredit with Othello?

4. What does Iago advise Cassio to do to restore himself with Othello?

5. Why does he give him this advice?

Act Three

1. In Scene Three, Othello says of Desdemona, "Perdition catch my soul/But I do love thee! And when I love thee not,/Chaos is come again." What does this suggest about his character?

2. What are the steps by which Iago induces Othello to believe in Desdemona's infidelity?

3. Why do you think Othello responds so readily to Iago's hints about Desdemona and Cassio?

4. How does Iago respond to Othello's demand for visual proof of Desdemona's infidelity?

5. In Scene Four, how does Othello's manner toward Desdemona change when he has become convinced of her infidelity?

Act Four

1. In Scene One, what prompts Othello to faint? What does this suggest about his state of mind?

2. How does Iago use Cassio's relationship with Bianca to further arouse Othello's jealousy and rage?

3. How does Lodovico interpret Othello's behavior toward Desdemona?

4. In Scene Two, how does Desdemona respond when Othello accuses her of being unfaithful? How does Emilia repond?

5. In Scene Three, how do Desdemona and Emilia differ in their views of infidelity?

Act Five

1. In Scene One, what is Iago's motive for killing Roderigo?

2. At the beginning of Scene Two, Othello repeatedly refers to an unspecified "cause" for killing Desdemona. If you judge by his words in this scene, what is Othello's specific motive in murdering her?

3. At what point does Othello recognize he has been tricked by Iago?

4. Why do you think Iago refuses to explain his actions?

5. How does Othello attempt to explain his fall?

ANALYZING THE PLAY

1. The conflict in a play is the struggle between opposing forces that gives movement to the dramatic plot. What is the fundamental conflict in *Othello*?

2. The climax—or crisis—in the plot is the turning point in the struggle when one of the contending forces gets the upper hand. In *Othello*, where does this turning point occur?

3. According to Aristotle, a tragic hero is one whose fall was brought about "not by vice and depravity, but by some error or frailty." What faults in his character cause Othello's fall?

4. How do you interpret Iago's villainy? What seems to motivate him? Does he seem a human being with understandable motives or simply a fiend?

5. Modern interpretations of *Othello* have emphasized the importance of Iago. In what sense could he be said to be the central character in the play?

Molière ▶

The Misanthrope

BY MOLIÈRE

During the Renaissance, theater developed later and more slowly in France than in England. Although the form of Italian improvisational theater known as the commedia dell'arte was popular in Paris from the beginning of the 1600s, regular comedy and tragedy did not flourish in France until the late 1620s. French playhouses of this period were often converted indoor tennis courts, which produced long, narrow theaters with galleries on three sides and a pit in front providing standing room. Raised at one end was a shallow, curtainless stage. Scenery was minimal, but costumes, by contrast, were very elaborate.

French Neoclassical Drama

Unlike English dramatists, French playwrights were strongly influenced by the critical theories of the Greek philosopher Aristotle. French neoclassical drama stressed the dramatic unities of time, place, and action: a play was to present only one principal action occupying only one day and showing only what could be observed by a spectator sitting in one place. Following these rules, playwrights such as Pierre Corneille (1606–1684), Jean Racine (1639–1699), and Molière (1622–1673) produced a Golden Age of French neoclassical drama. This era reached its peak in 1680 with the establishment of the Comédie Française—the first national theater in existence.

Actor and Playwright

Molière was the stage name of Jean-Baptiste Poquelin, the son of the upholsterer at the French court. Over his family's objections, he began his career in the theater as an actor in a theatrical company that toured the provinces performing farces in the style of the commedia dell'arte. This experience shaped his dramatic style when he returned to Paris with his company in the late 1650s and began to write his own plays. During the next 15 years, he wrote, directed, and performed in over 30 plays, while also serving as the manager of his theater company. Worn out by overwork, he died at fifty-one, suffering a fatal hemorrhage onstage while performing the title role in his last comedy, The Imaginary Invalid.

Molière's Comic Style

Molière's comedy was influenced by the commedia dell'arte, *but in his hands its stock characters become fully rounded individuals. Molière's humor is tolerant, expressing, as one critic observes, "an unusual warmth; not sentiment, not tenderness, but a feeling for and appreciation of the central dignity and worth of human beings." Nevertheless, his plays are also sharply satirical, particularly of the middle class, attacking influential groups such as doctors and lawyers. While delighting the royal court and gaining Molière the patronage of King Louis XIV, his satire also made him many enemies. His attack on religious hypocrisy,* Tartuffe, *caused so much anger that it was banned from the stage for five years after its first performance.* The Misanthrope *is often regarded as Molière's masterpiece. In its central character, Alceste, he presents someone probably much like himself, a sensitive, lonely man taking a disillusioned look at the cruelties and follies of the world.*

CHARACTERS

Alceste, in love with Célimène
Philinte, Alceste's friend
Oronte, in love with Célimène
Célimène, Alceste's beloved
Eliante, Célimène's cousin
Arsinoé, a friend of Célimène's

Acaste, marquess
Clitandre, marquess
Basque, Célimène's servant
A Guard of the Marshalsea
Dubois, Alceste's valet

The scene throughout is in Célimène's house at Paris.

Act One, Scene One

[Philinte, Alceste]

Philinte. Now, what's got into you?

Alceste [*seated*].   Kindly leave me alone.

Philinte. Come, come, what is it? This **lugubrious**[1] tone . . .

Alceste. Leave me, I said; you spoil my solitude.

Philinte. Oh, listen to me, now, and don't be rude.

5 **Alceste.** I choose to be rude, Sir, and to be hard of hearing.

Philinte. These ugly moods of yours are not endearing;
Friends though we are, I really must insist . . .

Alceste [*abruptly rising*]. Friends? Friends, you say? Well, cross me off
your list.
I've been your friend till now, as you well know;

10 But after what I saw a moment ago
I tell you flatly that our ways must part.
I wish no place in a dishonest heart.

---

[1] **lugubrious**—mournful, gloomy (with sense of exaggeration).

Philinte. Why, what have I done, Alceste? Is this quite just?

Alceste. My God, you ought to die of self-disgust.

15   I call your conduct inexcusable, Sir,

    And every man of honor will concur.

    I see you almost hug a man to death,

    Exclaim for joy until you're out of breath,

    And supplement these loving demonstrations

20   With endless offers, vows, and protestations;[2]

    Then when I ask you "Who was that?", I find

    That you can barely bring his name to mind!

    Once the man's back is turned, you cease to love him,

    And speak with absolute indifference of him!

25   By God, I say it's base and scandalous

    To falsify the heart's affections thus;

    If I caught myself behaving in such a way,

    I'd hang myself for shame, without delay.

Philinte. It hardly seems a hanging matter to me;

30   I hope that you will take it graciously

    If I extend myself a slight **reprieve**,[3]

    And live a little longer, by your leave.

Alceste. How dare you joke about a crime so grave?[4]

Philinte. What crime? How else are people to behave?

35 **Alceste.** I'd have them be sincere, and never part

    With any word that isn't from the heart.

Philinte. When someone greets us with a show of pleasure,

    It's but polite to give him equal measure,

    Return his love the best that we know how,

40   And trade him offer for offer, vow for vow.

Alceste. No, no, this formula you'd have me follow,

    However fashionable, is false and hollow,

    And I despise the frenzied operations

    Of all these barterers of protestations,

45   These lavishers of meaningless embraces,

    These utterers of obliging commonplaces,[5]

    Who court and flatter everyone on earth

---

[2] protestations—emphatic declarations.

[3] **reprieve**—delay in carrying out a sentence.

[4] grave—serious.

[5] commonplaces—trite remarks.

And praise the fool no less than the man of worth.
Should you rejoice that someone fondles you,

50 Offers his love and service, swears to be true,
And fills your ears with praises of your name,
When to the first damned fop[6] he'll say the same?
No, no: no self-respecting heart would dream
Of prizing so promiscuous an esteem;[7]

55 However high the praise, there's nothing worse
Than sharing honors with the universe.
Esteem is founded on comparison:
To honor all men is to honor none.
Since you embrace this indiscriminate vice,

60 Your friendship comes at far too cheap a price;
I spurn the easy tribute of a heart
Which will not set the worthy man apart:
I choose, Sir, to be chosen; and in fine,[8]
The friend of mankind is no friend of mine.

65 **Philinte.** But in polite society, custom decrees
That we show certain outward courtesies. . . .

Alceste. Ah, no! we should condemn with all our force
Such false and artificial intercourse.[9]
Let men behave like men; let them display

70 Their inmost hearts in everything they say;
Let the heart speak, and let our sentiments
Not mask themselves in silly compliments.

Philinte. In certain cases it would be uncouth
And most absurd to speak the naked truth;

75 With all respect for your exalted notions,
It's often best to veil one's true emotions.
Wouldn't the social fabric come undone
If we were wholly frank with everyone?
Suppose you met with someone you couldn't bear;

80 Would you inform him of it then and there?

Alceste. Yes.

---

[6] fop—person obsessed with details of dress.

[7] so promiscuous an esteem—so indiscriminate an expression of respect.

[8] in fine—in conclusion.

[9] intercourse—communication.

Philinte.   Then you'd tell old Emilie it's pathetic
The way she daubs[10] her features with cosmetic
And plays the gay coquette[11] at sixty-four?

Alceste. I would.

Philinte.   And you'd call Dorilas a bore,

85   And tell him every ear at court is lame
From hearing him brag about his noble name?

Alceste. Precisely.

Philinte.   Ah, you're joking.

Alceste.   *Au contraire*:[12]
In this regard there's none I'd choose to spare.
All are corrupt; there's nothing to be seen

90   In court or town but aggravates my spleen.[13]
I fall into deep gloom and melancholy
When I survey the scene of human folly,
Finding on every hand base[14] flattery,
Injustice, fraud, self-interest, treachery. . . .

95   Ah, it's too much; mankind has grown so base,
I mean to break with the whole human race.

Philinte. This philosophic rage is a bit extreme;
You've no idea how comical you seem;
Indeed, we're like those brothers in the play

100   Called *School for Husbands*,[15] one of whom was prey . . .

Alceste. Enough, now! None of your stupid similes.[16]

Philinte. Then let's have no more **tirades**,[17] if you please.
The world won't change, whatever you say or do;
And since plain speaking means so much to you,

105   I'll tell you plainly that by being frank
You've earned the reputation of a crank,[18]
And that you're thought ridiculous when you rage
And rant against the manners of the age.

---

[10] daubs—paints crudely.

[11] gay coquette—pleasure-seeking flirt.

[12] *Au contraire*—on the contrary.

[13] aggravates my spleen—arouses my anger.

[14] base—morally low.

[15] *School for Husbands*—play by Molière.

[16] similes—comparisons.

[17] **tirades**—angry speeches.

[18] crank—eccentric.

Alceste. So much the better; just what I wish to hear.

110 No news could be more grateful to my ear.

All men are so detestable in my eyes,

I should be sorry if they thought me wise.

Philinte. Your hatred's very sweeping, is it not?

Alceste. Quite right: I hate the whole degraded lot.

115 **Philinte.** Must all poor human creatures be embraced,

Without distinction, by your vast distaste?

Even in these bad times, there are surely a few . . .

Alceste. No, I include all men in one dim view:

Some men I hate for being rogues; the others

120 I hate because they treat the rogues like brothers,

And, lacking a virtuous scorn for what is vile,

Receive the villain with a **complaisant**[19] smile.

Notice how tolerant people choose to be

Toward that bold rascal who's at law with me.

125 His social polish can't conceal his nature;

One sees at once that he's a treacherous creature;

No one could possibly be taken in

By those soft speeches and that sugary grin.

The whole world knows the shady means by which

130 The low-brow's[20] grown so powerful and rich,

And risen to a rank so bright and high

That virtue can but blush, and merit sigh.

Whenever his name comes up in conversation,

None will defend his wretched reputation;

135 Call him knave,[21] liar, scoundrel, and all the rest,

Each head will nod, and no one will protest.

And yet his smirk is seen in every house,

He's greeted everywhere with smiles and bows,

And when there's any honor that can be got

140 By pulling strings, he'll get it, like as not.

My God! It chills my heart to see the ways

Men come to terms with evil nowadays;

Sometimes, I swear, I'm moved to flee and find

Some desert land unfouled by humankind.

---

[19] **complaisant**—eager to please.

[20] low-brow—uncultured person.

[21] knave—rascal.

145　**Philinte.** Come, let's forget the follies of the times
　　　And pardon mankind for its petty crimes;
　　　Let's have an end of rantings and of railings,[22]
　　　And show some **leniency**[23] toward human failings.
　　　This world requires a pliant rectitude;[24]
150　　Too stern a virtue makes one stiff and rude;
　　　Good sense views all extremes with detestation,
　　　And bids us to be noble in moderation.
　　　The rigid virtues of the ancient days
　　　Are not for us; they jar with all our ways
155　　And ask of us too lofty a perfection.
　　　Wise men accept their times without objection,
　　　And there's no greater folly, if you ask me,
　　　Than trying to reform society.
　　　Like you, I see each day a hundred and one
160　　Unhandsome deeds that might be better done,
　　　But still, for all the faults that meet my view,
　　　I'm never known to storm and rave like you.
　　　I take men as they are, or let them be,
　　　And teach my soul to bear their frailty;
165　　And whether in court or town, whatever the scene,
　　　My phlegm's[25] as philosophic as your spleen.
　　　Alceste. This phlegm which you so eloquently commend,
　　　Does nothing ever rile it up, my friend?
　　　Suppose some man you trust should treacherously
170　　Conspire to rob you of your property,
　　　And do his best to wreck your reputation?
　　　Wouldn't you feel a certain indignation?
　　　Philinte. Why, no. These faults of which you so complain
　　　Are part of human nature, I maintain,
175　　And it's no more a matter for disgust
　　　That men are knavish, selfish and unjust,
　　　Than that the vulture dines upon the dead,
　　　And wolves are furious, and apes ill-bred.

---

[22] railings—harsh criticisms.

[23] **leniency**—softness.

[24] pliant rectitude—adaptable righteousness.

[25] phlegm—calmness.

Alceste. Shall I see myself betrayed, robbed, torn to bits,

180   And not . . . Oh, let's be still and rest our wits.

Enough of reasoning, now. I've had my fill.

Philinte. Indeed, you would do well, Sir, to be still.

Rage less at your opponent, and give some thought

To how you'll win this lawsuit that he's brought.

185 **Alceste.** I assure you I'll do nothing of the sort.

Philinte. Then who will plead your case before the court?

Alceste. Reason and right and justice will plead for me.

Philinte. Oh, Lord. What judges do you plan to see?

Alceste. Why, none. The justice of my cause is clear.

190 **Philinte.** Of course, man; but there's politics to fear. . . .

Alceste. No, I refuse to lift a hand. That's flat.

I'm either right, or wrong.

Philinte.   Don't count on that.

Alceste. No, I'll do nothing.

Philinte.   Your enemy's influence

Is great, you know . . .

Alceste.   That makes no difference.

195 **Philinte.** It will; you'll see.

Alceste.   Must honor bow to guile?[26]

If so, I shall be proud to lose the trial.

Philinte. Oh, really . . .

Alceste.   I'll discover by this case

Whether or not men are sufficiently base

And **impudent**[27] and villainous and perverse[28]

200   To do me wrong before the universe.

Philinte. What a man!

Alceste.   Oh, I could wish, whatever the cost,

Just for the beauty of it, that my trial were lost.

Philinte. If people heard you talking so, Alceste,

They'd split their sides. Your name would be a jest.

205 **Alceste.** So much the worse for jesters.

Philinte.   May I enquire

Whether this rectitude you so admire,

---

[26] guile—trickery.

[27] **impudent**—disrespectful.

[28] perverse—willfully wrong.

And these hard virtues you're enamored of
Are qualities of the lady whom you love?
It much surprises me that you, who seem
210   To view mankind with furious disesteem,
Have yet found something to enchant your eyes
Amidst a species which you so despise.
And what is more amazing, I'm afraid,
Is the most curious choice your heart has made.
215   The honest Eliante is fond of you,
Arsinoé, the prude, admires you too;
And yet your spirit's been perversely led
To choose the flighty Célimène instead,
Whose brittle malice[29] and coquettish ways
220   So typify the manners of our days.
How is it that the traits you most **abhor**[30]
Are bearable in this lady you adore?
Are you so blind with love that you can't find them?
Or do you contrive, in her case, not to mind them?

225   **Alceste.** My love for that young widow's not the kind
That can't perceive defects; no, I'm not blind.
I see her faults, despite my **ardent**[31] love,
And all I see I fervently reprove.[32]
And yet I'm weak; for all her falsity,
230   That woman knows the art of pleasing me,
And though I never cease complaining of her,
I swear I cannot manage not to love her.
Her charm outweighs her faults; I can but aim
To cleanse her spirit in my love's pure flame.

235   **Philinte.** That's no small task; I wish you all success.
You think then that she loves you?

Alceste.   Heavens, yes!
I wouldn't love her did she not love me.

Philinte. Well, if her taste for you is plain to see,
Why do these rivals cause you such despair?

---

[29] **brittle malice**—cold ill-will.

[30] **abhor**—hate, detest.

[31] **ardent**—passionate.

[32] **fervently reprove**—strongly criticize.

240 **Alceste.** True love, Sir, is possessive, and cannot bear
To share with all the world. I'm here today
To tell her she must send that mob away.

Philinte. If I were you, and had your choice to make,
Eliante, her cousin, would be the one I'd take;

245 That honest heart, which cares for you alone,
Would harmonize far better with your own.

Alceste. True, true: each day my reason tells me so;
But reason doesn't rule in love, you know.

Philinte. I fear some bitter sorrow is in store;

250 This love . . .

Act One, Scene Two

[Oronte, Alceste, Philinte]

Oronte [*to* Alceste]. The servants told me at the door
That Eliante and Célimène were out,
But when I heard, dear Sir, that you were about,
I came to say, without exaggeration,

5 That I hold you in the vastest admiration,
And that it's always been my dearest desire
To be the friend of one I so admire.
I hope to see my love of merit requited,[33]
And you and I in friendship's bond united.

10 I'm sure you won't refuse—if I may be frank
A friend of my devotedness—and rank.

[*During this speech of* Oronte's Alceste *is abstracted, and seems unaware that
he is being spoken to. He only breaks off his reverie*[34] *when* Oronte *says:*]
It was for you, if you please, that my words were intended.

Alceste. For me, Sir?

Oronte.   Yes, for you. You're not offended?

Alceste. By no means. But this much surprises me . . . .

15 The honor comes most unexpectedly. . . .

Oronte. My high regard should not astonish you;
The whole world feels the same. It is your due.

Alceste. Sir . . .

---

[33] *requited*—returned.

[34] *reverie*—daydream.

Oronte.   Why, in all the State there isn't one
          Can match your merits; they shine, Sir, like the sun.
20 **Alceste.** Sir . . .
     Oronte.   You are higher in my estimation
          Than all that's most illustrious in the nation.
     Alceste. Sir . . .
     Oronte.   If I lie, may heaven strike me dead!
          To show you that I mean what I have said,
          Permit me, Sir, to embrace you most sincerely,
25   And swear that I will prize our friendship dearly.
          Give me your hand. And now, Sir, if you choose,
          We'll make our vows.
     Alceste.   Sir . . .
     Oronte.   What! You refuse?
     Alceste. Sir, it's a very great honor you extend:
          But friendship is a sacred thing, my friend;
30   It would be profanation[35] to bestow
          The name of friend on one you hardly know.
          All parts are better played when well-rehearsed;
          Let's put off friendship, and get acquainted first.
          We may discover it would be unwise
35   To try to make our natures harmonize.
     Oronte. By heaven! You're **sagacious**[36] to the core;
          This speech has made me admire you even more.
          Let time, then, bring us closer day by day;
          Meanwhile, I shall be yours in every way.
40   If, for example, there should be anything
          You wish at court, I'll mention it to the King.
          I have his ear, of course; it's quite well known
          That I am much in favor with the throne.
          In short, I am your servant. And now, dear friend,
45   Since you have such fine judgment, I intend
          To please you, if I can, with a small sonnet
          I wrote not long ago. Please comment on it,
          And tell me whether I ought to publish it.
     Alceste. You must excuse me, Sir; I'm hardly fit
50   To judge such matters.

---

[35] profanation—defilement, desecration.
[36] **sagacious**—wise.

Oronte. Why not?

Alceste. I am, I fear,
Inclined to be unfashionably sincere.

Oronte. Just what I ask; I'd take no satisfaction
In anything but your sincere reaction.
I beg you not to dream of being kind.

55 **Alceste.** Since you desire it, Sir, I'll speak my mind.

Oronte. *Sonnet. It's a sonnet. . . . Hope . . .* The poem's addressed
To a lady who wakened hopes within my breast.
Hope . . . this is not the **pompous**[37] sort of thing,
Just modest little verses, with a tender ring.

60 **Alceste.** Well, we shall see.

Oronte. *Hope . . .* I'm anxious to hear
Whether the style seems properly smooth and clear,
And whether the choice of words is good or bad.

Alceste. We'll see, we'll see.

Oronte. Perhaps I ought to add
That it took me only a quarter-hour to write it.

65 **Alceste.** The time's irrelevant, Sir: kindly recite it.

Oronte [*reading*].

Hope comforts us awhile, 'tis true,
Lulling our cares with careless laughter,
And yet such joy is full of rue,[38]
My Phyllis, if nothing follows after.

70 **Philinte.** I'm charmed by this already; the style's delightful.

Alceste [*sotto voce,*[39] *to* Philinte]. How can you say that? Why, the thing
is frightful.

Oronte. *Your fair face smiled on me awhile,*
But was it kindness so to enchant me?
'Twould have been fairer not to smile,
75 *If hope was all you meant to grant me.*

Philinte. What a clever thought! How handsomely you phrase it!

Alceste [*sotto voce, to* Philinte]. You know the thing is trash. How dare
you praise it?

Oronte. *If it's to be my passion's fate*
Thus everlastingly to wait,

---

[37] **pompous**—exaggeratedly formal, overly dignified.

[38] *rue*—sorrow.

[39] *sotto voce*—in a whisper.

80 *Then death will come to set me free:*
For death is fairer than the fair;
Phyllis, to hope is to despair
When one must hope eternally.

Philinte. The close is exquisite—full of feeling and grace.

85 **Alceste** [*sotto voce, aside*]. Oh, blast the close; you'd better close your face
Before you send your lying soul to hell.

Philinte. I can't remember a poem I've liked so well.

Alceste [*sotto voce, aside*]. Good Lord!

Oronte [*to* Philinte].   I fear you're flattering me a bit.

Philinte. Oh, no!

Alceste [*sotto voce, aside*]. What else d'you call it, you hypocrite?

90 **Oronte** [*to* Alceste]. But you, Sir, keep your promise now: don't shrink
From telling me sincerely what you think.

Alceste. Sir, these are delicate matters; we all desire
To be told that we've the true poetic fire.
But once, to one whose name I shall not mention,
95 I said, regarding some verse of his invention,
That gentlemen should rigorously control
That itch to write which often afflicts the soul;
That one should curb the heady inclination
To publicize one's little **avocation**;[40]
100 And that in showing off one's works of art
One often plays a very clownish part.

Oronte. Are you suggesting in a **devious**[41] way
That I ought not . . .

Alceste.   Oh, that I do not say.
Further, I told him that no fault is worse
105 Than that of writing frigid, lifeless verse,
And that the merest whisper of such a shame
Suffices[42] to destroy a man's good name.

Oronte. D'you mean to say my sonnet's dull and **trite**?[43]

Alceste. I don't say that. But I went on to cite
110 Numerous cases of once-respected men
Who came to grief by taking up the pen.

---

[40] **avocation**—hobby.

[41] **devious**—not straightforward; shifty.

[42] Suffices—is enough.

[43] **trite**—commonplace.

Oronte. And am I like them? Do I write so poorly?

Alceste. I don't say that. But I told this person, "Surely
You're under no necessity to compose;

115   Why you should wish to publish, heaven knows.
There's no excuse for printing **tedious**[44] rot
Unless one writes for bread, as you do not.
Resist temptation, then, I beg of you;
Conceal your pastimes from the public view;

120   And don't give up, on any provocation,
Your present high and courtly reputation,
To purchase at a greedy printer's shop
The name of silly author and scribbling fop."
These were the points I tried to make him see.

125   **Oronte.** I sense that they are also aimed at me;
But now—about my sonnet—I'd like to be told . . .

Alceste. Frankly, that sonnet should be pigeonholed.
You've chosen the worst models to imitate.
The style's unnatural. Let me illustrate:

130   For. example, *Your fair face smiled on me awhile,*
Followed by, *'Twould have been fairer not to smile!*
Or this: *such joy is full of rue;*
Or this: *For death is fairer than the fair;*
Or, *Phyllis, to hope is to despair*

135   *When one must hope eternally!*
This artificial style, that's all the fashion,
Has neither taste, nor honesty, nor passion;
It's nothing but a sort of wordy play,
And nature never spoke in such a way.

140   What, in this shallow age, is not debased?
Our fathers, though less refined, had better taste;
I'd barter all that men admire today
For one old love-song I shall try to say:
  If the King had given me for my own

145   *Paris, his citadel,*
  And I for that must leave alone
  Her whom I love so well,
  I'd say then to the Crown,

---

[44] **tedious**—tiresome.

>   *Take back your glittering town;*
> 150   *My darling is more fair, I swear,*
>   *My darling is more fair.*

> The rhyme's not rich, the style is rough and old,
> But don't you see that it's the purest gold
> Beside the tinsel nonsense now preferred,
> 155 And that there's passion in its every word?

>   *If the King had given me for my own*
>   *Paris, his citadel,*
>   *And I for that must leave alone*
>   *Her whom I love so well,*
> 160   *I'd say then to the Crown,*
>   *Take back your glittering town;*
>   *My darling is more fair, I swear,*
>   *My darling is more fair.*

> There speaks a loving heart. [*To* Philinte.] You're laughing, eh?
> 165 Laugh on, my precious wit. Whatever you say,
> I hold that song's worth all the bibelots[45]
> That people hail today with ah's and oh's.

Oronte. And I maintain my sonnet's very good.

Alceste. It's not at all surprising that you should.
170 You have your reasons; permit me to have mine
For thinking that you cannot write a line.

Oronte. Others have praised my sonnet to the skies.

Alceste. I lack their art of telling pleasant lies.

Oronte. You seem to think you've got no end of wit.

175 **Alceste.** To praise your verse, I'd need still more of it.

Oronte. I'm not in need of your approval, Sir.

Alceste. That's good; you couldn't have it if you were.

Oronte. Come now, I'll lend you the subject of my sonnet;
I'd like to see you try to improve upon it.

180 **Alceste.** I might, by chance, write something just as shoddy;
But then I wouldn't show it to everybody.

Oronte. You're most opinionated and conceited.

Alceste. Go find your flatterers, and be better treated.

Oronte. Look here, my little fellow, pray watch your tone.

185 **Alceste.** My great big fellow, you'd better watch your own.

---

[45] bibelots—trinkets.

Philinte [*stepping between them*]. Oh, please, please, gentlemen! This will
    never do.

Oronte. The fault is mine, and I leave the field to you.
    I am your servant, Sir, in every way.

Alceste. And I, Sir, am your most abject valet.[46]

Act One, Scene Three

[Philinte, Alceste]

Philinte. Well, as you see, sincerity in excess
    Can get you into a very pretty mess;
    Oronte was hungry for appreciation. . . .

Alceste. Don't speak to me.

Philinte.   What?

Alceste.   No more conversation.

5 **Philinte.** Really, now . . .

Alceste.   Leave me alone.

Philinte.   If I . . .

Alceste.   Out of my sight!

Philinte. But what . . .

Alceste.   I won't listen.

Philinte.   But . . .

Alceste.   Silence!

Philinte.   Now, is it polite . . .

Alceste. By heaven, I've had enough. Don't follow me.

Philinte. Ah, you're just joking. I'll keep you company.

Act Two, Scene One

[Alceste, Célimène]

Alceste. Shall I speak plainly, Madam? I confess
    Your conduct gives me infinite distress,
    And my resentment's grown too hot to smother.
    Soon, I foresee, we'll break with one another.

5   If I said otherwise, I should deceive you;
    Sooner or later, I shall be forced to leave you,

---

[46] abject valet—humble servant.

And if I swore that we shall never part,
I should misread the omens[1] of my heart.
Célimène. You kindly saw me home, it would appear,
10   So as to pour invectives[2] in my ear.
Alceste. I've no desire to quarrel. But I **deplore**[3]
Your inability to shut the door
On all these suitors who **beset**[4] you so.
There's what annoys me, if you care to know.
15   **Célimène.** Is it my fault that all these men pursue me?
Am I to blame if they're attracted to me?
And when they gently beg an audience,
Ought I to take a stick and drive them hence?
Alceste. Madam, there's no necessity for a stick;
20   A less responsive heart would do the trick.
Of your attractiveness I don't complain;
But those your charms attract, you then **detain**[5]
By a most melting and receptive manner,
And so enlist their hearts beneath your banner.
25   It's the agreeable hopes which you excite
That keep these lovers round you day and night;
Were they less liberally smiled upon,
That sighing troop would very soon be gone.
But tell me, Madam, why it is that lately
30   This man Clitandre interests you so greatly?
Because of what high merits do you deem
Him worthy of the honor of your esteem?
Is it that your admiring glances linger
On the splendidly long nail of his little finger?
35   Or do you share the general deep respect
For the blond wig he chooses to affect?
Are you in love with his embroidered hose?
Do you adore his ribbons and his bows?
Or is it that this paragon[6] bewitches

---

[1] omens—signs through which the future can be read.

[2] invectives—abuse.

[3] **deplore**—regret.

[4] **beset**—trouble.

[5] **detain**—delay.

[6] paragon—model of excellence.

Your tasteful eye with his vast German breeches?[7]
Perhaps his giggle, or his falsetto[8] voice,
Makes him the latest gallant of your choice?

Célimène. You're much mistaken to resent him so.
Why I put up with him you surely know:
My lawsuit's very shortly to be tried,
And I must have his influence on my side.

Alceste. Then lose your lawsuit, Madam, or let it drop;
Don't torture me by humoring such a fop.

Célimène. You're jealous of the whole world, Sir.

Alceste. That's true,
Since the whole world is well-received by you.

Célimène. That my good nature is so unconfined
Should serve to pacify your jealous mind;
Were I to smile on one, and scorn the rest,
Then you might have some cause to be distressed.

Alceste. Well, if I mustn't be jealous, tell me, then,
Just how I'm better treated than other men.

Célimène. You know you have my love. Will that not do?

Alceste. What proof have I that what you say is true?

Célimène. I would expect, Sir, that my having said it
Might give the statement a sufficient credit.

Alceste. But how can I be sure that you don't tell
The selfsame thing to other men as well?

Célimène. What a gallant speech! How flattering to me!
What a sweet creature you make me out to be!
Well then, to save you from the pangs of doubt,
All that I've said I hereby cancel out;
Now, none but yourself shall make a monkey of you:
Are you content?

Alceste. Why, why am I doomed to love you?
I swear that I shall bless the blissful hour
When this poor heart's no longer in your power!
I make no secret of it: I've done my best
To exorcise[9] this passion from my breast;

---

[7] breeches—trousers.

[8] falsetto—high in pitch.

[9] exorcise—expel.

But thus far all in vain; it will not go;
It's for my sins that I must love you so.

75 **Célimène.** Your love for me is matchless, Sir; that's clear.

Alceste. Indeed, in all the world it has no peer;
Words can't describe the nature of my passion,
And no man ever loved in such a fashion.

Célimène. Yes, it's a brand-new fashion, I agree:
80 You show your love by castigating[10] me,
And all your speeches are enraged and rude.
I've never been so furiously wooed.

Alceste. Yet you could calm that fury, if you chose.
Come, shall we bring our quarrels to a close?
85 Let's speak with open hearts, then, and begin . . .

Act Two, Scene Two

[Célimène, Alceste, Basque]

Célimène. What is it?

Basque.   Acaste is here.

Célimène.   Well, send him in.

Act Two, Scene Three

[Célimène, Alceste]

Alceste. What! Shall we never be alone at all?
You're always ready to receive a call,
And you can't bear, for ten ticks of the clock,
Not to keep open house for all who knock.

5 **Célimène.** I couldn't refuse him: he'd be most put out.

Alceste. Surely that's not worth worrying about.

Célimène. Acaste would never forgive me if he guessed
That I consider him a dreadful pest.

Alceste. If he's a pest, why bother with him then?

10 **Célimène.** Heavens! One can't antagonize such men;
Why, they're the chartered gossips of the court,
And have a say in things of every sort.
One must receive them, and be full of charm;

---

[10] castigating—criticizing sharply.

They're no great help, but they can do you harm,

15 And though your influence be ever so great,
They're hardly the best people to alienate.

Alceste. I see, dear lady, that you could make a case
For putting up with the whole human race;
These friendships that you calculate so nicely . . .

Act Two, Scene Four

[Alceste, Célimène, Basque]

Basque. Madam, Clitandre is here as well.

Alceste. Precisely.

Célimène. Where are you going?

Alceste. Elsewhere.

Célimène. Stay.

Alceste. No, no.

Célimène. Stay, Sir.

Alceste. I can't.

Célimène. I wish it.

Alceste. No, I must go.
I beg you, Madam, not to press the matter;

5 You know I have no taste for idle chatter.

Célimène. Stay: I command you.

Alceste. No, I cannot stay.

Célimène. Very well; you have my leave to go away.

Act Two, Scene Five

[Eliante, Philinte, Acaste, Clitandre, Alceste, Célimène, Basque]

Eliante [to Célimène]. The Marquesses[11] have kindly come to call.
Were they announced?

Célimène. Yes. Basque, bring chairs for all.

[Basque *provides the chairs, and exits.*]

[*To* Alceste.] You haven't gone?

Alceste. No; and I shan't depart
Till you decide who's foremost in your heart.

5 **Célimène.** Oh, hush.

Alceste. It's time to choose; take them, or me.

---

[11] Marquesses—noblemen.

Célimène. You're mad.

Alceste. I'm not, as you shall shortly see.

Célimène. Oh?

Alceste. You'll decide.

Célimène. You're joking now, dear friend.

Alceste. No, no; you'll choose; my patience is at an end.

Clitandre. Madam, I come from court, where poor Cléonte
10 Behaved like a perfect fool, as is his wont.[12]
Has he no friend to counsel him, I wonder,
And teach him less unerringly to blunder?

Célimène. It's true, the man's a most accomplished dunce;
His **gauche**[13] behavior charms the eye at once;
15 And every time one sees him, on my word,
His manner's grown a trifle more absurd.

Acaste. Speaking of dunces, I've just now conversed
With old Damon, who's one of the very worst;
I stood a lifetime in the broiling sun
20 Before his dreary monologue was done.

Célimène. Oh, he's a wondrous talker, and has the power
To tell you nothing hour after hour:
If, by mistake, he ever came to the point,
The shock would put his jawbone out of joint.

25 **Eliante** [*to* Philinte]. The conversation takes its usual turn,
And all our dear friends' ears will shortly burn.[14]

Clitandre. Timante's a character, Madam.

Célimène. Isn't he, though?
A man of mystery from top to toe,
Who moves about in a romantic mist
30 On secret missions which do not exist.
His talk is full of eyebrows and grimaces;
How tired one gets of his momentous faces;
He's always whispering something confidential
Which turns out to be quite inconsequential;
35 Nothing's too slight for him to mystify;
He even whispers when he says "good-by."

Acaste. Tell us about Géralde.

---

[12] wont—habit, custom.

[13] **gauche**—clumsy.

[14] ears will shortly burn—because they are being talked about.

Célimène. That tiresome ass.
He mixes only with the titled class,
And fawns on[15] dukes and princes, and is bored
40 With anyone who's not at least a lord.
The man's obsessed with rank, and his discourses
Are all of hounds and carriages and horses;
He uses Christian names with all the great,
And the word Milord, with him, is out of date.

45 **Clitandre.** He's very taken with Bélise, I hear.

Célimène. She is the dreariest company, poor dear.
Whenever she comes to call, I grope about
To find some topic which will draw her out,
But, owing to her dry and faint replies,
50 The conversation wilts, and droops, and dies.
In vain one hopes to animate her face
By mentioning the ultimate commonplace;
But sun or shower, even hail or frost
Are matters she can instantly exhaust.
55 Meanwhile her visit, painful though it is,
Drags on and on through mute eternities,
And though you ask the time, and yawn, and yawn,
She sits there like a stone and won't be gone.

Acaste. Now for Adraste.

Célimène. Oh, that conceited elf
60 Has a gigantic passion for himself;
He rails against the court, and cannot bear it
That none will recognize his hidden merit;
All honors given to others give offense
To his imaginary excellence.

65 **Clitandre.** What about young Cléon? His house, they say,
Is full of the best society, night and day.

Célimène. His cook has made him popular, not he:
It's Cléon's table that people come to see.

Eliante. He gives a splendid dinner, you must admit.

70 **Célimène.** But must he serve himself along with it?
For my taste, he's a most **insipid**[16] dish
Whose presence sours the wine and spoils the fish.

---

[15] fawns on—flatters.

[16] **insipid**—tasteless, bland.

Philinte. Damis, his uncle, is admired no end.
What's your opinion, Madam?
Célimène.   Why, he's my friend.

75 **Philinte.** He seems a decent fellow, and rather clever.
Célimène. He works too hard at cleverness, however.
I hate to see him sweat and struggle so
To fill his conversation with bons mots.[17]
Since he's decided to become a wit

80 His taste's so pure that nothing pleases it;
He scolds at all the latest books and plays,
Thinking that wit must never stoop to praise,
That finding fault's a sign of intellect,
That all appreciation is abject,

85 And that by damning everything in sight
One shows oneself in a distinguished light.
He's scornful even of our conversations:
Their **trivial**[18] nature sorely tries his patience;
He folds his arms, and stands above the battle,

90 And listens sadly to our childish prattle.[19]
Acaste. Wonderful, Madam! You've hit him off precisely.
Clitandre. No one can sketch a character so nicely.
Alceste. How bravely, Sirs, you cut and thrust at all
These absent fools, till one by one they fall:

95 But let one come in sight, and you'll at once
Embrace the man you lately called a dunce,
Telling him in a tone sincere and fervent
How proud you are to be his humble servant.
Clitandre. Why pick on us? Madame's been speaking, Sir,

100 And you should quarrel, if you must, with her.
Alceste. No, no, by God, the fault is yours, because
You lead her on with laughter and applause,
And make her think that she's the more delightful
The more her talk is scandalous and spiteful.

105 Oh, she would stoop to malice far, far less
If no such claque[20] approved her cleverness.

---

[17] bons mots—witty remarks.
[18] **trivial**—unimportant.
[19] prattle—silly talk.
[20] claque—admirers.

It's flatterers like you whose foolish praise
Nourishes all the vices of these days.

Philinte. But why protest when someone ridicules
110   Those you'd condemn, yourself, as knaves or fools?

Célimène. Why, Sir? Because he loves to make a fuss.
You don't expect him to agree with us,
When there's an opportunity to express
His heaven-sent spirit of contrariness?
115   What other people think, he can't abide;
Whatever they say, he's on the other side;
He lives in deadly terror of agreeing;
'Twould make him seem an ordinary being.
Indeed, he's so in love with contradiction,
120   He'll turn against his most profound conviction
And with a furious eloquence deplore it,
If only someone else is speaking for it.

Alceste. Go on, dear lady, mock me as you please;
You have your audience in ecstasies.

125 **Philinte.** But what she says is true: you have a way
Of bridling at whatever people say;
Whether they praise or blame, your angry spirit
Is equally unsatisfied to hear it.

Alceste. Men, Sir, are always wrong, and that's the reason
130   That righteous anger's never out of season;
All that I hear in all their conversation
Is flattering praise or reckless condemnation.

Célimène. But . . .

Alceste.   No, no, Madam, I am forced to state
That you have pleasures which I deprecate,[21]
135   And that these others, here, are much to blame
For nourishing the faults which are your shame.

Clitandre. I shan't defend myself, Sir; but I vow
I'd thought this lady faultless until now.

Acaste. I see her charms and graces, which are many;
140   But as for faults, I've never noticed any.

Alceste. I see them, Sir; and rather than ignore them,
I strenuously criticize her for them.

---

[21] deprecate—disapprove of.

The more one loves, the more one should object
To every blemish, every least defect.
145   Were I this lady, I would soon get rid
Of lovers who approved of all I did,
And by their slack indulgence and applause
Endorsed my follies and excused my flaws.

Célimène. If all hearts beat according to your measure,
150   The dawn of love would be the end of pleasure;
And love would find its perfect consummation
In ecstasies of rage and reprobation.[22]

Eliante. Love, as a rule, affects men otherwise,
And lovers rarely love to criticize.
155   They see their lady as a charming blur,
And find all things commendable in her.
If she has any blemish, fault, or shame,
They will redeem it by a pleasing name.
The pale-faced lady's lily-white, perforce;[23]
160   The swarthy[24] one's a sweet brunette, of course;
The spindly[25] lady has a slender grace;
The fat one has a most majestic pace;
The plain one, with her dress in disarray,
They classify as *beauté négligée;*[26]
165   The hulking one's a goddess in their eyes,
The dwarf, a concentrate of Paradise;
The haughty lady has a noble mind;
The mean one's witty, and the dull one's kind;
The chatterbox has liveliness and verve,
170   The mute one has a virtuous reserve.
So lovers manage, in their passion's cause,
To love their ladies even for their flaws.

Alceste. But I still say . . .

Célimène.   I think it would be nice
To stroll around the gallery once or twice.
175   What! You're not going, Sirs?

---

[22] reprobation—condemnation.

[23] perforce—by necessity.

[24] swarthy—dark.

[25] spindly—very thin.

[26] *beauté négligée*—casual beauty.

Clitandre and Acaste.　　　No, Madam, no.

Alceste. You seem to be in terror lest they go.
　　Do what you will, Sirs; leave, or linger on,
　　But I shan't go till after you are gone.

Acaste. I'm free to linger, unless I should perceive

180　　*Madame* is tired, and wishes me to leave.

Clitandre. And as for me, I needn't go today
　　Until the hour of the King's *coucher.*[27]

Célimène [*to* Alceste]. You're joking, surely?

Alceste. Not in the least; we'll see

185　　Whether you'd rather part with them, or me.

Act Two, Scene Six

[Alceste, Célimène, Eliante, Acaste, Philinte, Clitandre, Basque]

Basque [*to* Alceste]. Sir, there's a fellow here who bids me state
　　That he must see you, and that it can't wait.

Alceste. Tell him that I have no such pressing affairs.

Basque. It's a long tailcoat that this fellow wears,

5　　With gold all over.

Célimène [*to* Alceste]. You'd best go down and see.
　　Or—have him enter.

Act Two, Scene Seven

[Alceste, Célimène, Eliante, Acaste, Philinte, Clitandre, A Guard *of the Marshalsea*[28]]

Alceste [*confronting the guard*]. Well, what do you want with me?
　　Come in, Sir.

Guard.　　　I've a word, Sir, for your ear.

Alceste. Speak it aloud, Sir; I shall strive to hear.

Guard. The Marshals have instructed me to say
　　You must report to them without delay.

5　　**Alceste.** Who? Me, Sir?

Guard.　　　Yes, Sir; you.

Alceste.　　　　　But what do they want?

---

[27] *coucher*—reception held by a king before retiring to bed.

[28] *Marshalsea*—a court (actually located in London) that dealt with disputes between servants of the king.

Philinte [*to* Alceste]. To scotch[29] your silly quarrel with Oronte.

Célimène [*to* Philinte]. What quarrel?

Philinte.   Oronte and he have fallen out

    Over some verse he spoke his mind about;

    The Marshals wish to arbitrate the matter.

10   **Alceste.** Never shall I **equivocate**[30] or flatter!

Philinte. You'd best obey their summons; come, let's go.

Alceste. How can they mend our quarrel, I'd like to know?

    Am I to make a cowardly retraction,

    And praise those jingles to his satisfaction?

15   I'll not **recant**;[31] I've judged that sonnet rightly.

    It's bad.

Philinte.   But you might say so more politely. . . .

Alceste. I'll not back down; his verses make me sick.

Philinte. If only you could be more politic!

    But come, let's go.

Alceste.   I'll go, but I won't unsay

20   A single word.

Philinte.   Well, let's be on our way.

Alceste. Till I am ordered by my lord the King

    To praise that poem, I shall say the thing

    Is scandalous, by God, and that the poet

    Ought to be hanged for having the nerve to show it.

    [*To* Clitandre *and* Acaste, *who are laughing.*]

25   By heaven, Sirs, I really didn't know

    That I was being humorous.

Célimène.   Go, Sir, go;

    Settle your business.

Alceste.   I shall, and when I'm through,

    I shall return to settle things with you.

Act Three, Scene One

[Clitandre, Acaste]

Clitandre. Dear Marquess, how contented you appear;

    All things delight you, nothing mars your cheer.

---

[29] scotch—end.

[30] **equivocate**—use misleading language.

[31] **recant**—take back a statement made earlier.

Can you, in perfect honesty, declare
That you've a right to be so debonair?[1]

5   **Acaste.** By Jove, when I survey myself, I find
No cause whatever for distress of mind.
I'm young and rich; I can in modesty
Lay claim to an exalted pedigree;
And owing to my name and my condition

10   I shall not want for honors and position.
Then as to courage, that most precious trait,
I seem to have it, as was proved of late
Upon the field of honor, where my bearing,
They say, was very cool and rather daring.

15   I've wit, of course; and taste in such perfection
That I can judge without the least reflection,
And at the theater, which is my delight,
Can make or break a play on opening night,
And lead the crowd in hisses or bravos,

20   And generally be known as one who knows.
I'm clever, handsome, gracefully polite;
My waist is small, my teeth are strong and white;
As for my dress, the world's astonished eyes
Assure me that I bear away the prize.

25   I find myself in favor everywhere,
Honored by men, and worshiped by the fair;
And since these things are so, it seems to me
I'm justified in my complacency.

      Clitandre. Well, if so many ladies hold you dear,

30   Why do you press a hopeless courtship here?

      Acaste. Hopeless, you say? I'm not the sort of fool
That likes his ladies difficult and cool.
Men who are awkward, shy, and peasantish
May pine for heartless beauties, if they wish,

35   Grovel before them, bear their cruelties,
Woo them with tears and sighs and bended knees,
And hope by dogged faithfulness to gain
What their poor merits never could obtain.
For men like me, however, it makes no sense

---

[1] debonair—comfortable, contented.

40   To love on trust, and foot the whole expense.
         Whatever any lady's merits be,
         I think, thank God, that I'm as choice as she;
         That if my heart is kind enough to burn
         For her, she owes me something in return;
45   And that in any proper love affair
         The partners must invest an equal share.

Clitandre. You think, then, that our hostess favors you?

Acaste. I've reason to believe that that is true.

Clitandre. How did you come to such a mad conclusion?
50   You're blind, dear fellow. This is sheer **delusion**.[2]

Acaste. All right, then: I'm deluded and I'm blind.

Clitandre. Whatever put the notion in your mind?

Acaste. Delusion.

Clitandre.   What persuades you that you're right?

Acaste. I'm blind.

Clitandre.   But have you any proofs to cite?
55 **Acaste.** I tell you I'm deluded.

Clitandre.   Have you, then,
         Received some secret pledge from Célimène?

Acaste. Oh, no: she scorns me.

Clitandre.   Tell me the truth, I beg.

Acaste. She just can't bear me.

Clitandre.   Ah, don't pull my leg.
         Tell me what hope she's given you, I pray.
60 **Acaste.** I'm hopeless, and it's you who win the day.
         She hates me thoroughly, and I'm so vexed
         I mean to hang myself on Tuesday next.

Clitandre. Dear Marquess, let us have an armistice[3]
         And make a treaty. What do you say to this?
65   If ever one of us can plainly prove
         That Célimène encourages his love,
         The other must abandon hope, and yield,
         And leave him in possession of the field.

Acaste. Now, there's a bargain that appeals to me;
70   With all my heart, dear Marquess, I agree.
         But hush.

---

[2] **delusion**—false belief.

[3] armistice—cease-fire.

Act Three, Scene Two

[Célimène, Acaste, Clitandre]

Célimène. Still here?

Clitandre. 'Twas love that stayed our feet.

Célimène. I think I heard a carriage in the street.
Whose is it? D'you know?

Act Three, Scene Three

[Célimène, Acaste, Clitandre, Basque]

Basque. Arsinoé is here,
Madame.

Célimène. Arsinoé, you say? Oh, dear.

Basque. Eliante is entertaining her below.

Célimène. What brings the creature here, I'd like to know?

Acaste. They say she's dreadfully prudish, but in fact

5   I think her piety . . .

Célimène. It's all an act.
At heart she's worldly, and her poor success
In snaring men explains her prudishness.
It breaks her heart to see the beaux and gallants[4]
Engrossed by other women's charms and talents,

10   And so she's always in a jealous rage
Against the faulty standards of the age.
She lets the world believe that she's a prude
To justify her loveless solitude,
And strives to put a brand of moral shame

15   On all the graces that she cannot claim.
But still she'd love a lover; and Alceste
Appears to be the one she'd love the best.
His visits here are poison to her pride;
She seems to think I've lured him from her side;

20   And everywhere, at court or in the town,
The spiteful, envious woman runs me down.
In short, she's just as stupid as can be,
Vicious and arrogant in the last degree,
And . . .

---

[4] beaux and gallants—fashionable men.

Act Three, Scene Four

[Arsinoé, Célimène, Clitandre, Acaste]

Célimène. Ah! What happy chance has brought you here?
　　I've thought about you ever so much, my dear.
Arsinoé. I've come to tell you something you should know.
Célimène. How good of you to think of doing so!
[Clitandre *and* Acaste *go out, laughing.*]

Act Three, Scene Five

[Arsinoé, Célimène]

Arsinoé. It's just as well those gentlemen didn't tarry.
Célimène. Shall we sit down?
Arsinoé. 　　　　　　　　That won't be necessary.
　　Madam, the flame of friendship ought to burn
　　Brightest in matters of the most concern,
5　　And as there's nothing which concerns us more
　　Than honor, I have hastened to your door
　　To bring you, as your friend, some information
　　About the status of your reputation.
　　I visited, last night, some virtuous folk,
10　　And, quite by chance, it was of you they spoke;
　　There was, I fear, no tendency to praise
　　Your light behavior and your dashing ways.
　　The quantity of gentlemen you see
　　And your by now notorious coquetry
15　　Were both so vehemently criticized
　　By everyone, that I was much surprised.
　　Of course, I needn't tell you where I stood;
　　I came to your defense as best I could,
　　Assured them you were harmless, and declared
20　　Your soul was absolutely unimpaired.
　　But there are some things, you must realize,
　　One can't excuse, however hard one tries,
　　And I was forced at last into conceding
　　That your behavior, Madam, is misleading,
25　　That it makes a bad impression, giving rise

To ugly gossip and obscene surmise,[5]
And that if you were more *overtly*[6] good,
You wouldn't be so much misunderstood.
Not that I think you've been unchaste[7]—no! no!

30   The saints preserve me from a thought so low!
But mere good conscience never did suffice:
One must avoid the outward show of vice.
Madam, you're too intelligent, I'm sure,
To think my motives anything but pure

35   In offering you this counsel—which I do
Out of a zealous interest in you.

   Célimène.   Madam, I haven't taken you amiss;
I'm very much obliged to you for this;
And I'll at once discharge the obligation

40   By telling you about your reputation.
You've been so friendly as to let me know
What certain people say of me, and so
I mean to follow your benign example
By offering you a somewhat similar sample.

45   The other day, I went to an affair
And found some most distinguished people there
Discussing piety, both false and true.
The conversation soon came round to you.
Alas! Your prudery and bustling zeal

50   Appeared to have a very slight appeal.
Your affectation of a grave demeanor,[8]
Your endless talk of virtue and of honor,
The aptitude of your suspicious mind
For finding sin where there is none to find,

55   Your towering self-esteem, that pitying face
With which you contemplate the human race,
Your sermonizings and your sharp aspersions[9]
On people's pure and innocent diversions—
All these were mentioned, Madam, and, in fact,

---

[5] obscene surmise—indecent inference.

[6] *overtly*—openly.

[7] unchaste—immodest.

[8] demeanor—manner.

[9] aspersions—unfavorable remarks.

60   Were roundly[10] and concertedly attacked.
     "What good," they said, "are all these outward shows,
     When everything belies[11] her pious pose?
     She prays **incessantly**;[12] but then, they say,
     She beats her maids and cheats them of their pay;
65   She shows her zeal in every holy place,
     But still she's vain enough to paint her face;
     She holds that naked statues are immoral,
     But with a naked *man* she'd have no quarrel."
     Of course, I said to everybody there
70   That they were being viciously unfair;
     But still they were disposed to criticize you,
     And all agreed that someone should advise you
     To leave the morals of the world alone,
     And worry rather more about your own.
75   They felt that one's self-knowledge should be great
     Before one thinks of setting others straight;
     That one should learn the art of living well
     Before one threatens other men with hell,
     And that the Church is best equipped, no doubt,
80   To guide our souls and root our vices out.
     Madam, you're too intelligent, I'm sure,
     To think my motives anything but pure
     In offering you this counsel—which I do
     Out of a zealous interest in you.
85   **Arsinoé.** I dared not hope for gratitude, but I
     Did not expect so acid a reply;
     I judge, since you've been so extremely tart,
     That my good counsel pierced you to the heart.
     Célimène. Far from it, Madam. Indeed, it seems to me
90   We ought to trade advice more frequently.
     One's vision of oneself is so defective
     That it would be an excellent corrective.
     If you are willing, Madam, let's arrange
     Shortly to have another frank exchange

---

[10] roundly—thoroughly.

[11] belies—contradicts.

[12] **incessantly**—continuously.

95   In which we'll tell each other, *entre nous*,[13]
          What you've heard tell of me, and I of you.

Arsinoé. Oh, people never censure[14] you, my dear;
          It's me they criticize. Or so I hear.

Célimène. Madam, I think we either blame or praise
100   According to our taste and length of days.
          There is a time of life for coquetry,
          And there's a season, too, for prudery.
          When all one's charms are gone, it is, I'm sure,
          Good strategy to be devout and pure:
105   It makes one seem a little less forsaken.
          Some day, perhaps, I'll take the road you've taken:
          Time brings all things. But I have time aplenty,
          And see no cause to be a prude at twenty.

Arsinoé. You give your age in such a gloating tone
110   That one would think I was an ancient crone;[15]
          We're not so far apart, in sober truth,
          That you can mock me with a boast of youth!
          Madam, you baffle me. I wish I knew
          What moves you to provoke me as you do.

115 **Célimène.** For my part Madam, I should like to know
          Why you abuse me everywhere you go.
          Is it my fault, dear lady, that your hand
          Is not, alas, in very great demand?
          If men admire me, if they pay me court
120   And daily make me offers of the sort
          You'd dearly love to have them make to you,
          How can I help it? What would you have me do?
          If what you want is lovers, please feel free
          To take as many as you can from me.

125 **Arsinoé.** Oh, come. D'you think the world is losing sleep
          Over that flock of lovers which you keep,
          Or that we find it difficult to guess
          What price you pay for their devotedness?
          Surely you don't expect us to suppose
130   Mere merit could attract so many beaux?

---

[13] *entre nous*—between ourselves.

[14] censure—criticize.

[15] crone—old woman.

It's not your virtue that they're dazzled by;
Nor is it virtuous love for which they sigh.
You're fooling no one, Madam; the world's not blind;
There's many a lady heaven has designed
135   To call men's noblest, tenderest feelings out,
Who has no lovers dogging her about;
From which it's plain that lovers nowadays
Must be acquired in bold and shameless ways,
And only pay one court for such reward
140   As modesty and virtue can't afford.
Then don't be quite so puffed up, if you please,
About your **tawdry**[16] little victories,
Try, if you can, to be a shade less vain,
And treat the world with somewhat less disdain.
145   If one were envious of your amours,
One soon could have a following like yours;
Lovers are no great trouble to collect
If one prefers them to one's self-respect.

Célimène. Collect them then, my dear; I'd love to see
150   You demonstrate that charming theory;
Who knows, you might . . .

Arsinoé.   Now, Madam, that will do;
It's time to end this trying interview.
My coach is late in coming to your door,
Or I'd have taken leave of you before.

155 **Célimène.** Oh, please don't feel that you must rush away;
I'd be delighted, Madam, if you'd stay.
However, lest my conversation bore you,
Let me provide some better company for you;
This gentleman, who comes most apropos,[17]
160   Will please you more than I could do, I know.

Act Three, Scene Six

[Alceste, Célimène, Arsinoé]

Célimène. Alceste, I have a little note to write
Which simply must go out before tonight;

---

[16] **tawdry**—gaudy.
[17] apropos—opportunely.

Please entertain *Madame;* I'm sure that she
Will overlook my incivility.

Act Three, Scene Seven

[Alceste, Arsinoé]

Arsinoé. Well, Sir, our hostess graciously contrives
    For us to chat until my coach arrives;
    And I shall be forever in her debt
    For granting me this little tête-à-tête.[18]
5   We women very rightly give our hearts
    To men of noble character and parts,
    And your especial merits, dear Alceste,
    Have roused the deepest sympathy in my breast.
    Oh, how I wish they had sufficient sense
10   At court, to recognize your excellence!
    They wrong you greatly, Sir. How it must hurt you
    Never to be rewarded for your virtue!

Alceste. Why, Madam, what cause have I to feel aggrieved?
    What great and brilliant thing have I achieved?
15   What service have I rendered to the King
    That I should look to him for anything?

Arsinoé. Not everyone who's honored by the State
    Has done great services. A man must wait
    Till time and fortune offer him the chance.
20   Your merit, Sir, is obvious at a glance,
    And . . .

Alceste.   Ah, forget my merit; I'm not neglected.
    The court, I think, can hardly be expected
    To mine men's souls for merit, and unearth
    Our hidden virtues and our secret worth.

25 **Arsinoé.** *Some* virtues, though, are far too bright to hide;
    Yours are acknowledged, Sir, on every side.
    Indeed, I've heard you warmly praised of late
    By persons of considerable weight.

Alceste. This fawning age has praise for everyone,
30   And all distinctions, Madam, are undone.

---

[18] tête-à-tête—private talk.

All things have equal honor nowadays,
And no one should be gratified by praise.
To be admired, one only need exist,
And every lackey's[19] on the honors list.

35   **Arsinoé.** I only wish, Sir, that you had your eye
On some position at court, however high;
You'd only have to hint at such a notion
For me to set the proper wheels in motion;
I've certain friendships I'd be glad to use
40   To get you any office you might choose.

    Alceste. Madam, I fear that any such ambition
Is wholly foreign to my disposition.
The soul God gave me isn't of the sort
That prospers in the weather of a court.
45   It's all too obvious that I don't possess
The virtues necessary for success.
My one great talent is for speaking plain;
I've never learned to flatter or to **feign;**[20]
And anyone so stupidly sincere
50   Had best not seek a courtier's career.
Outside the court, I know, one must dispense
With honors, privilege, and influence;
But still one gains the right, foregoing these,
Not to be tortured by the wish to please.
55   One needn't live in dread of snubs and slights,
Nor praise the verse that every idiot writes,
Nor humor silly Marquesses, nor bestow
Politic sighs on Madam So-and-So.

    Arsinoé. Forget the court, then; let the matter rest.
60   But I've another cause to be distressed
About your present situation, Sir.
It's to your love affair that I refer.
She whom you love, and who pretends to love you,
Is, I regret to say, unworthy of you.

65   **Alceste.** Why, Madam! Can you seriously intend
To make so grave a charge against your friend?

---

[19] lackey—servant.

[20] **feign**—pretend.

Arsinoé. Alas, I must. I've stood aside too long
    And let that lady do you grievous wrong;
    But now my debt to conscience shall be paid:
70   I tell you that your love has been betrayed.
Alceste. I thank you, Madam; you're extremely kind.
    Such words are soothing to a lover's mind.
Arsinoé. Yes, though she is my friend, I say again
    You're very much too good for Célimène.
75   She's wantonly misled you from the start.
Alceste. You may be right; who knows another's heart?
    But ask yourself if it's the part of charity
    To shake my soul with doubts of her sincerity.
Arsinoé. Well, if you'd rather be a dupe[21] than doubt her,
80   That's your affair. I'll say no more about her.
Alceste. Madam, you know that doubt and vague suspicion
    Are painful to a man in my position;
    It's most unkind to worry me this way
    Unless you've some real proof of what you say.
85 **Arsinoé.** Sir, say no more: all doubt shall be removed,
    And all that I've been saying shall be proved.
    You've only to escort me home, and there
    We'll look into the heart of this affair.
    I've ocular[22] evidence which will persuade you
90   Beyond a doubt, that Célimène's betrayed you.
    Then, if you're saddened by that revelation,
    Perhaps I can provide some consolation.

Act Four, Scene One

[Eliante, Philinte]
Philinte. Madam, he acted like a stubborn child;
    I thought they never would be reconciled;
    In vain we reasoned, threatened, and appealed;
    He stood his ground and simply would not yield.
5   The Marshals, I feel sure, have never heard
    An argument so splendidly absurd.

---

[21] dupe—deceived person.

[22] ocular—visual.

"No, gentlemen," said he, "I'll not retract.
His verse is bad: extremely bad, in fact.
Surely it does the man no harm to know it.
10   Does it disgrace him, not to be a poet?
A gentleman may be respected still,
Whether he writes a sonnet well or ill.
That I dislike his verse should not offend him;
In all that touches honor, I commend him;
15   He's noble, brave, and virtuous—but I fear
He can't in truth be called a sonneteer.
I'll gladly praise his wardrobe; I'll endorse
His dancing, or the way he sits a horse;
But, gentlemen, I cannot praise his rhyme.
20   In fact, it ought to be a capital crime
For anyone so sadly unendowed
To write a sonnet, and read the thing aloud."
At length he fell into a gentler mood
And, striking a concessive[1] attitude,
25   He paid Oronte the following courtesies:
"Sir, I regret that I'm so hard to please,
And I'm profoundly sorry that your lyric
Failed to provoke me to a panegyric."[2]
After these curious words, the two embraced,
30   And then the hearing was adjourned—in haste.
Eliante. His conduct has been very singular lately;
Still, I confess that I respect him greatly.
The honesty in which he takes such pride
Has—to my mind—its noble, heroic side.
35   In this false age, such **candor**[3] seems outrageous;
But I could wish that it were more contagious.
Philinte. What most intrigues me in our friend Alceste
Is the grand passion that rages in his breast.
The sullen humors he's compounded of
40   Should not, I think, dispose his heart to love;
But since they do, it puzzles me still more
That he should choose your cousin to adore.

---

[1] concessive—conciliatory.

[2] panegyric—expression of praise.

[3] **candor**—frankness, truthfulness.

Eliante. It does, indeed, belie the theory
That love is born of gentle sympathy,
45 And that the tender passion must be based
On sweet accords of temper and of taste.
Philinte. Does she return his love, do you suppose?
Eliante. Ah, that's a difficult question, Sir. Who knows?
How can we judge the truth of her devotion?
50 Her heart's a stranger to its own emotion.
Sometimes it thinks it loves, when no love's there;
At other times it loves quite unaware.
Philinte. I rather think Alceste is in for more
Distress and sorrow than he's bargained for;
55 Were he of my mind, Madam, his affection
Would turn in quite a different direction,
And we would see him more responsive to
The kind regard which he receives from you.
Eliante. Sir, I believe in frankness, and I'm inclined,
60 In matters of the heart, to speak my mind.
I don't oppose his love for her; indeed,
I hope with all my heart that he'll succeed,
And were it in my power, I'd rejoice
In giving him the lady of his choice.
65 But if, as happens frequently enough
In love affairs, he meets with a rebuff[4]—
If Célimène should grant some rival's suit—
I'd gladly play the role of substitute;
Nor would his tender speeches please me less
70 Because they'd once been made without success.
Philinte. Well, Madam, as for me, I don't oppose
Your hopes in this affair; and heaven knows
That in my conversations with the man
I plead your cause as often as I can.
75 But if those two should marry, and so remove
All chance that he will offer you his love,
Then I'll declare my own, and hope to see
Your gracious favor pass from him to me.

---

[4] rebuff—refusal.

In short, should you be cheated of Alceste,

80   I'd be most happy to be second best.

Eliante. Philinte, you're teasing.

Philinte.   Ah, Madam, never fear;

No words of mine were ever so sincere,

And I shall live in fretful expectation

Till I can make a fuller declaration.

Act Four, Scene Two

[Alceste, Eliante, Philinte]

Alceste. Avenge me, Madam! I must have satisfaction,

Or this great wrong will drive me to distraction!

Eliante. Why, what's the matter? What's upset you so?

Alceste. Madam, I've had a mortal, mortal blow.

5   If Chaos repossessed the universe,

I swear I'd not be shaken any worse.

I'm ruined. . . . I can say no more. . . . My soul. . .

Eliante. Do try, Sir, to regain your self-control.

Alceste. Just heaven! Why were so much beauty and grace

10   Bestowed on one so vicious and so base?

Eliante. Once more, Sir, tell us. . . .

Alceste.   My world has gone to wrack;[5]

I'm—I'm betrayed; she's stabbed me in the back:

Yes, Célimène (who would have thought it of her?)

Is false to me, and has another lover.

15   **Eliante.** Are you quite certain? Can you prove these things?

Philinte. Lovers are prey to wild imaginings

And jealous fancies. No doubt there's some mistake. . . .

Alceste. Mind your own business, Sir, for heaven's sake.

[*To* Eliante.] Madam, I have the proof that you demand

20   Here in my pocket, penned by her own hand.

Yes, all the shameful evidence one could want

Lies in this letter written to Oronte—

Oronte! whom I felt sure she couldn't love,

And hardly bothered to be jealous of.

---

[5] wrack—ruin.

25 **Philinte.** Still, in a letter, appearances may deceive;
     This may not be so bad as you believe.

   Alceste. Once more I beg you, Sir, to let me be;
     Tend to your own affairs; leave mine to me.

   Eliante. Compose yourself; this anguish that you feel . . .

30 **Alceste.** Is something, Madam, you alone can heal.
     My outraged heart, beside itself with grief,
     Appeals to you for comfort and relief.
     Avenge me on your cousin, whose unjust
     And faithless nature has deceived my trust;

35   Avenge a crime your pure soul must detest.

   Eliante. But how, Sir?

   Alceste.   Madam, this heart within my breast
     Is yours; pray take it; redeem my heart from her,
     And so avenge me on my torturer.
     Let her be punished by the fond emotion,

40   The ardent love, the bottomless devotion,
     The faithful worship which this heart of mine
     Will offer up to yours as to a shrine.

   Eliante. You have my sympathy, Sir, in all you suffer;
     Nor do I scorn the noble heart you offer;

45   But I suspect you'll soon be **mollified**,[6]
     And this desire for vengeance will subside.
     When some beloved hand has done us wrong
     We thirst for retribution—but not for long;
     However dark the deed that she's committed,

50   A lovely culprit's very soon acquitted.
     Nothing's so stormy as an injured lover,
     And yet no storm so quickly passes over.

   Alceste. No, Madam, no—this is no lovers' spat;
     I'll not forgive her; it's gone too far for that;

55   My mind's made up; I'll kill myself before
     I waste my hopes upon her any more.
     Ah, here she is. My wrath intensifies.
     I shall confront her with her tricks and lies,
     And crush her utterly, and bring you then

60   A heart no longer slave to Célimène.

---

[6] **mollified**—soothed.

Act Four, Scene Three

[Célimène, Alceste]

Alceste [*aside*]. Sweet heaven, help me to control my passion.

Célimène [*aside to* Alceste]. Oh, Lord. Why stand there staring in that
      fashion?
    And what d'you mean by those dramatic sighs,
    And that **malignant**[7] glitter in your eyes?

5   **Alceste.** I mean that sins which cause the blood to freeze
    Look innocent beside your treacheries;
    That nothing Hell's or Heaven's wrath could do
    Ever produced so bad a thing as you.

Célimène. Your compliments were always sweet and pretty.

10   **Alceste.** Madam, it's not the moment to be witty.
    No, blush and hang your head; you've ample reason,
    Since I've the fullest evidence of your treason.
    Ah, this is what my sad heart prophesied;
    Now all my anxious fears are verified;

15   My dark suspicion and my gloomy doubt
    Divined the truth, and now the truth is out.
    For all your trickery, I was not deceived;
    It was my bitter stars that I believed.
    But don't imagine that you'll go scot-free;

20   You shan't misuse me with **impunity**.[8]
    I know that love's irrational and blind;
    I know the heart's not subject to the mind,
    And can't be reasoned into beating faster;
    I know each soul is free to choose its master;

25   Therefore had you but spoken from the heart,
    Rejecting my attentions from the start,
    I'd have no grievance, or at any rate
    I could complain of nothing but my fate.
    Ah, but so falsely to encourage me—

30   That was a treason and a treachery
    For which you cannot suffer too severely,
    And you shall pay for that behavior dearly.
    Yes, now I have no pity, not a shred;

---

[7] **malignant**—threatening.

[8] **impunity**—freedom from punishment.

My temper's out of hand; I've lost my head;
35   Shocked by the knowledge of your double-dealings,
       My reason can't restrain my savage feelings;
       A righteous wrath deprives me of my senses,
       And I won't answer for the consequences.
       Célimène. What does this outburst mean? Will you please explain?
40   Have you, by any chance, gone quite insane?
       Alceste. Yes, yes, I went insane the day I fell
       A victim to your black and fatal spell,
       Thinking to meet with some sincerity
       Among the treacherous charms that beckoned me.
45   **Célimène.** Pooh. Of what treachery can you complain?
       Alceste. How sly you are, how cleverly you feign!
       But you'll not victimize me any more.
       Look: here's a document you've seen before.
       This evidence, which I acquired today,
50   Leaves you, I think, without a thing to say.
       Célimène. Is this what sent you into such a fit?
       Alceste. You should be blushing at the sight of it.
       Célimène. Ought I to blush? I truly don't see why.
       Alceste. Ah, now you're being bold as well as sly;
55   Since there's no signature, perhaps you'll claim . . .
       Célimène. I wrote it, whether or not it bears my name.
       Alceste. And you can view with **equanimity**[9]
       This proof of your disloyalty to me!
       Célimène. Oh, don't be so outrageous and extreme.
60   **Alceste.** You take this matter lightly, it would seem.
       Was it no wrong to me, no shame to you,
       That you should send Oronte this billet-doux?[10]
       Célimène. Oronte! Who said it was for him?
       Alceste.   Why, those
       Who brought me this example of your prose.
65   But what's the difference? If you wrote the letter
       To someone else, it pleases me no better.
       My grievance and your guilt remain the same.
       Célimène. But need you rage, and need I blush for shame,
       If this was written to a *woman* friend?

---

[9] **equanimity**—calmness.
[10] billet-doux—love letter.

70 **Alceste.** Ah! Most ingenious. I'm impressed no end;
And after that incredible **evasion**[11]
Your guilt is clear. I need no more persuasion.
How dare you try so clumsy a deception?
D'you think I'm wholly wanting in perception?
75 Come, come, let's see how brazenly you'll try
To bolster[12] up so **palpable**[13] a lie:
Kindly construe this ardent closing section
As nothing more than sisterly affection!
Here, let me read it. Tell me, if you dare to,
80 That this is for a woman . . .
Célimène. I don't care to.
What right have you to badger and berate me,
And so highhandedly interrogate me?
Alceste. Now, don't be angry; all I ask of you
Is that you justify a phrase or two . . .
85 **Célimène.** No, I shall not. I utterly refuse,
And you may take those phrases as you choose.
Alceste. Just show me how this letter could be meant
For a woman's eyes, and I shall be content.
Célimène. No, no, it's for Oronte; you're perfectly right.
90 I welcome his attentions with delight,
I prize his character and his intellect,
And everything is just as you suspect.
Come, do your worst now; give your rage free rein;
But kindly cease to bicker and complain.
95 **Alceste** [*aside*]. Good God! Could anything be more inhuman?
Was ever a heart so mangled by a woman?
When I complain of how she has betrayed me,
She bridles, and commences to upbraid[14] me!
She tries my tortured patience to the limit;
100 She won't deny her guilt; she glories in it!
And yet my heart's too faint and cowardly
To break these chains of passion, and be free,
To scorn her as it should, and rise above

---

[11] **evasion**—deceptive strategy.

[12] bolster—support.

[13] **palpable**—obvious.

[14] upbraid—criticize sharply.

This unrewarded, mad, and bitter love.

105 [*To* Célimène.] Ah, traitress, in how confident a fashion
You take advantage of my helpless passion,
And use my weakness for your faithless charms
To make me once again throw down my arms!
But do at least deny this black transgression;[15]

110 Take back that mocking and perverse confession;
Defend this letter and your innocence,
And I, poor fool, will aid in your defense.
Pretend, pretend, that you are just and true,
And I shall make myself believe in you.

115 **Célimène.** Oh, stop it. Don't be such a jealous dunce,
Or I shall leave off loving you at once.
Just why should I *pretend?* What could impel me
To stoop so low as that? And kindly tell me
Why, if I loved another, I shouldn't merely

120 Inform you of it, simply and sincerely!
I've told you where you stand, and that admission
Should altogether clear me of suspicion;
After so generous a guarantee,
What right have you to harbor doubts of me?

125 Since women are (from natural reticence[16])
Reluctant to declare their sentiments,
And since the honor of our sex requires
That we conceal our amorous desires,
Ought any man for whom such laws are broken

130 To question what the oracle[17] has spoken?
Should he not rather feel an obligation
To trust that most obliging declaration?
Enough, now. Your suspicions quite disgust me;
Why should I love a man who doesn't trust me?

135 I cannot understand why I continue,
Fool that I am, to take an interest in you.
I ought to choose a man less prone to doubt,
And give you something to be vexed about.

---

[15] transgression—offense.

[16] reticence—shyness.

[17] oracle—prophet.

Alceste. Ah, what a poor enchanted fool I am;
140   These gentle words, no doubt, were all a sham;
    But destiny requires me to entrust
    My happiness to you, and so I must.
    I'll love you to the bitter end, and see
    How false and treacherous you dare to be.
145 **Célimène.** No, you don't really love me as you ought.
Alceste. I love you more than can be said or thought;
    Indeed, I wish you were in such distress
    That I might show my deep devotedness.
    Yes, I could wish that you were wretchedly poor,
150   Unloved, uncherished, utterly obscure;
    That fate had set you down upon the earth
    Without possessions, rank, or gentle birth;
    Then, by the offer of my heart, I might
    Repair the great injustice of your plight;
155   I'd raise you from the dust, and proudly prove
    The purity and vastness of my love.
Célimène. This is a strange benevolence indeed!
    God grant that I may never be in need. . . .
    Ah, here's Monsieur Dubois, in quaint disguise.

Act Four, Scene Four

[Célimène, Alceste, Dubois]
Alceste. Well, why this costume? Why those frightened eyes?
    What ails you?
Dubois.   Well, Sir, things are most mysterious.
Alceste. What do you mean?
Dubois.   I fear they're very serious.
Alceste. What?
Dubois.   Shall I speak more loudly?
5 **Alceste.** Yes; speak out.
Dubois.   Isn't there someone here, Sir?
Alceste. Speak, you lout![18]
    Stop wasting time.
Dubois.   Sir, we must slip away.

---

[18] lout—oaf.

Alceste. How's that?

Dubois.   We must decamp[19] without delay.

Alceste. Explain yourself.

Dubois.   I tell you we must fly.

10 **Alceste.** What for?

Dubois.   We mustn't pause to say good-by.

Alceste. Now what d'you mean by all of this, you clown?

Dubois. I mean, Sir, that we've got to leave this town.

Alceste. I'll tear you limb from limb and joint from joint
If you don't come more quickly to the point.

15 **Dubois.** Well, Sir, today a man in a black suit,
Who wore a black and ugly scowl to boot,
Left us a document scrawled in such a hand
As even Satan couldn't understand.
It bears upon your lawsuit, I don't doubt;

20 But all hell's devils couldn't make it out.

Alceste. Well, well, go on. What then? I fail to see
How this event obliges us to flee.

Dubois. Well, Sir: an hour later, hardly more,
A gentleman who's often called before

25 Came looking for you in an anxious way.
Not finding you, he asked me to convey
(Knowing I could be trusted with the same)
The following message. . . . Now, what *was* his name?

Alceste. Forget his name, you idiot. What did he say?

30 **Dubois.** Well, it was one of your friends, Sir, anyway.
He warned you to begone, and he suggested
That if you stay, you may well be arrested.

Alceste. What? Nothing more specific? Think, man, think!

Dubois. No, Sir. He had me bring him pen and ink,

35 And dashed you off a letter which, I'm sure,
Will render things distinctly less obscure.

Alceste. Well—let me have it!

Célimène.   What *is* this all about?

Alceste. God knows; but I have hopes of finding out.
How long am I to wait, you blitherer?

---

[19] decamp—depart.

Dubois [*after a protracted*[20] *search for the letter*].
40   I must have left it on your table, Sir.
Alceste. I ought to . . .
Célimène.   No, no, keep your self-control;
         Go find out what's behind his rigmarole.[21]
Alceste. It seems that fate, no matter what I do,
         Has sworn that I may not converse with you;
45   But, Madam, pray permit your faithful lover
         To try once more before the day is over.

Act Five, Scene One

[Alceste, Philinte]
Alceste. No, it's too much. My mind's made up, I tell you.
Philinte. Why should this blow, however hard, compel you . . .
Alceste. No, no, don't waste your breath in argument;
         Nothing you say will alter my intent;
5   This age is vile, and I've made up my mind
         To have no further commerce with mankind.
         Did not truth, honor, decency, and the laws
         Oppose my enemy and approve my cause?
         My claims were justified in all men's sight;
10   I put my trust in equity and right;
         Yet, to my horror and the world's disgrace,
         Justice is mocked, and I have lost my case!
         A scoundrel whose dishonesty is notorious
         Emerges from another lie victorious!
15   Honor and right condone[1] his brazen fraud,
         While rectitude and decency applaud!
         Before his smirking face, the truth stands charmed,
         And virtue conquered, and the law disarmed!
         His crime is sanctioned by a court decree!
20   And not content with what he's done to me,
         The dog now seeks to ruin me by stating
         That I composed a book now circulating,
         A book so wholly criminal and vicious

---

[20] *protracted*—lengthy.
[21] rigmarole—nonsense.
[1] condone—overlook.

That even to speak its title is seditious!²

25 Meanwhile Oronte, my rival, lends his credit
To the same libelous³ tale, and helps to spread it!
Oronte! a man of honor and of rank,
With whom I've been entirely fair and frank;
Who sought me out and forced me, willy-nilly,

30 To judge some verse I found extremely silly;
And who, because I properly refused
To flatter him, or see the truth abused,
Abets⁴ my enemy in a rotten slander!
There's the reward of honesty and candor!

35 The man will hate me to the end of time
For failing to commend his wretched rhyme!
And not this man alone, but all humanity
Do what they do from interest and vanity;
They prate of honor, truth, and righteousness,

40 But lie, betray, and swindle nonetheless.
Come then: man's villainy is too much to bear;
Let's leave this jungle and this jackal's lair.
Yes! treacherous and savage race of men,
You shall not look upon my face again.

45 **Philinte.** Oh, don't rush into exile prematurely;
Things aren't as dreadful as you make them, surely.
It's rather obvious, since you're still at large,
That people don't believe your enemy's charge.
Indeed, his tale's so patently⁵ untrue

50 That it may do more harm to him than you.

Alceste. Nothing could do that scoundrel any harm:
His frank corruption is his greatest charm,
And, far from hurting him, a further shame
Would only serve to magnify his name.

55 **Philinte.** In any case, his bald prevarication⁶
Has done no injury to your reputation,
And you may feel secure in that regard.

---

² seditious—rebellious.

³ libelous—damaging to reputation.

⁴ Abets—aids in a crime.

⁵ patently—obviously, plainly.

⁶ prevarication—lie.

As for your lawsuit, it should not be hard
To have the case reopened, and contest
60   This judgment . . .

Alceste.   No, no, let the verdict rest.
Whatever cruel penalty it may bring,
I wouldn't have it changed for anything.
It shows the times' injustice with such **clarity**[7]
That I shall pass it down to our **posterity**[8]
65   As a great proof and signal demonstration
Of the black wickedness of this generation.
It may cost twenty thousand francs; but I
Shall pay their twenty thousand, and gain thereby
The right to storm and rage at human evil,
70   And send the race of mankind to the devil.

Philinte. Listen to me. . . .

Alceste.   Why? What can you possibly say?
Don't argue, Sir; your labor's thrown away.
Do you propose to offer lame excuses
For men's behavior and the times' abuses?

75   **Philinte.** No, all you say I'll readily concede:
This is a low, dishonest age indeed;
Nothing but trickery prospers nowadays,
And people ought to mend their shabby ways.
Yes, man's a beastly creature; but must we then
80   Abandon the society of men?
Here in the world, each human frailty
Provides occasion for philosophy,
And that is virtue's noblest exercise;
If honesty shone forth from all men's eyes,
85   If every heart were frank and kind and just,
What could our virtues do but gather dust
(Since their employment is to help us bear
The villainies of men without despair)?
A heart well-armed with virtue can endure. . . .

90   **Alceste.** Sir, you're a matchless reasoner, to be sure;
Your words are fine and full of **cogency**;[9]

---

[7] **clarity**—clearness.

[8] **posterity**—descendents.

[9] cogency—force.

But don't waste time and eloquence on me.
My reason bids me go, for my own good.
My tongue won't lie and flatter as it should;

95   God knows what frankness it might next commit,
And what I'd suffer on account of it.
Pray let me wait for Célimène's return
In peace and quiet. I shall shortly learn,
By her response to what I have in view,

100   Whether her love for me is feigned or true.

Philinte. Till then, let's visit Eliante upstairs.

Alceste. No, I am too weighed down with somber cares.
Go to her, do; and leave me with my gloom
Here in the darkened corner of this room.

105 **Philinte.** Why, that's no sort of company, my friend;
I'll see if Eliante will not descend.

Act Five, Scene Two

[Célimène, Oronte, Alceste]

Oronte. Yes, Madam, if you wish me to remain
Your true and ardent lover, you must deign
To give me some more positive assurance.
All this suspense is quite beyond endurance.

5   If your heart shares the sweet desires of mine,
Show me as much by some convincing sign;
And here's the sign I urgently suggest:
That you no longer tolerate Alceste,
But sacrifice him to my love, and sever

10   All your relations with the man forever.

Célimène. Why do you suddenly dislike him so?
You praised him to the skies not long ago.

Oronte. Madam, that's not the point. I'm here to find
Which way your tender feelings are inclined.

15   Choose, if you please, between Alceste and me,
And I shall stay or go accordingly.

Alceste [*emerging from the corner*]. Yes, Madam, choose; this
            gentleman's demand
Is wholly just, and I support his stand.
I too am true and ardent; I too am here

20   To ask you that you make your feelings clear.

      No more delays, now; no equivocation;

      The time has come to make your declaration.

     Oronte. Sir, I've no wish in any way to be

      An obstacle to your **felicity**.[10]

25   **Alceste.** Sir, I've no wish to share her heart with you;

      That may sound jealous, but at least it's true.

     Oronte. If, weighing us, she leans in your direction . . .

     Alceste. If she regards you with the least affection . . .

     Oronte. I swear I'll yield her to you there and then.

30   **Alceste.** I swear I'll never see her face again.

     Oronte. Now, Madam, tell us what we've come to hear.

     Alceste. Madam, speak openly and have no fear.

     Oronte. Just say which one is to remain your lover.

     Alceste. Just name one name, and it will all be over.

35   **Oronte.** What! Is it possible that you're undecided?

     Alceste. What! Can your feelings possibly be divided?

     Célimène. Enough: this inquisition's gone too far:

      How utterly unreasonable you are!

      Not that I couldn't make the choice with ease;

40   My heart has no conflicting sympathies;

      I know full well which one of you I favor,

      And you'd not see me hesitate or waver.

      But how can you expect me to reveal

      So cruelly and bluntly what I feel?

45   I think it altogether too unpleasant

      To choose between two men when both are present;

      One's heart has means more subtle and more kind

      Of letting its affections be divined,

      Nor need one be uncharitably plain

50   To let a lover know he loves in vain.

     Oronte. No, no, speak plainly; I for one can stand it.

      I beg you to be frank.

     Alceste.   And I demand it.

      The simple truth is what I wish to know,

      And there's no need for softening the blow.

55   You've made an art of pleasing everyone,

---

[10] **felicity**—happiness.

But now your days of coquetry are done:
You have no choice now, Madam, but to choose,
For I'll know what to think if you refuse;
I'll take your silence for a clear admission
60   That I'm entitled to my worst suspicion.
Oronte. I thank you for this **ultimatum**,[11] Sir,
And I may say I heartily concur.
Célimène. Really, this foolishness is very wearing:
Must you be so unjust and overbearing?
65   Haven't I told you why I must demur?[12]
Ah, here's Eliante; I'll put the case to her.

Act Five, Scene Three

[Eliante, Philinte, Célimène, Oronte, Alceste]
Célimène. Cousin, I'm being persecuted here
By these two persons, who, it would appear,
Will not be satisfied till I confess
Which one I love the more, and which the less,
5   And tell the latter to his face that he
Is henceforth banished from my company.
Tell me, has ever such a thing been done?
Eliante. You'd best not turn to me; I'm not the one
To back you in a matter of this kind:
10   I'm all for those who frankly speak their mind.
Oronte. Madam, you'll search in vain for a defender.
Alceste. You're beaten, Madam, and may as well surrender.
Oronte. Speak, speak, you must; and end this awful strain.
Alceste. Or don't, and your position will be plain.
15   **Oronte.** A single word will close this painful scene.
Alceste. But if you're silent, I'll know what you mean.

---

[11] **ultimatum**—final demand.
[12] demur—object.

Act Five, Scene Four

[Arsinoé, Célimène, Eliante, Alceste, Philinte, Acaste, Clitandre, Oronte]

Acaste [*to* Célimène]. Madam, with all due deference,[13] we two
    Have come to pick a little bone with you.

Clitandre [*to* Oronte *and* Alceste]. I'm glad you're present, Sirs; as you'll
       soon learn,
    Our business here is also your concern.

5   **Arsinoé** [*to* Célimène]. Madam, I visit you so soon again
    Only because of these two gentlemen,
    Who came to me indignant and aggrieved
    About a crime too base to be believed.
    Knowing your virtue, having such confidence in it,
10   I couldn't think you guilty for a minute,
    In spite of all their telling evidence;
    And, rising above our little difference,
    I've hastened here in friendship's name to see
    You clear yourself of this great calumny.[14]

15   **Acaste.** Yes, Madam, let us see with what composure
    You'll manage to respond to this disclosure.
    You lately sent Clitandre this tender note.

Clitandre. And this one, for Acaste, you also wrote.

Acaste [*to* Oronte *and* Alceste]. You'll recognize this writing, Sirs, I think;
20   The lady is so free with pen and ink
    That you must know it all too well, I fear.
    But listen: this is something you should hear.
    "How absurd you are to condemn my lightheartedness in society, and
    to accuse me of being happiest in the company of others. Nothing
25   could be more unjust; and if you do not come to me instantly and
    beg pardon for saying such a thing, I shall never forgive you as long
    as I live. Our big bumbling friend the Viscount[15] . . ."
    What a shame that he's not here.
    "Our big bumbling friend the Viscount, whose name stands first in
30   your complaint, is hardly a man to my taste; and ever since the day I
    watched him spend three-quarters of an hour spitting into a well, so
    as to make circles in the water, I have been unable to think highly of

---

[13] deference—respect.

[14] calumny—false charge.

[15] Viscount—nobleman.

him. As for the little Marquess . . ."
In all modesty, gentlemen, that is I.

35 "As for the little Marquess, who sat squeezing my hand for such a
long while yesterday, I find him in all respects the most trifling
creature alive; and the only things of value about him are his cape
and his sword. As for the man with the green ribbons . . ."
[*To* Alceste.] It's your turn now, Sir.

40 "As for the man with the green ribbons, he amuses me now and
then with his bluntness and his bearish ill-humor; but there are
many times indeed when I think him the greatest bore in the
world. And as for the sonneteer . . ."
[*To* Oronte.] Here's your helping.

45 "And as for the sonneteer, who has taken it into his head to be
witty, and insists on being an author in the teeth of opinion, I simply cannot be bothered to listen to him, and his prose wearies me
quite as much as his poetry. Be assured that I am not always so
well-entertained as you suppose; that I long for your company,

50 more than I dare to say, at all these entertainments to which people
drag me; and that the presence of those one loves is the true and
perfect seasoning to all one's pleasures."

Clitandre. And now for me.
"Clitandre, whom you mention, and who so pesters me with his

55 saccharine[16] speeches, is the last man on earth for whom I could
feel any affection. He is quite mad to suppose that I love him, and
so are you, to doubt that you are loved. Do come to your senses;
exchange your suppositions for his; and visit me as often as possible, to help me bear the annoyance of his unwelcome attentions."

60 It's a sweet character that these letters show,
And what to call it, Madam, you well know.
Enough. We're off to make the world acquainted
With this sublime self-portrait that you've painted.

Acaste. Madam, I'll make you no farewell oration;

65 No, you're not worthy of my indignation.
Far choicer hearts than yours, as you'll discover,
Would like this little Marquess for a lover.

---

[16] saccharine—sweet.

Act Five, Scene Five

[Célimène, Eliante, Arsinoé, Alceste, Oronte, Philinte]

Oronte. So! After all those loving letters you wrote,
    You turn on me like this, and cut my throat!
    And your dissembling,[17] faithless heart, I find,
    Has pledged itself by turns to all mankind!
5   How blind I've been! But now I clearly see;
    I thank you, Madam, for enlightening me.
    My heart is mine once more, and I'm content;
    The loss of it shall be your punishment.
    [*To* Alceste]
    Sir, she is yours; I'll seek no more to stand
10   Between your wishes and this lady's hand.

Act Five, Scene Six

[Célimène, Eliante, Arsinoé, Alceste, Philinte]

Arsinoé [*to* Célimène]. Madam, I'm forced to speak. I'm far too stirred
    To keep my counsel, after what I've heard.
    I'm shocked and staggered by your want of morals.
    It's not my way to mix in others' quarrels;
5   But really, when this fine and noble spirit,
    This man of honor and surpassing merit,
    Laid down the offering of his heart before you,
    How *could* you . . .

Alceste.   Madam, permit me, I implore you,
    To represent myself in this debate.
10   Don't bother, please, to be my advocate.
    My heart, in any case, could not afford
    To give your services their due reward;
    And if I chose, for consolation's sake,
    Some other lady, t'would not be you I'd take.
15 **Arsinoé.** What makes you think you could, Sir? And how dare you
    Imply that I've been trying to ensnare you?
    If you can for a moment entertain
    Such flattering fancies, you're extremely vain.
    I'm not so interested as you suppose

[17] dissembling—false.

20   In Célimène's discarded gigolos.[18]
Get rid of that absurd illusion, do.
Women like me are not for such as you.
Stay with this creature, to whom you're so attached;
I've never seen two people better matched.

Act Five, Scene Seven

[Célimène, Eliante, Alceste, Philinte]

Alceste [*to* Célimène]. Well, I've been still throughout this exposé,
Till everyone but me has said his say.
Come, have I shown sufficient self-restraint?
And may I now . . .

Célimène.   Yes, make your just complaint.

5   Reproach me freely, call me what you will;
You've every right to say I've used you ill.
I've wronged you, I confess it; and in my shame
I'll make no effort to escape the blame.
The anger of those others I could despise;

10   My guilt toward you I sadly recognize.
Your wrath is wholly justified, I fear;
I know how culpable[19] I must appear,
I know all things bespeak my treachery,
And that, in short, you've grounds for hating me.

15   Do so; I give you leave.

Alceste.   Ah, traitress—how,
How should I cease to love you, even now?
Though mind and will were passionately bent
On hating you, my heart would not consent.
[*To* Eliante *and* Philinte.]
Be witness to my madness, both of you;

20   See what infatuation drives one to;
But wait; my folly's only just begun,
And I shall prove to you before I'm done
How strange the human heart is, and how far
From rational we sorry creatures are.

---

[18] gigolos—paid male escorts.

[19] culpable—guilty.

[*To* Célimène.]

25   Woman, I'm willing to forget your shame,
      And clothe your treacheries in a sweeter name;
      I'll call them youthful errors, instead of crimes,
      And lay the blame on these corrupting times.
      My one condition is that you agree
30   To share my chosen fate, and fly with me
      To that wild, trackless, solitary place
      In which I shall forget the human race.
      Only by such a course can you atone
      For those atrocious letters; by that alone
35   Can you remove my present horror of you,
      And make it possible for me to love you.

Célimène. What! *I* renounce the world at my young age,
      And die of boredom in some hermitage?

Alceste. Ah, if you really loved me as you ought,
40   You wouldn't give the world a moment's thought;
      Must you have me, and all the world beside?

Célimène. Alas, at twenty one is terrified
      Of solitude. I fear I lack the force
      And depth of soul to take so stern a course.
45   But if my hand in marriage will content you,
      Why, there's a plan which I might well consent to,
      And . . .

Alceste.   No, I detest you now. I could excuse
      Everything else, but since you thus refuse
      To love me wholly, as a wife should do,
50   And see the world in me, as I in you,
      Go! I reject your hand, and disenthrall[20]
      My heart from your enchantments, once for all.

Act Five, Scene Eight

[Eliante, Alceste, Philinte]

Alceste [*to* Eliante]. Madam, your virtuous beauty has no peer;
      Of all this world, you only are sincere;
      I've long esteemed you highly, as you know;

---

[20] disenthrall—free from a spell.

Permit me ever to esteem you so,
5   And if I do not now request your hand,
Forgive me, Madam, and try to understand.
I feel unworthy of it; I sense that fate
Does not intend me for the married state,
That I should do you wrong by offering you
10 My shattered heart's unhappy residue,
And that in short . . .

Eliante.   Your argument's well taken:
Nor need you fear that I shall feel forsaken.
Were I to offer him this hand of mine,
Your friend Philinte, I think, would not decline.

15 **Philinte.** Ah, Madam, that's my heart's most cherished goal,
For which I'd gladly give my life and soul.

Alceste [*to* Eliante *and* Philinte]. May you be true to all you now profess,
And so deserve unending happiness.
Meanwhile, betrayed and wronged in everything,
20 I'll flee this bitter world where vice is king,
And seek some spot unpeopled and apart
Where I'll be free to have an honest heart.

Philinte. Come, Madam, let's do everything we can
To change the mind of this unhappy man.

UNDERSTANDING THE PLAY

Act One

1. In Scene One, of what does Alceste accuse Philinte? How does Philinte defend himself?

2. What attitude does Alceste express toward winning his upcoming court case?

3. Why does Philinte feel that Alceste's love for Célimène is inconsistent with his general views on human beings?

4. In Scene Two, why does Oronte bring his sonnet to Alceste? What results from this?

Act Two

1. In Scene One, how does Célimène react to Alceste's complaints about her behavior toward other men?

2. In Scene Five, how do Célimène, Acaste, and Clitandre discuss their acquaintances?

3. In lines 111–122, how does Célimène analyze Alceste's character?

4. In Scene Seven, what results from Alceste's quarrel with Oronte?

Act Three

1. In Scene One, what do Clitandre and Acaste agree to do concerning Célimène?

2. In Scene Three, how does Célimène analyze Arsinoé's character?

3. In Scene Five, how does Arsinoé advise Célimène? How does Célimène respond?

4. In Scene Seven, why does Arsinoé criticize Célimène to Alceste?

Act Four

1. In Scene One, what attitude does Eliante express toward Alceste's love for Célimène? How does Philinte feel toward Eliante?

2. In Scene Two, why does Alceste offer his love to Eliante? How does she respond?

3. In Scene Three, how does Célimène react to Alceste's charge of unfaithfulness?

4. In Scene Four, why does Alceste's servant Dubois say he and his master must flee?

Act Five

1. In Scene One, what has been the result of Alceste's court case?

2. In Scene Two, what demand do Alceste and Oronte make of Célimène?

3. In Scene Four, what do Célimène's notes to Acaste and Clitandre reveal?

4. In Scene Seven, what does Alceste offer Célimène? How does she respond?

ANALYZING THE PLAY

1. The conflict in a play is the struggle between opposing forces that gives movement to the dramatic plot. What is the fundamental conflict in *The Misanthrope*?

2. What are Alceste's strengths and weaknesses? What are Célimène's?

3. How does Molière adhere to the dramatic unities in *The Misanthrope*?

4. The German critic Schlegel said *The Misanthrope* was improbable because someone like Alceste would never have fallen in love with Célimène or had Philinte as a friend. What is your opinion?

5. With which character's point of view do you think Molière most closely sympathizes? Why?

Performing at the Globe

BY JOSEPH PAPP AND ELIZABETH KIRKLAND

American theatrical producer and director Joseph Papp (1921–1991) was the founder of the New York Shakespeare Festival. In the following excerpt from their book Shakespeare Alive!, *he and Elizabeth Kirkland describe how plays were rehearsed and performed at Shakespeare's Globe Theater.*

Unlike their twentieth-century successors, Shakespearean actors don't have time to go into a long period of rehearsal, crafting every line to perfection under the seasoned eye of a director. If anyone guides the actors through the play, explaining his sense of how it should be performed, it may be the playwright himself. . . .

Rehearsal itself isn't really an issue, it appears, simply because there is never time for it to become one. The average time span between the day a company receives a new play from a playwright and the first performance is about two weeks. Whether the company rehearses as the comical players do in *A Midsummer Night's Dream,* "by moonlight" in a forest clearing, where "This green plot shall be our stage, this hawthorn brake our tiring-house,"[1] or on the stage of the Globe in the remaining hour or two of daylight after that afternoon's

performance, not much time can be spent working out the details.

But, like everything else in the theater, the few rehearsals that do take place are a collaborative effort. Bottom and Quince and Company again provide a delightful illustration of this. They all agree on the length and form of a prologue to introduce their play. They discuss the possible effects of their presentation on the ladies in the audience, and they resolve the problems that come up in the course of the rehearsal by mutual consent. . . .

While the actors are running around onstage trying to pull the play together in two weeks, the stationer or printer they take their business to is busy printing up playbills to advertise "A New Play, to be played at the Globe on Bankside the Tuesday next." The hired men post these

---

[1] tiring-house—dressing room. (*Tiring* is a shortened form of *attiring*, "dressing.")

signs all over town to lure audiences to their theater. Competition with the other forms of popular entertainment is heated indeed, and a less-than-scrupulous actor might feel perfectly within his rights to post his sign on top of an ad for the bear-baiting at the nearby arena. But this isn't really necessary, for a new play is guaranteed to draw big crowds, even if its title and author aren't announced ahead of time. . . .

Opening day arrives almost before anyone can turn around. Up goes the company's silken flag on the pole above the playhouse. Backstage the book-keeper hangs the "plot," a big piece of thick paper pasted on cardboard that dangles from a nail in the tiring-room. It is crucial to a smooth-running performance, for it contains all the essential information about which actor is playing which parts, when actors enter and exit, what props they should be carrying, at what point specific sound effects are needed, and other necessary stage business.

As the actors scan this plot for last-minute reminders, the audiences flock in. The gatherers, or ticket-takers make sure that no one tries to sneak in without paying his penny. The fruit and nut sellers, having laid in all extra supply for the bigger and more enthusiastic opening day crowds wander about the theater hawking their wares. There is a general hubbub as apprentices jostle one another to sit near their friends or an attractive girl, bricklayers happily rub elbows with perfumed ladies, and jealous playwrights stand, quill in hand, ready to borrow a catch phrase or two. . . .

As the flourish of the trumpet and the beat of the drum waft out over the heads of the groundlings,[2] the crowd grows quiet and settles in for "the two hours' traffic of our stage," as Shakespeare refers to it in his Prologue to *Romeo and Juliet.* (It is still a mystery how a four-hour play like *Hamlet* could be played in two hours.) Over that time there's plenty of action to hold the attention of the most impatient apprentice. There is dancing and singing; there are processions, tournaments, battles, betrothals, and lots more—all as run-of-the-mill in all Elizabethan theater as car chases, bedroom scenes, and shoot-outs are in today's adventure movies.

The costumes are a stunning component of the spectacle, colorful and lavish, richly embroidered with pearls and golden thread, and made of the finest materials. They are a company's most important possession, and the single biggest expenditure in the production budget, along with the playbooks. . . . No expense is spared in collecting the most beautiful garments. Luckily, most of the costumes actually turn out to be less expensive than they look. Many costumes, in fact are cast-offs from rich nobles, bought secondhand from their servants. . . .

But a good play is more than just a pretty picture; it requires good acting as well. And the audience at the Globe sees plenty of that. The actors in Shakespeare's company are the cream of the crop—talented versatile entertainers who combine the legs and lungs of

---

[2] groundlings—audience standing on the ground in the Pit, the area in front of the stage in an Elizabethan theater.

an Olympic athlete, the vocal chords of a rock star, the quick wit of a standup comic, and the memory of a computer.

The audience listens, rapt, to the actors' stirring delivery of their lines—in a somewhat more artificial style than a modern audience might be comfortable with, and at a decibel level high enough to compete with the cries of the watermen on the river, the creaking of coach wheels rolling by, and the suburban bustle of Southwark.

But although their speech might be more rhetorical or formalized, it is lively and natural. We have only to look at the evidence of Shakespeare's plays to understand that his actors couldn't be anything but natural and life-like. And indeed, Shakespeare shows what his conception of good acting is when he has Hamlet instruct the Players in the essentials of the art of performing. Hamlet counsels them to speak nimbly but with feeling, to gesture gently and to remember above all that the purpose of acting is—and always will be—"to hold . . . the mirror up to nature."

QUESTIONS TO CONSIDER

1. How were rehearsals handled by an Elizabethan theater company?

2. What elements contributed to the "entertainment value" offered an audience at the Globe?

The Rehearsal at Versailles

BY MOLIÈRE

In his one-act play, The Rehearsal at Versailles, *the French dramatist Molière presents a glimpse of himself as director, rehearsing the actors of his company before a performance for the king at his palace at Versailles.*

Molière. Actors—impossible creatures to handle—

Mlle[1] Béjart. We're all here. What do you want with us?

Mlle du Parc. What do you have in mind?

Mlle de Brie. What are we doing?

Molière. We have our costumes on. Let's get ready to start. The King will be here in two hours; we can make good use of the time by blocking out the business[2] and improving the readings.

La Grange. How can we act parts we haven't learned?

Mlle du Parc. I honestly don't remember one word I'm supposed to say.

Mlle de Brie. I'll have to be prompted from start to finish.

Mlle Béjart. I'll have to hold my script.

Mlle Molière. So will I.

Mlle Hervé. I have practically no lines to speak.

Mlle Du Croisy. Nor have I, but I won't be responsible if I fluff them.

Du Croisy. One hundred francs for anybody who wants my part.

Brecourt. Flog me twenty times before I play mine.

Molière. Look at the way you're all quivering over a few simple parts. What would you do if you were me?

Mlle Béjart. Who feels sorry for you? You wrote the play; you're not afraid of drying up.

---

[1] **Mlle**—abbreviation for the title *Mademoiselle*, "Miss."
[2] blocking out the business—coordinating actors' movements relating to props, costumes, and make-up.

Molière. A bad memory's not the only thing I'm afraid of. If the play fails, it's my failure. To stage a comedy for this kind of an audience is no joke. These are not easy people to amuse or impress. They laugh only when they feel like it. What author wouldn't tremble at facing this severe a test? I should be the one who wants to back out.

Mlle Béjart. If you're nervous, it's your own fault. You should have taken the proper precautions and given yourself more than a week to put the thing together.

Molière. How could I help it? The King gave me an order.

Mlle Béjart. How? By excusing yourself respectfully. By explaining that it's impossible in such a short time. Any other author would have refused to commit himself so heavily. What happens to your reputation if the play goes over badly? Think how your rivals will gloat about it.

Mlle de Brie. She's right. You should have politely asked the King to excuse you, or to give you more time.

Molière. A King expects prompt obedience; he doesn't like obstacles thrown up at him. He wants his entertainment when he asks for it; he doesn't wish to be kept waiting. As far as he's concerned, the faster it's prepared the better. We can't study our personal feelings; we're here to satisfy him, and when he gives us an opportunity we must seize it and do our best to give him pleasure in return. It's better to make a clumsy attempt than not to make an attempt until too late. Even if we don't entirely succeed it'll be to our credit that we complied with his orders. And now, please, the rehearsal.

Mlle Béjart. How are we supposed to rehearse when we don't know our parts?

Molière. But you will, I promise; not thoroughly, perhaps, but you do know what the play's about and you can improvise, since it's in prose. . . . Now, you, Mademoiselle du Parc—

Mlle du Parc. I'm going to be awful in this part, and I don't see why you always make me play a fashionable lady.

Molière. You said the same thing in the last play, yet you pulled it off marvelously. Everybody said you couldn't have been better. You'll do it again, I promise you. You just don't realize how good you are.

Mlle du Parc. How's that possible? Nobody is less of a fashionable lady than I am.

Molière. Exactly. That proves what a fine actress you are, capturing a person who is totally unlike you. Now, I want you all to get inside your characters, to become them. Du Croisy, you're the playwright, and you must fill out personality. He's a pedant[3] moving in high society and trying to hold on to what he thinks is his integrity. Pompous tone of voice. Rigorous pronunciation which doesn't miss a single syllable; can practically hear every letter spelled out.

Brecourt, your part is exactly the same as that of Dorante in the last play, an honest man at Court. Look thoughtful, speak in a natural voice, and **gesticulate**[4] as little as possible. . . .

Mademoiselle Béjart, you're one of those women who think that because they don't make love they can do anything else. They sit back proudly on their prudery, looking down on every newcomer, each one telling herself that other women's virtues don't compare with her miserable honor—which nobody wants to take from her anyway. Imagine her face in front of you so that you can catch the right expressions.

Mademoiselle de Brie, you play one of those women who thinks she's good as long as nobody knows she's bad. If there's no scandal there can't be any sin. When she has an affair afoot she pursues it quietly, and she calls the young men who come wooing her "my innocent friends." Steep yourself in this character. . . .

Mademoiselle du Croisy, you're one of those people who pay nasty compliments to everybody; you never miss a chance to drop a sweet insult out of the side of your mouth, and you can't bear to hear anybody speak well of her neighbor. I think you can carry this off well.

Finally, Mademoiselle Hervé, you're similar to the servant in *Two Precious Maidens Ridiculed*.[5] You join in the conversation now and again and borrow your mistress' jargon.

I've told you all about the important characteristics, and I hope I've impressed them on you. Now we'll run through the text and see how it goes. . . .

---

[3] pedant—fussy scholar.

[4] **gesticulate**—make gestures while speaking, especially for emphasis.

[5] *Two Precious Maidens Ridiculed*—play by Molière.

QUESTIONS TO CONSIDER

1. If you judge by *The Rehearsal at Versailles*, what special problems were faced by an acting company in Molière's time?

2. As a director, how does Molière relate to his actors?

On Stage

Renaissance and Neoclassical Theater

In the late 1500s and early 1600s, there was a golden age of theater in Europe that rivaled that of ancient Greece. In England, Renaissance drama reached its height in the plays of William Shakespeare; in France, in those of Molière. Both dramatists were involved in all aspects of theater— as playwrights, actors, and managers of professional companies.

▲

One influence on Renaissance drama was *commedia dell'arte,* a form of improvisational theater that originated in Italy in the 1500s, using stock characters (such as the famous Harlequin figure shown here) and situations for which performers made up dialogue.

◀ An artist's reconstruction of Shakespeare's own theater, the Globe, shows the audience in the gallery and the performers on stage.

A typical playhouse in Shakespeare's London, the Swan Theater (shown here in a drawing from 1596) featured a thrust stage surrounded by galleries for the audience. The area directly in front of the stage provided standing room for those who couldn't afford a seat in the galleries.
▼

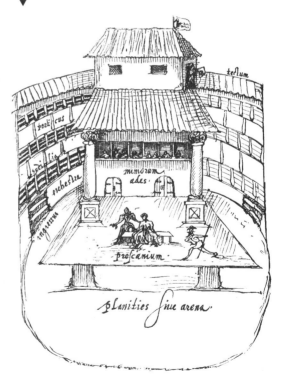

▲

An artist's reconstruction suggests what a performance of *A Midsummer Night's Dream* might have looked like in Shakespeare's day.

◀ This scene is from a stage production of *A Midsummer Night's Dream* by German director Max Reinhardt, who also directed a 1935 movie version of the play.

Demetrius (Robert Williams) and Lysander (Del Parker) are shown competing for the affection of Helena (Grace Chaporan) in a scene from a 1957 production of *A Midsummer Night's Dream* at the Antioch Shakespeare Festival in Ohio.

▲

(Left) One version of Bottom's transformation is shown in a 1996 production of *A Midsummer Night's Dream* at the Guthrie Theater in Minneapolis. (Right) A more abstract approach to Bottom's make-up is shown in a 1991 production at Seattle's Intiman Theatre.

In this 1998 production of *A Midsummer Night's Dream* by Boston's Huntington Theatre Company, Puck is presented as a half-goat creature reminiscent of the Greek god Pan. ▶

▲

In this scene from the 1942 production of *Othello* starring
Paul Robeson, Iago (Jose Ferrer) begins to plant doubts in
Othello's mind about his wife's faithfulness.

In the final scene from the 1942 production, Othello prepares
to murder his wife Desdemona (Uta Hagen). ▶

▲

In the 1991 production of *Othello* at the New York Shakespeare Festival, Othello
was played by Raul Julia, Desdemona by Kathryn Meisle, Iago by Christopher Walken,
and Emilia by Mary Beth Hurt.

▲
Othello (Ezra Knight) threatens Iago (Allen Gilmore) in this 1995 production of *Othello* by The Acting Company.

◀ The elaborate theatrical costumes of Molière's theater, shown here in a scene from his first successful comedy, *The Ridiculous Damsels,* reflected the fashions of the time.

Typical of French theaters in Molière's time, Paris's Hôtel de Bourgogne had a long, narrow auditorium, with two galleries running along the walls and a narrow stage (shown here in an engraving from the 1600s) across one end.

▼

Alceste (Stephen Lang) and Célimène (Nancy Bell) appear in the elaborate theatrical costumes of Molière's own time in this 1996 production of *The Misanthrope* at the McCarter Theatre in Princeton, New Jersey. ▶

◀ In this 1993 Long Wharf Theatre production of *The Misanthrope*, actors playing Alceste (Nicholas Woodeson) and Philinte (David Manis) are costumed in the fashion of the early 1800s.

Part Three

Modern Drama

Reality and Dreams

Realist playwrights such as Henrik Ibsen and Anton Chekhov created modern drama by presenting human life as it actually existed. Later, antirealist dramatists such as Federico García Lorca revealed the fragmented inner life of humanity through fantasies, hallucinations, and nightmares.

An Enemy of the People HENRIK IBSEN

The Sea Gull ANTON CHEKHOV

Blood Wedding FEDERICO GARCÍA LORCA

◀ Act One of *The Sea Gull* is shown in a 1997 production at the Yale School of Drama.

Henrik Ibsen ▶

An Enemy of the People

BY HENRIK IBSEN

Throughout most of the 1800s, very little dramatic literature of high quality was produced. During this period, most theater was simply entertainment for a new urban mass audience. This theater was more concerned with sensationalism and spectacular crowd-pleasing stage effects than with exploring important ideas or presenting great drama. The typical theatrical form of the period was the melodrama, characterized by exaggerated sentiment, romantic plots, and elaborate staging. The acting style of 19th-century theater was also exaggerated and artificial, employing declamatory vocal techniques and conventionalized gestures and poses.

Naturalism

The movement away from this artificial, escapist theater began in France in the 1870s with the French literary movement known as naturalism. Basing their views on contemporary scientific theory, naturalists believed that human character was completely shaped by heredity and environment. Naturalist writers such as Émile Zola (1840–1902) felt that plays should be rigorously detailed "case studies." These "slices of life" should present their subjects with absolute fidelity, displaying no more artistic structure than life does. The influence of naturalism spread after André Antoine (1858–1943) founded the Théâtre Libre (Free Theater) in Paris, where the works of Zola and other contemporary playwrights were performed. This marked the beginning of the Independent Theater Movement, which spread to other European countries.

Founder of Modern Realism

Among the first works performed by these independent theater companies were the plays of Norwegian dramatist Henrik Ibsen (1828–1906). Ibsen's early plays were verse dramas dealing with a romantic past. These were followed by his most influential works, four prose plays presenting realistic pictures of small-town life in contemporary Norway: The Pillars of Society, A Doll's House, Ghosts, *and* An Enemy of the People. *The impact of these plays was enormous and can be said to mark the beginning of modern realistic drama. Realism had its origin in naturalism and differed from it chiefly in how closely a dramatist attempted to reproduce the details of actual life. Like Zola, Ibsen was interested in contemporary scientific and political ideas, but he did not imitate the naturalists' formless "slice-of-life" approach. Ibsen's plays are realistic presentations of problems of everyday life rendered in ordinary language; but they are also carefully plotted and well-structured, displaying a thorough mastery of stagecraft.*

A Majority of One

At the heart of An Enemy of the People *(1882) is the character of Dr. Thomas Stockmann, an individual who, like his creator, sees the need to stir up his community. During the time he was writing* An Enemy of the People, *Ibsen asserted in a letter, "The minority is always right," and then went on to say, "I mean the minority in the vanguard that pushes on to points which the majority has not yet reached. I believe that that man is in the right who is most closely in league with the future."*

CHARACTERS

Doctor Thomas Stockmann, medical officer of the Baths
Mrs. Stockmann, his wife
Petra, their daughter, a teacher
Eilif and Morten, their sons, thirteen and ten years old, respectively
Peter Stockmann, the doctor's elder brother, Burgomaster[1] and chief of police, chairman of the Baths Committee, etc.

Morten Kiil, master tanner, Mrs. Stockmann's adoptive father
Hovstad, editor of the *People's Messenger*
Billing, on the staff of the paper
Horster, a ship's captain
Aslaksen, a printer
Participants in a meeting of citizens: all sorts and conditions of men, some women, and a band of schoolboys

The action passes in a town on the South Coast of Norway.

Act One

[*Evening.* Dr. Stockmann's *sitting room; simply but neatly decorated and furnished. In the wall to the right are two doors, the further one leading to the hall, the nearer one to the Doctor's study. In the opposite wall, facing the hall door, a door leading to the other rooms of the house. Against the middle of this wall stands the stove; further forward a sofa with a mirror above it, and in front of it an oval table with a cover. On the table a lighted lamp, with a shade. In the back wall an open door leading to the dining room, in which is seen a supper table, with a lamp on it.*

Billing *is seated at the supper table, with a napkin under his chin.* Mrs. Stockmann *is standing by the table and placing before him a dish with a large joint of roast beef. The other seats round the table are empty; the table is in disorder, as after a meal.*]

Mrs. Stockmann. If you come an hour late, Mr. Billing, you must put up with a cold supper.

---

[1] Burgomaster—magistrate.

Billing [*eating*]. It is excellent—really first rate.

Mrs. Stockmann. You know how Stockmann insists on regular meal-hours—

Billing. Oh, I don't mind at all. I almost think I enjoy my supper more when I can sit down to it like this, alone and undisturbed.

Mrs. Stockmann. Oh, well, if you enjoy it— [*Listening in the direction of the hall.*] I believe this is Mr. Hovstad coming too.

Billing. Very likely.

[Burgomaster Stockmann *enters, wearing an overcoat and an official gold-laced cap, and carrying a stick.*]

Burgomaster. Good evening, sister-in-law.

Mrs. Stockmann [*coming forward into the sitting room*]. Oh, good evening; is it you? It is good of you to look in.

Burgomaster. I was just passing, and so— [*Looks towards the drawing room.*] Ah, I see you have company.

Mrs. Stockmann [*rather embarrassed*]. Oh no, not at all; it's the merest chance. [*Hurriedly.*] Won't you sit down and have a little supper?

Burgomaster. I? No, thank you. Good gracious! hot meat in the evening! That wouldn't suit my digestion.

Mrs. Stockmann. Oh, for once in a way—

Burgomaster. No, no,—much obliged to you. I stick to tea and bread and butter. It's more wholesome in the long run—and rather more economical, too.

Mrs. Stockmann [*smiling*]. You mustn't think Thomas and I are mere spendthrifts, either.

Burgomaster. You are not, sister-in-law; far be it for me to say that. [*Pointing to the Doctor's study.*] Is he not at home?

Mrs. Stockmann. No, he has gone for a little turn[2] after supper—with the boys.

Burgomaster. I wonder if that is a good thing to do? [*Listening.*] There he is, no doubt.

Mrs. Stockmann. No, that is not he. [*A knock.*] Come in! [Hovstad *enters from the hall.*]

Mrs. Stockmann. Ah, it's Mr. Hovstad—

Hovstad. You must excuse me; I was detained at the printer's. Good evening, Burgomaster.

---

[2] turn—walk.

Burgomaster [*bowing rather stiffly*]. Mr. Hovstad? You come on business, I presume?

Hovstad. Partly. About an article for the paper.

Burgomaster. So I supposed. I hear my brother is an extremely **prolific**[3] contributor to the *People's Messenger.*

Hovstad. Yes, when he wants to unburden his mind on one thing or another, he gives the *Messenger* the benefit.

Mrs. Stockmann [*to* Hovstad]. But will you not—? [*Points to the dining room.*]

Burgomaster. Well, well, I am far from blaming him for writing for the class of readers he finds most in sympathy with him. And, personally, I have no reason to bear your paper any ill will, Mr. Hovstad.

Hovstad. No, I should think not.

Burgomaster. One may say, on the whole, that a fine spirit of mutual tolerance prevails in our town—an excellent public spirit. And that is because we have a great common interest to hold us together—an interest in which all right-minded citizens are equally concerned—

Hovstad. Yes—the Baths.

Burgomaster. Just so. We have our magnificent new Baths. Mark my words! The whole life of the town will center around the Baths, Mr. Hovstad. There can be no doubt of it!

Mrs. Stockmann. That is just what Thomas says.

Burgomaster. How marvelously the place has developed, even in this couple of years! Money has come into circulation, and brought life and movement with it. Houses and ground rents rise in value every day.

Hovstad. And there are fewer people out of work.

Burgomaster. That is true. There is a gratifying **diminution**[4] in the burden imposed on the well-to-do classes by the **poor-rates**;[5] and they will be still further lightened if only we have a really good summer this year— a rush of visitors—plenty of **invalids**,[6] to give the Baths a reputation.

Hovstad. I hear there is every prospect of that.

Burgomaster. Things look most promising. Inquiries about apartments and so forth keep on pouring in.

Hovstad. Then the Doctor's paper will come in very opportunely.

Burgomaster. Has he been writing again?

---

[3] **prolific**—productive.

[4] diminution—lessening.

[5] poor-rates—taxes payed by members of a community to support the poor.

[6] **invalids**—people in poor health.

Hovstad. This is a thing he wrote in the winter; enlarging on the virtues of the Baths, and on the excellent sanitary conditions of the town. But at that time I held it over.

Burgomaster. Ah—I suppose there was something not quite **judicious**[7] about it?

Hovstad. Not at all. But I thought it better to keep it till the spring, when people are beginning to look about them, and think of their summer quarters—

Burgomaster. You were right, quite right, Mr. Hovstad.

Mrs. Stockmann. Yes, Thomas is really **indefatigable**[8] where the Baths are concerned.

Burgomaster. It is his duty as one of the staff.

Hovstad. And of course he was really their creator.

Burgomaster. Was he? Indeed! I gather that certain persons are of that opinion. But I should have thought that I, too, had a modest share in that undertaking.

Mrs. Stockmann. Yes, that is what Thomas is always saying.

Hovstad. No one dreams of denying it, Burgomaster. You set the thing going, and put it on a practical basis; everybody knows that. I only meant that the original idea was the Doctor's.

Burgomaster. Yes, my brother has certainly had ideas enough in his time—worse luck! But when it comes to realizing them, Mr. Hovstad, we want men of another stamp. I should have thought that in this house at any rate—

Mrs. Stockmann. Why, my dear brother-in-law—

Hovstad. Burgomaster, how can you—?

Mrs. Stockmann. Do go in and have some supper, Mr. Hovstad; my husband is sure to be home directly.

Hovstad. Thanks; just a mouthful, perhaps.

[*He goes into the dining room.*]

Burgomaster [*speaking in a low voice*]. It is extraordinary how people who spring direct from the peasant class never can get over their want of tact.

Mrs. Stockmann. But why should you care? Surely you and Thomas can share the honor, like brothers.

Burgomaster. Yes, one would suppose so; but it seems a share of the honor is not enough for some persons.

---

[7] **judicious**—prudent.

[8] **indefatigable**—tireless.

Mrs. Stockmann. What nonsense! You and Thomas always get on so well together. [*Listening.*] There, I think I hear him.

[*Goes and opens the door to the hall.*]

Dr. Stockmann [*laughing and talking loudly, outside*]. Here's another visitor for you, Katrina. Isn't it capital,[9] eh? Come in, Captain Horster. Hang your coat on that peg. What! you don't wear an overcoat? Fancy, Katrina, I caught him in the street, and I could hardly get him to come in.

[Captain Horster *enters and bows to* Mrs. Stockmann.]

Dr. Stockmann [*in the doorway*]. In with you, boys. They're famishing[10] again! Come along, Captain Horster; you must try our roast beef—

[*He forces* Horster *into the dining room.* Eilif *and* Morten *follow them.*]

Mrs. Stockmann. But, Thomas, don't you see—

Dr. Stockmann [*turning round in the doorway*]. Oh, is that you, Peter!

[*Goes up to him and holds out his hand.*] Now this is really capital.

Burgomaster. Unfortunately, I have only a moment to spare—

Dr. Stockmann. Nonsense! We shall have some toddy[11] in a minute. You're not forgetting the toddy, Katrina?

Mrs. Stockmann. Of course not; the water's boiling.

[*She goes into the dining room.*]

Burgomaster. Toddy too—!

Dr. Stockmann. Yes; sit down, and let's make ourselves comfortable.

Burgomaster. Thanks; I never join in drinking parties.

Dr. Stockmann. But this isn't a party.

Burgomaster. I don't know what else— [*Looks towards the dining room.*] It's extraordinary how they can get through all that food.

Dr. Stockmann [*rubbing his hands*]. Yes, doesn't it do one good to see young people eat? Always hungry! That's as it should be. They need good, solid meat to put **stamina**[12] into them! It is they that have got to whip up the ferment[13] of the future, Peter.

Burgomaster. May I ask what there is to be "whipped up," as you call it?

Dr. Stockmann. You'll have to ask the young people that—when the time comes. We shan't see it, of course. Two old fogies like you and me—

---

[9] capital—very good, excellent.

[10] famishing—starving.

[11] toddy—beverage made of liquor, such as whiskey or brandy, mixed with hot water, sugar, and other flavorings.

[12] **stamina**—strength.

[13] ferment—agitation.

Burgomaster. Come, come! Surely that is a very extraordinary expression to use—

Dr. Stockmann. Oh, you mustn't mind my nonsense, Peter. I'm in such glorious spirits, you see. I feel so unspeakably happy in the midst of all this growing, germinating[14] life. Isn't it a marvelous time we live in! It seems as though a whole new world were springing up around us.

Burgomaster. Do you really think so?

Dr. Stockmann. Of course, you can't see it as clearly as I do. You have passed your life in the midst of it all; and that deadens the impression. But I who had to vegetate all those years in that little hole in the north, hardly ever seeing a soul that could speak a stimulating word to me—all this affects me as if I had suddenly dropped into the heart of some teeming metropolis.

Burgomaster. Well, metropolis—

Dr. Stockmann. Oh, I know well enough that things are on a small scale here, compared with many other places. But there's life here—there's promise—there's an infinity of things to work and strive for; and that is the main point. [*Calling.*] Katrina, haven't there been any letters?

Mrs. Stockmann [*in the dining room*]. No, none at all.

Dr. Stockmann. And then a good income, Peter! That's a thing one learns to appreciate when one has lived on starvation wages—

Burgomaster. Good heavens—!

Dr. Stockmann. Oh yes, I can tell you we often had hard times of it up there. And now we can live like princes! Today, for example, we had roast beef for dinner; and we've had some of it for supper too. Won't you have some? Come along—just look at it, at any rate—

Burgomaster. No, no; certainly not—

Dr. Stockmann. Well then, look here—do you see we've bought a table cover?

Burgomaster. Yes, so I observed.

Dr. Stockmann. And a lampshade, too. Do you see? Katrina has been saving up for them. They make the room look comfortable, don't they? Come over here. No, no, no, not there. So—yes! Now you see how it concentrates the light—. I really think it has quite an artistic effect. Eh?

Burgomaster. Yes, when one can afford such luxuries—

---

[14] germinating—sprouting, growing.

Dr. Stockmann. Oh, I can afford it now. Katrina says I make almost as much as we spend.

Burgomaster. Ah—almost!

Dr. Stockmann. Besides, a man of science must live in some style. Why, I believe a mere sheriff spends much more a year than I do.

Burgomaster. Yes, I should think so! A member of the superior magistracy—

Dr. Stockmann. Well then, even a common shipowner! A man of that sort will get through many times as much.

Burgomaster. That is natural, in your relative positions.

Dr. Stockmann. And after all, Peter, I really don't squander any money. But I can't deny myself the delight of having people about me. I *must* have them. After living so long out of the world, I find it a necessity of life to have bright, cheerful, freedom-loving, hard-working young fellows around me—and that's what they are, all of them, that are sitting there eating so heartily. I wish you knew more of Hovstad—

Burgomaster. Ah, that reminds me—Hovstad was telling me that he is going to publish another article of yours.

Dr. Stockmann. An article of mine?

Burgomaster. Yes, about the Baths. An article you wrote last winter.

Dr. Stockmann. Oh, that one? But I don't want that to appear for the present.

Burgomaster. Why not? It seems to me this is the very time for it.

Dr. Stockmann. Very likely—under ordinary circumstances—
[*Crosses the room.*]

Burgomaster [*following him with his eyes*]. And what is unusual in the circumstances now?

Dr. Stockmann [*standing still*]. The fact is, Peter, I really cannot tell you just now; not this evening, at all events. There may prove to be a great deal that is unusual in the circumstances. On the other hand, there may be nothing at all. Very likely it's only my fancy.

Burgomaster. Upon my word, you are very **enigmatical.**[15] Is there anything in the wind? Anything I am to be kept in the dark about? I should think, as Chairman of the Bath Committee—

Dr. Stockmann. And I should think that I—Well, well, don't let us get our backs up, Peter.

Burgomaster. God forbid! I am not in the habit of "getting my back up," as you express it. But I must absolutely insist that all arrangements

---

[15] **enigmatical**—puzzling.

shall be made and carried out in a businesslike manner, and through the properly constituted authorities. I cannot be a party to crooked or underhand courses.

Dr. Stockmann. Have *I* ever been given to crooked or underhand courses?

Burgomaster. At any rate you have an ingrained propensity[16] to taking your own course. And that, in a well-ordered community, is almost as inadmissible.[17] The individual must subordinate himself to society, or, more precisely, to the authorities whose business it is to watch over the welfare of society.

Dr. Stockmann. Maybe. But what the devil has that to do with me?

Burgomaster. Why this is the very thing, my dear Thomas, that it seems you will never learn. But take care; you will have to pay for it—sooner or later. Now I have warned you. Good-bye.

Dr. Stockmann. Are you stark mad? You're on a totally wrong track—

Burgomaster. I am not often on the wrong track. Moreover, I must protest against— [*Bowing towards dining room.*] Good-bye, sister-in-law; good-day to you, gentlemen.

[*He goes.*]

Mrs. Stockmann [*entering the sitting room*]. Has he gone?

Dr. Stockmann. Yes, and in a fine temper, too.

Mrs. Stockmann. Why, my dear Thomas, what have you been doing to him now?

Dr. Stockmann. Nothing at all. He can't possibly expect me to account to him for everything—before the time comes.

Mrs. Stockmann. What have you to account to him for?

Dr. Stockmann. H'm;—never mind about that, Katrina.—It's very odd the postman doesn't come.

[Hovstad, Billing *and* Horster *have risen from table and come forward into the sitting room.* Eilif *and* Morten *presently follow.*]

Billing [*stretching himself*]. Ah! Strike me dead if one doesn't feel a new man after such a meal.

Hovstad. The Burgomaster didn't seem in the best of tempers this evening.

Dr. Stockmann. That's his stomach. He has a very poor digestion.

Hovstad. I fancy it's the staff of the *Messenger* he finds it hardest to stomach.

Mrs. Stockmann. I thought you got on well enough with him.

---

[16] ingrained propensity—deep-seated inclination.

[17] inadmissible—unacceptable.

Hovstad. Oh, yes; but it's only a sort of **armistice**[18] between us.

Billing. That's it! That word sums up the situation.

Dr. Stockmann. We must remember that Peter is a lonely bachelor, poor devil! He has no home to be happy in; only business, business. And then all that cursed weak tea he goes and pours down his throat! Now then, chairs round the table, boys! Katrina, shan't we have the toddy now?

Mrs. Stockmann [*going toward the dining room*]. I am just getting it.

Dr. Stockmann. And you, Captain Horster, sit beside me on the sofa. So rare a guest as you—. Sit down, gentlemen, sit down.

[*The men sit round the table;* Mrs. Stockmann *brings in a tray with kettle, glasses, decanters, etc.*]

Mrs. Stockmann. Here you have it: here's arrack,[19] and this is rum, and this cognac. Now, help yourselves.

Dr. Stockmann [*taking a glass*]. So we will. [*While the toddy is being mixed.*] And now out with the cigars. Eilif, I think you know where the box is. And Morten, you may fetch my pipe. [*The boys go into the room on the right.*] I have a suspicion that Eilif sneaks a cigar now and then, but I pretend not to notice. [*Calls.*] And my smoking cap, Morten! Katrina, can't you tell him where I left it. Ah, he's got it. [*The boys bring in the things.*] Now, friends, help yourselves. I stick to my pipe, you know;—this one has been on many a stormy journey with me, up there in the north. [*They clink glasses.*] Your health! Ah, I can tell you it's better fun to sit cosily here, safe from wind and weather.

Mrs. Stockmann [*who sits knitting*]. Do you sail soon, Captain Horster?

Horster. I hope to be ready for a start by next week.

Mrs. Stockmann. And you're going to America?

Horster. Yes, that's the intention.

Billing. But then you'll miss the election of the new Town Council.

Horster. Is there to be an election again?

Billing. Didn't you know?

Horster. No, I don't trouble myself about those things.

Billing. But I suppose you take an interest in public affairs?

Horster. No, I don't understand anything about them.

Billing. All the same, one ought at least to vote.

Horster. Even those who don't understand anything about it?

---

[18] **armistice**—cease-fire, truce.

[19] arrack—liquor distilled from rum.

Billing. Understand? Why, what do you mean by that? Society is like a ship: every man must put his hand to the helm.

Horster. That may be all right on shore; but at sea it wouldn't do at all.

Hovstad. It's remarkable how little sailors care about public affairs as a rule.

Billing. Most extraordinary.

Dr. Stockmann. Sailors are like birds of passage; they are at home both in the south and in the north. So it behooves[20] the rest of us to be all the more energetic, Mr. Hovstad. Will there be anything of public interest in the *People's Messenger* tomorrow?

Hovstad. Nothing of local interest. But the day after tomorrow I think of printing your article—

Dr. Stockmann. Oh confound it, that article! No, you'll have to hold it over.

Hovstad. Really? We happen to have plenty of space, and I should say this was the very time for it—

Dr. Stockmann. Yes, yes, you may be right; but you must hold it over all the same. I shall explain to you by-and-by.

[Petra, *wearing a hat and cloak, and with a number of exercise-books*[21] *under her arm, enters from the hall.*]

Petra. Good evening.

Dr. Stockmann. Good evening, Petra. Is that you?

[*General greetings.* Petra *puts her cloak, hat, and books on a chair by the door.*]

Petra. Here you all are, enjoying yourselves, while I've been out slaving.

Dr. Stockmann. Well then, you come and enjoy yourself too.

Billing. May I mix you a little—?

Petra [*coming towards the table*]. Thank you, I'd rather help myself—you always make it too strong. By the way, father, I have a letter for you.

[*Goes to the chair where her things are lying.*]

Dr. Stockmann. A letter! From whom?

Petra [*searching in the pocket of her cloak*]. I got it from the postman just as I was going out—

Dr. Stockmann [*rising and going towards her*]. And you only bring it to me now?

Petra. I really hadn't time to run up again. Here it is.

Dr. Stockmann [*seizing the letter*]. Let me see, let me see, child. [*Reads the address.*] Yes; this is it—!

Mrs. Stockmann. Is it the one you have been so anxious about, Thomas?

---

20 behooves—is necessary for.

21 exercise-books—booklets in which students write school exercises.

Dr. Stockmann. Yes it is. I must go at once. Where shall I find a light, Katrina? Is there no lamp in my study again!

Mrs. Stockmann. Yes—the lamp is lighted. It's on the writing table.

Dr. Stockmann. Good, good. Excuse me one moment—

[*He goes into the room on the right.*]

Petra. What can it be, mother?

Mrs. Stockmann. I don't know. For the last few days he has been continually on the lookout for the postman.

Billing. Probably a country patient—

Petra. Poor father! He'll soon have far too much to do. [*Mixes her toddy.*] Ah, this will taste good!

Hovstad. Have you been teaching in the night school as well today?

Petra [*sipping from her glass*]. Two hours.

Billing. And four hours in the morning at the institute—

Petra [*sitting down by the table*]. Five hours.

Mrs. Stockmann. And I see you have exercises to correct this evening.

Petra. Yes, a heap of them.

Horster. It seems to me you have plenty to do, too.

Petra. Yes; but I like it. You feel so delightfully tired after it.

Billing. Do you like that?

Petra. Yes, for then you sleep so well.

Morten. I say, Petra, you must be a great sinner.

Petra. A sinner?

Morten. Yes, if you work so hard. Mr. Rörlund[22] says work is a punishment for our sins.

Eilif [*contemptuously*]. Bosh! What a silly you are, to believe such stuff as that.

Mrs. Stockmann. Come come, Eilif.

Billing [*laughing*]. Capital, capital!

Hovstad. Should you not like to work so hard, Morten?

Morten. No, I shouldn't.

Hovstad. Then what will you do with yourself in the world?

Morten. I should like to be a Viking.

Eilif. But then you'd have to be a heathen.[23]

Morten. Well, so I would.

Billing. There I agree with you, Morten! I say just the same thing.

---

[22] Mr. Rörlund—character in Ibsen's play *The Pillars of Society.*

[23] heathen—pagan.

Mrs. Stockmann [*making a sign to him*]. No, no, Mr. Billing, I'm sure you don't.

Billing. Strike me dead but I do, though. I am a heathen, and I'm proud of it. You'll see we shall all be heathens soon.

Morten. And shall we be able to do anything we like then?

Billing. Well, you see, Morten—

Mrs. Stockmann. Now run away, boys; I'm sure you have lessons to prepare for tomorrow.

Eilif. You might let me stay just a little longer—

Mrs. Stockmann. No, you must go too. Be off, both of you.

[*The boys say good-night and go into the room on the left.*]

Hovstad. Do you really think it can hurt the boys to hear these things?

Mrs. Stockmann. Well, I don't know; I don't like it.

Petra. Really, mother, I think you are quite wrong there.

Mrs. Stockmann. Perhaps. But I don't like it—not here, at home.

Petra. There's no end of hypocrisy both at home and at school. At home you must hold your tongue, and at school you have to stand up and tell lies to the children.

Horster. Have you to tell lies?

Petra. Yes; do you think we don't have to tell them many and many a thing we don't believe ourselves?

Billing. Ah, that's too true.

Petra. If only I could afford it, I should start a school myself, and things should be very different there.

Billing. Oh, afford it—!

Horster. If you really think of doing that, Miss Stockmann, I shall be delighted to let you have a room at my place. You know my father's old house is nearly empty; there's a great big dining room on the ground floor—

Petra [*laughing*]. Oh, thank you very much—but I'm afraid it won't come to anything.

Hovstad. No, I fancy Miss Petra is more likely to go over to journalism. By the way, have you had time to look into the English novel you promised to translate for us?

Petra. Not yet. But you shall have it in good time.

[Dr. Stockmann *enters from his room, with the letter open in his hand.*]

Dr. Stockmann [*flourishing the letter*]. Here's news, I can tell you, that will waken up the town!

Billing. News?

Mrs. Stockmann. What news?

Dr. Stockmann. A great discovery, Katrina!

Hovstad. Indeed?

Mrs. Stockmann. Made by you?

Dr. Stockmann. Precisely—by me! [*Walks up and down.*] Now let them go on accusing me of fads and crack-brained notions. But they won't dare to! Ha-ha! I tell you they won't dare!

Petra. Do tell us what it is, father.

Dr. Stockmann. Well, well, give me time, and you shall hear all about it. If only I had Peter here now! This just shows how we men can go about forming judgments like the blindest moles—

Hovstad. What do you mean, Doctor?

Dr. Stockmann [*stopping beside the table*]. Isn't it the general opinion that our town is a healthy place?

Hovstad. Of course.

Dr. Stockmann. A quite exceptionally healthy place, indeed—a place to be warmly recommended, both to invalids and people in health—

Mrs. Stockmann. My dear Thomas—

Dr. Stockmann. And assuredly we haven't failed to recommend and belaud[24] it. I've sung its praises again and again, both in the *Messenger* and in pamphlets—

Hovstad. Well, what then?

Dr. Stockmann. These Baths, that we have called the pulse of the town, its vital nerve, and—and the devil knows what else—

Billing. "Our city's **palpitating**[25] heart," I once ventured to call them in a **convivial**[26] moment—

Dr. Stockmann. Yes, I daresay. Well—do you know what they really are, these mighty, magnificent, belauded Baths, that have cost so much money—do you know what they are?

Hovstad. No, what are they?

Mrs. Stockmann. Do tell us.

Dr. Stockmann. Simply a pestiferous[27] hole.

Petra. The Baths, father?

Mrs. Stockmann [*at the same time*]. Our Baths!

Hovstad [*also at the same time*]. But, Doctor—!

---

[24] belaud—praise.

[25] **palpitating**—beating.

[26] **convivial**—festive.

[27] pestiferous—unhealthy, diseased.

Billing. Oh, it's incredible!

Dr. Stockmann. I tell you the whole place is a poisonous whited sepulcher;[28] **noxious**[29] in the highest degree! All that filth up there in the Mill Dale—the stuff that smells so horribly—taints the water in the feed pipes of the Pump Room; and the same accursed poisonous refuse oozes out by the beach—

Hovstad. Where the sea baths are?

Dr. Stockmann. Exactly.

Hovstad. But how are you so sure of all this, Doctor?

Dr. Stockmann. I've investigated the whole thing as **conscientiously**[30] as possible. I've long had my suspicions about it. Last year we had some extraordinary cases of illness among the patients—both typhoid and gastric attacks[31]—

Mrs. Stockmann. Yes, I remember.

Dr. Stockmann. We thought at the time that the visitors had brought the infection with them; but afterwards—last winter—I began to question that. So I set about testing the water as well as I could.

Mrs. Stockmann. It was *that* you were working so hard at!

Dr. Stockmann. Yes, you may well say I've worked, Katrina. But here, you know, I hadn't the necessary scientific appliances: so I sent samples both of our drinking water and of our sea water to the University, for exact analysis by a chemist.

Hovstad. And you have received his report?

Dr. Stockmann [*showing letter*]. Here it is! And it proves beyond dispute the presence of putrefying organic matter[32] in the water—millions of infusoria.[33] It's absolutely **pernicious**[34] to health, whether used internally or externally.

Mrs. Stockmann. What a blessing you found it out in time.

Dr. Stockmann. Yes, you may well say that.

Hovstad. And what do you intend to do now, Doctor?

Dr. Stockmann. Why, to set things right, of course.

---

[28] whited sepulcher—whitewashed tomb, that is, someone or something beautiful on the outside, but ugly within; an allusion to the Gospel of Matthew 28:27.

[29] **noxious**—harmful.

[30] **conscientiously**—thoroughly.

[31] typhoid and gastric attacks—Typhoid fever is an acute infectious disease caused by contaminated food and water; gastric attacks are stomach problems.

[32] putrefying organic matter—rotting animal or vegetable material.

[33] infusoria—microorganisms

[34] **pernicious**—deadly.

Hovstad. You think it can be done, then?

Dr. Stockmann. It *must* be done. Else the whole Baths are useless; ruined. But there's no fear. I am quite clear as to what is required.

Mrs. Stockmann. But my dear Thomas, why should you have made such a secret of all this?

Dr. Stockmann. Would you have had me rush all over the town and chatter about it, before I was quite certain? No, thank you; I'm not so mad as that.

Petra. But to us at home—

Dr. Stockmann. I couldn't say a word to a living soul. But tomorrow you may look in at the Badger's—

Mrs. Stockmann. Oh, Thomas!

Dr. Stockmann. Well well, at your grandfather's. The old fellow *will* be astonished! He thinks I'm not quite right in my head—yes, and plenty of others think the same, I've noticed. But now these good people shall see—yes, they shall see now! [*Walks up and down rubbing his hands.*] What a stir there will be in the town, Katrina! Just think of it! All the water pipes will have to be relaid.

Hovstad [*rising*]. All the water pipes—?

Dr. Stockmann. Why, of course. The intake is too low down; it must be moved much higher up.

Petra. So you were right, after all.

Dr. Stockmann. Yes, do you remember, Petra? I wrote against it when they were beginning the works. But no one would listen to me then. Now, you may be sure, I shall give them my full broadside[35]—for of course I've prepared a statement for the Directors; it has been lying ready a whole week; I've only been waiting for this report. [*Points to letter.*] But now they shall have it at once. [*Goes into his room and returns with a manuscript in his hand.*] See! Four closely written sheets! And I'll enclose the report. A newspaper, Katrina! Get me something to wrap them up in. There—that's it. Give it to—to—[*Stamps.*]—what the devil's her name? Give it to the girl, I mean, and tell her to take it at once to the Burgomaster.

[Mrs. Stockmann *goes out with the packet through the dining room.*]

Petra. What do you think Uncle Peter will say, father?

Dr. Stockmann. What should he say? He can't possibly be otherwise than pleased that so important a fact has been brought to light.

---

[35] broadside—forceful attack; an allusion to the simultaneous firing of all the cannons on one side of a warship.

Hovstad. I suppose you will let me put a short announcement of your discovery in the *Messenger*.

Dr. Stockmann. Yes, I shall be much obliged if you will.

Hovstad. It is highly desirable that the public should know about it as soon as possible.

Dr. Stockmann. Yes, certainly.

Mrs. Stockmann [*returning*]. She's gone with it.

Billing. Strike me dead if you won't be the first man[36] in the town, Doctor!

Dr. Stockmann [*walks up and down in high glee*]. Oh, nonsense! After all, I have done no more than my duty. I've been a lucky treasure hunter, that's all. But all the same—

Billing. Hovstad, don't you think the town ought to get up a torchlight procession in honor of Dr. Stockmann?

Hovstad. I shall certainly propose it.

Billing. And I'll talk it over with Aslaksen.

Dr. Stockmann. No, my dear friends; let all such claptrap alone. I won't hear of anything of the sort. And if the Directors should want to raise my salary, I won't accept it. I tell you, Katrina, I will not accept it.

Mrs. Stockmann. You are quite right, Thomas.

Petra [*raising her glass*]. Your health, father!

Hovstad and Billing. Your health, your health, Doctor!

Horster [*clinking glasses with the Doctor*]. I hope you may have nothing but joy of your discovery.

Dr. Stockmann. Thanks, thanks, my dear friends! I can't tell you how happy I am—! Oh, what a blessing it is to feel that you have deserved well of your native town and your fellow citizens. Hurrah, Katrina!

[*He puts both his arms round her neck, and whirls her round with him.* Mrs. Stockmann *screams and struggles. A burst of laughter, applause, and cheers for the* Doctor. *The boys thrust their heads in at the door.*]

Act Two

[*The* Doctor's *sitting room. The dining room door is closed. Morning.*]

Mrs. Stockmann [*enters from the dining room with a sealed letter in her hand, goes to the foremost door on the right, and peeps in*]. Are you there, Thomas?

Dr. Stockmann [*within*]. Yes, I have just come in. [*Enters*] What is it?

---

[36] first man—most important person.

Mrs. Stockmann. A letter from your brother. [*Hands it to him.*]

Dr. Stockmann. Aha, let us see. [*Opens the envelope and reads.*] "The manuscript sent me is returned herewith—" [*Reads on, mumbling to himself.*] H'm—

Mrs. Stockmann. Well, what does he say?

Dr. Stockmann [*putting the paper in his pocket*]. Nothing; only that he'll come up himself about midday.

Mrs. Stockmann. Then be sure you remember to stay at home.

Dr. Stockmann. Oh, I can easily manage that; I've finished my morning's visits.

Mrs. Stockmann. I am very curious to know how he takes it.

Dr. Stockmann. You'll see he won't be over-pleased that it is I that have made the discovery, and not he himself.

Mrs. Stockmann. Ah, that's just what I'm afraid of.

Dr. Stockmann. Of course at bottom he'll be glad. But still—Peter is damnably unwilling that anyone but himself should do anything for the good of the town.

Mrs. Stockmann. Do you know, Thomas, I think you might stretch a point, and share the honor with him. Couldn't it appear that it was he that put you on the track—?

Dr. Stockmann. By all means, for aught I care. If only I can get things put straight—

[Old Morten Kiil *puts his head in at the hall door, and asks slyly:*]

Morten Kiil. Is it—is it true?

Mrs. Stockmann [*going toward him*]. Father—is that you?

Dr. Stockmann. Hallo, father-in-law! Good morning, good morning.

Mrs. Stockmann. Do come in.

Morten Kiil. Yes, if it's true; if not, I'm off again.

Dr. Stockmann. If what is true?

Morten Kiil. This crazy business about the waterworks. Now is it true?

Dr. Stockmann. Why, of course it is. But how came *you* to hear of it?

Morten Kiil [*coming in*]. Petra looked in on her way to the school—

Dr. Stockmann. Oh, did she?

Morten Kiil. Ay ay—and she told me—. I thought she was only making game of[1] me; but that's not like Petra either.

Dr. Stockmann. No, indeed; how could you think so?

---

[1] making game of—teasing.

Morten Kiil. Oh, you can never be sure of anybody. You may be made a fool of before you know where you are. So it is true, after all?

Dr. Stockmann. Most certainly it is. Do sit down, father-in-law. [*Forces him down on the sofa.*] Now isn't it a real blessing for the town—?

Morten Kiil [*suppressing his laughter*]. A blessing for the town?

Dr. Stockmann. Yes, that I made this discovery in time—

Morten Kiil [*as before*]. Ay, ay, ay!—Well, I could never have believed that you would play monkey tricks with your very own brother.

Dr. Stockmann. Monkey tricks!

Mrs. Stockmann. Why, father dear—

Morten Kiil [*resting his hands and chin on the top of his stick and blinking slyly at the* Doctor]. What was it again? Wasn't it that some animals had got into the water pipes?

Dr. Stockmann. Yes; infusorial animals.

Morten Kiil. And any number of these animals had got in, Petra said— whole swarms of them.

Dr. Stockmann. Certainly; hundreds of thousands.

Morten Kiil. But no one can see them—isn't that it?

Dr. Stockmann. Quite right; no one can see them.

Morten Kiil [*with a quiet, chuckling laugh*]. I'll be damned if that isn't the best thing I've heard of you yet.

Dr. Stockmann. What do you mean?

Morten Kiil. But you'll never in this world make the Burgomaster take in anything of the sort.

Dr. Stockmann. Well, that we shall see.

Morten Kiil. Do you really think he'll be so crazy?

Dr. Stockmann. I hope the whole town will be so crazy.

Morten Kiil. The whole town! Well, I don't say but it may. But it serves them right; it'll teach them a lesson. They wanted to be so much cleverer than we old fellows. They hounded me out of the Town Council. Yes; I tell you they hounded me out like a dog, that they did. But now it's their turn. Just you keep up the game with them, Stockmann.

Dr. Stockmann. Yes, but, father-in-law—

Morten Kiil. Keep it up, I say. [*Rising.*] If you can make the Burgomaster and his gang eat humble pie, I'll give a hundred crowns² straight away to the poor.

Dr. Stockmann. Come, that's good of you.

---

² crowns—The name of the monetary unit in Norway, the krone, means "crown."

Morten Kiil. Of course I've little enough to throw away; but if you can manage that, I shall certainly remember the poor at Christmastime, to the tune of fifty crowns.

[Hovstad *enters from hall.*]

Hovstad. Good morning! [*Pausing.*] Oh! I beg your pardon—

Dr. Stockmann. Not at all. Come in, come in.

Morten Kiil [*chuckling again*]. He! Is he in it too?

Hovstad. What do you mean?

Dr. Stockmann. Yes, of course he is.

Morten Kiil. I might have known it! It's to go into the papers. Ah, you're the one, Stockmann! Do you two lay your heads together;[3] I'm off.

Dr. Stockmann. Oh no; don't go yet, father-in-law.

Morten Kiil. No, I'm off now. Play them all the monkey tricks you can think of. Devil take me but you shan't lose by it. [*He goes,* Mrs. Stockmann *accompanying him.*]

Dr. Stockmann [*laughing*]. What do you think—? The old fellow doesn't believe a word of all this about the waterworks.

Hovstad. Was that what he—?

Dr. Stockmann. Yes; that was what we were talking about. And I daresay you have come on the same business?

Hovstad. Yes. Have you a moment to spare, Doctor?

Dr. Stockmann. As many as you like, my dear fellow.

Hovstad. Have you heard anything from the Burgomaster?

Dr. Stockmann. Not yet. He'll be here presently.

Hovstad. I have been thinking the matter over since last evening.

Dr. Stockmann. Well?

Hovstad. To you, as a doctor and a man of science, this business of the waterworks appears an isolated affair. I daresay it hasn't occurred to you that a good many other things are bound up with it?

Dr. Stockmann. Indeed! In what way? Let us sit down, my dear fellow.—No; there, on the sofa.

[Hovstad *sits on sofa; the* Doctor *in an easy chair on the other side of the table.*]

Dr. Stockmann. Well, so you think—?

Hovstad. You said yesterday that the water is polluted by impurities in the soil.

Dr. Stockmann. Yes, undoubtedly; the mischief comes from that poisonous swamp up in the Mill Dale.

---

[3] lay your heads together—conspire.

Hovstad. Excuse me, Doctor, but I think it comes from a very
different swamp.

Dr. Stockmann. What swamp may that be?

Hovstad. The swamp in which our whole municipal life is rotting.

Dr. Stockmann. The devil, Mr. Hovstad! What notion is this you've got
hold of?

Hovstad. All the affairs of the town have gradually drifted into the
hands of a pack of bureaucrats—

Dr. Stockmann. Come now, they're not all bureaucrats.

Hovstad. No; but those who are not are the friends and **adherents**[4] of
those who are. We are entirely under the thumb of a ring of wealthy
men, men of old family and position in the town.

Dr. Stockmann. Yes, but they are also men of ability and insight.

Hovstad. Did they show ability and insight when they laid the water
pipes where they are?

Dr. Stockmann. No; that, of course, was a piece of stupidity. But that
will be set right now.

Hovstad. Do you think it will go so smoothly?

Dr. Stockmann. Well, smoothly or not, it will have to be done.

Hovstad. Yes, if the press exerts its influence.

Dr. Stockmann. Not at all necessary, my dear fellow; I am sure
my brother—

Hovstad. Excuse me, Doctor, but I must tell you that I think of taking
the matter up.

Dr. Stockmann. In the paper?

Hovstad. Yes. When I took over the *People's Messenger,* I was determined
to break up the ring of **obstinate**[5] old blockheads who held everything
in their hands.

Dr. Stockmann. But you told me yourself what came of it. You nearly
ruined the paper.

Hovstad. Yes, at that time we had to draw in our horns,[6] that's true
enough. The whole Bath scheme might have fallen through if these
men had been sent about their business. But now the Baths are
an accomplished fact, and we can get on without these august
personages.[7]

---

[4] **adherents**—supporters.

[5] **obstinate**—stubborn.

[6] draw in our horns—retreat.

[7] august personages—admired people of distinction (said ironically).

Dr. Stockmann. Get on without them, yes; but still we owe them a great deal.

Hovstad. The debt shall be duly acknowledged. But a journalist of my democratic tendencies cannot let such an opportunity slip through his fingers. We must explode the tradition of official infallibility.[8] That rubbish must be got rid of, like every other superstition.

Dr. Stockmann. There I am with you with all my heart, Mr. Hovstad. If it's a superstition, away with it!

Hovstad. I should be sorry to attack the Burgomaster, as he is your brother. But I know you think with me—the truth before all other considerations.

Dr. Stockmann. Why, of course. [*Vehemently.*] But still—! but still—!

Hovstad. You mustn't think ill of me. I am neither more self-interested nor more ambitious than other men.

Dr. Stockmann. Why, my dear fellow—who says you are?

Hovstad. I come of humble folk, as you know; and I have had ample opportunities of seeing what the lower classes really require. And that is to have a share in the direction of public affairs, Doctor. That is what develops ability and knowledge and self-respect—

Dr. Stockmann. I understand that perfectly.

Hovstad. Yes; and I think a journalist **incurs**[9] a heavy responsibility if he lets slip a chance of helping to **emancipate**[10] the downtrodden masses. I know well enough that our **oligarchy**[11] will denounce me as an agitator, and so forth; but what do I care? If only my conscience is clear, I—

Dr. Stockmann. Just so, just so, my dear Mr. Hovstad. But still—devil take it—! [*A knock at the door.*] Come in!

[Aslaksen, *the printer, appears at the door leading to the hall. He is humbly but respectably dressed in black, wears a white necktie, slightly crumpled, and has a silk hat and gloves in his hand.*]

Aslaksen [*bowing*]. I beg pardon, Doctor, for making so bold—

Dr. Stockmann [*rising*]. Hallo! If it isn't Mr. Aslaksen!

Aslaksen. Yes, it's me, Doctor.

Hovstad [*rising*]. Is it me you want, Aslaksen?

Aslaksen. No, not at all. I didn't know you were here. No, it's the Doctor himself—

---

[8] infallibility—inability to make an error.

[9] **incurs**—sustains.

[10] **emancipate**—liberate.

[11] **oligarchy**—rule by a small elite.

Dr. Stockmann. Well, what can I do for you?

Aslaksen. Is it true, what Mr. Billing tells me, that you're going to get us a better set of waterworks?

Dr. Stockmann. Yes, for the Baths.

Aslaksen. Of course, of course. Then I just looked in to say that I'll back up the movement with all my might.

Hovstad [*to the Doctor*]. You see!

Dr. Stockmann. I'm sure I thank you heartily; but—

Aslaksen. You may find it no such bad thing to have us small middle-class men at your back. We form what you may call a solid majority in the town—when we really make up our minds, that's to say. And it's always well to have the majority with you, Doctor.

Dr. Stockmann. No doubt, no doubt; but I can't conceive that any special measures will be necessary in this case. I should think in so clear and straightforward a matter—

Aslaksen. Yes, but all the same, it can do no harm. I know the local authorities very well—the powers that be are not very ready to adopt suggestions from outsiders. So I think it wouldn't be amiss if we made some sort of a demonstration.

Hovstad. Precisely my opinion.

Dr. Stockmann. A demonstration, you say? But in what way would you demonstrate?

Aslaksen. Of course with great moderation, Doctor. I always insist upon moderation; for moderation is a citizen's first virtue—at least that's my way of thinking.

Dr. Stockmann. We all know that, Mr. Aslaksen.

Aslaksen. Yes, I think my moderation is generally recognized. And this affair of the waterworks is very important for us small middle-class men. The Baths bid fair[12] to become, as you might say, a little gold mine for the town. We shall all have to live by the Baths, especially we houseowners. So we want to support the Baths all we can; and as I am Chairman of the Houseowners' Association—

Dr. Stockmann. Well—?

Aslaksen. And as I'm an active worker for the Temperance Society[13]— of course you know, Doctor, that I'm a temperance man?

Dr. Stockmann. To be sure, to be sure.

---

[12] bid fair—promise.

[13] Temperance Society—organization opposing use of alcoholic beverages.

Aslaksen. Well, you'll understand that I come in contact with a great many people. And as I'm known to be a prudent and law-abiding citizen, as you yourself remarked, Doctor, I have certain influence in the town, and hold some power in my hands—though I say it that shouldn't.

Dr. Stockmann. I know that very well, Mr. Aslaksen.

Aslaksen. Well then, you see—it would be easy for me to get up an address, if it came to a pinch.

Dr. Stockmann. An address?

Aslaksen. Yes, a kind of vote of thanks to you, from the citizens of the town, for your action in a matter of such general concern. Of course it will have to be drawn up with all fitting moderation, so as to give no offense to the authorities and parties in power. But so long as we're careful about that, no one can take it ill, I should think.

Hovstad. Well, even if they didn't particularly like it—

Aslaksen. No, no, no; no offense to the powers that be, Mr. Hovstad. No opposition to people that can take it out of us again so easily. I've had enough of that in my time; no good ever comes of it. But no one can object to the free but temperate expression of a citizen's opinion.

Dr. Stockmann [*shaking his hand*]. I can't tell you, my dear Mr. Aslaksen, how heartily it delights me to find so much support among my fellow townsmen. I'm so happy—so happy! Come, you'll have a glass of sherry? Eh?

Aslaksen. No, thank you; I never touch spirituous liquors.

Dr. Stockmann. Well, then, a glass of beer—what do you say to that?

Aslaksen. Thanks, not that either, Doctor. I never take anything so early in the day. And now I'll be off round the town, and talk to some of the Houseowners, and prepare public opinion.

Dr. Stockmann. It's extremely kind of you, Mr. Aslaksen; but I really cannot get it into my head that all these preparations are necessary. The affair seems to me so simple and self-evident.

Aslaksen. The authorities always move slowly, Doctor—God forbid I should blame them for it—

Hovstad. We'll stir them up in the paper tomorrow, Aslaksen.

Aslaksen. No violence, Mr. Hovstad. Proceed with moderation, or you'll do nothing with them. Take my advice; I've picked up experience in the school of life.—And now I'll say good morning, Doctor. You know now that at least you have us small middle-class men behind you, solid as a wall. You have the solid majority on your side, Doctor.

Dr. Stockmann. Many thanks, my dear Mr. Aslaksen. [*Holds out his hand.*] Good-bye, good-bye.

Aslaksen. Are you coming to the office, Mr. Hovstad?

Hovstad. I shall come on presently. I have still one or two things to arrange.

Aslaksen. Very well. [*Bows and goes.* Dr. Stockmann *accompanies him into the hall.*]

Hovstad [*as the* Doctor *reenters*]. Well, what do you say to that, Doctor? Don't you think it is high time we should give all this weak-kneed, half-hearted cowardice a good shaking-up?

Dr. Stockmann. Are you speaking of Aslaksen?

Hovstad. Yes, I am. He's a decent enough fellow, but he's one of those who are sunk in the swamp. And most people here are just like him; they are for ever wavering and wobbling from side to side; what with scruples and misgivings,[14] they never dare advance a step.

Dr. Stockmann. Yes, but Aslaksen seems to me thoroughly well-intentioned.

Hovstad. There is one thing I value more than good intentions, and that is an attitude of manly self-reliance.

Dr. Stockmann. There I am quite with you.

Hovstad. So I am going to seize this opportunity, and try whether I can't for once put a little grit into their good intentions. The worship of authority must be rooted up in this town. This gross, inexcusable blunder of the waterworks must be brought home clearly to every voter.

Dr. Stockmann. Very well. If you think it's for the good of the community, so be it; but not till I have spoken to my brother.

Hovstad. At all events, I shall be writing my editorial in the meantime. And if the Burgomaster won't take the matter up—

Dr. Stockmann. But how can you conceive his refusing?

Hovstad. Oh, it's not inconceivable. And then—

Dr. Stockmann. Well then, I promise you—; look here—in that case you may print my paper—put it in just as it is.

Hovstad. May I? Is that a promise?

Dr. Stockmann [*handing him the manuscript*]. There it is; take it with you. You may as well read it in any case; you can return it to me afterwards.

Hovstad. Very good; I shall do so. And now, good-bye, Doctor.

Dr. Stockmann. Good-bye, good-bye. You'll see it will all go smoothly, Mr. Hovstad—as smoothly as possible.

---

[14] scruples and misgivings—cautions and doubts.

Hovstad. H'm—we shall see. [*Bows and goes out through the hall.*]

Dr. Stockmann [*going to the dining room door and looking in*]. Katrina! Hallo! are you back, Petra?

Petra [*entering*]. Yes, I've just got back from school.

Mrs. Stockmann [*entering*]. Hasn't he been here yet?

Dr. Stockmann. Peter? No; but I have been having a long talk with Hovstad. He's quite enthusiastic about my discovery. It turns out to be of much wider import than I thought at first. So he has placed his paper at my disposal, if I should require it.

Mrs. Stockmann. Do you think you will?

Dr. Stockmann. Not I! But at the same time, one cannot but be proud to know that the enlightened, independent press is on one's side. And what do you think? I have had a visit from the Chairman of the Houseowners' Association too.

Mrs. Stockmann. Really? What did he want?

Dr. Stockmann. To assure me of his support. They will all stand by me at a pinch. Katrina, do you know what I have behind me?

Mrs. Stockmann. Behind you? No. What have you behind you?

Dr. Stockmann. The solid majority!

Mrs. Stockmann. Oh! Is that good for you, Thomas?

Dr. Stockmann. Yes, indeed; I should think it was good. [*Rubbing his hands as he walks up and down.*] Great God! what a delight it is to feel oneself in such brotherly unison with one's fellow townsmen!

Petra. And to do so much that's good and useful, father!

Dr. Stockmann. And all for one's native town, too!

Mrs. Stockmann. There's the bell.

Dr. Stockmann. That must be he. [*Knock at the door.*] Come in! [*Enter Burgomaster Stockmann from the hall.*]

Burgomaster. Good morning.

Dr. Stockmann. I'm glad to see you, Peter.

Mrs. Stockmann. Good morning, brother-in-law. How are you?

Burgomaster. Oh, thanks, so-so. [*To the* Doctor.] Yesterday evening, after office hours, I received from you a dissertation[15] upon the state of the water at the Baths.

Dr. Stockmann. Yes. Have you read it?

Burgomaster. I have.

Dr. Stockmann. And what do you think of the affair?

---

[15] dissertation—lengthy, formal report.

Burgomaster. H'm— [*With a sidelong glance.*]

Mrs. Stockmann. Come, Petra.

[*She and* Petra *go into the room on the left.*]

Burgomaster [*after a pause*]. Was it necessary to make all these investigations behind my back?

Dr. Stockmann. Yes, till I was absolutely certain, I—

Burgomaster. And are you absolutely certain now?

Dr. Stockmann. My paper must surely have convinced you of that.

Burgomaster. Is it your intention to submit this statement to the Board of Directors, as a sort of official document?

Dr. Stockmann. Of course. Something must be done in the matter, and that promptly.

Burgomaster. As usual, you use very strong expressions in your statement. Amongst other things, you say that what we offer our visitors is a slow poison.

Dr. Stockmann. Why, Peter, what else can it be called? Only think— poisoned water both internally and externally! And that to poor invalids who come to us in all confidence, and pay us handsomely to cure them!

Burgomaster. And then you announce as your conclusion that we must build a sewer to carry off the **alleged**[16] impurities from the Mill Dale, and must relay all the water pipes.

Dr. Stockmann. Yes. Can you suggest any other plan?—I know of none.

Burgomaster. I found a pretext[17] for looking in at the town engineer's this morning, and—in a half-jesting way—I mentioned these alterations as things we might possibly have to consider, at some future time.

Dr. Stockmann. At some future time!

Burgomaster. Of course he smiled at what he thought my extravagance. Have you taken the trouble to think what your proposed alterations would cost? From what the engineer said, I gathered that the expenses would probably amount up to several hundred thousand crowns.

Dr. Stockmann. So much as that?

Burgomaster. Yes. But that is not the worst. The work would take at least two years.

Dr. Stockmann. Two years! Do you mean to say two whole years?

Burgomaster. At least. And what are we to do with the Baths in the meanwhile? Are we to close them? We should have no alternative.

---

[16] **alleged**—stated without proof.

[17] pretext—excuse.

Do you think anyone would come here, if it got around that the water was pestilential?[18]

Dr. Stockmann. But, Peter, that's precisely what it is.

Burgomaster. And all this now, just now, when the Baths are doing so well! Neighboring towns, too, are not without their claims to rank as health resorts. Do you think they would not at once set to work to divert the full stream of visitors to themselves? Undoubtedly they would; and we should be left stranded. We should probably have to give up the whole costly undertaking; and so you would have ruined your native town.

Dr. Stockmann. I—ruined—!

Burgomaster. It is only through the Baths that the town has any future worth speaking of. You surely know that as well as I do.

Dr. Stockmann. Then what do you think should be done?

Burgomaster. I have not succeeded in convincing myself that the condition of the water at the Baths is as serious as your statement represents.

Dr. Stockmann. I tell you it's if anything worse—or will be in the summer, when the hot weather sets in.

Burgomaster. I repeat that I believe you exaggerate greatly. A competent physician should know what measures to take—he should be able to obviate[19] deleterious[20] influences, and to counteract them in case they should make themselves unmistakably felt.

Dr. Stockmann. Indeed—? And then—?

Burgomaster. The existing waterworks are, once for all, a fact, and must naturally be treated as such. But when the time comes, the Directors will probably not be indisposed[21] to consider whether it may not be possible, without unreasonable pecuniary sacrifices,[22] to introduce certain improvements.

Dr. Stockmann. And do you imagine I could ever be a party to such dishonesty?

Burgomaster. Dishonesty?

Dr. Stockmann. Yes, it would be dishonesty—a fraud, a lie, an absolute crime against the public, against society as a whole!

---

[18] pestilential—unhealthy, diseased.

[19] obviate—dispose of.

[20] deleterious—harmful.

[21] indisposed—unwilling.

[22] pecuniary sacrifices—money losses.

Burgomaster. I have not, as I before remarked, been able to convince myself that there is really any such **imminent**[23] danger.

Dr. Stockmann. You have! You must have! I know that my demonstration is absolutely clear and convincing. And you understand it perfectly, Peter, only you won't admit it. It was you who insisted that both the Bath buildings and the waterworks should be placed where they now are; and it's *that*—it's that damned blunder that you won't confess. Pshaw! Do you think I don't see through you?

Burgomaster. And even if it were so? If I do watch over my reputation with a certain anxiety, I do it for the good of the town. Without moral authority I cannot guide and direct affairs in the way I consider most conducive to the general welfare. Therefore—and on various other grounds—it is of great importance to me that your statement should not be submitted to the Board of Directors. It must be kept back, for the good of the community. Later on I will bring up the matter for discussion, and we will do the best we can, quietly; but not a word, not a whisper, of this unfortunate business must come to the public ears.

Dr. Stockmann. But it can't be prevented now, my dear Peter.

Burgomaster. It must and shall be prevented.

Dr. Stockmann. It can't be, I tell you; far too many people know about it already.

Burgomaster. Know about it! Who? Surely not those fellows on the *People's Messenger*—?

Dr. Stockmann. Oh yes; they know. The liberal, independent press will take good care that you do your duty.

Burgomaster [after a short pause]. You are an amazingly reckless man, Thomas. Have not you reflected what the consequences of this may be to yourself?

Dr. Stockmann. Consequences?—Consequences to me?

Burgomaster. Yes—to you and yours.

Dr. Stockmann. What the devil do you mean?

Burgomaster. I believe I have always shown myself ready and willing to lend you a helping hand.

Dr. Stockmann. Yes, you have, and I thank you for it.

Burgomaster. I ask for no thanks. Indeed, I was in some measure forced to act as I did—for my own sake. I always hoped I should be able to keep you a little in check, if I helped to improve your pecuniary position.

---

[23] **imminent**—immediate.

Dr. Stockmann. What! So it was only for your own sake—!

Burgomaster. In a measure, I say. It is painful for a man in an official position, when his nearest relative goes and compromises himself time after time.

Dr. Stockmann. And you think I do that?

Burgomaster. Yes, unfortunately, you do, without knowing it. Yours is a **turbulent,**[24] unruly, rebellious spirit. And then you have an unhappy propensity[25] for rushing into print upon every possible and impossible occasion. You no sooner hit upon an idea than you must needs write a newspaper article or a whole pamphlet about it.

Dr. Stockmann. Isn't it a citizen's duty, when he has conceived a new idea, to communicate it to the public?

Burgomaster. Oh, the public has no need for new ideas. The public gets on best with the good old recognized ideas it has already.

Dr. Stockmann. You say that right out!

Burgomaster. Yes, I must speak frankly to you for once. Hitherto I have tried to avoid it, for I know how irritable you are; but now I must tell you the truth, Thomas. You have no conception how much you injure yourself by your officiousness.[26] You complain of the authorities, ay, of the Government itself—you attack them and maintain that you have been slighted, persecuted. But what else can you expect, with your impossible disposition?

Dr. Stockmann. Oh, indeed! So I am impossible, am I?

Burgomaster. Yes, Thomas, you are an impossible man to work with. I know that from experience. You have no consideration for anyone or anything; you seem quite to forget that you have me to thank for your position as medical officer of the Baths—

Dr. Stockmann. It was mine by right! Mine, and no one else's! I was the first to discover the town's capabilities as a watering-place;[27] I saw them, and, at that time, I alone. For years I fought single-handed for this idea of mine; I wrote and wrote—

Burgomaster. No doubt; but then the right time had not come. Of course, in that out-of-the-world corner, you could not judge of that.

---

[24] **turbulent**—restless.

[25] propensity—tendency, inclination.

[26] officiousness—eagerness.

[27] watering-place—health resort.

As soon as the propitious[28] moment arrived, I—and others—took the matter in hand—

Dr. Stockmann. Yes, and you went and bungled the whole of my glorious plan. Oh, we see now what a set of wiseacres you were!

Burgomaster. All I can see is that you are again seeking an outlet for your **pugnacity.**[29] You want to make an onslaught[30] on your superiors—that is an old habit of yours. You cannot endure any authority over you; you look askance[31] at anyone who holds a higher post than your own; you regard him as a personal enemy—and then you care nothing what kind of weapon you use against him. But now I have shown you how much is at stake for the town, and consequently for me too. And therefore I warn you, Thomas, that I am **inexorable**[32] in the demand I am about to make of you!

Dr. Stockmann. What demand?

Burgomaster. As you have not had the sense to refrain from chattering to outsiders about this delicate business, which should have been kept an official secret, of course it cannot now be hushed up. All sorts of rumors will get around, and unfriendly persons will invent all sorts of additions to them. It will therefore be necessary for you publicly to contradict these rumors.

Dr. Stockmann. I! How? I don't understand you?

Burgomaster. We expect that, after further investigation, you will come to the conclusion that the affair is not nearly so serious or pressing as you had at first imagined.

Dr. Stockmann. Aha! So you expect that?

Burgomaster. Furthermore, we expect you to express your confidence that the Board of Directors will thoroughly and conscientiously carry out all measures for the remedying of any possible defects.

Dr. Stockmann. Yes, but that you'll never be able to do, so long as you go on tinkering and patching. I tell you that, Peter; and it's my deepest, sincerest conviction—

Burgomaster. As an official, you have no right to hold any individual conviction.

Dr. Stockmann [*starting*]. No right to—?

---

[28] propitious—favorable.

[29] **pugnacity**—combativeness, belligerence.

[30] onslaught—attack.

[31] askance—with disapproval.

[32] **inexorable**—relentless.

Burgomaster. As an official, I say. In your private capacity, of course, it is another matter. But as a subordinate official of the Baths, you have no right to express any conviction at issue with that of your superiors.

Dr. Stockmann. This is too much! I, a doctor, a man of science, have no right to—!

Burgomaster. The matter in question is not a purely scientific one; it is a complex affair; it has both a technical and an economic side.

Dr. Stockmann. What the devil do I care what it is! I will be free to speak my mind upon any subject under the sun!

Burgomaster. As you please—so long as it does not concern the Baths. With them we forbid you to meddle.

Dr. Stockmann [*shouts*]. You forbid—! You! A set of—

Burgomaster. *I* forbid it—*I*, your chief; and when I issue an order, you have simply to obey.

Dr. Stockmann [*controlling himself*]. Upon my word, Peter, if you weren't my brother—

Petra [*tears open the door*]. Father, you shan't submit to this!

Mrs. Stockmann [*following her*]. Petra, Petra!

Burgomaster. Ah! So we have been listening!

Mrs. Stockmann. The partition is so thin, we couldn't help—

Petra. I stood and listened on purpose.

Burgomaster. Well, on the whole, I am not sorry—

Dr. Stockmann [*coming nearer to him*]. You spoke to me of forbidding and obeying—

Burgomaster. You have forced me to adopt that tone.

Dr. Stockmann. And am I to make myself lie, in a public declaration?

Burgomaster. We consider it absolutely necessary that you should issue a statement in the terms indicated.

Dr. Stockmann. And if I do not obey?

Burgomaster. Then we shall ourselves put forth a statement to reassure the public.

Dr. Stockmann. Well and good; then I shall write against you. I shall stick to my point and prove that I am right, and you wrong. And what will you do then?

Burgomaster. Then I shall be unable to prevent your dismissal.

Dr. Stockmann. What—!

Petra. Father! Dismissal!

Mrs. Stockmann. Dismissal!

Burgomaster. Your dismissal from the Baths. I shall be compelled to move that notice be given you at once, and that you have henceforth no connection whatever with the Baths.

Dr. Stockmann. You would dare to do that!

Burgomaster. It is you who are playing the daring game.

Petra. Uncle, this is a shameful way to treat a man like father!

Mrs. Stockmann. Do be quiet, Petra!

Burgomaster [*looking at* Petra]. Aha! We have opinions of our own already, eh? To be sure, to be sure! [*To* Mrs. Stockmann.] Sister-in-law, you are presumably the most rational member of this household. Use all your influence with your husband; try to make him realize what all this will involve both for his family—

Dr. Stockmann. My family concerns myself alone!

Burgomaster. —both for his family, I say, and for the town he lives in.

Dr. Stockmann. It is I that have the real good of the town at heart! I want to lay bare the evils that, sooner or later, must come to light. Ah! You shall see whether I love my native town.

Burgomaster. You, who, in your blind **obstinacy**,[33] want to cut off the town's chief source of prosperity!

Dr. Stockmann. That source is poisoned, man! Are you mad? We live by trafficking filth and corruption! The whole of our flourishing social life is rooted in a lie!

Burgomaster. Idle fancies—or worse. The man who scatters broadcast such offensive insinuations[34] against his native place must be an enemy of society.

Dr. Stockmann [*going towards him*]. You dare to—!

Mrs. Stockmann [*throwing herself between them*]. Thomas!

Petra [*seizing her father's arm*]. Keep calm, father!

Burgomaster. I will not expose myself to violence. You have had your warning now. Reflect upon what is due to yourself and to your family. Good-bye. [*He goes.*]

Dr. Stockmann [*walking up and down*]. And I must put up with such treatment! In my own house, Katrina! What do you say to that!

Mrs. Stockmann. Indeed, it's a shame and a disgrace, Thomas—

Petra. Oh, if I could only get hold of uncle—!

---

[33] **obstinacy**—stubbornness.

[34] **insinuations**—hints, suggestions.

Dr. Stockmann. It's my own fault. I ought to have stood up against them long ago—to have shown my teeth—and used them too!—And to be called an enemy of society! Me! I won't bear it; by Heaven, I won't!

Mrs. Stockmann. But my dear Thomas, after all, your brother has the power—

Dr. Stockmann. Yes, but I have the right.

Mrs. Stockmann. Ah yes, right, right! What good does it do to have the right, if you haven't any might?

Petra. Oh, mother—how can you talk so?

Dr. Stockmann. What! No good, in a free community, to have right on your side? What an absurd idea, Katrina! And besides—haven't I the free and independent press before me—and the solid majority at my back? That is might enough, I should think!

Mrs. Stockmann. Why, good heavens, Thomas! you're surely not thinking of—?

Dr. Stockmann. What am I not thinking of?

Mrs. Stockmann. —of setting yourself up against your brother, I mean.

Dr. Stockmann. What the devil would you have me do, if not stick to what is right and true?

Petra. Yes, that's what I should like to know!

Mrs. Stockmann. But it will be of no earthly use. If they won't, they won't.

Dr. Stockmann. Ho-ho, Katrina! just wait a while, and you shall see whether I can fight my battles to the end.

Mrs. Stockmann. Yes, to the end of getting your dismissal; that is what will happen.

Dr. Stockmann. Well then, I shall at any rate have done my duty towards the public, towards society—I who am called an enemy of society!

Mrs. Stockmann. But towards your family, Thomas? Towards us at home? Do you think *that* is doing your duty towards those who are dependent on you?

Petra. Oh, mother, don't always think first of us.

Mrs. Stockmann. Yes, it's easy for you to talk; you can stand alone if need be.—But remember the boys, Thomas; and think a little of yourself too, and of me—

Dr. Stockmann. You're surely out of your senses, Katrina! If I were to be such a pitiful coward as to knuckle under to this Peter and his confounded crew—should I ever have another happy hour in all my life?

Mrs. Stockmann. I don't know about that; but God preserve us from the happiness we shall all of us have if you persist in defying them. There you will be again, with nothing to live on, with no regular income. I should have thought we had had enough of that in the old days. Remember them, Thomas; think of what it all means.

Dr. Stockmann [*struggling with himself and clenching his hands*]. And this is what these jacks-in-office can bring upon a free and honest man! Isn't it revolting, Katrina?

Mrs. Stockmann. Yes, no doubt they are treating you shamefully. But God knows there's plenty of injustice one must just submit to in this world.—Here are the boys, Thomas. Look at them! What is to become of them? Oh no, no! you can never have the heart—

[Eilif *and* Morten, *with schoolbooks, have meanwhile entered.*]

Dr. Stockmann. The boys—! [*With a sudden access of firmness and decision.*] Never, though the whole earth should crumble, will I bow my neck beneath the yoke.[35]

[*Goes towards his room.*]

Mrs. Stockmann [*following him*]. Thomas—what are you going to do?

Dr. Stockmann [*at the door*]. I must have the right to look my boys in the face when they have grown into free men.

[*Goes into his room.*]

Mrs. Stockmann [*bursts into tears*]. Ah, God help us all!

Petra. Father is true to the core. He will never give in!

[*The boys ask wonderingly what it all means;* Petra *signs to them to be quiet.*]

Act Three

[*The Editor's Room of the* People's Messenger. *In the background, to the left, an entrance door; to the right another door, with glass panes, through which can be seen the composing room. A door in the right-hand wall. In the middle of the room a large table covered with papers, newspapers, and books. In front, on the left, a window, and by it a desk with a high stool. A couple of armchairs beside the table; some other chairs along the walls. The room is dingy and cheerless, the furniture shabby, the armchairs dirty and torn. In the composing room are seen a few compositors at work; further back, a hand press in operation.*

Hovstad *is seated at the desk, writing. Presently* Billing *enters from the right, with the* Doctor's *manuscript in his hand.*]

Billing. Well, I must say—!

Hovstad [*writing*]. Have you read it through?

---

[35] bow . . . yoke—humble myself.

Billing [*laying the manuscript on the desk*]. Yes, I should think I had.

Hovstad. Don't you think the Doctor comes out strong?

Billing. Strong! Why, strike me dead if he isn't crushing! Every word falls like a—well, like a sledgehammer.

Hovstad. Yes, but these fellows won't collapse at the first blow.

Billing. True enough; but we'll keep on hammering away, blow after blow, till the whole officialdom comes crashing down. As I sat in there reading that article, I seemed to hear the revolution thundering afar.

Hovstad [*turning round*]. Hush! Don't let Aslaksen hear that.

Billing [*in a lower voice*]. Aslaksen's a white-livered, cowardly fellow, without a spark of manhood in him. But this time you'll surely carry your point? Eh? You'll print the Doctor's paper?

Hovstad. Yes, if only the Burgomaster doesn't give in—

Billing. That would be damned annoying.

Hovstad. Well, whatever happens, fortunately we can't turn the situation to account. If the Burgomaster won't agree to the Doctor's proposal, we'll have all the small middle-class down upon him—all the Houseowner's Association, and the rest of them. And if he does agree to it, he'll fall out with the whole crew of big shareholders in the Baths, who have hitherto been his main support—

Billing. Yes, of course; for no doubt they'll have to fork out a lot of money—

Hovstad. You may take your oath of that. And then, don't you see, when the ring is broken up, we'll din[1] it into the public day by day that the Burgomaster is incompetent in every respect, and that all responsible positions in the town, the whole municipal government in short, must be entrusted to men of liberal ideas.

Billing. Strike me dead if that isn't the square truth! I see it—I see it: we are on the eve of a revolution!

[*A knock at the door.*]

Hovstad. Hush! [*Calls.*] Come in!

[Dr. Stockmann *enters from the back, left.*]

Hovstad [*going towards him*]. Ah, here is the Doctor. Well?

Dr. Stockmann. Print away, Mr. Hovstad!

Hovstad. So it has come to that?

Billing. Hurrah!

Dr. Stockmann. Print away, I tell you. To be sure it has come to that. Since they will have it so, they must. War is declared, Mr. Billing!

---

[1] din—repeat.

Billing. War to the knife, say I! War to the death, Doctor!

Dr. Stockmann. This article is only the beginning. I have four or five others sketched out in my head already. But where do you keep Aslaksen?

Billing [*calling into the printing room*]. Aslaksen! just come here a moment.

Hovstad. Four or five more articles, eh?? On the same subject?

Dr. Stockmann. Oh no—not at all, my dear fellow. No; they will deal with quite different matters. But they're all of a piece with the waterworks and sewer question. One thing leads to another. It's just like beginning to pick at an old house, don't you know?

Billing. Strike me dead, but that's true! You feel you can't leave off till you've pulled the whole lumber heap² to pieces.

Aslaksen [*enters from the printing room*]. Pulled to pieces! Surely the Doctor isn't thinking of pulling the Baths to pieces?

Hovstad. Not at all. Don't be alarmed.

Dr. Stockmann. No, we were talking of something quite different. Well, what do you think of my article, Mr. Hovstad?

Hovstad. I think it's simply a masterpiece—

Dr. Stockmann. Yes, isn't it? I'm glad you think so—very glad.

Hovstad. It's so clear and to the point. One doesn't in the least need to be a specialist to understand the **gist**³ of it. I am certain every intelligent man will be on your side.

Aslaksen. And all the prudent ones too, I hope?

Billing. Both the prudent and imprudent—in fact, almost the whole town.

Aslaksen. Then I suppose we may venture to print it.

Dr. Stockmann. I should think so!

Hovstad. It shall go in tomorrow.

Dr. Stockmann. Yes, plague take it, not a day must be lost. Look here, Mr. Aslaksen, this is what I wanted to ask you: won't you take personal charge of the article?

Aslaksen. Certainly I will.

Dr. Stockmann. Be as careful as if it were gold. No printers' errors; every word is important. I shall look in again presently; perhaps you'll be able to let me see a proof.—Ah! I can't tell you how I long to have the thing in print—to see it launched—

Billing. Yes, like a thunderbolt!

Dr. Stockmann. —and submitted to the judgment of every intelligent citizen. Oh, you have no idea what I have had to put up with today.

---

² lumber heap—pile of rubbish.

³ **gist**—central idea.

I've been threatened with all sorts of things. I was to be robbed of my clearest rights as a human being—

Billing. What! Your rights as a human being!

Dr. Stockmann. —I was to humble myself, and eat the dust; I was to set my personal interests above my deepest, holiest convictions—

Billing. Strike me dead, but that's too outrageous!

Hovstad. Oh, what can you expect from that quarter?

Dr. Stockmann. But they shall find they were mistaken in me; they shall learn that in black and white, I promise them! I shall throw myself into the breach[4] every day in the *Messenger*, bombard them with one explosive article after another—

Aslaksen. Yes, but look here—

Billing. Hurrah! It's war! War!

Dr. Stockmann. I shall smite[5] them to the earth, I shall crush them, I shall level their entrenchments to the ground in the eyes of all right-thinking men! That's what I shall do!

Aslaksen. But above all things be temperate, Doctor; bombard with moderation—

Billing. Not at all, not at all! Don't spare the dynamite!

Dr. Stockmann [*going on imperturbably*]. For now it's no mere question of waterworks and sewers, you see. No, the whole community must be purged, disinfected—

Billing. *There* sounds the word of salvation!

Dr. Stockmann. All the old bunglers must be sent packing, you understand. And that in every possible department! Such endless vistas have opened out before me today. I am not quite clear about everything yet, but I shall see my way presently. It's young and vigorous standard bearers we must look for, my friends; we must have new captains at all the outposts.

Billing. Hear, hear!

Dr. Stockmann. And if only we hold together, it will go so smoothly, so smoothly! The whole revolution will glide off the stocks[6] just like a ship. Don't you think so?

Hovstad. For my part, I believe we have now every prospect of placing our municipal affairs in the right hands.

---

[4] throw . . . breach—attack.

[5] smite—strike.

[6] glide . . . stocks—slide like a ship down the framework that holds it while under construction.

Aslaksen. And if only we proceed with moderation, I really don't think there can be any danger.

Dr. Stockmann. Who the devil cares whether there's danger or not! What I do, I do in the name of truth and for conscience' sake.

Hovstad. You are a man to be backed up, Doctor.

Aslaksen. Yes, there's no doubt the Doctor is a true friend to the town; he's what I call a friend of society.

Billing. Strike me dead if Dr. Stockmann isn't a Friend of the People, Aslaksen!

Aslaksen. I have no doubt the Houseowners' Association will soon adopt that expression.

Dr. Stockmann [*shaking their hands, deeply moved*]. Thanks, thanks, my dear, faithful friends; it does me good to hear you. My respected brother called me something very different. Never mind! Trust me to pay him back with interest! But I must be off now to see a poor devil of a patient. I shall look in again, though. Be sure you look after the article, Mr. Aslaksen; and, whatever you do, don't leave out any of my exclamation points! Rather put in a few more! Well, good-bye for the present, good-bye, good-bye.

[*Mutual salutations while they accompany him to the door. He goes out.*]

Hovstad. He will be invaluable to us.

Aslaksen. Yes, so long as he confines himself to this matter of the Baths. But if he goes further, it will scarcely be advisable to follow him.

Hovstad. H'm—that entirely depends on—

Billing. You're always so confoundedly timid, Aslaksen.

Aslaksen. Timid? Yes, when it's a question of attacking local authorities, I am timid, Mr. Billing; I have learnt caution in the school of experience, let me tell you. But start me on the higher politics, confront me with the Government itself, and then see if I'm timid.

Billing. No, you're not; but that's just where your inconsistency comes in.

Aslaksen. The fact is, I am keenly alive to my responsibilities. If you attack the Government, you at least do society no harm; for the men attacked don't care a straw, you see—they stay where they are all the same. But *local* authorities can be turned out; and then we might get some incompetent set into power, to the irreparable injury both of houseowners and other people.

Hovstad. But the education of citizens by self-government—do you never think of *that*?

Aslaksen. When a man has solid interests to protect, he can't think of everything, Mr. Hovstad.

Hovstad. Then I hope I may never have solid interests to protect.

Billing. Hear, hear!

Aslaksen [*smiling*]. H'm! [*Points to the desk.*] Governor Stensgård[7] sat in that editorial chair before you.

Billing [*spitting*]. Pooh! A turncoat[8] like that!

Hovstad. I am no weathercock[9]—and never will be.

Aslaksen. A politician should never be too sure of anything on earth, Mr. Hovstad. And as for you, Mr. Billing, you ought to take in a reef[10] or two, I should say, now that you are applying for the secretaryship to the Town Council.

Billing. I—

Hovstad. Is that so, Billing?

Billing. Well, yes—but, devil take it, you understand, I'm only doing it to spite their high-mightinesses.

Aslaksen. Well, that has nothing to do with me. But if I am to be accused of cowardice and inconsistency, I should just like to point out *this:* my political record is open to every one. I have not changed at all, except in becoming more moderate. My heart still belongs to the people; but I don't deny that my reason inclines somewhat towards the authorities—the local ones, I mean.

[*Goes into the printing room.*]

Billing. Don't you think we should try to get rid of him, Hovstad?

Hovstad. Do you know of anyone else that will pay for our paper and printing?

Billing. What a confounded nuisance it is to have no capital![11]

Hovstad [*sitting down by the desk*]. Yes, if we only had that—

Billing. Suppose you applied to Dr. Stockmann?

Hovstad [*turning over his papers*]. What would be the good? He hasn't a penny.

Billing. No; but he has a good man behind him—old Morten Kiil— "The Badger," as they call him.

Hovstad [*writing*]. Are you so sure he has money?

---

[7] Governor Stensgård—character in Ibsen's play *The League of Youth.*

[8] turncoat—traitor.

[9] weathercock—person constantly changing his or her views.

[10] take in a reef—shorten the sails on a ship before a storm, that is, be more prudent.

[11] capital—financial resources, money.

Billing. Yes, strike me dead if he hasn't! And part of it must certainly go to Stockmann's family. He's bound to provide for—for the children at any rate.

Hovstad [*half turning*]. Are you counting on *that?*

Billing. Counting? How should I be counting on it?

Hovstad. Best not! And that secretaryship you shouldn't count on either; for I can assure you you won't get it.

Billing. Do you think I don't know that? A refusal is the very thing I want. Such a **rebuff**[12] fires the spirit of opposition in you, gives you a fresh supply of **gall**,[13] as it were; and that's just what you need in a godforsaken hole like this, where anything really stimulating so seldom happens.

Hovstad [*writing*]. Yes, Yes.

Billing. Well—they shall soon hear from me!—Now I'll go and write the appeal to the Houseowners' Association.

[*Goes into the room on the right.*]

Hovstad [*sits at his desk, biting his penholder, and says slowly:*] H'm—so that's the way of it.—[*A knock at the door.*] Come in.

[*Petra enters from the back, left.*]

Hovstad [*rising*]. What! Is it you? Here?

Petra. Yes; please excuse me—

Hovstad [*offering her an armchair*]. Won't you sit down?

Petra. No, thanks; I must go again directly.

Hovstad. Perhaps you bring a message from your father—?

Petra. No, I have come on my own account. [*Takes a book from the pocket of her cloak.*] Here is that English story.

Hovstad. Why have you brought it back?

Petra. Because I won't translate it.

Hovstad. But you promised—

Petra. Yes; but then I hadn't read it. I suppose you have not read it either?

Hovstad. No; you know I can't read English; but—

Petra. Exactly; and that's why I wanted to tell you that you must find something else. [*Putting the book on the table.*] This will never do for the *Messenger.*

Hovstad. Why not?

Petra. Because it flies in the face of all your convictions.

Hovstad. Well, for that matter—

---

[12] **rebuff**—rejection.

[13] **gall**—resentment.

Petra. You don't understand me. It makes out that a supernatural power looks after the so-called good people in this world, and turns everything to their advantage at last; while all the so-called bad people are punished.

Hovstad. Yes, but that's all right. That's the very thing the public like.

Petra. And would *you* supply the public with such stuff? You don't believe a word of it yourself. You know well enough that things do not really happen like that.

Hovstad. Of course not; but an editor can't always do as he likes. He has often to humor people's fancies in minor matters. After all, politics is the chief thing in life—at any rate for a newspaper; and if I want the people to follow me along the path of emancipation and progress, I mustn't scare them away. If they find a moral story like this down in the cellar,[14] they are all the more ready to take in what we tell them above—they feel themselves safer.

Petra. For shame! You're not such a hypocrite as to set traps like that for your readers. You're not a spider.

Hovstad [*smiling*]. Thanks for your good opinion. It's true that the idea is Billing's not mine.

Petra. Mr. Billing's!

Hovstad. Yes, at least he was talking in that strain the other day. It was Billing that was so anxious to get the story into the paper; I don't even know the book.

Petra. But how can Mr. Billing, with his advanced views—

Hovstad. Well, Billing is many-sided. He's applying for the secretaryship to the Town Council, I hear.

Petra. I don't believe that, Mr. Hovstad. How could he descend to such a thing?

Hovstad. That you must ask *him.*

Petra. I could never have thought it of Billing!

Hovstad [*looking more closely at her*]. No? Is it such a surprise to you?

Petra. Yes. And yet—perhaps not. Oh, I don't know—

Hovstad. We journalists are not worth much, Miss Petra.

Petra. Do you really say that?

Hovstad. I think so, now and then.

Petra. Yes, in the little everyday squabbles—that I can understand. But now that you have taken up a great cause—

---

[14] cellar—bottom of the page, where newspapers sometimes ran lighter articles or stories.

Hovstad. You mean this affair of your father's?

Petra. Of course. I should think you must feel yourself worth more than the general run of people now.

Hovstad. Yes, today I do feel something of the sort.

Petra. Yes, surely you must. Oh, it's a glorious career you have chosen! To be the pioneer of unrecognized truths and new and daring ways of thought!—even, if that were all, to stand forth fearlessly in support of an injured man—

Hovstad. Especially when the injured man is—I hardly know how to put it—

Petra. You mean when he is so upright and true?

Hovstad [*in a low voice*]. I mean—especially when he is your father.

Petra [*suddenly taken aback*]. *That?*

Hovstad. Yes, Petra—Miss Petra.

Petra. So that is your chief thought, is it? Not the cause itself? Not the truth? Not father's great, warm heart?

Hovstad. Oh, that too, of course.

Petra. No, thank you; you said too much that time, Mr. Hovstad. Now I shall never trust you again, in anything.

Hovstad. Can you be so hard on me because it's mainly for your sake—?

Petra. What I blame you for is that you have not acted straightforwardly towards father. You have talked to him as if you cared only for the truth and the good of the community. You have trifled with both father and me. You are not the man you pretended to be. And that I will never forgive you—never.

Hovstad. You shouldn't say that so bitterly, Miss Petra—least of all now.

Petra. Why not now?

Hovstad. Because your father cannot do without my help.

Petra [*measuring him from head to foot*]. So you are capable of *that*, too? Oh, shame!

Hovstad. No, no. I spoke without thinking. You mustn't believe that of me.

Petra. I know what to believe. Good-bye.

[Aslaksen *enters from printing room, hurriedly and mysteriously.*]

Aslaksen. What do you think, Mr. Hovstad—[*Seeing* Petra.] Ow, that's awkward—

Petra. Well, there is the book. You must give it to someone else. [*Going towards the main door.*]

Hovstad [*following her*]. But, Miss Petra—

Petra. Good-bye. [*She goes.*]

Aslaksen. I say, Mr. Hovstad!

Hovstad. Well well; what is it?

Aslaksen. The Burgomaster's out there, in the printing office.

Hovstad. The Burgomaster?

Aslaksen. Yes. He wants to speak to you; he came in by the back way— he didn't want to be seen, you understand.

Hovstad. What can be the meaning of this? Stop, I'll go myself—

[*Goes toward the printing room, opens the door, bows and invites the* Burgomaster *to enter.*]

Hovstad. Keep a lookout, Aslaksen, that no one—

Aslaksen. I understand. [*Goes into the printing room.*]

Burgomaster. You didn't expect to see me here, Mr. Hovstad.

Hovstad. No, I cannot say that I did.

Burgomaster [*looking about him*]. You are very comfortably installed here—capital quarters.

Hovstad. Oh—

Burgomaster. And here have I come, without notice or permission, to take up your time—

Hovstad. You are very welcome, Burgomaster; I am at your service. Let me take your cap and stick. [*He does so, and puts them on a chair.*] And won't you be seated?

Burgomaster [*sitting down by the table*]. Thanks. [Hovstad *also sits by the table.*] I have been much—very much worried today, Mr. Hovstad.

Hovstad. Really? Well, I suppose with all your various duties, Burgomaster—

Burgomaster. It is the Doctor that has been causing me annoyance today.

Hovstad. Indeed! The Doctor?

Burgomaster. He has written a sort of memorandum to the Directors about some alleged shortcomings in the Baths.

Hovstad. Has he really?

Burgomaster. Yes; hasn't he told you? I thought he said—

Hovstad. Oh yes, by-the-bye, he did mention something—

Aslaksen [*from the printing office*]. I've just come for the manuscript—

Hovstad [*in a tone of vexation*]. Oh!—there it is on the desk.

Aslaksen [*finding it*]. All right.

Burgomaster. Why, *that* is the very thing—

Aslaksen. Yes, this is the Doctor's article, Burgomaster.

Hovstad. Oh, is *that* what you were speaking of?

Burgomaster. Precisely. What do you think of it?

Hovstad. I have no technical knowledge of the matter, and I've only glanced through it.

Burgomaster. And yet you are going to print it!

Hovstad. I can't very well refuse a signed communication—

Aslaksen. I have nothing to do with the editing of the paper, Burgomaster—

Burgomaster. Of course not.

Aslaksen. I merely print what is placed in my hands.

Burgomaster. Quite right, quite right.

Aslaksen. So I must— [*Goes towards the printing room.*]

Burgomaster. No, stop a moment, Mr. Aslaksen. With your permission, Mr. Hovstad—

Hovstad. By all means, Burgomaster.

Burgomaster. You are a discreet and thoughtful man, Mr. Aslaksen.

Aslaksen. I am glad you think so, Burgomaster.

Burgomaster. And a man of very wide influence.

Aslaksen. Well—chiefly among the lower middle-class.

Burgomaster. The small taxpayers form the majority—here as everywhere.

Aslaksen. That's very true.

Burgomaster. And I have no doubt that you know the general feeling among them. Am I right?

Aslaksen. Yes, I think I may say that I do, Burgomaster.

Burgomaster. Well—since our townsfolk of the poorer class appear to be so heroically eager to make sacrifices—

Aslaksen. How so?

Hovstad. Sacrifices?

Burgomaster. It is a pleasing evidence of public spirit—a most pleasing evidence. I admit it is more than I should quite have expected. But, of course, you know public feeling better than I do.

Aslaksen. Yes but, Burgomaster—

Burgomaster. And assuredly it is no small sacrifice the town will have to make.

Hovstad. The town?

Aslaksen. But I don't understand— It's the Baths—

Burgomaster. At a rough provisional estimate, the alterations the Doctor thinks desirable will come to two or three hundred thousand crowns.

Aslaksen. That's a lot of money; but—

Burgomaster. Of course we shall be obliged to raise a municipal loan.

Hovstad [*rising*]. You surely can't mean that the town—?

Aslaksen. Would you come upon the taxes? Upon the scanty savings of the lower middle-class?

Burgomaster. Why, my dear Mr. Aslaksen, where else are the funds to come from?

Aslaksen. The proprietors of the Baths must see to that.

Burgomaster. The proprietors are not in a position to go to any further expense.

Aslaksen. Are you quite sure of that, Burgomaster?

Burgomaster. I have positive information. So if these extensive alterations are called for, the town itself will have to bear the cost.

Aslaksen. Oh, plague take it all—I beg your pardon!—but this is quite another matter, Mr. Hovstad.

Hovstad. Yes, it certainly is.

Burgomaster. The worst of it is, that we shall be obliged to close the establishment for a couple of years.

Hovstad. To close it? Completely?

Aslaksen. For two years!

Burgomaster. Yes, the work will require that time—at least.

Aslaksen. But, damn it all! we can't stand that, Burgomaster. What are we houseowners to live on in the meantime?

Burgomaster. It's extremely difficult to say, Mr. Aslaksen. But what would you have us do? Do you think a single visitor will come here if we go about making them imagine that the water is poisoned, that the place is pestilential, that the whole town—

Aslaksen. And it's all nothing but imagination?

Burgomaster. With the best will in the world, I have failed to convince myself that it is anything else.

Aslaksen. In that case it's simply inexcusable of Dr. Stockmann—I beg your pardon, Burgomaster, but—

Burgomaster. I'm sorry to say you are only speaking the truth, Mr. Aslaksen. Unfortunately, my brother has always been noted for his rashness.

Aslaksen. And yet you want to back him up in this, Mr. Hovstad!

Hovstad. But who could possibly imagine that—?

Burgomaster. I have drawn up a short statement of the facts, as they appear from a sober-minded standpoint; and I have **intimated**[15] that any drawbacks that may possibly exist can no doubt be remedied by measures compatible with the finances of the Baths.

---

[15] **intimated**—suggested.

Hovstad. Have you the article with you, Burgomaster?

Burgomaster [*feeling in his pockets*]. Yes; I brought it with me, in case you—

Aslaksen [*quickly*]. Plague take it, there he is!

Burgomaster. Who? My brother?

Hovstad. Where? where?

Aslaksen. He's coming through the composing room.

Burgomaster. Most unfortunate! I don't want to meet him here, and yet there are several things I want to talk to you about.

Hovstad [*pointing to the door on the right*]. Go in there for a moment.

Burgomaster. But—?

Hovstad. You'll find nobody but Billing there.

Aslaksen. Quick, quick, Burgomaster; he's just coming.

Burgomaster. Very well, then. But try to get rid of him quickly.

[*He goes out by the door on the right, which* Aslaksen *opens, and closes behind him.*]

Hovstad. Pretend to be busy, Aslaksen.

[*He sits down and writes.* Aslaksen *turns over a heap of newspapers on a chair, right.*]

Dr. Stockmann [*entering from the composing room*]. Here I am back again. [*Puts down his hat and stick.*]

Hovstad [*writing*]. Already, Doctor? Make haste with what we were speaking of, Aslaksen. We've no time to lose today.

Dr. Stockmann [*to Aslaksen*]. No proof yet, I hear.

Aslaksen [*without turning round*]. No; how could you expect it?

Dr. Stockmann. Of course not; but you understand my impatience. I can have no rest or peace until I see the thing in print.

Hovstad. H'm; it will take a good while yet. Don't you think so, Aslaksen?

Aslaksen. I'm afraid it will.

Dr. Stockmann. All right, all right, my good friend; then I shall look in again. I'll look in twice if necessary. With so much at stake—the welfare of the whole town—one mustn't grudge a little trouble. [*Is on the point of going but stops and comes back.*] Oh, by the way—there's one other thing I must speak to you about.

Hovstad. Excuse me; wouldn't some other time—?

Dr. Stockmann. I can tell you in two words. You see it's this: when people read my article in the paper tomorrow, and find I have spent the whole winter working quietly for the good of the town—

Hovstad. Yes but, Doctor—

Dr. Stockmann. I know what you're going to say. You don't think it was a bit more than my duty—my simple duty as a citizen. Of course I know that, as well as you do. But you see, my fellow townsmen—good Lord! the poor souls think so much of me—

Aslaksen. Yes, the townspeople have hitherto thought very highly of you, Doctor.

Dr. Stockmann. That's exactly why I'm afraid that—. What I wanted to say was this: when all this comes to them—especially to the poorer classes—as a summons to take the affairs of the town into their own hands for the future—

Hovstad [*rising*]. H'm, Doctor, I won't conceal from you—

Dr. Stockmann. Aha! I thought there was something brewing! But I won't hear of it. If they are getting up anything of that sort—

Hovstad. Of what sort?

Dr. Stockmann. Well, anything of any sort—a procession with banners, or a banquet, or a subscription for a testimonial,[16] or whatever it may be—you must give me your solemn promise to put a stop to it. And you too, Mr. Aslaksen; do you hear?

Hovstad. Excuse me, Doctor; we may as well tell you the whole truth first as last—

[Mrs. Stockmann *enters from the back, left.*]

Mrs. Stockmann [*seeing the* Doctor]. Ah! just as I thought!

Hovstad [*going toward her*]. Mrs. Stockmann, too?

Dr. Stockmann. What the devil do *you* want here, Katrina?

Mrs. Stockmann. You know very well what I want.

Hovstad. Won't you sit down? Or perhaps—

Mrs. Stockmann. Thanks, please don't trouble. And you must forgive my following my husband here; remember, I am the mother of three children.

Dr. Stockmann. Stuff and nonsense! We all know that well enough.

Mrs. Stockmann. Well, it doesn't look as if you thought very much about your wife and children today, or you wouldn't be so ready to plunge us all into ruin.

Dr. Stockmann. Are you quite mad, Katrina! Has a man with a wife and children no right to proclaim the truth? Has he no right to be an active and useful citizen? Has he no right to do his duty by the town he lives in?

Mrs. Stockmann. Everything in moderation, Thomas!

Aslaksen. That's just what I say. Moderation in everything.

---

[16] subscription for a testimonial—collection for a tribute.

Mrs. Stockmann. You are doing us a great wrong, Mr. Hovstad, in enticing my husband away from house and home, and befooling him in this way.

Hovstad. I am not befooling anyone—

Dr. Stockmann. Befooling! Do you think I should let myself be befooled?

Mrs. Stockmann. Yes, that's just what you do. I know very well that you are the cleverest man in the town; but you're very easily made a fool of, Thomas. [*To* Hovstad.] Remember that he loses his post at the Baths if you print what he has written—

Aslaksen. What!

Hovstad. Well now, really, Doctor—

Dr. Stockmann [*laughing*]. Ha ha! just let them try—! No no, my dear, they'll think twice about that. I have the solid majority behind me, you see!

Mrs. Stockmann. That's just the misfortune, that you should have such a horrid thing behind you.

Dr. Stockmann. Nonsense, Katrina;—you go home and look after your house, and let me take care of society. How can you be in such a fright when you see me so confident and happy? [*Rubbing his hands and walking up and down.*] Truth and the People must win the day; you may be perfectly sure of that. Oh! I can see all our free-souled citizens standing shoulder to shoulder like a conquering army—! [*Stopping by a chair.*] Why, what the devil is *that?*

Aslaksen [*looking at it*]. Oh Lord!

Hovstad [*the same*]. H'm—

Dr. Stockmann. Why, here's the topknot of authority!

[*He takes the Burgomaster's official cap carefully between the tips of his fingers and holds it up.*]

Mrs. Stockmann. The Burgomaster's cap!

Dr. Stockmann. And here's the staff of office, too! But how in the devil's name did they—?

Hovstad. Well then—

Dr. Stockmann. Ah, I understand! He has been here to talk you over. Ha, ha! He reckoned without his host that time! And when he caught sight of me in the printing room—[*Bursts out laughing.*]—he took to his heels, eh, Mr. Aslaksen?

Aslaksen [*hurriedly*]. Exactly; he took to his heels, Doctor.

Dr. Stockmann. Made off without his stick and—. No, *that* won't do! Peter never left anything behind him. But where the devil have you stowed him? Ah—in here, of course. Now you shall see, Katrina!

Mrs. Stockmann. Thomas—I implore you—!

Aslaksen. Take care, Doctor!

[Dr. Stockmann *has put on the Burgomaster's cap and grasped his stick; he now goes up to the door, throws it open, and makes a military salute. The* Burgomaster *enters, red with anger. Behind him comes* Billing.]

Burgomaster. What is the meaning of these antics?

Dr. Stockmann. Respect, my good Peter! Now, it's I that am in power in this town. [*He struts up and down.*]

Mrs. Stockmann [*almost in tears*]. Oh, Thomas!

Burgomaster [*following him*]. Give me my cap and stick!

Dr. Stockmann [*as before*]. You may be Chief of Police, but I am Burgomaster. I am master of the whole town I tell you!

Burgomaster. Put down my cap, I say. Remember it is an official cap, as by law prescribed!

Dr. Stockmann. Pshaw! Do you think the awakening lion of the democracy will let itself be scared by a gold-laced cap? There's to be a revolution in the town tomorrow, let me tell you. You threatened me with dismissal; but now *I* dismiss *you*—dismiss you from all your offices of trust—. You think I can't do it?—Oh, yes, I can! I have the irresistible forces of society on my side. Hovstad and Billing will thunder in the *People's Messenger,* and Aslaksen will take the field at the head of the Houseowners' Association—

Aslaksen. No, Doctor, I shall not.

Dr. Stockmann. Why, of course you will—

Burgomaster. Aha! Perhaps Mr. Hovstad would like to join the agitation after all?

Hovstad. No, Burgomaster.

Aslaksen. No, Mr. Hovstad isn't such a fool as to ruin both himself and the paper for the sake of a delusion.

Dr. Stockmann [*looking about him*]. What does all this mean?

Hovstad. You have presented your case in a false light, Doctor; therefore I am unable to give you my support.

Billing. And after what the Burgomaster has been so kind as to explain to me, I—

Dr. Stockmann. In a false light! Well, I am responsible for that. Just you print my article, and I promise you I shall prove it up to the hilt.

Hovstad. I shall not print it. I cannot, and will not, and dare not print it.

Dr. Stockmann. You dare not? What nonsense is this? You are editor; and I suppose it's the editor that controls a paper.

Aslaksen. No, it's the subscribers, Doctor.

Burgomaster. Fortunately.

Aslaksen. It's public opinion, the enlightened majority, the houseowners and all the rest. It's *they* who control a paper.

Dr. Stockmann [*calmly*]. And all these powers I have against me?

Aslaksen. Yes, you have. It would mean absolute ruin for the town if your article were inserted.

Dr. Stockmann. So *that* is the way of it!

Burgomaster. My hat and stick!

[Dr. Stockmann *takes off the cap and lays it on the table along with the stick.*]

Burgomaster [*taking them both*]. Your term of office has come to an untimely end.

Dr. Stockmann. The end is not yet. [*To Hovstad.*] So you are quite determined not to print my article in the *Messenger?*

Hovstad. Quite; for the sake of your family, if for no other reason.

Mrs. Stockmann. Oh, be kind enough to leave his family out of the question, Mr. Hovstad.

Burgomaster [*takes a manuscript front his pocket*]. When this appears, the public will be in possession of all necessary information; it is an authentic statement. I place it in your hands.

Hovstad [*taking the manuscript*]. Good. It shall appear in due course.

Dr. Stockmann. And not mine! You imagine you can kill me and the truth by a conspiracy of silence! But it won't be so easy as you think. Mr. Aslaksen, will you be good enough to print my article at once, as a pamphlet? I'll pay for it myself, and be my own publisher. I'll have four hundred copies—no, five—six hundred.

Aslaksen. No. If you offered me its weight in gold, I dare not lend my press to such a purpose, Doctor. I daren't fly in the face of public opinion. You won't get it printed anywhere in the whole town.

Dr. Stockmann. Then give it me back.

Hovstad [*handing him the manuscript*]. By all means.

Dr. Stockmann [*taking up his hat and cane*]. It shall be made public all the same. I shall read it at a great mass meeting; all my fellow citizens shall hear the voice of truth!

Burgomaster. Not a single society in the town would let you their hall for such a purpose.

Aslaksen. Not one, I'm quite certain.

Billing. No, strike me dead if they would!

Mrs. Stockmann. That would be too disgraceful! Why do they turn against you like this, every one of them?

Dr. Stockmann [*irritated*]. I'll tell you why. It's because in this town all the men are old women—like you. They all think of nothing but their families, not of the general good.

Mrs. Stockmann [*taking his arm*]. Then I'll show them that an—an old woman can be a man for once in a way. For *now* I'll stand by you, Thomas.

Dr. Stockmann. Bravely said, Katrina! I swear by my soul and conscience the truth shall out! If they won't let me a hall, I'll hire a drum and march through the town with it; and I'll read my paper at every street corner.

Burgomaster. You can scarcely be such a raving lunatic as that?

Dr. Stockmann. I am.

Aslaksen. You would not get a single man in the whole town to go with you.

Billing. No, strike me dead if you would!

Mrs. Stockmann. Don't give in, Thomas. I'll ask the boys to go with you.

Dr. Stockmann. That's a splendid idea!

Mrs. Stockmann. Morten will be delighted; and Eilif will go too, I daresay.

Dr. Stockmann. Yes, and so will Petra! And you yourself, Katrina!

Mrs. Stockmann. No no, not I. But I'll stand at the window and watch you—that I will.

Dr. Stockmann [*throwing his arms about her and kissing her*]. Thank you for that! Now, my good sirs, we're ready for the fight! Now we shall see whether your **despicable**[17] tactics can stop the mouth of the patriot who wants to purge society!

[*He and his wife go out together by the door in the back, left.*]

Burgomaster [*shaking his head dubiously*]. Now he has turned *her* head too!

Act Four

[*A large old-fashioned room in* Captain Horster's *house. An open folding door in the background leads to an anteroom. In the wall on the left are three windows. About the middle of the opposite wall is a platform, and on it a small table, two candles, a water bottle and glass, and a bell. For the rest, the room is lighted by* sconces[1] *placed between the windows. In front, on the left, is a table with a candle on it, and by it a chair. In front, to the right, a door, and near it a few chairs.*]

---

[17] **despicable**—contemptible.

[1] *sconces*—brackets for candles.

Large assemblage[2] of all classes of townsfolk. In the crowd are a few women and schoolboys. More and more people gradually stream in from the back until the room is quite full.]

First Citizen [*to another standing near him*]. So you're here too, Lamstad?

Second Citizen. I never miss a public meeting.

A Bystander. I suppose you've brought your whistle?

Second Citizen. Of course I have; haven't you?

Third Citizen. I should think so. And Skipper Evensen said he'd bring a thumping big horn.

Second Citizen. He's a good 'un, is Evensen! [*Laughter in the group.*]

A Fourth Citizen [*joining them*]. I say, what's it all about? What's going on here tonight?

Second Citizen. Why, it's Dr. Stockmann that's going to lecture against the Burgomaster.

Fourth Citizen. But the Burgomaster's his brother.

First Citizen. That makes no difference. Dr. Stockmann's not afraid of him.

Third Citizen. But he's all wrong; the *People's Messenger* says so.

Second Citizen. Yes, he must be wrong this time; for neither the Houseowners' Association nor the Citizens' Club would let him have a hall.

First Citizen. They wouldn't even lend him the hall at the Baths.

Second Citizen. No, you may be sure they wouldn't.

A Man [*in another group*]. Now, who's the one to follow in this business, eh?

Another Man [*in the same group*]. Just keep your eye on Aslaksen, and do as he does.

Billing [*with a portfolio under his arm, makes his way through the crowd*]. Excuse me, gentlemen. Will you allow me to pass? I'm here to report for the *People's Messenger*. Many thanks. [*Sits by the table on the left.*]

A Working Man. Who's he?

Another Working Man. Don't you know him? It's that fellow Billing, that writes for Aslaksen's paper.

[Captain Horster *enters by the door in front on the right, escorting* Mrs. Stockmann *and* Petra. Eilif *and* Morten *follow them.*]

Horster. This is where I thought you might sit; you can so easily slip out if anything should happen.

Mrs. Stockmann. Do you think there will be any disturbance?

---

[2] *assemblage*—assembly, gathering.

Horster. One can never tell—with such a crowd. But there's no occasion for anxiety.

Mrs. Stockmann [*sitting down*]. How kind it was of you to offer Stockmann this room.

Horster. Since no one else would, I—

Petra [*who has also seated herself*]. And it was brave too, Captain Horster.

Horster. Oh, I don't see where the bravery comes in.

[Hovstad *and* Aslaksen *enter at the same moment, but make their way through the crowd separately.*]

Aslaksen [*going up to* Horster]. Hasn't the Doctor come yet?

Horster. He's waiting in there.

[*A movement at the door in the background.*]

Hovstad [*to* Billing]. There's the Burgomaster! Look!

Billing. Yes, strike me dead if he hasn't put in an appearance after all!

[Burgomaster Stockmann *makes his way blandly through the meeting, bowing politely to both sides, and takes his stand by the wall on the left. Soon afterwards,* Dr. Stockmann *enters by the door on the right. He wears a black frockcoat and white necktie. Faint applause, met by a subdued hissing. Then silence.*]

Dr. Stockmann [*in a low tone*]. How do you feel, Katrina?

Mrs. Stockmann. Quite comfortable, thank you. [*In a low voice.*] Now do keep your temper, Thomas.

Dr. Stockmann. Oh, I shall keep myself well in hand. [*Looks at his watch, ascends the platform, and bows.*] It's a quarter past the hour, so I shall begin—[*Takes out his manuscript.*]

Aslaksen. But surely a chairman must be elected first.

Dr. Stockmann. No, that's not at all necessary.

Several Gentlemen [*shouting*]. Yes, yes.

Burgomaster. I should certainly say that a chairman ought to be elected.

Dr. Stockmann. But I've called this meeting to give a lecture, Peter!

Burgomaster. Dr. Stockmann's lecture may possibly lead to differences of opinion.

Several Voices in the Crowd. A chairman! A chairman!

Hovstad. The general voice of the meeting seems to be for a chairman!

Dr. Stockmann [*controlling himself*]. Very well then; let the meeting have its way.

Aslaksen. Will not the Burgomaster take the chair?

Three Gentlemen [*clapping*]. Bravo! Bravo!

Burgomaster. For reasons you will easily understand, I must decline. But, fortunately, we have among us one whom I think we can all accept. I allude to the president of the Houseowners' Association, Mr. Aslaksen.

Many Voices. Yes, yes! Bravo Aslaksen! Hurrah for Aslaksen!

[Dr. Stockmann *takes his manuscript and descends from the platform.*]

Aslaksen. Since my fellow citizens repose this trust in me, I cannot refuse—

[*Applause and cheers.* Aslaksen *ascends the platform.*]

Billing [*writing*]. So—"Mr. Aslaksen was elected by acclamation—"

Aslaksen. And now, as I have been called to the chair, I take the liberty of saying a few brief words. I am a quiet, peace-loving man; I am in favor of discreet moderation, and of—and of moderate discretion. Every one who knows me, knows that.

Many Voices. Yes, yes, Aslaksen!

Aslaksen. I have learnt in the school of life and of experience that moderation is the virtue in which the individual citizen finds his best advantage—

Burgomaster. Hear, hear!

Aslaksen. —and it is discretion and moderation, too, that best serve the community. I could therefore suggest to our respected fellow citizen, who has called this meeting, that he should endeavor to keep within the bounds of moderation.

A Man [*by the door*]. Three cheers for the Temperance Society!

A Voice. Go to the devil!

Voices. Hush! hush!

Aslaksen. No interruptions, gentlemen!—Does anyone wish to offer any observations?

Burgomaster. Mr. Chairman!

Aslaksen. Burgomaster Stockman will address the meeting.

Burgomaster. On account of my close relationship—of which you are probably aware—to the present medical officer of the Baths, I should have preferred not to speak here this evening. But my position as chairman of the Baths, and my care for the vital interests of this town, force me to move a resolution. I may doubtless assume that not a single citizen here present thinks it desirable that untrustworthy and exaggerated statements should get around as to the sanitary condition of the Baths and of our town.

Many Voices. No, no, no! Certainly not! We protest!

Burgomaster. I therefore beg to move, "That this meeting declines to hear the proposed lecture or speech on the subject by the medical officer of the Baths."

Dr. Stockmann [*flaring up*]. Declines to hear—! What do you mean?

Mrs. Stockmann [*coughing*]. H'm! h'm!

Dr. Stockmann [*controlling himself*]. So I am not to be heard?

Burgomaster. In my statement in the *People's Messenger* I have made the public acquainted with the essential facts, so that all well-disposed citizens can easily form their own judgment. From that statement it will be seen that the medical officer's proposal— besides amounting to a vote of censure upon the leading men of the town—at bottom only means saddling the taxpayers with an unnecessary outlay of at least a hundred thousand crowns.

[*Sounds of protest and some hissing.*]

Aslaksen [*ringing the bell*]. Order, gentlemen! I must beg leave to support the Burgomaster's resolution. I quite agree with him that there is something beneath the surface of the Doctor's agitation. In all his talk about the Baths, it is really a revolution he is aiming at; he wants to effect a redistribution of power. No one doubts the excellence of Dr. Stockmann's intentions—of course there cannot be two opinions as to that. I, too, am in favor of self-government by the people, if only it doesn't cost the taxpayers too much. But in this case it would do so; and therefore I'll be hanged if—excuse me—in short, I cannot go with Dr. Stockmann upon this occasion. You can buy even gold too dear; that's my opinion.

[*Loud applause on all sides.*]

Hovstad. I, too feel bound to explain my attitude. Dr. Stockmann's agitation seemed at first to find favor in several quarters, and I supported it as impartially as I could. But it presently appeared that we had been misled by a false representation of the facts—

Dr. Stockmann. False—!

Hovstad. Well then, an untrustworthy representation. This the Burgomaster's report has proved. I trust no one here present doubts my liberal principles; the attitude of the *Messenger* on all great political questions is well known to you all. But I have learned from men of judgment and experience that in purely local matters a paper must observe a certain amount of caution.

Aslaksen. I entirely agree with the speaker.

Hovstad. And in the matter under discussion it is quite evident that Dr. Stockmann has public opinion against him. But, gentlemen, what is an editor's clearest and most **imperative**[3] duty? Is it not to work in harmony with his readers? Has he not in some sort received a tacit mandate[4] to further assiduously[5] and unweariedly the interests of his constituents?[6] Or am I mistaken in this?

Many Voices. No, no, no! Hovstad is right!

Hovstad. It has cost me a bitter struggle to break with a man in whose house I have of late been a frequent guest—with a man who, up to this day, has enjoyed the unqualified goodwill of his fellow citizens—with a man whose only, or, at any rate, whose chief fault is that he consults his heart rather than his head.

A Few Scattered Voices. That's true! Hurrah for Dr. Stockmann!

Hovstad. But my duty towards the community has **constrained**[7] me to break with him. Then, too, there is another consideration that impels me to oppose him, and, if possible, to block the ill-omened path upon which he is entering: consideration for his family—

Dr. Stockmann. Keep to the waterworks and sewers!

Hovstad. —consideration for his wife and his unprotected[8] children.

Morten. Is that us, mother?

Mrs. Stockmann. Hush!

Aslaksen. I will now put the Burgomaster's resolution to the vote.

Dr. Stockmann. You need not. I have no intention of saying anything this evening of all the filth at the Baths. No! You shall hear something quite different.

Burgomaster [*half aloud*]. What next, I wonder?

A Drunken Man [*at the main entrance*]. I'm a taxpayer, so I've a right to my opinion! And it's my full, firm, **incomprehensible**[9] opinion that—

Several Voices. Silence up there!

Others. He's drunk! Turn him out!

[*The drunken man is turned out.*]

Dr. Stockmann. Can I speak?

Aslaksen [*ringing the bell*]. Dr. Stockmann will address the meeting.

---

[3] **imperative**—commanding.

[4] tacit mandate—implied authorization.

[5] assiduously—industriously.

[6] constituents—those represented by another; here, newspaper readers.

[7] **constrained**—forced.

[8] unprotected—literally, "unprovided for."

[9] **incomprehensible**—not understandable (presumably a blunder for some other word, such as *incontrovertible*, "impossible to dispute").

Dr. Stockmann. A few days ago, I should have liked to see anyone venture upon such an attempt to gag me as has been made here tonight! I would have fought like a lion for my sacred rights! But now I care little enough; for now I have more important things to speak of.

[*The people crowd closer round him.* Morten Kiil *comes in sight among the bystanders.*]

Dr. Stockmann [*continuing*]. I have been pondering a great many things during these last days—thinking such a multitude of thoughts, that at last my head was positively in a whirl—

Burgomaster [*coughing*]. H'm—!

Dr. Stockmann. But presently things seemed to straighten themselves out, and I saw them clearly in all their bearings. That is why I stand here this evening. I am about to make great revelations, my fellow citizens! I am going to announce to you a far-reaching discovery, beside which the trifling fact that our waterworks are poisoned, and that our health resort is built on pestilential ground, sinks into insignificance.

Many Voices [*shouting*]. Don't speak about the Baths! We won't listen to that! No more of that!

Dr. Stockmann. I have said I would speak of the great discovery I have made within the last few days—the discovery that all our sources of spiritual life are poisoned, and that our whole society rests upon a pestilential basis of falsehood.

Several Voices [*in astonishment and half aloud*]. What's he saying?

Burgomaster. Such an insinuation—!

Aslaksen [*with his hand on the bell*]. I must call upon the speaker to moderate his expressions.

Dr. Stockmann. I have loved my native town as dearly as any man can love the home of his childhood. I was young when I left our town, and distance, homesickness and memory threw, as it were, a glamour over the place and its people.

[*Some applause and cries of approval.*]

Dr. Stockmann. Then for years I was imprisoned in a horrible hole, far away in the north. As I went about among the people scattered here and there over the stony wilderness, it seemed to me, many a time, that it would have been better for these poor famishing creatures to have had a cattle doctor to attend them, instead of a man like me.

[*Murmurs in the room.*]

Billing [*laying down his pen*]. Strike me dead if I've ever heard—!

Hovstad. What an insult to an estimable[10] peasantry!

Dr. Stockmann. Wait a moment!—I don't think anyone can reproach me with forgetting my native town up there. I sat brooding like an eider duck, and what I hatched was—the plan of the Baths.

[*Applause and expressions of dissent.*]

Dr. Stockmann. And when, at last, fate ordered things so happily that I could come home again—then, fellow citizens, it seemed to me that I hadn't another desire in the world. Yes, one desire I had: an eager, constant, burning desire to be of service to my birthplace, and to its people.

Burgomaster [*gazing into vacancy*]. A strange method to select—!

Dr. Stockmann. So I went about revelling in my happy illusions. But yesterday morning—no, it was really two nights ago—my mind's eyes were opened wide, and the first thing I saw was the colossal stupidity of the authorities—

[*Noise, cries, and laughter. Mrs. Stockmann coughs repeatedly.*]

Burgomaster. Mr. Chairman!

Aslaksen [*ringing his bell*]. In virtue of my position—!

Dr. Stockmann. It's petty to catch me up on a word, Mr. Aslaksen! I only mean that I became alive to the extraordinary muddle our leading men had been guilty of, down at the Baths. I cannot for the life of me abide leading men—I've seen enough of them in my time. They are like goats in a young plantation:[11] they do harm at every point; they block the path of a free man wherever he turns—and I should be glad if we could exterminate them like other noxious animals—

[*Uproar in the room.*]

Burgomaster. Mr. Chairman, are such expressions permissible?

Aslaksen [*with his hand on the bell*]. Dr. Stockmann—

Dr. Stockmann. I can't conceive how it is that I have only now seen through these gentry; for haven't I had a magnificent example before my eyes here every day—my brother Peter—slow of understanding, **tenacious**[12] in prejudice—

[*Laughter, noise, and whistling. Mrs. Stockmann coughs. Aslaksen rings violently.*]

The Drunken Man [*who has come in again*]. Is it me you're alluding to? Sure enough, my name's Petersen; but devil take me if—

Angry Voices. Out with that drunken man! Turn him out!

[*The man is again turned out.*]

---

[10] estimable—worthy of respect.

[11] young plantation—recently planted crop.

[12] **tenacious**—stubborn.

Burgomaster. Who is that person?

A Bystander. I don't know him, Burgomaster.

Another. He doesn't belong to the town.

A Third. I believe he's a timber-dealer from—

[*The rest is inaudible.*]

Aslaksen. The man was evidently intoxicated.—Continue, Dr. Stockmann; but pray endeavor to be moderate.

Dr. Stockmann. Well, fellow citizens, I shall say no more about our leading men. If anyone imagines, from what I have just said, that it's these gentlemen I want to make short work of tonight, he is mistaken— altogether mistaken. For I cherish the comfortable conviction that these laggards,[13] these relics of a decaying order of thought, are **diligently**[14] cutting their own throats. They need no doctor to hasten their end. And it is not people of that sort that constitute the real danger to society; it is not they who are most active in poisoning the sources of our spiritual life and making a plague spot of the ground beneath our feet; it is not *they* who are the most dangerous enemies of truth and freedom in our society.

Cries from All Sides. Who, then? Who is it? Name, name!

Dr. Stockmann. Yes, you may be sure I shall name them! For *this* is the great discovery I made yesterday: [*In a louder tone.*] The most dangerous foe to truth and freedom in our midst is the solid majority. Yes, it's the confounded, solid, liberal majority—that, and nothing else! There, I've told you.

[*Immense disturbance in the room. Most of the audience are shouting, stamping, and whistling. Several elderly gentlemen exchange furtive*[15] *glances and seem to be enjoying the scene.* Mrs. Stockmann *rises in alarm.* Eilif *and* Morten *advance threateningly toward the schoolboys, who are making noises.* Aslaksen *rings the bell and calls for order.* Hovstad *and* Billing *both speak, but nothing can be heard. At last quiet is restored.*]

Aslaksen. I must request the speaker to withdraw his ill-considered expressions.

Dr. Stockmann. Never, Mr. Aslaksen! For it's this very majority that robs me of my freedom, and wants to forbid me to speak the truth.

Hovstad. The majority always has right on its side.

Billing. Yes, and truth too, strike me dead!

---

[13] laggards—sluggish people.

[14] **diligently**—earnestly.

[15] furtive—sly.

Dr. Stockmann. The majority never has right on its side. Never I say! That is one of the social lies that a free, thinking man is bound to rebel against. Who make up the majority in any given country? Is it the wise men or the fools? I think we must agree that the fools are in a terrible, overwhelming majority, all the wide world over. But how in the devil's name can it ever be right for the fools to rule over the wise men?

[*Uproar and yells.*]

Dr. Stockmann. Yes, yes, you can shout me down, but you cannot gainsay[16] me. The majority has *might*—unhappily—but *right* it has not. It is I, and the few, the individuals, that are in the right. The minority is always right.

[*Renewed uproar.*]

Hovstad. Ha ha! Dr. Stockmann has turned aristocrat since the day before yesterday!

Dr. Stockmann. I have said that I have no words to waste on the little, narrow-chested, short-winded crew that lie in our wake. Pulsating[17] life has nothing more to do with them. I am speaking of the few, the individuals among us, who have made all the new, germinating truths their own. These men stand, as it were, at the outposts, so far in the van[18] that the solid majority has not yet reached them and *there* they fight for truths that are too lately born into the world's consciousness to have won over the majority.

Hovstad. So the Doctor's a revolutionist now!

Dr. Stockmann. Yes, by Heaven, I am, Mr. Hovstad! I am going to revolt against the lie that truth belongs exclusively to the majority. What sort of truths do the majority rally round? Truths so stricken in years that they are sinking into decrepitude.[19] When a truth is so old as that, gentlemen, it's in a fair way to become a lie.

[*Laughter and jeers.*]

Dr. Stockmann. Yes, yes, you may believe me or not, as you please; but truths are by no means the wiry Methusalehs[20] some people think them. A normally constituted truth lives—let us say—as a rule, seventeen or eighteen years; at the outside twenty; very seldom more. And

---

[16] gainsay—contradict.

[17] Pulsating—throbbing.

[18] van—vanguard, forward section of an army.

[19] decrepitude—decay.

[20] Methusalehs—Methusaleh is an extraordinarily long-lived person in the Old Testament.

truths so patriarchal[21] as that are always shockingly **emaciated**;[22] yet it's not till then that the majority takes them up and recommends them to society as wholesome food. I can assure you there's not much nutriment in that sort of fare;[23] you may take my word as a doctor for that. All these majority truths are like last year's salt pork; they're like **rancid**,[24] moldy ham, producing all the moral scurvy[25] that devastates society.

Aslaksen. It seems to me that the honorable speaker is wandering rather far from the subject.

Burgomaster. I beg to endorse the Chairman's remark.

Dr. Stockmann. Why you're surely mad, Peter! I'm keeping as closely to my text as I possibly can; for my text is precisely this—that the masses, the majority, this devil's own solid majority—it's that, I say, that's poisoning the sources of our spiritual life, and making a plague spot of the ground beneath our feet.

Hovstad. And you make this charge against the great, independent majority, just because they have the sense to accept only certain and acknowledged truths?

Dr. Stockmann. Ah, my dear Mr. Hovstad, don't talk about certain truths! The truths acknowledged by the masses, the multitude, were certain truths to the vanguard in our grandfathers' days. We, the vanguard of today, don't acknowledge them any longer; and I don't believe there exists any other certain truth but this—that no society can live a healthy life upon truths so old and marrowless.[26]

Hovstad. But instead of all this vague talk, suppose you were to give us some specimens of these old marrowless truths that we are living upon. [*Approval from several quarters.*]

Dr. Stockmann. Oh, I could give you no end of samples from the rubbish heap; but, for the present, I shall keep to one acknowledged truth, which is a hideous lie at bottom, but which Mr. Hovstad, and the *Messenger*, and all adherents of the *Messenger*, live on all the same.

---

[21] patriarchal—ancient. The patriarchs are ancestors of the Jews whose stories are narrated in the Old Testament. Methusaleh was a patriarch.

[22] **emaciated**—extraordinarily thin from starvation.

[23] nutriment . . . fare—nourishment in that kind of food.

[24] **rancid**—stale.

[25] scurvy—disease resulting from vitamin shortage.

[26] marrowless—without vitality.

Hovstad. And that is—?

Dr. Stockmann. That is the doctrine you have inherited from your fore-fathers, and go on thoughtlessly proclaiming far and wide—the doctrine that the multitude, the vulgar herd, the masses, are the pith[27] of the people—that they *are* the people—that the common man, the ignorant, undeveloped member of society, has the same right to sanction and to condemn, to counsel and to govern, as the intellectually distinguished few.

Billing. Well, now, strike me dead—!

Hovstad [*shouting at the same time*]. Citizens, please note this!

Angry Voices. Ho-ho! Aren't we the people? Is it only the grand folks that are to govern?

A Working Man. Out with the fellow that talks like that!

Others. Turn him out!

A Citizen [*shouting*]. Blow your horn, Evensen.

[*The deep notes of a horn are heard; whistling, and terrific noise in the room.*]

Dr. Stockmann [*when the noise has somewhat subsided*]. Now do be reasonable! Can't you bear even for once in a way to hear the voice of truth? I don't ask you all to agree with me on the instant. But I certainly should have expected Mr. Hovstad to back me up, as soon as he had collected himself a bit. Mr. Hovstad sets up to be a freethinker—

Several Voices [*subdued and wondering*]. Freethinker, did he say? What? Mr. Hovstad a freethinker?

Hovstad [*shouting*]. Prove it, Dr. Stockmann. When have I said so in print?

Dr. Stockmann [*reflecting*]. No, upon my soul, you're right there; you've never had the frankness to do that. Well, well, I won't put you on the rack, Mr. Hovstad. Let me be the freethinker then. And now I'll make it clear to you all, and on scientific grounds too, that the *Messenger* is leading you shamefully by the nose, when it tells you that you, the masses, the crowd, are the true pith of the people. I tell you that's only a newspaper lie. The masses are nothing but the raw material that must be fashioned into a People.

[*Murmurs, laughter, and disturbance in the room.*]

Dr. Stockmann. Is it not so with all other living creatures? What a difference between a cultivated and an uncultivated breed of animals! Just look at a common barn door hen. What meat do you get from such a skinny carcass? Not much, I can tell you! And what sort of eggs does

---

[27] pith—substance.

she lay? A decent crow or raven can lay nearly as good. Then take a cultivated Spanish or Japanese hen, or take a fine pheasant or turkey—ah! then you'll see the difference! And now look at the dog, our near relation. Think first of an ordinary vulgar cur—I mean one of those wretched, ragged, plebeian[28] mongrels that haunt the gutters, and soil the sidewalks. Then place such a mongrel by the side of a poodle dog, descended through many generations from an aristocratic stock, who have lived on delicate food, and heard harmonious voices and music. Do you think the brain of the poodle isn't very differently developed from that of the mongrel? Yes, you may be sure it is! It's well-bred poodle pups like this that jugglers train to perform the most marvelous tricks. A common peasant cur could never learn anything of the sort—not if he tried till doomsday.

[*Noise and laughter are heard all round.*]

A Citizen [*shouting*]. Do you want to make dogs of us now?

Another Man. We're not animals, Doctor!

Dr. Stockmann. Yes, on my soul, but we *are* animals, my good sir! We're one and all of us animals, whether we like it or not. But truly there are few enough aristocratic animals among us. Oh, there's a terrible difference between poodle men and mongrel men! And the ridiculous part of it is, that Mr. Hovstad quite agrees with me so long as it's four-legged animals we're talking of—

Hovstad. Oh, beasts are only beasts.

Dr. Stockmann. Well and good—but no sooner do I apply the law to two-legged animals, than Mr. Hovstad stops short; then he daren't hold his own opinions, or think out his own thoughts; then he turns the whole principle upside down, and proclaims in the *People's Messenger* that the barn door hen and the gutter mongrel are precisely the finest specimens in the **menagerie**.[29] But that's always the way, so long as the commonness still lingers in your system, and you haven't worked your way up to spiritual distinction.

Hovstad. I make no pretense[30] to any sort of distinction. I come of simple peasant folk, and I am proud that my root should lie deep down among the common people, who are here being insulted.

Workmen. Hurrah for Hovstad. Hurrah! hurrah!

---

[28] plebeian—low-class.

[29] **menagerie**—collection of animals.

[30] pretense—claim.

Dr. Stockmann. The sort of common people I am speaking of are not found among the lower classes alone; they crawl and swarm all around us—up to the very summits of society. Just look at your own smug, respectable Burgomaster! Why, my brother Peter belongs as clearly to the common people as any man that walks on two legs— [*Laughter and hisses.*]

Burgomaster. I protest against such personalities.[31]

Dr. Stockmann [*imperturbably*[32]] —and that not because, like myself, he's descended from a good-for-nothing old pirate from Pomerania, or thereabouts—for that's our ancestry—

Burgomaster. An absurd tradition! Utterly groundless.

Dr. Stockmann. —but he is so because he thinks the thoughts and holds the opinions of his official superiors. Men who do that, belong intellectually speaking, to the common people; and that is why my distinguished brother Peter is at bottom so undistinguished,—and consequently so illiberal.

Burgomaster. Mr. Chairman—!

Hovstad. So that the distinguished people in this country are the Liberals? That's quite a new light on the subject.

[*Laughter.*]

Dr. Stockmann. Yes, that is part of my new discovery. And this, too, follows: that liberality of thought is almost precisely the same thing as morality. Therefore I say it's absolutely unpardonable of the *Messenger* to proclaim, day out, day in, the false doctrine that it's the masses, the multitude, the solid majority, that monopolize liberality and morality,—and that vice and corruption and all sorts of spiritual uncleanness ooze out of culture, as all that filth oozes down to the Baths from the Mill Dale tanworks![33] [*Noise and interruptions.*]

Dr. Stockmann [*goes on imperturbably, smiling in his eagerness*]. And yet this same *Messenger* can preach about elevating the masses and the multitude to a higher level of well-being! Why, devil take it, if the *Messenger*'s own doctrine holds good, the elevation of the masses would simply mean hurling them straight to **perdition**![34] But, happily, the notion that culture demoralizes is nothing but an old traditional lie. No it's stupidity, poverty, the ugliness of life, that do

---

[31] personalities—personal attacks.

[32] *imperturbably*—calmly.

[33] tanworks—tannery, site where leather is processed, or tanned.

[34] **perdition**—destruction.

the devil's work! In a house that isn't aired and swept every day—my wife maintains that the floors ought to be scrubbed too, but perhaps that is going too far;—well,—in such a house, I say, within two or three years, people lose the power of thinking or acting morally. Lack of oxygen enervates[35] the conscience. And there seems to be precious little oxygen in many and many a house in this town, since the whole solid majority is unscrupulous enough to want to found its future upon a quagmire[36] of lies and fraud.

Aslaksen. I cannot allow so gross an insult to be leveled against a whole community.

A Gentleman. I move that the Chairman order the speaker to sit down.

Eager Voices. Yes, yes! That's right! Sit down! Sit down!

Dr. Stockmann [*flaring up*]. Then I shall proclaim the truth at every street corner! I shall write to newspapers in other towns! The whole country shall know how matters stand here!

Hovstad. It almost seems as if the Doctor's object were to ruin the town.

Dr. Stockmann. Yes, so well do I love my native town that I would rather ruin it than see it flourishing upon a lie.

Aslaksen. That's plain speaking.

[*Noise and whistling.* Mrs. Stockmann *coughs in vain; the* Doctor *no longer heeds her.*]

Hovstad [*shouting amid the tumult*]. The man who would ruin a whole community must be an enemy to his fellow citizens!

Dr. Stockmann [*with growing excitement*]. What does it matter if a lying community is ruined! Let it be leveled to the ground, say I! All men who live upon a lie ought to be exterminated like vermin! You'll end by poisoning the whole country; you'll bring it to such a pass that the whole country will deserve to perish. And if ever it comes to that, I shall say, from the bottom of my heart: Perish the country! Perish all its people!

A Man [*in the crowd*]. Why, he talks like a regular enemy of the people!

Billing. Strike me dead but there spoke the people's voice!

The Whole Assembly [*shouting*]. Yes! yes! yes! He's an enemy of the people! He hates his country! He hates the whole people!

Aslaksen. Both as a citizen of this town and as a human being, I am deeply shocked at what it has been my lot to hear tonight.

---

[35] enervates—weakens.

[36] quagmire—bog.

Dr. Stockmann has unmasked himself in a manner I should never have dreamt of. I must reluctantly subscribe to the opinion just expressed by some estimable citizens; and I think we ought to formulate this opinion in a resolution. I therefore beg to move, "That this meeting declares the medical officer of the Baths, Dr. Thomas Stockmann, to be an enemy of the people."

[*Thunders of applause and cheers. Many form a circle round the* Doctor *and hoot at him.* Mrs. Stockmann *and* Petra *have risen.* Morten *and* Eilif *fight the other schoolboys, who have also been hooting. Some grown-up persons separate them.*]

Dr. Stockmann [*to the people hooting*]. Ah, fools that you are! I tell you that—

Aslaksen [*ringing*]. The Doctor is out of order in speaking. A formal vote must be taken; but out of consideration for personal feelings, it will be taken in writing and without names. Have you any blank paper, Mr. Billing?

Billing. Here's both blue and white paper—

Aslaksen. Capital; that will save time. Cut it up into slips. That's it. [*To the meeting.*] Blue means no, white means aye. I myself will go round and collect the votes.

[The Burgomaster *leaves the room.* Aslaksen *and a few others go round with pieces of paper in hats.*]

A Gentleman [*to* Hovstad]. What can be the matter with the Doctor? What does it all mean?

Hovstad. Why, you know what a hare-brained creature he is.

Another Gentleman [*to* Billing]. I say, you're often at his house. Have you ever noticed if the fellow drinks?

Billing. Strike me dead if I know what to say. The toddy's always on the table when anyone looks in.

A Third Gentleman. No, I should rather say he went off his head at times.

First Gentleman. I wonder if there's madness in the family?

Billing. I shouldn't be surprised.

A Fourth Gentleman. No, it's pure **malice**.[37] He wants to be revenged for something or other.

Billing. He was certainly talking about a rise in his salary the other day; but he didn't get it.

All the Gentlemen [*together*]. Aha! That explains everything.

---

[37] **malice**—ill will.

The Drunken Man [*in the crowd*]. I want a blue one, I do! And I'll have a white one too.

Several People. There's the tipsy man again! Turn him out.

Morten Kiil [*approaching the* Doctor]. Well, Stockmann, you see now what such monkey tricks lead to?

Dr. Stockmann. I have done my duty.

Morten Kiil. What was that you said about the Mill Dale tanneries?

Dr. Stockmann. You heard what I said—that all the filth comes from them.

Morten Kiil. From my tannery as well?

Dr. Stockmann. I'm sorry to say yours is the worst of all.

Morten Kiil. Are you going to put *that* in the papers, too?

Dr. Stockmann. I can't gloze[38] anything over.

Morten Kiil. This may cost you dear, Stockmann! [*He goes out.*]

A Fat Gentleman [*goes up to* Horster, *without bowing to the ladies*]. Well, Captain, so you lend your house to enemies of the people.

Horster. I suppose I can do as I please with my own property, Sir.

The Gentleman. Then of course you can have no objection if I follow your example?

Horster. What do you mean, Sir?

The Gentleman. You shall hear from me tomorrow.

[*Turns away and goes out.*]

Petra. Wasn't that the owner of your ship, Captain Horster?

Horster. Yes, that was Mr. Vik.

Aslaksen [*with the voting papers in his hands, ascends the platform and rings*]. Gentlemen! I have now to announce the result of the vote. All the voters, with one exception—

A Young Gentleman. That's the tipsy man!

Aslaksen. With the exception of one intoxicated person, this meeting of citizens unanimously declares the medical officer of the Baths, Dr. Thomas Stockmann, to be an enemy of the people. [*Cheers and applause.*] Three cheers for our fine old municipality! [*Cheers.*] Three cheers for our able and energetic Burgomaster, who has so loyally set family prejudice aside! [*Cheers.*] The meeting is dissolved. [*He descends.*]

Billing. Three cheers for the Chairman!

All. Hurrah for Aslaksen!

Dr. Stockmann. My hat and coat, Petra. Captain, have you room for passengers to the new world?

---

[38] gloze—gloss over, diminish.

Horster. For you and yours, Doctor, we'll make room.

Dr. Stockmann [*while* Petra *helps him to put on his coat*]. Good. Come Katrina, come boys!

[*He gives his wife his arm.*]

Mrs. Stockmann [*in a low voice*]. Thomas, dear, let us go out by the back way.

Dr. Stockmann. No back ways, Katrina! [*In a loud voice.*] You shall hear from the enemy of the people, before he shakes the dust from his feet! I am not so forbearing as a certain person; I don't say: I forgive you, for you know not what you do.[39]

Aslaksen [*shouts*]. That is a **blasphemous**[40] comparison, Dr. Stockmann!

Billing. Strike me—! This is more than a serious man can stand!

A Coarse Voice. And he threatens us into the bargain!

Angry Cries. Let's smash his windows! Duck him in the fiord![41]

A Man [*in the crowd*]. Blow your horn, Evensen! Blow, man, blow!

[*Horn-blowing, whistling, and wild shouting. The* Doctor, *with his family, goes toward the door.* Horster *clears the way for them.*]

All [*yelling after them as they go out*]. Enemy of the people! Enemy of the people! Enemy of the people!

Billing. Strike me dead if I'd care to drink toddy at Stockmann's tonight!

[*The people throng towards the door; the shouting is taken up by others outside; from the street are heard cries of "Enemy of the people! Enemy of the people!"*]

Act Five

[Dr. Stockmann's *Study. Bookshelves and glass cases with various collections along the walls. In the back, a door leading to the hall; in front, on the left, a door to the sitting room. In the wall to the right are two windows, all the panes of which are smashed. In the middle of the room is the* Doctor's *writing table, covered with books and papers. The room is in disorder. It is forenoon.*

Dr. Stockmann, *in dressing gown, slippers, and skullcap, is bending down and raking with an umbrella under one of the cabinets; at last he rakes out a stone.*]

Dr. Stockmann [*speaking through the sitting room doorway*]. Katrina, I've found another!

Mrs. Stockmann [*in the sitting room*]. Oh, I'm sure you'll find plenty more.

---

[39] certain person . . . what you do—an allusion to Jesus, who asked God to forgive those who crucified him because "they know not what they do."

[40] **blasphemous**—extremely irreverent.

[41] fiord—inlet of the sea.

Dr. Stockmann [*placing the stone on a pile of others on the table*]. I shall keep these stones as sacred relics. Eilif and Morten shall see them every day, and when I die they shall be **heirlooms**.[1] [*Raking under the bookcase.*] Hasn't—what the devil is her name?—the girl—hasn't she been for the glazier[2] yet?

Mrs. Stockmann [*coming in*]. Yes, but he said he didn't know whether he would be able to come today.

Dr. Stockmann. I believe, if the truth were told, he daren't come.

Mrs. Stockmann. Well, Randina, too, had an idea he was afraid to come, because of the neighbors. [*Speaks through the sitting room doorway.*] What is it, Randina?—Very well. [*Goes out, and returns immediately.*] Here is a letter for you, Thomas.

Dr. Stockmann. Let me see. [*Opens the letter and reads.*] Aha!

Mrs. Stockmann. Who is it from?

Dr. Stockmann. From the landlord. He gives us notice.

Mrs. Stockmann. Is it possible? He is such a nice man—

Dr. Stockmann [*looking at the letter*]. He daren't do otherwise, he says. He is very unwilling to do it; but he daren't do otherwise—on account of his fellow citizens—out of respect for public opinion—is in dependent position—doesn't dare to offend certain influential men—

Mrs. Stockmann. There, you see, Thomas.

Dr. Stockmann. Yes, yes, I see well enough; they are all cowards, every one of them, in this town; no one dares do anything for fear of all the rest. [*Throws the letter on the table.*] But it's all the same to us, Katrina. We will shape our course for the new world, and then—

Mrs. Stockmann. But are you sure this idea of going abroad is altogether wise, Thomas?

Dr. Stockmann. Would you have me stay here, where they have pilloried[3] me as an enemy of the people, branded me, smashed my windows! And look here, Katrina, they've torn a hole in my black trousers, too.

Mrs. Stockmann. Oh dear; and these are the best you have!

Dr. Stockmann. A man should never put on his best trousers when he goes out to battle for freedom and truth. Well, I don't care so much about the trousers; them you can always patch up for me. But that the

---

[1] **heirlooms**—valued possessions left to heirs.

[2] glazier—worker who repairs windows.

[3] pilloried—publicly abused.

mob, the rabble, should dare to attack me as if they were my equals—
that is what I can't, for the life of me, stomach!

Mrs. Stockmann. Yes, they have behaved abominably to you here,
Thomas; but is that any reason for leaving the country altogether?

Dr. Stockmann. Do you think the plebeians aren't just as **insolent**[4] in
other towns? Oh yes, they are, my dear; it's six of one and half a
dozen of the other. Well, never mind; let the curs yelp; *that's* not the
worst; the worst is that every one, all over the country, is the slave of
his party. Not that I suppose—very likely it's no better in the free
West either; the solid majority, and enlightened public opinion, and
all the other devil's trash is rampant[5] there too. But you see the conditions are larger there than here; they may kill you, but they don't
slow-torture you; they don't screw up a free soul in a vice, as they do
at home here. And then, if need be, you can keep out of it all. [*Walks
up and down.*] If I only knew of any primeval forest, or a little South
Sea island to be sold cheap—

Mrs. Stockmann. Yes, but the boys, Thomas.

Dr. Stockmann [*comes to a standstill*]. What an extraordinary woman you
are, Katrina! Would you rather have the boys grow up in such a society as ours? Why, you could see for yourself yesterday evening that
one half of the population is stark mad, and if the other half hasn't
lost its wits, that's only because they are brute beasts who haven't
any wits to lose.

Mrs. Stockmann. But really, my dear Thomas, you do say such imprudent things.

Dr. Stockmann. What! Isn't it the truth that I tell them? Don't they turn
all ideas upside down? Don't they stir up right and wrong into one
hotch potch?[6] Don't they call lies everything that I know to be the
truth? But the maddest thing of all is to see crowds of grown men,
calling themselves Liberals, go about persuading themselves and
others that they are friends of freedom! Did you ever hear anything
like it, Katrina?

Mrs. Stockmann. Yes, yes, no doubt. But—

[Petra *enters from the sitting room.*]

Mrs. Stockmann. Back from school already?

Petra. Yes; I have been dismissed.

---

[4] **insolent**—rude, disrespectful.

[5] rampant—unrestrained.

[6] hotch potch—hodgepodge, jumble.

Mrs. Stockmann. Dismissed?

Dr. Stockmann. You too!

Petra. Mrs. Busk gave me notice, and so I thought it best to leave there and then.

Dr. Stockmann. You did perfectly right!

Mrs. Stockmann. Who could have thought Mrs. Busk was such a bad woman!

Petra. Oh mother, Mrs. Busk isn't bad at all; I saw clearly how sorry she was. But she dared not do otherwise, she said; and so I am dismissed.

Dr. Stockmann [*laughing and rubbing his hands*]. She dared not do otherwise—just like the rest! Oh, it's delicious.

Mrs. Stockmann. Oh well, after that frightful scene last night—

Petra. It wasn't only that. What do you think, father—?

Dr. Stockmann. Well?

Petra. Mrs. Busk showed me no fewer than three letters she had received this morning—

Dr. Stockmann. Anonymous, of course?

Petra. Yes.

Dr. Stockmann. They never dare give their names, Katrina!

Petra. And two of them stated that a gentleman who is often at our house said at the club last night that I held extremely advanced opinions upon various things—

Dr. Stockmann. Of course you didn't deny it.

Petra. Of course not. You know Mrs. Busk herself is pretty advanced in her opinions when we're alone together; but now that this has come out about me, she dared not keep me on.

Mrs. Stockmann. Someone that is often at our house, too. There, you see, Thomas, what comes of all your hospitality.

Dr. Stockmann. We won't live any longer in such a pigsty! Pack up as quickly as you can, Katrina; let's get away—the sooner the better.

Mrs. Stockmann. Hush! I think there is someone in the passage. See who it is, Petra.

Petra [*opening the door*]. Oh, is it you, Captain Horster? Please come in.

Horster [*from the hall*]. Good morning. I thought I might just look in and ask how you are.

Dr. Stockmann [shaking his hand]. Thanks; that's very good of you.

Mrs. Stockmann. And thank you for helping us through the crowd last night, Captain Horster.

Petra. How did you ever get home again?

Horster. Oh, that was all right. I am tolerably able-bodied, you know; and those fellows' bark is worse than their bite.

Dr. Stockmann. Yes, isn't it extraordinary, this piggish cowardice? Come here, and let me show you something! Look, here are all the stones they threw in at us. Only look at them! Upon my soul there aren't more than two decent-sized lumps in the whole heap; the rest are nothing but pebbles—mere gravel. They stood down there, and yelled, and swore they'd half kill me;—but as for really doing it—no, there's mighty little fear of *that* in this town!

Horster. You may thank your stars for that this time, Doctor.

Dr. Stockmann. So I do, of course. But it's depressing all the same; for if ever it should come to a serious national struggle, you may be sure public opinion would be for taking to its heels, and the solid majority would scamper for their lives like a flock of sheep, Captain Horster. That is what's so melancholy to think of; it grieves me to the heart.—But devil take it—it's foolish of me to feel anything of the sort! They have called me an enemy of the people; well then, let me *be* an enemy of the people!

Mrs. Stockmann. That you'll never be, Thomas.

Dr. Stockmann. You'd better not take your oath of it, Katrina. A bad name may act like a pin scratch in the lung. And that confounded word—I can't get rid of it; it has sunk deep into my heart; and there it lies gnawing and sucking like an acid. And no magnesia⁷ can cure me.

Petra. Pooh; you should only laugh at them, father.

Horster. People will think differently yet, Doctor.

Mrs. Stockmann. Yes, Thomas, that's as certain as that you are standing here.

Dr. Stockmann. Yes, perhaps, when it is too late. Well, as they make their bed so they must lie! Let them go on wallowing here in their pigsty, and learn to repent having driven a patriot into exile. When do you sail, Captain Horster?

Horster. Well—that's really what I came to speak to you about—

Dr. Stockmann. What? Anything wrong with the ship?

Horster. No; but the fact is, I shan't be sailing in her.

Petra. Surely you have not been dismissed?

Horster [*smiling*]. Yes, I have.

Petra. You too!

---

⁷ magnesia—preparation of magnesium hydroxide, used as an antacid.

Mrs. Stockmann. There, you see, Thomas.

Dr. Stockmann. And for the truth's sake! Oh, if I could possibly have imagined such a thing—

Horster. You mustn't be troubled about this; I shall soon find a berth with some other company, elsewhere.

Dr. Stockmann. And this is that man Vik! A wealthy man, independent of everyone! Faugh!

Horster. Oh, for that matter, he's a very well-meaning man. He said himself he would gladly have kept me on if only he dared—

Dr. Stockmann. But he didn't dare? Of course not!

Horster. It's not so easy, he said, when you belong to a party—

Dr. Stockmann. My gentleman has hit it there! A party is like a sausage machine; it grinds all the brains together in one mash; and that's why we see nothing but porridge-heads and pulp-heads all around!

Mrs. Stockmann. Now really, Thomas!

Petra [*to* Horster]. If only you hadn't seen us home, perhaps it would not have come to this.

Horster. I don't regret it.

Petra [*gives him her hand*]. Thank you for that!

Horster [*to* Dr. Stockmann]. And then, too, I wanted to tell you this: if you are really determined to go abroad, I've thought of another way—

Dr. Stockmann. That's good—if only we can get off quickly—

Mrs. Stockmann. Hush! Isn't that a knock?

Petra. I believe it is uncle.

Dr. Stockmann. Aha! [*Calls.*] Come in.

Mrs. Stockmann. My dear Thomas, now do promise me—

[*The* Burgomaster *enters from the hall.*]

Burgomaster [*in the doorway*]. Oh, you are engaged. Then I'd better—

Dr. Stockmann. No no; come in.

Burgomaster. But I wanted to speak to you alone.

Mrs. Stockmann. We can go into the sitting room.

Horster. And I shall look in again presently.

Dr. Stockmann. No no; go with the ladies, Captain Horster; I must hear more about—

Horster. All right, then I'll wait.

[*He follows* Mrs. Stockmann *and* Petra *into the sitting room. The* Burgomaster *says nothing, but casts glances at the windows.*]

Dr. Stockmann. I daresay you find it rather drafty here today? Put on your cap.

Burgomaster. Thanks, if I may. [*Does so.*] I fancy I caught cold yesterday evening. I stood there shivering—

Dr. Stockmann. Really. On my soul, now, I found it quite warm enough.

Burgomaster. I regret that it was not in my power to prevent these nocturnal[8] excesses.

Dr. Stockmann. Have you anything else in particular to say to me?

Burgomaster [*producing a large letter*]. I have this document for you from the Directors of the Baths.

Dr. Stockmann. My dismissal?

Burgomaster. Yes; dated from today. [*Places the letter on the table.*] We are very sorry—but frankly, we dared not do otherwise, on account of public opinion.

Dr. Stockmann [*smiling*]. Dared not? I've heard that phrase already today.

Burgomaster. I beg you to realize your position clearly. For the future, you cannot count upon any sort of practice in the town.

Dr. Stockmann. Devil take the practice! But how can you be so sure of that?

Burgomaster. The Houseowners' Association is sending round a circular from house to house, in which all well-disposed citizens are called upon not to employ you; and I dare swear that not a single head of a family will venture to refuse his signature; he simply *dare* not.

Dr. Stockmann. Well well; I don't doubt that. But what then?

Burgomaster. If I might advise, I would suggest that you should leave the town for a time—

Dr. Stockmann. Yes, I've had some such idea in my mind already.

Burgomaster. Good. And when you have had six months or so for mature deliberation, if you could make up your mind to acknowledge your error, with a few words of regret—

Dr. Stockmann. I might perhaps be reinstated, you think?

Burgomaster. Perhaps it's not quite out of the question.

Dr. Stockmann. Yes, but how about public opinion? You daren't, on account of public opinion.

Burgomaster. Opinion is extremely variable. And, to speak candidly, it is of the greatest importance for us to have such an admission under your own hand.

Dr. Stockmann. Yes, I daresay it would be mightily convenient for you! But you remember what I've said to you before about such foxes' tricks!

---

[8] nocturnal—nighttime.

Burgomaster. At that time your position was infinitely more favorable; at that time you thought you had the whole town at your back—

Dr. Stockmann. Yes, and now I have the whole town *on* my back [*Flaring up.*] But no—not if I had the devil and his dam[9] on my back—! Never—never, I tell you!

Burgomaster. The father of a family has no right to act as you are doing. You have no right to do it, Thomas.

Dr. Stockmann. I have no right! There's only one thing in the world that a free man has no right to do; and do you know what that is?

Burgomaster. No.

Dr. Stockmann. Of course not; but *I* will tell you. A free man has no right to wallow in filth like a cur; he has no right to act so that he ought to spit in his own face!

Burgomaster. That sounds extremely **plausible;**[10] and if there were not another explanation of your obstinacy—but we all know there is—

Dr. Stockmann. What do you mean by that?

Burgomaster. You understand well enough. But as your brother, and as a man who knows the world, I warn you not to build too confidently upon prospects and expectations that may very likely come to nothing.

Dr. Stockmann. Why, what on earth are you driving at?

Burgomaster. Do you really want me to believe that you are ignorant of the terms of old Morten Kiil's will?

Dr. Stockmann. I know that the little he has is to go to a home for old and needy artisans.[11] But what has that got to do with me?

Burgomaster. To begin with, "the little he has" is no trifle. Morten Kiil is a tolerably wealthy man.

Dr. Stockmann. I have never had the least notion of that!

Burgomaster. H'm—really? Then I suppose you have no notion that a not inconsiderable part of his fortune is to go to your children, you and your wife having a life interest in it. Has he not told you that?

Dr. Stockmann. No, I'll be hanged if he has! On the contrary, he has done nothing but grumble about being so preposterously overtaxed. But are you really sure of this, Peter?

Burgomaster. I have it from a thoroughly trustworthy source.

Dr. Stockmann. Why, good heavens, then Katrina's provided for—and the children too! Oh, I must tell her—[*Calls.*] Katrina, Katrina!

---

[9] dam—mother.

[10] **plausible**—believable, convincing.

[11] artisans—skilled workers.

Burgomaster [*holding him back*]. Hush! don't say anything about it yet.

Mrs. Stockmann [*opening the door*]. What is it?

Dr. Stockmann. Nothing my dear; go in again.

[Mrs. Stockmann *closes the door.*]

Dr. Stockmann [*pacing up and down*]. Provided for! Only think—all of them provided for! And for life! After all, it's a grand thing to feel yourself secure!

Burgomaster. Yes, but that is just what you are not. Morten Kiil can revoke his will any day or hour he chooses.

Dr. Stockmann. But he won't, my good Peter. The Badger is only too delighted to see me fall foul of you and your wiseacre friends.

Burgomaster [*starts and looks searchingly at him*]. Aha! That throws a new light on a good many things.

Dr. Stockmann. What things?

Burgomaster. So the whole affair has been a carefully concocted intrigue. Your recklessly violent onslaught—in the name of truth—upon the leading men of the town—

Dr. Stockmann. Well, what of it?

Burgomaster. It was nothing but a preconcerted requital[12] for that **vindictive**[13] old Morten Kiil's will.

Dr. Stockmann [*almost speechless*]. Peter—you are the most abominable plebeian I have ever known in all my born days.

Burgomaster. All is over between us. Your dismissal is **irrevocable**[14]— for now we have a weapon against you. [*He goes out.*]

Dr. Stockmann. Shame! shame! shame! [*Calls.*] Katrina! The floor must be scrubbed after him! Tell her to come here with a pail—what's her name? confound it—the girl with the smudge on her nose—

Mrs. Stockmann [*in the sitting room doorway*]. Hush, hush! Thomas!

Petra [*also in the doorway*]. Father, here's grandfather; he wants to know if he can speak to you alone.

Dr. Stockmann. Yes, of course he can. [*By the door.*] Come in, father-in-law. [Morten Kiil *enters. Dr. Stockmann closes the door behind him.*]

Dr. Stockmann. Well, what is it? Sit down.

Morten Kiil. I won't sit down. [*Looking about him.*] It looks cheerful here today, Stockmann.

Dr. Stockmann. Yes, don't you think so?

---

[12] preconcerted requital—prearranged return.

[13] **vindictive**—revengeful.

[14] **irrevocable**—final, unchangeable.

Morten Kiil. Sure enough. And you've plenty of fresh air too; you've got your fill of that oxygen you were talking about yesterday. You must have a rare good conscience today, I should think.

Dr. Stockmann. Yes, I have.

Morten Kiil. So I should suppose. [*Tapping himself on the breast.*] But do you know what *I* have got here?

Dr. Stockmann. A good conscience too, I hope.

Morten Kiil. Pooh! No; something far better than that.

[*Takes out a large pocketbook, opens it, and shows* Stockmann *a bundle of papers.*]

Dr. Stockmann [*looking at him in astonishment*]. Shares in the Baths!

Morten Kiil. They weren't difficult to get today.

Dr. Stockmann. And you've gone and bought these up—?

Morten Kiil. All I had the money to pay for.

Dr. Stockmann. Why, my dear sir,—just when things are in such a desperate way at the Baths—

Morten Kiil. If you behave like a reasonable being, you can soon set the Baths all right again.

Dr. Stockmann. Well, you can see for yourself I'm doing all I can. But the people of this town are mad!

Morten Kiil. You said yesterday that the worst filth came from my tannery. Now, if that's true, then my grandfather, and my father before me, and I myself, have for ever so many years been poisoning the town with filth, like three destroying angels. Do you think I'm going to sit quiet under such a **reproach?**[15]

Dr. Stockmann. Unfortunately, you can't help it.

Morten Kiil. No, thank you. I hold fast to my good name. I've heard that people call me "the Badger." A badger's a sort of a pig, I know; but I'm determined to give them the lie. I will live and die a clean man.

Dr. Stockmann. And how will you manage *that?*

Morten Kiil. *You* shall make me clean, Stockmann.

Dr. Stockmann. I!

Morten Kiil. Do you know what money I've used to buy these shares with? No, you can't know; but now I'll tell you. It's the money Katrina and Petra and the boys are to have after my death. For, you see, I've laid by something after all.

Dr. Stockmann [*flaring up*]. And you've taken Katrina's money and done *this* with it!

---

[15] **reproach**—shame, disgrace.

Morten Kiil. Yes; the whole of it is invested in the Baths now. And now I want to see if you're really so stark, staring mad, after all, Stockmann. If you go on making out that these beasts and other abominations dribble down from my tannery, it'll be just as if you were to flay broad stripes of Katrina's skin—and Petra's too, and the boys! No decent father would ever do that—unless he were a madman.

Dr. Stockmann [*walking up and down*]. Yes, but I *am* a madman; I *am* a madman!

Morten Kiil. You surely can't be so raving, ramping mad where your wife and children are concerned.

Dr. Stockmann [*stopping in front of him*]. Why couldn't you have spoken to me before you went and bought all that rubbish?

Morten Kiil. What's done can't be undone.

Dr. Stockmann [*walking restlessly about*]. If only I weren't so certain about the affair—! But I am absolutely convinced that I'm right.

Morten Kiil [*weighing the pocket-book in his hand*]. If you stick to this lunacy, these aren't worth much.

[*Puts the book into his pocket.*]

Dr. Stockmann. But, devil take it! surely science ought to be able to hit upon some antidote, some sort of prophylactic—[16]

Morten Kiil. Do you mean something to kill the beasts?

Dr. Stockmann. Yes, or at least to make them harmless.

Morten Kiil. Couldn't you try ratsbane?

Dr. Stockmann. Oh, nonsense, nonsense!—But since everyone declares it's nothing but imagination, why imagination let it be! Let them have it their own way! Haven't the ignorant, narrowhearted curs **reviled**[17] me as an enemy of the people?—and weren't they on the point of tearing the clothes off my back?

Morten Kiil. And they've smashed all your windows for you too!

Dr. Stockmann. Yes, and then there's one's duty to one's family! I must talk that over with Katrina; such things are more in her line.

Morten Kiil. That's right! You just follow the advice of a sensible woman.

Dr. Stockmann [*turning upon him angrily*]. How could you act so **preposterously**![18] Risking Katrina's money, and putting me to this horrible torture! When I look at you, I seem to see the devil himself—!

---

[16] antidote . . . prophylactic—cure . . . preventative measure.

[17] **reviled**—abused.

[18] **preposterously**—absurdly.

Morten Kiil. Then I'd better be off. But I must hear from you, yes or no, by two o'clock. If it's *no,* all the shares go to the Hospital—and that this very day.

Dr. Stockmann. And what will Katrina get?

Morten Kiil. Not a penny.

[*The door leading to the hall opens.* Hovstad *and* Aslaksen *are seen outside it.*]

Morten Kiil. Hullo! look at these two.

Dr. Stockmann [*staring at them*]. What! Do *you* actually venture to come here?

Hovstad. Why, to be sure we do.

Aslaksen. You see, we've something to discuss with you.

Morten Kiil [*whispers*]. Yes or no—by two o'clock.

Aslaksen [*with a glance at* Hovstad]. Aha!

[Morten Kiil *goes out.*]

Dr. Stockmann. Well, what do you want with me? Be brief.

Hovstad. I can quite understand that you resent our attitude at the meeting yesterday—

Dr. Stockmann. Your attitude, you say? Yes, it was a pretty attitude! I call it the attitude of cowards—of old women—Shame upon you!

Hovstad. Call it what you will; but we *could* not act otherwise.

Dr. Stockmann. You *dared* not, I suppose? Isn't that so?

Hovstad. Yes, if you like to put it so.

Aslaksen. But why didn't you just say a word to us beforehand? The merest hint to Mr. Hovstad or to me—

Dr. Stockmann. A hint? What about?

Aslaksen. About what was really behind it all.

Dr. Stockmann. I don't in the least understand you.

Aslaksen [*nods confidentially*]. Oh yes, you do, Dr. Stockmann.

Hovstad. It's no good making a mystery of it any longer.

Dr. Stockmann [*looking from one to the other*]. Why, what in the devil's name—!

Aslaksen. May I ask—isn't your father-in-law going about the town buying up all the Bath stock?

Dr. Stockmann. Yes, he has been buying Bath stock today but—

Aslaksen. It would have been more prudent to let somebody else do that—someone not so closely connected with you.

Hovstad. And then you ought not to have appeared in the matter under your own name. No one need have known that the attack on the

Baths came from you. You should have taken me into your counsels, Dr. Stockmann.

Dr. Stockmann [*stares straight in front of him; a light seems to break in upon him, and he says as though thunderstruck*]. Is this possible? Can such things be?

Aslaksen [*smiling*]. It's plain enough that they can. But they ought to be managed delicately, you understand.

Hovstad. And there ought to be more people in it; for the responsibility always falls more lightly when there are several to share it.

Dr. Stockmann [*calmly*]. In one word, gentlemen—what is it you want?

Aslaksen. Mr. Hovstad can best—

Hovstad. No, you explain, Aslaksen.

Aslaksen. Well, it's this: now that we know how the matter really stands, we believe we can venture to place the *People's Messenger* at your disposal.

Dr. Stockmann. You can venture to *now*, eh? But how about public opinion? Aren't you afraid of bringing down a storm upon us?

Hovstad. We must manage to ride out the storm.

Aslaksen. And you must be ready to put about quickly, Doctor. As soon as your attack has done its work—

Dr. Stockmann. As soon as my father-in-law and I have bought up the shares at a discount, you mean?

Hovstad. I presume it is mainly on scientific grounds that you want to take the management of the Baths into your own hands.

Dr. Stockmann. Of course; it was on scientific grounds that I got the old Badger to stand in with me. And then we'll tinker up the waterworks a little, and potter about a bit down at the beach, without its costing the town sixpence. That ought to do the business? Eh?

Hovstad. I think so—if you have the *Messenger* to back you up.

Aslaksen. In a free community the press is a power, Doctor.

Dr. Stockmann. Yes, indeed; and so is public opinion. And you, Mr. Aslaksen—I suppose you will answer for the Houseowners' Association?

Aslaksen. Both for the Houseowners' Association and the Temperance Society. You may make your mind easy.

Dr. Stockmann. But, gentlemen—really I'm quite ashamed to mention such a thing—but—what return—?

Hovstad. Of course, we should prefer to give you our support for nothing. But the *Messenger* is not very firmly established; it's not getting on as it ought to; and I should be very sorry to have to stop the paper just now, when there's so much to be done in general politics.

Dr. Stockmann. Naturally; that would be very hard for a friend of the people like you. [*Flaring up.*] But I—I am an enemy of the people! [*Striding about the room.*] Where's my stick? Where the devil is my stick?

Hovstad. What do you mean?

Aslaksen. Surely you wouldn't—

Dr. Stockmann [*standing still*]. And suppose I don't give you a single penny out of all my shares? You must remember we rich folk don't like parting with our money.

Hovstad. And you must remember that this business of the shares can be represented in two ways.

Dr. Stockmann. Yes, you are the man for that; if I don't come to the rescue of the *Messenger*, you'll manage to put a vile complexion on the affair; you'll hunt me down, I suppose—bait me—try to throttle me as a dog throttles a hare!

Hovstad. That's a law of nature—every animal fights for its own subsistence.[19]

Aslaksen. And must take its food where it can find it, you know.

Dr. Stockmann. Then see if you can't find some out in the gutter; [*Striding about the room.*] for now, by heaven! we shall see which is the strongest animal of us three. [*Finds his umbrella and brandishes it.*] Now, look here—!

Hovstad. You surely don't mean to assault us!

Aslaksen. I say, be careful with that umbrella!

Dr. Stockmann. Out at the window with you, Mr. Hovstad!

Hovstad [*by the hall door*]. Are you utterly crazy?

Dr. Stockmann. Out at the window, Mr. Aslaksen! Jump I tell you! Be quick about it!

Aslaksen [*running round the writing table*]. Moderation, Doctor; I'm not at all strong; I can't stand much— [*Screams.*] Help! help!

[Mrs. Stockmann, Petra, *and* Horster *enter from sitting room.*]

Mrs. Stockmann. Good heavens, Thomas! what *can* be the matter?

Dr. Stockmann [*brandishing the umbrella*]. Jump! I tell you! Out into the gutter!

Hovstad. An unprovoked assault! I call you to witness, Captain Horster. [*Rushes off through the hall.*]

---

[19] **subsistence**—survival.

Aslaksen [*bewildered*]. If one only knew the local situation— [*He slinks out by the sitting room door.*]

Mrs. Stockmann [*holding back the* Doctor]. Now, do restrain yourself, Thomas!

Dr. Stockmann [*throwing down the umbrella*]. I'll be hanged if they haven't got off after all.

Mrs. Stockmann. Why, what can they have wanted with you?

Dr. Stockmann. I'll tell you afterwards; I have other things to think of now. [*Goes to the table and writes on a visiting card.*] Look here, Katrina: what's written here?

Mrs. Stockmann. Three big *Noes;* what does that mean?

Dr. Stockmann. That I'll tell you afterwards, too. [*Handing the card.*] There, Petra; let smudgy-face run to the Badger's with this as fast as she can. Be quick!

[Petra *goes out through the hall with the card.*]

Dr. Stockmann. Well, if I haven't had visits today from all the emissaries of the devil! But now I'll sharpen my pen against them till it becomes a goad; I'll dip it in gall and venom; I'll hurl my inkstand straight at their skulls.

Mrs. Stockmann. You forget we are going away, Thomas.

[Petra *returns.*]

Dr. Stockmann. Well?

Petra. She has gone.

Dr. Stockmann. Good. Going away, do you say? No, I'll be damned if we do; we stay where we are, Katrina!

Petra. Stay!

Mrs. Stockmann. Here in the town?

Dr. Stockmann. Yes, here; the field of battle is here; here the fight must be fought; here I will conquer! As soon as my trousers are mended, I shall go out into the town and look for a house; we must have a roof over our heads for the winter.

Horster. That you can have in my house.

Dr. Stockmann. Can I?

Horster. Yes, there's no difficulty about that. I have room enough, and I'm hardly ever at home myself.

Mrs. Stockmann. Oh, how kind of you, Captain Horster.

Petra. Thank you!

Dr. Stockmann [*shaking his hand*]. Thanks, thanks! So that is off my mind. And this very day I shall set to work in earnest. Oh, there's no end of work to be done here, Katrina! It's a good thing I shall have all my time at my disposal now; for you must know I've had notice from the Baths—

Mrs. Stockmann [*sighing*]. Oh yes, I was expecting that.

Dr. Stockmann. —And now they want to take away my practice as well. But let them! The poor I shall keep anyhow—those that can't pay; and, good Lord! it's they that need me most. But by heaven! I'll make them listen to me; I'll preach to them in season and out of season, as the saying goes.

Mrs. Stockmann. My dear Thomas, I should have thought you had learnt what good preaching does.

Dr. Stockmann. You really are absurd, Katrina. Am I to let myself be beaten off the field by public opinion, and the solid majority, and all that sort of devilry? No, thank you! Besides, my point is so simple, so clear and straightforward. I only want to drive it into the heads of these curs that the Liberals are the craftiest foes free men have to face; that party programs wring the necks of all young and living truths; that considerations of **expediency**[20] turn justice and morality upside down, until life here becomes simply unlivable. Come, Captain Horster, don't you think I shall be able to make the people understand that?

Horster. Maybe; I don't know much about these things myself.

Dr. Stockmann. Well, you see—this is the way of it! It's the party leaders that must be exterminated. For a party leader is just like a wolf, you see—like a ravening[21] wolf; he must devour a certain number of smaller animals a year, if he's to exist at all. Just look at Hovstad and Aslaksen! How many small animals they polish off—or at least mangle and maim, so that they're fit for nothing else but to be houseowners and subscribers to the *People's Messenger!* [*Sits on the edge of the table.*] Just come here, Katrina—see how bravely the sun shines today! And how the blessed fresh spring air blows in upon me!

Mrs. Stockmann. Yes, if only we could live on sunshine and spring air, Thomas.

Dr. Stockmann. Well, you'll have to pinch and save to eke them out— and then we shall get on all right. That's what troubles me least. No, what *does* trouble me is that I don't see any man free enough and high-minded enough to dare to take up my work after me.

---

[20] **expediency**—self-interest.

[21] ravening—predatory.

Petra. Oh, don't think about that, father; you have time enough before you.—Why, see, there are the boys already.

[Eilif *and* Morten *enter from the sitting room.*]

Mrs. Stockmann. Have you a holiday today?

Morten. No; but we had a fight with the other fellows in playtime—

Eilif. That's not true; it was the other fellows that fought us.

Morten. Yes, and then Mr. Rörlund said we had better stop at home for a few days.

Dr. Stockmann [*snapping his fingers and springing down from the table*]. Now I have it! Now I have it, on my soul! You shall never set foot in school again!

The Boys. Never go to school!

Mrs. Stockmann. Why, Thomas—

Dr. Stockmann. Never, I say! I shall teach you myself—that's to say, I won't teach you any mortal thing—

Morten. Hurrah!

Dr. Stockmann. —but I shall help you to grow into free, high-minded men.—Look here, you'll have to help me, Petra.

Petra. Yes, father, you may be sure I will.

Dr. Stockmann. And we'll have our school in the room where they reviled me as an enemy of the people. But we must have more pupils. I must have at least a dozen boys to begin with.

Mrs. Stockmann. You'll never get them in this town.

Dr. Stockmann. We shall see. [*To the boys.*] Don't you know any street urchins—any regular ragamuffins—?

Morten. Yes, father, I know lots!

Dr. Stockmann. That's all right; bring me a few of them. I shall experiment with the street-curs for once in a way; there are sometimes excellent heads amongst them.

Morten. But what are we to do when we've grown into free and high-minded men?

Dr. Stockmann. Drive all the wolves out to the far west, boys!

[Eilif *looks rather doubtful;* Morten *jumps about shouting "Hurrah!"*]

Mrs. Stockmann. If only the wolves don't drive you out, Thomas.

Dr. Stockmann. Are you quite mad, Katrina! Drive me out! Now that I am the strongest man in the town?

Mrs. Stockmann. The strongest—now?

Dr. Stockmann. Yes, I venture to say this: that now I am one of the strongest men in the whole world.

Morten. I say, what fun!

Dr. Stockmann [*in a subdued voice*]. Hush; you mustn't speak about it yet: but I have made a great discovery.

Mrs. Stockmann. What, another?

Dr. Stockmann. Yes, of course! [*Gathers them about him, and speaks confidentially.*] This is what I have discovered, you see: the strongest man in the world is he who stands most alone.

Mrs. Stockmann [*shakes her head, smiling*]. Ah, Thomas dear—!

Petra [*grasping his hands cheerily*]. Father!

UNDERSTANDING THE PLAY

Act One

1. How have the Baths affected life in the community?

2. How do Dr. Stockmann and his brother differ in personality?

3. What has Dr. Stockmann discovered about the Baths?

4. What do he and his family and friends think will be the result of the publication of his discovery?

5. What is the mood of Dr. Stockmann and his family at the end of Act One?

Act Two

1. How do Morten Kiil, Hovstad, and Aslaksen differ in their reasons for supporting Dr. Stockmann?

2. Why does the Burgomaster oppose his brother's recommendations?

3. Why does Dr. Stockmann believe his brother opposes him?

4. What alternatives does the Burgomaster offer his brother?

5. How does Mrs. Stockmann view the situation? How does Petra view it?

Act Three

1. How do Hovstad and Billing hope to use Dr. Stockmann?

2. Why does Petra object to the English story she has been asked to translate?

3. How does the Burgomaster change the minds of Hovstad and Billing toward Dr. Stockmann's proposal?

4. How does Dr. Stockmann behave when he believes he has the upper hand? What does this suggest about his character?

5. How does Mrs. Stockmann's attitude change during Act Three?

Act Four

1. What is the atmosphere at the beginning of the town meeting?

2. Why does Dr. Stockmann oppose majority rule?

3. What is your opinion of Dr. Stockmann's analogy between human development and the breeding of animals?

4. What do Dr. Stockmann's remarks reveal about him?

5. How does the behavior of his fellow townspeople at the meeting support Dr. Stockmann's views?

Act Five

1. What immediate consequences for Dr. Stockmann's family and friends result from his being declared "an enemy of the people"?

2. What significance does the phrase "dare not" acquire in Act Five? What do you think it represents to Dr. Stockmann?

3. Why does Dr. Stockmann change his mind about leaving the community?

4. How do Dr. Stockmann's views about educating street urchins compare with his opinion of "mongrels" in Act Three?

5. What does he finally believe to be the basis of his strength?

ANALYZING THE PLAY

1. The conflict in a play is the struggle between opposing forces that gives movement to the dramatic plot. What is the fundamental conflict in *An Enemy of the People?*

2. The peripeteia—or reversal of fortune—in a drama is a sudden, unexpected turn of events. In *An Enemy of the People,* where does this turn of events take place?

3. The mood of a literary work is the general atmosphere or prevailing emotional quality. How would you describe the mood of *An Enemy of the People?* What elements contribute to this mood?

4. What attitude do you think Ibsen had toward the press?

5. What view do you think Ibsen took of the possibility of achieving social reform through the democratic process?

Anton Chekhov ▶

The Sea Gull

BY ANTON CHEKHOV

The success of Russian writer Anton Chekhov (1860–1904) as a dramatist owes a great deal to the Moscow Art Theater, one of the independent theaters inspired by André Antoine's Théâtre Libre. (For general background on 19th-century drama, see the introduction for An Enemy of the People, *page 380.) Perhaps the most influential company in theater history, the Moscow Art Theater was founded in 1898 by Konstantin Stanislavsky (1863–1938) and Vladimir Nemirovich-Danchenko (1859–1943). Rejecting the exaggerated vocal delivery and mannerisms of most 19th-century actors, Stanislavksy insisted that acting must be based on artistic "inner truth." One of the first productions of the Moscow Art Theater was a revival of Chekhov's* The Sea Gull, *which had been a flop when first performed two years earlier by a conventional theater company. The new production revealed the subtlety of Chekhov's play and established his reputation as a dramatist.*

Doctor and Writer

The grandson of a peasant, Chekhov nevertheless received a good education and eventually became a doctor. While still in medical school, he had begun to write humorous sketches and short stories for a variety of publications that made him widely popular. He was less successful with some critics, who disapproved of his apparent lack of political and social opinions and unwillingness to pass judgments and present morals in his fiction. Although much of Chekhov's later writing presents human misery and despair, humor always remains an important element. Even when his plays, such as The Sea Gull, Uncle Vanya, Three Sisters, *and* The Cherry Orchard, *were successfully produced by the Moscow Art Theater, Chekhov remained dissatisfied with the rehearsals and performances he saw. He insisted that his plays were intended as comedies, not tragedies, and required a very light and natural style of acting.*

Artistic Conflict

At the center of The Sea Gull *(1895) is generational conflict, but this conflict is often expressed in terms of a dispute over theatrical style. The play's main character, Konstantin Treplev, is a young man who wants to be a writer and is in frustrated revolt against the conventional realism of the theater represented by his mother, a famous actress. He sneers at the artificiality of "the room with three walls," that is, the representational style of theater in which actors are supposed to be living real lives that the audience is observing through an invisible "fourth wall." Konstantin also objects to the 19th-century tradition of the "well-made" play that typically featured a formulaic, often melodramatic, study of middle-class domestic life in which some problem was neatly resolved in a conventionally moral ending. Konstantin's own ideas of theater resemble those of symbolist drama, which developed in the 1890s, and in which the dramatic action, characters, setting, and language are all reflections of the playwright's inner life. As he observes, "One must depict life not as it is, and not as it ought to be, but as we see it in our dreams."*

CHARACTERS

Irina Nikolayevna Arkadin (Madame Arkadin), an actress
Konstantin Gavrilovitch Treplev, her son, a young man
Pyotr Nikolayevitch Sorin, her brother
Nina Mihailovna Zaretchny, a young girl, the daughter of a wealthy landowner
Ilya Afanasyevitch Shamraev, a retired lieutenant, Sorin's steward[1]

Polina Andreyevna, his wife
Masha, his daughter
Boris Alexeyevitch Trigorin, a literary man
Yevgeny Sergeyevitch Dorn, a doctor
Semyon Semyonovitch Medvedenko, a schoolmaster
Yakov, a laborer
A Man **Cook**
A **Housemaid**

The action takes place in Sorin's house and garden. Between the Third and Fourth Acts there is an interval of two years.

Act One

[*Part of the park on* Sorin's *estate. Wide avenue leading away from the spectators into the depths of the park towards the lake is blocked up by a platform roughly put together for private theatricals, so that the lake is not visible. To right and left of the platform, bushes. A few chairs, a little table.*

The sun has just set. Yakov *and other laborers are at work on the platform behind the curtain; there is the sound of coughing and hammering.* Masha *and* Medvedenko *enter on the left, returning from a walk.*]

Medvedenko. Why do you always wear black?

Masha. I am in mourning for my life. I am unhappy.

Medvedenko. Why? [*Pondering.*] I don't understand . . . You are in good health; though your father is not very well off, he has got enough. My life is much harder than yours. I only get twenty-three rubles[2] a month, and from that they deduct something for the pension fund, and yet I don't wear mourning. [*They sit down.*]

Masha. It isn't money that matters. A poor man may be happy.

---

[1] steward—estate manager.

[2] rubles—The ruble is the Russian monetary unit.

Medvedenko. Theoretically, yes; but in practice it's like this: there are my two sisters and my mother and my little brother and I, and my salary is only twenty-three rubles. We must eat and drink, mustn't we? One must have tea and sugar. One must have tobacco. It's a tight fit.

Masha [*looking round at the platform*]. The play will soon begin.

Medvedenko. Yes. Miss Zaretchny will act: it is Konstantin Gavrilitch's play. They are in love with each other and today their souls will be united in the effort to realize the same artistic effect. But your soul and mine have not a common point of contact. I love you. I am so wretched I can't stay at home. Every day I walk four miles here and four miles back and I meet with nothing but **indifference**[3] from you. I can quite understand it. I am without means and have a big family to keep. . . . Who would care to marry a man who hasn't a penny to bless himself with?

Masha. Oh, nonsense! [*Takes a pinch of snuff.*] Your love touches me, but I can't **reciprocate**[4] it—that's all. [*Holding out the snuffbox to him.*] Help yourself.

Medvedenko. I don't feel like it [*a pause*].

Masha. How stifling it is! There must be a storm coming. . . . You're always discussing theories or talking about money. You think there is no greater misfortune than poverty, but to my mind it is a thousand times better to go in rags and be a beggar than . . . But you wouldn't understand that, though. . . .

[*Sorin and Treplev enter on the right.*]

Sorin [*leaning on his walking-stick*]. I am never quite myself in the country, my boy, and, naturally enough, I shall never get used to it. Last night I went to bed at ten and woke up this morning at nine feeling as though my brain were glued to my skull, through sleeping so long. [*Laughs.*] And after dinner I accidentally dropped off again, and now I am utterly shattered and feel as though I were in a nightmare, in fact. . . .

Treplev. Yes, you really ought to live in town. [*Catches sight of Masha and Medvedenko.*] When the show begins, my friends, you will be summoned, but you mustn't be here now. You must please go away.

Sorin [*to Masha*]. Marya Ilyinishna, will you be so good as to ask your papa to tell them to take the dog off the chain?—it howls. My sister could not sleep again last night.

---

[3] **indifference**—lack of interest.

[4] **reciprocate**—return.

Masha. Speak to my father yourself; I am not going to. Please don't ask me. [*To* Medvedenko.] Come along!

Medvedenko [*to* Treplev]. So you will send and let us know before it begins. [*Both go out.*]

Sorin. So I suppose the dog will be howling all night again. What a business it is! I have never done as I liked in the country. In old days I used to get leave for twenty-eight days and come here for a rest and so on, but they worried me so with all sorts of trifles that before I had been here two days I was longing to be off again. [*Laughs.*] I've always been glad to get away from here. . . . But now I am on the retired list, and I have nowhere else to go, as a matter of fact. I've got to live here whether I like it or not. . . .

Yakov [*to* Treplev]. We are going to have a swim, Konstantin Gavrilitch.

Treplev. Very well; but don't be more than ten minutes [*looks at his watch*]. It will soon begin.

Yakov. Yes, sir. [*Goes out.*]

Treplev [*looking round the stage*]. Here is our theater. The curtain, then the first wing,⁵ then the second, and beyond that—open space. No scenery of any sort. There is an open view of the lake and the horizon. We shall raise the curtain at exactly half-past eight, when the moon rises.

Sorin. Magnificent.

Treplev. If Nina is late it will spoil the whole effect. It is time she was here. Her father and her stepmother keep a sharp eye on her, and it is as hard for her to get out of the house as to escape from prison. [*Puts his uncle's cravat⁶ straight.*] Your hair and your beard are very untidy. They need clipping or something. . . .

Sorin [*combing out his beard*]. It's the tragedy of my life. Even as a young man I looked as though I had been drinking for days or something of the sort. I was never a favorite with the ladies. [*Sitting down.*] Why is your mother out of humor?

Treplev. Why? Because she is bored. [*Sitting down beside him.*] She is jealous. She is set against me, and against the performance, and against my play because Nina is acting in it, and she is not. She does not know my play, but she hates it.

Sorin [*laughs*]. What an idea!

---

⁵ wing—left or right side of a stage immediately outside the acting area, usually unseen by the audience.

⁶ cravat—scarf.

Treplev. She is annoyed to think that even on this little stage Nina will have a triumph and not she. [*Looks at his watch.*] My mother is a psychological freak. Unmistakably talented, intelligent, capable of sobbing over a book, she will reel off all Nekrassov[7] by heart; nursing the sick she is an angel; but just try praising Duse[8] in her presence! O-ho! You must praise no one but herself, you must write about her, make a fuss over her, be in raptures over her extraordinary acting in *La Dame aux Camélias* or the *Ferment of Life*;[9] but she has none of this narcotic in the country, she is bored and cross, and we are all her enemies—we are all in fault. Then she is superstitious—she is afraid of three candles, of the number thirteen. She is stingy. She has got seventy thousand rubles in a bank at Odessa—I know that for a fact—but ask her to lend you some money, and she will burst into tears.

Sorin. You imagine your mother does not like your play, and you are already upset and all that. Don't worry; your mother adores you.

Treplev [*pulling the petals off a flower*]. Loves me, loves me not; loves me, loves me not; loves me, loves me not. [*Laughs.*] You see, my mother does not love me. I should think not! She wants to live, to love, to dress like a girl; and I am twenty-five, and I am a continual reminder that she is no longer young. When I am not there she is only thirty-two, but when I am there she is forty-three, and for that she hates me. She knows, too, that I have no belief in the theater. She loves the stage, she imagines she is working for humanity, for the holy cause of art, while to my mind the modern theater is nothing but tradition and conventionality. When the curtain goes up, and by artificial light, in a room with three walls,[10] these great geniuses, the devotees of holy art, represent how people eat, drink, love, move about, and wear their jackets; when from these commonplace sentences and pictures they try to draw a moral—a petty moral, easy of comprehension and convenient for domestic use; when in a thousand variations I am offered the same thing over and over again—I run away as Maupassant ran away from the Eiffel Tower[11] which weighed upon his brain with its vulgarity.

---

[7] Nekrassov—Nikolay Alexseyevich Nekrassov (1821–1878), Russian poet who created sympathetic but frequently sentimental pictures of peasant life.

[8] Duse—Eleonora Duse (1859–1924), Italian actress celebrated for her tragic roles.

[9] *La Dame Aux Camélias* . . . *The Ferment of Life*, two 19th-century melodramas that demand virtuoso performances from the actresses in the leading roles.

[10] room with three walls—stage.

[11] Maupassant . . . Eiffel Tower—Guy de Maupassant (1850–1893) was a French writer of fiction; the Eiffel Tower was created for the 1889 Paris World's Fair.

Sorin. You can't do without the stage.

Treplev. We need new forms of expression. We need new forms, and if we can't have them we had better have nothing. [*Looks at his watch.*] I love my mother—I love her very much—but she leads a senseless sort of life, always taken up with this literary gentleman, her name is always trotted out in the papers—and that wearies me. And sometimes the simple egoism[12] of an ordinary mortal makes me feel sorry that my mother is a celebrated actress, and I fancy that if she were an ordinary woman I should be happier. Uncle, what could be more hopeless and stupid than my position? She used to have visitors, all celebrities—artists and authors—and among them all I was the only one who was nothing, and they only put up with me because I was her son. Who am I? What am I? I left the University in my third year—owing to circumstances "for which we accept no responsibility," as the editors say; I have no talents, I haven't a penny of my own, and on my passport I am described as an artisan[13] of Kiev. You know my father was an artisan of Kiev, though he too was a well-known actor. So, when in her drawing room all these artists and authors graciously noticed me, I always fancied from their faces that they were taking the measure of my insignificance—I guessed their thoughts and suffered from the humiliation. . . .

Sorin. And, by the way, can you tell me, please, what sort of man this literary gentleman is? There's no making him out. He never says anything.

Treplev. He is an intelligent man, good-natured and rather melancholy, you know. A very decent fellow. He is still a good distance off forty, but he is already celebrated and has enough and to spare of everything. As for his writings . . . what shall I say? They are charming, full of talent, but . . . after Tolstoy or Zola[14] you do not care to read Trigorin.

Sorin. Well, I am fond of authors, my boy. At one time I had a passionate desire for two things: I wanted to get married, and I wanted to become an author; but I did not succeed in doing either. Yes, it is pleasant to be even a small author, as a matter of fact.

---

[12] egoism—self-centeredness.

[13] artisan—skilled worker. Treplev is unfavorably contrasting his mere "artisan" status with that of the artists whom his mother entertains.

[14] Tolstoy or Zola—Nikolai Tolstoy (1828–1910) was one of the greatest Russian writers of the 1800s; Émile Zola (1840–1902), French novelist and dramatist, was a leader of the naturalist school (see page 380).

Treplev [*listens*]. I hear steps. . . . [*Embraces his uncle.*] I cannot live without her. . . . The very sound of her footsteps is lovely. . . . I am wildly happy. [*Goes quickly to meet* Nina Zaretchny *as she enters.*] My enchantress—my dream. . . .

Nina [*in agitation*]. I am not late. . . . Of course I am not late. . . .

Treplev [*kissing her hands*]. No, no, no!

Nina. I have been uneasy all day. I was so frightened. I was afraid father would not let me come. . . . But he has just gone out with my stepmother. The sky is red, the moon is just rising, and I kept urging on the horse. [*Laughs.*] But I am glad. [*Shakes* Sorin's *hand warmly.*]

Sorin [*laughs*]. Your eyes look as though you have been crying. . . . Fie,[15] fie! That's not right!

Nina. Oh, it was nothing. . . . You see how out of breath I am. I have to go in half an hour. We must make haste. I can't stay, I can't! For God's sake don't keep me! My father doesn't know I am here.

Treplev. It really is time to begin. We must go and call the others.

Sorin. I'll go this minute. [*Goes to the right, singing* "To France two grenadiers." *Looks round.*] Once I sang like that, and a deputy prosecutor said to me, "You have a powerful voice, your Excellency"; then he thought a little and added, "but not a pleasant one." [*Laughs and goes off.*]

Nina. My father and his wife won't let me come here. They say it is so Bohemian[16] here . . . they are afraid I shall go on the stage. . . . But I feel drawn to the lake here like a sea gull. . . . My heart is full of you. [*Looks round.*]

Treplev. We are alone.

Nina. I fancy there is someone there.

Treplev. There's nobody. [*They kiss.*]

Nina. What tree is this?

Treplev. An elm.

Nina. Why is it so dark?

Treplev. It's evening; everything is getting dark. Don't go away early, I entreat[17] you!

Nina. I must.

Treplev. And if I come to you, Nina, I'll stand in the garden all night, watching your window.

---

[15] Fie—expression of disapproval.

[16] Bohemian—unconventional.

[17] **entreat**—beg.

Nina. You can't; the watchman would notice you. Trésor is not used to you, and he would bark.

Treplev. I love you!

Nina. Sh-h. . . .

Treplev [*hearing footsteps*]. Who is there? You, Yakov?

Yakov [*behind the stage*]. Yes, sir.

Treplev. Take your places. It's time to begin. Is the moon rising?

Yakov. Yes, sir.

Treplev. Have you got the methylated spirit?[18] Have you got the sulphur? When the red eyes appear there must be a smell of sulphur. [*To* Nina.] Go, it's all ready. Are you nervous?

Nina. Yes, awfully! Your mother is all right—I am not afraid of her— but there's Trigorin . . . I feel frightened and ashamed of acting before him . . . a celebrated author. . . . Is he young?

Treplev. Yes.

Nina. How wonderful his stories are.

Treplev [*coldly*]. I don't know. I haven't read them.

Nina. It is difficult to act in your play. There are no living characters in it.

Treplev. Living characters! One must depict life not as it is, and not as it ought to be, but as we see it in our dreams.

Nina. There is very little action in your play—nothing but speeches. And to my mind there ought to be love in a play. [*Both go behind the stage.*]

[*Enter* Polina Andreyevna *and* Dorn.]

Polina. It is getting damp. Go back and put on your galoshes.

Dorn. I am hot.

Polina. You don't take care of yourself. It's **obstinacy**.[19] You are a doctor, and you know perfectly well that damp air is bad for you, but you want to make me miserable; you sat out on the **verandah**[20] all yesterday evening on purpose. . . .

Dorn [*hums*]. "Do not say that youth is ruined."

Polina. You were so absorbed in conversation with Irina Nikolayevna . . . you did not notice the cold. Own up . . . you are attracted by her.

Dorn. I am fifty-five.

Polina. Nonsense! That's not old for a man. You look very young for your age, and are still attractive to women.

Dorn. Well, what would you have?

---

[18] methylated spirit—wood alcohol, used as a fuel.

[19] **obstinacy**—stubbornness.

[20] **verandah**—porch.

Polina. All you men are ready to fall down and worship an actress, all of you!

Dorn [*hums*]. "Before thee once again I stand." If artists are liked in society and treated differently from merchants, for example, that's only in the nature of things. It's idealism.

Polina. Women have always fallen in love with you and thrown themselves on your neck. Is that idealism too?

Dorn [*shrugs his shoulders*]. Well, in the attitude of women to me there has been a great deal that was good. What they principally loved in me was a first-rate doctor. You remember that ten or fifteen years ago I was the only decent obstetrician[21] in the district. Then, too, I have always been an honest man.

Polina [*seizes him by the hand*]. Dearest!

Dorn. Sh-h! They are coming.

[*Enter* Madame Arkadin *arm in arm with* Sorin, Trigorin, Shamraev, Medvedenko *and* Masha.]

Shamraev. In the year 1873 she acted marvellously at the fair at Poltava. It was a delight! She acted exquisitely! Do you happen to know, madam, where Pavel Semyonitch Tchadin, a comic actor, is now? His Rasplyuev was inimitable, even finer than Sadovsky's,[22] I assure you, honored lady. Where is he now?

Madame Arkadin. You keep asking me about antediluvians.[23] How should I know? [*Sits down.*]

Shamraev [*with a sigh*]. Pashka Tchadin! There are no such actors now. The stage has gone down, Irina Nikolayevna! In old days there were mighty oaks, but now we see nothing but stumps.

Dorn. There are few actors of brilliant talents nowadays, that's true; but the average level of acting is far higher than it was.

Shamraev. I can't agree with you. But, of course, it's a matter of taste. *De gustibus aut bene aut nihil.*[24]

[Treplev *comes out from behind the stage.*]

Madame Arkadin [*to her son*]. My dear son, when is it going to begin?

Treplev. In a minute. I beg you to be patient.

---

[21] obstetrician—doctor who specializes in caring for women during childbirth.

[22] Tchadin . . . Sadovsky—These Russians made their reputations performing low comedy.

[23] antediluvians—ancients, those who lived "before the flood."

[24] *De gustibus . . . nihil*—Shamraev pompously confuses two Latin phrases: *De gustibus non disputandum est* ("There's no disputing about taste") and *De mortuis aut bene aut nihil* ("If you can't speak well of the dead, say nothing").

Madame Arkadin [*recites from* Hamlet[25]]. "Oh, Hamlet, speak no more!
    Thou turn'st mine eyes into my very soul;
    And there I see such black and grained spots
    As will not leave their tinct."[26]

Treplev [*from* Hamlet]. "And let me wring your heart, for so I shall,
    If it be made of penetrable stuff."

[*A horn is sounded behind the stage.*]

Treplev. Ladies and gentlemen; we begin! I beg you to attend [*a pause*].
    I begin. [*Taps with a stick and recites aloud.*] Oh, you venerable old
    shadows that float at nighttime over this lake, lull us to sleep and
    let us dream of what will be in two hundred thousand years!

Sorin. There will be nothing in two hundred thousand years.

Treplev. Then let them present that nothing to us.

Madame Arkadin. Let them. We are asleep.

[*The curtain rises; the view of the lake is revealed; the moon is above the horizon, its reflection in the water;* Nina Zaretchny, *all in white, is sitting on a big stone.*]

Nina. Men, lions, eagles and partridges, horned deer, geese, spiders,
    silent fish that dwell in the water, starfishes and creatures which can-
    not be seen by the eye—all living things, all living things, all living
    things, having completed their cycle of sorrow, are extinct. . . . For
    thousands of years the earth has borne[27] no living creature on its sur-
    face, and this poor moon lights its lamp in vain. On the meadow the
    cranes no longer waken with a cry, and there is no sound of the May
    beetles in the lime trees. It is cold, cold, cold! Empty, empty, empty!
    Dreadful, dreadful, dreadful! [*A pause.*] The bodies of living creatures
    have vanished into dust, and eternal matter has transformed them
    into rocks, into water, into clouds, while the souls of all have melted
    into one. That world-soul I am—I. . . . In me is the soul of Alexander
    the Great, of Caesar, of Shakespeare and of Napoleon, and of the
    lowest leech.[28] In me the consciousness of men is blended with
    the instincts of the animals, and I remember all, all, all! And I live
    through every life over again in myself! [*Will-of-the-wisps*[29] *appear.*]

---

[25] Hamlet—Madame Arkadin and her son quote from Shakespeare's *Hamlet*, Act Three, Scene Four, in which Hamlet accuses his mother of having betrayed the memory of her late husband by hastily marrying his brother.

[26] tinct—tincture, color.

[27] borne—carried.

[28] leech—bloodsucking worm.

[29] *Will-of-the-wisps*—glowing lights seen over marshes at night.

Madame Arkadin [*softly*]. It's something decadent.[30]

Treplev [*in an imploring and reproachful*[31] *voice*]. Mother!

Nina. I am alone. Once in a hundred years I open my lips to speak, and my voice echoes mournfully in the void, and no one hears. . . . You too, pale lights, hear me not. . . . The stagnant[32] marsh begets you before daybreak and you wander until dawn, but without thought, without will, without the tremor of life. For fear that life should spring up in you the father of eternal matter, the devil, keeps the atoms in you, as in the stones and in the water, in continual flux, and you are changing perpetually. For in all the universe nothing remains permanent and unchanged but the spirit. [*A pause.*] Like a prisoner cast into a deep, empty well I know not where I am and what awaits me. All is hidden from me but that in the cruel, persistent struggle with the devil—the principle of the forces of matter—I am destined to conquer, and, after that, matter and spirit will be blended in glorious harmony and the Kingdom of the Cosmic Will will come. But that will come only little by little, through long, long thousands of years when the moon and the bright Sirius[33] and the earth are changed to dust. . . . Till then—terror, terror. . . . [*A pause; two red spots appear upon the background of the lake.*] Here my powerful foe, the devil, is approaching. I see his dreadful crimson eyes. . . .

Madame Arkadin. There's a smell of sulphur. Is that as it should be?

Treplev. Yes.

Madame Arkadin [*laughs*]. Oh, it's a stage effect!

Treplev. Mother!

Nina. He is dreary without man—

Polina [*to* Dorn]. You have taken your hat off. Put it on or you will catch cold.

Madame Arkadin. The doctor has taken his hat off to the devil, the father of eternal matter.

Treplev [*firing up, aloud*]. The play is over! Enough! Curtain!

Madame Arkadin. What are you cross about?

Treplev. Enough! The curtain! Let down the curtain! [*Stamping.*] Curtain! [*The curtain falls.*] I am sorry! I lost sight of the fact that only a few of the elect may write plays and act in them. I have infringed the

---

[30] decadent—artificial, fantastical, bizarre.

[31] *imploring and reproachful*—pleading and disapproving.

[32] stagnant—foul because unmoving, as standing water.

[33] Sirius—brightest star in the sky; located in the constellation Canis Major.

monopoly.[34] I . . . I . . . [*Tries to say something more, but with a wave of his hand goes out on left.*]

Madame Arkadin. What's the matter with him?

Sorin. Irina, you really must have more consideration for youthful vanity, my dear.

Madame Arkadin. What did I say to him?

Sorin. You hurt his feelings.

Madame Arkadin. He told us beforehand that it was a joke, and I regarded his play as a joke.

Sorin. All the same . . .

Madame Arkadin. Now it appears that he has written a great work. What next! So he has got up this performance and smothered us with sulphur not as a joke but as a protest. . . . He wanted to show us how to write and what to act. This is getting tiresome! These continual sallies[35] at my expense—these continual pinpricks would put anyone out of patience, say what you like. He is a vain, whimsical boy!

Sorin. He meant to give you pleasure.

Madame Arkadin. Really? He did not choose an ordinary play, however, but made us listen to this decadent **delirium**.[36] For the sake of a joke I am ready to listen to delirium, but here we have pretensions[37] to new forms and a new view of art. To my thinking it's no question of new forms at all, but simply bad temper.

Trigorin. Everyone writes as he likes and as he can.

Madame Arkadin. Let him write as he likes and as he can, only let him leave me in peace.

Dorn. Jupiter![38] you are angry. . . .

Madame Arkadin. I am not Jupiter—I am a woman. [*Lights a cigarette.*] I am not angry—I am only vexed that a young man should spend his time so drearily.[39] I did not mean to hurt his feelings.

Medvedenko. No one has any grounds to separate spirit from matter, seeing that spirit itself may be a combination of material atoms. [*With animation, to* Trigorin.] But you know someone ought to write a play on how we poor teachers live, and get it acted. We have a hard, hard life.

---

[34] infringed the monopoly—violated the exclusive right.

[35] sallies—jests.

[36] **delirium**—madness.

[37] pretensions—claims.

[38] Jupiter—king of the gods.

[39] drearily—dismally, sadly.

Madame Arkadin. That's true, but don't let us talk either of plays or of atoms. It is such a glorious evening! Do you hear? There is singing! [*Listens.*] How nice it is!

Polina. It's on the other side of the lake. [*A pause.*]

Madame Arkadin [*to Trigorin*]. Sit down beside me. Ten or fifteen years ago there were sounds of music and singing on that lake continually almost every night. There are six country houses on the shores of the lake. I remember laughter, noise, shooting, and love affairs without end. . . . The *jeune premier*[40] and the idol of all those six households was in those days our friend here, the doctor, [*Motions with her head toward* Dorn.] Yevgeny Sergeitch. He is fascinating still, but in those days he was irresistible. But my conscience is beginning to trouble me. Why did I hurt my poor boy's feelings? I feel worried. [*Aloud.*] Kostya![41] Son! Kostya!

Masha. I'll go and look for him.

Madame Arkadin. Please do, my dear.

Masha [*going to the left*]. Aa-oo! Konstantin Gavrilitch! Aa-oo! [*Goes off.*]

Nina [*coming out from behind the stage*]. Apparently there will be no going on, and I may come out. Good evening! [*Kisses* Madame Arkadin *and* Polina Andreyevna.]

Sorin. Bravo! Bravo!

Madame Arkadin. Bravo! Bravo! We admired you. With such an appearance, with such a lovely voice, you really cannot stay in the country; it is a sin. You must have talent. Do you hear? It's your duty to go on the stage.

Nina. Oh, that's my dream! [*Sighing.*] But it will never be realized.

Madame Arkadin. Who knows? Here, let me introduce Boris Alexeyevitch Trigorin.

Nina. Oh, I am so glad. . . . [*Overcome with embarrassment.*] I am always reading your . . .

Madame Arkadin [*making her sit down beside them*]. Don't be shy, my dear. He is a celebrity, but he has a simple heart. You see, he is shy himself.

Dorn. I suppose we may raise the curtain; it's rather **uncanny**.[42]

Shamraev [*aloud*]. Yakov, pull up the curtain, my lad. [*The curtain goes up.*]

Nina [*to Trigorin*]. It is a queer play, isn't it?

---

[40] *jeune premier*—young leading man in an acting company.

[41] Kostya—nickname for Konstantin.

[42] **uncanny**—weird.

The Sea Gull 479

Trigorin. I did not understand it at all. But I enjoyed it. You acted so genuinely. And the scenery was delightful. [*A pause.*] There must be a lot of fish in that lake.

Nina. Yes.

Trigorin. I love angling. There is nothing I enjoy so much as sitting on the bank of a river in the evening and watching the float.

Nina. But I should have thought that for anyone who has known the enjoyment of creation, no other enjoyment can exist.

Madame Arkadin [*laughing*]. Don't talk like that. When people say nice things to him he is utterly floored.

Shamraev. I remember one evening in the opera theater in Moscow the celebrated Silva took the lower C![43] As it happened, there was sitting in the gallery the bass of our church choir, and all at once—imagine our intense astonishment—we heard from the gallery "Bravo, Silva!" a whole octave[44] lower—like this: [*In a deep bass.*] "Bravo, Silva!" The audience sat spellbound. [*A pause.*]

Dorn. The angel of silence has flown over us.[45]

Nina. It's time for me to go. Good-bye.

Madame Arkadin. Where are you off to? Why so early? We won't let you go.

Nina. My father expects me.

Madame Arkadin. What a man, really. . . . [*Kisses her.*] Well, there is no help for it. I am sorry—I am sorry to let you go.

Nina. If you knew how grieved I am to go.

Madame Arkadin. Someone ought to see you home, my little dear.

Nina [*frightened*]. Oh, no, no!

Sorin [*to her, in an **imploring**[46] voice*]. Do stay!

Nina. I can't, Pyotr Nikolayevitch.

Sorin. Stay for an hour. What is there in that?

Nina [*thinking a minute, tearfully*]. I can't! [*Shakes hands and hurriedly goes off.*]

Madame Arkadin. Unfortunate girl she is, really. They say her mother left her father all her immense property—every penny of it—and now the girl has got nothing, as her father has already made a will leaving everything to his second wife. It's monstrous!

---

[43] celebrated Silva . . . lower C—famous operatic bass sang a very low note.

[44] octave—range of eight notes.

[45] The angel . . . over us—Dorn is alluding to an embarrassed or irritated quiet following Shamraev's story, which is an overfamiliar anecdote that had been told about many basses.

[46] *imploring*—pleading.

Dorn. Yes, her father is a pretty thorough scoundrel, one must do him the justice to say so.

Sorin [*rubbing his cold hands*]. Let us go too, it's getting damp. My legs ache.

Madame Arkadin. They seem like wooden legs, you can hardly walk. Let us go, unlucky old man! [*Takes his arm.*]

Shamraev [*offering his arm to his wife*]. Madame?

Sorin. I hear that dog howling again. [*To Shamraev.*] Be so kind, Ilya Afanasyitch, as to tell them to let it off the chain.

Shamraev. It's impossible, Pyotr Nikolayevitch, I am afraid of thieves getting into the barn. Our millet[47] is there. [*To Medvedenko who is walking beside him.*] Yes, a whole octave lower: "Bravo, Silva! " And he not a singer—simply a church chorister!

Medvedenko. And what salary does a chorister get? [*All go out except* Dorn.]

Dorn [*alone*]. I don't know, perhaps I know nothing about it, or have gone off my head, but I liked the play. There is something in it. When that girl talked about loneliness and afterwards when the devil's eyes appeared, I was so excited that my hands trembled. It is fresh, naïve. . . . Here he comes, I believe. I want to say all the nice things I can to him.

Treplev [*enters*]. They have all gone.

Dorn. I am here.

Treplev. Mashenka is looking for me all over the park. Insufferable[48] creature she is!

Dorn. Konstantin Gavrilitch, I liked your play extremely. It's a strange thing, and I haven't heard the end, and yet it made a strong impression! You are a gifted man—you must persevere.[49]

[Treplev *presses his hand warmly and embraces him impulsively.*]

Dorn. Fie, what an hysterical[50] fellow! There are tears in his eyes! What I mean is this. You have taken a subject from the realm of abstract ideas. So it should be, for a work of art ought to express a great idea. A thing is only fine when it is serious. How pale you are!

Treplev. So you tell me to persevere?

Dorn. Yes. . . . But write only of what is important and eternal. You know, I have had varied experiences of life, and have enjoyed it; I am satisfied, but if it had been my lot to know the spiritual heights which

---

[47] millet—type of grain.

[48] Insufferable—unendurable.

[49] persevere—persist, continue.

[50] hysterical—emotional.

artists reach at the moment of creation, I should, I believe, have despised my bodily self and all that appertains to it and left all things earthly as far behind as possible.

Treplev. Excuse me, where is Nina?

Dorn. And another thing. In a work of art there ought to be a clear definite idea. You ought to know what is your aim in writing, for if you go along that picturesque route without a definite goal you will be lost and your talent will be your ruin.

Treplev [*impatiently*]. Where is Nina?

Dorn. She has gone home.

Treplev [*in despair*]. What am I to do? I want to see her . . . I must see her. . . . I must go. . . .

[*Enter Masha.*]

Dorn [*to Treplev*]. Calm yourself, my boy.

Treplev. But I am going all the same. I must go.

Masha. Come indoors, Konstantin Gavrilitch. Your mother wants you. She is worried.

Treplev. Tell her that I have gone away. And I beg you—all of you— leave me in peace! Let me alone! Don't follow me about!

Dorn. Come, come, come, dear boy. . . . You can't go on like that. . . . That's not the thing.

Treplev [*in tears*]. Good-bye, doctor. Thank you. . . . [*Goes off.*]

Dorn [*with a sigh*]. Youth! youth!

Masha. When people have nothing better to say, they say, "Youth! youth!" . . . [*Takes a pinch of snuff.*]

Dorn [*takes her snuff box from her and flings it into the bushes*]. That's disgusting! [*A pause.*] I believe they are playing the piano indoors. We must go in.

Masha. Wait a little.

Dorn. What is it?

Masha. I want to tell you once more. I have a longing to talk. . . . [*Growing agitated.*] I don't care for my father . . . but I feel drawn to you. For some reason I feel with all my heart that you are very near me. . . . Help me. Help me, or I shall do something silly, I shall make a mock of my life and ruin it. . . . I can't go on. . . .

Dorn. What is it? Help you in what?

Masha. I am miserable. No one, no one knows how miserable I am! [*Laying her head on his breast, softly.*] I love Konstantin!

Dorn. How hysterical they all are! How hysterical! And what a lot of love. . . . Oh, the sorcery of the lake! [*Tenderly.*] But what can I do, my child? What? What?

[*Curtain.*]

Act Two

[*A croquet lawn. The house with a big verandah in the background on the right, on the left is seen the lake with the blazing sun reflected in it.*

Flower beds. Midday. Hot. Madame Arkadin, Dorn *and* Masha *are sitting on a garden seat in the shade of an old lime tree on one side of the croquet lawn.* Dorn *has an open book on his knee.*]

Madame Arkadin [*to* Masha]. Come, let us stand up. [*They both get up.*] Let us stand side by side. You are twenty-two and I am nearly twice as old. Yevgeny Sergeitch, which of us looks the younger?

Dorn. You, of course.

Madame Arkadin. There! And why is it? Because I work, I feel I am always on the go, while you stay always in the same place and have no life at all. . . . And it is my rule never to look into the future. I never think about old age or death. What is to be, will be.

Masha. And I feel as though I had been born long, long ago; I trail my life along like an endless train. . . . And often I have not the slightest desire to go on living. [*Sits down.*] Of course, that's all nonsense. I must shake myself and throw it all off.

Dorn [*hums quietly*]. "Tell her, my flowers."

Madame Arkadin. Then I am as particular as an Englishman. I keep myself in hand, as they say, my dear, and am always dressed and have my hair done *comme il faut.*[1] Do I allow myself to go out of the house even into the garden in a dressing gown, or without my hair being done? Never! What has preserved me is that I have never been a dowdy,[2] I have never let myself go, as some women do . . . [*Walks about the lawn with her arms akimbo[3].*] Here I am, as brisk as a bird. I could take the part of a girl of fifteen.

Dorn. Nevertheless, I shall go on. [*Takes up the book.*] We stopped at the corn merchant and the rats. . . .

---

[1] *comme il faut*—French phrase meaning "as it should be."

[2] dowdy—shabby woman.

[3] *akimbo*—with hands on hips and arms bent outward.

Madame Arkadin. And the rats. Read. [*Sits down.*] But give it to me, I'll read. It is my turn. [*Takes the book and looks in it.*] And rats. . . . Here it is. . . . [*Reads.*] "And of course for society people to spoil novelists and to attract them to themselves is as dangerous as for a corn merchant to rear rats in his granaries. And yet they love them. And so, when a woman has picked out an author whom she desires to captivate, she lays siege to him by means of compliments, flattery and favors . . ." Well, that may be so with the French, but there is nothing like that with us, we have no set rules. Among us, before a woman sets to work to captivate an author, she is generally head over ears in love herself, if you please. To go no further, take Trigorin and me. . . .

[*Enter* Sorin, *leaning on his stick and with him* Nina; Medvedenko *wheels an empty bathchair*[4] *in after them.*]

Sorin [*in a caressing tone, as to a child*]. Yes? We are delighted, aren't we? We are happy today at last? [*To his sister.*] We are delighted! Our father and stepmother have gone off to Tver, and we are free now for three whole days.

Nina [*sits down beside* Madame Arkadin *and embraces her*]. I am happy! Now I belong to you.

Sorin [*sits down in his bathchair*]. She looks quite a beauty today.

Madame Arkadin. Nicely dressed and interesting. . . . That's a good girl [*kisses* Nina]. But we mustn't praise you too much for fear of ill luck. Where is Boris Alexeyevitch?

Nina. He is in the bathing house, fishing.

Madame Arkadin. I wonder he doesn't get sick of it! [*Is about to go on reading.*]

Nina. What is that?

Madame Arkadin. Maupassant's "Sur l'eau," my dear. [*Reads a few lines to herself.*] Well, the rest isn't interesting or true. [*Shuts the book.*] I feel uneasy. Tell me, what's wrong with my son? Why is he so depressed and ill-humored? He spends whole days on the lake and I hardly ever see him.

Masha. His heart is troubled. [*To* Nina, *timidly.*] Please, do read us something out of his play!

Nina [*shrugging her shoulders*]. Would you like it? It's so uninteresting.

Masha [*restraining her enthusiasm*]. When he reads anything himself his eyes glow and his face turns pale. He has a fine mournful voice, and the gestures of a poet.

---

[4] *bathchair*—wheelchair.

[*There is a sound of* Sorin *snoring.*]

Dorn. Good night!

Madame Arkadin. Petrusha!

Sorin. Ah?

Madame Arkadin. Are you asleep?

Sorin. Not a bit of it. [*A pause.*]

Madame Arkadin. You do nothing for your health, brother, and that's
not right.

Sorin. I should like to take something, but the doctor won't give me
anything.

Dorn. Take medicine at sixty!

Sorin. Even at sixty one wants to live!

Dorn [*with vexation*]. Oh, very well, take valerian drops![5]

Madame Arkadin. It seems to me it would do him good to go to some
mineral springs.

Dorn. Well, he might go. And he might not.

Madame Arkadin. What is one to make of that?

Dorn. There's nothing to make of it. It's quite clear. [*A pause.*]

Medvedenko. Pyotr Nikolayevitch ought to give up smoking.

Sorin. Nonsense!

Dorn. No, it's not nonsense. Wine and tobacco destroy the personality.
After a cigar or a glass of vodka, you are not Pyotr Nikolayevitch
any more but Pyotr Nikolayevitch plus somebody else; your ego is
diffused[6] and you feel towards yourself as to a third person.

Sorin [*laughs*]. It's all very well for you to argue! You've lived your life,
but what about me? I have served in the Department of Justice for
twenty-eight years, but I haven't lived yet, I've seen and done nothing as a matter of fact, and very naturally I want to live very much.
You've had enough and you don't care, and so you are inclined to be
philosophical, but I want to live, and so I drink sherry at dinner and
smoke cigars and so on. That's all it comes to.

Dorn. One must look at life seriously, but to go in for cures at sixty and
to regret that one hasn't enjoyed oneself enough in one's youth is
frivolous,[7] if you will forgive my saying so.

Masha [*gets up*]. It must be lunchtime [*walks with a lazy, lagging step*]. My
leg is gone to sleep. [*Goes off.*]

---

[5] valerian drops—drug once used as a sedative.

[6] ego is diffused—personality is dispersed or scattered.

[7] **frivolous**—silly.

Dorn. She will go and have a couple of glasses before lunch.

Sorin. She has no personal happiness, poor thing.

Dorn. Nonsense, your Excellency.

Sorin. You argue like a man who has had all he wants.

Madame Arkadin. Oh, what can be more boring than this sweet country boredom! Hot, still, no one ever doing anything, everyone airing their theories. . . . It's nice being with you, my friends, charming to listen to you, but . . . to sit in a hotel room somewhere and learn one's part is ever so much better.

Nina [*enthusiastically*]. Delightful! I understand you.

Sorin. Of course, it's better in town. You sit in your study, the footman[8] lets no one in unannounced, there's a telephone . . . in the streets there are cabs and everything. . . .

Dorn [*hums*]. "Tell her, my flowers."

[*Enter* Shamraev, *and after him* Polina Andreyevna.]

Shamraev. Here they are! Good morning! [*Kisses* Madame Arkadin's *hand and then* Nina's.] Delighted to see you in good health. [*To* Madame Arkadin.] My wife tells me that you are proposing to drive into town with her today. Is that so?

Madame Arkadin. Yes, we are thinking of it.

Shamraev. Hm! that's splendid, but how are you going, honored lady? They are carting the rye today; all the men are at work. What horses are you to have, allow me to ask?

Madame Arkadin. What horses? How can I tell which?

Sorin. We've got carriage horses.

Shamraev [*growing excited*]. Carriage horses! But where am I to get collars[9] for them? Where am I to get collars? It's a strange thing! It passes my understanding! Honored lady! forgive me, I am full of reverence for your talent. I would give ten years of my life for you, but I cannot let you have the horses!

Madame Arkadin. But if I have to go! It's a queer thing!

Shamraev. Honored lady! you don't know what farming means.

Madame Arkadin [*flaring up*]. That's the old story! If that's so, I go back to Moscow today. Give orders for horses to be hired for me at the village, or I'll walk to the station.

Shamraev [*flaring up*]. In that case I resign my position! You must look for another steward [*goes off*].

---

[8] footman—servant.

[9] collars—horse-collars, part of the harness used to enable a horse to pull a vehicle.

Madame Arkadin. It's like this every summer; every summer I am insulted here! I won't set my foot in the place again. [*Goes off at left where the bathing shed is supposed to be; a minute later she can be seen entering the house.* Trigorin *follows her, carrying fishing rods and tackle, and a pail.*]

Sorin [*flaring up*]. This is insolence! It's beyond everything. I am thoroughly sick of it. Send all the horses here this minute!

Nina [*to* Polina Andreyevna]. To refuse Irina Nikolayevna, the famous actress! Any wish of hers, any whim even, is of more consequence than all your farming. It's positively incredible!

Polina [*in despair*]. What can I do? Put yourself in my position: what can I do?

Sorin [*to* Nina]. Let us go to my sister. We will all entreat her not to go away. Won't we? [*Looking in the direction in which* Shamraev *has gone.*] Insufferable man! Despot![10]

Nina [*preventing him from getting up*]. Sit still, sit still. We will wheel you in. [*She and* Medvedenko *push the bathchair.*] Oh, how awful it is!

Sorin. Yes, yes, it's awful. But he won't leave, I'll speak to him directly. [*They go out;* Dorn *and* Polina Andreyevna *are left alone on the stage.*]

Dorn. People are tiresome. Your husband ought to be simply kicked out, but it will end in that old woman Pyotr Nikolayevitch and his sister begging the man's pardon. You will see!

Polina. He has sent the carriage horses into the fields too! And there are misunderstandings like this every day. If you only knew how it upsets me! It makes me ill; see how I am trembling. . . . I can't endure his rudeness. [*In an imploring voice.*] Yevgeny, dearest, light of my eyes, my darling, let me come to you. . . . Our time is passing, we are no longer young, and if only we could lay aside concealment and lying for the end of our lives, anyway. . . . [*A pause.*]

Dorn. I am fifty-five; it's too late to change my life.

Polina. I know you refuse me because there are other women too who are as near to you. You can't take them all to live with you. I understand. Forgive me, you are tired of me.

[Nina *appears near the house; she is picking flowers.*]

Dorn. No, it's all right.

Polina. I am wretched from jealousy. Of course you are a doctor, you can't avoid women. I understand.

Dorn [*to* Nina, *who comes up to them*]. How are things going?

---

[10] Despot—tyrant.

Nina. Irina Nikolayevna is crying and Pyotr Nikolayevitch has an attack of asthma.

Dorn [*gets up*]. I'd better go and give them both valerian drops.

Nina [*gives him the flowers*]. Please take these.

Dorn. *Merci bien.*[11] [*Goes towards the house.*]

Polina [*going with him*]. What charming flowers! [*Near the house, in a smothered voice.*] Give me those flowers! Give me those flowers! [*On receiving them tears the flowers to pieces and throws them away; both go into the house.*]

Nina [*alone*]. How strange it is to see a famous actress cry, and about such a trivial thing! And isn't it strange? A famous author, adored by the public, written about in all the papers, his photographs for sale, his works translated into foreign languages—and he spends the whole day fishing and is delighted that he has caught two gudgeon.[12] I thought famous people were proud, unapproachable, that they despised the crowd, and by their fame and the glory of their name, as it were, revenged themselves on the vulgar herd for putting rank and wealth above everything. But here they cry and fish, play cards, laugh and get cross like everyone else!

Treplev [*comes in without a hat on, with a gun and a dead sea gull*]. Are you alone here?

Nina. Yes.

[Treplev *lays the sea gull at her feet.*]

Nina. What does that mean?

Treplev. I was so mean as to kill this bird today. I lay it at your feet.

Nina. What is the matter with you? [*Picks up the bird and looks at it.*]

Treplev [*after a pause*]. Soon I shall kill myself in the same way.

Nina. You have so changed, I hardly know you.

Treplev. Yes, ever since the day when I hardly knew you. You have changed to me, your eyes are cold, you feel me in the way.

Nina. You have become irritable of late, you express yourself so incomprehensibly, as it were in symbols. This bird is a symbol too, I suppose, but forgive me, I don't understand it. [*Lays the sea gull on the seat.*] I am too simple to understand you.

Treplev. This began from that evening when my play came to grief so stupidly. Women never forgive failure. I have burnt it all; every scrap of it. If only you knew how miserable I am! Your growing cold to me

---

[11] *Merci bien*—French phrase meaning "thank you very much."
[12] gudgeon—small fish often used as bait.

is awful, incredible, as though I had woken up and found this lake had suddenly dried up or sunk into the earth. You have just said that you are too simple to understand me. Oh, what is there to understand? My play was not liked, you despise my inspiration, you already consider me commonplace, insignificant, like so many others. . . . [*Stamping.*] How well I understand it all, how I understand it! I feel as though I had a nail in my brain, damnation take it together with my vanity which is sucking away my life, sucking it like a snake . . . [*sees* Trigorin, *who comes in reading a book*]. Here comes the real genius, walking like Hamlet and with a book too. [*Mimics.*] "Words, words, words." . . . The sun has scarcely reached you and you are smiling already, your eyes are melting in its rays. I won't be in your way. [*Goes off quickly.*]

Trigorin [*making notes in his book*]. Takes snuff and drinks vodka. Always in black. The schoolmaster is in love with her. . . .

Nina. Good morning, Boris Alexeyevitch!

Trigorin. Good morning. Circumstances have turned out so unexpectedly that it seems we are setting off today. We are hardly likely to meet again. I am sorry. I don't often have the chance of meeting young girls, youthful and charming; I have forgotten how one feels at eighteen or nineteen and can't picture it to myself, and so the young girls in my stories and novels are usually false. I should like to be in your shoes just for one hour to find out how you think, and altogether what sort of person you are.

Nina. And I should like to be in your shoes.

Trigorin. What for?

Nina. To know what it feels like to be a famous, gifted author. What does it feel like to be famous? How does it affect you, being famous?

Trigorin. How? Nohow, I believe. I have never thought about it. [*After a moment's thought.*] It's one of two things: either you exaggerate my fame, or it never is felt at all.

Nina. But if you read about yourself in the newspapers?

Trigorin. When they praise me I am pleased, and when they abuse me I feel out of humor for a day or two.

Nina. What a wonderful world! If only you knew how I envy you! How different people's lots in life are! Some can scarcely get through their dull, obscure existence, they are all just like one another, they are all unhappy; while others—you, for instance—you are one out of a million, have an interesting life full of brightness and significance. You are happy.

Trigorin. I? [*Shrugging his shoulders.*] Hm. . . . You talk of fame and happiness, of bright interesting life, but to me all those fine words, if you will forgive my saying so, are just like a sweetmeat[13] which I never taste. You are very young and very good-natured.

Nina. Your life is splendid!

Trigorin. What is there particularly nice in it? [*Looks at his watch*] I must go and write directly. Excuse me, I mustn't stay . . . [*laughs*]. You have stepped on my favorite corn, as the saying is, and here I am beginning to get excited and a little cross. Let us talk though. We will talk about my splendid bright life. . . . Well, where shall we begin? [*After thinking a little.*] There are such things as fixed ideas, when a man thinks days and night, for instance, of nothing but the moon. And I have just such a moon. I am haunted day and night by one persistent thought: I ought to be writing, I ought to be writing, I ought . . . I have scarcely finished one novel when, for some reason, I must begin writing another, then a third, after the third a fourth. I write incessantly, posthaste,[14] and I can't write in any other way. What is there splendid and bright in that, I ask you? Oh, it's an absurd life! Here I am with you; I am excited, yet every moment I remember that my unfinished novel is waiting for me. Here I see a cloud that looks like a grand piano. I think that I must put into a story somewhere that a cloud sailed by that looked like a grand piano. There is a scent of heliotrope.[15] I hurriedly make a note: a sickly smell, a widow's flower, to be mentioned in the description of a summer evening. I catch up myself and you at every sentence, every word, and make haste to put those sentences and words away into my literary treasure house—it may come in useful! When I finish work I race off to the theater or to fishing; if only I could rest in that and forget myself. But no, there's a new subject rolling about in my head like a heavy iron cannon ball, and I am drawn to my writing table and must make haste again to go on writing and writing. And it's always like that, always. And I have no rest from myself, and I feel that I am eating up my own life, and that for the sake of the honey I give to someone in space I am stripping the pollen from my best flowers, tearing up the flowers themselves and trampling on their roots. Don't you think I am mad? Do my friends and acquaintances treat me as though I were sane?

---

[13] sweetmeat—sweet cake or candy.

[14] incessantly, posthaste—without stopping, with the greatest speed.

[15] heliotrope—plant with fragrant purple flowers.

"What are you writing? What are you giving us?" It's the same thing again and again, and it seems to me as though my friends' notice, their praises, their enthusiasm—that it's all a sham, that they are deceiving me as an invalid and I am somehow afraid that they will steal up to me from behind, snatch me and carry me off and put me in a madhouse. And in those years, the best years of my youth, when I was beginning, my writing was unmixed torture. A small writer, particularly when he is not successful, seems to himself clumsy, awkward, unnecessary; his nerves are strained and overwrought. He can't resist hanging about people connected with literature and art, unrecognized and unnoticed by anyone, afraid to look anyone boldly in the face, like a passionate gambler without any money. I hadn't seen my reader, but for some reason I always imagined him hostile, and mistrustful. I was afraid of the public, it alarmed me, and when I had to produce my first play it always seemed to me that all the dark people felt hostile and all the fair ones were coldly indifferent. Oh, how awful it was! What agony it was!

Nina. But surely inspiration and the very process of creation give you moments of exalted happiness?

Trigorin. Yes. While I am writing I enjoy it. And I like reading my proofs, but . . . as soon as it is published I can't endure it, and I see that it is all wrong, a mistake, that it ought not to have been written at all, and I feel vexed and sick about it. . . . [*Laughing.*] And the public reads it and says: "Yes, charming, clever. Charming, but very inferior to Tolstoy," or, "It's a fine thing, but Turgenev's *Fathers and Sons*[16] is finer." And it will be the same to my dying day, only charming and clever, charming and clever—and nothing more. And when I die, my friends, passing by my tomb, will say, "Here lies Trigorin. He was a good writer, but inferior to Turgenev."

Nina. Forgive me, but I refuse to understand you. You are simply spoiled by success.

Trigorin. What success? I have never liked myself; I dislike my own work. The worst of it is that I am in a sort of delirium, and often don't understand what I am writing. I love this water here, the trees, the sky. I feel nature; it arouses in me a passionate, irresistible desire to write. But I am not simply a landscape painter; I am also a citizen. I love my native country, my people; I feel that if I am a writer I am in

---

[16] Turgenev's *Fathers and Sons*—famous novel (1862) by Russian writer Ivan Turgenev (1818–1883) that, like *The Sea Gull*, presents generational conflict.

duty bound to write of the people, of their sufferings, of their future, to talk about science and the rights of man and so on, and so on, and I write about everything. I am hurried and flustered, and on all sides they whip me up and are angry with me; I dash about from side to side like a fox beset by hounds. I see life and culture continually getting farther and farther away while I fall farther and farther behind like a peasant too late for the train; and what it comes to is that I feel I can only describe scenes and in everything else I am false to the marrow of my bones.

Nina. You are overworked and have not the leisure nor the desire to appreciate your own significance. You may be dissatisfied with yourself, but for others you are great and splendid! If I were a writer like you, I should give up my whole life to the common herd, but I should know that there could be no greater happiness for them than to rise to my level, and they would harness themselves to my chariot.

Trigorin. My chariot, what next! Am I an Agamemnon,[17] or what? [*Both smile.*]

Nina. For such happiness as being a writer or an artist I would be ready to endure poverty, disappointment, the dislike of those around me; I would live in a garret[18] and eat nothing but rye bread, I would suffer from being dissatisfied with myself, from recognizing my own imperfections, but I should ask in return for fame . . . real, resounding fame. . . . [*Covers her face with her hands.*] It makes me dizzy. . . . Oh! [*The voice of* Madame Arkadin *from the house.*]

Madame Arkadin. Boris Alexeyevitch!

Trigorin. They are calling for me. I suppose it's to pack. But I don't want to leave here. [*Looks round at the lake.*] Just look how glorious it is! It's splendid!

Nina. Do you see the house and garden on the other side of the lake?

Trigorin. Yes.

Nina. That house was my dear mother's. I was born there. I have spent all my life beside this lake and I know every little islet on it.

Trigorin. It's very delightful here! [*Seeing the sea gull.*] And what's this?

Nina. A sea gull. Konstantin Gavrilitch shot it.

Trigorin. A beautiful bird. Really, I don't want to go away. Try and persuade Irina Nikolayevna to stay. [*Makes a note in his book.*]

---

[17] Agamemnon—legendary king of Argos, leader of the Greeks in the Trojan War.

[18] garret—attic.

Nina. What are you writing?

Trigorin. Oh, I am only making a note. A subject struck me. [*Putting away the notebook.*] A subject for a short story: a young girl, such as you, has lived all her life beside a lake; she loves the lake like a sea gull, and is as free and happy as a sea gull. But a man comes by chance, sees her, and having nothing better to do, destroys her like that sea gull here. [*A pause.*]

[Madame Arkadin *appears at the window.*]

Madame Arkadin. Boris Alexeyevitch, where are you?

Trigorin. I am coming [*Goes and looks back at* Nina. *To* Madame Arkadin *at the window*] What is it?

Madame Arkadin. We are staying.

[Trigorin *goes into the house.*]

Nina [*advances to the footlights; after a few moments' meditation*]. It's a dream! [*Curtain.*]

Act Three

[*The dining room in* Sorin's *house. Doors on right and on left. A sideboard.*[1] *A medicine cupboard. A table in the middle of the room. A portmanteau*[2] *and hat boxes; signs of preparation for departure.* Trigorin *is having lunch;* Masha *stands by the table.*]

Masha. I tell all this to you as a writer. You may make use of it. I am telling you the truth: if he had hurt himself seriously I would not have gone on living another minute. But I have pluck[3] enough all the same. I just made up my mind that I would tear this love out of my heart, tear it out by the roots.

Trigorin. How are you going to do that?

Masha. I am going to be married. To Medvedenko.

Trigorin. That's the schoolmaster?

Masha. Yes.

Trigorin. I don't understand what's the object of it.

Masha. To love without hope, to spend whole years waiting for something. . . . But when I marry, there will be no time left for love, new cares will smother all the old feelings. And, anyway, it will be a change, you know. Shall we have another?

---

[1] *sideboard*—cabinet with drawers and shelves for holding glasses, cups, plates, tableware, napkins, and so on.

[2] *portmanteau*—suitcase, trunk.

[3] pluck—courage.

Trigorin. Won't that be too much?

Masha. Oh, come! [*Fills two glasses.*] Don't look at me like that! Women drink much oftener than you imagine. Only a small proportion drink openly as I do, the majority drink in secret. Yes. And it's always vodka or brandy. [*Clinks glasses.*] My best wishes! You are a good-hearted man; I am sorry to be parting from you. [*They drink.*]

Trigorin. I don't want to go myself.

Masha. You should beg her to stay.

Trigorin. No, she won't stay now. Her son is behaving very tactlessly. First, he shoots himself, and now they say he is going to challenge me to a duel. And whatever for? He sulks, and snorts, and preaches new forms of art. . . . But there is room for all—new and old—why quarrel about it?

Masha. Well, there's jealousy too. But it is nothing to do with me.

[*A pause.* Yakov *crosses from right to left with a portmanteau.* Nina *enters and stands by the window.*]

Masha. My schoolmaster is not very brilliant, but he is a good-natured man, and poor, and he is very much in love with me. I am sorry for him. And I am sorry for his old mother. Well, let me wish you all happiness. Don't remember evil against me. [*Shakes hands with him warmly.*] I am very grateful for your friendly interest. Send me your books and be sure to put in an inscription. Only don't write, "To my honored friend," but write simply, "To Marya who belongs nowhere and has no object in life." Good-bye! [*Goes out.*]

Nina [*stretching out her arm towards* Trigorin, *with her fist clenched*]. Odd or even?

Trigorin. Even.

Nina [*with a sigh*]. Wrong. I had only one pea in my hand. I was trying my fortune whether to go on the stage or not. I wish someone would advise me.

Trigorin. It's impossible to advise in such a matter. [*A pause.*]

Nina. We are parting and . . . perhaps we shall never meet again. Won't you please take this little medallion as a parting gift? I had your initials engraved on one side of it . . . and on the other the title of your book, "Days and Nights."

Trigorin. How exquisite! [*Kisses the medallion.*] A charming present!

Nina. Think of me sometimes.

Trigorin. I shall think of you. I shall think of you as you were on that sunny day—do you remember?—a week ago, when you were wearing a light dress . . . we were talking . . . there was a white sea gull lying on the seat.

Nina [*pensively*]. Yes, a sea gull. . . . [*A pause.*] We can't talk any more, there's someone coming. . . . Let me have two minutes before you go, I entreat you. . . . [*Goes out on the left.*]

[*At the same instant* Madame Arkadin, Sorin *in a dress coat with a star of some order on it, then* Yakov, *occupied with the luggage, enter on the right.*]

Madame Arkadin. Stay at home, old man. With your rheumatism you ought not to go gadding about.[4] [*To Trigorin.*] Who was that went out? Nina?

Trigorin. Yes.

Madame Arkadin. *Pardon*, we interrupted you. [*Sits down.*] I believe I have packed everything. I am worn out.

Trigorin [*reads on the medallion*]. "'Days and Nights,' page 121, lines 11 and 12."

Yakov [*clearing the table*]. Am I to pack your fishing things too, sir?

Trigorin. Yes, I shall want them again. You can give away the books.

Yakov. Yes, Sir.

Trigorin [*to himself*]. Page 121, lines 11 and 12. What is there in those lines? [*To* Madame Arkadin.] Are there copies of my books in the house?

Madame Arkadin. Yes, in my brother's study, in the corner bookcase.

Trigorin. Page 121 . . . [*Goes out.*]

Madame Arkadin. Really, Petrusha, you had better stay at home.

Sorin. You are going away; it will be deary for me at home without you.

Madame Arkadin. And what is there in the town?

Sorin. Nothing particular, but still . . . [*Laughs.*] There will be the laying of the foundation stone of the Zemstvo-hall and all that sort of thing. One longs to shake oneself free from this stagnant existence, if only for an hour or two. I've been too long on the shelf like some old cigarette holder. I have ordered the horses for one o'clock; we'll set off at the same time.

Madame Arkadin [*after a pause*]. Come, stay here, don't be bored and don't catch cold. Look after my son. Take care of him. Give him good advice. [*A pause.*] Here I am going away and I shall never know why Konstantin tried to shoot himself. I fancy jealousy was the chief cause, and the sooner I get Trigorin away from here, the better.

---

[4] gadding about—traveling aimlessly.

Sorin. What can I say? There were other reasons too. It's easy to understand; he is young, intelligent, living in the country, in the wilds,
with no money, no position and no future. He has nothing to do.
He is ashamed of his idleness and afraid of it. I am very fond of him
indeed, and he is attached to me, yet in spite of it all he feels he is
superfluous in the house, that he is a dependant, a poor relation. It's
easy to understand, it's *amour-propre*.[5] . . .

Madame Arkadin. He is a great anxiety to me! [*Pondering.*] He might go
into the service, perhaps.

Sorin [*begins to whistle, then irresolutely*]. I think that quite the best thing
would be if you were to . . . let him have a little money. In the first
place he ought to be able to be dressed like other people and all that.
Just look at him, he's been going about in the same wretched jacket
for the last three years and he has no overcoat. . . . [*Laughs.*] It would
do him no harm to have a little fun . . . to go abroad or something. . . .
It wouldn't cost much.

Madame Arkadin. But all the same . . . I might manage the suit, perhaps,
but as for going abroad . . . No, just at the moment I can't even
manage the suit. [*Resolutely.*] I have no money!

[Sorin *laughs.*]

Madame Arkadin. No!

Sorin [*begins to whistle*]. Quite so. Forgive me, my dear, don't be cross. I
believe you. . . . You are a generous, noblehearted woman.

Madame Arkadin [*weeping*]. I have no money.

Sorin. If I had money, of course I would give him some myself, but I
have nothing, not a penny. [*Laughs.*] My steward takes all my pension
and spends it all on the land and the cattle and the bees, and my
money is all wasted. The bees die, and the cows die, they never let
me have horses. . . .

Madame Arkadin. Yes, I have money, but you see I am an actress; my
dresses alone are enough to ruin me.

Sorin. You are a kind, good creature . . . I respect you. . . . Yes . . . but
there, I got a touch of it again. . . . [*Staggers.*] I feel dizzy. [*Clutches at
the table.*] I feel ill and all that.

Madame Arkadin [*alarmed*]. Petrusha! [*Trying to support him.*] Petrusha,
my dear! [*Calling.*] Help! help!

[*Enter* Treplev *with a bandage round his head and* Medvedenko.]

---

[5] *amour-propre*—French phrase meaning "self-esteem," "self-respect."

Madame Arkadin. He feels faint!

Sorin. It's all right, it's all right! [*Smiles and drinks some water.*] It's passed off . . . and all that.

Treplev [*to his mother*]. Don't be frightened, mother, it's not serious. Uncle often has these attacks now. [*To his uncle.*] You must lie down, uncle.

Sorin. For a little while, yes. . . . But I am going to the town all the same. . . . I'll lie down a little and then set off. . . . It's quite natural. [*Goes out leaning on his stick.*]

Medvedenko [*gives him his arm*]. There's a riddle: in the morning on four legs, at noon on two, in the evening on three.[6] . . .

Sorin [*laughs*]. Just so. And at night on the back. Thank you, I can manage alone. . . .

Medvedenko. Oh come, why stand on ceremony! [*Goes out with* Sorin.]

Madame Arkadin. How he frightened me!

Treplev. It is not good for him to live in the country. He gets depressed. If you would be generous for once, mother, and lend him fifteen hundred or two thousand rubles, he could spend a whole year in town.

Madame Arkadin. I have no money. I am an actress, not a banker. [*A pause.*]

Treplev. Mother, change my bandage. You do it so well.

Madame Arkadin. [*takes out of the medicine cupboard some iodoform[7] and a box with bandaging material*] The doctor is late.

Treplev. He promised to be here at ten, and it is midday already.

Madame Arkadin. Sit down. [*Takes the bandage off his head.*] It's like a turban. Yesterday a stranger asked in the kitchen what nationality you were. But you have almost completely healed. There is the merest trifle left. [*Kisses him on the head.*] You won't do anything naughty again while I am away, will you?

Treplev. No, mother. It was a moment of mad despair when I could not control myself. It won't happen again. [*Kisses her hand.*] You have such clever hands. I remember, long ago, when you were still acting at the Imperial Theater—I was little then—there was a fight in our yard and a washerwoman, one of the tenants, was badly beaten. Do you remember? She was picked up senseless . . . you looked after her, took her remedies and washed her children in a tub. Don't you remember?

Madame Arkadin. No. [*Puts on a fresh bandage.*]

---

[6] riddle . . . three—famous riddle of the sphinx in Greek mythology that is answered by Oedipus. The solution is "man," who crawls as an infant, walks upright on two legs as an adult, and needs a cane when old.

[7] *iodoform*—antiseptic.

Treplev. Two ballet dancers lived in the same house as we did at the time. . . . They used to come to you and have coffee. . . .

Madame Arkadin. I remember that.

Treplev. They were very pious. [*A pause.*] Just lately, these last days, I have loved you as tenderly and completely as when I was a child. I have no one left now but you. Only why, why do you give yourself up to the influence of that man?

Madame Arkadin. You don't understand him, Konstantin. He is a very noble character. . . .

Treplev. And yet when he was told I was going to challenge him, the nobility of his character did not prevent him from funking it.[8] He is going away. **Ignominious**[9] flight!

Madame Arkadin. What nonsense! It is I who am asking him to go.

Treplev. A very noble character! Here you and I are almost quarrelling over him, and at this very moment he is somewhere in the drawing room or the garden laughing at us . . . developing[10] Nina, trying to convince her finally that he is a genius.

Madame Arkadin. You take a pleasure in saying unpleasant things to me. I respect that man and beg you not to speak ill of him before me.

Treplev. And I don't respect him. You want me to think him a genius too, but forgive me, I can't tell lies, his books make me sick.

Madame Arkadin. That's envy. There's nothing left for people who have pretension[11] without talent but to attack real talent. Much comfort in that, I must say!

Treplev [*ironically*]. Real talent! [*Wrathfully.*] I have more talent than all of you put together if it comes to that! [*Tears the bandage off his head.*] You, with your hackneyed conventions, have usurped the supremacy in art and consider nothing real and legitimate but what you do yourselves; everything else you stifle and suppress. I don't believe in you! I don't believe in you or in him!

Madame Arkadin. Decadent!

Treplev. Get away to your charming theater and act there in your **paltry**,[12] stupid plays!

---

[8] funking it—being cowardly.

[9] **Ignominious**—shameful.

[10] developing—influencing.

[11] pretension—claim.

[12] **paltry**—unimportant.

Madame Arkadin. I have never acted in such plays. Let me alone! You are not capable of writing even a wretched burlesque![13] You are nothing but a Kiev shopman! living on other people!

Treplev. You miser!

Madame Arkadin. You ragged beggar!

[Treplev s*its down and weeps quietly.*]

Madame Arkadin. Nonentity![14] [*Walking up and down in agitation.*] Don't cry. . . . You mustn't cry [*weeps*]. Don't . . . [*Kisses him on the forehead, on the cheeks and on the head.*] My dear child, forgive me. . . . Forgive your sinful mother. Forgive me, you know I am wretched.

Treplev [*puts his arms round her*]. If only you knew! I have lost everything! She does not love me, and now I cannot write . . . all my hopes are gone. . . .

Madame Arkadin. Don't despair . . . Everything will come right. He is going away directly, she will love you again. [*Wipes away his tears.*] Give over.[15] We have made it up now.

Treplev [*kisses her hands*]. Yes, mother.

Madame Arkadin [*tenderly*]. Make it up with him too. You don't want a duel, do you?

Treplev. Very well. Only, mother, do allow me not to meet him. It's painful to me—it's more than I can bear. [*Enter* Trigorin.] Here he is . . . I am going. . . . [*Rapidly puts away the dressings in the cupboard.*] The doctor will do the bandaging now.

Trigorin [*looking in a book*]. Page 121 . . . lines 11 and 12. Here it is. [*Reads.*] "If ever my life can be of use to you, come and take it."

[Treplev *picks up the bandage from the floor and goes out.*]

Madame Arkadin [*looking at her watch*]. The horses will soon be here.

Trigorin [*to himself*]. "If ever my life can be of use to you, come and take it."

Madame Arkadin. I hope all your things are packed?

Trigorin [*impatiently*]. Yes, yes. [*Musing*] Why is it that I feel so much sorrow in that appeal from a pure soul and that it wrings my heart so painfully? "If ever my life can be of use to you, come and take it." [*To* Madame Arkadin] Let us stay one day longer.

[Madame Arkadin *shakes her head.*]

Trigorin. Let us stay!

---

[13] burlesque—comic skit.

[14] **Nonentity**—nobody.

[15] Give over—stop (here, crying).

Madame Arkadin. Darling, I know what keeps you here. But have control over yourself. You are a little intoxicated, try to be sober.

Trigorin. You be sober too, be sensible and reasonable, I implore you; look at it all as a true friend should. [*Presses her hand.*] You are capable of sacrifice. Be a friend to me, let me be free!

Madame Arkadin [*in violent agitation*]. Are you so enthralled?[16]

Trigorin. I am drawn to her! Perhaps it is just what I need.

Madame Arkadin. The love of a provincial girl? Oh, how little you know yourself!

Trigorin. Sometimes people sleep as they talk—that's how it is with me, I am talking to you and yet I am asleep and dreaming of her. . . . I am possessed by sweet, marvelous dreams. . . . Let me be free. . . .

Madame Arkadin [*trembling*]. No, no! I am an ordinary woman, you can't talk like that to me. Don't torture me, Boris. It terrifies me.

Trigorin. If you cared to, you could be not ordinary. Love—youthful, charming, poetical, lifting one into a world of dreams—that's the only thing in life that can give happiness! I have never yet known a love like that. . . . In my youth I never had time, I was always hanging about the editors' offices, struggling with want. Now it is here, that love, it has come, it beckons to me. What sense is there in running away from it?

Madame Arkadin [*wrathfully*]. You have gone mad!

Trigorin. Well, let me?

Madame Arkadin. You are all in a conspiracy together to torment me today! [*Weeps.*]

Trigorin [*clutching at his heart*]. She does not understand! She won't understand!

Madame Arkadin. Am I so old and ugly that you don't mind talking of other women to me? [*Puts her arms round him and kisses him.*] Oh, you are mad! My wonderful, splendid darling. . . . You are the last page of my life! [*Falls on her knees.*] My joy, my pride, my bliss! . . . [*Embraces his knees.*] If you forsake me even for one hour I shall not survive it, I shall go mad, my marvelous, magnificent one, my master. . . .

Trigorin. Someone may come in. [*Helps her to get up.*]

Madame Arkadin. Let them, I am not ashamed of my love for you. [*Kisses his hands.*] My treasure, you desperate boy, you want to be mad, but I won't have it, I won't let you. . . . [*Laughs.*] You are mine . . . mine. . . .

---

[16] enthralled—enslaved.

This forehead is mine, and these eyes, and this lovely silky hair is mine too . . . you are mine all over. You are so gifted, so clever, the best of all modern writers, you are the one hope of Russia. . . . You have so much truthfulness, simplicity, freshness, healthy humor. . . . In one touch you can give all the essential characteristics of a person or a landscape, your characters are living. One can't read you without delight! You think this is exaggerated? That I am flattering you? But look into my eyes . . . look. . . . Do I look like a liar? You see, I am the only one who can appreciate you; I am the only one who tells you the truth, my precious, wonderful darling. . . . Are you coming? Yes? You won't abandon me? . . .

Trigorin. I have no will of my own . . . I have never had a will of my own. . . . Flabby, feeble, always submissive—how can a woman care for such a man? Take me, carry me off, but don't let me move a step away from you. . . .

Madame Arkadin [*to herself*]. Now he is mine! [*In an easy tone as though nothing had happened.*] But, of course, if you like, you can stay. I'll go by myself and you can come afterwards, a week later. After all, why should you be in a hurry?

Trigorin. No, we may as well go together.

Madame Arkadin. As you please. Let us go together then. [*A pause.*] [Trigorin *makes a note.*]

Madame Arkadin. What are you writing?

Trigorin. I heard a good name this morning, "The Maiden's Forest." It may be of use. [*Stretches.*] So we are to go then? Again there will be railway carriages, stations, refreshment bars, mutton chops, conversations. . . .

Shamraev [*enters*]. I have the honor to announce, with regret, that the horses are ready. It's time, honored lady, to set off for the station; the train comes in at five minutes past two. So please do me a favor, Irina Nikolayevna, do not forget to inquire what has become of the actor Suzdaltsev. Is he alive and well? We used to drink together at one time. . . . In "The Plundered Mail" he used to play incomparably. . . . I remember the tragedian Izmaïlov, also a remarkable personality, acted with him in Elisavetograd. . . . Don't be in a hurry, honored lady, you need not start for five minutes. Once they were acting conspirators in a melodrama and when they were suddenly discovered Izmaïlov had to say, "We are caught in a trap," but he said, "We are caught in a tap!" [*Laughs.*] A tap!

[*While he is speaking* Yakov *is busy looking after the luggage. The maid brings* Madame Arkadin *her hat, her coat, her umbrella and her gloves; they all help* Madame Arkadin *to put on her things. The man-cook looks in at the door on left and after some hesitation comes in. Enter* Polina Andreyevna, *then* Sorin *and* Medvedenko.]

Polina [*with a basket*]. Here are some plums for the journey. . . . Very sweet ones. You may be glad to have something nice. . . .

Madame Arkadin. You are very kind, Polina Andreyevna.

Polina. Good-bye, my dear! If anything has not been to your liking, forgive it. [*Weeps.*]

Madame Arkadin [*embraces her*]. Everything has been nice, everything! But you mustn't cry.

Polina. The time flies so fast!

Madame Arkadin. There's no help for it.

Sorin [*in a greatcoat with a cape to it, with his hat on and a stick in his hand, enters from door on left, crossing the stage*]. Sister, it's time to start, or you may be too late after all. I am going to get into the carriage. [*Goes out.*]

Medvedenko. And I shall walk to the station . . . to see you off. I'll be there in no time. . . . [*Goes out.*]

Madame Arkadin. Good-bye, dear friends. . . . If we are all alive and well, we shall meet again next summer. [*The* maid, the cook *and* Yakov *kiss her hand.*] Don't forget me. [*Gives the cook a ruble.*] Here's a ruble for the three of you.[17]

The Cook. We humbly thank you, madam! Good journey to you! We are very grateful for your kindness!

Yakov. May God give you good luck!

Shamraev. You might rejoice our hearts with a letter! Good-bye, Boris Alexeyevitch!

Madame Arkadin. Where is Konstantin? Tell him that I am starting; I must say good-bye. Well, don't remember evil against me. [*To Yakov.*] I gave the cook a ruble. It's for the three of you.

[*All go out on right. The stage is empty. Behind the scenes the noise that is usual when people are being seen off. The maid comes back to fetch the basket of plums from the table and goes out again.*]

Trigorin [*coming back*]. I have forgotten my stick. I believe it is out there, on the verandah. [*Goes and, at door on left meets* Nina *who is coming in.*] Is that you? We are going. . . .

---

[17] a ruble for the three of you—a very stingy tip.

Nina. I felt that we should see each other once more. [*Excitedly.*] Boris
Alexeyevitch, I have come to a decision, the die is cast,[18] I am going
on the stage. I shall be gone from here tomorrow; I am leaving my
father, I am abandoning everything, I am beginning a new life. Like
you, I am going . . . to Moscow. We shall meet there.

Trigorin [*looking round*]. Stay at the "Slavyanksky Bazaar" . . . Let me
know at once . . . Molchanovka, Groholsky House. . . . I am in a
hurry. . . . [*A pause.*]

Nina. One minute more. . . .

Trigorin [*in an undertone*]. You are so lovely. . . . Oh, what happiness to
think that we shall see each other soon! [*She sinks on his breast.*] I shall
see again those wonderful eyes, that inexpressibly beautiful tender
smile . . . those soft features, the expression of angelic purity. . . . My
darling . . . [*A prolonged kiss.*]

[*Curtain.*]

[*Between the Third and Fourth Acts there is an interval of two years.*]

Act Four

[*One of the drawing rooms in* Sorin's *house, which has been turned into a study
for* Konstantin Treplev. *On the right and left, doors leading to inner apartments. In the middle, glass door leading on to the verandah. Besides the usual
drawing room furniture there is, in corner on right, a writing table, near door on
left, a sofa, a bookcase and books in windows and on the chairs. Evening. There is
a single lamp alight with a shade on it. It is half dark. There is the sound of the
trees rustling, and the wind howling in the chimney. A watchman is tapping.*[1]
Enter Medvedenko *and* Masha.]

Masha [*calling*]. Konstantin Gavrilitch! Konstantin Gavrilitch! [*Looking
round.*] No, there is no one here. The old man keeps asking every
minute, where is Kostya, where is Kostya? He cannot live without
him. . . .

Medvedenko. He is afraid of being alone. [*Listening.*] What awful
weather! This is the second day of it.

Masha [*turns up the lamp*]. There are waves on the lake. Great big ones.

Medvedenko. How dark it is in the garden! We ought to have told them
to break up that stage in the garden. It stands as bare and ugly as a

---

[18] die is cast—risk is taken. (*Die* is the singular of *dice*.)

[1] *watchman is tapping*—that is, with his stick as a warning as he makes his nightly rounds.

skeleton, and the curtain flaps in the wind. When I passed it yesterday evening, it seemed as though someone were crying in it.

Masha. What next . . . [*A pause.*]

Medvedenko. Let us go home, Masha.

Masha [*shakes her head*]. I shall stay here for the night.

Medvedenko [*in an imploring voice*]. Masha, do come! Our baby must be hungry.

Masha. Nonsense. Matryona will feed him. [*A pause.*]

Medvedenko. I am sorry for him. He has been three nights now without his mother.

Masha. You are a bore. In old days you used at least to discuss general subjects, but now it is only home, baby, home, baby—that's all one can get out of you.

Medvedenko. Come along, Masha!

Masha. Go by yourself.

Medvedenko. Your father won't let me have a horse.

Masha. Yes, he will. You ask, and he will.

Medvedenko. Very well, I'll ask. Then you will come tomorrow?

Masha [*taking a pinch of snuff*]. Very well, tomorrow. How you pester me.

[*Enter* Treplev *and* Polina Andreyevna; Treplev *brings in pillows and a quilt, and* Polina Andreyevna *sheets and pillowcases; they lay them on the sofa, then* Treplev *goes to his table and sits down.*]

Masha. What's this for, mother?

Polina. Pyotr Nikolayevitch asked us to make a bed for him in Kostya's room.

Masha. Let me do it. [*Makes the bed.*]

Polina [*sighing*]. Old people are like children [*goes up to the writing table, and leaning on her elbow, looks at the manuscript; a pause*].

Medvedenko. Well, I am going then. Good-bye, Masha. [*Kisses his wife's hand.*] Good-bye, mother. [*Tries to kiss his mother-in-law's hand.*]

Polina [*with vexation*]. Come, if you are going, go.

Medvedenko. Good-bye, Konstantin Gavrilitch.

[Treplev *gives him his hand without speaking;* Medvedenko *goes out.*]

Polina [*looking at the manuscript*]. No one would have guessed or thought that you would have become a real author, Kostya. And now, thank God, they send you money from the magazines. [*Passes her hand over his hair.*] And you have grown good-looking too. . . . Dear, good Kostya, do be a little kinder to my Mashenka!

Masha [*as she makes the bed*]. Leave him alone, mother.

Polina [*to* Treplev]. She is a nice little thing. [*A pause.*] A woman wants nothing, you know, Kostya, so long as you give her a kind look. I know from myself.

[Treplev *gets up from the table and walks away without speaking.*]

Masha. Now you have made him angry. What **induced**[2] you to pester him?

Polina. I feel so sorry for you, Mashenka.

Masha. Much use that is!

Polina. My heart aches for you. I see it all, you know, I understand it all.

Masha. It's all foolishness. There is no such thing as hopeless love except in novels. It's of no consequence. The only thing is one mustn't let oneself go and keep expecting something, waiting for the tide to turn. . . . When love gets into the heart there is nothing to be done but to clear it out. Here they promised to transfer my husband to another district. As soon as I am there, I shall forget it all. . . . I shall tear it out of my heart.

[*Two rooms away a melancholy waltz is played.*]

Polina. That's Kostya playing. He must be depressed.

Masha [*noiselessly dances a few waltz steps*]. The great thing, mother, is not to have him before one's eyes. If they only give my Semyon his transfer, trust me, I shall get over it in a month. It's all nonsense.

[*Door on left opens.* Dorn *and* Medvedenko *wheel in* Sorin *in his chair.*]

Medvedenko. I have six of them at home now. And flour is two kopeks[3] per pound.

Dorn. You've got to look sharp to make both ends meet.

Medvedenko. It's all very well for you to laugh. You've got more money than you know what to do with.

Dorn. Money? After thirty years of practice, my boy, troublesome work during which I could not call my soul my own by day or by night, I only succeeded in saving two thousand rubles, and that I spent not long ago abroad. I have nothing.

Masha [*to her husband*]. You have not gone?

Medvedenko [*guiltily*]. Well, how can I when they won't let me have a horse?

Masha [*with bitter vexation in an undertone*]. I can't bear the sight of you.

[*The wheelchair remains in the left half of the room;* Polina Andreyevna, Masha *and* Dorn *sit down beside it,* Medvedenko *moves mournfully to one side.*]

Dorn. What changes there have been here! The drawing room has been turned into a study.

---

[2] **induced**—persuaded.

[3] kopeks—A kopek is equal to 1/100 of a ruble.

Masha. It is more convenient for Konstantin Gavrilitch to work here. Whenever he likes, he can walk out into the garden and think there. [*A watchman taps.*]

Sorin. Where is my sister?

Dorn. She has gone to the station to meet Trigorin. She will be back directly.

Sorin. Since you thought it necessary to send for my sister, I must be dangerously ill. [*After a silence.*] It's a queer thing, I am dangerously ill and here they don't give me any medicines.

Dorn. Well, what would you like to have? Valerian drops? Soda? Quinine?

Sorin. Ah, he is at his moralizing again! What an infliction it is! [*With a motion of his head towards the sofa.*] Is that bed for me?

Polina. Yes, it's for you, Pyotr Nikolayevitch.

Sorin. Thank you.

Dorn [*hums*]. "The moon is floating in the midnight sky."

Sorin. I want to give Kostya a subject for a story. It ought to be called "The Man who Wished"—*L'homme qui a voulu*. In my youth I wanted to become a literary man—and didn't; I wanted to speak well—and I spoke horribly badly, [*Mimicking himself.*] "and all the rest of it, and all that, and so on, and so forth" . . . and I would go plodding on and on, trying to sum up till I was in a regular perspiration; I wanted to get married—and I didn't; I always wanted to live in town and here I am ending my life in the country—and so on.

Dorn. I wanted to become an actual civil councillor—and I have.

Sorin [*laughs*]. That I had no hankerings after. That happened of itself.

Dorn. To be expressing dissatisfaction with life at sixty-two is really ungracious, you know.

Sorin. What a persistent fellow he is! You might understand that one wants to live!

Dorn. That's just frivolity. It's the law of nature that every life must have an end.

Sorin. You argue like a man who has had enough. You are satisfied and so you are indifferent to life, nothing matters to you. But even you will be afraid to die.

Dorn. The dread of death is an animal fear. One must overcome it. A rational fear of death is only possible for those who believe in eternal life and are conscious of their sins. And you, in the first place, don't believe, and, in the second, what sins have you to worry about? You have served in the courts of justice for twenty-five years—that's all.

Sorin [*laughs*]. Twenty-eight. . . .

[Treplev *comes in and sits down on a stool at* Sorin's *feet.* Masha *never takes her eyes off him.*]

Dorn. We are hindering Konstantin Gavrilitch from working.

Treplev. Oh no, it doesn't matter. [*A pause.*]

Medvedenko. Allow me to ask you, doctor, what town did you like best abroad?

Dorn. Genoa.

Treplev. Why Genoa?

Dorn. The life in the streets is so wonderful there. When you go out of the hotel in the evening, the whole street is packed with people. You wander aimlessly zigzagging about among the crowd, backwards and forwards; you live with it, are psychologically at one with it and begin almost to believe that a world soul[4] is really possible, such as was acted by Nina Zaretchny in your play. And, by the way, where is she now? How is she getting on?

Treplev. I expect she is quite well.

Dorn. I was told that she was leading a rather peculiar life. How was that?

Treplev. That's a long story, doctor.

Dorn. Well, tell it us shortly. [*A pause.*]

Treplev. She ran away from home and had an affair with Trigorin. You know that?

Dorn. I know.

Treplev. She had a child. The child died. Trigorin got tired of her and went back to his old ties, as might have been expected. Though, indeed, he had never abandoned them, but in his weak-willed way contrived to keep both going. As far as I can make out from what I have heard, Nina's private life was a complete failure.

Dorn. And the stage?

Treplev. I fancy that was worse still. She made her début[5] at some holiday place near Moscow, then went to the provinces. All that time I did not lose sight of her, and wherever she went I followed her. She always took big parts, but she acted crudely, without taste, screamingly, with violent gestures. There were moments when she uttered a cry successfully or died successfully, but they were only moments.

Dorn. Then she really has some talent?

Treplev. It was difficult to make it out. I suppose she has. I saw her but she would not see me, and the servants would not admit me at the hotel. I

---

[4] world soul—universal spirit animating the earth and all its inhabitants.

[5] début—first public appearance.

understood her state of mind and did not insist on seeing her [*a pause*]. What more can I tell you? Afterwards, when I was back at home, I had some letters from her—warm, intelligent, interesting letters. She did not complain, but I felt that she was profoundly unhappy; every line betrayed sick overstrained nerves. And her imagination is a little unhinged. She signed herself the Sea Gull. In Pushkin's *Mermaid*[6] the miller says that he is a raven, and in the same way in her letters she kept repeating that she was a sea gull. Now she is here.

Dorn. Here? How do you mean?

Treplev. In the town, staying at an inn. She has been there for five days. I did go to see her, and Marya Ilyinishna here went too, but she won't see anyone. Semyon Semyonitch declares he saw her yesterday afternoon in the fields a mile and a half from here.

Medvedenko. Yes, I saw her. She went in that direction, towards the town. I bowed to her and asked her why she did not come to see us. She said she would come.

Treplev. She won't come. [*A pause.*] Her father and stepmother refuse to recognize her. They have put watchmen about so that she may not even go near the house. [*Walks away with the doctor towards the writing table.*] How easy it is to be a philosopher on paper, doctor, and how difficult it is in life!

Sorin. She was a charming girl.

Dorn. What?

Sorin. She was a charming girl, I say. Actual Civil Councillor Sorin was positively in love with her for a time.

Dorn. The old Lovelace.[7]

[Shamraev's *laugh is heard.*]

Polina. I fancy our people have come back from the station. . . .

Treplev. Yes, I hear mother.

[*Enter Madame Arkadin, Trigorin and with them Shamraev.*]

Shamraev [*as he enters*]. We all grow old and **dilapidated**[8] under the influence of the elements, while you, honored lady, are still young . . . a light blouse, sprightliness, grace. . . .

Madame Arkadin. You want to bring me ill luck again, you tiresome man!

---

[6] Pushkin's *Mermaid*—famous play by Alexander Pushkin (1799–1837), Russia's greatest poet.

[7] Lovelace—fashionable seducer who is the chief male character in the novel *Clarissa Harlowe* (1749), by English writer Samuel Richardson (1689–1761).

[8] **dilapidated**—ruinous; decayed.

Trigorin. How do you do, Pyotr Nikolayevitch! So you are still poorly? That's bad! [*Seeing* Masha, *joyfully.*] Marya Ilyinishna!

Masha. You know me, do you? [*Shakes hands.*]

Trigorin. Married?

Masha. Long ago.

Trigorin. Are you happy? [*Bows to* Dorn *and* Medvedenko, *then hesitatingly approaches* Treplev.] Irina Nikolayevna has told me that you have forgotten the past and are no longer angry.

[Treplev *holds out his hand.*]

Madame Arkadin [*to her son*]. Boris Alexeyevitch has brought the magazine with your new story in it.

Treplev [*taking the magazine, to* Trigorin]. Thank you, you are very kind. [*They sit down.*]

Trigorin. Your admirers send their greetings to you. . . . In Petersburg and Moscow there is great interest in your work and I am continually being asked questions about you. People ask what you are like, how old you are, whether you are dark or fair. Everyone imagines, for some reason, that you are no longer young. And no one knows your real name, as you always publish under a **pseudonym**.[9] You are as mysterious as the Iron Mask.[10]

Treplev. Will you be able to make a long stay?

Trigorin. No, I think I must go back to Moscow tomorrow. I am obliged to. I am in a hurry to finish my novel, and besides, I have promised something for a collection of tales that is being published. It's the old story, in fact.

[*While they are talking* Madame Arkadin *and* Polina Andreyevna *put a card table in the middle of the room and open it out.* Shamraev *lights candles and sets chairs. A game of lotto*[11] *is brought out of the cupboard.*]

Trigorin. The weather has not given me a friendly welcome. There is a cruel wind. If it has dropped by tomorrow morning I shall go to the lake to fish. And I must have a look at the garden and that place where—you remember?—your play was acted. I've got a subject for a story, I only want to revive my recollections of the scene in which it is laid.

Masha [*to her father*]. Father, let my husband have a horse! He must get home.

---

[9] **pseudonym**—assumed name, such as a pen name.

[10] Iron Mask—"the Man in the Iron Mask," a mysterious prisoner confined for over 40 years by French king Louis XIV (1638–1715); in his novel *The Iron Mask*, French writer Alexandre Dumas (1802–1870) presents him as the king's twin brother.

[11] *lotto*—game like bingo.

Shamraev [*mimicking*]. Must get home—a horse! [*Sternly.*] You can see for yourself: they have just been to the station. I can't send them out again.

Masha. But there are other horses. [*Seeing that her father says nothing, waves her hand.*] There's no doing anything with you.

Medvedenko. I can walk, Masha. Really. . . .

Polina [*with a sigh*]. Walk in such weather . . . [*Sits down to the card table.*] Come, friends.

Medvedenko. It is only four miles. Good-bye [*kisses his wife's hand*]. Good-bye, mother. [*His mother-in-law reluctantly holds out her hand for him to kiss.*] I wouldn't trouble anyone, but the baby . . . [*Bows to the company.*] Good-bye. . . . [*Goes out with a guilty step.*]

Shamraev. He can walk right enough. He's not a general.

Polina [*tapping on the table*]. Come, friends. Don't let us waste time, we shall soon be called to supper.

[Shamraev, Masha *and* Dorn *sit down at the table.*]

Madame Arkadin [*to* Trigorin]. When the long autumn evenings come on, they play lotto here. Look, it's the same old lotto that we had when our mother used to play with us, when we were children. Won't you have a game before supper? [*Sits down to the table with* Trigorin.] It's a dull game, but it is not so bad when you are used to it. [*Deals three cards to everyone.*]

Treplev [*turning the pages of the magazine*]. He has read his own story, but he has not even cut mine. [*Puts the magazine down on the writing table, then goes towards door on left; as he passes his mother he kisses her on the head.*]

Madame Arkadin. And you, Kostya?

Treplev. Excuse me, I would rather not . . . I am going out. [*Goes out.*]

Madame Arkadin. The stake is ten kopeks. Put it down for me, doctor, will you?

Dorn. Right.

Masha. Has everyone put down their stakes? I begin . . . Twenty-two.

Madame Arkadin. Yes.

Masha. Three!

Dorn. Right!

Masha. Did you play three? Eight! Eighty-one! Ten!

Shamraev. Don't be in a hurry!

Madame Arkadin. What a reception I had in Harkov! My goodness! I feel dizzy with it still.

Masha. Thirty-four!

[*A melancholy waltz is played behind the scenes.*]

Madame Arkadin. The students gave me an **ovation**.[12] . . . Three baskets of flowers . . . two wreaths and this, see. [*Unfastens a brooch on her throat and lays it on the table.*]

Shamraev. Yes, that is a thing. . . .

Masha. Fifty!

Dorn. Exactly fifty?

Madame Arkadin. I had a wonderful dress. . . . Whatever I don't know, I do know how to dress.

Polina. Kostya is playing the piano; he is depressed, poor fellow.

Shamraev. He is awfully abused in the newspapers.

Masha. Seventy-seven!

Madame Arkadin. As though that mattered!

Trigorin. He never quite comes off. He has not yet hit upon his own medium. There is always something queer and vague, at times almost like delirium. Not a single living character.

Masha. Eleven!

Madame Arkadin [*looking round at* Sorin]. Petrusha, are you bored? [*A pause.*] He is asleep.

Dorn. The actual civil councillor is asleep.

Masha. Seven! Ninety!

Trigorin. If I lived in such a place, beside a lake, do you suppose I should write? I should overcome this passion and should do nothing but fish.

Masha. Twenty-eight!

Trigorin. Catching perch is so delightful!

Dorn. Well, I believe in Konstantin Gavrilitch. There is something in him! There is something in him! He thinks in images; his stories are vivid, full of color and they affect me strongly. The only pity is that he has not got definite aims. He produces an impression and that's all, but you can't get far with nothing but an impression. Irina Nikolayevna, are you glad that your son is a writer?

Madame Arkadin. Only fancy, I have not read anything of his yet. I never have time.

Masha. Twenty-six!

[Treplev comes *in quietly and sits down at his table.*]

Shamraev [*to* Trigorin]. We have still got something here belonging to you, Boris Alexeyevitch.

Trigorin. What's that?

---

[12] **ovation**—prolonged applause.

Shamraev. Konstantin Gavrilitch shot a sea gull and you asked me to get it stuffed for you.

Trigorin. I don't remember! [*Pondering.*] I don't remember!

Masha. Sixty-six! One!

Treplev [*flinging open the window, listens*]. How dark it is! I don't know why I feel so uneasy.

Madame Arkadin. Kostya, shut the window, there's a draft.

[Treplev *shuts the window.*]

Masha. Eighty-eight!

Trigorin. The game is mine!

Madame Arkadin [*gaily*]. Bravo, bravo!

Shamraev. Bravo!

Madame Arkadin. That man always has luck in everything. [*Gets up.*] And now let us go and have something to eat. Our great man has not dined today. We will go on again after supper. [To *her son.*] Kostya, leave your manuscripts and come to supper.

Treplev. I don't want any, mother, I am not hungry.

Madame Arkadin. As you like. [*Wakes* Sorin.] Petrusha, supper! [*Takes* Shamraev's *arm.*] I'll tell you about my reception in Harkov.

[Polina Andreyevna *puts out the candles on the table. Then she and* Dorn *wheel the chair. All go out by door on left; only* Treplev, *sitting at the writing table, is left on the stage.*]

Treplev [*settling himself to write; runs through what he has written already*]. I have talked so much about new forms and now I feel that little by little I am falling into a convention myself. [*Reads.*] "The placard on the wall proclaimed. . . . The pale face in its setting of dark hair." Proclaimed, setting. That's stupid. [*Scratches out.*] I will begin where the hero is awakened by the patter of the rain, and throw out all the rest. The description of the moonlight evening is long and overelaborate. Trigorin has worked out methods for himself, it's easy for him now. . . . With him the broken bottle neck glitters on the dam and the mill wheel casts a black shadow—and there you have the moonlight night, while I have the **tremulous**[13] light, and the soft twinkling of the stars, and the far away strains of the piano dying away in the still fragrant air. . . . It's agonizing. [*A pause.*] I come more and more to the conviction that it is not a question of new and old forms, but that what matters is that a man should write without thinking about forms at all,

---

[13] **tremulous**—quivering.

write because it springs freely from his soul. [*There is a tap at the window nearest to the table.*] What is that? [*Looks out of window.*] There is nothing to be seen. . . . [*Opens the glass door and looks out into the garden.*] Someone ran down the steps. [*Calls*] Who is there? [*Goes out and can be heard walking rapidly along the verandah; returns half a minute later with* Nina Zaretchny.] Nina, Nina!

[Nina *lays her head on his breast and weeps with subdued sobs.*]

Treplev [*moved*]. Nina! Nina! It's you . . . you. . . . It's as though I had foreseen it, all day long my heart has been aching and restless. [*Takes off her hat and cape.*] Oh, my sweet, my precious, she has come at last. Don't let us cry, don't let us!

Nina. There is someone here.

Treplev. No one.

Nina. Lock the doors, someone may come in.

Treplev. No one will come in.

Nina. I know Irina Nikolayevna is here. Lock the doors.

Treplev [*locks the door on right, goes to door on left*]. There is no lock on this one. I'll put a chair against it. [*Puts an armchair against the door.*] Don't be afraid, no one will come.

Nina [*looking intently into his face*]. Let me look at you. [*Looking round.*] It's warm, it's nice. . . . In old days this was the drawing room. Am I very much changed?

Treplev. Yes . . . You are thinner and your eyes are bigger. Nina, how strange it is that I should be seeing you. Why would not you let me see you? Why haven't you come all this time? I know you have been here almost a week. . . . I have been to you several times every day; I stood under your window like a beggar.

Nina. I was afraid that you might hate me. I dream every night that you look at me and don't know me. If only you knew! Ever since I came I have been walking here . . . by the lake. I have been near your house many times and could not bring myself to enter it. Let us sit down. [*They sit down.*] Let us sit down and talk and talk. It's nice here, it's warm and snug. Do you hear the wind? There's a passage in Turgenev, "Well for the man on such a night who sits under the shelter of home, who has a warm corner in safety." I am a sea gull. . . . No, that's not it. [*Rubs her forehead.*] What was I saying? Yes . . . Turgenev . . . "And the Lord help all homeless wanderers!" . . . It doesn't matter. [*Sobs.*]

Treplev. Nina, you are crying again. . . . Nina!

Nina. Never mind, it does me good . . . I haven't cried for two years. Yesterday, late in the evening, I came into the garden to see whether our stage was still there. It is still standing. I cried for the first time after two years and it eased the weight on my heart and made it lighter. You see, I am not crying now. [*Takes him by the hand.*] And so now you are an author. . . . You are an author, I am an actress. . . . We too have been drawn into the whirlpool. I lived joyously like a child— I woke up singing in the morning; I loved you and dreamed of fame, and now? Early tomorrow morning I must go to Yelets third class[14] . . . with peasants, and at Yelets the cultured tradesmen will pester me with attentions. Life is a coarse business!

Treplev. Why to Yelets?

Nina. I have taken an engagement for the whole winter. It is time to go.

Treplev. Nina, I cursed you, I hated you, I tore up your letters and photographs, but I was conscious every minute that my soul is bound to yours for ever. It's not in my power to leave off loving you, Nina. Ever since I lost you and began to get my work published my life has been unbearable—I am wretched. . . . My youth was, as it were, torn away all at once and it seems to me as though I have lived for ninety years already. I call upon you, I kiss the earth on which you have walked; wherever I look I see your face, that tender smile that lighted up the best days of my life. . . .

Nina [*distractedly*]. Why does he talk like this, why does he talk like this?

Treplev. I am alone in the world, warmed by no affection. I am as cold as though I were in a cellar, and everything I write is dry, hard and gloomy. Stay here, Nina, I entreat you, or let me go with you!

[Nina *rapidly puts on her hat and cape.*]

Treplev. Nina, why is this? For God's sake, Nina! [*Looks at her as she puts her things on; a pause.*]

Nina. My horses are waiting at the gate. Don't see me off, I'll go alone. . . . [*Through her tears.*] Give me some water. . . .

Treplev [*gives her some water*]. Where are you going now?

Nina. To the town. [*A pause.*] Is Irina Nikolayevna here?

Treplev. Yes. . . . Uncle was taken worse on Thursday and we telegraphed for her.

Nina. Why do you say that you kissed the earth on which I walked? I ought to be killed. [*Bends over table.*] I am so tired! If I could rest . . . if

---

[14] third class—cheapest railroad fare.

I could rest! [*Raising her head.*] I am a sea gull. . . . No, that's not it. I am an actress. Oh, well! [*Hearing* Madame Arkadin *and* Trigorin *laughing, she listens, then runs to door on left and looks through the keyhole.*] He is here too. . . . [*Turning back to* Treplev.] Oh, well . . . it doesn't matter . . . no. . . . He did not believe in the stage, he always laughed at my dreams and little by little I left off believing in it too, and lost heart. . . . And then I was fretted by love and jealousy, and continually anxious over my little one. . . . I grew petty and trivial, I acted stupidly. . . . I did not know what to do with my arms, I did not know how to stand on the stage, could not control my voice. You can't understand what it feels like when one knows one is acting disgracefully. I am a sea gull. No, that's not it. . . . Do you remember you shot a sea gull? A man came by chance, saw it and, just to pass the time, destroyed it. . . . A subject for a short story. . . . That's not it, though. [*Rubs her forehead.*] What was I saying? . . . I am talking of the stage. Now I am not like that. I am a real actress, I act with enjoyment, with enthusiasm, I am intoxicated when I am on the stage and feel that I am splendid. And since I have been here, I keep walking about and thinking, thinking and feeling that my soul is getting stronger every day. Now I know, I understand, Kostya, that in our work—in acting or writing—what matters is not fame, not glory, not what I dreamed of, but knowing how to be patient. To bear one's cross and have faith. I have faith and it all doesn't hurt so much, and when I think of my vocation I am not afraid of life.

Treplev [*mournfully*]. You have found your path, you know which way you are going, but I am still floating in a chaos of dreams and images, not knowing what use it is to anyone. I have no faith and don't know what my vocation is.

Nina [*listening*]. 'Sh-sh . . . I am going. Good-bye. When I become a great actress, come and look at me. Will you promise? But now . . . [*presses his hand*] it's late. I can hardly stand on my feet. . . . I am worn out and hungry. . . .

Treplev. Stay, I'll give you some supper.

Nina. No, no. . . . Don't see me off, I will go by myself. My horses are close by. . . . So she brought him with her? Well, it doesn't matter. When you see Trigorin, don't say anything to him. . . . I love him! I love him even more than before. . . . A subject for a short story . . . I love him, I love him passionately, I love him to despair. It was nice in old days, Kostya! Do you remember? How clear, warm, joyous and pure life was, what feelings we had—feelings like tender, exquisite flowers. . . . Do you remember? [*Recites.*] "Men, lions, eagles, and partridges, horned deer, geese, spiders, silent fish that dwell in the water, starfishes, and creatures which cannot be seen by the eye—all living things, all living things, all living things, have completed their cycle of sorrow, are extinct. . . . For thousands of years the earth has borne no living creature on its surface, and this poor moon lights its lamp in vain. On the meadow the cranes no longer waken with a cry and there is no sound of the May beetles in the lime trees . . ." [*Impulsively embraces* Treplev *and runs out of the glass door.*]

Treplev [*after a pause*]. It will be a pity if someone meets her in the garden and tells mother. It may upset mother. . . .

[*He spends two minutes in tearing up all his manuscripts and throwing them under the table; then unlocks the door on right and goes out.*]

Dorn [*trying to open the door on left*]. Strange. The door seems to be locked. . . . [*Comes in and puts the armchair in its place.*] An obstacle race.

[*Enter* Madame Arkadin *and* Polina Andreyevna, *behind them* Yakov *carrying a tray with bottles;* Masha; *then* Shamraev *and* Trigorin.]

Madame Arkadin. Put the claret and the beer for Boris Alexeyevitch here on the table. We will play as we drink it. Let us sit down, friends.

Polina [*to* Yakov]. Bring tea too at the same time. [*Lights the candles and sits down to the card table.*]

Shamraev [*leads* Trigorin *to the cupboard*]. Here's the thing I was speaking about just now [*takes the stuffed sea gull from the cupboard*]. This is what you ordered.

Trigorin [*looking at the sea gull*]. I don't remember it. [*Musing.*[15]] I don't remember.

[*The sound of a shot coming from right of stage; everyone starts.*]

Madame Arkadin [*frightened*]. What's that?

Dorn. That's nothing. It must be something in my medicine chest that has gone off. Don't be anxious. [*Goes out at door on right, comes back in half a minute.*] That's what it is. A bottle of ether[16] has exploded. [*Hums.*] "I stand before thee enchanted again. . . ."

Madame Arkadin [*sitting down to the table*]. Oh, how frightened I was. It reminded me of how . . . [*Hides her face in her hands.*] It made me quite dizzy. . . .

---

[15] *Musing*—thinking.

[16] ether—flammable liquid used as an anesthetic.

Dorn [*turning over the leaves of the magazine, to* Trigorin]. There was an article in this two months ago—a letter from America—and I wanted to ask you, among other things [*Puts his arm round* Trigorin's *waist and leads him to the footlights.*] as I am very much interested in the question. . . . [*In a lower tone, dropping his voice.*] Get Irina Nikolayevna away somehow. The fact is, Konstantin Gavrilitch has shot himself. . . . [*Curtain.*]

UNDERSTANDING THE PLAY

Act One

1. Asked why she always wears black, Masha replies, "I am in mourning for my life." What do you think she means?

2. What impression of his mother does Treplev give to his uncle?

3. What views about theater does Treplev express? What do you think motivates him in his view?

4. How does the account of Trigorin that Treplev gives to his uncle differ from the one he gives to Nina? Why do you think they differ?

5. How does Madame Arkadin's behavior at her son's play support the impression of her he gives to his uncle?

Act Two

1. How are Madame Arkadin and Masha contrasted in their approaches to life? How are Sorin and Dorn contrasted?

2. Nina assumes Treplev's gift of the dead sea gull is symbolic. (A symbol is a person, place, object or activity that stands for something beyond itself.) What do you think the sea gull means?

3. How does Trigorin present the creative life?

4. How do Trigorin's observations about the "small writer" reflect Treplev's situation?

5. What is foreshadowed by the story idea Trigorin sketches out at the end of Act Two?

Act Three

1. Why has Masha decided to marry Medvedenko? What do you think their marriage will be like?

2. What does Madame Arkadin's unwillingness to give money to her son or brother convey about her feelings toward them and toward her career?

3. When Madame Arkadin argues with her son about Trigorin, why does it take the form of a dispute about theater?

4. With whom does Madame Arkadin's behavior seem the most sincere—her son or Trigorin? Why do you think so?

5. At the end of Act Three, Nina has decided to become an actress. Assuming that Madame Arkadin reflects the type of personality required to be a success in the theater, how would you estimate Nina's chances?

Act Four

1. What impression do you get of Masha and Medvedenko's marriage? How closely does this impression agree with what you anticipated in Act Three?

2. Why do you think Nina has come to see herself as "the Sea Gull"?

3. What is the dramatic function of the lotto game?

4. What do you think prompts Treplev to shoot himself?

ANALYZING THE PLAY

1. Chekhov described *The Sea Gull* as a comedy. What comic elements do you find in this play?

2. The conflict in a play is the struggle between opposing forces that gives movement to the dramatic plot. What is the fundamental conflict in *The Sea Gull*?

3. The climax—or crisis—in the plot is the turning point in the struggle when one of the contending forces gets the upper hand. In *The Sea Gull,* where does this turning point occur?

4 How much are Treplev and Nina victims of circumstance and how much are they to blame for their own problems?

5. Like his creator Chekhov, Dorn is a doctor. In what ways do you think Dorn might serve as an authorial voice in *The Sea Gull*?

6. Boredom is a persistent problem for the characters in Chekhov's dramas. Which characters in *The Sea Gull* seem to suffer most acutely from boredom? Which seem least affected by it?

Federico García Lorca ▶

Blood Wedding

BY FEDERICO GARCÍA LORCA

Beginning with the works of Ibsen (see page 380), realism has been the dominant mode in modern drama. However, other anti-realist approaches to theater have coexisted with it. One of these was symbolist drama, developed in the 1890s, in which the dramatic action, characters, setting, and language are all reflections of the playwright's inner life. A more extreme form of symbolism was expressionism, which developed during World War I. Influenced by the horrors of the war and the insights of psychoanalysis, expressionist theater sought to reveal the fragmented inner life of humanity through the presentations of fantasies, hallucinations, and nightmares. Both symbolism and expressionism influenced the drama of Spanish poet and playwright Federico García Lorca (1898–1936).

A Rich Heritage

Born near the Spanish city of Granada, Lorca came from Andalusia, a region whose culture fuses Spanish, Arabic, and Gypsy elements. These varied cultures all contributed to the richness of his poetry and drama. Even as a child, Lorca had already begun creating plays, using a toy theater or costuming family members and servants. Because he developed simultaneously as a dramatist and a poet, many of the same elements characterize his work in both literary forms, including his love for traditional and popular poetry and his preoccupations with the naïve, with fantasy, and with violence. In addition to the traditional cultures of Andalusia, other important influences on Lorca's work were modern movements in poetry, music, and art. Besides being a poet, Lorca was also a talented pianist and painter, and all these arts find expression in his plays.

Theater and Politics

In the early 1930s, with the sponsorship of the government, Lorca organized a touring theater company and traveled throughout Spain performing all kinds of plays for mostly peasant audiences. The company's varied repertoire and the necessity of applying himself to all aspects of production deepened both Lorca's knowledge of theater and his understanding of the culture of rural Spain. Like the ancient Greek dramatists, Lorca felt that theater served an important social function: "A theater that is sensitive and well ordered in all its branches, from tragedy to vaudeville, can in a few years change the sensibility of a people; and a shattered theater, in which hoofs substitute for wings, can debase and benumb an entire nation." Between 1936 and 1939 the Spanish Civil War was fought between the Loyalist supporters of Spain's left-wing Republic and the right-wing followers of General Francisco Franco. Although Lorca's poetry and drama were not overtly political, he became an early victim of the brutal violence that was convulsing Spanish society. Arrested in August 1936 by Franco's partisans, he was executed without trial, becoming, ironically, a political martyr.

A Rural Tragedy

Lorca's source for Blood Wedding (1933) was a news item about an event that had taken place in his homeland of Andalusia. On her wedding day, a bride had fled with the man whom she secretly loved. When she and her lover were overtaken, her husband and lover killed each other. Lorca transformed this simple event into a tragedy whose fateful inevitability and menacing, doom-laden atmosphere recalls Greek drama.

CHARACTERS

The **Mother**
The **Bride**
The **Mother-in-Law**
Leonardo's Wife
The **Servant Woman**
The **Neighbor Woman**
Young Girls

Leonardo
The **Bridegroom**
The **Bride's Father**
The **Moon**
Woodcutters
Young Men

Act One, Scene One

[*A room painted yellow.*]
Bridegroom [*entering*]. Mother.
Mother. What?
Bridegroom. I'm going.
Mother. Where?
Bridegroom. To the vineyard.
[*He starts to go.*]
Mother. Wait.
Bridegroom. You want something?
Mother. Your breakfast, son.
Bridegroom. Forget it. I'll eat grapes. Give me the knife.
Mother. What for?
Bridegroom [*laughing*]. To cut the grapes with.
Mother [*muttering as she looks for the knife*]. Knives, knives. Cursed be all knives, and the scoundrel who invented them.
Bridegroom. Let's talk about something else.
Mother. And guns and pistols and the smallest little knife—and even hoes and pitchforks.

Bridegroom. All right.

Mother. Everything that can slice a man's body. A handsome man, full of young life, who goes out to the vineyards or to his own olive groves—his own because he's inherited them . . .

Bridegroom [*lowering his head*]. Be quiet.

Mother. . . . and then that man doesn't come back. Or if he does come back it's only for someone to cover him over with a palm leaf or a plate of rock salt so he won't bloat.[1] I don't know how you dare carry a knife on your body—or how I let this serpent [*She takes a knife from a kitchen chest.*] stay in the chest.

Bridegroom. Have you had your say?

Mother. If I lived to be a hundred I'd talk of nothing else. First your father; to me he smelled like a carnation and I had him for barely three years. Then your brother. Oh, is it right—how can it be—that a small thing like a knife or a pistol can finish off a man—a bull of a man? No, I'll never be quiet. The months pass and the hopelessness of it stings in my eyes and even to the roots of my hair.

Bridegroom [*forcefully*]. Let's quit this talk!

Mother. No. No. Let's not quit this talk. Can anyone bring me your father back? Or your brother? Then there's the jail. What do they mean, jail? They eat there, smoke there, play music there! My dead men choking with weeds, silent, turning to dust. Two men like two beautiful flowers. The killers in jail, carefree, looking at the mountains.

Bridegroom. Do you want me to go kill them?

Mother. No . . . If I talk about it it's because . . . Oh, how can I help talking about it, seeing you go out that door? It's . . . I don't like you to carry a knife. It's just that . . . that I wish you wouldn't go out to the fields.

Bridegroom [*laughing*]. Oh, come now!

Mother. I'd like it if you were a woman. Then you wouldn't be going out to the arroyo[2] now and we'd both of us embroider flounces[3] and little woolly dogs.

Bridegroom [*He puts his arm around his* Mother *and laughs.*]. Mother, what if I should take you with me to the vineyards?

Mother. What would an old lady do in the vineyards? Were you going to put me down under the young vines?

---

[1] cover . . . bloat—folk practices used to keep a dead body from swelling up.

[2] arroyo—narrow canyon, ravine.

[3] flounces—ornamental trimmings, such as for a skirt.

Bridegroom [*lifting her in his arms*]. Old lady, old lady—you little old, little old lady!

Mother. Your father, he used to take me. That's the way with men of good stock; good blood. Your grandfather left a son on every corner. That's what I like. Men, men; wheat, wheat.

Bridegroom. And I, Mother?

Mother. You, what?

Bridegroom. Do I need to tell you again?

Mother [*seriously*]. Oh!

Bridegroom. Do you think it's bad?

Mother. No.

Bridegroom. Well, then?

Mother. I don't really know. Like this, suddenly, it always surprises me. I know the girl is good. Isn't she? Well behaved. Hard working. Kneads her bread, sews her skirts, but even so when I say her name I feel as though someone had hit me on the forehead with a rock.

Bridegroom. Foolishness.

Mother. More than foolishness. I'll be left alone. Now only you are left me—I hate to see you go.

Bridegroom. But you'll come with us.

Mother. No. I can't leave your father and brother here alone. I have to go to them every morning and if I go away it's possible one of the Félix family, one of the killers, might die—and they'd bury him next to ours. And that'll never happen! Oh, no! That'll never happen! Because I'd dig them out with my nails and, all by myself, crush them against the wall.

Bridegroom [*sternly*]. There you go again.

Mother. Forgive me. [*Pause.*] How long have you known her?

Bridegroom. Three years. I've been able to buy the vineyard.

Mother. Three years. She used to have another sweetheart, didn't she?

Bridegroom. I don't know. I don't think so. Girls have to look at what they'll marry.

Mother. Yes. I looked at nobody. I looked at your father, and when they killed him I looked at the wall in front of me. One woman with one man, and that's all.

Bridegroom. You know my girl's good.

Mother. I don't doubt it. All the same, I'm sorry not to have known what her mother was like.

Bridegroom. What difference does it make now?

Mother [*looking at him*]. Son.

Bridegroom. What is it?

Mother. That's true! You're right! When do you want me to ask for her?

Bridegroom [*happily*]. Does Sunday seem all right to you?

Mother [*seriously*]. I'll take her the bronze earrings, they're very old—and you buy her . . .

Bridegroom. You know more about that . . .

Mother. . . . you buy her some open-work stockings—and for you, two suits—three! I have no one but you now!

Bridegroom. I'm going. Tomorrow I'll go see her.

Mother. Yes, yes—and see if you can make me happy with six grandchildren—or as many as you want, since your father didn't live to give them to me.

Bridegroom. The first-born for you!

Mother. Yes, but have some girls. I want to embroider and make lace, and be at peace.

Bridegroom. I'm sure you'll love my wife.

Mother. I'll love her.

[*She starts to kiss him but changes her mind.*]

Go on. You're too big now for kisses. Give them to your wife.

[*Pause. To herself.*] When she is your wife.

Bridegroom. I'm going.

Mother. And that land around the little mill—work it over. You've not taken good care of it.

Bridegroom. You're right. I will.

Mother. God keep you.

[*The* Son *goes out. The* Mother *remains seated—her back to the door. A* Neighbor Woman *with a kerchief on her head appears in the door.*]

Come in.

Neighbor. How are you?

Mother. Just as you see me.

Neighbor. I came down to the store and stopped in to see you. We live so far away!

Mother. It's twenty years since I've been up to the top of the street.

Neighbor. You're looking well.

Mother. You think so?

Neighbor. Things happen. Two days ago they brought in my neighbor's son with both arms sliced off by the machine.

[*She sits down.*]

Mother. Rafael?

Neighbor. Yes. And there you have him. Many times I've thought your son and mine are better off where they are—sleeping, resting—not running the risk of being left helpless.

Mother. Hush. That's all just something thought up—but no consolation.

Neighbor [*sighing*]. Ay!

Mother [*sighing*]. Ay!

[*Pause.*]

Neighbor [*sadly*]. Where's your son?

Mother. He went out.

Neighbor. He finally bought the vineyard!

Mother. He was lucky.

Neighbor. Now he'll get married.

Mother [*As though reminded of something, she draws her chair near the Neighbor.*]. Listen.

Neighbor [*in a confidential manner*]. Yes. What is it?

Mother. You know my son's sweetheart?

Neighbor. A good girl!

Mother. Yes, but . . .

Neighbor. But who knows her really well? There's nobody. She lives out there alone with her father—so far away—fifteen miles from the nearest house. But she's a good girl. Used to being alone.

Mother. And her mother?

Neighbor. Her mother I *did* know. Beautiful. Her face glowed like a saint's—but *I* never liked her. She didn't love her husband.

Mother [*sternly*]. Well, what a lot of things certain people know!

Neighbor. I'm sorry. I didn't mean to offend—but it's true. Now, whether she was decent or not nobody said. That wasn't discussed. She was **haughty.**[4]

Mother. There you go again!

Neighbor. You asked me.

Mother. I wish no one knew anything about them—either the live one or the dead one—that they were like two thistles no one even names but cuts off at the right moment.

Neighbor. You're right. Your son is worth a lot.

Mother. Yes—a lot. That's why I look after him. They told me the girl had a sweetheart some time ago.

---

[4] **haughty**—proud.

Neighbor. She was about fifteen. He's been married two years now—to a cousin of hers, as a matter of fact. But nobody remembers about their engagement.

Mother. How do you remember it?

Neighbor. Oh, what questions you ask!

Mother. We like to know all about the things that hurt us. Who was the boy?

Neighbor. Leonardo.

Mother. What Leonardo?

Neighbor. Leonardo Félix.

Mother. Félix!

Neighbor. Yes, but—how is Leonardo to blame for anything? He was eight years old when those things happened.

Mother. That's true. But I hear that name—Félix—and it's all the same. [*Muttering*] Félix, a slimy mouthful. [*She spits.*]

It makes me spit—spit so I won't kill!

Neighbor. Control yourself. What good will it do?

Mother. No good. But you see how it is.

Neighbor. Don't get in the way of your son's happiness. Don't say anything to him. You're old. So am I. It's time for you and me to keep quiet.

Mother. I'll say nothing to him.

Neighbor [*kissing her*]. Nothing.

Mother [*calmly*]. Such things . . . !

Neighbor. I'm going. My men will soon be coming in from the fields.

Mother. Have you ever known such a hot sun?

Neighbor. The children carrying water out to the reapers are black with it. Goodbye, woman.

Mother. Goodbye.

[*The* Mother *starts toward the door at the left. Halfway there she stops and slowly crosses herself.*]

[*Curtain.*]

Act One, Scene Two

[*A room painted rose with copperware and wreaths of common flowers. In the center of the room is a table with a tablecloth. It is morning.*

Leonardo's Mother-in-Law *sits in one corner holding a child in her arms and rocking it. His* Wife *is in the other corner mending stockings.*]

Mother-in-Law. Lullaby, my baby
once there was a big horse
who didn't like water.
The water was black there
under the branches.
When it reached the bridge
it stopped and it sang.
Who can say, my baby,
what the stream holds
with its long tail
in its green parlor?

Wife [*softly*]. Carnation, sleep and dream,
the horse won't drink from the stream.

Mother-in-Law. My rose, asleep now lie,
the horse is starting to cry.
His poor hooves were bleeding,
his long mane was frozen,
and deep in his eyes
stuck a silvery dagger.
Down he went to the river,
Oh, down he went down!
And his blood was running,
Oh, more than the water.

Wife. Carnation, sleep and dream,
the horse won't drink from the stream.

Mother-in-Law. My rose, asleep now lie,
the horse is starting to cry.

Wife. He never did touch
the **dank**[5] river shore
though his muzzle was warm
and with silvery flies.
So, to the hard mountains
he could only whinny
just when the dead stream
covered his throat.
Ay-y-y, for the big horse
who didn't like water!

---

[5] **dank**—unpleasantly wet and cold.

Ay-y-y, for the snow-wound,
big horse of the dawn!

Mother-in-Law. Don't come in! Stop him
and close up the window
with branches of dreams
and a dream of branches.

Wife. My baby is sleeping.

Mother-in-Law. My baby is quiet.

Wife. Look, horse, my baby
has him a pillow.

Mother-in-Law. His cradle is metal.

Wife. His quilt a fine fabric.

Mother-in-Law. Lullaby, my baby.

Wife. Ay-y-y, for the big horse
who didn't like water!

Mother-in-Law. Don't come near, don't come in!
Go away to the mountains
and through the gray valleys,
that's where your mare is.

Wife [*looking at the baby*]. My baby is sleeping.

Mother-in-Law. My baby is resting.

Wife [*softly*]. Carnation, sleep and dream,
The horse won't drink from the stream.

Mother-in-Law [*getting up, very softly*]. My rose, asleep now lie
for the horse is starting to cry.

[*She carries the child out. Leonardo enters.*]

Leonardo. Where's the baby?

Wife. He's sleeping.

Leonardo. Yesterday he wasn't well. He cried during the night.

Wife. Today he's like a dahlia.[6] And you? Were you at the blacksmith's?

Leonardo. I've just come from there. Would you believe it? For more than
two months he's been putting new shoes on the horse and they're
always coming off. As far as I can see he pulls them off on the stones.

Wife. Couldn't it just be that you use him so much?

Leonardo. No. I almost never use him.

Wife. Yesterday the neighbors told me they'd seen you on the far side of
the plains.

---

[6] dahlia—flower with showy blossoms.

Leonardo. Who said that?

Wife. The women who gather capers.[7] It certainly surprised me. Was it you?

Leonardo. No. What would I be doing there, in that wasteland?

Wife. That's what I said. But the horse was streaming sweat.

Leonardo. Did you see him?

Wife. No. Mother did.

Leonardo. Is she with the baby?

Wife. Yes. Do you want some lemonade?

Leonardo. With good cold water.

Wife. And then you didn't come to eat!

Leonardo. I was with the wheat weighers. They always hold me up.

Wife [*very tenderly, while she makes the lemonade*]. Did they pay you a good price?

Leonardo. Fair.

Wife. I need a new dress and the baby a bonnet with ribbons.

Leonardo [*getting up*]. I'm going to take a look at him.

Wife. Be careful. He's asleep.

Mother-in-Law [*coming in*]. Well! Who's been racing the horse that way? He's down there, worn out, his eyes popping from their sockets as though he'd come from the ends of the earth.

Leonardo [*acidly*]. I have.

Mother-in-Law. Oh, excuse me! He's your horse.

Wife [*timidly*]. He was at the wheat buyers.

Mother-in-Law. He can burst for all of me!

[*She sits down. Pause.*]

Wife. Your drink. Is it cold?

Leonardo. Yes.

Wife. Did you hear they're going to ask for my cousin?

Leonardo. When?

Wife. Tomorrow. The wedding will be within a month. I hope they're going to invite us.

Leonardo [*gravely*[8]]. I don't know.

Mother-in-Law. His mother, I think, wasn't very happy about the match.

Leonardo. Well, she may be right. She's a girl to be careful with.

Wife. I don't like to have you thinking bad things about a good girl.

---

[7] capers—buds of a Mediterranean shrub, pickled and used for garnish or as a seasoning.

[8] *gravely*—seriously.

Mother-in-Law [*meaningfully*]. If he does, it's because he knows her. Didn't you know he courted her for three years?

Leonardo. But I left her.

[*To his* Wife.] Are you going to cry now? Quit that!

[*He **brusquely**[9] pulls her hands away from her face.*]

Let's go see the baby.

[*They go in with their arms around each other. A* Girl *appears. She is happy. She enters running.*]

Girl. Señora.

Mother-in-Law. What is it?

Girl. The groom came to the store and he's bought the best of everything they had.

Mother-in-Law. Was he alone?

Girl. No. With his Mother. Stern, tall.

[*She imitates her.*]

And such extravagance!

Mother-in-Law. They have money.

Girl. And they bought some open-work stockings! Oh, such stockings! A woman's dream of stockings! Look: a swallow here,

[*She points to her ankle.*] a ship here,

[*She points to her calf.*] and here,

[*She points to her thigh.*] a rose!

Mother-in-Law. Child!

Girl. A rose with the seeds and the stem! Oh! All in silk.

Mother-in-Law. Two rich families are being brought together.

[Leonardo *and his* Wife *appear.*]

Girl. I came to tell you what they're buying.

Leonardo [*loudly*]. We don't care.

Wife. Leave her alone.

Mother-in-Law. Leonardo, it's not that important.

Girl. Please excuse me.

[*She leaves, weeping.*]

Mother-in-Law. Why do you always have to make trouble with people?

Leonardo. I didn't ask for your opinion.

[*He sits down.*]

Mother-in-Law. Very well.

[*Pause.*]

---

[9] **brusquely**—roughly, abruptly.

Wife [*to* Leonardo]. What's the matter with you? What idea've you got boiling there inside your head? Don't leave me like this, not knowing anything.

Leonardo. Stop that.

Wife. No. I want you to look at me and tell me.

Leonardo. Let me alone.

[*He rises.*]

Wife. Where are you going, love?

Leonardo [*sharply*]. Can't you shut up?

Mother-in-Law [*energetically, to her daughter*]. Be quiet!

[Leonardo *goes out.*]

    The baby!

[*She goes into the bedroom and comes out again with the baby in her arms. The wife has remained standing, unmoving.*]

Mother-in-Law. His poor hooves were bleeding,

    his long mane was frozen,

    and deep in his eyes

    stuck a silvery dagger.

    Down he went to the river,

    Oh, down he went down!

    And his blood was running,

    Oh, more than the water.

Wife [*turning slowly, as though dreaming*].

    Carnation, sleep and dream,

    the horse is drinking from the stream.

Mother-in-Law. My rose, asleep now lie

    the horse is starting to cry.

Wife. Lullaby, my baby.

Mother-in-Law. Ay-y-y, for the big horse

    who didn't like water!

Wife [*dramatically*]. Don't come near, don't come in!

    Go away to the mountains!

    Ay-y-y, for the snow-wound,

    big horse of the dawn!

Mother-in-Law [*weeping*]. My baby is sleeping . . .

Wife [*weeping, as she slowly moves closer*]. My baby is resting . . .

Mother-in-Law. Carnation, sleep and dream,

    the horse won't drink from the stream.

Wife [*weeping, and leaning on the table*]. My rose, asleep now lie,
  the horse is starting to cry.
[*Curtain.*]

Act One, Scene Three

[*Interior of the cave where the* Bride *lives. At the back is a cross of large rose-colored flowers. The round doors have lace curtains with rose-colored ties. Around the walls, which are of a white and hard material, are round fans, blue jars, and little mirrors.*]

Servant. Come right in . . .

[*She is very* **affable**,[10] *full of humble* **hypocrisy**.[11] *The* Bridegroom *and his* Mother *enter. The* Mother *is dressed in black satin and wears a lace mantilla;[12] the* Bridegroom *in black corduroy with a great golden chain.*]

  Won't you sit down? They'll be right here.

[*She leaves. The* Mother *and* Son *are left sitting motionless as statues. Long pause.*]

Mother. Did you wear the watch?

Bridegroom. Yes.

[*He takes it out and looks at it.*]

Mother. We have to be back on time. How far away these people live!

Bridegroom. But this is good land.

Mother. Good; but much too lonesome. A four hour trip and not one
  house, not one tree.

Bridegroom. This is the wasteland.

Mother. Your father would have covered it with trees.

Bridegroom. Without water?

Mother. He would have found some. In the three years we were married
  he planted ten cherry trees, [*remembering*] those three walnut trees by
  the mill, a whole vineyard and a plant called Jupiter which had scar-
  let flowers—but it dried up.

[*Pause.*]

Bridegroom [*referring to the* Bride]. She must be dressing.

[*The* Bride's Father *enters. He is very old, with shining white hair. His head is bowed. The* Mother *and the* Bridegroom *rise. They shake hands in silence.*]

Father. Was it a long trip?

Mother. Four hours.

[*They sit down.*]

---

[10] **affable**—friendly, pleasant.

[11] **hypocrisy**—false show (here, of humility).

[12] *mantilla*—shawl.

Father. You must have come the longest way.

Mother. I'm too old to come along the cliffs by the river.

Bridegroom. She gets dizzy.

[*Pause.*]

Father. A good hemp[13] harvest.

Bridegroom. A really good one.

Father. When I was young this land didn't even grow hemp. We've had to punish it, even weep over it, to make it give us anything useful.

Mother. But now it does. Don't complain. I'm not here to ask you for anything.

Father [*smiling*]. You're richer than I. Your vineyards are worth a fortune. Each young vine a silver coin. But—do you know?—what bothers me is that our lands are separated. I like to have everything together. One thorn I have in my heart, and that's the little orchard there, stuck in between my fields—and they won't sell it to me for all the gold in the world.

Bridegroom. That's the way it always is.

Father. If we could just take twenty teams of oxen and move your vineyards over here, and put them down on that hillside, how happy I'd be!

Mother. But why?

Father. What's mine is hers and what's yours is his. That's why. Just to see it all together. How beautiful it is to bring things together!

Bridegroom. And it would be less work.

Mother. When I die, you could sell ours and buy here, right alongside.

Father. Sell, sell? Bah! Buy, my friend, buy everything. If I had had sons I would have bought all this mountainside right up to the part with the stream. It's not good land, but strong arms can make it good, and since no people pass by, they don't steal your fruit and you can sleep in peace.

[*Pause.*]

Mother. You know what I'm here for.

Father. Yes.

Mother. And?

Father. It seems all right to me. They have talked it over.

Mother. My son has money and knows how to manage it.

Father. My daughter too.

---

[13] hemp—plant grown for fiber used in making rope and coarse cloth.

Mother. My son is handsome. He's never known a woman. His good name is cleaner than a sheet spread out in the sun.

Father. No need to tell you about my daughter. At three, when the morning star shines, she prepares the bread. She never talks: soft as wool, she embroiders all kinds of fancy work and she can cut a strong cord with her teeth.

Mother. God bless her house.

Father. May God bless it.

[*The* Servant *appears with two trays. One with drinks and the other with sweets.*]

Mother [*to the* Son]. When would you like the wedding?

Bridegroom. Next Thursday.

Father. The day on which she'll be exactly twenty-two years old.

Mother. Twenty-two! My oldest son would be that age if he were alive. Warm and manly as he was, he'd be living now if men hadn't invented knives.

Father. One mustn't think about that.

Mother. Every minute. Always a hand on your breast.

Father. Thursday, then? Is that right?

Bridegroom. That's right.

Father. You and I and the bridal couple will go in a carriage to the church which is very far from here; the wedding party on the carts and horses they'll bring with them.

Mother. Agreed.

[*The* Servant *passes through.*]

Father. Tell her she may come in now.

[*To the* Mother.] I shall be much pleased if you like her.

[*The* Bride *appears. Her hands fall in a modest pose and her head is bowed.*]

Mother. Come here. Are you happy?

Bride. Yes, señora.

Father. You shouldn't be so solemn. After all, she's going to be your mother.

Bride. I'm happy. I've said "yes" because I wanted to.

Mother. Naturally.

[*She takes her by the chin.*]

Look at me.

Father. She resembles my wife in every way.

Mother. Yes? What a beautiful glance! Do you know what it is to be married, child?

Bride [*seriously*]. I do.

Mother. A man, some children and a wall two yards thick for everything else.

Bridegroom. Is anything else needed?

Mother. No. Just that you all live—that's it! Live long!

Bride. I'll know how to keep my word.

Mother. Here are some gifts for you.

Bride. Thank you.

Father. Shall we have something?

Mother. Nothing for me.

[*To the* Son.] But you?

Bridegroom. Yes, thank you.

[*He takes one sweet, the* Bride *another.*]

Father [*to the* Bridegroom]. Wine?

Mother. He doesn't touch it.

Father. All the better.

[*Pause. All are standing.*]

Bridegroom [*to the* Bride]. I'll come tomorrow.

Bride. What time?

Bridegroom. Five.

Bride. I'll be waiting for you.

Bridegroom. When I leave your side I feel a great emptiness, and something like a knot in my throat.

Bride. When you are my husband you won't have it any more.

Bridegroom. That's what I tell myself.

Mother. Come. The sun doesn't wait.

[*To the* Father.] Are we agreed on everything?

Father. Agreed.

Mother [*to the* Servant]. Goodbye, woman.

Servant. God go with you!

[*The* Mother *kisses the* Bride *and they begin to leave in silence.*]

Mother [*at the door*]. Goodbye, daughter.

[*The* Bride *answers with her hand.*]

Father. I'll go out with you.

[*They leave.*]

Servant. I'm bursting to see the presents.

Bride [*Sharply*]. Stop that!

Servant. Oh, child, show them to me.

Bride. I don't want to.

Servant. At least the stockings. They say they're all open work. Please!

Bride. I said no.

Servant. Well, my Lord. All right then. It looks as if you didn't want to get married.

Bride [*biting her hand in anger*]. Ay-y-y!

Servant. Child, child! What's the matter with you? Are you sorry to give up your queen's life? Don't think of bitter things. Have you any reason to? None. Let's look at the presents.

[*She takes the box.*]

Bride [*holding her by the wrists*]. Let go.

Servant. Ay-y-y, girl!

Bride. Let go, I said.

Servant. You're stronger than a man.

Bride. Haven't I done a man's work? I wish I were.

Servant. Don't talk like that.

Bride. Quiet, I said. Let's talk about something else.

[*The light is fading from the stage. Long pause.*]

Servant. Did you hear a horse last night?

Bride. What time?

Servant. Three.

Bride. It might have been a stray horse—from the herd.

Servant. No. It carried a rider.

Bride. How do you know?

Servant. Because I saw him. He was standing by your window. It shocked me greatly.

Bride. Maybe it was my fiancé. Sometimes he comes by at that time.

Servant. No.

Bride. You saw him?

Servant. Yes.

Bride. Who was it?

Servant. It was Leonardo.

Bride [*strongly*]. Liar! You liar! Why should he come here?

Servant. He came.

Bride. Shut up! Shut your cursed mouth.

[*The sound of a horse is heard.*]

Servant [*at the window*]. Look. Lean out. Was it Leonardo?

Bride. It was!

[*Quick Curtain.*]

Act Two, Scene One

[*The entrance hall of the Bride's house. A large door in the back. It is night. The* Bride *enters wearing ruffled white petticoats full of laces and embroidered bands, and a sleeveless white bodice.*[1] *The* Servant *is dressed the same way.*]

Servant. I'll finish combing your hair out here.

Bride. It's too warm to stay in there.

Servant. In this country it doesn't even cool off at dawn.

[*The* Bride *sits on a low chair and looks into a little hand mirror. The* Servant *combs her hair.*]

Bride. My mother came from a place with lots of trees—from a fertile country.

Servant. And she was so happy!

Bride. But she wasted away here.

Servant. Fate.

Bride. As we're all wasting away here. The very walls give off heat. Ay-y-y! Don't pull so hard.

Servant. I'm only trying to fix this wave better. I want it to fall over your forehead.

[*The* Bride *looks at herself in the mirror.*] How beautiful you are! Ay-y-y!

[*She kisses her passionately.*]

Bride [*seriously*]. Keep right on combing.

Servant [*combing*]. Oh, lucky you—going to put your arms around a man; and kiss him; and feel his weight.

Bride. Hush.

Servant. And the best part will be when you'll wake up and you'll feel him at your side and when he caresses your shoulders with his breath, like a little nightingale's feather.

Bride [*sternly*]. Will you be quiet.

Servant. But, child! What *is* a wedding? A wedding is just that and nothing more. Is it the sweets—or the bouquets of flowers? No. It's a shining bed and a man and a woman.

Bride. But you shouldn't talk about it.

Servant. Oh, *that's* something else again. But fun enough too.

Bride. Or bitter enough.

Servant. I'm going to put the orange blossoms on from here to here, so the wreath will shine out on top of your hair.

---

[1] *bodice*—part of a woman's dress above the waistline.

[*She tries on the sprigs of orange blossom.*]

Bride [*looking at herself in the mirror*]. Give it to me.

[*She takes the wreath, looks at it and lets her head fall in discouragement.*]

Servant. Now what's the matter?

Bride. Leave me alone.

Servant. This is no time for you to start feeling sad.

[*Encouragingly.*] Give me the wreath.

[*The* Bride *takes the wreath and hurls it away.*]

    Child! You're just asking God to punish you, throwing the wreath on the floor like that. Raise your head! Don't you want to get married? Say it. You can still withdraw.

[*The* Bride *rises.*]

Bride. Storm clouds. A chill wind that cuts through my heart. Who hasn't felt it?

Servant. You love your sweetheart, don't you?

Bride. I love him.

Servant. Yes, yes. I'm sure you do.

Bride. But this is a very serious step.

Servant. You've got to take it.

Bride. I've already given my word.

Servant. I'll put on the wreath.

Bride [*She sits down.*]. Hurry. They should be arriving by now.

Servant. They've already been at least two hours on the way.

Bride. How far is it from here to the church?

Servant. Five leagues[2] by the stream, but twice that by the road.

[*The* Bride *rises and the* Servant *grows excited as she looks at her*]

Servant. Awake, O Bride, awaken,

    On your wedding morning waken!

    The world's rivers may all

    Bear along your bridal Crown!

Bride [*smiling*]. Come now.

Servant [*enthusiastically kissing her and dancing around her*].

    Awake,

    with the fresh bouquet

    of flowering laurel.[3]

    Awake,

---

[2] Five leagues—15 miles (a league equals three miles).

[3] laurel—tree whose dark green, glossy leaves are used to make ornaments.

by the trunk and branch
of the laurels!

[*The banging of the front door latch is heard.*]

Bride. Open the door! That must be the first guests.

[*She leaves. The* Servant *opens the door.*]

Servant [*in astonishment*]. You!

Leonardo. Yes, me. Good morning.

Servant. The first one!

Leonardo. Wasn't I invited?

Servant. Yes.

Leonardo. That's why I'm here.

Servant. Where's your wife?

Leonardo. I came on my horse. She's coming by the road.

Servant. Didn't you meet anyone?

Leonardo. I *passed* them on my horse.

Servant. You're going to kill that horse with so much racing.

Leonardo. When he dies, he's dead!

[*Pause.*]

Servant. Sit down. Nobody's up yet.

Leonardo. Where's the bride?

Servant. I'm just on my way to dress her.

Leonardo. The bride! She ought to be happy!

Servant [*changing the subject*]. How's the baby?

Leonardo. What baby?

Servant. Your son.

Leonardo [*remembering, as though in a dream*]. Ah!

Servant. Are they bringing him?

Leonardo. No.

[*Pause. Voices sing distantly.*]

Voices. Awake, O Bride, awaken,
    on your wedding morning waken!

Leonardo. Awake, O Bride, awaken,
    on your wedding morning waken!

Servant. It's the guests. They're still quite a way off.

Leonardo. The bride's going to wear a big wreath, isn't she? But it ought not to be so large. One a little smaller would look better on her. Has the groom already brought her the orange blossom that must be worn on the breast?

Bride [*appearing, still in petticoats and wearing the wreath*]. He brought it.

Servant [*sternly*]. Don't come out like that.

Bride. What does it matter? [*Seriously.*] Why do you ask if they brought the orange blossom? Do you have something in mind?

Leonardo. Nothing. What would I have in mind? [*Drawing near her.*] You, you know me; you know I don't. Tell me so. What have I ever meant to you? Open your memory, refresh it. But two oxen and an ugly little hut are almost nothing. That's the thorn.

Bride. What have you come here to do?

Leonardo. To see your wedding.

Bride. Just as I saw yours!

Leonardo. Tied up by you, done with your two hands. Oh, they can kill me but they can't spit on me. But even money, which shines so much, spits sometimes.

Bride. Liar!

Leonardo. I don't want to talk. I'm hot-blooded and I don't want to shout so all these hills will hear me.

Bride. My shouts would be louder.

Servant. You'll have to stop talking like this.

[*To the* Bride.] You don't have to talk about what's past.

[*The* Servant *looks around uneasily at the doors.*]

Bride. She's right. I shouldn't even talk to you. But it offends me to the soul that you come here to watch me, and spy on my wedding, and ask about the orange blossom with something on your mind. Go and wait for your wife at the door.

Leonardo. But, can't you and I even talk?

Servant [*with rage*]. No! No, you can't talk.

Leonardo. Ever since I got married I've been thinking night and day about whose fault it was, and every time I think about it, out comes a new fault to eat up the old one; but always there's a fault left!

Bride. A man with a horse knows a lot of things and can do a lot to ride roughshod over a girl stuck out in the desert. But I have my pride. And that's why I'm getting married. I'll lock myself in with my husband and then I'll have to love him above everyone else.

Leonardo. Pride won't help you a bit.

[*He draws near to her.*]

Bride. Don't come near me!

Leonardo. To burn with desire and keep quiet about it is the greatest punishment we can bring on ourselves. What good was pride to me—and not seeing you, and letting you lie awake night after night?

No good! It only served to bring the fire down on me! You think that time heals and walls hide things, but it isn't true, it isn't true! When things get that deep inside you there isn't anybody can change them.

Bride [*trembling*]. I can't listen to you. I can't listen to your voice. It's as though I'd drunk a bottle of anise[4] and fallen asleep wrapped in a quilt of roses. It pulls me along, and I know I'm drowning—but I go on down.

Servant [*seizing* Leonardo *by the lapels*]. You've got to go right now!

Leonardo. This is the last time I'll ever talk to her. Don't you be afraid of anything.

Bride. And I know I'm crazy and I know my breast rots with longing; but here I am—calmed by hearing him, by just seeing him move his arms.

Leonardo. I'd never be at peace if I didn't tell you these things.
I got married. Now you get married.

Servant. But she *is* getting married!

[*Voices are heard singing, nearer.*]

Voices. Awake, O Bride, awaken,
    On your wedding morning waken!

Bride. Awake, O Bride, awaken,

[*She goes out, running toward her room.*]

Servant. The people are here now.
    [*To* Leonardo] Don't you come near her again.

Leonardo. Don't worry.

[*He goes out to the left. Day begins to break.*]

First Girl [*entering*]. Awake, O Bride, awaken,
    the morning you're to marry;
    sing round and dance round;
    balconies a wreath must carry.

Voices. Bride, awaken!

Servant [*creating enthusiasm*]. Awake,
    with the green bouquet
    of love in flower.
    Awake,
    by the trunk and the branch
    of the laurels!

Second Girl [*entering*]. Awake,
    with her long hair,

---

[4] anise—liquor flavored with aniseed.

snowy sleeping gown,
patent leather boots with silver—
her forehead jasmines[5] crown.

Servant. Oh, shepherdess,
the moon begins to shine!

First Girl. Oh, gallant,[6]
leave your hat beneath the vine!

First Young Man [*entering, holding his hat on high*].
Bride, awaken,
for over the fields
the wedding draws nigh
with trays heaped with dahlias
and cakes piled high.

Voices. Bride, awaken!

Second Girl. The bride
has set her white wreath in place
and the groom
ties it on with a golden lace.

Servant. By the orange tree,
sleepless the bride will be.

Third Girl [*entering*]. By the citron vine,[7]
gifts from the groom will shine.

[*Three* Guests *come in.*]

First Youth. Dove, awaken!
In the dawn
shadowy bells are shaken.

Guest. The bride, the white bride
today a maiden,
tomorrow a wife.

First Girl. Dark one, come down
trailing the train of your silken gown.

Guest. Little dark one, come down,
cold morning wears a dewy crown.

First Guest. Awaken, wife, awake,
orange blossoms the breezes shake.

---

[5] jasmines—fragrant flowers of various shrubs and vines.

[6] gallant—elegant young man.

[7] citron vine—small tree that bears pale yellow fruit resembling lemons.

Servant. A tree I would embroider her
    with garnet[8] sashes wound,
    And on each sash a cupid,
    with "Long Live" all around.

Voices. Bride, awaken.

First Youth. The morning you're to marry!

Guest. The morning you're to marry
    how elegant you'll seem;
    worthy, mountain flower,
    of a captain's dream.

Father [*entering*]. A captain's wife
    the groom will marry.
    He comes with his oxen the treasure to carry!

Third Girl. The groom
    is like a flower of gold.
    When he walks,
    blossoms at his feet unfold.

Servant. Oh, my lucky girl!

Second Youth. Bride, awaken.

Servant. Oh, my elegant girl!

First Girl. Through the windows
    hear the wedding shout.

Second Girl. Let the bride come out.

First Girl. Come out, come out!

Servant. Let the bells
    ring and ring out clear!

First Youth. For here she comes!
    For now she's near!

Servant. Like a bull, the wedding
    is arising here!

[*The* Bride *appears. She wears a black dress in the style of 1900, with a bustle and large train[9] covered with pleated gauzes[10] and heavy laces. Upon her hair, brushed in a wave over her forehead, she wears an orange blossom wreath. Guitars sound. The* Girls *kiss the* Bride.]

Third Girl. What scent did you put on your hair?

Bride [*laughing*]. None at all.

---

[8] garnet—deep red.

[9] *bustle and large train*—padded back and elongated skirt.

[10] *pleated gauzes*—sheer fabrics with many folds.

Second Girl [*looking at her dress*]. This cloth is what you can't get.

First Youth. Here's the groom!

Bridegroom. *Salud!*[11]

First Girl [*putting a flower behind his ear*]. The groom
    is like a flower of gold.

Second Girl. Quiet breezes from his eyes unfold.

[*The* Groom *goes to the* Bride.]

Bride. Why did you put on those shoes?

Bridegroom. They're gayer than the black ones.

Leonardo's Wife [*entering and kissing the* Bride]. *Salud!*

[*They all speak excitedly.*]

Leonardo [*entering as one who performs a duty*].
    The morning you're to marry
    We give you a wreath to wear.

Leonardo's Wife. So the fields may be made happy
    with the dew dropped from your hair!

Mother [*to the* Father]. Are those people here, too?

Father. They're part of the family. Today is a day of forgiveness!

Mother. I'll put up with it, but I don't forgive.

Bridegroom. With your wreath, it's a joy to look at you!

Bride. Let's go to the church quickly.

Bridegroom. Are you in a hurry?

Bride. Yes. I want to be your wife right now so that I can be with you
    alone, not hearing any voice but yours.

Bridegroom. That's what I want!

Bride. And not seeing any eyes but yours. And for you to hug me so
    hard, that even though my dead mother should call me, I wouldn't be
    able to draw away from you.

Bridegroom. My arms are strong. I'll hug you for forty years without
    stopping.

Bride [*taking his arm, dramatically*]. Forever!

Father. Quick now! Round up the teams and carts! The sun's already out.

Mother. And go along carefully! Let's hope nothing goes wrong.

[*The great door in the background opens.*]

Servant [*weeping*]. As you set out from your house,
    Oh, maiden white,

---

[11] *Salud*—"Health," a Spanish greeting or toast.

remember you leave shining
with a star's light.

First Girl. Clean of body, clean of clothes
from her home to church she goes.

[*They start leaving.*]

Second Girl. Now you leave your home
for the church!

Servant. The wind sets flowers
on the sands.

Third Girl. Ah, the white maid!

Servant. Dark winds are the lace
of her mantilla.

[*They leave. Guitars, castanets*[12] *and tambourines are heard.* Leonardo *and his* Wife *are left alone.*]

Wife. Let's go.

Leonardo. Where?

Wife. To the church. But not on your horse. You're coming with me.

Leonardo. In the cart?

Wife. Is there anything else?

Leonardo. I'm not the kind of man to ride in a cart.

Wife. Nor I the wife to go to a wedding without her husband. I can't stand any more of this!

Leonardo. Neither can I!

Wife. And why do you look at me that way? With a thorn in each eye.

Leonardo. Let's go!

Wife. I don't know what's happening. But I think, and I don't want to think. One thing I do know. I'm already cast off by you. But I have a son. And another coming. And so it goes. My mother's fate was the same. Well, I'm not moving from here.

[Voices *outside.*]

Voices. As you set out from your home
and to the church go
remember you leave shining
with a star's glow.

Wife [*weeping*]. Remember you leave shining
with a star's glow!

---

[12] *castanets*—small percussion instrument held in the hand.

I left my house like that too. They could have stuffed the whole countryside in my mouth. I was that trusting.

Leonardo [*rising*]. Let's go!

Wife. But you with me!

Leonardo. Yes.

[*Pause.*]

Start moving!

[*They leave.*]

Voices. As you set out from your home
and to the church go,
remember you leave shining
with a star's glow.

[*Slow Curtain.*]

Act Two, Scene Two

[*The exterior of the* Bride's *Cave Home, in white gray and cold blue tones. Large cactus trees. Shadowy and silver tones. Panoramas of light tan tablelands, everything hard like a landscape in popular ceramics.*]

Servant [*arranging glasses and trays on a table*].

A-turning,
the wheel was a-turning
and the water was flowing,
for the wedding night comes.
May the branches part
and the moon be arrayed
at her white balcony rail.
[*In a loud voice*] Set out the tablecloths!
[*In a pathetic voice*] A-singing
bride and groom were singing
and the water was flowing
for their wedding night comes.
Oh, rime-frost, flash!—
and almonds bitter
fill with honey!
[*In a loud voice*] Get the wine ready!
[*In a poetic tone*] Elegant girl,
most elegant in the world,
see the way the water is flowing,

for your wedding night comes.
Hold your skirts close in
under the bridegroom's wing
and never leave your house,
for the Bridegroom is a dove
with his breast a firebrand
and the fields wait for the whisper
of spurting blood.
A-turning
the wheel was a-turning
and the water was flowing
and your wedding night comes.
Oh, water, sparkle!

Mother [*entering*]. At last!

Father. Are we the first ones?

Servant. No. Leonardo and his wife arrived a while ago. They drove like demons. His wife got here dead with fright. They made the trip as though they'd come on horseback.

Father. That one's looking for trouble. He's not of good blood.

Mother. What blood would you expect him to have? His whole family's blood. It comes down from his great grandfather, who started in killing, and it goes on down through the whole evil breed of knife wielding and false smiling men.

Father. Let's leave it at that!

Servant. But how can she leave it at that?

Mother. It hurts me to the tips of my veins. On the forehead of all of them I see only the hand with which they killed what was mine. Can you really see me? Don't I seem mad to you? Well, it's the madness of not having shrieked out all my breast needs to. Always in my breast there's a shriek standing tiptoe that I have to beat down and hold in under my shawls. But the dead are carried off and one has to keep still. And then, people find fault.

[*She removes her shawl.*]

Father. Today's not the day for you to be remembering these things.

Mother. When the talk turns on it, I have to speak. And more so today. Because today I'm left alone in my house.

Father. But with the expectation of having someone with you.

Mother. That's my hope: grandchildren.

[*They sit down.*]

Father. I want them to have a lot of them. This land needs hands that aren't hired. There's a battle to be waged against weeds, the thistles, the big rocks that come from one doesn't know where. And those hands have to be the owner's, who **chastises**[13] and dominates, who makes the seeds grow. Lots of sons are needed.

Mother. And some daughters! Men are like the wind! They're forced to handle weapons. Girls never go out into the street.

Father [*happily*]. I think they'll have both.

Mother. My son will cover her well. He's of good seed. His father could have had many sons with me.

Father. What I'd like is to have all this happen in a day. So that right away they'd have two or three boys.

Mother. But it's not like that. It takes a long time. That's why it's so terrible to see one's own blood spilled out on the ground. A fountain that spurts for a minute, but costs us years. When I got to my son, he lay fallen in the middle of the street. I wet my hands with his blood and licked them with my tongue—because it was my blood. You don't know what that's like. In a glass and topaz shrine I'd put the earth moistened by his blood.

Father. Now you must hope. My daughter is wide-hipped and your son is strong.

Mother. That's why I'm hoping.

[*They rise.*]

Father. Get the wheat trays ready!

Servant. They're all ready.

Leonardo's Wife [*entering*]. May it be for the best!

Mother. Thank you.

Leonardo. Is there going to be a celebration?

Father. A small one. People can't stay long.

Servant. Here they are!

[*Guests begin entering in gay groups. The* Bride *and* Groom *come in arm-in-arm.* Leonardo *leaves.*]

Bridegroom. There's never been a wedding with so many people!

Bride [*sullen*]. Never.

Father. It was brilliant.

Mother. Whole branches of families came.

Bridegroom. People who never went out of the house.

---

[13] **chastises**—punishes.

Mother. Your father sowed well, and now you're reaping it.

Bridegroom. There were cousins of mine whom I no longer knew.

Mother. All the people from the seacoast.

Bridegroom [*happily*]. They were frightened of the horses.

[*They talk.*]

Mother [*to the* Bride]. What are you thinking about?

Bride. I'm not thinking about anything.

Mother. Your blessings weigh heavily.

[*Guitars are heard.*]

Bride. Like lead.

Mother [*stern*]. But they shouldn't weigh so. Happy as a dove you
   ought to be.

Bride. Are you staying here tonight?

Mother. No. My house is empty.

Bride. You ought to stay!

Father [*to the* Mother]. Look at the dance they're forming. Dances
   of the far away seashore.

[Leonardo *enters and sits down. His* Wife *stands rigidly behind him.*]

Mother. They're my husband's cousins. Stiff as stones at dancing.

Father. It makes me happy to watch them. What a change for
   this house!

[*He leaves.*]

Bridegroom [*to the* Bride]. Did you like the orange blossom?

Bride [*looking at him fixedly*]. Yes.

Bridegroom. It's all of wax. It will last forever. I'd like you to
   have had them all over your dress.

Bride. No need of that.

[Leonardo *goes off to the right.*]

First Girl. Let's go and take out your pins.

Bride [*to the Groom*]. I'll be right back.

Leonardo's Wife. I hope you'll be happy with my cousin!

Bridegroom. I'm sure I will.

Leonardo's Wife. The two of you here; never going out; building
   a home. I wish I could live far away like this, too!

Bridegroom. Why don't you buy land? The mountainside is
   cheap and children grow up better.

Leonardo's Wife. We don't have any money. And at the rate
   we're going . . . !

Bridegroom. Your husband is a good worker.

Leonardo's Wife. Yes, but he likes to fly around too much; from one thing to another. He's not a patient man.

Servant. Aren't you having anything? I'm going to wrap up some wine cakes for your Mother. She likes them so much.

Bridegroom. Put up three dozen for her.

Leonardo's Wife. No, no. A half-dozen's enough for her!

Bridegroom. But today's a day!

Leonardo's Wife [*to the* Servant]. Where's Leonardo?

Bridegroom. He must be with the guests.

Leonardo's Wife. I'm going to go see.

[*She leaves.*]

Servant [*looking off at the dance*]. That's beautiful there.

Bridegroom. Aren't you dancing?

Servant. No one will ask me.

[Two Girls *pass across the back of the stage; during this whole scene the background should be an animated crossing of figures.*]

Bridegroom [*happily*]. They just don't know anything. Lively old girls like you dance better than the young ones.

Servant. Well! Are you tossing me a compliment, boy? What a family yours is! Men among men! As a little girl I saw your grandfather's wedding. What a figure! It seemed as if a mountain were getting married.

Bridegroom. I'm not as tall.

Servant. But there's the same twinkle in your eye. Where's the girl?

Bridegroom. Taking off her wreath.

Servant. Ah! Look. For midnight, since you won't be sleeping, I have prepared ham for you, and some large glasses of old wine. On the lower shelf of the cupboard. In case you need it.

Bridegroom [*smiling*]. I won't be eating at midnight.

Servant [*slyly*]. If not you, maybe the Bride.

[*She leaves.*]

First Youth [*entering*]. You've got to come have a drink with us!

Bridegroom. I'm waiting for the bride.

Second Youth. You'll have her at dawn!

First Youth. That's when it's best!

Second Youth. Just for a minute.

Bridegroom. Let's go.

[*They leave. Great excitement is heard. The* Bride *enters. From the opposite side* Two Girls *come running to meet her.*]

First Girl. To whom did you give the first pin; me or this one?

Bride. I don't remember.

First Girl. To me, you gave it to me here.

Second Girl. To me, in front of the altar.

Bride [*uneasily, with a great inner struggle*]. I don't know anything about it.

First Girl. It's just that I wish you'd . . .

Bride [*interrupting*]. Nor do I care. I have a lot to think about.

Second Girl. Your pardon.

[Leonardo *crosses at the rear of the stage.*]

Bride. [*She sees* Leonardo.] And this is an upsetting time.

First Girl. We wouldn't know anything about that!

Bride. You'll know about it when your time comes. This step is a very hard one to take.

First Girl. Has she offended you?

Bride. No. You must pardon me.

Second Girl. What for? But *both* the pins are good for getting married, aren't they?

Bride. Both of them.

First Girl. Maybe now one will get married before the other.

Bride. Are you so eager?

Second Girl [*shyly*]. Yes.

Bride. Why?

First Girl. Well . . .

[*She embraces the* Second Girl. *Both go running off. The* Groom *comes in very slowly and embraces the* Bride *from behind.*]

Bride [*in sudden fright*]. Let go of me!

Bridegroom. Are you frightened of me?

Bride. Ay-y-y! It's you?

Bridegroom. Who else would it be?

[*Pause*]

Your father or me.

Bride. That's true!

Bridegroom. Of course, your father would have hugged you more gently.

Bride [*darkly*]. Of course!

Bridegroom [*embracing her strongly and a little bit brusquely*]. Because he's old.

Bride [*curtly*[14]]. Let me go!

Bridegroom. Why?

---

[14] **curtly**—briefly, abruptly.

[*He lets her go.*]

Bride. Well . . . the people. They can see us.

[*The* Servant *crosses at the back of the stage again without looking at the* Bride *and* Groom.]

Bridegroom. What of it? It's consecrated now.

Bride. Yes, but let me be . . . Later.

Bridegroom. What's the matter with you? You look frightened!

Bride. I'm all right. Don't go.

[Leonardo's Wife *enters.*]

Leonardo's Wife. I don't mean to intrude . . .

Bridegroom. What is it?

Leonardo's Wife. Did my husband come through here?

Bridegroom. No.

Leonardo's Wife. Because I can't find him, and his horse isn't in the stable either.

Bridegroom [*happily*]. He must be out racing it.

[*The* Wife *leaves, troubled. The* Servant *enters.*]

Servant. Aren't you two proud and happy with so many good wishes?

Bridegroom. I wish it were over with. The bride is a little tired.

Servant. That's no way to act, child.

Bride. It's as though I'd been struck on the head.

Servant. A bride from these mountains must be strong.
[*To the* Groom.] You're the only one who can cure her, because she's yours.

[*She goes running off.*]

Bridegroom [*embracing the* Bride]. Let's go dance a little.

[*He kisses her.*]

Bride [*worried*]. No. I'd like to stretch out on my bed a little.

Bridegroom. I'll keep you company.

Bride. Never! With all these people here? What would they say? Let me be quiet for a moment.

Bridegroom. Whatever you say! But don't be like that tonight!

Bride [*at the door*]. I'll be better tonight.

Bridegroom. That's what I want.

[*The* Mother *appears.*]

Mother. Son.

Bridegroom. Where've you been?

Mother. Out there—in all that noise. Are you happy?

Bridegroom. Yes.

Mother. Where's your wife?

Bridegroom. Resting a little. It's a bad day for brides!

Mother. A bad day? The only good one. To me it was like coming into my own.

[*The* Servant *enters and goes toward the* Bride's *room.*]

Like the breaking of new ground; the planting of new trees.

Bridegroom. Are you going to leave?

Mother. Yes. I ought to be at home.

Bridegroom. Alone.

Mother. Not alone. For my head is full of things: of men, and fights.

Bridegroom. But now the fights are no longer fights.

[*The* Servant *enters quickly; she disappears at the rear of the stage, running.*]

Mother. While you live, you have to fight.

Bridegroom. I'll always obey you!

Mother. Try to be loving with your wife, and if you see she's acting foolish or touchy, caress her in a way that will hurt her a little: a strong hug, a bite and then a soft kiss. Not so she'll be angry, but just so she'll feel you're the man, the boss, the one who gives orders. I learned that from your father. And since you don't have him, I have to be the one to tell you about these strong defenses.

Bridegroom. I'll always do as you say.

Father [*entering*]. Where's my daughter?

Bridegroom. She's inside.

[*The* Father *goes to look for her.*]

First Girl. Get the bride and groom! We're going to dance a round!

First Youth [*to the* Bridegroom]. You're going to lead it.

Father [*entering*]. She's not there.

Bridegroom. No?

Father. She must have gone up to the railing.

Bridegroom. I'll go see!

[*He leaves. A hubbub of excitement and guitars is heard.*]

First Girl. They've started it already!

[*She leaves.*]

Bridegroom [*entering*]. She isn't there.

Mother [*uneasily*]. Isn't she?

Father. But where could she have gone?

Servant [*entering*]. But where's the girl, where is she?

Mother [*seriously*]. That we don't know.

[*The* Bridegroom *leaves. Three guests enter.*]

Father [*dramatically*]. But, isn't she in the dance?

Servant. She's not in the dance.

Father [*with a start*]. There are a lot of people. Go look!

Servant. I've already looked.

Father [*tragically*]. Then where is she?

Bridegroom [*entering*]. Nowhere. Not anywhere.

Mother [*to the* Father]. What does this mean? Where is your daughter?

[Leonardo's Wife *enters.*]

Leonardo's Wife. They've run away! They've run away! She and Leonardo. On the horse. With their arms around each other, they rode off like a shooting star!

Father. That's not true! Not my daughter!

Mother. Yes, your daughter! Spawn of a wicked mother, and he, he too. But now she's my son's wife!

Bridegroom [*entering*]. Let's go after them! Who has a horse?

Mother. Who has a horse? Right away! Who has a horse? I'll give him all I have—my eyes, my tongue even. . . .

Voice. Here's one.

Mother [*to the* Son]. Go! After them!

[*He leaves with two young men.*]

    No. Don't go. Those people kill quickly and well . . . but yes, run, and I'll follow!

Father. It couldn't be my daughter. Perhaps she's thrown herself in the well.

Mother. Decent women throw themselves in water; not that one! But now she's my son's wife. Two groups. There are two groups here.

[*They all enter.*]

    My family and yours. Everyone set out from here. Shake the dust from your heels! We'll go help my son.

[*The people separate into two groups.*]

    For he has his family: his cousins from the sea, and all who came from inland. Out of here! On all roads. The hour of blood has come again. Two groups! You with yours and I with mine. After them! After them!

[*Curtain.*]

Act Three, Scene One

[*A forest. It is nighttime. Great moist tree trunks. A dark atmosphere. Two violins are heard. Three* Woodcutters *enter.*]

First Woodcutter. And have they found them?

Second Woodcutter. No. But they're looking for them everywhere.

Third Woodcutter. They'll find them.

Second Woodcutter. Sh-h-h!

Third Woodcutter. What?

Second Woodcutter. They seem to be coming closer on all the roads at once.

First Woodcutter. When the moon comes out they'll see them.

Second Woodcutter. They ought to let them go.

First Woodcutter. The world is wide. Everybody can live in it.

Third Woodcutter. But they'll kill them.

Second Woodcutter. You have to follow your passion. They did right to run away.

First Woodcutter. They were deceiving themselves but at the last blood was stronger.

Third Woodcutter. Blood!

First Woodcutter. You have to follow the path of your blood.

Second Woodcutter. But blood that sees the light of day is drunk up by the earth.

First Woodcutter. What of it? Better dead with the blood drained away than alive with it rotting.

Third Woodcutter. Hush!

First Woodcutter. What? Do you hear something?

Third Woodcutter. I hear the crickets, the frogs, the night's ambush.

First Woodcutter. But not the horse.

Third Woodcutter. No.

First Woodcutter. By now he must be loving her.

Second Woodcutter. Her body for him; his body for her.

Third Woodcutter. They'll find them and they'll kill them.

First Woodcutter. But by then they'll have mingled their bloods. They'll be like two empty jars, like two dry arroyos.

Second Woodcutter. There are many clouds and it would be easy for the moon not to come out.

Third Woodcutter. The bridegroom will find them with or without the moon. I saw him set out. Like a raging star. His face the color of ashes. He looked the fate of all his clan.

First Woodcutter. His clan of dead men lying in the middle of the street.

Second Woodcutter. There you have it!

Third Woodcutter. You think they'll be able to break through the circle?

Second Woodcutter. It's hard to. There are knives and guns for ten leagues 'round.

Third Woodcutter. He's riding a good horse.

Second Woodcutter. But he's carrying a woman.

First Woodcutter. We're close by now.

Second Woodcutter. A tree with forty branches. We'll soon cut it down.

Third Woodcutter. The moon's coming out now.
Let's hurry.

[*From the left shines a brightness.*]

First Woodcutter. O rising moon!
Moon among the great leaves.

Second Woodcutter. Cover the blood with jasmines!

First Woodcutter. O lonely moon!
Moon among the great leaves.

Second Woodcutter. Silver on the bride's face.

Third Woodcutter. O evil moon!
Leave for their love a branch in shadow.

First Woodcutter. O sorrowing moon!
Leave for their love a branch in shadow.

[*They go out. The* Moon *appears through the shining brightness at the left. The* Moon *is a young woodcutter with a white face. The stage takes on an intense blue radiance.*]

Moon. Round swan in the river
and a cathedral's eye,
false dawn on the leaves,
they'll not escape; these things am I!
Who is hiding? And who sobs
in the thornbrakes of the valley?
The moon sets a knife
abandoned in the air
which being a leaden threat
yearns to be blood's pain.
Let me in! I come freezing
down to walls and windows!
Open roofs, open breasts
where I may warm myself!

I'm cold! My ashes
of **somnolent**[1] metals
seek the fire's crest
on mountains and streets.
But the snow carries me
upon its **mottled**[2] back
and pools soak me
in their water, hard and cold.
But this night there will be
red blood for my cheeks,
and for the reeds that cluster
at the wide feet of the wind.
Let there be neither shadow nor bower,[3]
and then they can't get away!
O let me enter a breast
where I may get warm!
A heart for me!
Warm! That will spurt
over the mountains of my chest;
let me come in, oh let me!

[*To the branches.*] I want no shadows. My rays
must get in everywhere,
even among the dark trunks I want
the whisper of gleaming lights,
so that this night there will be
sweet blood for my cheeks,
and for the reeds that cluster
at the wide feet of the wind.
Who is hiding? Out, I say!
No! They will not get away!
I will light up the horse
with a fever bright as diamonds.

[*He disappears among the trunks, and the stage goes back to its dark lighting.
An* Old Woman *comes out completely covered by thin green cloth. She is bare-
footed. Her face can barely be seen among the folds. This character does not
appear in the cast.*]

---

[1] **somnolent**—sleepy.

[2] **mottled**—spotted, blotched.

[3] **bower**—shelter of leafy branches.

Beggar Woman. That moon's going away, just when they's near.
    They won't get past here. The river's whisper
    and the whispering tree trunks will muffle
    the torn flight of their shrieks.
    It has to be here, and soon. I'm worn out.
    The coffins are ready, and white sheets
    wait on the floor of the bedroom
    for heavy bodies with torn throats.
    Let not one bird awake, let the breeze,
    gathering their moans in her skirt,
    fly with them over black tree tops
    or bury them in soft mud.
[*Impatiently.*] Oh, that moon! That moon!
[*The* Moon *appears. The intense blue light returns.*]

Moon. They're coming. One band through the ravine and the other along
    the river. I'm going to light up the boulders. What do you need?

Beggar Woman. Nothing.

Moon. The wind blows hard now, with a double edge.

Beggar Woman. Light up the waistcoat and open the buttons; the knives
    will know the path after that.

Moon. But let them be a long time a-dying. So the blood will slide its del-
    icate hissing between my fingers. Look how my ashen valleys already
    are waking in longing for this fountain of shuddering gushes!

Beggar Woman. Let's not let them get past the arroyo. Silence!

Moon. There they come!
[*He goes. The stage is left dark.*]

Beggar Woman. Quick! Lots of light! Do you hear me? They can't
    get away!
[*The* Bridegroom *and the* First Youth *enter. The* Beggar Woman *sits down
and covers herself with her cloak.*]

Bridegroom. This way.

First Youth. You won't find them.

Bridegroom [*angrily*]. Yes, I'll find them.

First Youth. I think they've taken another path.

Bridegroom. No. Just a moment ago I felt the galloping.

First Youth. It could have been another horse.

Bridegroom [*intensely*]. Listen to me. There's only one horse in the whole
    world, and this one's it. Can't you understand that? If you're going to
    follow me, follow me without talking.

First Youth. It's only that I want to . . .

Bridegroom. Be quiet. I'm sure of meeting them there. Do you see this arm? Well, it's not my arm. It's my brother's arm, and my father's, and that of all the dead ones in my family. And it has so much strength that it can pull this tree up by the roots, if it wants to. And let's move on, because here I feel the clenched teeth of all my people in me so that I can't breathe easily.

Beggar Woman [*whining*]. Ay-y-y!

First Youth. Did you hear that?

Bridegroom. You go that way and then circle back.

First Youth. This is a hunt.

Bridegroom. A hunt. The greatest hunt there is.

[*The* Youth *goes off. The* Bridegroom *goes rapidly to the left and stumbles over the* Beggar Woman, *Death.*]

Beggar Woman. Ay-y-y!

Bridegroom. What do you want?

Beggar Woman. I'm cold.

Bridegroom. Which way are you going?

Beggar Woman [*always whining like a beggar*]. Over there, far away . . .

Bridegroom. Where are you from?

Beggar Woman. Over there . . . very far away.

Bridegroom. Have you seen a man and a woman running away on a horse?

Beggar Woman [*awakening*]. Wait a minute . . .

[*She looks at him.*]

Handsome young man.

[*She rises.*]

But you'd be much handsomer sleeping.

Bridegroom. Tell me; answer me. Did you see them?

Beggar Woman. Wait a minute . . . What broad shoulders! How would you like to be laid out on them and not have to walk on the soles of your feet which are so small?

Bridegroom [*shaking her*]. I asked you if you saw them! Have they passed through here?

Beggar Woman [*energetically*]. No. They haven't passed; but they're coming from the hill. Don't you hear them?

Bridegroom. No.

Beggar Woman. Do you know the road?

Bridegroom. I'll go, whatever it's like!

Beggar Woman. I'll go along with you. I know this country.

Bridegroom [*impatiently*]. Well, let's go! Which way?

Beggar Woman [*dramatically*]. This way!

[*They go rapidly out. Two violins, which represent the forest, are heard distantly. The* Woodcutters *return. They have their axes on their shoulders. They move slowly among the tree trunks.*]

First Woodcutter. O rising death!

　Death among the great leaves.

Second Woodcutter. Don't open the gush of blood!

First Woodcutter. O lonely death!

　Death among the dried leaves.

Third Woodcutter. Don't lay flowers over the wedding!

Second Woodcutter. O sad death!

　Leave for their love a green branch.

First Woodcutter. O evil death!

　Leave for their love a branch of green!

[*They go out while they are talking.* Leonardo *and the* Bride *appear.*]

Leonardo. Hush!

Bride. From here I'll go on alone.

　You go now! I want you to turn back.

Leonardo. Hush, I said!

Bride. With your teeth, with your hands, anyway you can,

　take from my clean throat

　the metal of this chain,

　and let me live forgotten

　back there in my house in the ground.

　And if you don't want to kill me

　as you would kill a tiny snake,

　set in my hands, a bride's hands,

　the barrel of your shotgun.

　Oh, what lamenting, what fire,

　sweeps upward through my head!

　What glass splinters are stuck in my tongue!

Leonardo. We've taken the step now; hush!

　because they're close behind us,

　and I must take you with me.

Bride. Then it must be by force!

Leonardo. By force? Who was it first

　went down the stairway?

Bride. I went down it.

Leonardo. And who was it put
    a new bridle on the horse?
Bride. I myself did it. It's true.
Leonardo. And whose were the hands
    strapped spurs to my boots?
Bride. The same hands, these that are yours,
    but which when they see you would like
    to break the blue branches
    and sunder the purl of your veins.
    I love you! I love you! But leave me!
    For if I were able to kill you
    I'd wrap you 'round in a shroud
    with the edges bordered in violets.
    Oh, what lamenting, what fire,
    sweeps upward through my head!
Leonardo. What glass splinters are stuck in my tongue!
    Because I tried to forget you
    and put a wall of stone
    between your house and mine.
    It's true. You remember?
    And when I saw you in the distance
    I threw sand in my eyes.
    But I was riding a horse
    and the horse went straight to your door.
    And the silver pins of your wedding
    turned my red blood black.
    And in me our dream was choking
    my flesh with its poisoned weeds.
    Oh, it isn't my fault—
    the fault is the earth's—
    and this fragrance that you exhale
    from your breasts and your braids.
Bride. Oh, how untrue! I want
    from you neither bed nor food,
    yet there's not a minute each day
    that I don't want to be with you,
    because you drag me, and I come,
    then you tell me to go back
    and I follow you,

like chaff[4] blown on the breeze.
I have left a good, honest man,
and all his people,
with the wedding feast half over
and wearing my bridal wreath.
But you are the one will be punished
and that I don't want to happen.
Leave me alone now! You run away!
There is no one who will defend you.

Leonardo. The birds of early morning
are calling among the trees.
The night is dying
on the stone's ridge.
Let's go to a hidden corner
where I may love you forever,
for to me the people don't matter,
nor the **venom**[5] they throw on us.

[*He embraces her strongly.*]

Bride. And I'll sleep at your feet,
to watch over your dreams.
Naked, looking over the fields,
as though I were a bitch.
Because that's what I am! Oh, I look at you
and your beauty sears me.

Leonardo. Fire is stirred by fire.
The same tiny flame
will kill two wheat heads together.
Let's go!

Bride. Where are you taking me?

Leonardo. Where they cannot come,
these men who surround us.
Where I can look at you!

Bride [*sarcastically*]. Carry me with you from fair to fair,
a shame to clean women,
so that people will see me

---

[4] chaff—waste separated from grain during threshing.

[5] **venom**—poison.

with my wedding sheets
on the breeze like banners.

Leonardo. I, too, would want to leave you
if I thought as men should,
But wherever you go, I go.
You're the same. Take a step. Try.
Nails of moonlight have fused
my waist and your thighs.

[*This whole scene is* violent, full of great sensuality.]

Bride. Listen!

Leonardo. They're coming.

Bride.   Run!
It's fitting that I should die here,
with water over my feet,
with thorns upon my head.
And fitting the leaves should mourn me,
a woman lost and virgin.

Leonardo. Be quiet. Now they're appearing.

Bride.   Go now!

Leonardo. Quiet. Don't let them hear us.

[*The* Bride *hesitates.*]

Bride. Both of us!

Leonardo [*embracing her*]. Any way you want!
If they separate us, it will be
because I am dead.

Bride.
                    And I dead too.

[*They go out in each other's arms.*

The Moon *appears very slowly. The stage takes on a strong blue light. The two violins are heard. Suddenly two long, ear-splitting shrieks are heard, and the music of the two violins is cut short. At the second shriek The* Beggar Woman *appears and stands with her back to the audience. She opens her cape and stands in the center of the stage like a great bird with immense wings. The* Moon *halts. The curtain comes down in absolute silence.*]

[*Curtain.*]

Act Three, Scene Two

[*The Final Scene*
A white dwelling with arches and thick walls. To the right and left are white
stairs. At the back, a great arch and a wall of the same color. The floor also
should be shining white. This simple dwelling should have the monumental
feeling of a church. There should not be a single gray nor any shadow, not even
what is necessary for perspective.
Two Girls *dressed in dark blue are winding a red skein.*[6]]

First Girl. Wool, red wool,
    what would you make?

Second Girl. Oh, jasmine for dresses,
    fine wool like glass.
    At four o'clock born,
    at ten o'clock dead.
    A thread from this wool yarn,
    a chain 'round your feet
    a knot that will tighten
    the bitter white wreath.

Little Girl [*singing*]. Were you at the wedding?

First Girl. No.

Little Girl. Well, neither was I!
    What could have happened
    'midst the shoots of the vineyards?
    What could have happened
    'neath the branch of the olive?
    What really happened
    that no one came back?
    Were you at the wedding?

Second Girl. We told you once, no.

Little Girl [*leaving*]. Well, neither was I!

Second Girl. Wool, red wool,
    what would you sing?

First Girl. Their wounds turning waxen
    balm-myrtle[7] for pain.
    Asleep in the morning,
    and watching at night.

---

[6] *skein*—loose ball of yarn.

[7] balm-myrtle—preparation of the balm plant used as a medication.

Little Girl [*in the doorway*]. And then, the thread stumbled
  on the flinty stones,
  but mountains, blue mountains,
  are letting it pass.
  Running, running, running,
  and finally to come
  to stick in a knife blade,
  to take back the bread.

[*She goes out.*]

Second Girl. Wool, red wool,
  what would you tell?

First Girl. The lover is silent,
  crimson the groom,
  at the still shoreline
  I saw them laid out.

[*She stops and looks at the skein.*]

Little Girl [*appearing in the doorway*].
  Running, running, running,
  the thread runs to here.
  All covered with clay
  I feel them draw near.
  Bodies stretched stiffly
  in ivory sheets!

[*The* Wife *and* Mother-in-Law *of Leonardo appear. They are anguished.*]

First Girl. Are they coming yet?

Mother-in-Law [*harshly*]. We don't know.

Second Girl. What can you tell us about the wedding?

First Girl. Yes, tell me.

Mother-in-Law [*curtly*]. Nothing.

Leonardo's Wife. I want to go back and find out all about it.

Mother-in-Law [*sternly*]. You, back to your house.
  Brave and alone in your house.
  To grow old and to weep.
  But behind closed doors.
  Never again. Neither dead nor alive.
  We'll nail up our windows
  and let rains and nights
  fall on the bitter weeds.

Leonardo's Wife. What could have happened?

Mother-in-Law. It doesn't matter what.
> Put a veil over your face.
> Your children are yours,
> that's all. On the bed
> put a cross of ashes
> where his pillow was.

[*They go out.*]

Beggar Woman [*at the door*]. A crust of bread, little girls.

Little Girl. Go away!

[*The* Girls *huddle close together.*]

Beggar Woman. Why?

Little Girl. Because you whine; go away!

First Girl. Child!

Beggar Woman. I might have asked for your eyes! A cloud
> of birds is following me. Will you have one?

Little Girl. I want to get away from here!

Second Girl [*to the* Beggar Woman]. Don't mind her!

First Girl. Did you come by the road through the arroyo?

Beggar Woman. I came that way!

First Girl [*timidly*]. Can I ask you something?

Beggar Woman. I saw them: they'll be here soon; two torrents
> still at last, among the great boulders,
> two men at the horse's feet.
> Two dead men in the night's splendor.

[*With pleasure.*] Dead, yes, dead.

First Girl. Hush, old woman, hush!

Beggar Woman. Crushed flowers for eyes, and their teeth
> two fistfuls of hard-frozen snow.
> Both of them fell, and the Bride returns
> with bloodstains on her skirt and hair.
> And they come covered with two sheets
> carried on the shoulders of two tall boys.
> That's how it was; nothing more. What was fitting.
> Over the golden flower, dirty sand.

[*She goes. The* Girls *bow their heads and start going out rhythmically.*]

First Girl. Dirty sand.

Second Girl. Over the golden flower.

Little Girl. Over the golden flower
> they're bringing the dead from the arroyo.

Dark the one,
dark the other.
What shadowy nightingale flies and weeps
over the golden flower!

[*She goes. The stage is left empty. The* Mother *and a* Neighbor Woman *appear.
The* Neighbor *is weeping.*]

Mother. Hush.

Neighbor. I can't.

Mother. Hush, I said.

[*At the door*] Is there nobody here?

[*She puts her hands to her forehead.*]

My son ought to answer me. But now my son is an
armful of shriveled flowers. My son is a fading voice
beyond the mountains now.

[*With rage, to the* Neighbor.]

Will you shut up? I want no wailing in this house.
Your tears are only tears from your eyes, but when I'm alone
mine will come—from the soles of my feet, from my roots—
burning more than blood.

Neighbor. You come to my house; don't you stay here.

Mother. I want to be here. Here. In peace. They're all dead now: and at
midnight I'll sleep, sleep without terror of guns or knives. Other
mothers will go to their windows, lashed by rain, to watch for their
sons' faces. But not I. And of my dreams I'll make a cold ivory dove
that will carry camellias[8] of white frost to the graveyard. But no; not
graveyard, not graveyard: the couch of earth, the bed that shelters
them and rocks them in the sky.

[*A woman dressed in black enters, goes toward the right, and there kneels. To
the* Neighbor.]

Take your hands from your face. We have terrible days ahead. I want
to see no one. The earth and I. My grief and I. And these four walls.
Ay-y-y! Ay-y-y!

[*She sits down, overcome.*]

Neighbor. Take pity on yourself!

Mother [*pushing back her hair*]. I must be calm.

[*She sits down.*]

---

[8] camellias—blossoms of shrub with white flowers.

Because the neighbor women will come and I don't want them to see me so poor. So poor! A woman without even one son to hold to her lips.

[*The* Bride *appears. She is without her wreath and wears a black shawl.*]

Neighbor [*with rage, seeing the* Bride]. Where are you going?

Bride. I'm coming here.

Mother [*to the* Neighbor]. Who is it?

Neighbor. Don't you recognize her?

Mother. That's why I asked who it was. Because I don't want to recognize her, so I won't sink my teeth in her throat. You snake!

[*She moves wrathfully on the* Bride, *then stops. To the* Neighbor.]

Look at her! There she is, and she's crying, while I stand here calmly and don't tear her eyes out. I don't understand myself. Can it be I didn't love my son? But, where's his good name? Where is it now? Where is it?

[*She beats the* Bride *who drops to the floor.*]

Neighbor. For God's sake!

[*She tries to separate them.*]

Bride [*to the* Neighbor]. Let her; I came here so she'd kill me and they'd take me away with them.

[*To the* Mother.] But not with her hands; with grappling hooks, with a sickle—and with force—until they break on my bones. Let her! I want her to know I'm clean, that I may be crazy, but that they can bury me without a single man ever having seen himself in the whiteness of my breasts.

Mother. Shut up, shut up; what do I care about that?

Bride. Because I ran away with the other one; I ran away!

[*With anguish.*] You would have gone, too. I was a woman burning with desire, full of sores inside and out, and your son was a little bit of water from which I hoped for children, land, health; but the other one was a dark river, choked with brush, that brought near me the undertone of its rushes and its whispered song. And I went along with your son who was like a little boy of cold water—and the other sent against me hundreds of birds who got in my way and left white frost on my wounds, my wounds of a poor withered woman, of a girl caressed by fire. I didn't want to; remember that! I didn't want to. Your son was my destiny and I have not betrayed him, but the other one's arm dragged me along like the pull of the sea, like the head toss of a mule, and he would have dragged me always, always, always—even if I were an old woman and all your son's sons held me by the hair!

[*A* Neighbor *enters.*]

Mother. She is not to blame; nor am I!

[*Sarcastically.*] Who is, then? It's a delicate, lazy, sleepless woman who throws away an orange blossom wreath and goes looking for a piece of bed warmed by another woman!

Bride. Be still! Be still! Take your revenge on me; here I am! See how soft my throat is; it would be less work for you than cutting a dahlia in your garden. But never that! Clean, clean as a new-born little girl. And strong enough to prove it to you. Light the fire. Let's stick our hands in; you, for your son, I, for my body. *You'll* draw yours out first.

[*Another* Neighbor *enters.*]

Mother. But what does your good name matter to me? What does your death matter to me? What does anything about anything matter to me? Blessed be the wheat stalks, because my sons are under them; blessed be the rain, because it wets the face of the dead. Blessed be God, who stretches us out together to rest.

[*Another* Neighbor *enters.*]

Bride. Let me weep with you.

Mother. Weep. But at the door.

[*The* Girl *enters. The* Bride *stays at the door. The* Mother *is at the center of the stage.*]

Leonardo's Wife [*entering and going to the left*].

He was a beautiful horseman,
now he's a heap of snow.
He rode to fairs and mountains
and women's arms.
Now, the night's dark moss
crowns his forehead.

Mother. A sunflower to your mother,
a mirror of the earth.
Let them put on your breast
the cross of bitter rosebay;[9]
and over you a sheet
of shining silk;
between your quiet hands
let water form its lament.

Wife. Ay-y-y, four gallant boys
come with tired shoulders!

---

[9] rosebay—blossoms of rhododendron, shrub with pink, purple, or white flowers.

Bride. Ay-y-y, four gallant boys
   carry death on high!
Mother. Neighbors.
Little Girl [*at the door*]. They're bringing them now.
Mother. It's the same thing.
   Always the cross, the cross.
Women. Sweet nails,
   cross adored,
   sweet name
   of Christ our Lord.
Bride. May the cross protect both the quick and the dead.
Mother. Neighbors: with a knife,
   with a little knife,
   on their appointed day, between two and three,
   these two men killed each other for love.
   With a knife,
   with a tiny knife
   that barely fits the hand,
   but that slides in clean
   through the astonished flesh
   and stops at the place
   where trembles, enmeshed,
   the dark root of a scream.
Bride. And this is a knife,
   a tiny knife
   that barely fits the hand;
   fish without scales, without river,
   so that on their appointed day, between two and three,
   with this knife,
   two men are left stiff,
   with their lips turning yellow.
Mother. And it barely fits the hand
   but it slides in clean
   through the astonished flesh
   and stops there, at the place
   where trembles enmeshed
   the dark root of a scream.
[*The* Neighbors, *kneeling on the floor, sob.*]
[*Curtain.*]

UNDERSTANDING THE PLAY

Act One

1. In Scene One, how does the playwright immediately establish an atmosphere of menace?

2. How did the Bridegroom's father and brother die?

3. At the beginning of Scene Two, what dramatic function is served by the lullaby?

4. In what different ways does the news brought by the girl affect Leonardo, his wife, and her mother?

5. In Scene Three, how does the Bride react to the prospect of her marriage while the Bridegroom and his mother are there? How does she react after they leave?

Act Two

1. At the opening of Scene One, what is the Bride's mood?

2. What seems to have kept her from marrying Leonardo in the past?

3. As the scene closes, why is she so anxious to be wed?

4. In Scene Two, how do the Mother and Father differ in their hopes for grandchildren?

5. How do the different characters respond to the flight of Leonardo and the Bride?

Act Three

1. In Scene One, what different attitudes toward the fleeing lovers are expressed by the Woodcutters?

2. The Third Woodcutter observes of the Bridegroom's face when he set out to find his runaway bride, "He looked the fate of all his clan." What do you think he means?

3. What attitude toward the fleeing lovers is shared by the Moon and the Beggar Woman?

4. How does Leonardo appear to feel about what he has done? How does the Bride feel?

5. In Scene Two, why does the Bride return to confront the Mother?

ANALYZING THE PLAY

1. The conflict in a play is the struggle between opposing forces that gives movement to the dramatic plot. What is the fundamental conflict in *Blood Wedding*?

2. What view of the situation of women in the traditional culture of rural Spain is presented in this play?

3. Lorca was a talented painter. How does color symbolism function in *Blood Wedding*? (Notice the colors of the settings in the opening stage direction for each scene. What pattern do these colors form?)

4. What different functions does imagery of blood serve in the play?

5. How is fantasy introduced into the play? What dramatic effect does this have?

On *An Enemy of the People*

BY GEORGE BERNARD SHAW

One of the earliest defenders of the modern realistic drama being produced by Henrik Ibsen was the Irish-born playwright George Bernard Shaw (1856–1950), who in his study The Quintessence of Ibsenism *(1891) concentrated on the Norwegian dramatist's "social plays," such as* An Enemy of the People.

As *An Enemy of the People* contains one or two references to Democracy which are anything but respectful, it is necessary to examine Ibsen's criticism of it with precision. Democracy is really only an arrangement by which the governed are allowed to choose (as far as any choice is possible, which in capitalistic society is not saying much) the members of the representative bodies which control the executive. It has never been proved that this is the best arrangement; and it has been made effective only to the very limited extent short of which the dissatisfaction which it **appeases**[1] might take the form af actual violence. Now when men had to submit to kings, they consoled themselves by making it an article of faith that the king was always right, idealizing him as a Pope, in fact. In the same way we who have to submit to majorities . . . make it **blasphemy**[2] against Democracy to deny that the majority is always right, although that, as Ibsen says, is a lie. It is a scientific fact that the majority, however eager it may be for the reform of old abuses, is always wrong in its opinion of new developments, or rather is always unfit for them (for it can hardly be said to be wrong in opposing developments for which it is not yet fit). The pioneer is a tiny minority of the force he heads; and so though it is easy to be in a minority and yet be wrong, it is absolutely impossible to be in the majority and yet be right as to the newest social prospects. We should never progress at all if it were possible for each of us to stand still on democratic principles until we saw whither all the rest were moving, as our statesmen declare themselves bound to do when they are called upon to lead. Whatever clatter we may

[1] **appeases**—satisfies, relieves.
[2] **blasphemy**—disrespect of something sacred.

make for a time with our filing through feudal serf collars and kicking off old mercantilist fetters,[3] we shall never march a step forward except at the heels of "the strongest man, he who is able to stand alone" and to turn his back on "the [solid] Liberal majority." All of which is no disparagement[4] of parliaments and adult suffrage, but simply a wholesome reduction of them to their real place in the social economy as pure machinery: machinery which has absolutely no principles except the principles of mechanics, and no motive power in itself whatsoever. The idealization of public organizations is as dangerous as that of kings or priests. We need to be reminded that though there is in the world a vast number of buildings in which a certain ritual is conducted before crowds called congregations by a functionary called a priest, who is subject to a central council controlling all such functionaries on a few points, there is not therefore any such thing in the concrete as the ideal Catholic Church, nor ever was, nor ever will be. There may, too, be a highly elaborate organization of public affairs; but there is no such thing as the ideal State. . . . All abstractions invested with collective consciousness or collective authority, set above the individual, and exacting duty from him on pretence of acting or thinking with greater validity than he, are man-eating idols red with human sacrifices.

This position must not be confounded with Anarchism, or the idealization of the repudiation of Governments. Ibsen did not refuse to pay the tax collector, but may be supposed to have regarded him, not as the vicar[5] of an abstraction called THE STATE, but simply as the man sent round by a committee of citizens . . . to collect the money for the police or the paving and lighting of the streets.

---

[3] filing . . . fetters—removing outdated social or economic restrictions.

[4] disparagement—belittling, slighting.

[5] vicar—representative.

QUESTIONS TO CONSIDER

1. According to Shaw, why did Ibsen find democracy unsatisfactory?

2. Why can there be no such thing as an ideal state?

Stanislavsky and the Bearer Bonds

BY DAVID MAMET

The first great interpreter of the drama of Anton Chekhov was Konstantin Stanislavsky (1863–1938), the founder of the Moscow Art Theater. In the following essay, American playwright David Mamet (1947–   ) discusses the origin of Stanislavsky's concept of theatrical realism. Stanislavsky has been particularly influential in the United States, where adaptations of his ideas eventually led to the "method" style of acting practiced by such American actors as Marlon Brando and Dustin Hoffman.

Stanislavsky once asked his students to determine how to act the following scene: An accountant brings home from his office a fortune in negotiable bearer bonds, which he must catalogue. Living with him is his wife, their newborn child, and his wife's idiot brother.

He arrives home while his wife is bathing the baby. The idiot brother is seated by the fireplace staring into the fire.

The accountant wants to get started on his work before dinner so he sits down at the table, strips the wrappers off, which he throws in the fire, and starts cataloguing the bonds.

His wife calls from the next room, "Come and see how cute the baby is." The accountant gets up and goes into the next room. The idiot brother takes the bearer bonds and begins throwing them into the fire and laughing. The laughter draws the accountant back into the room. As he sees what is happening, he thrusts the brother out of the way, in an attempt to get the remaining bonds out of the fire before they burn. The brother hits his head on an andiron and dies. The wife comes running into the room and sees her brother dead. She then screams, "Oh my God, the baby!" and runs back into the other room, followed by her husband, where they both discover the baby drowned in the bath.

Stanislavsky told his students that when they know how to analyze and perform that scene, that *then* they would know how to act. . . .

New artistic vision grows in absolute contravention of this accepted thought. This is its fertile soil. In Berlin, in the 1870s, Stanislavsky saw a traveling troupe of players whose performance was the opposite of the formalized presentational theater of the day. They were the protégés of the Duke of Saxe-Meiningen.[1] This troupe treated each new play as a new problem in psychology; and rather than (in the accepted procedure) handing each actor only his or her lines, and assembling the cast several nights before the performance, said cast to act in support of the star around whom the performance was built, the Saxe-Meiningen troupe saw the play as an exercise in psychology. They analyzed the play in its entirety, and each individual part, to find the unifying theme, and then related that theme to congruent events in the life of the individual player, so that the actor trained to bring to the stage the message of the play, the actions of the character *as he believed it to relate to his own life.*

This was a revolutionary departure, and Stanislavsky, the son of a wealthy manufacturer, was sufficiently moved to forsake his class, adopt a foreign stage name (his family name was Alekseyev; "Stanislavsky" was the name of a Polish vaudeville performer), and embrace a despised profession.

Stanislavsky's obsession with "theatrical truth" grew and changed over the next forty years.

His axiom was to attempt to "Bring to the Stage the Life of the Human Soul" and, like many other artists, his attempts became more and more formal as he tried to codify his gains in knowledge, up until the point where they started becoming more and more mystical. He started out extending the set off the stage, so that the actor would not have to be shocked by the transition from the "real" into the "artificial," and, at the end of his career, he had his company sitting in a circle and endeavoring to transmit *prana*,[2] or rays of energy, to each other.

All his work was to the one end: to bring to the stage the life of the soul. As his vision of that life changed, he discarded the old and moved on.

---

[1] Duke of Saxe-Meiningen—German nobleman (1826–1914) who formed a private theater company and is generally considered the first modern director.

[2] *prana*—Hindu concept of the principle of life.

QUESTIONS TO CONSIDER

1. Why was the Saxe-Meiningen troupe revolutionary?

2. What was Stanislavsky's ideal of theatrical realism?

On *Blood Wedding*

BY ARTURO BAREA

In the following excerpt from his book Lorca: The Poet and His People, *Arturo Barea (1897–1957) discusses traditional Spanish attitudes toward sex and honor that infuse* Blood Wedding.

The mother is the incarnation[1] of this tragedy. A strong woman who enjoyed life with her husband, she has become dominated by the fear of the extinction of her blood—fear of death, not for herself but for the seed—and by an anxiety to see her physical existence continued, perpetuated by her son's children. This constant fear fills her with a sense of doom. Vengeance of her "blood" follows from her possessive, death-haunted love: to let the enemy's seed survive one's own would mean final death.

Centuries of Moorish[2] and medieval-Catholic breeding, centuries of a social order in which women were valued only for the sons they produced, created this attitude. The code which sprang from it is still valid in Spain. Lorca's "mother," who likes men to be lusty and wild because it means more sons, is deeply convinced that procreation and fecundity[3] are the object, not the correlate,[4] of married sexual love. Her son must marry to give her, the mother, grandchildren: ". . . and see to it that you

make me happy by giving me six grandchildren, or as many as you like, since your father did not have the time to make me more sons."

She glories in man's procreative strength: "Your grandfather left a son at every corner," she says proudly to her son. But she believes that a man must not only beget children but also engender life around him, be fecund in every sense. . . .

This moral conviction that men and women must be fecund and that the man and husband is the master because he is the instrument of fecundation has the deepest possible psychological and social roots. In peasant communities it is kept alive in its ancient form by a powerful economic fact: there must be sons to work the land and to defend the property. In Spain

---

[1] incarnation—personification.

[2] Moorish—relating to the medieval Islamic culture of Spain.

[3] fecundity—fruitfulness.

[4] correlate—effect.

this law was reinforced by the rules of the Moorish harem, rules which influenced the non-Moorish society of the country and survived the expulsion of the Moors. It was adjusted, exalted, and perpetuated in the stern teachings of the Church, which made it sinful for husband and wife to enjoy each other, but righteous to multiply. The code of honor which demands the taking of life and the preservation of virginity, not for the sake of "virtue" or love but for the sake of the purity of the "blood," is part of this tradition; it provides the sanctions against sexual offenses and protects the property of the family.

This code and the elements that went into its making were by no means confined to Spain. But the interesting point is that the code is still real to Spaniards, including those who have rationally repudiated it. . . .

In fact, blood feud and its code of honor are things of this age, not merely of the past, to Spaniards. The modern laws have prosecuted and suppressed **vendettas**,[5] but they were powerless against family feuds which lasted through generations and destroyed generations. The same fierce possessive love and haunting fear of extinction which drive the mother in Lorca's tragedy, drove many women during the Spanish Civil War and, through children steeped in hatred against the murderers of their "blood," threaten to breed relentless feuds for generations to come.

On this hard soil, the code of the blood is stronger than love. The mother in *Blood Wedding* admits no justification for the betrayal of the law of purity. A woman must have no lover. Contemptuously she says of the girl who followed her beloved: "Honest women, clean women, go into the water. But not she." This rule is accepted by the girl herself. She knows that she did wrong in following the other man, whom she could never marry, and in wanting to live with him. She accepts the law that the honor of the family and her own honor are safe only if her virginity is left intact for her husband to convert it into maternity.

---

[5] **vendettas**—feuds.

QUESTIONS TO CONSIDER

1. Why is the mother the "incarnation" of the tragedy in *Blood Wedding*?

2. Why is "the code of the blood stronger than love"?

On Stage

Modern Theater

A theater revolution began in the 1870s that eventually went in two very different directions. One tendency, represented by naturalism and realism, resulted in a heightened emphasis on exactly reproducing the appearance of the exterior world in sets, costumes, and props. The stage was conceived of as a "room with three walls" in which actors are supposed to be living real lives that the audience is observing through an invisible "fourth wall." Reacting against this approach were such antirealist movements as symbolism and expressionism, in which dramatic action, characters, setting, and language were intended to reflect states of mind.

▲

This production of Chekhov's early play *Ivanov* shows the "box set" representing the interior of a room that is typical of naturalist and realist theater.

▲
This production of Lorca's play *Blood Wedding* displays the antirealist staging typical of symbolist or expressionist theater.

Frederic March, playing Dr. Stockmann, in a 1950 adaptation by American playwright Arthur Miller of *An Enemy of the People,* defies the will of the community. ▶

Dr. Stockmann (Sam Tsoutsavas) listens to one of the townspeople in this scene from a 1992 production of *An Enemy of the People* by the Long Wharf Theatre in New Haven, Connecticut.
▼

 Konstantin Stanislavsky, founder of the Moscow Art Theater, is shown as Trigorin in the company's historic production of Chekhov's *The Sea Gull.*

The first act of *The Sea Gull* is shown in a 1938 New York production.
▼

Another scene from the Playmakers Rep production shows the actress Annalee Jeffries playing Madame Arkadin.

▲

In a 1996 production of *The Sea Gull* by the Playmakers Rep Company in Raleigh, North Carolina, Nina (Alyssa Breshahan) is shown performing Konstantin's play within a play in Act One.

▲
A scene from Sidney Lumet's 1968 film version of
Chekhov's *The Sea Gull* shows Masha (Kathleen
Widdoes), Nina (Vanessa Redgrave), Madame Arkadin
(Simone Signoret), and Sorin (Harry Andrews),
gathered on the lawn in Act Two.

David Warner is shown as Konstantin in another
scene from Lumet's film. ▶

▲
The Mother (Gloria Foster) encounters her son's bride-to-be (Elizabeth Peña) in Act One, Scene Three of Lorca's *Blood Wedding* in a 1992 New York Shakespeare Festival production.

In this photo from the 1992 production of *Blood Wedding*, the
Mother caresses the face of the Bridegroom (Al Rodrigo) on his
wedding day.

◀ The somber Bride in her wedding dress, "covered with pleated gauzes and heavy laces," stands beside her Bridegroom.

In the final scene of *Blood Wedding*, the Mother is overcome by grief following her son's death.

Part Four

American Drama

Local Heroes

The 20th century was a richly creative period for American drama, during which playwrights such as Tennessee Williams and Lorraine Hansberry contributed great plays to world theater.

The Glass Menagerie TENNESSEE WILLIAMS

A Raisin in the Sun LORRAINE HANSBERRY

◀ The Younger family shares a happy moment in Act Three of *A Raisin in the Sun.*

Tennessee Williams ▶

The Glass Menagerie

BY TENNESSEE WILLIAMS

Perhaps because of a lingering Puritan suspicion that the theater encouraged immorality, drama developed more slowly in the United States than other literary forms, such as poetry and fiction. Throughout the 1800s, American drama largely imitated the escapist European theater of the time. Melodramas became highly popular in America during this period. These plays stressed suspense, sentiment, moralism, and stagecraft; literary merit was secondary. Beginning in the 1870s, a revolution began in European drama, producing a rich, new, dramatic literature expressed in a spectrum of new theatrical styles. These styles ranged from naturalism and realism (see page 380) to anti-realist styles such as symbolism and expressionism (see page 519).

Modern American Drama

In the early 20th century, American dramatists absorbed these modern theatrical styles and used them to create vigorously original dramas, beginning with the major plays of Eugene O'Neill (1888–1953) in the early 1920s. A later influence on American drama was epic realism, which developed in Germany in the 1920s and 1930s. Epic realism rejected the emphasis on creating convincing theatrical illusion that was typical of naturalism and realism. It also rejected the emphasis on heightened aesthetic emotion typical of symbolism and expressionism. Instead, epic realism was frankly theatrical: for example, actors often addressed the audience, and the staging sometimes called for the use of descriptive titles onstage, either carried by the actors on signs or projected on screens. American playwrights were frequently not content to follow exclusively any single style, but preferred to combine them. In The Glass Menagerie, Tennessee Williams has synthesized a number of theatrical styles, including realism, symbolism, expressionism, and epic realism.

A Theater with the Blues

Born Thomas Lanier Williams (1911–1983), Tennessee Williams was one of the most important figures in 20th-century American drama. Williams's first successful play, The Glass Menagerie (1944), is strongly autobiographical. The drab St. Louis neighborhood in which the play is set, Tom's distasteful job at the shoe warehouse, his bookishness and devotion to writing, his habitual moviegoing, his mother's genteel background, his sister's loneliness and absorption in her glass collection—all these Williams drew from his own experience. Reflecting compassionately on memories of his youth, he created a play that combines tenderness and humor, sweetness and sadness—in the phrase of his great contemporary Arthur Miller—"a theater with the blues."

Southern Belles

Most of Williams's plays are set in the American South and reflect some of that region's characteristic social values. One of these is a traditional idealization of women as physically delicate, culturally refined, highly moral, and greatly in need of male protection. The most famous embodiment of this tradition in Williams's drama is Blanche DuBois, the faded belle in A Streetcar Named Desire. In The Glass Menagerie the tradition of Southern womanhood is particularly evident in the character of the mother, Amanda, and her devotion to her memories of the vanished social glories of her girlhood.

CHARACTERS

Amanda Wingfield, the mother. A little woman of great but confused vitality clinging frantically to another time and place. Her characterization must be carefully created, not copied from type. She is not paranoiac, but her life is paranoia.[1] There is much to admire in Amanda, and as much to love and pity as there is to laugh at. Certainly she has endurance and a kind of heroism, and though her foolishness makes her unwittingly cruel at times, there is tenderness in her slight person.

Laura Wingfield, her daughter. Amanda, having failed to establish contact with reality, continues to live vitally in her illusions, but Laura's situation is even graver.

A childhood illness has left her crippled, one leg slightly shorter than the other, and held in a brace. This defect need not be more than suggested on the stage. Stemming from this, Laura's separation increases till she is like a piece of her own glass collection, too exquisitely fragile to move from the shelf.

Tom Wingfield, her son. And the narrator of the play. A poet with a job in a warehouse. His nature is not **remorseless**,[2] but to escape from a trap he has to act without pity.

Jim O'Connor, the gentleman caller. A nice, ordinary, young man.

---

[1] paranoiac . . . paranoia—Paranoia is a mental disorder characterized by elaborate delusions. Williams means that although Amanda is not insane, her life is defined by delusions.

[2] **remorseless**—merciless.

SCENE: An alley in St. Louis.
    Part One. Preparation for a Gentleman Caller.
    Part Two. The Gentleman Calls.
TIME: Now and the Past.

Part One
Scene One

[*The Wingfield apartment is in the rear of the building, one of those vast hive-like conglomerations*[3] *of cellular living units that flower as warty growths in over-crowded urban centers of lower middle-class population and are symptomatic of the impulse of this largest and fundamentally enslaved section of American society to avoid fluidity and differentiation and to exist and function as one interfused*[4] *mass of automatism.*[5]

    The apartment faces an alley and is entered by a fire escape, a structure whose name is a touch of accidental poetic truth, for all of these huge buildings are always burning with the slow and implacable[6] *fires of human desperation. The fire escape is included in the set—that is, the landing of it and steps descending from it.*

    The scene is memory and is therefore unrealistic. Memory takes a lot of poetic license. It omits some details; others are exaggerated, according to the emotional value of the articles it touches, for memory is seated predominantly in the heart. The interior is therefore rather dim and poetic.

    At the rise of the curtain, the audience is faced with the dark, grim rear wall of the Wingfield tenement. This building, which runs parallel to the footlights, is flanked on both sides by dark, narrow alleys which run into murky canyons of tangled clotheslines, garbage cans and the sinister latticework[7] *of neighboring fire escapes. It is up and down these side alleys that exterior entrances and exits are made during the play. At the end of* Tom's *opening commentary, the dark tenement wall slowly reveals (by means of a transparency*[8]*) the interior of the ground floor Wingfield apartment.*

    Downstage is the living room, which also serves as a sleeping room for Laura, *the sofa unfolding to make her bed. Upstage, center, and divided by a*

---

[3] *conglomerations*—clusters, masses.

[4] *interfused*—mingled.

[5] *automatism*—unconscious movements.

[6] *implacable*—relentless.

[7] *latticework*—diagonal or crisscross pattern.

[8] *transparency*—backdrop curtain that becomes transparent when lighted from behind. Also called a *scrim.*

wide arch or second proscenium with transparent faded portieres[9] *(or second curtain), is the dining room. In an old-fashioned whatnot*[10] *in the living room are seen scores of transparent glass animals. A blown-up photograph of the father hangs on the wall of the living room, facing the audience, to the left of the archway. It is the face of a very handsome young man in a doughboy's First World War cap.*[11] *He is gallantly smiling, ineluctably*[12] *smiling, as if to say, "I will be smiling forever."*

The audience hears and sees the opening scene in the dining room through both the transparent fourth wall of the building and the transparent gauze portieres of the dining-room arch. It is during this revealing scene that the fourth wall slowly ascends, out of sight. This transparent exterior wall is not brought down again until the very end of the play, during Tom's *final speech.*

The narrator is an undisguised convention of the play. He takes whatever license with dramatic convention as is convenient to his purposes.

Tom *enters dressed as a merchant sailor from the alley, stage left, and strolls across the front of the stage to the fire escape. There he stops and lights a cigarette. He addresses the audience.*]

Tom. Yes, I have tricks in my pocket, I have things up my sleeve. But I am the opposite of a stage magician. He gives you illusion that has the appearance of truth. I give you truth in the pleasant disguise of illusion. To begin with, I turn back time. I reverse it to that quaint period, the thirties, when the huge middle class of America was matriculating[13] in a school for the blind. Their eyes had failed them, or they had failed their eyes, and so they were having their fingers pressed forcibly down on the fiery Braille alphabet[14] of a dissolving economy. In Spain there was revolution. Here there was only shouting and confusion. In Spain there was Guernica.[15] Here there were disturbances of labor, sometimes pretty violent, in otherwise peaceful cities such as Chicago, Cleveland, St. Louis. . . . This is the social background of the play.

---

[9] *portieres*—heavy curtains hung across a doorway.

[10] *whatnot*—case for knickknacks.

[11] *doughboy's . . . cap*—Doughboy was a term for an American infantryman in World War I.

[12] *ineluctably*—unavoidably.

[13] *matriculating*—enrolling.

[14] Braille alphabet—alphabet for the blind.

[15] Spain . . . Guernica—In 1936 the right-wing followers of Spanish general Francisco Franco revolted against Spain's left-wing Republic, and a civil war was fought which ended with Franco's victory in 1939. One of the most notorious events of the Spanish Civil War was the destruction in 1937 of the ancient Basque town of Guernica by German bombers. The Germans were Franco's allies.

[*Music.*]

The play is memory. Being a memory play, it is dimly lighted, it is sentimental, it is not realistic. In memory everything seems to happen to music. That explains the fiddle in the wings. I am the narrator of the play, and also a character in it. The other characters are my mother, Amanda, my sister, Laura, and a gentleman caller who appears in the final scenes. He is the most realistic character in the play, being an **emissary**[16] from a world of reality that we were somehow set apart from. But since I have a poet's weakness for symbols, I am using this character also as a symbol; he is the long delayed but always expected something that we live for. There is a fifth character in the play who doesn't appear except in this larger-than-life photograph over the mantel. This is our father who left us a long time ago. He was a telephone man who fell in love with long distances; he gave up his job with the telephone company and skipped the light fantastic out of town. . . . The last we heard of him was a picture post-card from Mazatlan, on the Pacific coast of Mexico, containing a message of two words— "Hello—Good-bye!" and an address. I think the rest of the play will explain itself. . . .

[*Amanda's voice becomes audible through the portieres.*]

[*Screen Legend: "Où Sont Les Neiges."*[17]]

[*He divides the portieres and enters the upstage area.*

Amanda *and* Laura *are seated at a drop-leaf table. Eating is indicated by gestures without food or utensils.* Amanda *faces the audience.* Tom *and* Laura *are seated in profile.*

The interior has lit up softly and through the scrim we see Amanda *and* Laura *seated at the table in the upstage area.*]

Amanda [*calling*]. Tom?

Tom. Yes, Mother.

Amanda. We can't say grace until you come to the table!

Tom. Coming, Mother. [*He bows slightly and withdraws, reappearing a few moments later in his place at the table.*]

Amanda [*to her son*]. Honey, don't *push* with your *fingers.* If you have to push with something, the thing to push with is a crust of bread. And chew—chew! Animals have sections in their stomachs which enable

---

[16] **emissary**—agent sent on a mission to represent or advance the interests of another.

[17] *Screen Legend: "Où Sont Les Neiges"*—This stage direction indicates that a sign bearing the famous refrain ("Where are the snows of yesteryear?") from a poem by the medieval French poet François Villon (1431–1463?) is to be projected on a stage wall. The refrain expresses the transitory nature of all things, including human life.

them to digest food without mastication,[18] but human beings are supposed to chew their food before they swallow it down. Eat food leisurely, son, and really enjoy it. A well-cooked meal has lots of delicate flavors that have to be held in the mouth for appreciation. So chew your food and give your salivary glands a chance to function!

[Tom *deliberately lays his imaginary fork down and pushes his chair back from the table.*]

Tom. I haven't enjoyed one bite of this dinner because of your constant directions on how to eat it. It's you that makes me rush through meals with your hawk-like attention to every bite I take. Sickening—spoils my appetite—all this discussion of animals' secretion—salivary glands—mastication!

Amanda [*lightly*]. Temperament like a Metropolitan star![19] [*He rises and crosses downstage.*] You're not excused from the table.

Tom. I am getting a cigarette.

Amanda. You smoke too much.

[Laura *rises.*]

Laura. I'll bring in the blanc mange.[20]

[*He remains standing with his cigarette by the portieres during the following.*]

Amanda [*rising*]. No, sister, no, sister—you be the lady this time and I'll be the servant.

Laura. I'm already up.

Amanda. Resume your seat, little sister—I want you to stay fresh and pretty—for gentlemen callers!

Laura. I'm not expecting any gentlemen callers.

Amanda [*crossing out to kitchenette. Airily*]. Sometimes they come when they are least expected! Why, I remember one Sunday afternoon in Blue Mountain— [*Enters kitchenette.*]

Tom. I know what's coming!

Laura. Yes. But let her tell it.

Tom. Again?

Laura. She loves to tell it.

[Amanda *returns with bowl of dessert.*]

Amanda. One Sunday afternoon in Blue Mountain—your mother received—*seventeen!*—gentlemen callers! Why, sometimes there

---

[18] mastication—chewing.

[19] Metropolitan star—star of the Metropolitan Opera.

[20] blanc mange—milk pudding.

weren't chairs enough to accommodate them all. We had to send the servant over to bring in folding chairs from the parish house.

Tom [*remaining at portieres*]. How did you entertain those gentlemen callers?

Amanda. I understood the art of conversation!

Tom. I bet you could talk.

Amanda. Girls in those days knew how to talk, I can tell you.

Tom. Yes?

[*Image:* Amanda *As A Girl On A Porch Greeting Callers.*]

Amanda. They knew how to entertain their gentlemen callers. It wasn't enough for a girl to be possessed of a pretty face and a graceful figure—although I wasn't slighted in either respect. She also needed to have a nimble wit and a tongue to meet all occasions.

Tom. What did you talk about?

Amanda. Things of importance going on in the world! Never anything coarse or common or vulgar. [*She addresses* Tom *as though he were seated in the vacant chair at the table though he remains by portieres. He plays this scene as though he held the book.*[21]] My callers were gentlemen—all! Among my callers were some of the most prominent young planters of the Mississippi Delta—planters and sons of planters!

[Tom *motions for music and a spot of light on* Amanda. *Her eyes lift, her face glows, her voice becomes rich and elegiac.*[22]]

[*Screen Legend: "Où Sont Les Neiges."*]

There was young Champ Laughlin who later became vice-president of the Delta Planters Bank. Hadley Stevenson who was drowned in Moon Lake and left his widow one hundred and fifty thousand in Government bonds. There were the Cutrere brothers, Wesley and Bates. Bates was one of my bright particular beaux![23] He got in a quarrel with that wild Wainright boy. They shot it out on the floor of Moon Lake Casino. Bates was shot through the stomach. Died in the ambulance on his way to Memphis. His widow was also well-provided for, came into eight or ten thousand acres, that's all. She married him on the rebound—never loved her—carried my picture on him the night he died! And there was that boy that every girl in the Delta had set her cap for! That beautiful, brilliant young Fitzhugh boy from Green County!

Tom. What did he leave his widow?

---

[21] *book*—director's promptbook, containing the script of the play and the director's notes for the production.

[22] *elegiac*—gently mournful.

[23] *beaux*—sweethearts, boyfriends.

Amanda. He never married! Gracious, you talk as though all of my old admirers had turned up their toes to the daisies!

Tom. Isn't this the first you mentioned that still survives?

Amanda. That Fitzhugh boy went North and made a fortune—came to be known as the Wolf of Wall Street! He had the Midas touch, whatever he touched turned to gold! And I could have been Mrs. Duncan J. Fitzhugh, mind you! But—I picked your father!

Laura [*rising*]. Mother, let me clear the table.

Amanda. No dear, you go in front and study your typewriter chart. Or practice your shorthand a little. Stay fresh and pretty!—It's almost time for our gentlemen callers to start arriving. [*She flounces*[24] *girlishly toward the kitchenette.*] How many do you suppose we're going to entertain this afternoon?

[Tom *throws down the paper and jumps up with a groan.*]

Laura [*alone in the dining room*]. I don't believe we're going to receive any, Mother.

Amanda [*reappearing, airily*[25]]. What? No one—not one? You must be joking! [Laura *nervously echoes her laugh. She slips in a fugitive manner through the half-open portieres and draws them gently behind her. A shaft of very clear light is thrown on her face against the jaded tapestry of the curtains.*] [*Music:*[26] *"The Glass Menagerie" Under Faintly.*] [*Lightly.*] Not one gentleman caller? It can't be true! There must be a flood, there must have been a tornado!

Laura. It isn't a flood, it's not a tornado, Mother. I'm just not popular like you were in Blue Mountain. . . . [Tom *utters another groan.* Laura *glances at him with a faint, apologetic smile. Her voice catching a little.*] Mother's afraid I'm going to be an old maid.

[*The Scene Dims Out With "Glass Menagerie" Music.*]

Scene Two

"Laura, Haven't You Ever Liked Some Boy?"
[*On the dark stage the screen is lighted with the image of blue roses.*
    Gradually Laura's *figure becomes apparent and the screen goes out.*
    The music subsides.

---

[24] *flounces*—moves in an exaggerated manner.

[25] *airily*—light-heartedly.

[26] *Music*—In his "Production Notes" for the play, Williams observes, "A single recurring tune, 'The Glass Menagerie,' is used to give emphasis to suitable passages. The tune is like circus music . . . at some distance. . . . It expresses the surface vivacity of life with the underlying strain of immutable and inexpressable sorrow."

Laura *is seated in the delicate ivory chair at the small clawfoot table.*

She wears a dress of soft violet material for a kimono[27]*—her hair tied back from her forehead with a ribbon.*

She is washing and polishing her collection of glass.

Amanda *appears on the fire-escape steps. At the sound of her ascent,* Laura *catches her breath, thrusts the bowl of ornaments away and seats herself stiffly before the diagram of the typewriter keyboard as though it held her spellbound. Something has happened to* Amanda. *It is written in her face as she climbs to the landing: a look that is grim and hopeless and a little absurd.*

She has on one of those cheap or imitation velvety looking cloth coats with imitation fur collar. Her hat is five or six years old, one of those dreadful cloche hats[28] *that were worn in the late twenties, and she is clasping an enormous black patent-leather pocketbook with nickel clasp and initials. This is her fulldress outfit, the one she usually wears to the* D.A.R.[29]

Before entering she looks through the door.

She purses her lips, opens her eyes wide, rolls them upward and shakes her head.

Then she slowly lets herself in the door. Seeing her mother's expression Laura *touches her lips with a nervous gesture.*]

Laura. Hello, Mother, I was—[*She makes a nervous gesture toward the chart on the wall.* Amanda *leans against the shut door and stares at* Laura *with a martyred look.*]

Amanda. Deception? Deception? [*She slowly removes her hat and gloves, continuing the swift suffering stare. She lets the hat and gloves fall on the floor—a bit of acting.*]

Laura [*shakily*]. How was the D.A.R. meeting? [Amanda *slowly opens her purse and removes a dainty white handkerchief which she shakes out delicately and delicately touches to her lips and nostrils.*] Didn't you go to the D.A.R. meeting, Mother?

Amanda [*faintly, almost inaudibly*]. —No. —No. [*Then more forcibly.*] I did not have the strength—to go to the D.A.R. In fact, I did not have the courage! I wanted to find a hole in the ground and hide myself in it forever! [*She crosses slowly to the wall and removes the diagram of the typewriter keyboard. She holds it in front of her for a second, staring at it sweetly and sorrowfully—then bites her lips and tears it in two pieces.*]

---

[27] *kimono*—loose robe.

[28] *cloche hats*—close-fitting, bell-shaped women's hats.

[29] *D.A.R.*—Daughters of the American Revolution.

Laura [*faintly*]. Why did you do that, Mother? [Amanda *repeats the same procedure with the chart of the Gregg Alphabet.*[30]] Why are you—

Amanda. Why? Why? How old are you, Laura?

Laura. Mother, you know my age.

Amanda. I thought that you were an adult; it seems that I was mistaken. [*She crosses slowly to the sofa and sinks down and stares at* Laura.]

Laura. Please don't stare at me, Mother.

[Amanda *closes her eyes and lowers her head. Count ten.*]

Amanda. What are we going to do, what is going to become of us, what is the future?

[*Count ten.*]

Laura. Has something happened, Mother? [Amanda *draws a long breath and takes out the handkerchief again. Dabbing process.*] Mother, has—something happened?

Amanda. I'll be all right in a minute. I'm just bewildered—[*count five*]—by life. . . .

Laura. Mother, I wish that you would tell me what's happened.

Amanda. As you know, I was supposed to be inducted into my office at the D.A.R. this afternoon. [*Image: A Swarm of Typewriters.*] But I stopped off at Rubicam's Business College to speak to your teachers about your having a cold and ask them what progress they thought you were making down there.

Laura. Oh . . .

Amanda. I went to the typing instructor and introduced myself as your mother. She didn't know who you were. Wingfield, she said. We don't have any such student enrolled at the school! I assured her she did, that you had been going to classes since early in January. "I wonder," she said, "if you could be talking about that terribly shy little girl who dropped out of school after only a few days' attendance?" "No," I said, "Laura, my daughter, has been going to school every day for the past six weeks!" "Excuse me," she said. She took the attendance book out and there was your name, unmistakably printed, and all the dates you were absent until they decided that you had dropped out of school. I still said, "No, there must have been some mistake! There must have been some mix-up in the records!" And she said, "No—I remember her perfectly now. Her hand shook so that she couldn't hit the right keys! The first time we gave a speed-test, she broke down

---

[30] *Gregg Alphabet*—symbols used in taking shorthand.

completely—was sick at the stomach and almost had to be carried into the washroom! After that morning she never showed up anymore. We phoned the house but never got any answer"—while I was working at Famous and Barr, I suppose, demonstrating those—Oh! I felt so weak I could barely keep on my feet. I had to sit down while they got me a glass of water! Fifty dollars' tuition, all of our plans—my hopes and ambitions for you—just gone up the spout, just gone up the spout like that. [Laura *draws a long breath and gets awkwardly to her feet. She crosses to the victrola*[31] *and winds it up.*] What are you doing?

Laura. Oh! [*She releases the handle and returns to her seat.*]

Amanda. Laura, where have you been going when you've gone out pretending that you were going to business college?

Laura. I've just been going out walking.

Amanda. That's not true.

Laura. It is. I just went walking.

Amanda. Walking? Walking? In winter? Deliberately courting pneumonia in that light coat? Where did you walk to, Laura?

Laura. It was the lesser of two evils, Mother. [*Image: Winter Scene In Park.*] I couldn't go back. I—threw up—on the floor!

Amanda. From half past seven till after five every day you mean to tell me you walked around in the park, because you wanted to make me think that you were still going to Rubicam's Business College?

Laura. It wasn't as bad as it sounds. I went inside places to get warmed up.

Amanda. Inside where?

Laura. I went in the art museum and the birdhouses at the Zoo. I visited the penguins every day! Sometimes I did without lunch and went to the movies. Lately I've been spending most of my afternoons in the Jewel-box, that big glass house where they raise the tropical flowers.

Amanda. You did all this to deceive me, just for the deception? [Laura *looks down.*] Why?

Laura. Mother, when you're disappointed, you get that awful suffering look on your face, like the picture of Jesus' mother in the museum!

Amanda. Hush!

Laura. I couldn't face it.

[*Pause. A whisper of strings.*]

[*Legend: "The Crust Of Humility."*]

---

[31] *victrola*—early phonograph.

Amanda [*hopelessly fingering the huge pocketbook*]. So what are we going to do the rest of our lives? Stay home and watch the parades go by? Amuse ourselves with the glass **menagerie**,[32] darling? Eternally play those worn-out phonograph records your father left as a painful reminder of him? We won't have a business career—we've given that up because it gave us nervous indigestion! [*Laughs wearily.*] What is there left but dependence all our lives? I know so well what becomes of unmarried women who aren't prepared to occupy a position. I've seen such pitiful cases in the South—barely tolerated spinsters living upon the grudging patronage of sister's husband or brother's wife!—stuck away in some little mousetrap of a room— encouraged by one in-law to visit another—little birdlike women without any nest—eating the crust of humility all their life! Is that the future that we've mapped out for ourselves? I swear it's the only alternative I can think of! It isn't a very pleasant alternative, is it? Of course—some girls do marry. [Laura *twists her hands nervously.*] Haven't you ever liked some boy?

Laura. Yes I liked one once. [*Rises.*] I came across his picture a while ago.

Amanda [*with some interest*]. He gave you his picture?

Laura. No, it's in the yearbook.

Amanda [*disappointed*]. Oh—a high-school boy.

[*Screen Image:* Jim *As A High-School Hero Bearing A Silver Cup.*]

Laura. Yes. His name was Jim. [Laura *lifts the heavy annual from the claw-foot table.*] Here he is in *The Pirates of Penzance.*[33]

Amanda [*absently*]. The what?

Laura. The operetta the senior class put on. He had a wonderful voice and we sat across the aisle from each other Mondays, Wednesdays and Fridays in the Aud. Here he is with the silver cup for debating! See his grin?

Amanda [*absently*]. He must have had a jolly disposition.

Laura. He used to call me—Blue Roses.

[*Image: Blue Roses.*]

Amanda. Why did he call you such a name as that?

Laura. When I had that attack of pleurosis[34]—he asked me what was the matter when I came back. I said pleurosis—he thought that I said Blue Roses! So that's what he always called me after that. Whenever

---

[32] **menagerie**—collection of animals.

[33] *The Pirates of Penzance*—operetta (1879) by Gilbert and Sullivan.

[34] pleurosis—pleurisy, inflammation of the membrane that lines the chest cavity.

he saw me, he'd holler, "Hello, Blue Roses!" I didn't care for the girl he went out with. Emily Meisenbach. Emily was the best-dressed girl at Soldan. She never struck me, though, as being sincere . . . It says in the Personal Section—they're engaged. That's—six years ago! They must be married by now.

Amanda. Girls that aren't cut out for business careers usually wind up married to some nice man. [*Gets up with a spark of revival.*] Sister, that's what you'll do!

[Laura *utters a startled, doubtful laugh. She reaches quickly for a piece of glass.*]

Laura. But, Mother—

Amanda. Yes! [*Crossing to phonograph.*]

Laura [*in a tone of frightened apology*]. I'm—crippled!

[*Image: Screen.*]

Amanda. Nonsense! Laura, I've told you never, never to use that word. Why, you're not crippled, you just have a little defect—hardly noticeable, even! When people have some slight disadvantage like that, they cultivate other things to make up for it—develop charm—and **vivacity**[35]—and—*charm!* That's all you have to do! [*She turns again to the phonograph.*] One thing your father had *plenty of*—was *charm!*

[Tom *motions to the fiddle in the wings.*]

[*The Scene Fades Out With Music.*]

Scene Three

[*Legend On The Screen: "After The Fiasco—"*]

[Tom *speaks from the fire-escape landing.*]

Tom. After the fiasco at Rubicam's Business College, the idea of getting a gentleman caller for Laura began to play a more important part in Mother's calculations. It became an obsession. Like some archetype of the universal unconscious,[36] the image of the gentleman caller haunted our small apartment. . . . [*Image: Young Man At Door With Flowers.*] An evening at home rarely passed without some allusion to this image, this specter, this hope. . . . Even when he wasn't mentioned, his presence hung in Mother's preoccupied look and in my sister's frightened, apologetic manner—hung like a sentence passed upon the Wingfields! Mother was a woman of action as well as words. She

---

[35] **vivacity**—liveliness.

[36] archetype of the universal unconscious—according to one psychological theory, an ideal figure from collective human memory.

began to take logical steps in the planned direction. Late that winter and in the early spring—realizing that extra money would be needed to properly feather the nest and plume the bird—she conducted a vigorous campaign on the telephone, roping in subscribers to one of those magazines for matrons called *The Homemaker's Companion,* the type of journal that features the serialized sublimations of ladies of letters[37] who think in terms of delicate cup-like breasts, slim, tapering waists, rich, creamy thighs, eyes like wood-smoke in autumn, fingers that soothe and caress like strains of music, bodies as powerful as Etruscan sculpture.[38]

[*Screen Image: Glamor Magazine Cover.*]

[Amanda *enters with phone on long extension cord. She is spotted in the dim stage.*]

Amanda. Ida Scott? This is Amanda Wingfield! We *missed* you at the D.A.R. last Monday! I said to myself: She's probably suffering with that sinus condition! How is that sinus condition? Horrors! Heaven have mercy!—You're a Christian martyr, yes, that's what you are, a Christian martyr! Well, I just now happened to notice that your subscription to the *Companion's* about to expire! Yes, it expires with the next issue, honey!—just when that wonderful new serial by Bessie Mae Hopper is getting off to such an exciting start. Oh, honey, it's something that you can't miss! You remember how *Gone With the Wind* took everybody by storm? You simply couldn't go out if you hadn't read it. All everybody *talked* was Scarlett O'Hara. Well, this is a book that critics already compare to *Gone With the Wind.* It's the *Gone With the Wind* of the post-World War generation!—What?—Burning?—Oh, honey, don't let them burn, go take a took in the oven and I'll hold the wire! Heavens—I think she's hung up!

[*Dim Out.*]

[*Legend On Screen: "You Think I'm In Love With Continental Shoemakers?"*]

[*Before the stage is lighted, the violent voices of* Tom *and* Amanda *are heard. They are quarreling behind the portieres. In front of them stands* Laura *with clenched hands and panicky expression.*

A clear pool of light on her figure throughout this scene.]

Tom. What in Christ's name am I—

Amanda [*shrilly*]. Don't you use that—

Tom. Supposed to do!

---

[37] serialized sublimations of ladies of letters—Tom means women's magazine fiction in which sexual situations are heavily romanticized.

[38] Etruscan sculpture—art of a people of ancient Italy.

Amanda. Expression! Not in my—

Tom. Ohhh!

Amanda. Presence! Have you gone out of your senses?

Tom. I have, that's true, *driven* out!

Amanda. What is the matter with you, you—big—big—IDIOT!

Tom. Look—I've got *no thing,* no single thing—

Amanda. Lower your voice!

Tom. In my life here that I can call my OWN! Everything is—

Amanda. Stop that shouting!

Tom. Yesterday you confiscated my books! You had the nerve to—

Amanda. I took that horrible novel back to the library—yes! That hideous
book by that insane Mr. Lawrence.[39] [Tom *laughs wildly.*] I cannot
control the output of diseased minds or people who cater to them—
[Tom *laughs still more wildly.*] BUT I WON'T ALLOW SUCH FILTH
BROUGHT INTO MY HOUSE! No, no, no, no, no!

Tom. House, house! Who pays rent on it, who makes a slave of himself to—

Amanda [*fairly screeching*]. Don't you DARE to—

Tom. No, no, I mustn't say things! *I've* got to just—

Amanda. Let me tell you—

Tom. I don't want to hear any more! [*He tears the portieres open. The
upstage area is lit with a turgid[40] smoky red glow.*]

[Amanda's *hair is in metal curlers and she wears a very old bathrobe, much too
large for her slight figure, a relic of the faithless Mr. Wingfield.*

*An upright typewriter and a wild disarray of manuscripts are on the drop-
leaf table. The quarrel was probably* **precipitated**[41] *by* Amanda's *interruption of
his creative labor. A chair lying overthrown on the floor.*

Their gesticulating[42] shadows are cast on the ceiling by the fiery glow.]

Amanda. You *will* hear more, you—

Tom. No, I won't hear more, I'm going out!

Amanda. You come right back in—

Tom. Out, out out! Because I'm—

Amanda. Come back here, Tom Wingfield! I'm not through talking to you!

Tom. Oh, go—

Laura [*desperately*]. Tom!

---

[39] Mr. Lawrence—English writer D. H. Lawrence (1885–1930), notorious for his handling of sex in his fiction.

[40] *turgid*—bloated.

[41] **precipitated**—caused.

[42] *gesticulating*—gesturing.

Amanda. You're going to listen, and no more **insolence**[43] from you! I'm at the end of my patience! [*He comes back toward her.*]

Tom. What do you think I'm at? Aren't I supposed to have any patience to reach the end of, Mother? I know, I know. It seems unimportant to you, what I'm *doing*—what I *want* to do—having a little *difference* between them! You don't think that—

Amanda. I think you've been doing things that you're ashamed of. That's why you act like this. I don't believe that you go every night to the movies. Nobody goes to the movies night after night. Nobody in their right minds goes to the movies as often as you pretend to. People don't go to the movies at nearly midnight, and movies don't let out at two A.M. Come in stumbling. Muttering to yourself like a maniac! You get three hours' sleep and then go to work. Oh, I can picture the way you're doing down there. Moping, doping, because you're in no condition.

Tom [*wildly*]. No, I'm in no condition!

Amanda. What right have you got to jeopardize your job! Jeopardize the security of us all? How do you think we'd manage if you were—

Tom. Listen! You think I'm crazy *about* the *warehouse*? [*He bends fiercely toward her slight figure.*] You think I'm in love with the Continental Shoemakers? You think I want to spend fifty-five *years* down there in that—*celotex interior!* with—*fluorescent*—*tubes!* Look! I'd rather somebody picked up a crowbar and battered out my brains—than go back mornings! I *go!* Every time you come in yelling that . . . *"Rise and Shine!" "Rise and Shine!"* I say to myself "How *lucky dead* people are!" But I get up. I *go!* For sixty-five dollars a month I give up all that I dream of doing and being *ever!* And you say self—*self's* all I ever think of. Why, listen, if self is what I thought of, Mother, I'd be where he is—GONE! [*Pointing to father's picture.*] As far as the system of transportation reaches! [*He starts past her. She grabs his arm.*] Don't grab at me, Mother!

Amanda. Where are you going?

Tom. I'm going to the *movies!*

Amanda. I don't believe that lie!

Tom [*crouching toward her, overtowering her tiny figure. She backs away, gasping*]. I'm going to opium dens! Yes, opium dens, dens of vice and criminals' hangouts, Mother. I've joined the Hogan gang, I'm a hired

---

[43] **insolence**—rudeness.

assassin, I carry a tommy-gun in a violin case! I run a string of cat-houses[44] in the Valley! They call me Killer, Killer Wingfield, I'm leading a double life, a simple, honest warehouse worker by day, by night a dynamic *czar* of the *underworld, Mother.* I go to gambling casinos, I spin away fortunes on the roulette table! I wear a patch over one eye and a false mustache, sometimes I put on green whiskers. On those occasions they call me—*El Diablo!*[45] Oh, I could tell you things to make you sleepless! My enemies plan to dynamite this place. They're going to blow us all sky-high some night! I'll be glad, very happy, and so will you! You'll go up, up on a broomstick, over Blue Mountain with seventeen gentlemen callers! You ugly—babbling old—*witch.* . . . [*He goes through a series of violent, clumsy movements, seizing his overcoat, lunging to the door, pulling it fiercely open. The women watch him, **aghast.**[46] His arm catches in the sleeve of the coat as he struggles to pull it on. For a moment he is pinioned[47] by the bulky garment. With an outraged groan he tears the coat off again, splitting the shoulders of it, and hurls it across the room. It strikes against the shelf of* Laura's *glass collection, there is a tinkle of shattering glass.* Laura *cries out as if wounded.*]

[*Music Legend: "The Glass Menagerie."*]

Laura [*shrilly*]. My glass!—menagerie. . . . [*She covers her face and turns away.*]

[*But* Amanda *is still stunned and **stupefied**[48] by the "ugly witch" so that she barely notices this occurrence. Now she recovers her speech.*]

Amanda [*in an awful voice*]. I won't speak to you—until you apologize!

[*She crosses through portieres and draws them together behind her.* Tom *is left with* Laura. Laura *clings weakly to the mantel with her face averted.* Tom *stares at her stupidly for a moment. Then he crosses to shelf. Drops awkwardly to his knees to collect the fallen glass, glancing at* Laura *as if he would speak but couldn't.*]

[*"The Glass Menagerie" steals in as The Scene Dims Out.*]

Scene Four

[*The interior is dark. Faint in the alley.*

    A deep-voiced bell in a church is tolling the hour of five as the scene commences. Tom *appears at the top of the alley. After each solemn boom of the bell in*

---

[44] cat-houses—houses of prostitution.

[45] *El Diablo*—the Devil.

[46] **aghast**—shocked.

[47] *pinioned*—bound.

[48] **stupefied**—amazed.

the tower, he shakes a little noise-maker or rattle as if to express the tiny spasm of man in contrast to the sustained power and dignity of the Almighty. This and the unsteadiness of his advance make it evident that he has been drinking.

As he climbs the few steps to the fire-escape landing light steals up inside. Laura *appears in nightdress, observing* Tom's *empty bed in the front room.*

Tom *fishes in his pockets for the door key, removing a motley assortment of articles in the search, including a perfect shower of movie ticket stubs and an empty bottle. At last he finds the key, but just as he is about to insert it, it slips from his fingers. He strikes a match and crouches below the door.*]

Tom [*bitterly*]. One crack—and it falls through!

[Laura *opens the door.*]

Laura. Tom! Tom, what are you doing!

Tom. Looking for a door key.

Laura. Where have you been all this time?

Tom. I have been to the movies.

Laura. All this time at the movies?

Tom. There was a very long program. There was a Garbo[49] picture and a Mickey Mouse and a travelogue and a newsreel and a preview of coming attractions. And there was an organ solo and a collection for the milk fund—simultaneously—which ended up in a terrible fight between a fat lady and an usher!

Laura [*innocently*]. Did you have to stay through everything?

Tom. Of course! And, oh, I forgot! There was a big stage show! The headliner on this stage show was Malvolio the Magician. He performed wonderful tricks, many of them, such as pouring water back and forth between pitchers. First it turned to wine and then it turned to beer and then it turned to whiskey. I know it was whiskey it finally turned into because he needed somebody to come up out of the audience to help him, and I came up——both shows! It was Kentucky Straight Bourbon. A very generous fellow, he gave souvenirs. [*He pulls from his back pocket a shimmering rainbow-colored scarf.*] He gave me this. This is his magic scarf. You can have it, Laura. You wave it over a canary cage and you get a bowl of goldfish. You wave it over the goldfish bowl and they fly away canaries. . . . But the wonderfullest trick of all was the coffin trick. We nailed him into a coffin and he got out of the coffin without removing one nail. [*He has come inside.*] There is a trick that would come in handy for me—get me out of this 2 by 4 situation! [*Flops onto bed and starts removing shoes.*]

---

[49] Garbo—Swedish-born American film actress Greta Garbo (1905–1990).

Laura. Tom—Shhh!

Tom. What're you shushing me for?

Laura. You'll wake up Mother.

Tom. Goody, goody! Pay 'er back for all those "Rise an' Shines." [*Lies down, groaning.*] You know it don't take much intelligence to get yourself into a nailed–up coffin, Laura. But who . . . ever got himself out of one without removing one nail?

[*As if in answer, the father's grinning photograph lights up.*]

[*Scene Dims Out.*]

[*Immediately following: The church bell is heard striking six. At the sixth stroke the alarm clock goes off in* Amanda's *room, and after a few moments we hear her calling: "Rise and Shine! Rise and Shine! Laura, go tell your brother to rise and shine!"*]

Tom [*sitting up slowly*]. I'll rise—but I won't shine.

[*The light increases.*]

Amanda. Laura, tell your brother his coffee is ready.

[Laura *slips into front room.*]

Laura. Tom! it's nearly seven. Don't make Mother nervous. [*He stares at her stupidly. Beseechingly.*] Tom, speak to Mother this morning. Make up with her, apologize, speak to her!

Tom. She won't to me. It's her that started not speaking.

Laura. If you just say you're sorry she'll start speaking.

Tom. Her not speaking—is that such a tragedy?

Laura. Please—please!

Amanda [*calling from kitchenette*]. Laura, are you going to do what I asked you to do, or do I have to get dressed and go out myself?

Laura. Going, going—soon as I get on my coat! [*She pulls on a shapeless felt hat with nervous, jerky movement, pleadingly glancing at* Tom. *Rushes awkwardly for coat. The coat is one of* Amanda's *inaccurately made over, the sleeves too short for* Laura.] Butter and what else?

Amanda. [*entering upstage.*] Just butter. Tell them to charge it.

Laura. Mother, they make such faces when I do that.

Amanda. Sticks and stones may break my bones, but the expression on Mr. Garfinkel's face won't harm us! Tell your brother his coffee is getting cold.

Laura [*at door*]. Do what I asked you, will you, will you, Tom?

[*He looks sullenly away.*]

Amanda. Laura, go now or just don't go at all!

Laura [*rushing out*]. Going—going! [*A second later she cries out.* Tom *springs up and crosses to the door.* Amanda *rushes anxiously in.* Tom *opens the door.*]

Tom. Laura!

Laura. I'm all right. I slipped, but I'm all right.

Amanda [*peering anxiously after her*]. If anyone breaks a leg on those fire-escape steps, the landlord ought to be sued for every cent he possesses! [*She shuts door. Remembers she isn't speaking and returns to other room.*]

[*As* Tom *enters* **listlessly**[50] *for his coffee, she turns her back to him and stands rigidly facing the window on the gloomy gray vault of the areaway. Its light on her face with its aged but childish features is cruelly sharp, satirical as a Daumier print.*[51]]

[*Music Under: "Ave Maria."*]

[Tom *glances sheepishly*[52] *but sullenly at her averted*[53] *figure and slumps at the table. The coffee is scalding hot; he sips it and gasps and spits it back in the cup. At his gasp,* Amanda *catches her breath and half turns. Then catches herself and turns back to window.*

Tom *blows on his coffee, glancing sidewise at his mother. She clears her throat.* Tom *clears his. He starts to rise. Sinks back down again, scratches his head, clears his throat again.* Amanda *coughs.* Tom *raises his cup in both hands to blow on it, his eyes staring over the rim of it at his mother for several moments. Then he slowly sets the cup down and awkwardly and hesitantly rises from the chair.*]

Tom [*hoarsely*]. Mother. I—I apologize. Mother. [Amanda *draws a quick, shuddering breath. Her face works grotesquely. She breaks into childlike tears.*] I'm sorry for what I said, for everything that I said, I didn't mean it.

Amanda [*sobbingly*]. My devotion has made me a witch and so I make myself hateful to my children!

Tom. No, you *don't*.

Amanda. I worry so much, don't sleep, it makes me nervous!

Tom [*gently*]. I understand that.

Amanda. I've had to put up a solitary battle all these years. But you're my right-hand bower![54] Don't fall down, don't fail!

Tom [*gently*]. I try, Mother.

Amanda [*with great enthusiasm*]. Try and you will SUCCEED! [*The notion makes her breathless.*] Why, you—you're just *full* of natural endowments!

---

[50] **listlessly**—without energy.

[51] *Daumier print*—lithograph by French artist Honoré Daumier (1808–1879).

[52] *sheepishly*—with embarrassment.

[53] *averted*—turned away.

[54] right-hand bower—trump card.

Both of my children—they're *unusual* children! Don't you think I know it? I'm so—*proud!* Happy and—feel I've—so much to be thankful for but—Promise me one thing, son!

Tom. What, Mother?

Amanda. Promise, son, you'll—never be a drunkard!

Tom [*turns to her grinning*]. I will never be a drunkard, Mother.

Amanda. That's what frightened me so, that you'd be drinking! Eat a bowl of Purina!

Tom. Just coffee, Mother.

Amanda. Shredded wheat biscuit?

Tom. No. No, Mother, just coffee.

Amanda. You can't put in a day's work on an empty stomach. You've got ten minutes—don't gulp! Drinking too-hot liquids makes cancer of the stomach. . . . Put cream in.

Tom. No, thank you.

Amanda. To cool it.

Tom. No! No, thank you, I want it black.

Amanda. I know, but it's not good for you. We have to do all that we can to build ourselves up. In these trying times we live in, all that we have to cling to is—each other. . . . That's why it's so important to—Tom, I—I sent out your sister so I could discuss something with you. If you hadn't spoken I would have spoken to you. [*Sits down.*]

Tom [*gently*]. What is it, Mother, that you want to discuss?

Amanda. Laura!

[*Tom puts his cup down slowly.*]

[*Legend On Screen: "Laura."*]

[*Music: "The Glass Menagerie."*]

Tom. —Oh.—Laura . . .

Amanda [*touching his sleeve*]. You know how Laura is. So quiet but—still water runs deep! She notices things and I think she—broods about them. [*Tom looks up.*] A few days ago I came in and she was crying.

Tom. What about?

Amanda. You.

Tom. Me?

Amanda. She has an idea that you're not happy here.

Tom. What gave her that idea?

Amanda. What gives her any idea? However, you do act strangely. I—I'm not criticizing, understand *that!* I know your ambitions do not lie in the warehouse, that like everybody in the whole wide world—you've had to—make sacrifices, but—Tom—Tom— life's not easy, it calls for—Spartan endurance! There's so many things in my heart that I cannot describe to you! I've never told you but I—*loved* your father. . . .

Tom [*gently*]. I know that, Mother.

Amanda. And you—when I see you taking after his ways! Staying out late—and—well, you *had* been drinking the night you were in that— terrifying condition! Laura says that you hate the apartment and that you go out nights to get away from it! Is that true, Tom?

Tom. No. You say there's so much in your heart that you can't describe to me. That's true of me, too. There's so much in my heart that I can't describe to *you!* So let's respect each other's—

Amanda. But, why—*why*, Tom—are you always so *restless!* Where do you go to, nights?

Tom. I—go to the movies.

Amanda. Why do you go to the movies so much, Tom?

Tom. I go to the movies because—I like adventure. Adventure is something I don't have much of at work, so I go to the movies.

Amanda. But, Tom, you go to the movies *entirely* too *much!*

Tom. I like a lot of adventure.

[Amanda *looks baffled, then hurt. As the familiar inquisition resumes he becomes hard and impatient again. Amanda slips back into her querulous*[55] *attitude toward him.*]

[*Image On Screen: Sailing Vessel With Jolly Roger.*]

Amanda. Most young men find adventure in their careers.

Tom. Then most young men are not employed in a warehouse.

Amanda. The world is full of young men employed in warehouses and offices and factories.

Tom. Do all of them find adventure in their careers?

Amanda. They do or they do without it! Not everybody has a craze for adventure.

Tom. Man is by instinct a lover, a hunter, a fighter, and none of those instincts are given much play at the warehouse!

Amanda. Man is by instinct! Don't quote instinct to me! Instinct is something that people have got away from! It belongs to animals! Christian adults don't want it!

Tom. What do Christian adults want, then, Mother?

---

[55] *querulous*—peevish.

Amanda. Superior things! Things of the mind and the spirit! Only animals have to satisfy instincts! Surely your aims are somewhat higher than theirs! Than monkeys—pigs—

Tom. I reckon they're not.

Amanda. You're joking. However, that isn't what I wanted to discuss.

Tom [*rising*]. I haven't much time.

Amanda [*pushing his shoulder*]. Sit down.

Tom. You want me to punch in red at the warehouse, Mother?

Amanda. You have five minutes. I want to talk about Laura.

[*Legend: "Plans And Provisions."*]

Tom. All right! What about Laura?

Amanda. We have to be making plans and provisions for her. She's older than you, two years, and nothing has happened. She just drifts along doing nothing. It frightens me terribly how she just drifts along.

Tom. I guess she's the type that people call home girls.

Amanda. There's no such type, and if there is, it's a pity! That is unless the home is hers, with a husband!

Tom. What?

Amanda. Oh, I can see the handwriting on the wall as plain as I see the nose in front of my face! It's terrifying! More and more you remind me of your father! He was out all hours without explanation—Then *left! Goodbye!* And me with the bag to hold. I saw that letter you got from the Merchant Marine. I know what you're dreaming of. I'm not standing here blindfolded. Very well, then. Then *do* it. But not till there's somebody to take your place.

Tom. What do you mean!

Amanda. I mean that as soon as Laura has got somebody to take care of her, married, a home of her own, independent—why, then you'll be free to go wherever you please, on land, on sea, whichever way the wind blows! But until that time you've got to look out for your sister. I don't say me because I'm old and don't matter! I say for your sister because she's young and dependent. I put her in business college—a dismal failure! Frightened her so it made her sick to her stomach. I took her over to the Young People's League at the church. Another fiasco. She spoke to nobody, nobody spoke to her. Now all she does is fool with those pieces of glass and play those worn-out records. What kind of a life is that for a girl to lead!

Tom. What can I do about it?

Amanda. Overcome selfishness! Self, self, self is all that you ever think of. [Tom *springs up and crosses to get his coat. It is ugly and bulky. He pulls on a cap with earmuffs.*] Where is your muffler? Put your wool muffler on! [*He snatches it angrily from the closet and tosses it around his neck and pulls both ends tight.*] Tom! I haven't said what I had in mind to ask you.

Tom. I'm too late to—

Amanda [*catching his arm—very importunately.*[56] *Then shyly*]. Down at the warehouse, aren't there some—nice young men?

Tom. No!

Amanda. There *must* be—*some* . . .

Tom. Mother—

[*Gesture.*]

Amanda. Find one that's clean-living—doesn't drink and—ask him out for sister!

Tom. What?

Amanda. For sister! To *meet! Get acquainted!*

Tom [*stamping to door*]. Oh, my go-osh!

Amanda. Will you? [*He opens door. Imploringly.*] Will you? [*He starts down.*] Will you? Will you, dear?

Tom [*calling back*]. YES!

[Amanda *closes the door hesitantly and with a troubled but faintly hopeful expression.*]

[*Screen Image: Glamor Magazine Cover.*]

[*Spot* Amanda *at phone.*]

Amanda. Ella Cartwright? This is Amanda Wingfield! How are you, honey? How is that kidney condition? [*Count five.*] Horrors! [*Count five.*] You're a Christian martyr, yes, honey, that's what you are, a Christian martyr! Well, I just happened to notice in my little red book that your subscription to the *Companion* has just run out! I knew that you wouldn't want to miss out on the wonderful serial starting in this new issue. It's by Bessie Mae Hopper, the first thing she's written since *Honeymoon for Three.* Wasn't that a strange and interesting story! Well, this one is even lovelier, I believe. It has a sophisticated society background. It's all about the horsey set[57] on Long Island!

[*Fade Out.*]

---

[56] *importunately*—urgently.

[57] horsey set—rich, fashionable people (who are able to afford to keep horses).

Scene Five

[*Legend On Screen: "Annunciation."*]

[*Fade with music.*

It is early dusk of a spring evening. Supper has just been finished in the Wingfield apartment. Amanda *and* Laura *in light colored dresses are removing dishes from the table, in the upstage area, which is shadowy, their movements formalized almost as a dance or ritual, their moving forms as pale and silent as moths.*

Tom, *in white shirt and trousers, rises from the table and crosses toward the fire escape.*]

Amanda [*as he passes her*]. Son, will you do me a favor?

Tom. What?

Amanda. Comb your hair! You look so pretty when your hair is combed! [Tom *slouches on sofa with evening paper. Enormous caption "Franco Triumphs."*] There is only one respect in which I would like you to **emulate**[58] your father.

Tom. What respect is that?

Amanda. The care he always took of his appearance. He never allowed himself to look untidy. [*He throws down the paper and crosses to fire escape.*] Where are you going?

Tom. I'm going out to smoke.

Amanda. You smoke too much. A pack a day at fifteen cents a pack. How much would that amount to in a month! Thirty times fifteen is how much, Tom? Figure it out and you will be astounded at what you could save. Enough to give you a night-school course in accounting at Washington U! Just think what a wonderful thing that would be for you, son!

[Tom *is unmoved by the thought.*]

Tom. I'd rather smoke. [*He steps out on landing, letting the screen door slam.*]

Amanda [*sharply*]. I know! That's the tragedy of it. . . . [*Alone, she turns to look at her husband's picture.*]

[*Dance Music; "All The World Is Waiting For The Sunrise."*]

Tom [*to the audience*]. Across the alley from us was the Paradise Dance Hall. On evenings in spring the windows and doors were open and the music came outdoors. Sometimes the lights were turned out except for a large glass sphere that hung from the ceiling. It would turn slowly about and filter the dusk with delicate rainbow colors. Then the orchestra played

---

[58] emulate—imitate.

a waltz or a tango, something that had a slow and **sensuous**[59] rhythm. Couples would come outside, to the relative privacy of the alley. You could see them kissing behind ashpits and telephone poles. This was the compensation for lives that passed like mine, without any change or adventure. Adventure and change were **imminent**[60] in this year. They were waiting around the corner for all these kids. Suspended in the mist over Berchtesgaden,[61] caught in the folds of Chamberlain's umbrella[62]—In Spain there was Guernica! But here there was only hot swing music and liquor, dance halls, bars, and movies, and sex that hung in the gloom like a chandelier and flooded the world with brief, deceptive rainbows. . . . All the world was waiting for bombardments!

[Amanda *turns from the picture and comes outside.*]

Amanda [*sighing*] A fire-escape landing's a poor excuse for a porch.
[*She spreads a newspaper on a step and sits down, gracefully and demurely*[63] *as if she were settling into a swing on a Mississippi veranda.*] What are you looking at?

Tom. The moon.

Amanda. Is there a moon this evening?

Tom. It's rising over Garfinkel's Delicatessen.

Amanda. So it is! A little silver slipper of a moon. Have you made a wish on it yet?

Tom. Um-hum.

Amanda. What did you wish for?

Tom. That's a secret.

Amanda. A secret, huh? Well, I won't tell mine either. I will be just as mysterious as you.

Tom. I bet I can guess what yours is.

Amanda. Is my head so transparent?

Tom. You're not a **sphinx**.[64]

Amanda. No, I don't have secrets. I'll tell you what I wished for on the moon. Success and happiness for my precious children! I wish for

---

[59] **sensuous**—pleasing to the senses.

[60] **imminent**—likely to occur soon.

[61] **Berchtesgaden**—mountain retreat of Adolf Hitler (1889–1945), Nazi dictator of Germany.

[62] **Chamberlain's umbrella**—Neville Chamberlain (1869–1940) was British Prime Minister in 1938 when England agreed to the Munich Pact, which handed much of Czechoslovakia to Nazi Germany.

[63] *demurely*—shyly, coyly.

[64] **sphinx**—puzzling or mysterious person.

that whenever there's a moon, and when there isn't a moon, I wish for it, too.

Tom. I thought perhaps you wished for a gentleman caller.

Amanda. Why do you say that?

Tom. Don't you remember asking me to fetch one?

Amanda. I remember suggesting that it would be nice for your sister if you brought home some nice young man from the warehouse. I think I've made that suggestion more than once.

Tom. Yes, you have made it repeatedly.

Amanda. Well?

Tom. We are going to have one.

Amanda. What?

Tom. A gentleman caller!

[*The Annunciation Is Celebrated With Music.*]

[Amanda *rises.*]

[*Image On Screen: Caller With Bouquet.*]

Amanda. You mean you have asked some nice young man to come over?

Tom. Yep. I've asked him to dinner.

Amanda. You really did?

Tom. I did!

Amanda. You did, and did he—*accept?*

Tom. He did!

Amanda. Well, well—well, well! That's—lovely!

Tom. I thought that you would be pleased.

Amanda. It's definite, then?

Tom. Very definite.

Amanda. Soon?

Tom. Very soon.

Amanda. For heaven's sake, stop putting on and tell me some things, will you?

Tom. What things do you want me to tell you?

Amanda. Naturally I would like to know when he's *coming!*

Tom. He's coming tomorrow.

Amanda. *Tomorrow?*

Tom. Yep. Tomorrow.

Amanda. But, Tom!

Tom. Yes, Mother?

Amanda. Tomorrow gives me no time!

Tom. Time for what?

Amanda. Preparations! Why didn't you phone me at once, as soon as you asked him, the minute that he accepted? Then, don't you see, I could have been getting ready!

Tom. You don't have to make any fuss.

Amanda. Oh, Tom, Tom, Tom, of course I have to make a fuss! I want things nice, not sloppy! Not thrown together. I'll certainly have to do some fast thinking, won't I?

Tom. I don't see why you have to think at all.

Amanda. You just don't know. We can't have a gentleman caller in a pigsty! All my wedding silver has to be polished, the monogrammed table linen ought to be laundered! The windows have to be washed and fresh curtains put up. And how about clothes? We have to *wear* something, don't we?

Tom. Mother, this boy is no one to make a fuss over!

Amanda. Do you realize he's the first young man we've introduced to your sister? It's terrible, dreadful, disgraceful that poor little sister has never received a single gentleman caller! Tom, come inside! [*She opens the screen door.*]

Tom. What for?

Amanda. I want to ask you some things.

Tom. If you're going to make such a fuss, I'll call it off, I'll tell him not to come.

Amanda. You certainly won't do anything of the kind. Nothing offends people worse than broken engagements. It simply means I'll have to work like a Turk! We won't be brilliant, but we'll pass inspection. Come on inside. [Tom *follows, groaning.*] Sit down.

Tom. Any particular place you would like me to sit?

Amanda. Thank heavens I've got that new sofa! I'm also making payments on a floor lamp I'll have sent out! And put the chintz covers[65] on, they'll brighten things up! Of course I'd hoped to have these walls re-papered. . . . What is the young man's name?

Tom. His name is O'Connor.

Amanda. That, of course, means fish—tomorrow is Friday![66] I'll have that salmon loaf—with Durkee's dressing! What does he do? He works at the warehouse?

Tom. Of course! How else would I—

---

[65] chintz covers—furniture slipcovers made of a printed cotton fabric.

[66] fish . . . Friday—Amanda assumes that Jim O'Connor, being Irish, is also Catholic. Catholics were formerly required to abstain from eating meat on Fridays.

Amanda. Tom, he—doesn't drink?

Tom. Why do you ask me that?

Amanda. Your father *did!*

Tom. Don't get started on that!

Amanda. He *does* drink, then?

Tom. Not that I know of!

Amanda. Make sure, be certain! The last thing I want for my daughter's a boy who drinks!

Tom. Aren't you being a little premature? Mr. O'Connor has not yet appeared on the scene!

Amanda. But will tomorrow. To meet your sister, and what do I know about his character? Nothing! Old maids are better off than wives of drunkards!

Tom. Oh, my God!

Amanda. Be still!

Tom [*leaning forward to whisper*]. Lots of fellows meet girls whom they don't marry!

Amanda. Oh, talk sensibly, Tom—and don't be sarcastic! [*She has gotten a hairbrush.*]

Tom. What are you doing?

Amanda. I'm brushing that cowlick down! What is this young man's position at the warehouse?

Tom [*submitting grimly to the brush and the interrogation*]. This young man's position is that of a shipping clerk, Mother.

Amanda. Sounds to me like a fairly responsible job, the sort of a job *you* would be in if you just had more *get-up.* What is his salary? Have you got any idea?

Tom. I would judge it to be approximately eighty-five dollars a month.

Amanda. Well—not princely, but—

Tom. Twenty more than I make.

Amanda. Yes, how well I know! But for a family man, eighty-five dollars a month is not much more than you can just get by on. . . .

Tom. Yes, but Mr. O'Connor is not a family man.

Amanda. He might be, mightn't he? Some time in the future?

Tom. I see. Plans and provisions.

Amanda. You are the only young man that I know of who ignores the fact that the future becomes the present, the present the past, and the past turns into everlasting regret if you don't plan for it!

Tom. I will think that over and see what I can make of it.

Amanda. Don't be **supercilious**[67] with your mother! Tell me some more about this—what do you call him?

Tom. James D. O'Connor. The D. is for Delaney.

Amanda. Irish on *both* sides! *Gracious!* And doesn't drink?

Tom. Shall I call him up and ask him right this minute?

Amanda. The only way to find out about those things is to make discreet inquiries at the proper moment. When I was a girl in Blue Mountain and it was suspected that a young man drank, the girl whose attentions he had been receiving, if any girl *was,* would sometimes speak to the minister of his church, or rather her father would if her father was living, and sort of feel him out on the young man's character. That is the way such things are discreetly handled to keep a young woman from making a tragic mistake!

Tom. Then how did you happen to make a tragic mistake?

Amanda. That innocent look of your father's had everyone fooled! He *smiled*—the world was *enchanted!* No girl can do worse than put herself at the mercy of a handsome appearance! I hope that Mr. O'Connor is not too good-looking.

Tom. No, he's not too good-looking. He's covered with freckles and hasn't too much of a nose.

Amanda. He's not right-down homely, though?

Tom. Not right-down homely. Just medium homely, I'd say.

Amanda. Character's what to look for in a man.

Tom. That's what I've always said, Mother.

Amanda. You've never said anything of the kind and I suspect you would never give it a thought.

Tom. Don't be suspicious of me.

Amanda. At least I hope he's the type that's up and coming.

Tom. I think he really goes in for self-improvement.

Amanda. What reason have you to think so?

Tom. He goes to night school.

Amanda [*beaming*]. Splendid! What does he do, I mean study?

Tom. Radio engineering and public speaking!

Amanda. Then he has visions of being advanced in the world! Any young man who studies public speaking is aiming to have an executive job some day! And radio engineering? A thing for the future! Both of these facts are very illuminating. Those are the sort of things that a

---

[67] **supercilious**—disdainful.

mother should know concerning any young man who comes to call on her daughter. Seriously or—not.

Tom. One little warning. He doesn't know about Laura. I didn't let on that we had dark ulterior[68] motives. I just said, why don't you come have dinner with us? He said okay and that was the whole conversation.

Amanda. I bet it was! You're eloquent as an oyster. However, he'll know about Laura when he gets here. When he sees how lovely and sweet and pretty she is, he'll thank his lucky stars he was asked to dinner.

Tom. Mother, you mustn't expect too much of Laura.

Amanda. What do you mean?

Tom. Laura seems all those things to you and me because she's ours and we love her. We don't even notice she's crippled any more.

Amanda. Don't say crippled! You know that I never allow that word to be used!

Tom. But face facts, Mother. She is and—that not's all—

Amanda. What do you mean "not all"?

Tom. Laura is very different from other girls.

Amanda. I think the difference is all to her advantage.

Tom. Not quite all—in the eyes of others—strangers—she's terribly shy and lives in a world of her own and those things make her seem a little peculiar to people outside the house.

Amanda. Don't say peculiar.

Tom. Face the facts. She is.

[*The Dance-hall Music Changes To A Tango That Has A Minor And Somewhat Ominous Tone.*]

Amanda. In what way is she peculiar—may I ask?

Tom [*gently*]. She lives in a world of her own—a world of—little glass ornaments, Mother. . . . [*Gets up.* Amanda *remains holding brush, looking at him, troubled.*] She plays old phonograph records and—that's about all—[*He glances at himself in the mirror and crosses to door.*]

Amanda [*sharply*]. Where are you going?

Tom. I'm going to the movies. [*Out screen door.*]

Amanda. Not to the movies, every night to the movies! [*Follows quickly to screen door.*] I don't believe you always go to the movies! [*He is gone.* Amanda *looks worriedly after him for a moment. Then vitality and optimism return and she turns from the door. Crossing to portieres.*] Laura! Laura! [Laura *answers from kitchenette.*]

---

[68] ulterior—hidden.

Laura. Yes, Mother.

Amanda. Let those dishes go and come in front! [Laura *appears with dish towel. Gaily.*] Laura, come here and make a wish on the moon!

Laura [*entering*]. Moon—moon?

Amanda. A little silver slipper of a moon. Look over your left shoulder, Laura, and make a wish! [Laura *looks faintly puzzled as if called out of sleep.* Amanda *seizes her shoulders and turns her at an angle by the door.*] Now! Now, darling, *wish!*

Laura. What shall I wish for, Mother?

Amanda [*her voice trembling and her eyes suddenly filling with tears*]. Happiness! Good Fortune!

[*The violin rises and the stage dims out.*]

Part Two
Scene Six

[*Image: High-School Hero.*]

Tom. And so the following evening I brought Jim home to dinner. I had known Jim slightly in high school. In high school Jim was a hero. He had tremendous Irish good nature and vitality with the scrubbed and polished look of white chinaware. He seemed to move in a continual spotlight. He was a star in basketball, captain of the debating club, president of the senior class and the glee club and he sang the male lead in the annual light operas. He was always running or bounding, never just walking. He seemed always at the point of defeating the law of gravity. He was shooting with such **velocity**[1] through his adolescence that you would logically expect him to arrive at nothing short of the White House by the time he was thirty. But Jim apparently ran into more interference after his graduation from Soldan. His speed had definitely slowed. Six years after he left high school he was holding a job that wasn't much better than mine.

[*Image: Clerk.*]

He was the only one at the warehouse with whom I was on friendly terms. I was valuable to him as someone who could remember his former glory, who had seen him win basketball games and the silver cup in debating. He knew of my secret practice of retiring to a cabinet of the washroom to work on my poems when business was slack in the warehouse. He called me Shakespeare. And while the other boys

---

[1] **velocity**—speed.

in the warehouse regarded me with suspicious hostility, Jim took a humorous attitude toward me. Gradually his attitude affected the others, their hostility wore off and they also began to smile at me as people smile at an oddly fashioned dog who trots across their path at some distance.

I knew that Jim and Laura had known each other at Soldan, and I had heard Laura speak admiringly of his voice. I didn't know if Jim remembered her or not. In high school Laura had been as **unobtrusive**[2] as Jim had been astonishing. If he did remember Laura, it was not as my sister, for when I asked him to dinner, he grinned and said, "You know, Shakespeare, I never thought of you as having folks!"

He was about to discover that I did. . . .

[*Light Up Stage.*]

[*Legend On Screen: "The Accent Of A Coming Foot."*]

[*Friday evening. It is about five o'clock of a late spring evening which comes "scattering poems in the sky."*

A delicate lemony light is in the Wingfield apartment.

Amanda *has worked like a Turk in preparation for the gentleman caller. The results are astonishing. The new floor lamp with its rose-silk shade is in place, a colored paper lantern conceals the broken light fixture in the ceiling, new billowing white curtains are at the windows, chintz covers are on chairs and sofa, a pair of new sofa pillows make their initial appearance.*

Open boxes and tissue paper are scattered on the floor.

Laura *stands in the middle with lifted arms while* Amanda *crouches before her, adjusting the hem of the new dress, devout and ritualistic. The dress is colored and designed by memory. The arrangement of* Laura's *hair is changed; it is softer and more becoming. A fragile, unearthly prettiness has come out in* Laura: *she is like a piece of translucent[3] glass touched by light, given a momentary radiance, not actual, not lasting.*]

Amanda [*impatiently*]. Why are you trembling?

Laura. Mother, you've made me so nervous!

Amanda. How have I made you nervous!

Laura. By all this fuss! You make it seem so important!

Amanda. I don't understand you, Laura. You couldn't be satisfied with just sitting home, and yet whenever I try to arrange something for you, you seem to resist it. [*She gets up.*] Now take a look at yourself. No, wait! Wait just a moment—I have an idea!

---

[2] **unobtrusive**—inconspicuous, unnoticed.

[3] *translucent*—clear.

Laura. What is it now?

[Amanda *produces two powder puffs which she wraps in handkerchiefs and stuffs in* Laura's *bosom.*]

Laura. Mother, what are you doing?

Amanda. They call them "Gay Deceivers"!

Laura. I won't wear them!

Amanda. You will!

Laura. Why should I?

Amanda. Because, to be painfully honest, your chest is flat.

Laura. You make it seem like we were setting a trap.

Amanda. All pretty girls are a trap, a pretty trap, and men expect them to be. [*Legend. "A Pretty Trap."*] Now look at yourself, young lady. This is the prettiest you will ever be! I've got to fix myself now! You're going to be surprised by your mother's appearance! [*She crosses through portieres, humming gaily.*]

[Laura *moves slowly to the long mirror and stares solemnly at herself. A wind blows the white curtains inward in a slow, graceful motion and with a faint, sorrowful sighing.*]

Amanda. [*offstage*] It isn't dark enough yet. [*She turns slowly before the mirror with a troubled look.*]

[*Legend On Screen: "This Is My Sister. Celebrate Her With Strings!" Music.*]

Amanda [*laughing, off*]. I'm going to show you something. I'm going to make a spectacular appearance!

Laura. What is it, Mother?

Amanda. Possess your soul in patience—you will see! Something I've resurrected from that old trunk! Styles haven't changed so terribly much after all. . . . [*She parts the portieres.*] Now just look at your mother! [*She wears a girlish frock of yellowed voile*[4] *with a blue silk sash. She carries a bunch of jonquils*[5]—*the legend of her youth is nearly revived. Feverishly.*] This is the dress in which I led the cotillion.[6] Won the cakewalk twice at Sunset Hill, wore one spring to the Governor's ball in Jackson! See how I sashayed around the ballroom, Laura? [*She raises her skirt and does a mincing*[7] *step around the room.*] I wore it on Sundays for my gentlemen callers! I had it on the day I met your father—I had malaria fever all that spring. The change of climate from East Tennessee to the

---

[4] *voile*—light, sheer fabric.

[5] *jonquils*—spring flower with yellow blossoms.

[6] cotillion—formal ball, especially one at which young girls are introduced to society.

[7] *mincing*—dainty.

Delta—weakened resistance—I had a little temperature all the time—not enough to be serious—just enough to make me restless and giddy! Invitations poured in—parties all over the Delta!—"Stay in bed," said Mother, "you have fever!"—but I just wouldn't.—I took quinine but kept on going, going!—Evenings, dances!—Afternoons, long, long rides! Picnics—lovely!—So lovely, that country in May.—All lacy with dogwood, literally flooded with jonquils!—That was the spring I had the craze for jonquils. Jonquils became an absolute obsession. Mother said, "Honey, there's no more room for jonquils." And still I kept bringing in more jonquils. Whenever, wherever I saw them, I'd say, "Stop! Stop! I see jonquils!" I made the young men help me gather the jonquils! It was a joke, Amanda and her jonquils! Finally there were no more vases to hold them, every available space was filled with jonquils. No vases to hold them? All right, I'll hold them myself! And then I—[*She stops in front of the picture.*] [*Music.*] met your father! Malaria fever and jonquils and then—this—boy. . . . [*She switches on the rose-colored lamp.*] I hope they get here before it starts to rain. [*She crosses upstage and places the jonquils in bowl on table.*] I gave your brother a little extra change so he and Mr. O'Connor could take the service car home.

Laura [*with altered look*]. What did you say his name was?

Amanda. O'Connor.

Laura. What is his first name?

Amanda. I don't remember. Oh, yes, I do. It was—Jim!

[Laura *sways slightly and catches hold of a chair.*]

[*Legend On Screen: "Not Jim!"*]

Laura [*faintly*]. Not—Jim!

Amanda. Yes, that was it, it was Jim! I've never known a Jim that wasn't nice!

[*Music: Ominous.*]

Laura. Are you sure his name is Jim O'Connor?

Amanda. Yes. Why?

Laura. Is he the one that Tom used to know in high school?

Amanda. He didn't say so. I think he just got to know him at the warehouse.

Laura. There was a Jim O'Connor we both knew in high school—[*Then, with effort.*] If that is the one that Tom is bringing to dinner—you'll have to excuse me, I won't come to the table.

Amanda. What sort of nonsense is this?

Laura. You asked me once if I'd ever liked a boy. Don't you remember I showed you this boy's picture?

Amanda. You mean the boy you showed me in the yearbook?

Laura. Yes, that boy.

Amanda. Laura, Laura, were you in love with that boy?

Laura. I don't know, Mother. All I know is I couldn't sit at the table if it was him!

Amanda. It won't be him! It isn't the least bit likely. But whether it is or not, you will come to the table. You will not be excused.

Laura. I'll have to be, Mother.

Amanda. I don't intend to humor your silliness, Laura. I've had too much from you and your brother, both! So just sit down and compose yourself till they come. Tom has forgotten his key so you'll have to let them in, when they arrive.

Laura [*panicky*]. Oh, Mother—*you* answer the door!

Amanda [*lightly*]. I'll be in the kitchen—busy!

Laura. Oh, Mother, please answer the door, don't make me do it!

Amanda [*crossing into kitchenette*]. I've got to fix the dressing for the salmon. Fuss, fuss—silliness!—over a gentleman caller!

[*Door swings shut.* Laura *is left alone.*]

[*Legend: "Terror!"*]

[*She utters a low moan and turns off the lamp—sits stiffly on the edge of the sofa, knotting her fingers together.*]

[*Legend On Screen: "The Opening Of A Door!"*]

[Tom *and* Jim *appear on the fire-escape steps and climb to landing. Hearing their approach,* Laura *rises with a panicky gesture. She retreats to the portieres. The doorbell.* Laura *catches her breath and touches her throat. Low drums.*]

Amanda [*calling*]. Laura, sweetheart! The door!

[Laura *stares at it without moving.*]

Jim. I think we just beat the rain.

Tom. Uh-huh. [*He rings again, nervously.* Jim *whistles and fishes for a cigarette.*]

Amanda [*very, very gaily*]. Laura, that is your brother and Mr. O'Connor! Will you let them in, darling!

[*Laura crosses toward kitchenette door.*]

Laura [*breathlessly*]. Mother—you go to the door!

[Amanda *steps out of kitchenette and stares furiously at* Laura. *She points imperiously*[8] *at the door.*]

---

[8] *imperiously*—commandingly.

Laura. Please, please!

Amanda [*in a fierce whisper*]. What is the matter with you, you silly thing?

Laura [*desperately*]. Please, you answer it, *please!*

Amanda. I told you I wasn't going to humor you, Laura. Why have you chosen this moment to lose your mind?

Laura. Please, please, please, you go!

Amanda. You'll have to go to the door because I can't!

Laura [*despairingly*]. I can't either!

Amanda. Why?

Laura. I'm *sick!*

Amanda. I'm sick, too—of your nonsense! Why can't you and your brother be normal people? Fantastic whims and behavior! [Tom *gives a long ring.*] **Preposterous**[9] goings on! Can you give me one reason— [*Calls out lyrically.*] COMING! JUST ONE SECOND!—why should you be afraid to open a door? Now you answer it, Laura!

Laura. Oh, oh, oh . . . [*She returns through the portieres. Darts to the victrola and winds it frantically and turns it on.*]

Amanda. Laura Wingfield, you march right to that door!

Laura. Yes—yes, Mother!

[*A faraway, scratchy rendition of "Dardanella" softens the air and gives her strength to move through it. She slips to the door and draws it cautiously open. Tom enters with the caller, Jim O'Connor.*]

Tom. Laura, this is Jim. Jim, this is my sister, Laura.

Jim [*stepping inside*]. I didn't know that Shakespeare had a sister!

Laura [*retreating stiff and trembling from the door*]. How—how do you do?

Jim [*heartily extending his hand*]. Okay!

[Laura *touches it hesitantly with hers.*]

Jim. Your hand's cold, Laura!

Laura. Yes, well—I've been playing the victrola. . . .

Jim. Must have been playing classical music on it! You ought to play a little hot swing music to warm you up!

Laura. Excuse me—I haven't finished playing the victrola. . . .

[*She turns awkwardly and hurries into the front room. She pauses a second by the victrola. Then catches her breath and darts through the portieres like a frightened deer.*]

Jim [*grinning*]. What was the matter?

Tom. Oh—with Laura? Laura is—terribly shy.

---

[9] **Preposterous**—absurd.

Jim. Shy, huh? It's unusual to meet a shy girl nowadays. I don't believe you ever mentioned you had a sister.

Tom Well, now you know. I have one. Here is the *Post Dispatch.* You want a piece of it?

Jim. Uh-huh.

Tom. What piece? The comics?

Jim. Sports! [*Glances at it.*] Ole Dizzy Dean[10] is on his bad behavior.

Tom [*disinterest*]. Yeah? [*Lights cigarette and crosses back to fire-escape door.*]

Jim. Where are you going?

Tom. I'm going out on the terrace.

Jim [*goes after him*]. You know, Shakespeare—I'm going to sell you a bill of goods!

Tom. What goods?

Jim. A course I'm taking.

Tom. Huh?

Jim. In public speaking! You and me, we're not the warehouse type.

Tom. Thanks—that's good news. But what has public speaking got to do with it?

Jim. It fits you for—executive positions!

Tom. Awww.

Jim. I tell you it's done a helluva lot for me.

[*Image: Executive At Desk.*]

Tom. In what respect?

Jim. In every! Ask yourself what is the difference between you an' me and men in the office down front? Brains?—No!—Ability?—No! Then what? Just one little thing—

Tom. What is that one little thing?

Jim. Primarily it amounts to—social poise! Being able to square up to people and hold your own on any social level!

Amanda [*offstage*]. Tom?

Tom. Yes, Mother?

Amanda. Is that you and Mr. O'Connor?

Tom. Yes, Mother.

Amanda. Well, you just make yourselves comfortable in there.

Tom. Yes, Mother.

Amanda. Ask Mr. O'Connor if he would like to wash his hands.

Jim. Aw—no—thank you—I took care of that at the warehouse. Tom—

---

[10] Dizzy Dean—star pitcher for the St. Louis Cardinals in the 1930s.

Tom. Yes?

Jim. Mr. Mendoza was speaking to me about you.

Tom. Favorably?

Jim. What do you think?

Tom. Well—

Jim. You're going to be out of a job if you don't wake up.

Tom. I am waking up

Jim. You show no signs.

Tom. The signs are interior.

[*Image On Screen: The Sailing Vessel With Jolly Roger Again.*]

Tom. I'm planning to change. [*He leans over the rail speaking with quiet exhilaration.*[11] *The* ***incandescent***[12] *marquees and signs of the first-run movie houses light his face from across the alley. He looks like a voyager.*] I'm right at the point of committing myself to a future that doesn't include the warehouse and Mr. Mendoza or even a night-school course in public speaking.

Jim. What are you gassing[13] about?

Tom. I'm tired of the movies.

Jim. Movies!

Tom. Yes, movies! Look at them—[*A wave toward the marvels of Grand Avenue.*] All of those glamorous people—having adventures—hogging it all, gobbling the whole thing up! You know what happens? People go to the *movies* instead of *moving!* Hollywood characters are supposed to have all the adventures for everybody in America, while everybody in America sits in a dark room and watches them have them! Yes, until there's a war. That's when adventure becomes available to the masses! *Everyone's* dish, not only Gable's![14] Then the people in the dark room come out of the dark room to have some adventures themselves— Goody, goody—It's our turn now, to go to the South Sea Island—to make a safari—to be exotic, far-off—But I'm not patient. I don't want to wait till then. I'm tired of the *movies* and I am *about* to *move!*

Jim [*incredulously*[15]]. Move?

Tom. Yes!

Jim. When?

---

[11] ***exhilaration***—high spirits, elation.

[12] ***incandescent***—glowing, illuminated.

[13] gassing—talking boastfully.

[14] Gable's—Clark Gable (1901–1960) was an American movie star.

[15] incredulously—skeptically, disbelievingly.

Tom. Soon!

Jim. Where? Where?

[*Theme three music seems to answer the question, while* Tom *thinks it over. He searches among his pockets.*]

Tom. I'm starting to boil inside. I know I seem dreamy, but inside—well, I'm boiling! Whenever I pick up a shoe, I shudder a little thinking how short life is and what I am doing!—Whatever that means. I know it doesn't mean shoes—except as something to wear on a traveler's feet! [*Finds paper.*] Look—

Jim. What?

Tom. I'm a member.

Jim [*reading*]. The Union of Merchant Seamen.

Tom. I paid my dues this month, instead of the light bill.

Jim. You will regret it when they turn the lights off.

Tom. I won't be here.

Jim. How about your mother?

Tom. I'm like my father. . . . See how he grins! And he's been absent going on sixteen years!

Jim. You're just talking, you drip. How does your mother feel about it?

Tom. Shhh—Here comes Mother! Mother is not acquainted with my plans!

Amanda [*enters portieres*]. Where are you all?

Tom. On the terrace, Mother.

[*They start inside. She advances to them.* Tom *is distinctly shocked at her appearance. Even* Jim *blinks a little. He is making his first contact with girlish Southern vivacity and in spite of the night-school course in public speaking is somewhat thrown off the beam by the unexpected outlay of social charm.*

Certain responses are attempted by Jim *but are swept aside by* Amanda's *gay laughter and chatter.* Tom *is embarrassed but after the first shock* Jim *reacts very warmly. Grins and chuckles, is altogether won over.*]

[*Image:* Amanda *As A Girl.*]

Amanda [*coyly smiling, shaking her girlish ringlets[16]*]. Well, well, well, so this is Mr. O'Connor. Introductions entirely unnecessary. I've heard so much about you from my boy. I finally said to him, Tom—good gracious!—why don't you bring this paragon[17] to supper? I'd like to meet this nice young man at the warehouse!— Instead of just hearing him sing your praises so much! I don't know why my son

---

[16] *ringlets*—curled locks of hair.

[17] paragon—ideal.

is so standoffish—that's not Southern behavior! Let's sit down and—I think we could stand a little more air in here! Tom, leave the door open. I felt a nice fresh breeze a moment ago. Where has it gone? Mmm, so warm already! And not quite summer, even. We're going to burn up when summer really gets started. However, we're having—we're having a very light supper. I think light things are better fo' this time of year. The same as light clothes are. Light clothes an' light food are what warm weather calls fo'. You know our blood gets so thick during th' winter—it takes a while fo' us to *adjust* ou'selves!—when the season changes . . . It's come so quick this year. I wasn't prepared. All of a sudden—heavens! Already summer!—I ran to the trunk an' pulled out this light dress—Terribly old! Historical almost! But feels so good—so good an' co-ol, y'know. . . .

Tom. Mother—

Amanda Yes, honey?

Tom. How about—supper?

Amanda. Honey, you go ask Sister if supper is ready! You know that Sister is in full charge of supper! Tell her you hungry boys are waiting for it. [*To* Jim.] Have you met Laura?

Jim. She—

Amanda. Let you in? Oh, good, you've met already! It's rare for a girl as sweet an' pretty as Laura to be domestic! But Laura is, thank heavens, not only pretty but also very domestic. I'm not at all. I never was a bit. I never could make a thing but angel-food cake. Well, in the South we had so many servants. Gone, gone, gone. All **vestiges**[18] of gracious living! Gone completely! I wasn't prepared for what the future brought me. All of my gentlemen callers were sons of planters and so of course I assumed that I would be married to one and raise my family on a large piece of land with plenty of servants. But man proposes—and woman accepts the proposal!—To vary that old, old saying a little bit—I married no planter! I married a man who worked for the telephone company!—that gallantly smiling gentleman over there! [*Points to the picture.*] A telephone man who—fell in love with long-distance!—Now he travels and I don't even know where!—But what am I going on for about my—**tribulations**?[19] Tell me yours—I hope you don't have any! Tom?

[18] **vestiges**—traces.

[19] **tribulations**—troubles.

Tom [*returning*]. Yes, Mother?

Amanda. Is supper nearly ready?

Tom. It looks to me like supper is on the table.

Amanda. Let me look—[*She rises prettily and looks through portieres.*] Oh, lovely—But where is Sister?

Tom. Laura is not feeling well and she says that she thinks she'd better not come to the table.

Amanda. What?—Nonsense!—Laura? Oh, Laura!

Laura [*offstage, faintly*]. Yes, Mother.

Amanda. You really must come to the table. We won't be seated until you come to the table! Come in, Mr. O'Connor. You sit over there and I'll—Laura? Laura Wingfield! You're keeping us waiting, honey! We can't say grace until you come to the table!

[*The back door is pushed weakly open and* Laura *comes in. She is obviously quite faint, her lips trembling, her eyes wide and staring. She moves unsteadily toward the table.*]

[*Legend: "Terror!"*]

[*Outside a summer storm is coming abruptly. The white curtains billow inward at the windows and there is a sorrowful murmur and deep blue dusk.*

Laura *suddenly stumbles—She catches at a chair with a faint moan.*]

Tom. Laura!

Amanda. Laura! [*There is a clap of thunder.*] [*Legend: "Ah!"*] [*Despairingly*] Why, Laura, you *are* sick, darling! Tom, help your sister into the living room, dear! Sit in the living room, Laura—rest on the sofa. Well! [*To the gentleman caller.*] Standing over the hot stove made her ill!—I told her that it was just too warm this evening, but—[Tom *comes back in.* Laura *is on the sofa.*] Is Laura all right now?

Tom. Yes.

Amanda. What *is* that? Rain? A nice cool rain has come up! [*She gives the gentleman caller a frightened look.*] I think we may—have grace—now . . . [*Tom looks at her stupidly.*] Tom, honey—you say grace!

Tom. Oh . . . "For these and all thy mercies—" [*They bow their heads,* Amanda *stealing a nervous glance at* Jim. *In the living room* Laura, *stretched on the sofa, clenches her hand to her lips, to hold back a shuddering sob.*] God's Holy Name be praised—

[*The Scene Dims Out.*]

Scene Seven

[*A Souvenir.*]

[*Half an hour later. Dinner is just being finished in the upstage area which is concealed by the drawn portieres.*

As the curtain rises Laura *is still huddled upon the sofa, her feet drawn under her, her head resting on a pale blue pillow, her eyes wide and mysteriously watchful. The new floor lamp with its shade of rose-colored silk gives a soft, becoming light to her face, bringing out the fragile, unearthly prettiness which usually escapes attention. There is a steady murmur of rain, but it is slackening and stops soon after the scene begins; the air outside becomes pale and luminous as the moon breaks out. A moment after the curtain rises, the lights in both rooms flicker and go out.*]

Jim. Hey, there, Mr. Light Bulb!

[Amanda *laughs nervously.*]

[*Legend: "Suspension Of A Public Service."*]

Amanda. Where was Moses when the lights went out? Ha-ha. Do you know the answer to that one, Mr. O'Connor?

Jim. No, Ma'am, what's the answer?

Amanda. In the dark! [Jim *laughs appreciatively.*] Everybody sit still. I'll light the candles. Isn't it lucky we have them on the table? Where's a match? Which of you gentlemen can provide a match?

Jim. Here.

Amanda. Thank you, sir.

Jim. Not at all, Ma'am!

Amanda. I guess the fuse has burnt out. Mr. O'Connor, can you tell a burnt-out fuse? I know I can't and Tom is a total loss when it comes to mechanics. [*Sound: Getting Up: Voices Recede A Little To Kitchenette.*] Oh, be careful you don't bump into something. We don't want our gentleman caller to break his neck. Now wouldn't that be a fine howdy-do?

Jim. Ha-ha! Where is the fuse-box?

Amanda. Right here next to the stove. Can you see anything?

Jim. Just a minute.

Amanda. Isn't electricity a mysterious thing! Wasn't it Benjamin Franklin who tied a key to a kite? We live in such a mysterious universe, don't we? Some people say that science clears up all the mysteries for us. In my opinion it only creates more! Have you found it yet?

Jim. No, Ma'am. All these fuses look okay to me.

Amanda. Tom!

Tom. Yes, Mother?

Amanda. That light bill I gave you several days ago. The one I told you we got the notices about?

Tom. Oh.—Yeah.

[*Legend: "Ha!"*]

Amanda. You didn't neglect to pay it by any chance?

Tom. Why, I—

Amanda. Didn't! I might have known it!

Jim. Shakespeare probably wrote a poem on that light bill, Mrs. Wingfield.

Amanda. I might have known better than to trust him with it! There's such a high price for **negligence**[20] in this world!

Jim. Maybe the poem will win a ten-dollar prize.

Amanda. We'll just have to spend the remainder of the evening in the nineteenth century, before Mr. Edison made the Mazda lamp![21]

Jim. Candlelight is my favorite kind of light.

Amanda. That shows you're romantic! But that's no excuse for Tom. Well, we got through dinner. Very considerate of them to let us get through dinner before they plunged us into everlasting darkness, wasn't it, Mr. O'Connor?

Jim. Ha-ha!

Amanda. Tom, as a penalty for your carelessness you can help me with the dishes.

Jim. Let me give you a hand.

Amanda. Indeed you will not!

Jim. I ought to be good for something.

Amanda. Good for something? [*Her tone is rhapsodic.*[22]] *You?* Why, Mr. O'Connor, nobody, *nobody's* given me this much entertainment in years—as you have!

Jim. Aw, now, Mrs. Wingfield!

Amanda. I'm not exaggerating, not one bit! But Sister is all by her lonesome. You go keep her company in the parlor! I'll give you this lovely old candelabrum that used to be on the altar at the church of the Heavenly Rest. It was melted a little out of shape when the church burnt down. Lightning struck it one spring. Gypsy Jones was holding

---

[20] **negligence**—failure to act.

[21] Mazda lamp—incandescent light bulb.

[22] *rhapsodic*—enthusiastic.

a revival at the time and he **intimated**[23] that the church was destroyed because the Episcopalians gave card parties.

Jim. Ha-ha.

Amanda. And how about coaxing Sister to drink a little wine? I think it would be good for her! Can you carry both at once?

Jim. Sure. I'm Superman!

Amanda. Now, Thomas, get into this apron!

[*The door of kitchenette swings closed on* Amanda's *gay laughter; the flickering light approaches the portieres.*

Laura *sits up nervously as he enters. Her speech at first is low and breathless from the almost intolerable strain of being alone with a stranger.*]

[*The Legend: "I Don't Suppose You Remember Me At All!"*]

[*In her first speeches in this scene, before* Jim's *warmth overcomes her paralyzing shyness,* Laura's *voice is thin and breathless as though she has run up a steep flight of stairs.*

Jim's *attitude is gently humorous. In playing this scene it should be stressed that while the incident is apparently unimportant, it is to* Laura *the climax of her secret life.*]

Jim. Hello, there, Laura.

Laura [*faintly*]. Hello. [*She clears her throat.*]

Jim. How are you feeling now? Better?

Laura. Yes. Yes, thank you.

Jim. This is for you. A little dandelion wine. [*He extends it toward her with extravagant gallantry.*]

Laura. Thank you.

Jim. Drink it—but don't get drunk! [*He laughs heartily.* Laura *takes the glass uncertainly; laughs shyly.*] Where shall I set the candles!

Laura. Oh—oh, anywhere . . .

Jim. How about here on the floor? Any objections!

Laura. No.

Jim. I'll spread a newspaper under to catch the drippings. I like to sit on the floor. Mind if I do?

Laura. Oh, no.

Jim. Give me a pillow?

Laura. What?

Jim. A pillow!

Laura. Oh . . . [*Hands him one quickly.*]

---

[23] **intimated**—hinted.

Jim. How about you? Don't you like to sit on the floor?

Laura. Oh—yes.

Jim. Why don't you, then?

Laura. I—will.

Jim. Take a pillow! [Laura *does. Sits on the other side of the candelabrum.* Jim *crosses his legs and smiles engagingly at her.*] I can't hardly see you sitting way over there.

Laura. I can—see you.

Jim. I know, but that's not fair, I'm in the limelight. [Laura *moves her pillow closer.*] Good! Now I can see you! Comfortable?

Laura. Yes.

Jim. So am I. Comfortable as a cow. Will you have some gum?

Laura. No, thank you.

Jim. I think that I will indulge, with your permission. [*Musingly unwraps it and holds it up.*] Think of the fortune made by the guy that invented the first piece of chewing gum. Amazing, huh? The Wrigley Building is one of the sights of Chicago.—I saw it summer before last when I went up to the Century of Progress.[24] Did you take in the Century of Progress?

Laura. No, I didn't.

Jim. Well, it was quite a wonderful exposition.[25] What impressed me most was the Hall of Science. Gives you an idea of what the future will be in America, even more wonderful than the present time is! [*Pause. Smiling at her.*] Your brother tells me you're shy. Is that right, Laura?

Laura. I—don't know.

Jim. I judge you to be an old-fashioned type of girl. Well, I think that's a pretty good type to be. Hope you don't think I'm being too personal—do you?

Laura [*hastily, out of embarrassment*]. I believe I *will* take a piece of gum, if you—don't mind. [*Clearing her throat.*] Mr. O'Connor, have you—kept up with your singing?

Jim. Singing? Me?

Laura. Yes. I remember what a beautiful voice you had.

Jim. When did you hear me sing?

[*Voice Offstage In The Pause.*]

---

[24] Century of Progress—Chicago World's Fair (1933–1934).

[25] exposition—exhibition.

Voice [*offstage*].

> O blow, ye winds, heigh-ho,
> A-roving I will go!
> I'm off to my love
> With a boxing glove—
> Ten thousand miles away!

Jim. You say you've heard me sing?

Laura. Oh, yes! Yes, very often . . . I—don't suppose you remember me—at all?

Jim [*smiling doubtfully*]. You know I have an idea I've seen you before. I had that idea soon as you opened the door. It seemed almost like I was about to remember your name. But the name that I started to call you—wasn't a name! And so I stopped myself before I said it.

Laura. Wasn't it—Blue Roses?

Jim [*springs up, grinning*]. Blue Roses! My gosh, yes—Blue Roses! That's what I had on my tongue when you opened the door! Isn't it funny what tricks your memory plays? I didn't connect you with the high school somehow or other. But that's where it was; it was high school. I didn't even know you were Shakespeare's sister! Gosh, I'm sorry.

Laura. I didn't expect you to. You—barely knew me!

Jim. But we did have a speaking acquaintance, huh?

Laura. Yes, we—spoke to each other.

Jim. When did you recognize me?

Laura. Oh, right away!

Jim. Soon as I came in the door?

Laura. When I heard your name I thought it was probably you. I knew that Tom used to know you a little in high school. So when you came in the door—Well, then I was—sure.

Jim. Why didn't you say something, then?

Laura [*breathlessly*]. I didn't know what to say, I was—too surprised!

Jim. For goodness sakes! You know, this sure is funny!

Laura. Yes! Yes, isn't it, though . . .

Jim. Didn't we have a class in something together?

Laura. Yes, we did.

Jim. What class was that?

Laura. It was—singing—Chorus!

Jim. Aw!

Laura. I sat across the aisle from you in the Aud.

Jim. Aw.

Laura. Mondays, Wednesday and Fridays.

Jim. Now I remember—you always came in late.

Laura. Yes, it was so hard for me, getting upstairs. I had that brace on my leg—it clumped so loud!

Jim. I never heard any clumping.

Laura [*wincing at the recollection*]. To me it sounded like thunder!

Jim. Well, well, well. I never even noticed.

Laura. And everybody was seated before I came in. I had to walk in front of all those people. My seat was in the back row. I had to go clumping all the way up the aisle with everyone watching!

Jim. You shouldn't have been self-conscious.

Laura. I know, but I was. It was always such a relief when the singing started.

Jim. Aw, yes, I've placed you now! I used to call you Blue Roses. How was it that I got started calling you that?

Laura. I was out of school a little while with pleurosis. When I came back you asked me what was the matter. I said I had pleurosis—you thought I said Blue Roses. That's what you always called me after that!

Jim. I hope you didn't mind.

Laura. Oh, no—I liked it. You see, I wasn't acquainted with many— people. . . .

Jim. As I remember you sort of stuck by yourself.

Laura. I—I—never had much luck at—making friends.

Jim. I don't see why you wouldn't.

Laura. Well, I—started out badly.

Jim. You mean being—

Laura. Yes, it sort of—stood between me—

Jim. You shouldn't have let it!

Laura. I know, but it did, and—

Jim. You were shy with people!

Laura. I tried not to be but never could—

Jim. Overcome it?

Laura. No, I—I never could!

Jim. I guess being shy is something you have to work out of kind of gradually.

Laura [*sorrowfully*]. Yes—I guess it—

Jim. Takes time!

Laura. Yes—

Jim. People are not so dreadful when you know them. That's what you have to remember! And everybody has problems, not just you, but practically everybody has got some problems. You think of yourself as having the only problems, as being the only one who is disappointed. But just look around you and you will see lots of people as disappointed as you are. For instance, I hoped when I was going to high school that I would be further along at this time, six years later, than I am now—You remember that wonderful write-up I had in *The Torch?*

Laura. Yes! [*She rises and crosses to table.*]

Jim. It said I was bound to succeed in anything I went into! [*Laura returns with the annual.*] Holy Jeez! *The Torch!* [*He accepts it reverently. They smile across it with mutual wonder. Laura crouches beside him and they begin to turn through it. Laura's shyness is dissolving in his warmth.*]

Laura. Here you are in *Pirates of Penzance!*

Jim [*wistfully*]. I sang the baritone lead in that operetta.

Laura [*rapidly*]. So—*beautifully!*

Jim [*protesting*]. Aw—

Laura. Yes, yes—beautifully—beautifully!

Jim. You heard me?

Laura. All three times!

Jim. No!

Laura. Yes!

Jim. All three performances?

Laura [*looking down*]. Yes.

Jim. Why?

Laura. I—wanted to ask you to—autograph my program.

Jim. Why didn't you ask me to?

Laura. You were always surrounded by your own friends so much that I never had a chance to.

Jim. You should have just—

Laura. Well, I—thought you might think I was—

Jim. Thought I might think you was—what?

Laura. Oh—

Jim [*with reflective relish*]. I was beleaguered[26] by females in those days.

Laura. You were terribly popular!

Jim. Yeah—

---

[26] beleaguered—surrounded, besieged.

Laura. You had such a—friendly way—

Jim. I was spoiled in high school.

Laura. Everybody—liked you!

Jim. Including you?

Laura. I—yes, I—did, too—[*She gently closes the book in her lap.*]

Jim. Well, well, well!—Give me that program, Laura. [*She hands it to him. He signs it with a flourish.*] There you are—better late than never!

Laura. Oh, I—what a—surprise!

Jim. My signature isn't worth very much right now. But some day—maybe—it will increase in value! Being disappointed is one thing and being discouraged is something else. I am disappointed but I'm not discouraged. I'm twenty-three years old. How old are you?

Laura. I'll be twenty-four in June.

Jim. That's not old age!

Laura. No, but—

Jim. You finished high school?

Laura [*with difficulty*]. I didn't go back.

Jim. You mean you dropped out?

Laura. I made bad grades in my final examinations. [*She rises and replaces the book and the program. Her voice strained.*] How is—Emily Meisenbach getting along?

Jim. Oh, that kraut-head!

Laura. Why do you call her that?

Jim. That's what she was.

Laura. You're not still—going with her?

Jim. I never see her.

Laura. It said in the Personal Section that you were—engaged!

Jim. I know, but I wasn't impressed by that—propaganda!

Laura. It wasn't—the truth?

Jim. Only in Emily's optimistic opinion!

Laura. Oh—

[*Legend. "What Have You Done Since High School?"*]

[Jim *lights a cigarette and leans* **indolently**[27] *back on his elbows smiling at* Laura *with a warmth and charm which light her inwardly with altar candles. She remains by the table and turns in her hands a piece of glass to cover her* **tumult**.[28]]

---

[27] **indolently**—lazily.

[28] **tumult**—agitation.

Jim [*after several reflective puffs an a cigarette*]. What have you done since high school? [*She seems not to hear him.*] Huh? [Laura *looks up.*] I said what have you done since high school, Laura?

Laura. Nothing much.

Jim. You must have been doing something these six long years.

Laura. Yes.

Jim. Well, then, such as what?

Laura. I took a business course at business college—

Jim. How did that work out?

Laura. Well, not very—well—I had to drop out, it gave me—indigestion— [Jim *laughs gently.*]

Jim. What are you doing now?

Laura. I don't do anything—much. Oh, please don't think I sit around doing nothing! My glass collection takes up a good deal of my time. Glass is something you have to take good care of.

Jim. What did you say—about glass?

Laura. Collection I said—I have one—[*She clears her throat and turns away again, acutely shy.*]

Jim [*abruptly*]. You know what I judge to be the trouble with you! Inferiority complex! Know what that is? That's what they call it when someone low-rates himself! I understand it because I had it, too. Although my case was not so aggravated as yours seems to be. I had it until I took up public speaking, developed my voice, and learned that I had an aptitude for science. Before that time I never thought of myself as being outstanding in any way whatsoever! Now I've never made a regular study of it, but I have a friend who says I can analyze people better than doctors that make a profession of it. I don't claim that to be necessarily true, but I can sure guess a person's psychology, Laura! [*Takes out his gum.*] Excuse me, Laura. I always take it out when the flavor is gone. I'll use this scrap of paper to wrap it in. I know how it is to get it stuck on a shoe. Yep—that's what I judge to be your principal trouble. A lack of confidence in yourself as a person. You don't have the proper amount of faith in yourself. I'm basing that fact on a number of your remarks and also on certain observations I've made. For instance that clumping you thought was so awful in high school. You say that you even dreaded to walk into class. You see what you did? You dropped out of school, you gave up an education because of a clump, which as far as I know was practically nonexistent! A little physical defect is what you have. Hardly noticeable even! Magnified thousands of times by imagination! You know what my strong advice to you is? Think of yourself as *superior* in some way!

Laura. In what way would I think?

Jim. Why, man alive, Laura! just look about you a little. What do you see? A world full of common people! All of 'em born and all of 'em going to die! Which of them has one-tenth of your good points! Or mine! Or anyone else's, as far as that goes—Gosh! Everybody excels in some one thing. Some in many! [*Unconsciously glances at himself in the mirror.*] All you've got to do is discover in *what!* Take me, for instance. [*He adjusts his tie at the mirror.*] My interest happens to lie in electrodynamics. I'm taking a course in radio engineering at night school, Laura, on top of a fairly responsible job at the warehouse. I'm taking that course and studying public speaking.

Laura. Ohhhh.

Jim. Because I believe in the future of television! [*Turning back to her.*] I wish to be ready to go up right along with it. Therefore I'm planning to get in on the ground floor. In fact, I've already made the right connections and all that remains is for the industry itself to get under way! Full steam—[*His eyes are starry.*] *Knowledge*—Zzzzzp! *Money*—Zzzzzzp!—*Power!* That's the cycle democracy is built on! [*His attitude is convincingly dynamic. Laura stares at him, even her shyness eclipsed in her absolute wonder. He suddenly grins.*] I guess you think I think a lot of myself!

Laura. No—o-o-o, I—

Jim. Now how about you? Isn't there something you take more interest in than anything else?

Laura. Well, I do—as I said—have my—glass collection—

[*A peal of girlish laughter from the kitchen.*]

Jim. I'm not right sure I know what you're talking about. What kind of glass is it?

Laura. Little articles of it, they're ornaments mostly! Most of them are little animals made out of glass, the tiniest little animals in the world. Mother calls them a glass menagerie! Here's an example of one, if you'd like to see it! This one is one of the oldest. It's nearly thirteen. [*He stretches out his hand.*] [*Music: "The Glass Menagerie."*] Oh, be careful—if you breathe, it breaks!

Jim. I'd better not take it. I'm pretty clumsy with things.

Laura. Go on, I trust you with him! [*Places it in his palm.*] There now—you're holding him gently! Hold him over the light, he loves the light! You see how the light shines through him?

Jim. It sure does shine!

Laura. I shouldn't be partial, but he is my favorite one.

Jim. What kind of a thing is this one supposed to be?

Laura. Haven't you noticed the single horn on his forehead?

Jim. A unicorn,[29] huh?

Laura. Mmm-hmmm!

Jim. Unicorns, aren't they extinct in the modern world?

Laura. I know!

Jim. Poor little fellow, he must feel sort of lonesome.

Laura [*smiling*]. Well, if he does he doesn't complain about it. He stays on a shelf with some horses that don't have horns and all of them seem to get along nicely together.

Jim. How do you know?

Laura [*lightly*]. I haven't heard any arguments among them!

Jim [*grinning*]. No arguments, huh? Well, that's a pretty good sign! Where shall I set him?

Laura. Put him on the table. They all like a change of scenery once in a while!

Jim [*stretching*]. Well, well, well, well—Look how big my shadow is when I stretch!

Laura. Oh, oh, yes—it stretches across the ceiling!

Jim [*crossing to door*]. I think it's stopped raining. [*Opens fire-escape door.*] Where does the music come from?

Laura. From the Paradise Dance Hall across the alley.

Jim. How about cutting the rug a little, Miss Wingfield!

Laura. Oh, I—

Jim. Or is your program[30] filled up? Let me have a look at it. [*Grasps imaginary card.*] Why, every dance is taken! I'll just have to scratch some out. [*Waltz Music: "La Golondrina."*] Ahhh, a waltz! [*He executes some sweeping turns by himself, then holds his arms toward* Laura.]

Laura [*breathlessly*]. I—can't dance!

Jim. There you go, that inferiority stuff!

Laura. I've never danced in my life!

---

[29] unicorn—legendary horselike animal with a single horn in the center of its forehead.

[30] program—dance program, card on which participants at a social dance schedule their upcoming partners.

Jim. Come on, try!

Laura. Oh, but I'd step on you!

Jim. I'm not made out of glass.

Laura. How—how—how do we start?

Jim. Just leave it to me. You hold your arms out a little.

Laura. Like this?

Jim. A little bit higher. Right. Now don't tighten up, that's the main thing about it—relax.

Laura [*laughing breathlessly*]. It's hard not to.

Jim. Okay.

Laura. I'm afraid you can't budge me.

Jim. What do you bet I can't? [*He swings her into motion.*]

Laura. Goodness, yes, you can!

Jim. Let yourself go, now, Laura, just let yourself go.

Laura. I'm—

Jim. Come on!

Laura. Trying!

Jim. Not so stiff—Easy does it!

Laura. I know but I'm—

Jim. Loosen th' backbone! There now, that's a lot better.

Laura. Am I?

Jim. Lots, lots better! [*He moves her about the room in a clumsy waltz.*]

Laura. Oh, my!

Jim. Ha-ha!

Laura. Goodness, yes you can!

Jim. Ha-ha-ha! [*They suddenly bump into the table,* Jim *stops.*] What did we hit on?

Laura. Table.

Jim. Did something fall off it? I think—

Laura. Yes.

Jim. I hope that it wasn't the little glass horse with the horn!

Laura. Yes.

Jim. Aw, aw, aw. Is it broken?

Laura. Now it is just like all the other horses.

Jim. It's lost its—

Laura. Horn! It doesn't matter. Maybe it's a blessing in disguise.

Jim. You'll never forgive me. I bet that that was your favorite piece of glass.

Laura. I don't have favorites much. It's no tragedy, Freckles. Glass breaks so easily. No matter how careful you are. The traffic jars the shelves and things fall off them.

Jim. Still I'm awfully sorry that I was the cause.

Laura [*smiling*]. I'll just imagine he had an operation. The horn was removed to make him feel less—freakish! [*They both laugh.*] Now he will feel more at home with the other horses, the ones that don't have horns . . .

Jim. Ha-ha, that's very funny! [*Suddenly serious.*] I'm glad to see that you have a sense of humor. You know—you're—well—very different! Surprisingly different from anyone else I know! [*His voice becomes soft and hesitant with a genuine feeling.*] Do you mind me telling you that? [*Laura is abashed*[31] *beyond speech.*] You make me feel sort of—I don't know how to put it! I'm usually pretty good at expressing things, but—This is something that I don't know how to say! [*Laura touches her throat and clears it—turns the broken unicorn in her hands.*] [*Even softer.*] Has anyone ever told you that you were pretty? [*Pause: Music.*] [*Laura looks up slowly, with wonder, and shakes her head.*] Well, you are! In a very different way from anyone else. And all the nicer because of the difference, too. [*His voice becomes low and husky. Laura turns away, nearly faint with the novelty of her emotions.*] I wish you were my sister. I'd teach you to have some confidence in yourself. The different people are not like other people, but being different is nothing to be ashamed of. Because other people are not such wonderful people. They're one hundred times one thousand. You're one times one! They walk all over the earth. You just stay here. They're common as—weeds, but—you—well, you're—*Blue Roses!*

[*Image On Screen: Blue Roses.*]

[*Music Changes.*]

Laura. But blue is wrong for—roses . . .

Jim. It's right for you—You're —pretty!

Laura. In what respect am I pretty?

Jim. In all respects—believe me! Your eyes—your hair—are pretty! Your hands are pretty! [*He catches hold of her hand.*] You think I'm making this up because I'm invited to dinner and have to be nice. Oh, I could do that! I could put on an act for you, Laura, and say lots of things without being very sincere. But this time I am. I'm talking to you sincerely.

---

[31] *abashed*—self-conscious.

I happened to notice you had this inferiority complex that keeps you from feeling comfortable with people. Somebody needs to build your confidence up and make you proud instead of shy and turning away and—blushing—Somebody ought to—ought to—*kiss* you, Laura! [*His hand slips slowly up her arm to her shoulder.*] [*Music Swells Tumultuously.*] [*He suddenly turns her about and kisses her on the lips. When he releases her* Laura *sinks on the sofa with a bright, dazed look.* Jim *backs away and fishes in his pocket for a cigarette.*] [*Legend On Screen: "Souvenir."*] Stumble-john! [*He lights the cigarette, avoiding her look. There is a peal of girlish laughter from* Amanda *in the kitchen.* Laura *slowly raises and opens her hand. It still contains the little broken glass animal. She looks at it with a tender, bewildered expression.*] Stumble-john! I shouldn't have done that—That was way off the beam. You don't smoke, do you! [*She looks up, smiling, not hearing the question. He sits beside her a little gingerly.*[32] *She looks at him speechlessly—waiting. He coughs decorously*[33] *and moves a little farther aside as he considers the situation and senses her feelings, dimly, with perturbation.*[34] *Gently.*] Would you—care for a—mint? [*She doesn't seem to hear him but her look grows brighter even.*] Peppermint—Life Saver? My pocket's a regular drug store—wherever I go . . . [*He pops a mint in his mouth. Then gulps and decides to make a clean breast of it. He speaks slowly and gingerly.*] Laura, you know, if I had a sister like you, I'd do the same thing as Tom, I'd bring out fellows— introduce her to them. The right type of boys of a type to—appreciate her. Only—well—he made a mistake about me. Maybe I've got no call to be saying this. That may not have been the idea in having me over. But what if it was? There's nothing wrong about that. The only trouble is that in my case—I'm not in a situation to—do the right thing. I can't take down your number and say I'll phone. I can't call up next week and—ask for a date. I thought I had better explain the situation in case you misunderstood it and—hurt your feelings. . . . [*Pause. Slowly, very slowly,* Laura's *look changes, her eyes returning slowly from his to the ornament in her palm.*]

[Amanda *utters another gay laugh in the kitchen.*]

Laura [*faintly*]. You—won't—call again?

Jim. No, Laura, I can't. [*He rises from the sofa.*] As I was just explaining, I've—got strings on me, Laura, I've—been going steady! I go out

---

[32] *gingerly*—cautiously.

[33] *decorously*—politely.

[34] *perturbation*—agitation.

all the time with a girl named Betty. She's a home-girl like you, and Catholic, and Irish, and in a great many ways we—get along fine. I met her last summer on a moonlight boat trip up the river to Alton, on the *Majestic*. Well—right away from the start it was—love! [*Legend: Love!*] [Laura *sways slightly forward and grips the arm of the sofa. He fails to notice, now enrapt in his own comfortable being.*] Being in love has made a new man of me! [*Leaning stiffly forward, clutching the arm of the sofa,* Laura *struggles visibly with her storm. But* Jim *is* **oblivious**,[35] *she is a long way off.*] The power of love is really pretty tremendous! Love is something that— changes the whole world, Laura! [*The storm* **abates**[36] *a little and* Laura *leans back. He notices her again.*] It happened that Betty's aunt took sick, she got a wire and had to go to Centralia. So Tom—when he asked me to dinner—I naturally just accepted the invitation, not knowing that you—that he—that I—[*He stops awkwardly.*] Huh—I'm a stumble-john! [*He flops back on the sofa. The holy candles in the altar of* Laura's *face have been snuffed out! There is a look of almost infinite* **desolation**.[37] Jim *glances at her uneasily.*] I wish that you would— say something. [*She bites her lip which was trembling and then bravely smiles. She opens her hand again on the broken glass ornament. Then she gently takes his hand and raises it level with her own. She carefully places the unicorn in the palm of his hand, then pushes his fingers closed upon it.*] What are you—doing that for? You want me to have him?—Laura? [*She nods.*] What for?

Laura. A—souvenir . . .

[*She rises unsteadily and crouches beside the victrola to wind it up.*]

[*Legend On Screen: "Things Have A Way Of Turning Out So Badly."*]

[*Or Image: "Gentleman Caller Waving Good-bye!—Gaily."*]

[*At this moment* Amanda *rushes brightly back in the front room. She bears a pitcher of fruit punch in an old-fashioned cut-glass pitcher and a plate of macaroons. The plate has a gold border and poppies painted on it.*]

Amanda. Well, well, well! Isn't the air delightful after the shower? I've made you children a little liquid refreshment. [*Turns gaily to the gentleman caller.*] Jim, do you know that song about lemonade?
"Lemonade, lemonade
Made in the shade and stirred with a spade—
Good enough for any old maid!"

---

[35] **oblivious**—unconscious.

[36] **abates**—lessens.

[37] desolation—misery.

Jim [*uneasily*]. Ha-ha! No—I never heard it.

Amanda. Why, Laura! You look so serious!

Jim. We were having a serious conversation.

Amanda. Good! Now you're better acquainted!

Jim [*uncertainly*]. Ha-ha! Yes.

Amanda. You modern young people are much more serious-minded than my generation. I was so gay as a girl!

Jim. You haven't changed, Mrs. Wingfield.

Amanda. Tonight I'm **rejuvenated**![38] The gaiety of the occasion, Mr. O'Connor! [*She tosses her head with a peal of laughter. Spills lemonade.*] Oooo! I'm baptizing myself!

Jim. Here—let me—

Amanda [*setting the pitcher down*]. There now. I discovered we had some maraschino cherries. I dumped them in, juice and all!

Jim. You shouldn't have gone to that trouble, Mrs. Wingfield.

Amanda. Trouble, trouble? Why it was loads of fun! Didn't you hear me cutting up in the kitchen? I bet your ears were burning! I told Tom how **outdone**[39] with him I was for keeping you to himself so long a time! He should have brought you over much, much sooner! Well, now that you've found your way, I want you to be a very frequent caller! Not just occasional but all the time. Oh, we're going to have a lot of gay times together! I see them coming! Mmm, just breathe that air! So fresh, and the moon's so pretty! I'll skip back out—I know where my place is when young folks are having a—serious conversation!

Jim. Oh, don't go out, Mrs. Wingfield. The fact of the matter is I've got to be going.

Amanda. Going, now? You're joking! Why, it's only the shank of the evening, Mr. O'Connor!

Jim. Well, you know how it is.

Amanda. You mean you're a young workingman and have to keep workingmen's hours. We'll let you off early tonight. But only on the condition that next time you stay later. What's the best night for you? Isn't Saturday night the best night for you workingmen?

Jim. I have a couple of time clocks to punch, Mrs. Wingfield. One at morning, another one at night!

Amanda. My, but you *are* ambitious! You work at night, too?

---

[38] **rejuvenated**—restored to youthfulness; invigorated.

[39] outdone—puzzled.

Jim. No, Ma'am, not work but—Betty! [*He crosses deliberately to pick up his hat. The band at the Paradise Dance Hall goes into a tender waltz.*]

Amanda. Betty? Betty? Who's—Betty? [*There is an ominous cracking sound in the sky.*]

Jim. Oh, just a girl. The girl I go steady with! [*He smiles charmingly. The sky falls.*]

[*Legend: "The Sky Falls."*]

Amanda [*a long-drawn exhalation*[40]]. Ohhhh . . . Is it a serious romance, Mr. O'Connor?

Jim. We're going to be married the second Sunday in June.

Amanda. Ohhhh—how nice! Tom didn't mention that you were engaged to be married.

Jim. The cat's not out of the bag at the warehouse yet. You know how they are. They call you Romeo and stuff like that. [*He stops at the oval mirror to put on his hat. He carefully shapes the brim and the crown to give a discreetly dashing effect.*] It's been a wonderful evening, Mrs. Wingfield. I guess this is what they mean by Southern hospitality.

Amanda. It really wasn't anything at all.

Jim. I hope it don't seem like I'm rushing off. But I promised Betty I'd pick her up at the Wabash depot, an' by the time I get my jalopy down there her train'll be in. Some women are pretty upset if you keep 'em waiting.

Amanda. Yes, I know—The tyranny of women! [*Extends her hand.*] Goodbye, Mr. O'Connor. I wish you luck—and happiness—and success! All three of them, and so does Laura!—Don't you, Laura?

Laura. Yes!

Jim [*taking her hand*]. Goodbye, Laura. I'm certainly going to treasure that souvenir. And don't you forget the good advice I gave you. [*Raises his voice to a cheery shout.*] So long, Shakespeare! Thanks again, ladies—Good night!

[*He grins and ducks jauntily out.*]

Still bravely grimacing, Amanda *closes the door on the gentleman caller. Then she turns back to the room with a puzzled expression. She and* Laura *don't dare to face each other.* Laura *crouches beside the victrola to wind it.*]

Amanda [*faintly*]. Things have a way of turning out so badly. I don't believe that I would play the victrola. Well, well—well—Our gentleman caller was engaged to be married! Tom!

---

[40] exhalation—sigh.

Tom [*from back*]. Yes, Mother?

Amanda. Come in here a minute. I want to tell you something awfully funny.

Tom [*enters with macaroon and a glass of the lemonade*]. Has the gentleman caller gotten away already?

Amanda. The gentleman caller has made an early departure. What a wonderful joke you played on us!

Tom. How do you mean?

Amanda. You didn't mention that he was engaged to be married.

Tom. Jim? Engaged?

Amanda. That's what he just informed us.

Tom. I'll be jiggered! I didn't know about that.

Amanda. That seems very peculiar.

Tom. What's peculiar about it?

Amanda. Didn't you call him your best friend down at the warehouse?

Tom. He is, but how did I know?

Amanda. It seems extremely peculiar that you wouldn't know your best friend was going to be married!

Tom. The warehouse is where I work, not where I know things about people!

Amanda. You don't know things anywhere! You live in a dream; you manufacture illusions! [*He crosses to door.*] Where are you going?

Tom. I'm going to the movies.

Amanda. That's right, now that you've had us make such fools of ourselves. The effort, the preparations, all the expense! The new floor lamp, the rug, the clothes for Laura! All for what? To entertain some other girl's fiancé! Go to the movies, go! Don't think about us, a mother deserted, an unmarried sister who's crippled and has no job! Don't let anything interfere with your selfish pleasure! Just go, go, go—to the movies!

Tom. All right, I will! The more you shout about my selfishness to me the quicker I'll go, and I won't go to the movies!

Amanda. Go, then! Then go to the moon—you selfish dreamer!

[Tom *smashes his glass on the floor. He plunges out on the fire escape, slamming the door.* Laura *screams—cut by door.*

Dance-hall music up. Tom *goes to the rail and grips it desperately, lifting his face in the chill white moonlight penetrating the narrow abyss of the alley.*]

[*Legend On Screen: "And So Good-bye. . . "*]

[Tom's *closing speech is timed with the interior pantomime. The interior scene is played as though viewed through sound-proof glass.* Amanda *appears to be making a comforting speech to* Laura *who is huddled upon the sofa. Now that we cannot hear the mother's speech, her silliness is gone and she has dignity and tragic beauty.* Laura's *dark hair hides her face until at the end of the speech she lifts it to smile at her mother.* Amanda's *gestures are slow and graceful, almost dancelike, as she comforts the daughter. At the end of her speech she glances a moment at the father's picture—then withdraws through the portieres. At close of* Tom's *speech,* Laura *blows out the candles, ending the play.*]

Tom. I didn't go to the movies, I went much further—for time is the longest distance between two places—Not long after that I was fired for writing a poem on the lid of a shoe box. I left Saint Louis. I descended the steps of this fire escape for a last time and followed, from then on, in my father's footsteps, attempting to find in motion what was lost in space—I traveled around a great deal. The cities swept about me like dead leaves, leaves that were brightly colored but torn away from the branches. I would have stopped, but was pursued by something. It always came upon me unawares, taking me altogether by surprise. Perhaps it was a familiar bit of music. Perhaps it was only a piece of transparent glass. Perhaps I am walking along a street at night, in some strange city, before I have found companions. I pass the lighted window of a shop where perfume is sold. The window is filled with pieces of colored glass, tiny transparent bottles in delicate colors, like bits of a shattered rainbow. Then all at once my sister touches my shoulder. I turn around and look into her eyes . . . Oh, Laura, Laura, I tried to leave you behind me, but I am more faithful than I intended to be! I reach for a cigarette, I cross the street, I run into the movies or a bar, I buy a drink, I speak to the nearest stranger—anything that can blow your candles out! [Laura *bends over the candles.*]—for nowadays the world is lit by lightning! Blow out your candles, Laura—and so good-bye. . . .

[*She blows the candles out.*]

[*The Scene Dissolves.*]

UNDERSTANDING THE PLAY

Part One

1. What dramatic function is served by Tom's prologue?

2. What does their behavior at the dinner table in Scene One establish about Amanda, Tom, and Laura?

3. In Scene Two, Laura confesses that she has been "spending most of my afternoons in the Jewel-box, that big glass house where they raise tropical flowers." What does this preference convey about her?

4. How do Laura and her mother differ in their response to Laura's handicap?

5. In Scene Three, why do Tom and his mother fight? With whom do you sympathize more?

6. In Scene Four, how do Tom and his mother differ in their response to the need for adventure? How do they differ on the role of instinct?

7. How does Scene Five advance the action of the play?

8. How do Tom's observations about the state of the world in Scene Five reflect on the rest of the action?

Part Two

1. In Scene Six, why have Tom and Jim become friends?

2. Why is Laura distressed to learn the identity of the "gentleman caller"?

3. How does Amanda's speech and behavior alter after she encounters Jim?

4. In Scene Seven, what does Jim's behavior toward Laura reveal about him?

5. Amanda accuses Tom of being selfish. What is your opinion of him?

6. Why do you think Laura's image has haunted Tom?

ANALYZING THE PLAY

1. *The Glass Menagerie* is presented as a "memory play." In what different ways is this reflected in the play?

2. The conflict in a play is the struggle between opposing forces that gives movement to the dramatic plot. What is the fundamental conflict in *The Glass Menagerie?*

3. The mood of a literary work is the general atmosphere or prevailing emotion. What is the mood of *The Glass Menagerie?* How do music, lighting, and color effects help shape this mood?

4. A symbol is a person, place, object, or activity that stands for something beyond itself. What is the symbolism of blue roses? Laura's dress? the glass unicorn?

5. In what ways is *The Glass Menagerie* a realist play? In what ways is it antirealist?

Lorraine Hansberry ▶

A Raisin in the Sun

BY LORRAINE HANSBERRY

When it premiered in 1959, Lorraine Hansberry's A Raisin in the Sun *was the first drama by an African-American woman to be produced on Broadway. The play has since come to be regarded as a classic of the modern American theater. (For general background on modern American drama, see the introduction for* The Glass Menagerie, *page 588.)*

African-American Drama

The first significant African-American theater appeared in the 1920s and '30s in the context of the Harlem Renaissance. Among the important African-American writers who produced plays during this period were Zora Neale Hurston (1891–1960), Langston Hughes (1902–1967), and Wallace Thurman (1902–1934). The success of Hansberry's play was a watershed event in the history of American drama, marking the beginning of a vigorous black theater movement and leading the way for such playwrights as Charles Gordone (1925–1995), Amiri Baraka (1934–   ), August Wilson (1945–   ), and Ntozake Shange (1948–   ).

Young, Gifted, and Black

Born on the South Side of Chicago, Lorraine Hansberry (1930–1965) came from a middle-class, politically active African-American family. While still a child, she became acquainted with social conflict when her family challenged Chicago's segregated housing by moving into a white neighborhood. Hansberry began writing plays in high school, and she continued to pursue her interest in drama as a student at the University of Wisconsin. Moving to New York in 1950, she worked on Paul Robeson's radical black newspaper Freedom *and joined peace and civil rights movements. In 1953, Hansberry left journalism to concentrate on her career as a playwright. Before her early death from cancer at the age of 34, only two of Hansberry's plays had been produced,* A Raisin in the Sun *and* The Sign in Sidney Brustein's Window *(1964). To Be Young, Gifted, and Black, a collection of her journal entries, letters, speeches, and play excerpts made by Hansberry's former husband, Robert Nemiroff, appeared in 1969.*

Dreams Deferred

The title of Hansberry's A Raisin in the Sun *was drawn from Langston Hughes's well-known poem "Harlem," which questions whether the frustrated social aspirations of people might lead to violence. The play appeared at an expectant moment in the civil-rights movement. In 1954, the Supreme Court outlawed racial discrimination in education in its landmark ruling* Brown v. Board of Education. *A year later, African Americans in Montgomery, Alabama, had staged a successful boycott of the city's segregated buses. In 1957, schools in Little Rock, Arkansas, had been integrated with the help of federal marshals. The deeply felt desire for change that was going to produce social upheaval in the coming decade was reflected in Hansberry's drama about an African-American family in Chicago who want to better themselves.*

What happens to a dream deferred?

Does it dry up
Like a raisin in the sun?
Or fester like a sore—
And then run?
Does it stink like rotten meat?
Or crust and sugar over—
Like a syrupy sweet?

Maybe it just sags
Like a heavy load.

Or does it explode?
                    Langston Hughes, "Harlem"

CHARACTERS

Ruth Younger
Travis Younger
Walter Lee Younger (Brother)
Beneatha Younger
Lena Younger (Mama)
Joseph Asagai

George Murchison
Mrs. Johnson
Karl Lindner
Bobo
Moving Men

The action of the play is set in Chicago's South Side, sometime between World War II and the present.

Act One

Scene One Friday morning.
Scene Two The following morning.

Act Two

Scene One Later the same day.
Scene Two Friday night, a few weeks later.
Scene Three Saturday, moving day, one week later.

Act Three An hour later.

Act One, Scene One

[*The* Younger *living room would be a comfortable and well-ordered room if it were not for a number of indestructible contradictions to this state of being. Its furnishings are typical and undistinguished and their primary feature now is that they have clearly had to accommodate the living of too many people for too many years—and they are tired. Still, we can see that at some time, a time probably no longer remembered by the family (except perhaps for* Mama), *the furnishings of this room were actually selected with care and love and even hope—and brought to this apartment and arranged with taste and pride.*

That was a long time ago. Now the once loved pattern of the couch upholstery has to fight to show itself from under acres of crotcheted doilies and couch covers which have themselves finally come to be more important than the upholstery. And here a table or a chair has been moved to disguise the worn places in the carpet; but the carpet has fought back by showing its weariness, with depressing uniformity, elsewhere on its surface.

Weariness has, in fact, won in this room. Everything has been polished, washed, sat on, used, scrubbed too often. All pretenses but living itself have long since vanished from the very atmosphere of this room.

Moreover, a section of this room, for it is not really a room unto itself, though the landlord's lease would make it seem so, slopes backward to provide a small kitchen area, where the family prepares the meals that are eaten in the living room proper, which must also serve as dining room. The single window that has been provided for these "two" rooms is located in this kitchen area. The sole natural light the family may enjoy in the course of a day is only that which fights its way through this little window.

At left, a door leads to a bedroom which is shared by Mama *and her daughter,* Beneatha. *At right, opposite, is a second room (which in the beginning of the life of this apartment was probably a breakfast room), which serves as a bedroom for* Walter *and his wife,* Ruth.

Time: Sometime between World War II and the present.

Place: Chicago's South Side.

At rise: It is morning dark in the living room. Travis *is asleep on the make-down bed at center. An alarm clock sounds from within the bedroom at right, and presently* Ruth *enters from that room and closes the door behind her. She crosses sleepily toward the window. As she passes her sleeping son, she reaches down and shakes him a little. At the window she raises the shade and a dusky South Side morning light comes in feebly. She fills a pot with water and puts it on to boil. She calls to the boy, between yawns, in a slightly muffled voice.*

Ruth *is about thirty. We can see that she was a pretty girl, even exceptionally so, but now it is apparent that life has been little that she expected, and disappointment has already begun to hang in her face. In a few years, before thirty-five even, she will be known among her people as a "settled woman."*

She crosses to her son and gives him a good, final, rousing shake.]

Ruth. Come on now, boy, it's seven thirty! [*Her son sits up at last, in a stupor[1] of sleepiness.*] I say hurry up, Travis! You ain't the only person in the world got to use a bathroom! [*The child, a sturdy, handsome little boy of ten or eleven, drags himself out of the bed and almost blindly takes his towels and "today's clothes" from drawers and a closet and goes out to the bathroom, which is in an outside hall and which is shared by another family or families on the same floor.* Ruth *crosses to the bedroom door at right and opens it and calls in to her husband.*] Walter Lee! . . . It's after seven thirty! Lemme see you do some waking up in there now! [*She waits.*] You better get up from there, man! It's after seven thirty I tell you. [*She waits again.*] All right, you just go ahead and lay there and next thing you know Travis be finished and Mr. Johnson'll be in there and you'll be fussing and cussing round here like a mad man! And be late too! [*She waits, at the end of patience.*] Walter Lee—it's time for you to get up!

[*She waits another second and then starts to go into the bedroom, but is apparently satisfied that her husband has begun to get up. She stops, pulls the door to, and returns to the kitchen area. She wipes her face with a moist cloth and runs her fingers through her sleep-disheveled[2] hair in a vain effort and ties an apron around her housecoat. The bedroom door at right opens and her husband*

---

[1] *stupor*—sluggishness.
[2] *sleep-disheveled*—disordered from lying in bed.

stands in the doorway in his pajamas, which are rumpled and mismated. He is a lean, intense young man in his middle thirties, inclined to quick nervous movements and erratic[3] speech habits—and always in his voice there is a quality of indictment.[4]]

Walter. Is he out yet?

Ruth. What you mean *out*? He ain't hardly got in there good yet.

Walter [*wandering in, still more oriented to sleep than to a new day*]. Well, what was you doing all that yelling for if I can't even get in there yet? [*Stopping and thinking.*] Check coming today?

Ruth. They *said* Saturday and this is just Friday and I hopes to God you ain't going to get up here first thing this morning and start talking to me 'bout no money—'cause I 'bout don't want to hear it.

Walter. Something the matter with you this morning?

Ruth. No—I'm just sleepy as the devil. What kind of eggs you want?

Walter. Not scrambled. [*Ruth starts to scramble eggs.*] Paper come? [*Ruth points impatiently to the rolled up Tribune on the table, and he gets it and spreads it out and vaguely reads the front page.*] Set off another bomb yesterday.

Ruth [*maximum indifference[5]*]. Did they?

Walter [*looking up*]. What's the matter with you?

Ruth. Ain't nothing the matter with me. And don't keep asking me that this morning.

Walter. Ain't nobody bothering you. [*Reading the news of the day absently again.*] Say Colonel McCormick[6] is sick.

Ruth [*affecting tea-party interest*]. Is he now? Poor thing.

Walter [*sighing and looking at his watch*]. Oh, me. [*He waits.*] Now what is that boy doing in that bathroom all this time? He just going to have to start getting up earlier. I can't be being late to work on account of him fooling around in there.

Ruth [*turning on him*]. Oh, no he ain't going to be getting up no earlier no such thing! It ain't his fault that he can't get to bed no earlier nights 'cause he got a bunch of crazy good-for-nothing clowns sitting up running their mouths in what is supposed to be his bedroom after ten o'clock at night. . . .

---

[3] *erratic*—wandering, rambling.

[4] *indictment*—accusation.

[5] *indifference*—lack of interest.

[6] Colonel McCormick—Robert R. McCormick (1880–1955), publisher of the *Chicago Tribune*.

Walter. That's what you mad about, ain't it? The things I want to talk about with my friends just couldn't be important in your mind, could they?

[*He rises and finds a cigarette in her handbag on the table and crosses to the little window and looks out, smoking and deeply enjoying this first one.*]

Ruth [*almost matter of factly, a complaint too automatic to deserve emphasis*]. Why you always got to smoke before you eat in the morning?

Walter [*at the window*]. Just look at 'em down there. . . . Running and racing to work . . . [*He turns and faces his wife and watches her a moment at the stove, and then, suddenly*] You look young this morning, baby.

Ruth [*indifferently*]. Yeah?

Walter. Just for a second—stirring them eggs. It's gone now—just for a second it was—you looked real young again. [*He reaches for her, she crosses away. Then, drily.*] It's gone now—you look like yourself again.

Ruth. Man, if you don't shut up and leave me alone.

Walter [*looking out to the street again*]. First thing a man ought to learn in life is not to make love to no colored woman first thing in the morning. You all some eeeeevil people at eight o'clock in the morning.

[Travis *appears in the hall doorway, almost fully dressed and quite wide awake now, his towels and pajamas across his shoulders. He opens the door and signals for his father to make the bathroom in a hurry.*]

Travis [*watching the bathroom*]. Daddy, come on!

[Walter *gets his bathroom utensils and flies out to the bathroom.*]

Ruth. Sit down and have your breakfast, Travis.

Travis. Mama, this is Friday. [*Gleefully.*] Check coming tomorrow, huh?

Ruth. You get your mind off money and eat your breakfast.

Travis [*eating*]. This is the morning we supposed to bring the fifty cents to school.

Ruth. Well, I ain't got no fifty cents this morning.

Travis. Teacher say we have to.

Ruth. I don't care what teacher say. I ain't got it. Eat your breakfast, Travis.

Travis. I *am* eating.

Ruth. Hush up now and just eat!

[*The boy gives her an **exasperated**[7] look for her lack of understanding, and eats grudgingly.*]

Travis. You think Grandmama would have it?

---

[7] **exasperated**—extremely annoyed.

Ruth. No! And I want you to stop asking your grandmother for money, you hear me?

Travis [*outraged*]. Gaaaleee! I don't ask her, she just gimme it sometimes!

Ruth. Travis Willard Younger—I got too much on me this morning to be—

Travis. Maybe Daddy—

Ruth. *Travis!*

[*The boy hushes abruptly. They are both quiet and tense for several seconds.*]

Travis [*presently*]. Could I maybe go carry some groceries in front of the supermarket for a little while after school then?

Ruth. Just hush, I said. [Travis *jabs his spoon into his cereal bowl viciously, and rests his head in anger upon his fists.*] If you through eating, you can get over there and make up your bed.

[*The boy obeys stiffly and crosses the room, almost mechanically, to the bed and more or less carefully folds the covering. He carries the bedding into his mother's room and returns with his books and cap.*]

Travis [*sulking and standing apart from her unnaturally*]. I'm gone.

Ruth [*looking up from the stove to inspect him automatically*]. Come *here.* [He *crosses to her and she studies his head.*] If you don't take this comb and fix this here head, you better! [Travis *puts down his books with a great sigh of oppression,*[8] *and crosses to the mirror. His mother mutters under her breath about his "slubbornness."*] 'Bout to march out of here with that head looking just like chickens slept in it! I just don't know where you get your slubborn ways. . . . And get your jacket, too. Looks chilly out this morning.

Travis [*with conspicuously brushed hair and jacket*]. I'm gone.

Ruth. Get carfare and milk money—[*waving one finger*]—and not a single penny for no caps, you hear me?

Travis [*with sullen politeness*]. Yes'm.

[*He turns in outrage to leave. His mother watches after him as in his frustration he approaches the door almost comically. When she speaks to him her voice has become a very gentle tease.*]

Ruth [*mocking; as she thinks he would say it*]. Oh, Mama makes me so mad sometimes, I don't know what to do! [*She waits and continues to his back as he stands stock-still in front of the door.*] I wouldn't kiss that woman good-bye for nothing in this world this morning! [*The boy finally turns around and rolls his eyes at her, knowing the mood has changed and he is **vindicated**;*[9] *he does not, however, move toward her yet.*] Not for

---

[8] *oppression*—feeling of being oppressed.

[9] **vindicated**—cleared from an accusation.

nothing in this world! [*She finally laughs aloud at him and holds out her arms to him and we see that it is a way between them, very old and practiced. He crosses to her and allows her to embrace him warmly but keeps his face fixed with masculine rigidity. She holds him back from her presently and looks at him and runs her fingers over the features of his face. With utter gentleness—*] Now—whose little old angry man are you?

Travis [*the masculinity and gruffness start to fade at last*]. Aw gaalee— Mama . . .

Ruth [*mimicking*]. Aw—gaaaaalleeeee, Mama! [*She pushes him, with rough playfulness and finality, toward the door.*] Get on out of here or you going to be late.

Travis [*in the face of love, new aggressiveness*]. Mama, could I *please* go carry groceries?

Ruth. Honey, it's starting to get so cold evenings.

Walter [*coming in from the bathroom and drawing a make-believe gun from a make-believe holster and shooting at his son*]. What is it he wants to do?

Ruth. Go carry groceries after school at the supermarket.

Walter. Well, let him go . . .

Travis [*quickly, to the ally*]. I *have* to—she won't gimme the fifty cents. . . .

Walter [*to his wife only*]. Why not?

Ruth [*simply, and with flavor*]. 'Cause we don't have it.

Walter [*to Ruth only*]. What you tell the boys things like that for? [*Reaching down into his pants with a rather important gesture.*] Here, son—

[*He hands the boy the coin, but his eyes are directed to his wife's.* Travis *takes the money happily.*]

Travis. Thanks, Daddy.

[*He starts out.* Ruth *watches both of them with murder in her eyes.* Walter *stands and stares back at her with defiance, and suddenly reaches into his pocket again on an afterthought.*]

Walter [*without even looking at his son, still staring hard at his wife*]. In fact, here's another fifty cents. . . . Buy yourself some fruit today—or take a taxicab to school or something!

Travis. Whoopee—

[*He leaps up and clasps his father around the middle with his legs, and they face each other in mutual appreciation; slowly* Walter Lee *peeks around the boy to catch the violent rays from his wife's eyes and draws his head back as if shot.*]

Walter. You better get down now—and get to school, man.

Travis [*at the door*]. O.K. Good-bye. [*He exits.*]

Walter [*after him, pointing with pride*]. That's *my* boy. [*She looks at him with* *disgust and turns back to her work.*] You know what I was thinking 'bout in the bathroom this morning?

Ruth. No.

Walter. How come you always try to be so pleasant!

Ruth. What is there to be pleasant 'bout!

Walter. You want to know what I was thinking 'bout in the bathroom or not!

Ruth. I know what you thinking 'bout.

Walter [*ignoring her*]. 'Bout what me and Willy Harris was talking about last night.

Ruth [*immediately—a refrain*]. Willy Harris is a good-for-nothing loudmouth.

Walter. Anybody who talks to me has got to be a good-for-nothing loudmouth, ain't he? And what you know about who is just a good-for-nothing loudmouth? Charlie Atkins was just a "good-for-nothing loudmouth" too, wasn't he! When he wanted me to go in the dry-cleaning business with him. And now—he's grossing a hundred thousand a year. A hundred thousand dollars a year! You still call *him* a loudmouth!

Ruth [*bitterly*]. Oh, Walter Lee. . . . [*She folds her head on her arms over the table.*]

Walter [*rising and coming to her and standing over her*]. You tired, ain't you? Tired of everything. Me, the boy, the way we live—this beat-up hole—everything. Ain't you? [*She doesn't look up, doesn't answer.*] So tired—moaning and groaning all the time, but you wouldn't do nothing to help, would you? You couldn't be on my side that long for nothing, could you?

Ruth. Walter, please leave me alone.

Walter. A man needs for a woman to back him up. . .

Ruth. Walter—

Walter. Mama would listen to you. You know she listen to you more than she do me and Bennie. She think more of you. All you have to do is just sit down with her when you drinking your coffee one morning and talking 'bout things like you do and—[*He sits down beside her and demonstrates graphically what he thinks her methods and tone should be.*]—you just sip your coffee, see, and say easy like that you been thinking 'bout that deal Walter Lee is so interested in, 'bout the store and all, and sip some more coffee, like what you saying ain't really that important to you—And the next thing you know, she be listening good and asking you questions and when I come home—I can tell her the details. This ain't no fly-by-night proposition, baby. I mean we figured it out, me and Willy and Bobo.

Ruth [*with a frown*]. Bobo?

Walter. Yeah. You see, this little liquor store we got in mind cost seventy-five thousand and we figured the initial investment on the place be 'bout thirty thousand, see. That be ten thousand each. Course, there's a couple of hundred you got to pay so's you don't spend your life just waiting for them clowns to let your license get approved—

Ruth. You mean graft?

Walter [*frowning impatiently*]. Don't call it that. See there, that just goes to show you what women understand about the world. Baby, don't *nothing* happen for you in this world 'less you pay *somebody* off!

Ruth. Walter, leave me alone! [*She raises her head and stares at him vigorously—then says, more quietly.*] Eat your eggs, they gonna be cold.

Walter [*straightening up from her and looking off*]. That's it. There you are. Man say to his woman: I got me a dream. His woman say: Eat your eggs. [*Sadly, but gaining in power.*] Man say: I got to take hold of this here world, baby! And a woman will say: Eat your eggs and go to work. [*Passionately now.*] Man say: I got to change my life, I'm choking to death, baby! And his woman say—[*in utter anguish as he brings his fists down on his thighs*]—Your eggs is getting cold!

Ruth [*softly*]. Walter, that ain't none of our money.

Walter [*not listening at all or even looking at her*]. This morning, I was lookin' in the mirror and thinking about it. . . I'm thirty-five years old; I been married eleven years and I got a boy who sleeps in the living room—[*very, very quietly*]—and all I got to give him is stories about how rich white people live. . . .

Ruth. Eat your eggs, Walter.

Walter. DAMN MY EGGS . . . DAMN ALL THE EGGS THAT EVER WAS!

Ruth. Then go to work.

Walter [*looking up at her*]. See—I'm trying to talk to you 'bout myself—[*shaking his head with the repetition*]—and all you can say is eat them eggs and go to work.

Ruth [*wearily*]. Honey, you never say nothing new. I listen to you every day, every night and every morning, and you never say nothing new. [*Shrugging.*] So you would rather *be* Mr. Arnold than be his chauffeur. So—I would *rather* be living in Buckingham Palace.[10]

---

[10] Buckingham Palace—London residence of the English monarch.

Walter. That is just what is wrong with the colored woman in this world. . . . Don't understand about building their men up and making 'em feel like they somebody. Like they can do something.

Ruth [*drily, but to hurt*]. There *are* colored men who do things.

Walter. No thanks to the colored woman.

Ruth. Well, being a colored woman, I guess I can't help myself none.

[*She rises and gets the ironing board and sets it up and attacks a huge pile of rough-dried clothes, sprinkling them in preparation for the ironing and then rolling them into tight fat balls.*]

Walter [*mumbling*]. We one group of men tied to a race of women with small minds.

[*His sister* Beneatha *enters. She is about twenty, as slim and intense as her brother. She is not as pretty as her sister-in-law, but her lean, almost intellectual face has a handsomeness of its own. She wears a bright-red flannel nightie, and her thick hair stands wildly about her head. Her speech is a mixture of many things; it is different from the rest of the family's insofar as education has* **permeated**[11] *her sense of English—and perhaps the Midwest rather than the South has finally—at last—won out in her* **inflection**;[12] *but not altogether, because over all of it is a soft slurring and transformed use of vowels which is the decided influence of the South Side. She passes through the room without looking at either* Ruth *or* Walter *and goes to the outside door and looks, a little blindly, out to the bathroom. She sees that it has been lost to the Johnsons. She closes the door with a sleepy vengeance and crosses to the table and sits down a little defeated.*]

Beneatha. I am going to start timing those people.

Walter. You should get up earlier.

Beneatha [*her face in her hands; she is still fighting the urge to go back to bed*]. Really—would you suggest dawn? Where's the paper?

Walter [*pushing the paper across the table to her as he studies her almost clinically, as though he has never seen her before*]. You a horrible-looking chick at this hour.

Beneatha [*drily*]. Good morning, everybody.

Walter [*senselessly*]. How is school coming?

Beneatha [*in the same spirit*]. Lovely. Lovely. And you know, biology is the greatest. [*Looking up at him.*] I **dissected**[13] something that looked just like you yesterday.

---

[11] **permeated**—spread throughout, pervaded.

[12] **inflection**—pronunciation.

[13] **dissected**—cut apart for scientific study.

Walter. I just wondered if you've made up your mind and everything.

Beneatha [*gaining in sharpness and impatience*]. And what did I answer yesterday morning—and the day before that?

Ruth [*from the ironing board, like someone disinterested and old*]. Don't be so nasty, Bennie.

Beneatha [*still to her brother*]. And the day before that and the day before that!

Walter [*defensively*]. I'm interested in you. Something wrong with that? Ain't many girls who decide—

Walter *and* **Beneatha** [*in unison*]. —"to be a doctor."

[*Silence.*]

Walter. Have we figured out yet just exactly how much medical school is going to cost?

Ruth. Walter Lee, why don't you leave that girl alone and get out of here to work?

Beneatha [*exits to the bathroom and bangs on the door*]. Come on out of there, please!

[*She comes back into the room.*]

Walter [*looking at his sister intently*]. You know the check is coming tomorrow.

Beneatha [*turning on him with a sharpness all her own*]. That money belongs to Mama, Walter, and it's for her to decide how she wants to use it. I don't care if she wants to buy a house or a rocket ship or just nail it up somewhere and look at it. It's hers. Not ours—*hers*.

Walter [*bitterly*]. Now ain't that fine! You just got your mother's interest at heart, ain't you, girl? You such a nice girl—but if Mama got that money she can always take a few thousand and help you through school too—can't she?

Beneatha. I have never asked anyone around here to do anything for me!

Walter. No! And the line between asking and just accepting when the time comes is big and wide—ain't it!

Beneatha [*with fury*]. What do you want from me, Brother—that I quit school or just drop dead, which!

Walter. I don't want nothing but for you to stop acting holy 'round here. Me and Ruth done made some sacrifices for you—why can't you do something for the family?

Ruth. Walter, don't be dragging me in it.

Walter. You are in it—Don't you get up and go work in somebody's kitchen for the last three years to help put clothes on her back?

Ruth. Oh, Walter—that's not fair . . .

Walter. It ain't that nobody expects you to get on your knees and say thank you, Brother; thank you, Ruth; thank you, Mama—and thank you, Travis, for wearing the same pair of shoes for two semesters—

Beneatha [*dropping to her knees*]. Well—I *do*—all right?—thank everybody . . . And forgive me for ever wanting to be anything at all! [*Pursuing him on her knees across the floor.*] FORGIVE ME, FORGIVE ME, FORGIVE ME!

Ruth. Please stop it! Your mama'll hear you.

Walter. What fool told you you had to be a doctor? If you so crazy 'bout messing 'round with sick people—then go be a nurse like other women—or just get married and be quiet . . .

Beneatha. Well—you finally got it said. . . It took you three years but you finally got it said. Walter, give up; leave me alone—it's Mama's money.

Walter. *He was my father, too!*

Beneatha. So what? He was mine, too—and Travis' grandfather—but the insurance money belongs to Mama. Picking on me is not going to make her give it to you to invest in any liquor stores—[*underbreath, dropping into a chair*]—and I for one say, God bless Mama for that!

Walter [*to* Ruth]. See—did you hear? Did you hear!

Ruth. Honey, please go to work.

Walter. Nobody in this house is ever going to understand me.

Beneatha. Because you're a nut.

Walter. Who's a nut?

Beneatha. You—you are a nut. Thee is mad, boy.

Walter [*looking at his wife and his sister from the door, very sadly*]. The world's most backward race of people, and that's a fact.

Beneatha [*turning slowly in her chair*]. And then there are all those prophets who would lead us out of the wilderness—[Walter *slams out of the house.*]—into the swamps!

Ruth. Bennie, why you always gotta be pickin' on your brother? Can't you be a little sweeter sometimes?

[*Door opens.* Walter *walks in. He fumbles with his cap, starts to speak, clears throat, looks everywhere but at* Ruth. *Finally:*]

Walter [*to* Ruth]. I need some money for carfare.

Ruth [*looks at him, then warms; teasing, but tenderly*]. Fifty cents? [*She goes to her bag and gets money.*] Here, take a taxi!

[Walter *exits*. Mama *enters. She is a woman in her early sixties, full-bodied and strong. She is one of those women of a certain grace and beauty who wear it so* **unobtrusively**[14] *that it takes a while to notice. Her dark-brown face is surrounded by the total whiteness of her hair, and, being a woman who has adjusted to many things in life and overcome many more, her face is full of strength. She has, we can see, wit and faith of a kind that keep her eyes lit and full of interest and expectancy. She is, in a word, a beautiful woman. Her bearing is perhaps most like the noble bearing of the women of the Hereros of Southwest Africa*[15]—*rather as if she imagines that as she walks she still bears a basket or a vessel upon her head. Her speech, on the other hand, is as careless as her carriage*[16] *is precise— she is inclined to slur everything—but her voice is perhaps not so much quiet as simply soft.*]

Mama. Who that 'round here slamming doors at this hour?
[*She crosses through the room, goes to the window, opens it, and brings in a feeble little plant growing doggedly in a small pot on the windowsill. She feels the dirt and puts it back out.*]

Ruth. That was Walter Lee. He and Bennie was at it again.

Mama. My children and they tempers. Lord, if this little old plant don't get more sun than it's been getting it ain't never going to see spring again. [*She turns from the window.*] What's the matter with you this morning, Ruth? You looks right peaked.[17] You aiming to iron all them things? Leave some for me. I'll get to 'em this afternoon. Bennie honey, it's too drafty for you to be sitting 'round half dressed. Where's your robe?

Beneatha. In the cleaners.

Mama. Well, go get mine and put it on.

Beneatha. I'm not cold, Mama, honest.

Mama. I know—but you so thin. . .

Beneatha [*irritably*]. Mama, I'm not cold.

Mama [*seeing the make-down bed as* Travis *has left it*]. Lord have mercy, look at that poor bed. Bless his heart—he tries, don't he?
[*She moves to the bed* Travis *has sloppily made up.*]

Ruth. No—he don't half try at all 'cause he knows you going to come along behind him and fix everything. That's just how come he don't know how to do nothing right now—you done spoiled that boy so.

---

[14] **unobtrusively**—inconspicuously.

[15] *Hereros of Southwest Africa*—Bantu-speaking people of Namibia (formerly known as Southwest Africa).

[16] *carriage*—manner of holding and moving the head and body.

[17] peaked—sickly looking.

Mama [*folding bedding*]. Well—he's a little boy. Ain't supposed to know 'bout housekeeping. My baby, that's what he is. What you fix for his breakfast this morning?

Ruth [*angrily*]. I feed my son, Lena!

Mama. I ain't meddling—[*underbreath; busy bodyish*]—I just noticed all last week he had cold cereal, and when it starts getting this chilly in the fall a child ought to have some hot grits or something when he goes out in the cold—

Ruth [*furious*]. I gave him hot oats—is that all right!

Mama. I ain't meddling. [*Pause.*] Put a lot of nice butter on it? [*Ruth shoots her an angry look and does not reply.*] He likes lots of butter.

Ruth [*exasperated*]. Lena—

Mama [*to Beneatha. Mama is inclined to wander conversationally sometimes*]. What was you and your brother fussing 'bout this morning?

Beneatha. It's not important, Mama.

[*She gets up and goes to look out at the bathroom, which is apparently free, and she picks up her towels and rushes out.*]

Mama. What was they fighting about?

Ruth. Now you know as well as I do.

Mama [*shaking her head*]. Brother still worrying his self sick about that money?

Ruth. You know he is.

Mama. You had breakfast?

Ruth. Some coffee.

Mama. Girl, you better start eating and looking after yourself better. You almost thin as Travis.

Ruth. Lena—

Mama. Un-hunh?

Ruth. What are you going to do with it?

Mama. Now don't you start, child. It's too early in the morning to be talking about money. It ain't Christian.

Ruth. It's just that he got his heart set on that store—

Mama. You mean that liquor store that Willy Harris want him to invest in?

Ruth. Yes—

Mama. We ain't no business people, Ruth. We just plain working folks.

Ruth. Ain't nobody business people till they go into business. Walter Lee say colored people ain't never going to start getting ahead till they start gambling on some different kinds of things in the world— investments and things.

Mama. What done got into you, girl? Walter Lee done finally sold you on investing.

Ruth. No. Mama, something is happening between Walter and me. I don't know what it is—but he needs something—something I can't give him any more. He needs this chance, Lena.

Mama [*frowning deeply*]. But liquor, honey—

Ruth. Well—like Walter say—I spec people going to always be drinking themselves some liquor.

Mama. Well—whether they drinks it or not ain't none of my business. But whether I go into business selling it to 'em *is*, and I don't want that on my ledger[18] this late in life. [*Stopping suddenly and studying her daughter-in-law.*] Ruth Younger, what's the matter with you today? You look like you could fall over right there.

Ruth. I'm tired.

Mama. Then you better stay home from work today.

Ruth. I can't stay home. She'd be calling up the agency and screaming at them, "My girl didn't come in today—send me somebody! My girl didn't come in!" Oh, she just have a fit . . .

Mama. Well, let her have it. I'll just call her up and say you got the flu—

Ruth [*laughing*]. Why the flu?

Mama. 'Cause it sounds respectable to 'em. Something white people get, too. They know 'bout the flu. Otherwise they think you been cut up or something when you tell 'em you sick.

Ruth. I got to go in. We need the money.

Mama. Somebody would of thought my children done all but starved to death the way they talk about money here late. Child, we got a great big old check coming tomorrow.

Ruth [*sincerely, but also self-righteously*]. Now that's your money. It ain't got nothing to do with me. We all feel like that—Walter and Bennie and me—even Travis.

Mama [*thoughtfully, and suddenly very far away*]. Ten thousand dollars—

Ruth. Sure is wonderful.

Mama. Ten thousand dollars.

Ruth. You know what you should do, Miss Lena? You should take yourself a trip somewhere. To Europe or South America or someplace—

Mama [*throwing up her hands at the thought*]. Oh, child!

Ruth. I'm serious. Just pack up and leave! Go on away and enjoy

---

[18] ledger—account book; Mama means her conscience.

yourself some. Forget about the family and have yourself a ball for once in your life—

Mama [*drily*]. You sound like I'm just about ready to die. Who'd go with me? What I look like wandering 'round Europe by myself?

Ruth. Shoot—these here rich white women do it all the time. They don't think nothing of packing up they suitcases and piling on one of them big steamships and—swoosh!—they gone, child.

Mama. Something always told me I wasn't no rich white woman.

Ruth. Well—what are you going to do with it then?

Mama. I ain't rightly decided. [*Thinking. She speaks now with emphasis.*] Some of it got to be put away for Beneatha and her schoolin'—and ain't nothing going to touch that part of it. Nothing. [*She waits several seconds, trying to make up her mind about something, and looks at* Ruth *a little tentatively before going on.*] Been thinking that we maybe could meet the notes on a little old two-story somewhere, with a yard where Travis could play in the summertime, if we use part of the insurance for a down payment and everybody kind of pitch in. I could maybe take on a little day work again, few days a week—

Ruth. [*studying her mother-in-law* **furtively**[19] *and concentrating on her ironing, anxious to encourage without seeming to*] Well, Lord knows, we've put enough rent into this here rat trap to pay for four houses by now . . .

Mama [*looking up at the words "rat trap" and then looking around and leaning back and sighing—in a suddenly reflective mood—*]. "Rat trap"—yes, that's all it is. [*Smiling.*] I remember just as well the day me and Big Walter moved in here. Hadn't been married but two weeks and wasn't planning on living here no more than a year. [*She shakes her head at the dissolved dream.*] We was going to set away, little by little, don't you know, and buy a little place out in Morgan Park. We had even picked out the house. [*Chuckling a little.*] Looks right dumpy today. But Lord, child, you should know all the dreams I had 'bout buying that house and fixing it up and making me a little garden in the back—[*She waits and stops smiling.*] And didn't none of it happen.

[*Dropping her hands in a* **futile**[20] *gesture.*]

Ruth [*keeps her head down, ironing*]. Yes, life can be a barrel of disappointments, sometimes.

---

[19] **furtively**—secretly, stealthily.

[20] **futile**—pointless.

Mama. Honey, Big Walter would come in here some nights back then and slump down on that couch there and just look at the rug, and look at me and look at the rug and then back at me—and I'd know he was down then . . . really down. [*After a second very long and thoughtful pause; she is seeing back to times that only she can see.*] And then, Lord, when I lost that baby—little Claude—I almost thought I was going to lose Big Walter too. Oh, that man grieved hisself! He was one man to love his children.

Ruth. Ain't nothin' can tear at you like losin' your baby.

Mama. I guess that's how come that man finally worked hisself to death like he done. Like he was fighting his own war with this here world that took his baby from him.

Ruth. He sure was a fine man, all right. I always liked Mr. Younger.

Mama. Crazy 'bout his children! God knows there was plenty wrong with Walter Younger—hard-headed, mean, kind of wild with women—plenty wrong with him. But he sure loved his children. Always wanted them to have something—be something. That's where Brother gets all these notions, I reckon. Big Walter used to say, he'd get right wet in the eyes sometimes, lean his head back with the water standing in his eyes and say, "Seem like God didn't see fit to give the black man nothing but dreams—but He did give us children to make them dreams seem worth while." [*She smiles.*] He could talk like that, don't you know.

Ruth. Yes, he sure could. He was a good man, Mr. Younger.

Mama. Yes, a fine man—just couldn't never catch up with his dreams, that's all.

[Beneatha *comes in, brushing her hair and looking up to the ceiling, where the sound of a vacuum cleaner has started up.*]

Beneatha. What could be so dirty on that woman's rugs that she has to vacuum them every single day?

Ruth. I wish certain young women 'round here who I could name would take inspiration about certain rugs in a certain apartment I could also mention.

Beneatha [*shrugging*]. How much cleaning can a house need, for Christ's sakes.

Mama [*not liking the Lord's name used thus*]. Bennie!

Ruth. Just listen to her—just listen!

Beneatha. Oh, God!

Mama. If you use the Lord's name just one more time—

Beneatha [*a bit of a whine*]. Oh, Mama—

Ruth. Fresh—just fresh as salt, this girl!

Beneatha [*drily*]. Well—if the salt loses its savor[21]—

Mama. Now that will do. I just ain't going to have you 'round here
  reciting the scriptures in vain—you hear me?

Beneatha. How did I manage to get on everybody's wrong side by just
  walking into a room?

Ruth. If you weren't so fresh—

Beneatha. Ruth, I'm twenty years old.

Mama. What time you be home from school today?

Beneatha. Kind of late. [*With enthusiasm.*] Madeline is going to start my
  guitar lessons today.

[Mama *and* Ruth *look up with the same expression.*]

Mama. Your *what* kind of lessons?

Beneatha. Guitar.

Ruth. Oh, Father!

Mama. How come you done taken it in your mind to learn to play
  the guitar?

Beneatha. I just want to, that's all.

Mama [*smiling*]. Lord, child, don't you know what to do with yourself?
  How long it going to be before you get tired of this now—like you
  got tired of that little play-acting group you joined last year? [*Looking
  at* Ruth.] And what was it the year before that?

Ruth. The horseback-riding club for which she bought that fifty-five-
  dollar riding habit[22] that's been hanging in the closet ever since!

Mama [*to* Beneatha]. Why you got to flit so from one thing to another, baby?

Beneatha [*sharply*]. I just want to learn to play the guitar. Is there anything wrong with that?

Mama. Ain't nobody trying to stop you. I just wonders sometimes why
  you has to flit so from one thing to another all the time. You ain't never
  done nothing with all that camera equipment you brought home—

Beneatha. I don't flit! I—I experiment with different forms of expression—

Ruth. Like riding a horse?

Beneatha. —People have to express themselves one way or another.

Mama. What is it you want to express?

---

[21] savor—flavor. Beneatha is making a reference to the New Testament, where Jesus observes, "You are the salt of the
earth: but if the salt loses its savor, what shall be salted with it?" (Matthew 5:13).

[22] riding habit—formal clothes worn for riding.

Beneatha [*angrily*]. Me! [Mama *and* Ruth *look at each other and burst into* **raucous**²³ *laughter.*] Don't worry—I don't expect you to understand.

Mama [*to change the subject*]. Who you going out with tomorrow night?

Beneatha [*with displeasure*]. George Murchison again.

Mama [*pleased*]. Oh—you getting a little sweet on him?

Ruth. You ask me, this child ain't sweet on nobody but herself— [*Underbreath*] Express herself!

[*They laugh.*]

Beneatha. Oh—I like George all right, Mama. I mean I like him enough to go out with him and stuff, but—

Ruth [*for devilment*]. What does *and stuff* mean?

Beneatha. Mind your own business.

Mama. Stop picking at her now, Ruth. [*She chuckles—then a suspicious sudden look at her daughter as she turns in her chair for emphasis.*] What DOES it mean?

Beneatha [*wearily*]. Oh, I just mean I couldn't ever really be serious about George. He's—he's so shallow.

Ruth. Shallow—what do you mean he's shallow? He's *rich!*

Mama. Hush, Ruth.

Beneatha. I know he's rich. He knows he's rich, too.

Ruth. Well—what other qualities a man got to have to satisfy you, little girl?

Beneatha. You wouldn't even begin to understand. Anybody who married Walter could not possibly understand.

Mama [*outraged*]. What kind of way is that to talk about your brother?

Beneatha. Brother is a flip—let's face it.

Mama [*to* Ruth, *helplessly*]. What's a flip?

Ruth [*glad to add kindling*]. She's saying he's crazy.

Beneatha. Not crazy. Brother isn't really crazy yet—he—he's an elaborate neurotic.²⁴

Mama. Hush your mouth!

Beneatha. As for George. Well. George looks good—he's got a beautiful car and he takes me to nice places and, as my sister-in-law says, he is probably the richest boy I will ever get to know and I even like him sometimes—but if the Youngers are sitting around waiting to see if their little Bennie is going to tie up the family with the Murchisons, they are wasting their time.

---

²³ **raucous**—loud and boisterous.

²⁴ neurotic—in informal use, an anxious, fearful, or depressed person.

Ruth. You mean you wouldn't marry George Murchison if he asked you someday? That pretty, rich thing? Honey, I knew you was odd—

Beneatha. No I would not marry him if all I felt for him was what I feel now. Besides, George's family wouldn't really like it.

Mama. Why not?

Beneatha. Oh, Mama—The Murchisons are honest-to-God-real-*live*-rich colored people, and the only people in the world who are more snobbish than rich white people are rich colored people. I thought everybody knew that. I've met Mrs. Murchison. She's a scene!

Mama. You must not dislike people 'cause they well off, honey.

Beneatha. Why not? It makes just as much sense as disliking people 'cause they are poor, and lots of people do that.

Ruth [*a wisdom-of-the-ages manner; to* Mama]. Well, she'll get over some of this—

Beneatha. Get over it? What are you talking about, Ruth? Listen, I'm going to be a doctor. I'm not worried about who I'm going to marry yet—if I ever get married.

Mama *and* **Ruth.** *If!*

Mama. Now, Bennie—

Beneatha. Oh, I probably will . . . but first I'm going to be a doctor, and George, for one, still thinks that's pretty funny. I couldn't be bothered with that, I am going to be a doctor and everybody around here better understand that!

Mama [*kindly*]. 'Course you going to be a doctor, honey, God willing.

Beneatha [*drily*]. God hasn't got a thing to do with it.

Mama. Beneatha—that just wasn't necessary.

Beneatha. Well—neither is God. I get sick of hearing about God.

Mama. Beneatha!

Beneatha. I mean it! I'm just tired of hearing about God all the time. What has He got to do with anything? Does He pay tuition?

Mama. You 'bout to get your fresh little jaw slapped!

Ruth. That's just what she needs, all right!

Beneatha. Why? Why can't I say what I want to around here, like everybody else?

Mama. It don't sound nice for a young girl to say things like that—you wasn't brought up that way. Me and your father went to trouble to get you and Brother to church every Sunday.

Beneatha. Mama, you don't understand. It's all a matter of ideas, and God is just one idea I don't accept. It's not important, I am not going out and be immoral or commit crimes because I don't believe in God. I don't even think about it. It's just that I get tired of Him getting credit for all the things the human race achieves through its own stubborn effort. There simply is no blasted God—there is only man and it is *he* who makes miracles!

[Mama *absorbs this speech, studies her daughter and rises slowly and crosses to* Beneatha *and slaps her powerfully across the face. After, there is only silence and the daughter drops her eyes from her mother's face, and* Mama *is very tall before her.*]

Mama. Now—you say after me, in my mother's house there is still God. [*There is a long pause and* Beneatha *stares at the floor wordlessly.* Mama *repeats the phrase with precision and cool emotion.*] In my mother's house there is still God.

Beneatha. In my mother's house there is still God.

[*A long pause.*]

Mama [*walking away from* Beneatha, *too disturbed for triumphant posture; stopping and turning back to her daughter*]. There are some ideas we ain't going to have in this house. Not long as I am at the head of this family.

Beneatha. Yes, ma'am.

[Mama *walks out of the room.*]

Ruth [*almost gently, with profound understanding*]. You think you a woman, Bennie—but you still a little girl. What you did was childish—so you got treated like a child.

Beneatha. I see. [*Quietly.*] I also see that everybody thinks it's all right for Mama to be a tyrant. But all the tyranny in the world will never make her right!

[*She picks up her books and goes out. Pause.*]

Ruth [*goes to* Mama's *door*]. She said she was sorry.

Mama [*coming out, going to her plant*]. They frightens me, Ruth. My children.

Ruth. You got good children, Lena. They just a little off sometimes—but they're good.

Mama. No—there's something come down between me and them that don't let us understand each other and I don't know what it is. One done almost lost his mind thinking 'bout money all the time and the other done commence to talk about things I can't seem to understand in no form or fashion. What is it that's changing, Ruth?

Ruth [*soothingly, older than her years*]. Now . . . you taking it all too seriously.

You just got strong-willed children and it takes a strong woman like you to keep 'em in hand.

Mama [*looking at her plant and sprinkling a little water on it*]. They spirited all right, my children. Got to admit they got spirit—Bennie and Walter. Like this old plant that ain't never had enough sunshine or nothing—and look at it . . .

[*She has her back to* Ruth, *who has had to stop ironing and lean against something and put the back of her hand to her forehead.*]

Ruth [*trying to keep* Mama *from noticing*]. You . . . sure . . . loves that little old thing, don't you? . . .

Mama. Well, I always wanted me a garden like I used to see sometimes at the back of the houses down home. This plant is close as I ever got to having one. [*She looks out of the window as she replaces the plant.*] Lord, ain't nothing as dreary as the view from this window on a dreary day, is there? Why ain't you singing this morning, Ruth? Sing that "No Ways Tired." That song always lifts me up so—[*She turns at last to see that* Ruth *has slipped quietly into a chair, in a state of semiconsciousness.*] Ruth! Ruth honey—what's the matter with you . . . Ruth!

[*Curtain.*]

Act One, Scene Two

[*It is the following morning; a Saturday morning, and house cleaning is in progress at the Youngers'. Furniture has been shoved hither and yon and* Mama *is giving the kitchen-area walls a washing down.* Beneatha, *in dungarees, with a handkerchief tied around her face, is spraying insecticide into the cracks in the walls. As they work, the radio is on and a Southside disc-jockey program is inappropriately filling the house with a rather exotic saxophone blues.* Travis, *the sole idle one, is leaning on his arms, looking out of the window.*]

Travis. Grandmama, that stuff Bennie is using smells awful. Can I go downstairs, please?

Mama. Did you get all them chores done already? I ain't see you doing much.

Travis. Yes'm—finished early. Where did Mama go this morning?

Mama [*looking at* Beneatha]. She had to go on a little errand.

[*The phone rings.* Beneatha *runs to answer it and reaches it before* Walter, *who has entered from bedroom.*]

Travis. Where?

Mama. To tend to her business.

Beneatha. Haylo . . . [*Disappointed*] Yes, he is. [*She tosses the phone to* Walter, *who barely catches it.*] It's Willie Harris again.

Walter [*as privately as possible under* Mama's *gaze*]. Hello, Willie. Did you get the papers from the lawyer? . . . No, not yet. I told you the mailman doesn't get here till ten-thirty . . . No I'll come there . . . Yeah! Right away. [*He hangs up and goes for his coat.*]

Beneatha. Brother, where did Ruth go?

Walter [*as he exits*]. How should I know?

Travis. Aw come on, Grandma. Can I go outside?

Mama. Oh, I guess so. You better stay right in front of the house, though and keep a good lookout for the postman.

Travis. Yes'm. [*He darts into the bedroom for stickball and bat, reenters, and sees* Beneatha *on her knees spraying under sofa with behind upraised. He edges closer to the target, takes aim, and lets her have it. She screams.*] Leave them poor cockroaches alone, they ain't bothering you none! [*He runs as she swings the spray gun at him viciously and playfully.*] Grandma! Grandma!

Mama. Look out there, girl, before you be spilling some of that stuff on that child!

Travis [*safely behind the bastion²⁵ of* Mama]. That's right—look out now! [*He exits.*]

Beneatha [*drily*]. I can't imagine that it would hurt him—it has never hurt the roaches.

Mama. Well, little boys' hides ain't as tough as Southside roaches. You better get over there behind the bureau. I seen one marching out of there like Napoleon yesterday.

Beneatha. There's really only one way to get rid of them, Mama—

Mama. How?

Beneatha. Set fire to this building! Mama, where did Ruth go?

Mama [*looking at her with meaning*]. To the doctor, I think.

Beneatha. The doctor? What's the matter? [*They exchange glances.*] You don't think—

Mama [*with her sense of drama*]. Now I ain't saying what I think. But I ain't never been wrong 'bout a woman neither.

[*The phone rings.*]

Beneatha [*at the phone*]. Hay-lo . . . [*pause, and a moment of recognition*] Well—when did you get back! . . . And how was it? . . . Of course I've

---

²⁵ bastion—defense.

missed you—in my way. . . This morning? No . . . house cleaning and all that and Mama hates it if I let people come over when the house is like this. . . . You *have*? Well, that's different. . . . What is it—Oh, what the heck, come on over. . . . Right, see you then. *Arrivederci.*[26]

[*She hangs up.*]

Mama [*who has listened vigorously, as is her habit*]. Who is that you inviting over here with this house looking like this? You ain't got the pride you was born with!

Beneatha. Asagai doesn't care how houses look, Mama—he's an intellectual.

Mama. *Who?*

Beneatha. Asagai—Joseph Asagai. He's an African boy I met on campus. He's been studying in Canada all summer.

Mama. What's his name?

Beneatha. Asagai, Joseph. Ah-sah-guy . . . He's from Nigeria.[27]

Mama. Oh, that's the little country that was founded by slaves way back. . . .

Beneatha. No, Mama—that's Liberia.[28]

Mama. I don't think I never met no African before.

Beneatha. Well, do me a favor and don't ask him a whole lot of ignorant questions about Africans. I mean, do they wear clothes and all that—

Mama. Well, now, I guess if you think we so ignorant 'round here maybe you shouldn't bring your friends here—

Beneatha. It's just that people ask such crazy things. All anyone seems to know about when it comes to Africa is Tarzan—

Mama [*indignantly*]. Why should I know anything about Africa?

Beneatha. Why do you give money at church for the missionary work?

Mama. Well, that's to help save people.

Beneatha. You mean to save them from *heathenism*[29]—

Mama [*innocently*]. Yes.

Beneatha. I'm afraid they need more salvation from the British and the French.

[Ruth *comes in forlornly and pulls off her coat with dejection. They both turn to look at her.*]

---

[26] *Arrivederci*—Italian meaning "good-bye."

[27] Nigeria—country on the western coast of Africa, a former British colony that became independent in 1960.

[28] Liberia—country on the western coast of Africa, founded by freed American slaves in 1847.

[29] *heathenism*—paganism.

Ruth [*dispiritedly*]. Well, I guess from all the happy faces—everybody knows.

Beneatha. You pregnant?

Mama. Lord have mercy, I sure hope it's a little old girl. Travis ought to have a sister.

[*Beneatha and Ruth give her a hopeless look for this grandmotherly enthusiasm.*]

Beneatha. How far along are you?

Ruth. Two months.

Beneatha. Did you mean to? I mean did you plan it or was it an accident?

Mama. What do you know about planning or not planning?

Beneatha. Oh, Mama.

Ruth [*wearily*]. She's twenty years old, Lena.

Beneatha. Did you plan it, Ruth?

Ruth. Mind your own business.

Beneatha. It is my business—where is he going to live, on the *roof*? [*There is silence following the remark as the three women react to the sense of it.*] Gee—I didn't mean that, Ruth, honest. Gee, I don't feel like that at all. I—I think it is wonderful.

Ruth [*dully*]. Wonderful.

Beneatha. Yes—really.

Mama [*looking at Ruth, worried*]. Doctor say everything going to be all right?

Ruth [*far away*]. Yes—she says everything is going to be fine . . .

Mama [*immediately suspicious*]. "She"—What doctor you went to?

[*Ruth folds over, near hysteria.*]

Mama [*worriedly hovering over Ruth*]. Ruth honey—what's the matter with you—you sick?

[*Ruth has her fists clenched on her thighs and is fighting hard to suppress a scream that seems to be rising in her.*]

Beneatha. What's the matter with her, Mama?

Mama [*working her fingers in Ruth's shoulder to relax her*]. She be all right. Women gets right depressed sometimes when they get her way. [*Speaking softly, expertly, rapidly.*] Now you just relax. That's right . . . just lean back, don't think 'bout nothing at all . . . nothing at all—

Ruth. I'm all right . . .

[*The glassy-eyed look melts and then she collapses into a fit of heavy sobbing. The bell rings.*]

Beneatha. Oh, my God—that must be Asagai.

Mama [*to Ruth*]. Come on now, honey. You need to lie down and rest awhile . . . then have some nice hot food.

[*They exit,* Ruth's *weight on her mother-in-law.* Beneatha, *herself profoundly disturbed, opens the door to admit a rather dramatic-looking young man with a large package.*]

Asagai. Hello, Alaiyo—

Beneatha [*holding the door open and regarding him with pleasure*]. Hello . . . [*Long pause*] Well—come in. And please excuse everything. My mother was very upset about my letting anyone come here with the place like this.

Asagai [*coming into the room*]. You look disturbed too . . . Is something wrong?

Beneatha [*still at the door, absently*]. Yes . . . we've all got acute ghetto-itus. [*She smiles and comes toward him, finding a cigarette and sitting.*] So—sit down! No! Wait! [*She whips the spray gun off sofa where she had left it and puts the cushions back. At last perches on arm of sofa. He sits.*] How was Canada?

Asagai [*a sophisticate*]. Canadian.

Beneatha [*looking at him*]. I'm very glad you are back.

Asagai [*looking back at her in turn*]. Are you really?

Beneatha. Yes—very.

Asagai. Why—you were quite glad when I went away. What happened?

Beneatha. You went away.

Asagai. Ahhhhhhhh.

Beneatha. Before—you wanted to be so serious before there was time.

Asagai. How much time must there be before one knows what one feels?

Beneatha [*stalling this particular conversation, her hands pressed together in a deliberately childish gesture*]. What did you bring me?

Asagai [*handing her the package*]. Open it and see.

Beneatha [*eagerly opening the package and drawing out some records and the colorful robes of a Nigerian woman*]. Oh, Asagai! . . . You got them for me! . . . How beautiful . . . and the records too! [*She lifts out the robes and runs to the mirror with them and holds the drapery up in front of herself.*]

Asagai [*coming to her at the mirror*]. I shall have to teach you how to drape it properly. [*He flings the material about her for the moment and stands back to look at her.*] Ah—*Oh-pay-gay-day, oh-gbah-mu-shay.* [*a Yoruba*[30] *exclamation for admiration*] You wear it well . . . very well . . . mutilated hair and all.

Beneatha [*turning suddenly*]. My hair—what's wrong with my hair?

---

[30] *Yoruba*—language of a people of western Africa.

Asagai [*shrugging*]. Were you born with it like that?

Beneatha [*reaching up to touch it*]. No . . . of course not.

[*She looks back to the mirror, disturbed.*]

Asagai [*smiling*]. How then?

Beneatha. You know perfectly well how . . . as crinkly as yours . . . that's how.

Asagai. And it is ugly to you that way?

Beneatha [*quickly*]. Oh, no—not ugly . . . [*More slowly, apologetically*] But it's so hard to manage when it's well—raw.

Asagai. And so to accommodate that—you mutilate it every week?

Beneatha. It's not mutilation!

Asagai [*laughing aloud at her seriousness*]. Oh . . . please! I am only teasing you because you are so very serious about these things. [*He stands back from her and folds his arms across his chest as he watches her pulling at her hair and frowning in the mirror.*] Do you remember the first time you met me at school? . . . [*He laughs.*] You came up to me and said—and I thought you were the most serious little thing I had ever seen—you said: [*He imitates her.*] "Mr. Asagai—I want very much to talk with you. About Africa. You see, Mr. Asagai, I am looking for my *identity*!"

[*He laughs.*]

Beneatha [*turning to him, not laughing*]. Yes—

[*Her face is quizzical, profoundly disturbed.*]

Asagai [*still teasing and reaching out and taking her face in his hands and turning her profile to him*]. Well . . . it is true that this is not so much a profile of a Hollywood queen as perhaps a queen of the Nile— [*A mock dismissal of the importance of the question*] But what does it matter? Assimilationism[31] is so popular in your country.

Beneatha [*wheeling, passionately, sharply*]. I am not an assimilationist!

Asagai [*The protest hangs in the room for a moment and* Asagai *studies her, his laughter fading.*]. Such a serious one. [*There is a pause.*] So—you like the robes? You must take excellent care of them—they are from my sister's personal wardrobe.

Beneatha [*with incredulity*]. You—you sent all the way home—for me?

Asagai [*with charm*]. For you—I would do much more. . . . Well, that is what I came for. I must go.

Beneatha. Will you call me Monday?

---

[31] Assimilationism—cultural process by which minority groups adopt the customs and attitudes of the majority.

Asagai. Yes . . . We have a great deal to talk about. I mean about identity and time and all that.

Beneatha. Time?

Asagai. Yes. About how much time one needs to know what one feels.

Beneatha. You never understood that there is more than one kind of feeling which can exist between a man and a woman—or, at least, there should be.

Asagai [*shaking his head negatively but gently*]. No. Between a man and a woman there need be only one kind of feeling. I have that for you . . . Now even . . . right this moment. . .

Beneatha. I know—and by itself—it won't do. I can find that anywhere.

Asagai. For a woman it should be enough.

Beneatha. I know—because that's what it says in all the novels that men write. But it isn't. Go ahead and laugh—but I'm not interested in being someone's little episode in America or—[*with feminine vengeance*]—one of them! [Asagai *has burst into laughter again.*] That's funny . . . , huh!

Asagai. It's just that every American girl I have known has said that to me. White—black—in this you are all the same. And the same speech, too!

Beneatha [*angrily*]. Yuk, yuk, yuk!

Asagai. It's how you can be sure that the world's most liberated women are not liberated at all. You all talk about it too much!

[Mama *enters and is immediately all social charm because of the presence of a guest.*]

Beneatha. Oh—Mama—this is Mr. Asagai.

Mama. How do you do?

Asagai [*total politeness to an elder*]. How do you do, Mrs. Younger. Please forgive me for coming at such an outrageous hour on a Saturday.

Mama. Well, you are quite welcome. I just hope you understand that our house don't always look like this. [*Chatterish.*] You must come again. I would love to hear all about—[*not sure of the name*]—your country. I think it's so sad the way our American Negroes don't know nothing about Africa 'cept Tarzan and all that. And all that money they pour into these churches when they ought to be helping you people over there drive out them French and Englishmen done taken away your land.

[*The mother flashes a slightly superior look at her daughter upon completion of the recitation.*]

Asagai [*taken aback by this sudden and acutely unrelated expression of sympathy*]. Yes . . . yes. . .

Mama [*smiling at him suddenly and relaxing and looking him over*]. How many miles is it from here to where you come from?

Asagai. Many thousands.

Mama [*looking at him as she would* Walter]. I bet you don't half look after yourself, being away from your mama either. I spec you better come 'round here from time to time and get yourself some decent home-cooked meals . . .

Asagai [*moved*]. Thank you. Thank you very much. [*They are all quiet, then—*] Well . . . I must go. I will call you Monday, Alaiyo.

Mama. What's that he call you?

Asagai. Oh—"Alaiyo." I hope you don't mind. It is what you would call a nickname, I think. It is a Yoruba word. I am a Yoruba.

Mama [*looking at Beneatha*]. I—I thought he was from—

Asagai [*understanding*]. Nigeria is my country. Yoruba is my tribal origin—

Beneatha. You didn't tell us what Alaiyo means . . . for all I know, you might be calling me Little Idiot or something . . .

Asagai. Well . . . let me see . . . I do not know how just to explain it. . . The sense of a thing can be so different when it changes languages.

Beneatha. You're evading.

Asagai. No—really it is difficult. . . [*thinking*] It means . . . it means One for Whom Bread—Food—Is Not Enough. [*He looks at her.*] Is that all right?

Beneatha [*understanding, softly*]. Thank you.

Mama [*looking from one to the other and not understanding any of it*]. Well . . . that's nice. . . You must come see us again—Mr.—

Asagai. Ah-sah-guy . . .

Mama. Yes . . . Do come again.

Asagai. Goodbye.

[*He exits.*]

Mama [*after him*]. Lord, that's a pretty thing just went out here! [*Insinuatingly,*[32] *to her daughter*] Yes, I guess I see why we done commence to get so interested in Africa 'round here. Missionaries my aunt Jenny!

[*She exits.*]

Beneatha. Oh, Mama! . . .

[*She picks up the Nigerian dress and holds it up to her in front of the mirror again. She sets the headdress on haphazardly and then notices her hair again and clutches at it and then replaces the headdress and frowns at herself. Then she*

---

[32] *insinuatingly*—slyly.

starts to wriggle in front of the mirror as she thinks a Nigerian woman might.
Travis *enters and stands regarding her.*]

Travis. What's the matter girl, you cracking up?

Beneatha. Shut up.

[*She pulls the headdress off and looks at herself in the mirror and clutches at her hair again and squinches her eyes as if trying to imagine something. Then, suddenly, she gets her raincoat and kerchief and hurriedly prepares for going out.*]

Mama [*coming back into the room*]. She's resting now. Travis, baby, run next door and ask Miss Johnson to please let me have a little kitchen cleanser. This here can is empty as Jacob's kettle.

Travis. I just come in.

Mama. Do as you told. [*He exits and she looks at her daughter.*] Where you going?

Beneatha [*halting at the door*]. To become a queen of the Nile!

[*She exits in a breathless blaze of glory.* Ruth *appears in the bedroom doorway.*]

Mama. Who told you to get up?

Ruth. Ain't nothing wrong with me to be lying in no bed for. Where did Bennie go?

Mama [*drumming her fingers*]. Far as I could make out—to Egypt. [*Ruth just looks at her.*] What time is it getting to?

Ruth. Ten-twenty. And the mailman going to ring that bell this morning just like he done every morning for the last umpteen years.

[Travis *comes in with the cleanser can.*]

Travis. She say to tell you that she don't have much.

Mama [*angrily*]. Lord, some people I could name sure is tight-fisted! [*Directing her grandson.*] Mark two cans of cleanser down on the list there. If she that hard up for kitchen cleanser, I sure don't want to forget to get her none!

Ruth. Lena—maybe the woman is just short on cleanser—

Mama [*not listening*]. —Much baking powder as she done borrowed from me all these years, she could of done gone into the baking business!

[*The bell sounds suddenly and sharply and all three are stunned—serious and silent—mid-speech. In spite of all the other conversations and distractions of the morning, this is what they have been waiting for, even* Travis, *who looks helplessly from his mother to his grandmother.* Ruth *is the first to come to life again.*]

Ruth [*to* Travis]. Get down them steps, boy!

[Travis *snaps to life and flies out to get the mail.*]

Mama [*her eyes wide, her hand to her breast*]. You mean it done really come?

Ruth [*excitedly*]. Oh, Miss Lena!

Mama [*collecting herself*]. Well . . . I don't know what we all so excited about 'round here for. We known it was coming for months.

Ruth. That's a whole lot different from having it come and being able to hold it in your hands . . . a piece of paper worth ten thousand dollars. . . . [Travis *bursts back into the room. He holds the envelope high above his head, like a little dancer, his face is radiant and he is breathless. He moves to his grandmother with sudden slow ceremony and puts the envelope into her hands. She accepts it, and then merely holds it and looks at it.*] Come on! Open it . . . Lord have mercy, I wish Walter Lee was here!

Travis. Open it, Grandmama!

Mama [*staring at it*]. Now you all be quiet. It's just a check.

Ruth. Open it. . .

Mama [*still staring at it*]. Now don't act silly. . . We ain't never been no people to act silly 'bout no money—

Ruth [*swiftly*]. We ain't never had none before—OPEN IT!

[Mama *finally makes a good strong tear and pulls out the thin blue slice of paper and inspects it closely. The boy and his mother study it raptly over* Mama's *shoulders.*]

Mama. *Travis!* [*She is counting off with doubt.*] Is that the right number of zeros?

Travis. Yes'm . . . ten thousand dollars. Gaalee, Grandmama, you rich.

Mama [*She holds the check away from her, still looking at it. Slowly her face sobers into a mask of unhappiness.*]. Ten thousand dollars. [*She hands it to* Ruth.] Put it away somewhere, Ruth. [*She does not look at* Ruth; *her eyes seem to be seeing something somewhere very far off.*] Ten thousand dollars they give you. Ten thousand dollars.

Travis [*to his mother, sincerely*]. What's the matter with Grandmama—don't she want to be rich?

Ruth [*distractedly*]. You go out and play now, baby. [Travis *exits.* Mama *starts wiping dishes absently, humming intently to herself.* Ruth *turns to her, with kind exasperation.*] You're gone and got yourself upset.

Mama [*not looking at her*]. I spec if it wasn't for all you . . . I would just put that money away or give it to the church or something.

Ruth. Now what kind of talk is that. Mr. Younger would just be plain mad if he could hear you talking foolish like that.

Mama [*stopping and staring off*]. Yes . . . he sure would. [*Sighing.*] We got enough to do with that money, all right. [*She halts then, and turns and looks at her daughter-in-law hard;* Ruth *avoids her eyes and* Mama *wipes* *her hands with finality and starts to speak firmly to* Ruth.] Where did you go today, girl?

Ruth. To the doctor.

Mama [*impatiently*]. Now, Ruth . . . you know better than that. Old Doctor Jones is strange enough in his way but there ain't nothing 'bout him make somebody slip and call him "she"—like you done this morning.

Ruth. Well, that's what happened—my tongue slipped.

Mama. You went to see that woman, didn't you?

Ruth [*defensively, giving herself away*]. What woman you talking about?

Mama [*angrily*]. That woman who—

[Walter *enters in great excitement.*]

Walter. Did it come?

Mama [*quietly*]. Can't you give people a Christian greeting before you start asking about money?

Walter [*to Ruth*]. Did it come? [Ruth *unfolds the check and lays it quietly before him, watching him intently with thoughts of her own.* Walter *sits down and grasps it close and counts off the zeros.*] Ten thousand dollars—[*He turns suddenly, frantically, to his mother and draws some papers out of his breast pocket.*] Mama—look. Old Willy Harris put everything on paper—

Mama. Son—I think you ought to talk to your wife . . . I'll go on out and leave you alone if you want

Walter. I can talk to her later—Mama, look—

Mama. Son—

Walter. WILL SOMEBODY PLEASE LISTEN TO ME TODAY!

Mama [*quietly*]. I don't 'low no yellin' in this house, Walter Lee, and you know it—[Walter *stares at them in frustration and starts to speak several times.*] And there ain't going to be no investing in no liquor stores.

Walter. But, Mama, you ain't even looked at it.

Mama. I don't aim to have to speak on that again.

[*A long pause.*]

Walter. You ain't looked at it and you don't aim to have to speak on that again? You ain't even looked at it and *you* have decided . . . [*Crumpling his papers.*] Well, *you* tell that to my boy tonight when you put him to sleep on the living-room couch. . . . [*Turning to* Mama *and speaking directly to her.*] Yeah—and tell it to my wife, Mama, tomorrow when she has to go out of here to look after somebody else's kids. And tell it to *me*, Mama, every time we need a new pair of curtains and I have to watch *you* go out and work in somebody's kitchen. Yeah, you tell me then!

[Walter *starts out.*]

Ruth. Where you going?

Walter. I'm going out!

Ruth. Where?

Walter. Just out of this house somewhere—

Ruth [*getting her coat*]. I'll come too.

Walter. I don't want you to come!

Ruth. I got something to talk to you about, Walter.

Walter. That's too bad.

Mama [*still quietly*]. Walter Lee—[*She waits and he finally turns and looks at her.*] Sit down.

Walter. I'm a grown man, Mama.

Mama. Ain't nobody said you wasn't grown. But you still in my house and my presence. And as long as you are—you'll talk to your wife civil. Now sit down.

Ruth [*suddenly*]. Oh, let him go on out and drink himself to death! He makes me sick to my stomach! [*She flings her coat against him and exits to bedroom.*]

Walter [*violently, flinging the coat after her*]. And you turn mine too, baby! [*The door slams behind her.*] That was my greatest mistake—

Mama [*still quietly*]. Walter, what is the matter with you?

Walter. Matter with me? Ain't nothing the matter with *me*!

Mama. Yes there is. Something eating you up like a crazy man. Something more than me not giving you this money. The past few years I been watching it happen to you. You get all nervous acting and kind of wild in the eyes—[Walter *jumps impatiently at her words.*] I said sit there now, I'm talking to you!

Walter. Mama—I don't need no nagging at me today.

Mama. Seem like you getting to a place where you always tied up in some kind of knot about something. But if anybody ask you 'bout it you just yell at 'em and bust out the house and go out and drink somewheres. Walter Lee, people can't live with that. Ruth's a good, patient girl in her way—but you getting to be too much. Boy, don't make the mistake of driving that girl away from you.

Walter. Why—what she do for me?

Mama. She loves you.

Walter. Mama—I'm going out. I want to go off somewhere and be by myself for a while.

Mama. I'm sorry 'bout your liquor store, son. It just wasn't the thing for us to do. That's what I want to tell you about—

Walter. I got to go out, Mama—

[*He rises.*]

Mama. It's dangerous, son.

Walter. What's dangerous?

Mama. When a man goes outside his home to look for peace.

Walter [*beseechingly*]. Then why can't there never be no peace in this house then?

Mama. You done found it in some other house?

Walter. No—there ain't no woman! Why do women always think there's a woman somewhere when a man gets restless. [*Picks up the check*] Do you know what this money means to me? Do you know what this money can do for us? [*Puts it back*] Mama—Mama—I want so many things. . . .

Mama. Yes, son—

Walter. I want so many things that they are driving me kind of crazy. . . Mama—look at me.

Mama. I'm looking at you. You a good-looking boy. You got a job, a nice wife, a fine boy and—

Walter. A job. [*Looks at her.*] Mama, a job? I open and close car doors all day long. I drive a man around in his limousine and I say, "Yes, sir; no, sir; very good, sir; shall I take the Drive, sir?" Mama, that ain't no kind of job . . . that ain't nothing at all. [*Very quietly.*] Mama, I don't know if I can make you understand.

Mama. Understand what, baby?

Walter [*quietly*]. Sometimes it's like I can see the future stretched out in front of me—just plain as day. The future, Mama. Hanging over there at the edge of my days. Just waiting for me—a big, looming blank space—full of *nothing*. Just waiting for *me*. [*Pause. Kneeling beside her chair.*] Mama—sometimes when I'm downtown and I pass them cool, quiet-looking restaurants where them white boys are sitting back and talking 'bout things . . . sitting there turning deals worth millions of dollars . . . sometimes I see guys don't look much older than me—

Mama. Son—how come you talk so much 'bout money?

Walter [*with immense passion*]. Because it is life, Mama!

Mama [*quietly*]. Oh—[*Very quietly.*] So now it's life. Money is life. Once upon a time freedom used to be life—now it's money. I guess the world really do change . . .

Walter. No—it was always money, Mama. We just didn't know about it.

Mama. No . . . something has changed. [*She looks at him.*] You something new, boy. In my time we was worried about not being lynched and getting to the North if we could and how to stay alive and still have a pinch of dignity too. . . . Now here come you and Beneatha—talking 'bout things we ain't never even thought about hardly, me and your daddy. You ain't satisfied or proud of nothing we done. I mean that you had a home; that we kept you out of trouble till you was grown; that you don't have to ride to work on the back of nobody's streetcar—You my children—but how different we done become.

Walter. [*A long beat. He pats her hand and gets up.*] You just don't understand, Mama, you just don't understand.

Mama. Son—do you know your wife is expecting another baby? [Walter *stands, stunned, and absorbs what his mother has said*.] That's what she wanted to talk to you about. [Walter *sinks down into a chair*.] This ain't for me to be telling—but you ought to know. [*She waits.*] I think Ruth is thinking 'bout getting rid of that child.

Walter [*slowly understanding*]. No—no—Ruth wouldn't do that.

Mama. When the world gets ugly enough—a woman will do anything for her family. *The part that's already living.*

Walter. You don't know Ruth, Mama, if you think she would do that.

[Ruth *opens the bedroom door and stands there a little limp.*]

Ruth [*beaten*]. Yes I would too, Walter. [*Pause.*] I gave her a five-dollar down payment.

[*There is total silence as the man stares at his wife and the mother stares at her son.*]

Mama [*presently*]. Well—[*Tightly.*] Well—son, I'm waiting to hear you say something . . . I'm waiting to hear how you be your father's son. Be the man he was . . . [*Pause. The silence shouts.*] Your wife say she going to destroy your child. And I'm waiting to hear you talk like him and say we a people who give children life, not who destroys them—[*She rises.*] I'm waiting to see you stand up and look like your daddy and say we done give up one baby to poverty and that we ain't going to give up nary another one . . . I'm waiting.

Walter. Ruth— [*He can say nothing.*]

Mama. If you a son of mine, tell her! [Walter *picks up his keys and his coat and walks out. She continues, bitterly.*] You . . . you are a disgrace to your father's memory. Somebody get me my hat.

[*Curtain.*]

Act Two, Scene One

[*Time: Later the same day.*

At rise: Ruth *is ironing again. She has the radio going. Presently* Beneatha's *bedroom door opens and* Ruth's *mouth falls and she puts down the iron in fascination.*]

Ruth. What have we got on tonight!

Beneatha [*emerging grandly from the doorway so that we can see her thoroughly robed in the costume* Asagai *brought*]. You are looking at what a well-dressed Nigerian woman wears—[*She parades for* Ruth, *her hair completely hidden by the headdress; she is coquettishly fanning herself with an ornate oriental fan, mistakenly more like* Butterfly[1] *than any Nigerian that ever was.*] Isn't it beautiful? [*She promenades to the radio and, with an arrogant flourish, turns off the good loud blues that is playing.*] Enough of this assimilationist junk! [Ruth *follows her with her eyes as she goes to the phonograph and puts on a record and turns and waits ceremoniously for the music to come up. Then, with a shout—*] OCOMOGOSIAY![2]

[Ruth *jumps. The music comes up, a lovely Nigerian melody.* Beneatha *listens, enraptured, her eyes far away—"back to the past." She begins to dance.* Ruth *is dumbfounded.*]

Ruth. What kind of dance is that?

Beneatha. A folk dance.

Ruth [*Pearl Bailey*[3]]. What kind of folks do that, honey?

Beneatha. It's from Nigeria. It's a dance of welcome.

Ruth. Who you welcoming?

Beneatha. The men back to the village.

Ruth. Where they been?

Beneatha. How should I know—out hunting or something. Anyway, they are coming back now . . .

Ruth. Well, that's good.

Beneatha [*with the record*].

Alundi, alundi

Alundi alunya

Jop pu a jeepua

Ang gu soooooooooo

---

[1] *Butterfly*—Japanese woman who is the heroine of the opera *Madame Butterfly* (1904) by Giacomo Puccini.

[2] OCOMOGOSIAY—battle cry invented by combining syllables from several African languages.

[3] *Pearl Bailey*—African-American entertainer (1918–1990) whose style of speech Ruth is imitating.

Ai yai yae . . .
Ayehaye—alundi. . .[4]

[Walter *comes in during this performance; he has obviously been drinking. He leans against the door heavily and watches his sister, at first with distaste. Then his eyes look off—"back to the past"—as he lifts both his fists to the roof, screaming.*]

Walter. YEAH . . . AND ETHIOPIA STRETCH FORTH HER HANDS AGAIN! . . .

Ruth [*drily, looking at him*]. Yes—and Africa sure is claiming her own tonight. [*She gives them both up and starts ironing again.*]

Walter [*all in a drunken, dramatic shout*]. Shut up! . . . I'm digging them drums . . . them drums move me! . . . [*He makes his weaving way to his wife's face and leans in close to her.*] In my heart of hearts—[*he thumps his chest*]—I am much warrior!

Ruth [*without even looking up*]. In your heart of hearts you are much drunkard.

Walter [*coming away from her and starting to wander around the room, shouting*]. Me and Jomo[5] . . . [*Intently, in his sister's face. She has stopped dancing to watch him in this unknown mood.*] That's my man, Kenyatta. [*Shouting and thumping his chest*] FLAMING SPEAR! [*He is suddenly in possession of an imaginary spear and actively spearing enemies all over the room.*] OCOMOGOSIAY . . .

Beneatha [*to encourage* Walter, *thoroughly caught up with this side of him*]. OCOMOGOSIAY, FLAMING SPEAR!

Walter. THE LION IS WAKING . . . OWIMOWEH![6]

[*He pulls his shirt open and leaps up on the table and gestures with his spear.*]

Beneatha. OWIMOWEH!

Walter [*on the table, very far gone, his eyes pure glass sheets; he sees what we can not, that he is a leader of his people, a great chief, a descendant of Chaka,*[7] *and that the hour to march has come*]. Listen, my black brothers—

Beneatha. OCOMOGOSIAY!

Walter. —Do you hear the waters rushing against the shores of the coastlands—

Beneatha. OCOMOGOSIAY!

---

[4] *Alundi . . . alundi*—Yoruban harvest festival song.

[5] Jomo—Jomo Kenyatta (1893?–1978), Kenyan nationalist and first president of independent Kenya (1964–1978). The name *Jomo* means "flaming spear."

[6] OWIMOWEH—variation of a Zulu word meaning "lion."

[7] *Chaka*—or Shaka (1787?–1828), Zulu military leader; founder of the Zulu nation.

Walter. —Do you hear the screeching of the cocks in yonder hills beyond where the chiefs meet in council for the coming of the mighty war—

Beneatha. OCOMOGOSIAY!

[*And now the lighting shifts subtly to suggest the world of* Walter's *imagination, and the mood shifts from pure comedy. It is the inner* Walter *speaking; the South Side chauffeur has assumed an unexpected majesty.*]

Walter. —Do you hear the beating of the wings of the birds flying low over the mountains and the low places of our land—

Beneatha. OCOMOGOSIAY!

Walter. —Do you hear the singing of the women, singing the war songs of our fathers to the babies in the great houses . . . singing the sweet war songs? [*The doorbell rings.*] OH, DO YOU HEAR, MY *BLACK* BROTHERS!

Beneatha [*completely gone*]. We hear you, Flaming Spear—

[Ruth *shuts off the phonograph and opens the door.* George Murchison *enters.*]

Walter. Telling us to prepare for the GREATNESS OF THE TIME!

[*Lights back to normal. He turns and sees* George.] Black Brother!

[*He extends his hand for the fraternal clasp.*]

George. Black Brother, . . .

Ruth [*having had enough, and embarrassed for the family*]. Beneatha, you got company—what's the matter with you? Walter Lee Younger, get down off that table and stop acting like a fool. . .

[Walter *comes down off the table suddenly and makes a quick exit to the bathroom.*]

Ruth. He's had a little to drink . . . I don't know what her excuse is.

George [*to* Beneatha]. Look honey, we're going *to* the theater—we're not going to be *in* it . . . so go change, huh?

[Beneatha *looks at him and slowly, ceremoniously, lifts her hands and pulls off the headdress. Her hair is close-cropped and unstraightened.* George *freezes midsentence and* Ruth's *eyes all but fall out of her head.*]

George. What in the name of—

Ruth [*touching* Beneatha's *hair*]. Girl, you done lost your natural mind!? Look at your head!

George. What have you done to your head—I mean your hair!

Beneatha. Nothing—except cut it off.

Ruth. Now that's the truth—it's what ain't been done to it! You expect this boy to go out with you with your head all nappy like that?

Beneatha [*looking at* George]. That's up to George. If he's ashamed of his heritage—

George. Oh, don't be so proud of yourself, Bennie—just because you look eccentric.

Beneatha. How can something that's natural be eccentric?

George. That's what being eccentric means—being natural. Get dressed.

Beneatha. I don't like that, George.

Ruth. Why must you and your brother make an argument out of everything people say?

Beneatha. Because I hate assimilationist Negroes!

Ruth. Will somebody please tell me what assimila-whoever means!

George. Oh, it's just a college girl's way of calling people Uncle Toms—but that isn't what it means at all.

Ruth. Well, what does it mean?

Beneatha [*cutting* George *off and staring at him as she replies to* Ruth]. It means someone who is willing to give up his own culture and submerge himself completely in the dominant, and in this case, *oppressive* culture!

George. Oh, dear, dear, dear! Here we go! A lecture on the African past! On our Great West African Heritage! In one second we will hear all about the great Ashanti empires; the great Songhay civilizations; and the great sculpture of Benin—and then some poetry in the Bantu[8]— and the whole monologue will end with the word *heritage*! [*Nastily.*] Let's face it, baby, your heritage is nothing but a bunch of raggedy . . . spirituals and some grass huts!

Beneatha. *GRASS HUTS*! [Ruth *crosses to her and forcibly pushes her toward the bedroom.*] See there . . . you are standing there in your splendid ignorance talking about people who were the first to smelt iron on the face of the earth! [Ruth *is pushing her through the door.*] The Ashanti were performing surgical operations when the English— [Ruth *pulls the door to, with* Beneatha *on the other side, and smiles graciously at* George. Beneatha *opens the door and shouts the end of the sentence defiantly at* George.]—were still tattooing themselves with blue dragons! [*She goes back inside.*]

Ruth. Have a seat, George. [*They both sit.* Ruth *folds her hands rather primly on her lap, determined to demonstrate the civilization of the family.*] Warm, ain't it? I mean for September. [*Pause.*] just like they always say about

---

[8] Ashanti . . . Bantu—The Ashanti people of West Africa established a powerful empire in the 1800s and 1900s; the Songhay or Songhai Empire of West Africa was at the height of its power around 1500; formed in the late 1100s, the West African kingdom of Benin was famous for its bronze and ivory sculptures; Bantu is a group of more than 400 languages spoken in central and southern Africa.

Chicago weather: If it's too hot or cold for you, just wait a minute and it'll change. [*She smiles happily at this cliché of clichés.*] Everybody say it's got to do with them bombs and things they keep setting off. [*Pause.*] Would you like a nice cold beer?

George. No, thank you. I don't care for beer. [*He looks at his watch.*] I hope she hurries up.

Ruth. What time is the show?

George. It's an eight-thirty curtain. That's just Chicago, though. In New York standard curtain time is eight forty.

[*He is rather proud of this knowledge.*]

Ruth [*properly appreciating it*]. You get to New York a lot?

George [*offhand*]. Few times a year.

Ruth. Oh—that's nice. I've never been to New York.

[Walter *enters. We feel he has relieved himself, but the edge of unreality is still with him.*]

Walter. New York ain't got nothing Chicago ain't. Just a bunch of hustling people all squeezed up together—being "Eastern."

[*He turns his face into a screw of displeasure.*]

George. Oh—you've been?

Walter. *Plenty* of times.

Ruth [*shocked at the lie*]. Walter Lee Younger!

Walter [*staring her down*]. Plenty! [*Pause.*] What we got to drink in this house? Why don't you offer this man some refreshment? [*To George*] They don't know how to entertain people in this house, man.

George. Thank you—I don't really care for anything.

Walter [*feeling his head; sobriety coming*]. Where's Mama?

Ruth. She ain't come back yet.

Walter [*looking Murchison *over from head to toe, **scrutinizing**[9] *his carefully casual tweed sports jacket over cashmere V-neck sweater over soft eyelet shirt and tie, and soft slacks, finished off with white buckskin shoes*]. Why all you college boys wear them funny-looking white shoes?

Ruth. Walter Lee!

[George Murchison *ignores the remark.*]

Walter [*to Ruth*]. Well, they look crazy—white shoes, cold as it is.

Ruth [*crushed*]. You have to excuse him—

Walter. No he don't! Excuse me for what? What you always excusing me for! I'll excuse myself when I needs to be excused! [*A pause.*] They

---

[9] **scrutinizing**—inspecting critically.

look as funny as them black knee socks Beneatha wears out of here all the time.

Ruth. It's the college *style*, Walter.

Walter. Style . . . She looks like she got burnt legs or something!

Ruth. Oh, Walter—

Walter [*an irritable mimic*]. Oh, Walter! Oh, Walter! [*To* Murchison.] How's your old man making out? I understand you all going to buy that big hotel on the Drive? [*He finds a beer in the refrigerator, wanders over to* Murchison, *sipping and wiping his lips with the back of his hand, and straddling a chair backwards to talk to the other man.*] Shrewd move. Your old man is all right, man. [*Tapping his head and half winking for emphasis.*] I mean he knows how to operate. I mean he thinks *big*, you know what I mean, I mean for a *home*, you know? But I think he's kind of running out of ideas now. I'd like to talk to him. Listen, man, I got some plans that could turn this city upside down. I mean I think like he does. *Big*. Invest big, gamble big . . . lose *big* if you have to, you know what I mean. It's hard to find a man on this whole Southside who understands my kind of thinking—you dig? [*He scrutinizes* Murchison *again, drinks his beer, squints his eyes and leans in close, confidential, man to man.*] Me and you ought to sit down and talk sometimes, man. Man, I got me some ideas . . .

Murchison [*with boredom*]. Yeah—sometimes we'll have to do that, Walter.

Walter [*understanding the indifference, and offended*]. Yeah—well, when you get the time, man. I know you a busy little boy.

Ruth. Walter, please—

Walter [*bitterly, hurt*]. I know ain't nothing in this world as busy as you colored college boys with your fraternity pins and white shoes. . . .

Ruth [*covering her face with humiliation*]. Oh, Walter Lee—

Walter. I see you all the time—with the books tucked under your arms—going to your [*British A—a mimic*] "clahsses." And for what! What . . . you learning over there? Filling up your heads—[*counting off on his fingers*]—with the sociology and the psychology—but they teaching you how to be a man? How to take over and run the world? They teaching you how to run a rubber plantation or a steel mill? Naw—just to talk proper and read books and wear white shoes . . .

George [*looking at him with distaste, a little above it all*]. You're all wacked up with bitterness, man.

Walter [*intently, almost quietly, between the teeth, glaring at the boy*]. And you—ain't you bitter, man? Ain't you just about had it yet? Don't you see no stars gleaming that you can't reach out and grab? You happy?—You contented turkey—you happy? You got it made? Bitter? Man, I'm a volcano. Bitter? Here I am a giant— surrounded by ants! Ants who can't even understand what it is the giant is talking about.

Ruth [*passionately and suddenly*]. Oh, Walter—ain't you with nobody!

Walter [*violently*]. No! 'Cause ain't nobody with me! Not even my own mother!

Ruth. Walter, that's a terrible thing to say!

[Beneatha *enters, dressed for the evening in a cocktail dress and earrings, hair natural.*]

George. Well—hey, [*Crosses to* Beneatha; *thoughtful, with emphasis, since this is a reversal*] you look great.

Walter [*seeing his sister's hair for the first time*]. What's the matter with your head?

Beneatha [*tired of the jokes now*]. I cut it off, Brother.

Walter [*coming close to inspect it and walking around her*]. Well, I'll be damned. So that's what they mean by the African bush . . .

Beneatha. Ha, ha. Let's go, George.

George [*looking at her*]. You know something? I like it. It's sharp. I mean it really is. [*Helps her into her wrap.*]

Ruth. Yes—I think so, too. [*She goes to the mirror and starts to clutch at her hair.*]

Walter. Oh no! You leave yours alone, baby. You might turn out to have a pin-shaped head or something!

Beneatha. See you all later.

Ruth. Have a nice time.

George. Thanks. Good night. [*Half out the door, he reopens it. To* Walter.] Good night, Prometheus![10]

[Beneatha *and* George *exit.*]

Walter [*to* Ruth]. Who is Prometheus?

Ruth. I don't know. Don't worry about it.

Walter [*in fury, pointing after* George]. See there—they get to a point where they can't insult you man to man—they got to talk about something ain't nobody never heard of!

Ruth. How do you know it was an insult? [*To humor him.*] Maybe Prometheus is a nice fellow.

---

[10] Prometheus—in Greek mythology, a Titan who stole fire from heaven and gave it to mankind.

Walter. Prometheus! I bet there ain't even no such thing! I bet that simple-minded clown—

Ruth. Walter—

[*She stops what she is doing and looks at him.*]

Walter [*yelling*]. Don't start!

Ruth. Start what?

Walter. Your nagging! Where was I? Who was I with? How much money did I spend?

Ruth [*plaintively*[11]]. Walter Lee—why don't we just try to talk about it . . .

Walter [*not listening*]. I been out talking with people who understand me. People who care about the things I got on my mind.

Ruth [*wearily*]. I guess that means people like Willy Harris.

Walter. Yes, people like Willy Harris.

Ruth [*with a sudden flash of impatience*]. Why don't you all just hurry up and go into the banking business and stop talking about it!

Walter. Why? You want to know why? 'Cause we all tied up in a race of people that don't know how to do nothing but moan, pray and have babies!

[*The line is too bitter even for him and he looks at her and sits down.*]

Ruth. Oh, Walter . . . [*Softly*] Honey, why can't you stop fighting me?

Walter [*without thinking*]. Who's fighting you? Who even cares about you?

[*This line begins the retardation*[12] *of his mood.*]

Ruth. Well—[*She waits a long time, and then with resignation starts to put away her things.*] I guess I might as well go on to bed . . . [*More or less to herself*] I don't know where we lost it . . . but we have . . . [*Then, to him.*] I—I'm sorry about this new baby, Walter. I guess maybe I better go on and do what I started . . . I guess I just didn't realize how bad things was with us . . . I guess I just didn't really realize—[*She starts out to the bedroom and stops.*] You want some hot milk?

Walter. Hot milk?

Ruth. Yes—hot milk.

Walter. Why hot milk?

Ruth. 'Cause after all that liquor you come home with you ought to have something hot in your stomach.

Walter. I don't want no milk.

Ruth. You want some coffee then?

---

[11] *plaintively*—mournfully.

[12] *retardation*—diminishing.

Walter. No, I don't want no coffee. I don't want nothing hot to drink. [*Almost plaintively.*] Why you always trying to give me something to eat?

Ruth [*standing and looking at him helplessly*]. What else can I give you, Walter Lee Younger?

[*She stands and looks at him and presently turns to go out again. He lifts his head and watches her going away from him in a new mood which began to emerge when he asked her "Who cares about you?"*]

Walter. It's been rough, ain't it, baby? [*She hears and stops but does not turn around and he continues to her back.*] I guess between two people there ain't never as much understood as folks generally thinks there is. I mean like between me and you—[*She turns to face him.*] How we gets to the place where we scared to talk softness to each other. [*He waits, thinking hard himself.*] Why you think it got to be like that? [*He is thoughtful, almost as a child would be.*] Ruth, what is it gets into people ought to be close?

Ruth. I don't know, honey. I think about it a lot.

Walter. On account of you and me, you mean? The way things are with us. The way something done come down between us.

Ruth. There ain't so much between us, Walter . . . Not when you come to me and try to talk to me. Try to be with me . . . a little even.

Walter [*total honesty*]. Sometimes . . . sometimes . . . I don't even know how to try.

Ruth. Walter—

Walter. Yes?

Ruth [*coming to him, gently and with misgiving, but coming to him*]. Honey . . . life don't have to be like this. I mean sometimes people can do things so that things are better . . . You remember how we used to talk when Travis was born . . . about the way we were going to live . . . the kind of house . . . [*She is stroking his head.*] Well, it's all starting to slip away from us. . . .

[*He turns her to him and they look at each other and kiss, tenderly and hungrily. The door opens and* Mama *enters—*Walter *breaks away and jumps up. A beat.*]

Walter. Mama, where have you been?

Mama. My—them steps is longer than they used to be. Whew! [*She sits down and ignores him.*] How you feeling this evening, Ruth?

[Ruth *shrugs, disturbed at having been prematurely interrupted and watching her husband knowingly.*]

Walter. Mama, where have you been all day?

Mama [*still ignoring him and leaning on the table and changing to more comfortable shoes*]. Where's Travis?

Ruth. I let him go out earlier and he ain't come back yet. Boy, is he going to get it!

Walter. Mama!

Mama [*as if she has heard him for the first time*]. Yes, son?

Walter. Where did you go this afternoon?

Mama. I went downtown to tend to some business that I had to tend to.

Walter. What kind of business?

Mama. You know better than to question me like a child, Brother.

Walter [*rising and bending over the table*]. Where were you, Mama? [*Bringing his fists down and shouting*] Mama, you didn't go do something with that insurance money, something crazy?

[*The front door opens slowly, interrupting him, and* Travis *peeks his head in, less than hopefully.*]

Travis [*to his mother*]. Mama, I—

Ruth. "Mama I" nothing! You're going to get it, boy! Get on in that bedroom and get yourself ready!

Travis. But I—

Mama. Why don't you all never let the child explain hisself.

Ruth. Keep out of it now, Lena.

[Mama *clamps her lips together, and* Ruth *advances toward her son menacingly.*]

Ruth. A thousand times I have told you not to go off like that—

Mama [*holding out her arms to her grandson*]. Well—at least let me tell him something. I want him to be the first one to hear. . . . Come here, Travis. [*The boy obeys, gladly.*] Travis—[*She takes him by the shoulder and looks into his face.*] —you know that money we got in the mail this morning?

Travis. Yes'm—

Mama. Well—what do you think your grandmama gone and done with that money?

Travis. I don't know, Grandmama.

Mama [*putting her finger on his nose for emphasis*]. She went out and she bought you a house! [*The explosion comes from* Walter *at the end of the revelation and he jumps up and turns away from all of them in a fury.* Mama *continues, to* Travis.] You glad about the house? It's going to be yours when you get to be a man.

Travis. Yeah—I always wanted to live in a house.

Mama. All right, gimme some sugar then—[Travis *puts his arms around her neck as she watches her son over the boy's shoulder. Then, to* Travis, *after they embrace.*] Now when you say your prayers tonight, you thank God and your grandfather—'cause it was him who give you the house—in his way.

Ruth [*taking the boy from* Mama *and pushing him toward the bedroom*]. Now you get out of here and get ready for your beating.

Travis. Aw, Mama—

Ruth. Get on in there—[*Closing the door behind him and turning radiantly to her mother-in-law*] So you went and did it!

Mama [*quietly, looking at her son with pain*]. Yes, I did.

Ruth [*raising both arms classically*]. PRAISE GOD! [*Looks at* Walter *a moment, who says nothing. She crosses rapidly to her husband.*] Please, honey—let me be glad . . . you be glad too. [*She has laid her hands on his shoulders, but he shakes himself free of her roughly, without turning to face her.*] Oh, Walter . . . a home . . . a home . . . *a home.* [*She comes back to* Mama.] Well—where is it? How big is it? How much it going to cost?

Mama. Well—

Ruth. When we moving?

Mama [*smiling at her*]. First of the month.

Ruth [*throwing back her head with jubilance*]. *Praise God!*

Mama [*tentatively, still looking at her son's back turned against her and* Ruth]. It's—it's a nice house too . . . [*She cannot help speaking directly to him. An imploring quality in her voice, her manner, makes her almost like a girl now.*] Three bedrooms—nice big one for you and Ruth . . . Me and Beneatha still have to share our room, but Travis have one of his own—and [*with difficulty*] I figure if the—new baby—is a boy, we could get one of them double-decker outfits . . . And there's a yard with a little patch of dirt where I could maybe get to grow me a few flowers . . . And a nice big basement . . .

Ruth. Walter honey, be glad—

Mama [*still to his back, fingering things on the table*]. 'Course I don't want to make it sound fancier than it is. . . . It's just a plain little old house—but it's made good and solid—and it will be *ours.* Walter Lee—it makes a difference in a man when he can walk on floors that belong to *him* . . .

Ruth. Where is it?

Mama [*frightened at this telling*]. Well—well—it's out there in Clybourne Park—

[Ruth's *radiance fades abruptly, and* Walter *finally turns slowly to face his mother with incredulity and hostility.*]

Ruth. Where?

Mama [*matter-of-factly*]. Four o six Clybourne Street, Clybourne Park.

Ruth. Clybourne Park? Mama, there ain't no colored people living in Clybourne Park.

Mama [*almost idiotically*]. Well, I guess there's going to be some now.

Walter [*bitterly*]. So that's the peace and comfort you went out and bought for us today!

Mama [*raising her eyes to meet his finally*]. Son—I just tried to find the nicest place for the least amount of money for my family.

Ruth [*trying to recover from the shock*]. Well—well—'course I ain't one never been 'fraid of no crackers,[13] mind you—but—well, wasn't there no other houses nowhere?

Mama. Them houses they put up for colored in them areas way out all seem to cost twice as much as other houses. I did the best I could.

Ruth [*Struck senseless with the news, in its various degrees of goodness and trouble, she sits a moment, her fists propping her chin in thought, and then she starts to rise, bringing her fists down with vigor, the radiance spreading from cheek to cheek again.*]. Well—well!—All I can say is—if this is my time in life—MY TIME—to say goodbye— [*and she builds with momentum as she starts to circle the room with all exuberant, almost tearfully happy release.*]—to these . . . cracking walls!—[*She pounds the walls.*] —and these marching roaches!—[*She wipes at an imaginary army of marching roaches.*] —and this cramped little closet which ain't now or never was no kitchen! . . . then I say it loud and good, HALLELUJAH! AND GOODBYE MISERY! I DON'T NEVER WANT TO SEE YOUR UGLY FACE AGAIN! [*She laughs joyously, having practically destroyed the apartment, and flings her arms up and lets them come down happily, slowly, reflectively, over her abdomen, aware for the first time perhaps that the life therein pulses with happiness and not despair.*] Lena?

Mama [*moved, watching with happiness*]. Yes, honey?

Ruth [*looking off*]. Is there—is there a whole lot of sunlight?

Mama [*understanding*]. Yes, child, there's a whole lot of sunlight.

[*Long pause.*]

Ruth [*collecting herself and going to the door of the room* Travis *is in*]. Well—I guess I better see 'bout Travis. [*To* Mama.] Lord, I sure don't feel like whipping nobody today!

[*She exits.*]

---

[13] crackers—disparaging term for poor whites.

Mama [*The mother and son are left alone now and the mother waits a long time, considering deeply, before she speaks.*]. Son—you—you understand what I done, don't you? [Walter *is silent and sullen.*] I—I just seen my family falling apart today . . . just falling to pieces in front of my eyes . . . We couldn't of gone on like we was today. We was going backwards 'stead of forwards—talking 'bout not wanting babies and wishing each other was dead . . . When it gets like that in life—you just got to do something different, push on out and do something bigger . . . [*She waits.*] I wish you say something, son . . . I wish you'd say how deep inside you you think I done the right thing—

Walter [*crossing slowly to his bedroom door and finally turning there and speaking measuredly*]. What you need me to say you done right for? *You* the head of this family. You run our lives like you want to. It was your money and you did what you wanted with it. So what you need for me to say it was all right for? [*bitterly, to hurt her as deeply as he knows is possible*] So you butchered up a dream of mine—you—who always talking 'bout your children's dreams . . .

Mama. Walter Lee—

[*He just closes the door behind him.* Mama *sits alone, thinking heavily.*]
[*Curtain.*]

Act Two, Scene Two

[*Time: Friday night, a few weeks later.*
At rise: Packing crates mark the intention of the family to move. Beneatha *and* George *come in, presumably from an evening out again.*]

George. O.K. . . . O.K., whatever you say . . . [*They both sit on the couch. He tries to kiss her. She moves away.*] Look, we've had a nice evening; let's not spoil it, huh? . . .

[*He again turns her head and tries to nuzzle in and she turns away from him, not with distaste but with momentary lack of interest; in a mood to pursue what they were talking about.*]

Beneatha. I'm *trying* to talk to you.

George. We always talk.

Beneatha. Yes—and I love to talk.

George [*exasperated; rising*]. I know it and I don't mind it sometimes . . . I want you to cut it out, see—The moody stuff. I mean. I don't like it. You're a nice-looking girl . . . all over. That's all you need, honey, forget the atmosphere. Guys aren't going to go for the atmosphere—

they're going to go for what they see. Be glad for that. Drop the Garbo routine.[14] It doesn't go with you. As for myself, I want a nice—[*groping*]—simple—[*thoughtfully*]—sophisticated girl . . . not a poet— O.K.?

[*He starts to kiss her, she rebuffs[15] him again and he jumps up.*]

Beneatha. Why are you angry?

George. Because this is stupid! I don't go out with you to discuss the nature of "quiet desperation"[16] or to hear all about your thoughts— because the world will go on thinking what it thinks regardless—

Beneatha. Then why read books? Why go to school?

George [*with artificial[17] patience, counting on his fingers*]. It's simple. You read books—to learn facts—to get grades—to pass the course—to get a degree. That's all—it has nothing to do with thoughts.

[*A long pause.*]

Beneatha. I see. [*He starts to sit.*] Goodnight, George.

[George *looks at her a little oddly, and starts to exit. He meets* Mama *coming in.*]

George. Oh—hello, Mrs. Younger.

Mama. Hello, George, how you feeling?

George. Fine—fine, how are you?

Mama. Oh, a little tired. You know them steps can get you after a day's work. You all have a nice time tonight?

George. Yes—a fine time. Well, good night.

Mama. Good night. [*He exits.* Mama *closes the door behind her.*] Hello, honey. What you sitting like that for?

Beneatha. I'm just sitting.

Mama. Didn't you have a nice time?

Beneatha. No.

Mama. No? What's the matter?

Beneatha. Mama, George is a fool—honest. [*She rises.*]

Mama [*hustling around unloading the packages she has entered with. She stops*]. Is he, baby?

Beneatha. Yes.

[Beneatha *makes up* Travis's *bed as she talks.*]

Mama. You sure?

---

[14] Garbo routine—Greta Garbo (1905–1990), Swedish-born American film actress, was famous for her moodiness.

[15] *rebuffs*—repels.

[16] "quiet desperation" —reference to a famous line from Henry David Thoreau's *Walden*, "The mass of men lead lives of quiet desperation."

[17] *artificial*—not genuine.

Beneatha. Yes.

Mama. Well—I guess you better not waste your time with no fools.

[Beneatha *looks up at her mother, watching her put groceries in the refrigerator. Finally she gathers up her things and starts into the bedroom. At the door she stops and looks back at her mother.*]

Beneatha. Mama—

Mama. Yes, baby—

Beneatha. Thank you.

Mama. For what?

Beneatha. For understanding me this time.

[*She exits quickly and the mother stands, smiling a little, looking at the place where* Beneatha *just stood.* Ruth *enters.*]

Ruth. Now don't you fool with any of this stuff, Lena—

Mama. Oh, I just thought I'd sort a few things out. Is Brother here?

Ruth. Yes.

Mama [*with concern*]. Is he—

Ruth [*reading her eyes*]. Yes.

[Mama *is silent and someone knocks on the door.* Mama *and* Ruth *exchange weary and knowing glances and* Ruth *opens it to admit the neighbor,* Mrs. Johnson, *who is a rather squeaky wide-eyed lady of no particular age, with a newspaper under her arm.*]

Mama [*changing her expression to acute delight and a ringing cheerful greeting*]. Oh—hello there, Johnson.

Johnson [*This is a woman who decided long ago to be enthusiastic about EVERYTHING in life and is inclined to wave her wrist vigorously at the height of her exclamatory comments.*]. Hello there, yourself! H'you this evening, Ruth?

Ruth [*not much of a deceptive type*]. Fine, Mis' Johnson, h'you?

Johnson. Fine. [*Reaching out quickly, playfully, and patting* Ruth's *stomach.*] Ain't you starting to poke out none yet! [*She mugs with delight at the overfamiliar remark and her eyes dart around looking at the crates and packing preparation;* Mama's *face is a cold sheet of endurance.*] Oh, ain't we getting ready round here, though! Yessir! Lookathere! I'm telling you the Youngers is really getting ready to "move on up a little higher!"—Bless God!

Mama [*a little drily, doubting the total sincerity of the Blesser*]. Bless God.

Johnson. He's good, ain't He?

Mama. Oh yes, He's good.

Johnson. I mean sometimes He works in mysterious ways . . . but He works, don't He!

Mama [*the same*]. Yes, He does.

Johnson. I'm just soooooo happy for y'all. And this here child—[*about Ruth*] looks like she could just pop open with happiness, don't she. Where's all the rest of the family?

Mama. Bennie's gone to bed—

Johnson. Ain't no . . . [*The implication is pregnancy.*] sickness done hit you—I hope . . . ?

Mama. No—she just tired. She was out this evening.

Johnson [*All is a coo, an emphatic coo.*]. Aw—ain't that lovely. She still going out with the little Murchison boy?

Mama [*drily*]. Ummmm huh.

Johnson. That's lovely. You sure got lovely children, Younger. Me and Isaiah talks all the time 'bout what fine children you was blessed with. We sure do.

Mama. Ruth, give Mis' Johnson a piece of sweet potato pie and some milk.

Johnson. Oh honey, I can't stay hardly a minute—I just dropped in to see if there was anything I could do. [*Accepting the food easily.*] I guess y'all seen the news what's all over the colored paper this week . . .

Mama. No—didn't get mine yet this week.

Johnson [*lifting her head and blinking with the spirit of catastrophe*]. You mean you ain't read 'bout them colored people that was bombed out their place out there?

[Ruth *straightens with concern and takes the paper and reads it.* Johnson *notices her and feeds commentary.*]

Johnson. Ain't it something how bad these here white folks is getting here in Chicago! Lord, getting so you think you right down in Mississippi! [*With a tremendous and rather insincere sense of melodrama.*] 'Course I thinks it's wonderful how our folks keeps on pushing out. You hear some of these Negroes round here talking 'bout how they don't go where they ain't wanted and all that—but not me, honey! [*This is a lie.*] Wilhemenia Othella Johnson goes anywhere, any time she feels like it! [*with head movement for emphasis*] Yes I do! . . .

Mama. Don't you want some more pie?

Johnson. No—no thank you; this was lovely. I got to get on over home and have my midnight coffee. I hear some people say it don't let them sleep but I find I can't close my eyes right lessen I done had that laaaast cup of coffee . . . [*She waits. A beat. Undaunted.*] My Good-night coffee, I calls it!

Mama [*with much eye-rolling and communication between herself and* Ruth]. Ruth, why don't you give Mis' Johnson some coffee.

[Ruth *gives* Mama *an unpleasant look for her kindness.*]

Johnson [*accepting the coffee*]. Where's Brother tonight?

Mama. He's lying down.

Johnson. MMmmmmm, he sure gets his beauty rest, don't he? Good-looking man. Sure is a good-looking man! [*Reaching out to pat* Ruth's *stomach again*] I guess that's how come we keep on having babies around here. [*She winks at* Mama.] One thing 'bout Brother, he always know how to have a *good* time. And soooooo ambitious! I bet it was his idea y'all moving out to Clybourne Park. Lord—I bet this time next time y'all's names will have been in the papers plenty—[*holding up her hands to mark off each word of the headline she can see in front of her*] "NEGROES INVADE CLYBOURNE PARK—BOMBED!"

Mama [*She and* Ruth *look at the woman in amazement.*]. We ain't exactly moving out there to get bombed.

Johnson. Oh honey—you know I'm praying to God every day that don't nothing like that happen! But you have to think of life like it is—and these here Chicago peckerwoods[18] is some baaaad peckerwoods.

Mama [*wearily*]. We done thought about all that Mis' Johnson.

[Beneatha *comes out of the bedroom in her robe and passes through to the bathroom. Mrs. Johnson turns.*]

Johnson. Hello there, Bennie!

Beneatha [*crisply*]. Hello, Mrs. Johnson.

Johnson. How is school?

Beneatha [*crisply*]. Fine, thank you. [*She goes out.*]

Johnson [*insulted*]. Getting so she don't have much to say to nobody.

Mama. The child was on her way to the bathroom.

Johnson. I know—but sometimes she act like ain't got time to pass the time of day with nobody ain't been to college. Oh—I ain't criticizing her none. It's just—you know how some of our young people gets when they get a little education. [Mama *and* Ruth *say nothing, just look at her.*] Yes—well. Well, I guess I better get on home. [*Unmoving.*] 'Course I can understand how she must be proud and everything—being the only one in the family to make something of herself. I know

---

[18] peckerwoods—disparaging term for poor whites.

just being a chauffeur ain't never satisfied Brother none. He shouldn't feel like that, though. Ain't nothing wrong with being a chauffeur.

Mama. There's plenty wrong with it.

Johnson. What?

Mama. Plenty. My husband always said being any kind of servant wasn't a fit thing for a man to have to be. He always said a man's hands was made to make things, or to turn the earth with—not to drive nobody's car for 'em—or—[*She looks at her own hands.*] carry they slop jars. And my boy is just like him—he wasn't meant to wait on nobody.

Johnson [*rising, somewhat offended*]. Mmmmmmmmm. The Youngers is too much for me! [*She looks around.*] You sure are one proud-acting bunch of colored folks. Well—I always thinks like Booker T. Washington[19] said that time—"Education has spoiled many a good plow hand"—

Mama. Is that what old Booker T. said?

Johnson. He sure did.

Mama. Well, it sounds just like him. The fool.

Johnson [*indignantly*]. Well—he was one of our great men.

Mama. Who said so?

Johnson [*nonplussed*]. You know, me and you ain't never agreed about some things, Lena Younger. I guess I better be going—

Ruth [*quickly*]. Good night.

Johnson. Good night. Oh—[*thrusting it at her*] You can keep the paper! [*With a trill.*] 'Night.

Mama. Good night, Mis' Johnson

[Mrs. Johnson *exits.*]

Ruth. If ignorance was gold . . .

Mama. Shush. Don't talk about folks behind their backs.

Ruth. You do.

Mama. I'm old and corrupted. [Beneatha *enters.*] You was rude to Mis' Johnson, Beneatha, and I don't like it at all.

Beneatha [*at her door*]. Mama, if there are two things we, as a people, have got to overcome, one is the Klu Klux Klan—and the other is Mrs. Johnson. [*She exits.*]

Mama. Smart aleck.

[*The phone rings.*]

Ruth. I'll get it.

---

[19] Booker T. Washington—African American educator (1856–1915) and advocate of black economic self-development.

Mama. Lord, ain't this a popular place tonight.

Ruth [*at the phone*]. Hello—just a minute. [*Goes to the door.*] Walter, it's Mrs. Arnold. [*Waits; goes back to the phone; tense.*] Hello. Yes, this is his wife speaking . . . He's lying down now. Yes . . . well, he'll be in tomorrow. He's been very sick. Yes—I know we should have called, but we were so sure he'd be able to come in today. Yes—yes, I'm very sorry. Yes . . . Thank you very much. [*She hangs up.* Walter *is standing in the doorway of the bedroom behind her.*] That was Mrs. Arnold.

Walter [*indifferently*]. Was it?

Ruth. She said if you don't come in tomorrow that they are getting a new man . . .

Walter. Ain't that sad—ain't that crying sad.

Ruth. She said Mr. Arnold has had to take a cab for three days. . . . Walter, you ain't been to work for three days! [*This is a revelation to her.*] Where you been, Walter Lee Younger? [Walter *looks at her and starts to laugh.*] You're going to lose your job.

Walter. That's right . . .

Ruth. Oh, Walter, and with your mother working like a dog every day—

[*A steamy, deep blues pours into the room.*]

Walter. That's sad too—Everything is sad.

Mama. What you been doing for these three days, son?

Walter. Mama—you don't know all the things a man what got leisure can find to do in this city . . . What's this—Friday night? Well—Wednesday I borrowed Willy Harris' car and I went for a drive . . . just me and myself and I drove and drove . . . Way out . . . way past South Chicago, and I parked the car and I sat and looked at the steel mills all day long. I just sat in the car and looked at them big black chimneys for hours. Then I drove back and I went to the Green Hat. [*Pause.*] And Thursday—Thursday I borrowed the car again and I got in it and I pointed it the other way and I drove the other way—for hours—way, way up to Wisconsin, and I looked at the farms. I just drove and looked at the farms. Then I drove back and I went to the Green Hat. [*Pause.*] And today—today I didn't get the car. Today I just walked. All over the South side. And I looked at the Negroes and they looked at me and finally I just sat down on the curb at Thirty-ninth and South Parkway and I just sat there and watched the Negroes go by. And then I went to the Green Hat. You all sad? You all depressed? And you know where I am going right now—

[Ruth *goes out quietly.*]

Mama. Oh, Big Walter, is this the harvest of our days?

Walter. You know what I like about the Green Hat? I like this little cat they got there who blows a sax. . . . He blows. He talks to me. He ain't but 'bout five feet tall and he's got a conked[20] head and his eyes is always closed and he's all music—

Mama [*rising and getting some papers out of her handbag*]. Walter—

Walter. And there's this other guy who plays the piano . . . and they got a sound. I mean they can work on some music . . . They got the best little combo in the world in the Green Hat . . . You can just sit there and drink and listen to them three men play and you realize that don't nothing matter . . . but just being there—

Mama. I've helped do it to you, haven't I, son? Walter, I been wrong.

Walter. Naw—you ain't never been wrong about nothing, Mama.

Mama. Listen to me, now. I say I been wrong, son. That I been doing to you what the rest of the world been doing to you. [*She turns off the radio.*] Walter— [*She stops and he looks up slowly at her and she meets his eyes pleadingly.*] What you ain't never understood is that I ain't got nothing, don't own nothing, ain't never really wanted nothing that wasn't for you. There ain't nothing as precious to me. . . . There ain't nothing worth holding on to, money, dreams, nothing else—if it means—if it means it's going to destroy my boy. [*She takes an envelope out of her handbag and puts it in front of him and he watches without speaking or moving.*] I paid the man thirty-five hundred dollars down on the house. That leaves sixty-five hundred dollars. Monday morning I want you to take this money and take three thousand dollars and put it in a savings account for Beneatha's medical schooling. The rest you put in a checking account—with your name on it. And from now on any penny that come out of it or that go in it is for you to look after. For you to decide. [*She drops her hands a little helplessly.*] It ain't much, but it's all I got in the world and I'm putting it in your hands. I'm telling you to be the head of this family from now on like you supposed to be.

Walter [*stares at the money*]. You trust me like that, Mama?

Mama. I ain't never stop trusting you. Like I ain't never stop loving you. [*She goes out, and* Walter *sits looking at the money on the table as the music continues in its idiom,[21] pulsing in the room. Finally, in a decisive gesture, he*

---

[20] conked—with hair chemically straightened.

[21] idiom—style.

gets up, and, in mingled joy and desperation, picks up the money. At the same moment, Travis *enters for bed.*]

Travis. What's the matter, Daddy? You drunk?

Walter [*sweetly, more sweetly than we have ever known him*]. No, Daddy ain't drunk. Daddy ain't going to never be drunk again. . .

Travis. Well, good night, Daddy.

[*The* Father *has come from behind the couch and leans over, embracing his son.*]

Walter. Son, I feel like talking to you tonight.

Travis. About what?

Walter. Oh, about a lot of things. About you and what kind of man you going to be when you grow up. . . . Son—son, what do you want to be when you grow up?

Travis. A bus driver.

Walter [*laughing a little*]. A what? Man, that ain't nothing to want to be!

Travis. Why not?

Walter. 'Cause, man—it ain't big enough—you know what I mean.

Travis. I don't know then. I can't make up my mind. Sometimes Mama asks me that too. And sometimes when I tell her I just want to be like you—she says she don't want me to be like that and sometimes she says she does. . . .

Walter [*gathering him up in his arms*]. You know what, Travis? In seven years you going to be seventeen years old. And things is going to be very different with us in seven years, Travis. . . . One day when you are seventeen I'll come home—home from my office downtown somewhere—

Travis. You don't work in no office, Daddy.

Walter. No—but after tonight. After what your daddy gonna do tonight, there's going to be offices—a whole lot of offices. . . .

Travis. What you gonna do tonight, Daddy?

Walter. You wouldn't understand yet, son, but your daddy's gonna make a transaction . . . a business transaction that's going to change our lives . . . That's how come one day when you 'bout seventeen years old I'll come home and I'll be pretty tired, you know what I mean, after a day of conferences and secretaries getting things wrong the way they do . . . 'cause an executive's life is hard, man—[*The more he talks, the farther away he gets.*] And I'll pull the car up on the drive-way . . . just a plain black Chrysler, I think, with white walls—no—black tires. More elegant. Rich people don't have to be flashy . . . though I'll have to get something a little sportier for Ruth—maybe a

Cadillac convertible to do her shopping in. . . . And I'll come up the steps to the house and the gardener will be clipping away at the hedges and he'll say, "Good evening, Mr. Younger." And I'll say, "Hello, Jefferson, how are you this evening?" And I'll go inside and Ruth will come downstairs and meet me at the door and we'll kiss each other and she'll take my arm and we'll go up to your room to see you sitting on the floor with the catalogues of all the great schools in America around you. . . . All the great schools in the world! And— and I'll say, all right son—it's your seventeenth birthday, what is it you've decided? . . . Just tell me, where you want to go to school and you'll *go*. Just tell me, what it is you want to be—and you'll *be* it. . . . Whatever you want to be—Yessir! [*He holds his arms open for* Travis.] You just name it, son . . . [Travis *leaps into them.*] and I hand you the world!

[Walter's *voice has risen in pitch and hysterical promise and on the last line he lifts* Travis *high.*]

[*Blackout.*]

Act Two, Scene Three

[*Time: Saturday, moving day, one week later.*

Before the curtain rises, Ruth's *voice, a strident, dramatic church alto*[22] *cuts through the silence.*

It is, in the darkness, a triumphant surge, a penetrating statement of expectation: "Oh, Lord, I don't feel no ways tired! Children, oh, glory hallelujah!"

As the curtain rises we see that Ruth *is alone in the living room, finishing up the family's packing. It is moving day. She is nailing crates and tying cartons.* Beneatha *enters, carrying a guitar case, and watches her exuberant sister-in-law.*]

Ruth. Hey!

Beneatha. [*putting away the case*] Hi.

Ruth [*pointing at a package*]. Honey—look in that package there and see what I found on sale this morning at the South Center. [Ruth *gets up and moves to the package and draws out some curtains.*] Lookahere— hand-turned hems!

Beneatha. How do you know the window size out there?

Ruth [*who hadn't thought of that*]. Oh—Well, they bound to fit something in the whole house. Anyhow, they was too good a bargain to pass up.

---

[22] *strident . . . alto*—loud, low female singing voice.

[Ruth *slaps her head, suddenly remembering something.*] Oh, Bennie—I meant to put a special note on that carton over there. That's your mamma's good china and she wants me to be very careful with it.

Beneatha. I'll do it.

[Beneatha *finds a piece of paper and starts to draw large letters on it.*]

Ruth. You know what I'm going to do soon as I get in that new house?

Beneatha. What?

Ruth. Honey—I'm going to run me a tub of water up to here. . . . [*with her fingers practically up to her nostrils*] And I'm going to get in it—and I am going to sit . . . and sit . . . and sit in that hot water and the first person who knocks to tell *me* to hurry up and come out—

Beneatha. Gets shot at sunrise.

Ruth [*laughing happily*]. You said it, sister! [*Noticing how large* Beneatha *is absent-mindedly making the note.*] Honey, they ain't going to read that from no airplane.

Beneatha [*laughing herself*]. I guess I always think things have more emphasis if they are big, somehow.

Ruth [*looking up at her and smiling*]. You and your brother seem to have that as a philosophy of life. Lord, that man—done changed so 'round here. You know—you know what we did last night? Me and Walter Lee?

Beneatha. What?

Ruth [*smiling to herself*]. We went to the movies. [*Looking at* Beneatha *to see if she understands.*] We went to the movies. You know the last time me and Walter went to the movies together?

Beneatha. No.

Ruth. Me neither. That's how long it been. [*Smiling again.*] But we went last night. The picture wasn't much good, but that didn't seem to matter. We went—and we held hands.

Beneatha. Oh, Lord!

Ruth. We held hands—and you know what?

Beneatha. What?

Ruth. When we come out of the show it was late and dark and all the stores and things was closed up . . . and it was kind of chilly and there wasn't many people on the streets . . . and we was still holding hands, me and Walter.

Beneatha. You're killing me.

[Walter *enters with a large package. His happiness is deep in him; he cannot keep still with his new-found exuberance. He is singing and wiggling and snapping his fingers. He puts his package in a corner and puts a phonograph record, which he has brought in with him, on the record player. As the music comes up he dances over to* Ruth *and tries to get her to dance with him. She gives in at last to his raunchiness[23] and in a fit of giggling allows herself to be drawn into his mood. They dip and she melts into his arms in a classic, body-melding "slow drag."*]

Beneatha [*regarding them a long time as they dance, then drawing in her breath for a deeply exaggerated comment which she does not particularly mean*]. Talk about—olddddddddddd-fashioneddddddddd—Negroes!

Walter [*stopping momentarily*]. What kind of Negroes?

[*He says this in fun. He is not angry with her today, nor with anyone. He starts to dance with his wife again.*]

Beneatha. Old-fashioned.

Walter [*as he dances with* Ruth]. You know, when these *New Negroes* have their convention—[*pointing at his sister*]—that is going to be the chairman of the Committee on Unending Agitation. [*He goes on dancing, then stops.*] Race, race, race! . . . Girl, I do believe you are the first person in the history of the entire human race to successfully brainwash yourself. [Beneatha *breaks up and he goes on dancing. He stops again, enjoying his tease.*] Shoot, even the N double A C P takes a holiday sometimes! [Beneatha *and* Ruth *laugh. He dances with* Ruth *some more and starts to laugh and stops and pantomines someone over an operating table.*] I can just see that chick someday looking down at some poor cat on an operating table before she starts to slice him, saying . . . [*Pulling his sleeves back maliciously*] "By the way, what are your views on civil rights down there? . . ."

[*He laughs at her again and starts to dance happily. The bell sounds.*]

Beneatha. Sticks and stones may break my bones but . . . words will never hurt me!

[Beneatha *goes to the door and opens it as* Walter *and* Ruth *go on with the clowning.* Beneatha *is somewhat surprised to see a quiet-looking middle-aged white man in a business suit holding his hat and a briefcase in his hand and consulting a small piece of paper.*]

Man. Uh—how do you do, miss. I am looking for a Mrs.—[*He looks at the slip of paper*] Mrs. Lena Younger? [*He stops short, struck dumb at the sight of the oblivious* Walter *and* Ruth.]

Beneatha [*smoothing her hair with slight embarrassment*]. Oh—yes, that's my mother. Excuse me. [*She closes the door and turns to quiet the other two.*] Ruth! Brother! Somebody's here. [*Enunciating precisely but soundlessly:*

---

[23] *raunchiness*—sexiness.

"There's a white man at the door!" They stop dancing, Ruth *cuts off the phonograph,* Beneatha *opens the door. The* Man *casts a curious quick glance at all of them.*] Uh—come in please.

Man [*coming in*]. Thank you.

Beneatha. My mother isn't here just now. Is it business?

Man. Yes . . . well, of a sort.

Walter [*freely, the Man of the House*]. Have a seat. I'm Mrs. Younger's son. I look after most of her business matters.

[Ruth *and* Beneatha *exchange amused glances.*]

Man [*regarding* Walter, *and sitting*]. Well—my name is Karl Lindner . . .

Walter [*stretching out his hand*]. Walter Younger. This is my wife— [Ruth *nods politely.*]—and my sister.

Lindner. How do you do.

Walter [*amiably, as he sits himself easily on a chair, leaning with interest forward on his knees and looking expectantly into the newcomer's face*]. What can we do for you, Mr. Lindner!

Lindner [*some minor shuffling of the hat and briefcase on his knees*]. Well—I am a representative of the Clybourne Park Improvement Association—

Walter [*pointing*]. Why don't you sit your things on the floor?

Lindner. Oh—yes. Thank you. [*He slides the briefcase and hat under the chair.*] And as I was saying—I am from the Clybourne Park Improvement Association and we have had it brought to our attention at the last meeting that you people—or at least your mother—has bought a piece of residential property at—[*He digs for the slip of paper again*]—four o six Clybourne Street . . .

Walter. That's right. Care for something to drink? Ruth, get Mr. Lindner a beer.

Lindner [*upset for some reason*]. Oh—no, really. I mean thank you very much, but no thank you.

Ruth [*innocently*]. Some coffee?

Lindner. Thank you, nothing at all.

[Beneatha *is watching the man carefully.*]

Lindner. Well, I don't know how much you folks know about our organization. [*He is a gentle man; thoughtful and somewhat labored in his manner.*] It is one of those community organizations set up to look after—oh, you know, things like block upkeep and special projects and we also have what we call our New Neighbors Orientation Committee . . .

Beneatha [*drily*]. Yes—and what do they do?

Lindner [*turning a little to her and then returning the main force to* Walter]. Well—it's what you might call a sort of welcoming committee, I guess. I mean they, we, I'm the chairman of the committee—go around and see the new people who move into the neighborhood and sort of give them the lowdown on the way we do things out in Clybourne Park.

Beneatha [*with appreciation of the two meanings, which escape* Ruth *and* Walter]. Un-huh.

Lindner. And we also have the category of what the association calls— [*He looks elsewhere.*]—uh—special community problems . . .

Beneatha. Yes—and what are some of those?

Walter. Girl, let the man talk.

Lindner [*with understated relief*]. Thank you. I would sort of like to explain this thing in my own way. I mean I want to explain to you in a certain way.

Walter. Go ahead.

Lindner. Yes. Well. I'm going to try to get right to the point. I'm sure we'll all appreciate that in the long run.

Beneatha. Yes.

Walter. Be still now!

Lindner. Well—

Ruth [*still innocently*]. Would you like another chair—you don't look comfortable.

Lindner [*more frustrated than annoyed*]. No, thank you very much. Please. Well—to get right to the point I—[*A great breath, and he is off at last.*] I am sure you people must be aware of some of the incidents which have happened in various parts of the city when colored people have moved into certain areas—[Beneatha *exhales heavily and starts tossing a piece of fruit up and down in the air.*] Well—because we have what I think is going to be a unique type of organization in American community life—not only do we deplore[24] that kind of thing—but we are trying to do something about it. [Beneatha *stops tossing and turns with a new and quizzical interest to the man.*] We feel—[*gaining confidence in his mission because of the interest in the faces of the people he is talking to*]—we feel that most of the trouble in this world, when you come right down to it—[*He hits his knee for emphasis.*]—most of the trouble exists because people just don't sit down and talk to each other.

---

[24] deplore—regret.

Ruth [*nodding as she might in church, pleased with the remark*]. You can say that again, mister.

Lindner [*more encouraged by such affirmation*]. That we don't try hard enough in this world to understand the other fellow's problem. The other guy's point of view.

Ruth. Now that's right.

[Beneatha *and* Walter *merely watch and listen with genuine interest.*]

Lindner. Yes—that's the way we feel out in Clybourne Park. And that's why I was elected to come here this afternoon and talk to you people. Friendly like, you know, the way people should talk to each other and see if we couldn't find some way to work this thing out. As I say, the whole business is a matter of *caring* about the other fellow. Anybody can see that you are a nice family of folks, hard-working and honest I'm sure. [Beneatha *frowns slightly, quizzically, her head tilted regarding him.*] Today everybody knows what it means to be on the outside of *something*. And of course, there is always somebody who is out to take the advantage of people who don't always understand.

Walter. What do you mean?

Lindner. Well—you see our community is made up of people who've worked hard as the dickens for years to build up that little community. They're not rich and fancy people; just hard-working, honest people who don't really have much but those little homes and a dream of the kind of community they want to raise their children in. Now, I don't say we are perfect and there is a lot wrong in some of the things they want. But you've got to admit that a man, right or wrong, has the right to want to have the neighborhood he lives in a certain kind of way. And at the moment the overwhelming majority of our people out there feel that people get along better, take more of a common interest in the life of the community, when they share a common background. I want you to believe me when I tell you that race prejudice simply doesn't enter into it. It is a matter of the people of Clybourne Park believing, rightly or wrongly, as I say, that for the happiness of all concerned that our Negro families are happier when they live in their *own* communities.

Beneatha [*with a grand and bitter gesture*]. This, friends, is the Welcoming Committee!

Walter [*dumbfounded,*[25] *looking at* Lindner]. Is this what you came marching all the way over here to tell us?

Lindner. Well, now we've been having a fine conversation. I hope you'll hear me all the way through.

Walter [*tightly*]. Go ahead, man.

Lindner. You see—in the face of all things I have said, we are prepared to make your family a very generous offer . . .

Beneatha. Thirty pieces and not a coin less![26]

Walter. Yeah?

Lindner [*putting on his glasses and drawing a form out of the briefcase*]. Our association is prepared, through the collective effort of our people, to buy the house from you at a financial gain to your family.

Ruth. Lord have mercy, ain't this the living gall!

Walter. All right, you through?

Lindner. Well, I want to give you the exact terms of the financial arrangement—

Walter. We don't want to hear no exact terms of no arrangements. I want to know if you got any more to tell us 'bout getting together?

Lindner [*taking off his glasses*]. Well—I don't suppose that you feel. . . .

Walter. Never mind how I feel—you got any more to say 'bout how people ought to sit down and talk to each other? . . . Get out of my house, man.

[*He turns his back and walks to the door.*]

Lindner [*looking around at the hostile faces and reaching and assembling his hat and briefcase*]. Well—I don't understand why you people are reacting this way. What do you think you are going to gain by moving into a neighborhood where you just aren't wanted and where some elements—well—people can get awful worked up when they feel that their whole way of life and everything they've ever worked for is threatened.

Walter. Get out.

Lindner [*at the door, holding a small card*]. Well—I'm sorry it went like this.

Walter. Get out.

Lindner [*almost sadly, regarding* Walter]. You just can't force people to change their hearts, son.

---

[25] *dumbfounded*—astonished.

[26] Thirty . . . less—reference to the New Testament, where Judas Iscariot receives thirty pieces of silver for betraying Jesus.

[*He turns and puts his card on a table and exits.* Walter *pushes the door to with stinging hatred, and stands looking at it.* Ruth *just sits and* Beneatha *just stands. They say nothing.* Mama *and* Travis *enter.*]

Mama. Well—this all the packing got done since I left out of here this morning. I testify before God that my children got all the energy of the *dead.* What time the moving men due?

Beneatha. Four o'clock. You had a caller, Mama. [*She is smiling, teasingly.*]

Mama. Sure enough—who?

Beneatha [*her arms folded saucily*]. The Welcoming Committee.

[Walter *and* Ruth *giggle.*]

Mama [*innocently*]. Who?

Beneatha. The Welcoming Committee. They said they're sure going to be glad to see you when you get there.

Walter [*devilishly*]. Yeah, they said they can't hardly wait to see your face. [*Laughter.*]

Mama [*sensing their **facetiousness**[27]*]. What's the matter with you all?

Walter. Ain't nothing the matter with us. We just telling you 'bout the gentleman who came to see you this afternoon. From the Clybourne Park Improvement Association.

Mama. What he want?

Ruth [*in the same mood as* Beneatha *and* Walter]. To welcome you, honey.

Walter. He said they can't hardly wait. He said the one thing they don't have, that they just *dying* to have out there is a fine family of colored people! [*To* Ruth *and* Beneatha] Ain't that right!

Ruth and **Beneatha** [*mockingly*]. Yeah! He left his card—

Beneatha [*handing card to* Mama]. In case.

[Mama *reads and throws it on the floor—understanding and looking off as she draws her chair up to the table on which she has put her plant and some sticks and some cord.*]

Mama. Father, give us strength. [*Knowingly—and without fun.*] Did he threaten us?

Beneatha. Oh—Mama—they don't do it like that any more. He talked Brotherhood. He said everybody ought to learn how to sit down and hate each other with good Christian fellowship.

[*She and* Walter *shake hands to ridicule the remark.*]

Mama [*sadly*]. Lord, protect us. . . .

---

[27] **facetiousness**—humor.

Ruth. You should hear the money those folks raised to buy the house from us. All we paid and then some.

Beneatha. What they think we going to do—eat 'em?

Ruth. No, honey, marry 'em.

Mama [*shaking her head*]. Lord, Lord, Lord . . .

Ruth. Well—that's the way the crackers crumble. [*A beat*] Joke.

Beneatha [*laughingly noticing what her mother is doing*]. Mama, what are you doing?

Mama. Fixing my plant so it won't get hurt none on the way . . .

Beneatha. Mama, you going to take *that* to the new house?

Mama. Un-huh—

Beneatha. That raggedy-looking old thing?

Mama [*stopping and looking at her*]. It expresses ME!

Ruth [*with delight, to* Beneatha]. So there, Miss Thing!

[Walter *comes to* Mama *suddenly and bends down behind her and squeezes her in his arms with all his strength. She is overwhelmed by the suddenness of it and, though delighted, her manner is like that of* Ruth *with* Travis.]

Mama. Look out now, boy! You make me mess up my thing here!

Walter [*His face lit, he slips down on his knees beside her, his arms still around her.*]. Mama . . . you know what it means to climb up in the chariot?

Mama [*gruffly, very happy*]. Get on away from me now . . .

Ruth [*near the gift-wrapped package, trying to catch* Walter's *eye*]. Psst—

Walter. What the old song say, Mama . . .

Ruth. Walter—Now?

[*She is pointing at the package.*]

Walter [*speaking the lines, sweetly, playfully, in his mother's face*].
      I got wings . . . you got wings . . .
      All God's children got wings . . .

Mama. Boy—get out of my face and do some work . . .

Walter. *When I get to heaven gonna put on my wings.*
      Gonna fly all over God's heaven . . .

Beneatha [*teasingly, from across the room*]. Everybody talking 'bout heaven ain't going there!

Walter [*to* Ruth, *who is carrying the box across to them*]. I don't know, you think we ought to give her that . . . Seems to me she ain't been very appreciative around here.

Mama [*eyeing the box, which is obviously a gift*]. What is that?

Walter [*taking it from* Ruth *and putting it on the table in front of* Mama]. Well—what you all think? Should we give it to her?

Ruth. Oh—she was pretty good today.

Mama. I'll good you—

[*She turns her eyes to the box again.*]

Beneatha. Open it, Mama.

[*She stands up, looks at it, turns and looks at all of them, and then presses her hands together and does not open the package.*]

Walter [*sweetly*]. Open it, Mama. It's for you. [Mama *looks in his eyes. It is the first present in her life without its being Christmas. Slowly she opens her package and lifts out, one by one, a brand-new sparkling set of gardening tools.* Walter *continues, prodding.*] Ruth made up the note—read it . . .

Mama [*picking up the card and adjusting her glasses*]. "To our own Mrs. Miniver[28]—Love from Brother, Ruth and Beneatha." Ain't that lovely. . . .

Travis [*tugging at his father's sleeve*]. Daddy, can I give her mine now?

Walter. All right, son. [Travis *flies to get his gift.*]

Mama. Now I don't have to use my knives and forks no more . . .

Walter. Travis didn't want to go in with the rest of us, Mama. He got his own. [*Somewhat amused.*] We don't know what it is . . .

Travis [*racing back in the room with a large hatbox and putting it in front of his grandmother*]. Here!

Mama. Lord have mercy, baby. You done gone and bought your grand-mother a hat?

Travis [*very proud*]. Open it!

[*She does and lifts out an elaborate, but very elaborate, wide gardening hat, and all the adults break up at the sight of it.*]

Ruth. Travis, honey, what is that?

Travis [*who thinks it is beautiful and appropriate*]. It's a gardening hat! Like the ladies always have on in the magazines when they work in their gardens.

Beneatha [*giggling fiercely*]. Travis—we were trying to make Mama Mrs. Miniver—not Scarlett O'Hara![29]

Mama [*indignantly*]. What's the matter with you all! This here is a beautiful hat! [*Absurdly.*] I always wanted me one just like it!

[*She pops it on her head to prove it to her grandson, and the hat is **ludicrous**[30] and considerably oversized.*]

---

[28] Mrs. Miniver—garden-loving Englishwoman who is the title character in a best-selling novel (1940) by Jan Struther and a film (1942) based on it.

[29] Scarlett O'Hara—flamboyant main character in *Gone with the Wind*.

[30] **ludicrous**—hilarious because of absurdity.

Ruth. Hot dog! Go, Mama!

Walter [*doubled over with laughter*]. I'm sorry, Mama—but you look like you ready to go out and chop you some cotton sure enough!

[*They all laugh except* Mama, *out of deference to* Travis's *feelings.*]

Mama [*gathering the boy up to her*]. Bless your heart—this is the prettiest hat I ever owned—[Walter, Ruth, *and* Beneatha *chime in noisily, festively and insincerely congratulating* Travis *on his gift.*] What are we all standing around here for? We ain't finished packin' yet. Bennie, you ain't packed one book.

[*The bell rings.*]

Beneatha. That couldn't be the movers . . . it's not hardly two good yet—

[Beneatha *goes into her room.* Mama *starts for door.*]

Walter [*turning, stiffening*]. Wait—wait—I'll get it.

[*He stands and looks at the door.*]

Mama. You expecting company, son?

Walter [*just looking at the door*]. Yeah—yeah . . .

[Mama *looks at* Ruth, *and they exchange innocent and unfrightened glances.*]

Mama [*not understanding*]. Well, let them in, son.

Beneatha [*from her room*]. We need some more string.

Mama. Travis—you run to the hardware and get me some string cord.

[Mama *goes out and* Walter *turns and looks at* Ruth. Travis *goes to a dish for money.*]

Ruth. Why don't you answer the door, man?

Walter [*suddenly bounding across the floor to her*]. 'Cause sometimes it hard to let the future begin! [*Stooping down in her face.*]

   I got wings! You got wings!
   All God's children got wings!

[*He crosses to the door and throws it open. Standing there is a very slight little man in a not too prosperous business suit and with haunted frightened eyes and a hat pulled down tightly, brim up, around his forehead.* Travis *passes between the men and exits.* Walter *leans deep in the man's face, still in his jubilance.*]

   When I get to heaven gonna put on my wings,
   Gonna fly all over God's heaven . . .

[*The little man just stares at him.*]

   Heaven—

[*Suddenly he stops and looks past the little man into the empty hallway.*]

   Where's Willy, man?

Bobo. He ain't with me.

Walter [*not disturbed*]. Oh—come on in. You know my wife.

Bobo [*dumbly, taking off his hat*]. Yes—h'you, Miss Ruth.

Ruth [*quietly, a mood apart from her husband already, seeing* Bobo]. Hello, Bobo.

Walter. You right on time today . . . Right on time. That's the way! [*He slaps* Bobo *on his back.*] Sit down . . . lemme hear.

[Ruth *stands stiffly and quietly in back of them, as though somehow she senses death, her eyes fixed on her husband.*]

Bobo [*his frightened eyes on the floor, his hat in his hands*]. Could I please get a drink of water, before I tell you about it, Walter Lee?

[Walter *does not take his eyes off the man.* Ruth *goes blindly to the tap and gets a glass of water and brings it to* Bobo.]

Walter. There ain't nothing wrong, is there?

Bobo. Lemme tell you—

Walter. Man—didn't nothing go wrong?

Bobo. Lemme tell you—Walter Lee. [*Looking at* Ruth *and talking to her more than to* Walter.] You know how it was. I got to tell you how it was. I mean first I got tell you how it was all the way . . . I mean about the money I put in, Walter Lee. . .

Walter [*with taut agitation*]. What about the money you put in?

Bobo. Well—it wasn't much as we told you—me and Willy—[*He stops.*] I'm sorry, Walter. I got a bad feeling about it. I got a real bad feeling about it. . . .

Walter. Man, what you telling me about all this for? . . . Tell me what happened in Springfield. . . .

Bobo. Springfield.

Ruth [*like a dead woman*]. What was supposed to happen in Springfield?

Bobo [*to her*]. This deal that me and Walter went into with Willy—Me and Willy was going to go down to Springfield and spread some money 'round so's we wouldn't have to wait so long for the liquor license . . . That's what we were going to do. Everybody said that was the way you had to do, you understand, Miss Ruth?

Walter. Man—what happened down there?

Bobo [*a pitiful man, near tears*]. I'm trying to tell you, Walter.

Walter [*screaming at him suddenly*]. THEN TELL ME, DAMMIT . . . WHAT'S THE MATTER WITH YOU?

Bobo. Man . . . I didn't go to no Springfield, yesterday.

Walter [*halted, life hanging in the moment*]. Why not?

Bobo [*the long way, the hard way to tell*]. 'Cause I didn't have no reasons to . . .

Walter. Man, what are you talking about!

Bobo. I'm talking about the fact that when I got to the train station yesterday morning—eight o'clock like we planned . . . Man—*Willy didn't never show up.*

Walter. Why . . . where was he . . . where is he?

Bobo. That's what I'm trying to tell you . . . I don't know . . . I waited six hours . . . I called his house . . . and I waited . . . six hours . . . I waited in that train station six hours. . . . [*Breaking into tears.*] That was all the extra money I had in the world. . . . [*Looking up at* Walter *with tears running down his face.*] Man, *Willy is gone.*

Walter. Gone, what you mean Willy is gone? Gone where? You mean he went by himself. You mean he went off to Springfield by himself—to take care of getting the license—[*Turns and looks anxiously at* Ruth.] You mean maybe he didn't want too many people in on the business down there? [*Looks to* Ruth *again, as before.*] You know Willy got his own ways. [*Looks back to* Bobo.] Maybe you was late yesterday and he just went on down there without you. Maybe—maybe—he's been callin' you at home tryin' to tell you what happened or something. Maybe—maybe—he just got sick. He's somewhere—he's got to be somewhere. We just got to find him—me and you got to find him. [*Grabs* Bobo *senselessly by the collar and starts to shake him.*] We got to!

Bobo [*in sudden angry, frightened agony*]. What's the matter with you, Walter! *When a cat take off with your money he don't leave you no road maps!*

Walter [*turning madly, as though he is looking for Willy in the very room*]. Willy! . . . Willy . . . don't do it. . . Please don't do it . . . Man, not with that money . . . Man, please not with that money . . . Oh, God . . . Don't let it be true. . . . [*He is wandering around, crying out for Willy and looking for him or perhaps for help from God.*] Man . . . I trusted you . . . Man, I put my life in your hands. . . . [*He starts to crumple down on the floor as* Ruth *just covers her face in horror.* Mama *opens the door and comes into the room, with* Beneatha *behind her.*] Man . . . [*He starts to pound the floor with his fists, sobbing wildly.*] THAT MONEY IS MADE OUT OF MY FATHER'S FLESH—

Bobo [*standing over him helplessly*]. I'm sorry, Walter. . . . [*Only* Walter's *sobs reply.* Bobo *puts on his hat.*] I had my life staked on this deal, too . . . [*He exits.*]

Mama [*to* Walter]. Son— [*She goes to him, bends down to him, talks to his bent head.*] Son . . . Is it gone? Son, I gave you sixty-five hundred dollars. Is it gone? All of it? Beneatha's money too?

Walter [*lifting his head slowly*]. Mama . . . I never . . . went to the bank at all. . . .

Mama [*not wanting to believe him*]. You mean . . . your sister's school money . . . you used that too . . . Walter? . . .

Walter. Yessss! . . . All of it . . . It's all gone . . .

[*There is total silence. Ruth stands with her face covered with her hands; Beneatha leans forlornly against a wall, fingering a piece of red ribbon from the mother's gift. Mama stops and looks at her son without recognition and then, quite without thinking about it, starts to beat him senselessly in the face. Beneatha goes to them and stops it.*]

Beneatha. Mama!

[*Mama stops and looks at both of her children and rises slowly and wanders vaguely, aimlessly away from them.*]

Mama. I seen . . . him . . . night after night . . . come in . . . and look at that rug . . . and then look at me . . . the red showing in his eyes . . . the veins moving in his head. . . . I seen him grow thin and old before he was forty . . . working and working and working like somebody's old horse . . . killing himself . . . and you—you give it all away in a day—[*She raises her arms to strike him again.*]

Beneatha. Mama—

Mama. Oh, God . . . [*She looks up to Him.*] Look down here—and show me the strength.

Beneatha. Mama—

Mama [*plaintively*]. Strength . . .

Beneatha [*plaintively*]. Mama . . .

Mama. Strength!

[*Curtain.*]

Act Three, Scene One

[*An hour later.*

At curtain, there is a sullen light of gloom in the living room, gray light not unlike that which began the first scene of Act One. At left we can see Walter *within his room, alone with himself. He is stretched out on the bed, his shirt out and open, his arms under his head. He does not smoke, he does not cry out, he merely lies there, looking up at the ceiling, much as if he were alone in the world.*

In the living room Beneatha *sits at the table, still surrounded by the now almost* **ominous**[1] *packing crates. She sits looking off. We feel that this is a mood*

---

[1] **ominous**—menacing, threatening.

struck perhaps an hour before, and it lingers now, full of the empty sound of pro-
found disappointment. We see on a line from her brother's bedroom the sameness
of their attitudes. Presently the bell rings and Beneatha *rises without ambition*
or interest in answering. It is Asagai, *smiling broadly, striding into the room*
with energy and happy expectation and conversation.]

Asagai. I came over . . . I had some free time. I thought I might help with
the packing. Ah, I like the look of packing crates! A household in
preparation for a journey! It depresses some people . . . but for me . . .
it is another feeling. Something full of the flow of life, do you understand? Movement, progress . . . It makes me think of Africa.

Beneatha. Africa!

Asagai. What kind of a mood is this? Have I told you how deeply you
move me?

Beneatha. He gave away the money, Asagai . . .

Asagai. Who gave away what money?

Beneatha. The insurance money. My brother gave it away.

Asagai. Gave it away?

Beneatha. He made an investment! With a man even Travis wouldn't
have trusted with his most worn-out marbles.

Asagai. And it's gone?

Beneatha. Gone!

Asagai. I'm very sorry . . . And you, now?

Beneatha. Me? . . . Me? . . . Me I'm nothing . . . Me. When I was very
small . . . we used to take our sleds out in the wintertime and the only
hills we had were the ice-covered stone steps of some houses down
the street. And we used to fill them in with snow and make them
smooth and slide down them all day . . . and it was very dangerous
you know . . . far too steep . . . and sure enough one day a kid named
Rufus came down too fast and hit the sidewalk . . . and we saw his
face just split open right there in front of us . . . And I remember
standing there looking at his bloody open face thinking that was the
end of Rufus. But the ambulance came and they took him to the hospital and they fixed the broken bones and they sewed it all up . . . and
the next time I saw Rufus he just had a little line down the middle of
his face . . . I never got over that . . .

Asagai. What?

Beneatha. That was what one person could do for another, fix him up—
sew up the problem, make him all right again. That was the most
marvelous thing in the world . . . I wanted to do that. I always

thought it was the one concrete thing in the world that a human being could do. Fix up the sick, you know—and make them whole again. This was truly being God . . .

Asagai. You wanted to be God?

Beneatha. No—I wanted to cure. It used to be so important to me. I wanted to cure. It used to matter. I used to care. I mean about people and how their bodies hurt . . .

Asagai. And you've stopped caring?

Beneatha. Yes—I think so.

Asagai. Why?

Beneatha [bitterly]. Because it doesn't seem deep enough, close enough to what ails mankind—It was a child's way of seeing things—or an idealist's.

Asagai. Children see things very well sometimes—and idealists even better.

Beneatha. I know that's what you think. Because you are still where I left off—you still care. This is what you see for the world, for Africa. You with the dreams of the future will patch up all Africa—you are going to cure the Great Sore of Colonialism— [loftily, mocking it] with the Penicillin of Independence—!

Asagai. Yes!

Beneatha. Independence and then what? What about all the crooks and thieves and just plain idiots who will come into power and steal and plunder the same as before—only now they will be black and do it in the name of the new independence—WHAT ABOUT THEM?!

Asagai. That will be the problem for another time. First we must get there.

Beneatha. And where does it end?

Asagai. End? Who even spoke of an end? To life? To living?

Beneatha. An end to misery! To stupidity! Don't you see there isn't any real progress, Asagai, there is only one large circle that we march in, around and around, each of us with our own little picture in front of us—our own little mirage that we think is the future.

Asagai. That is the mistake.

Beneatha. What?

Asagai. What you just said—about the circle. It isn't a circle—it is simply a long line—as in geometry, you know, one that reaches into infinity. And because we cannot see the end—we also cannot see how it changes. And it is very odd but those who see the changes—

who dream, who will not give up—are called idealists . . . and those who see only the circle—we call *them* the "realists"!

Beneatha. Asagai, while I was sleeping in that bed in there, people went out and took the future right out of my hands! And nobody asked me, nobody consulted me—they just went out and changed my life!

Asagai. Was it your money?

Beneatha. What?

Asagai. Was it your money he gave away?

Beneatha. It belonged to all of us.

Asagai. But did you earn it? Would you have had it at all if your father had not died?

Beneatha. No.

Asagai. Then isn't there something wrong in a house—in a world—where all dreams, good or bad, must depend on the death of a man? I never thought to see *you* like this, Alaiyo. You! Your brother made a mistake and you are grateful to him so that now you can give up the ailing human race on account of it! You talk about what good is struggle, what good is anything! Where are we all going and why are we bothering?

Beneatha. AND YOU CANNOT ANSWER IT!

Asagai [*shouting over her*]. *I LIVE THE ANSWER!* [*Pause*] In my village at home it is the exceptional man who can even read a newspaper . . . or who ever sees a book at all. I will go home and much of what I will have to say will seem strange to the people of my village. . . . But I will teach and work and things will happen, slowly and swiftly. At times it will seem that nothing changes at all . . . and then again . . . the sudden dramatic events which make history leap into the future. And then quiet again. Retrogression[2] even. Guns, murder, revolution. And I even will have moments when I wonder if the quiet was not better than all that death and hatred. But I will look about my village at the illiteracy and disease and ignorance and I will not wonder long. And perhaps . . . perhaps I will be a great man. . . I mean perhaps I will hold on to the substance of truth and find my way always with the right course . . . and perhaps for it I will be butchered in my bed some night by the servants of empire . . .

Beneatha. *The martyr!*

---

[2] Retrogression—deterioration, decline.

Asagai [*He smiles*]. . . . or perhaps I shall live to be a very old man, respected and esteemed in my new nation. . . And perhaps I shall hold office and this is what I'm trying to tell you, Alaiyo; perhaps the things I believe now for my country will be wrong and outmoded, and I will not understand and do terrible things to have things my way or merely to keep my power. Don't you see that there will be young men and women—not British soldiers then, but my own black countrymen—to step out of the shadows some evening and slit my then useless throat? Don't you see they have always been there . . . that they always will be. And that such a thing as my own death will be an advance? They who might kill me even . . . actually **replenish**[3] all that I was.

Beneatha. Oh, Asagai, I know all that.

Asagai. Good! Then stop moaning and groaning and tell me what you plan to do.

Beneatha. Do?

Asagai. I have a bit of a suggestion.

Beneatha. What?

Asagai [*rather quietly for him*]. That when it is all over—that you come home with me—

Beneatha [*staring at him and crossing away with exasperation*]. Oh— Asagai—at this moment you decide to be romantic!

Asagai [*quickly understanding the misunderstanding*]. My dear, young creature of the New World—I do not mean across the city—I mean across the ocean: home—to Africa.

Beneatha [*slowly understanding and turning to him with murmured amazement*]. To Africa?

Asagai. Yes! . . . [*Smiling and lifting his arms playfully.*] Three hundred years later the African Prince rose up out of the seas and swept the maiden back across the middle passage[4] over which her ancestors had come—

Beneatha [*unable to play*]. To—to Nigeria?

Asagai. Nigeria. Home. [*Coming to her with genuine romantic* **flippancy**.[5]] I will show you our mountains and our stars; and give you cool drinks from gourds and teach you the old songs and the ways of our people—and, in time, we will pretend that—[*very softly*]—you have

---

[3] **replenish**—make complete again.

[4] middle passage—journey across the Atlantic Ocean to the Americas endured by enslaved Africans.

[5] **flippancy**—casualness.

only been away for a day—Say that you'll come—[*He swings her around and takes her full in his arms in a kiss which proceeds to passion.*]

Beneatha [*pulling away suddenly*]. You're getting me all mixed up—

Asagai. Why?

Beneatha. Too many things—too many things have happened today. I must sit down and think. I don't know what I feel about anything right this minute.

[*She promptly sits down and props her chin on her fist.*]

Asagai [*charmed*]. All right, I shall leave you. No—don't get up. [*Touching her, gently, sweetly.*] Just sit awhile and think . . . Never be afraid to sit awhile and think. [*He goes to door and looks at her.*] How often I have looked at you and said, "Ah—so this is what the New World hath finally wrought . . ."

[*He exits. Beneatha sits on alone. Presently* Walter *enters from his room and starts to rummage through things, feverishly looking for something. She looks up and turns in her seat.*]

Beneatha [*hissingly*]. Yes—just look at what the New World hath wrought! . . . Just look! [*She gestures with bitter disgust.*] There he is! *Monsieur le petit bourgeois noir*[6]—himself! There he is—Symbol of a Rising Class! Entrepreneur! Titan of the system! [Walter *ignores her completely and continues frantically and destructively looking for something and hurling things to floor and tearing things out of their place in his search.* Beneatha *ignores the eccentricity of his actions and goes on with the monologue of insult.*] Did you dream of yachts on Lake Michigan, Brother? Did you see yourself on that Great Day sitting down at the Conference Table, surrounded by all the mighty bald-headed men in America? All halted, waiting, breathless, waiting for your pronouncements on industry? Waiting for you—Chairman of the Board? [Walter *finds what he is looking for—a small piece of white paper—and pushes it in his pocket and puts on his coat and rushes out without even having looked at her. She shouts after him.*] I look at you and I see the final triumph of stupidity in the world!

[*The door slams and she returns to just sitting again.* Ruth *comes quickly out of* Mama's *room.*]

Ruth. Who was that?

Beneatha. Your husband.

Ruth. Where did he go?

---

[6] *Monsieur . . . noir*—French phrase meaning "Mister lower middle class black." The *petit bourgeoisie* are small business people, tradespeople, and craftworkers.

Beneatha. Who knows—maybe he has an appointment at U.S. Steel.

Ruth [*anxiously, with frightened eyes*]. You didn't say nothing bad to him, did you?

Beneatha. Bad? Say anything bad to him? No—I told him he was a sweet boy and full of dreams and everything is strictly peachy keen, as the ofay[7] kids say!

[Mama *enters from her bedroom. She is lost, vague, trying to catch hold, to make some sense of her former command of the world, but it still eludes her. A sense of waste overwhelms her* **gait**;[8] *a measure of apology rides on her shoulders. She goes to her plant, which has remained on the table, looks at it, picks it up and takes it to the window sill and sits it outside, and she stands and looks at it a long moment. Then she closes the window, straightens her body with effort and turns around to her children.*]

Mama. Well—ain't it a mess in here, though? [*A false cheerfulness, a beginning of something.*] I guess we all better stop moping around and get some work done. All this unpacking and everything we got to do. [Ruth *raises her head slowly in response to the sense of the line; and* Beneatha *in similar manner turns very slowly to look at her mother.*] One of you all better call the moving people and tell 'em not to come.

Ruth. Tell 'em not to come?

Mama. Of course, baby. Ain't no need in 'em coming all the way here and having to go back. They charges for that too. [*She sits down, fingers to her brow, thinking.*] Lord, ever since I was a little girl, I always remembers people saying, "Lena—Lena Eggleston, you aims too high all the time. You needs to slow down and see life a little more like it is. Just slow down some." That's what they always used to say down home—"Lord that Lena Eggleston is a high-minded thing. She'll get her due one day!"

Ruth. No, Lena . . .

Mama. Me and Big Walter just didn't never learn right.

Ruth. Lena, no! We gotta go. Bennie—tell her. . . . [*She rises and crosses to* Beneatha *with her arms outstretched.* Beneatha *doesn't respond.*] Tell her we can still move . . . the notes ain't but a hundred and twenty-five a month. We got four grown people in this house—we can work . . .

Mama [*to herself*]. Just aimed too high all the time—

---

[7] ofay—disparaging term for white person.

[8] **gait**—manner of walking.

Ruth [*turning and going to* Mama *fast—the words pouring out with urgency and desperation*]. Lena—I'll work . . . I'll work twenty hours a day in all the kitchens in Chicago . . . I'll strap my baby on my back if I have to and scrub all the floors in America and wash all the sheets in America if I have to—but we got to MOVE! We got to get OUT OF HERE!!

[Mama *reaches out absently and pats* Ruth's *hand.*]

Mama. No—I see things differently now. Been thinking 'bout some of the things we could do to fix this place up some. I seen a second-hand bureau over on Maxwell Street just the other day that could fit right there. [*She points to where the new furniture might go.* Ruth *wanders away from her.*] Would need some new handles on it and then a little varnish and then it look like something brand-new. And—we can put up them new curtains in the kitchen. . . . Why this place be looking fine. Cheer us all up so that we forget trouble ever came. . . . [*To* Ruth] And you could get some nice screens to put up in your room round the baby's bassinet[9]. . . . [*She looks at both of them, pleadingly.*] Sometimes you just got to know when to give up some things . . . and hold on to what you got.

[Walter *enters from the outside, looking spent*[10] *and leaning against the door, his coat hanging from him.*]

Mama. Where you been, son?

Walter [*breathing hard*]. Made a call.

Mama. To who, son?

Walter. To The Man. [*He heads for his room.*]

Mama. What man, baby?

Walter. The Man, Mama. Don't you know who The Man is?

Ruth. Walter Lee?

Walter. *The Man.* Like the guys in the streets say—The Man. Captain Boss—Mistuh Charley . . . Old Cap'n Please Mr. Bossman . . .

Beneatha [*suddenly*]. Lindner!

Walter. That's right! That's good. I told him to come right over.

Beneatha [*fiercely, understanding*]. For what? What do you want to see him for!

Walter [*looking at his sister*]. We going to do business with him.

Mama. What you talking 'bout, son?

---

[9] bassinet—baby's bed, crib.

[10] *spent*—exhausted.

Walter. Talking 'bout life, Mama. You all always telling me to see life like it is. Well—I laid in there on my back today . . . and I figured it out. Life just like it is. Who gets and who don't get. [*He sits down with his coat on and laughs.*] Mama, you know it's all divided up. Life is. Sure enough. Between the takers and the "tooken." [*He laughs.*] I've figured it out finally. [*He looks around at them.*] Yeah. Some of us always getting "tooken." [*He laughs.*] People like Willy Harris, they don't never get "tooken." And you know why the rest of us do? 'Cause we all mixed up. Mixed up bad. We get to looking 'round for the right and the wrong; and we worry about it and cry about it and stay up nights trying to figure out 'bout the wrong and the right of things all the time . . . And all the time, man, them takers is out there operating, just taking and taking. Willy Harris? Shoot—Willy Harris don't even count. He don't even count in the big scheme of things. But I'll say one thing for old Willy Harris . . . he's taught me something. He's taught me to keep my eye on what counts in this world. Yeah—[*shouting out a little*] Thanks, Willy!

Ruth. What did you call that man for, Walter Lee?

Walter. Called him to tell him to come on over to the show. Gonna put on a show for the man. Just what he wants to see. You see, Mama, the man came here today and he told us that them people out there where you want us to move—well they so upset they willing to pay us not to move out there. [*He laughs again.*] And—and oh, Mama— you would of been proud of the way me and Ruth and Bennie acted. We told him to get out . . . Lord have mercy! We told the man to get out. Oh, we was some proud folks this afternoon, yeah. [*He lights a cigarette.*] We were still full of that old-time stuff . . .

Ruth [*coming toward him slowly*]. You talking 'bout taking them people's money to keep us from moving in that house?

Walter. I ain't just talking 'bout it, baby—I'm telling you that's what's going to happen.

Beneatha. Oh, God! Where is the bottom! Where is the real honest-to-God bottom so he can't go any farther!

Walter. See—that's old stuff. You and that boy that was here today. You all want everybody to carry a flag and a spear and sing some marching songs, huh? You wanna spend your life looking into things and trying to find the right and the wrong part, huh? Yeah. You know what's going to happen to that boy someday—he'll find himself sitting in a dungeon, locked in forever—and the takers will have the key! Forget it, baby! There ain't no causes—there ain't nothing but taking in this world, and he who takes most is smartest—and it don't make a . . . bit of difference *how*.

Mama. You making something inside me cry, son. Some awful pain inside me.

Walter. Don't cry, Mama. Understand. That white man is going to walk in that door able to write checks for more money than we ever had. It's important to him and I'm going to help him . . . I'm going to put on the show, Mama.

Mama. Son—I come from five generations of people who was slaves and sharecroppers—but ain't nobody in my family never let nobody pay 'em no money that was a way of telling us we wasn't fit to walk the earth. We ain't never been that poor. [*Raising her eyes and looking at him.*] We ain't never been that—dead inside.

Beneatha. Well—we are dead now. All the talk about dreams and sunlight that goes on in this house. It's all dead now.

Walter. What's the matter with you all! I didn't make this world! It was give to me this way! . . . Yes, I want me some yachts someday! Yes, I want to hang some real pearls 'round my wife's neck. Ain't she supposed to wear no pearls? Somebody tell me—tell me, who decides which women is suppose to wear pearls in this world. I tell you I am a *man*—and I think my wife should wear pearls in this world!

[*This last line hangs a good while and* Walter *begins to move about the room. The word "Man" has penetrated his consciousness; he mumbles it to himself repeatedly between strange agitated pauses as he moves about.*]

Mama. Baby, how you going to feel on the inside?

Walter. Fine! . . . Going to feel fine . . . a man . . .

Mama. You won't have nothing left then, Walter Lee.

Walter [*coming to her*]. I'm going to feel fine, Mama. I'm going to look that man in the eyes and say—[*He falters.*]—and say, "All right, Mr. Lindner—[*He falters even more.*]—that's *your* neighborhood out there. You got the right to keep it like you want. You got the right to have it like you want. Just write the check and—the house is yours." And—and I am going to say—[*His voice almost breaks.*] And you—you people just put the money in my hand and you won't have to live next to this bunch of stinking . . ." [*He straightens up and moves away from his mother, walking around the room.*] Maybe—maybe I'll just get down on my black knees . . . [*He does so;* Ruth *and* Bennie *and* Mama *watch him in frozen horror.*] "Captain, Mistuh, Bossman. [*Groveling and grinning* *and wringing his hands in profoundly anguished imitation of the slow-wit-ted movie stereotype.*] A-hee-hee-hee! Oh, yassuh, boss! Yassssssuh! Great White—[*Voice breaking, he forces himself to go on.*]—Father, just gi' ussen de money, fo' God's sake, and we's—we's ain't gwine come out deh and dirty up yo' white folks neighborhood . . ." [*He breaks down completely.*] And I'll feel fine! Fine! FINE! [*He gets up and goes into the bedroom.*]

Beneatha. That is not a man. That is nothing but a toothless rat.

Mama. Yes—death done come in this here house. [*She is nodding, slowly, reflectively.*] Done come walking in my house—on the lips of my children. You what supposed to be my beginning again. You—what supposed to be my harvest. [*To Beneatha*] You—you mourning your brother?

Beneatha. He's no brother of mine.

Mama. What you say?

Beneatha. I said that that individual in that room is no brother of mine.

Mama. That's what I thought you said. You feeling like you better than he is today? [Beneatha *does not answer.*] Yes? What you tell him a minute ago? That he wasn't a man? Yes? You give him up for me? You done wrote his **epitaph**[11] too—like the rest of the world? Well, who give you the privilege?

Beneatha. Be on my side for once! You saw what he just did, Mama! You saw him—down on his knees. Wasn't it you who taught me—to despise any man who would do that. Do what he's going to do.

Mama. Yes—I taught you that. Me and your daddy. But I thought I taught you something else too . . . I thought I taught you to love him.

Beneatha. Love him? There is nothing left to love.

Mama. There is *always* something left to love. And if you ain't learned that, you ain't learned nothing. [*Looking at her.*] Have you cried for that boy today? I don't mean for yourself and for the family 'cause we lost the money. I mean for him; what he been through and what it done to him. Child, when do you think is the time to love somebody the most; when they done good and made things easy for everybody? Well, then, you ain't through learning because that ain't the time at all. It's when he's at his lowest and can't believe in hisself 'cause the world done whipped him so. When you starts measuring somebody, measure him right, child, measure him right. Make sure you done

---

[11] **epitaph**—inscription on a tombstone.

taken into account what hills and valleys he come through before he got to wherever he is.

[Travis *bursts into the room at the end of the speech, leaving the door open.*]

Travis. Grandmama—the moving men are downstairs! The truck just pulled up.

Mama [*turning and looking at him*]. Are they, baby? They downstairs?

[*She sighs and sits.* Lindner *appears in the doorway. He peers in and knocks lightly, to gain attention, and comes in. All turn to look at him.*]

Lindner [*hat and briefcase in hand*]. Uh—hello . . .

[Ruth *crosses mechanically to the bedroom door and opens it and lets it swing open freely and slowly as the lights come up on* Walter *within, still in his coat, sitting at the far corner of the room. He looks up and out through the room to* Lindner.]

Ruth. He's here.

[*A long minute passes and* Walter *slowly gets up.*]

Lindner [*coming to the table with efficiency, putting his briefcase on the table and starting to unfold papers and unscrew fountain pens*]. Well, I certainly was glad to hear from you people. [Walter *has begun the* **trek**[12] *out of the room, slowly and awkwardly, rather like a small boy, passing the back of his sleeve across his mouth from time to time.*] Life can really be so much simpler than people let it be most of the time. Well—with whom do I negotiate? You, Mrs. Younger, or your son here? [Mama *sits with her hands folded on her lap and her eyes closed as* Walter *advances.* Travis *goes close to* Lindner *and looks at the papers curiously.*] Just some official papers, sonny.

Ruth. Travis, you go downstairs.

Mama [*opening her eyes and looking into* Walter's]. No. Travis, you stay right here. And you make him understand what you doing, Walter Lee. You teach him good. Like Willy Harris taught you. You show where our five generations done come to. [Walter *looks from her to the boy, who grins at him innocently.*] Go ahead, son— [*She folds her hands and closes her eyes.*] Go ahead.

Walter [*at last crosses to* Lindner, *who is reviewing the contract*]. Well, Mr. Lindner. [Beneatha *turns away.*] We called you—[*There is a profound, simple groping quality in his speech.*]—because, well, me and my family—[*He looks around and shifts from one foot to the other.*] Well—we are very plain people . . .

---

[12] **trek**—journey.

Lindner. Yes—

Walter. I mean—I have worked as a chauffeur most of my life—and my wife here, she does domestic work in people's kitchens. So does my mother. I mean—we are plain people. . . .

Lindner. Yes, Mr. Younger—

Walter [*really like a small boy, looking down at his shoes and then up at the man*]. And—uh—well, my father, well, he was a laborer most of his life. . . .

Lindner [*absolutely confused*]. Uh, yes—yes, I understand. [*He turns back to the contract.*]

Walter [*a beat; staring at him*]. And my father—[*With sudden intensity*]— My father *almost beat a man to death* once because this man called him a bad name or something, you know what I mean?

Lindner [*looking up, frozen*]. No, I'm afraid I don't.

Walter [*a beat. The tension hangs, then* Walter *steps back from it.*]. Yeah. Well—what I mean is that we come from people who had a lot of *pride*. I mean—we are very proud people. And that's my sister over there and she's going to be a doctor—and we are very proud—

Lindner. Well—I am sure that is very nice, but—

Walter. What I am telling you is that we called you over here to tell you that we are very proud and that this—[*Signaling to* Travis] Travis, come here. [Travis *crosses and* Walter *draws him before him facing the man*]. This is my son, and he makes the sixth generation of our family in this country. And that we have all thought about your offer—

Lindner. Well good . . . good—

Walter. And we have decided to move into our house because my father—my father—he earned it for us brick by brick. [Mama *has her eyes closed and is rocking back and forth as though she were in church, with her head nodding the Amen yes.*] We don't want to make no trouble for nobody or fight no causes, and we will try to be good neighbors. And that's *all* we got to say about that. [*He looks the man absolutely in the eyes.*] We don't want your money. [*He turns and walks away.*]

Lindner [*looking around at all of them*]. I take it then—that you have decided to occupy . . .

Beneatha. That's what the man said.

Lindner [*to* Mama *in her **reverie**[13]*]. Then I would like to appeal to you, Mrs. Younger. You are older and wiser and understand things better I ·am sure . . .

---

[13] **reverie**—musing, daydream.

Mama. I am afraid you don't understand. My son said we was going to move and there ain't nothing left for me to say. [*Briskly.*] You know how these young folks is nowadays, mister. Can't do a thing with 'em. [*As he opens his mouth, she rises.*] Goodbye.

Lindner [*folding up his materials*]. Well—if you are that final about it . . . There is nothing left for me to say. [*He finishes. He is almost ignored by the family, who are concentrating on* Walter Lee. *At the door* Lindner *halts and looks around.*] I sure hope you people know what you're doing.

[*He shakes his head and exits.*]

Ruth [*looking around and coming to life*]. Well, for God's sake—if the moving men are here—LET'S GET THIS BLESSED FAMILY OUT OF HERE!

Mama [*into action*]. Ain't it the truth! Look at all this here mess. Ruth, put Travis' good jacket on him . . . Walter Lee, fix your tie and tuck your shirt in, you look just like somebody's hoodlum. Lord have mercy, where is my plant? [*She flies to get it amid the general bustling of the family, who are deliberately trying to ignore the nobility of the past moment.*] You all start on down . . . Travis child, don't go empty-handed . . . Ruth, where did I put that box with my skillets in it? I want to be in charge of it myself . . . I'm going to make us the biggest dinner we ever ate tonight . . . Beneatha, what's the matter with them stockings? Pull them things up, girl . . .

[*The family starts to file out as two moving men appear and begin to carry out the heavier pieces of furniture, bumping into the family as they move about.*]

Beneatha. Mama, Asagai—asked me to marry him today and go to Africa—

Mama [*in the middle of her getting-ready activity*]. He did? You ain't old enough to marry nobody—[*seeing the moving men lifting one of her chairs precariously*[14]] Darling, that ain't no bale of cotton, please handle it so we can sit in it again. I had that chair twenty-five years . . .

[*The movers sigh with exasperation and go on with their work.*]

Beneatha [*girlishly and unreasonably trying to pursue the conversation*]. To go to Africa, Mama—be a doctor in Africa . . .

Mama [*distracted*]. Yes, baby—

Walter. *Africa!* What he want you to go to Africa for?

Beneatha. To practice there . . .

Walter. Girl, if you don't get all them silly ideas out of your head! You better marry yourself a man with some loot . . .

---

[14] *precariously*—dangerously.

Beneatha [*angrily, precisely as in the first scene of the play*]. What have you got to do with who I marry!

Walter. Plenty. Now I think George Murchison—

Beneatha. *George Murchison!* I wouldn't marry him if he was Adam and I was Eve!

[*He and* Beneatha *go out yelling at each other vigorously, and the anger is loud and real till their voices diminish.* Ruth *stands at the door and turns to* Mama *and smiles knowingly.*]

Mama [*fixing her hat at last*]. Yeah—they something all right, my children . . .

Ruth. Yeah—they're something. Let's go, Lena.

Mama [*stalling, starting to look around at the house*]. Yes—I'm coming. Ruth—

Ruth. Yes?

Mama [*quietly, woman to woman*]. He finally come into his manhood today, didn't he? Kind of like a rainbow after the rain . . .

Ruth [*biting her lip lest her own pride explode in front of* Mama]. Yes, Lena.

[Walter's *voice calls for them raucously.*]

Walter [*offstage*]. Y'all come on! These people charges by the hour, you know!

Mama [*waving* Ruth *out vaguely*]. All right, honey—go on down. I be down directly.

[Ruth *hesitates, then exits.* Mama *stands, at last alone in the living room, her plant on the table before her as the lights start to come down. She looks around at all the walls and ceilings and suddenly, despite herself, while the children call below, a great heaving thing rises in her and she puts her fist to her mouth, takes a final desperate look, pulls her coat about her, pats her hat and goes out. The lights dim down. The door opens and she comes back in, grabs her plant, and goes out for the last time.*]

[*Curtain.*]

UNDERSTANDING THE PLAY

Act One

1. In Scene One, what does the setting of the Younger's apartment convey about them and their situation?

2. How are Walter and Beneatha alike in their ambitions? How are they different?

3. In Scene Two, what does Africa seem to represent to Beneatha? Why do you think she objects to being called an assimilationist?

4. Mama observes to Walter, "once upon a time freedom used to be life—now it's money." What does she mean?

5. At the end of Act One, why is Mama so disgusted with Walter?

Act Two

1. In Scene One, why do Walter and Beneatha both become caught up in their African masquerade?

2. In what ways does George reflect the snobbishness that Beneatha attributed to his family in Act One?

3. In Scene Two, what does Mrs. Johnson represent? What dramatic function does her visit serve?

4. How does Mama's willingness to entrust the family's savings to Walter affect him?

5. In Scene Three, why do you think Hansberry chose a character like Mr. Lindner to represent white racism?

Act Three

1. How does the loss of the money affect Walter? Beneatha? Mama?

2. How do Beneatha and Asagai disagree about the future—Africa's and hers?

3. Why does Walter decide to accept Lindner's offer? How does Walter's decision affect Mama?

4. What causes Walter to finally reject Lindner's offer?

5. At the play's end, how have the Youngers changed? What remains the same?

ANALYZING THE PLAY

1. The conflict in a play is the struggle between opposing forces that gives movement to the dramatic plot. What is the fundamental conflict in *A Raisin in the Sun*?

2. The peripeteia—or reversal of fortune—in a drama is a sudden, unexpected turn of events. In *A Raisin in the Sun,* where does this turn of events take place?

3. The tone of a literary work is the author's attitude, either stated or implied, toward his or her subject matter. What is the tone of *A Raisin in the Sun*?

4. How do gender and generational roles shape this play?

5. What role does religion have in *A Raisin in the Sun*? What role do African culture and politics have?

6. *A Raisin in the Sun* was written in the late 1950s, early in the civil rights movement. In what ways does the play reflect this era? In what ways is it still relevant to today?

Tragedy and the Common Man

BY ARTHUR MILLER

Shortly after the opening of his play Death of a Salesman *in February 1949, dramatist Arthur Miller wrote the following essay defending his belief in the possibility of creating tragedies about ordinary people.*

In this age few tragedies are written. It has often been held that the lack is due to a paucity[1] of heroes among us, or else that modern man has had the blood drawn out of his organs of belief by the skepticism of science, and the heroic attack on life cannot feed on an attitude of reserve and circumspection.[2] For one reason or another, we are often held to be below tragedy—or tragedy above us. The **inevitable**[3] conclusion is, of course, that the tragic mode is archaic, fit only for the very highly placed, the kings or the kingly, and where this admission is not made in so many words it is most often implied.

I believe that the common man is as apt a subject for tragedy in its highest sense as kings were. On the face of it this ought to be obvious in the light of modern psychiatry, which bases its analysis upon classic formulations, such as the Oedipus and Orestes complexes,[4] for instances,

which were enacted by royal beings, but which apply to everyone in similar emotional situations.

More simply, when the question of tragedy in art is not at issue, we never hesitate to attribute to the well-placed and the exalted the very same mental processes as the lowly. And finally, if the exaltation of tragic action were truly a property of the high-bred character alone, it is inconceivable that the mass of mankind should cherish tragedy above all other forms, let alone be capable of understanding it.

As a general rule, to which there may be exceptions unknown to me, I think the tragic feeling is evoked in us when we are

---

[1] paucity—scarcity.

[2] circumspection—prudence.

[3] **inevitable**—unavoidable.

[4] Oedipus and Orestes complexes—emotional obsessions with a mother or father, respectively.

in the presence of a character who is ready to lay down his life, if need be, to secure one thing—his sense of personal dignity. From Orestes to Hamlet, Medea to Macbeth, the underlying struggle is that of the individual attempting to gain his "rightful" position in his society.

Sometimes he is one who has been displaced from it, sometimes one who seeks to attain it for the first time, but the fateful wound from which the inevitable events spiral is the wound of indignity, and its dominant force is **indignation**.[5] Tragedy, then, is the consequence of a man's total compulsion to evaluate himself justly.

In the sense of having been initiated by the hero himself, the tale always reveals what has been called his "tragic flaw," a failing that is not peculiar to grand or elevated characters. Nor is it necessarily a weakness. The flaw, or crack in the character, is really nothing—and need be nothing— but his inherent unwillingness to remain passive in the face of what he conceives to be a challenge to his dignity, his image of his rightful status. Only the passive, only those who accept their lot without active retaliation, are "flawless." Most of us are in that category.

But there are among us today, as there always have been, those who act against the scheme of things that degrades them, and in the process of action everything we have accepted out of fear or insensitivity or ignorance is shaken before us and examined, and from this total onslaught by an individual against the seemingly stable cosmos surrounding us—from this total examination of the "unchangeable" environment—

comes the terror and the fear that is classically associated with tragedy.

More important, from this total questioning of what has previously been unquestioned, we learn. And such a process is not beyond the common man. In revolutions around the world, these past thirty years, he has demonstrated again and again this inner dynamic of all tragedy.

Insistence upon the rank of the tragic hero, or the so-called nobility of his character, is really but a clinging to the outward forms of tragedy. If rank or nobility of character was indispensable, then it would follow that the problems of those with rank were the particular problems of tragedy. But surely the right of one monarch to capture the domain from another no longer raises our passions, nor are our concepts of justice what they were to the mind of an Elizabethan king.

The quality in such plays that does shake us, however, derives from the underlying fear of being displaced, the disaster inherent in being torn away from our chosen image of what and who we are in this world. Among us today this fear is as strong, and perhaps stronger, than it ever was. In fact, it is the common man who knows this fear best.

Now, if it is true that tragedy is the consequence of a man's total compulsion to evaluate himself justly, his destruction in the attempt posits[6] a wrong or an evil environment. And this is precisely the morality of tragedy and its lesson. The discovery of

---

[5] **indignation**—anger aroused by injustice.

[6] posits—affirms the existence of.

the moral law, which is what the enlightenment of tragedy consists of, is not the discovery of some abstract or metaphysical quantity.

The tragic right is a condition of life, a condition in which the human personality is able to flower and realize itself. The wrong is the condition which suppresses man, perverts the flowing out of his love and creative instinct. Tragedy enlightens and it must, in that it points the heroic finger at the enemy of man's freedom. The thrust for freedom is the quality in tragedy which exalts. The revolutionary questioning of the stable environment is what terrifies. In no way is the common man debarred from such thoughts or such actions.

Seen in this light, our lack of tragedy may be partially accounted for by the turn which modern literature has taken toward the purely psychiatric view of life, or the purely sociological. If all our miseries, our indignities, are born and bred within our minds, then all action, let alone the heroic action, is obviously impossible.

And if society alone is responsible for the cramping of our lives, then the protagonist must needs be so pure and faultless as to force us to deny his validity as a character. From neither of these views can tragedy derive, simply because neither represents a balanced concept of life. Above all else, tragedy requires the finest appreciation by the writer of cause and effect.

No tragedy can therefore come about when its author fears to question absolutely everything, when he regards any institution, habit or custom as being either everlasting, **immutable**[7] or inevitable. In the tragic view

the need of man to wholly realize himself is the only fixed star, and whatever it is that hedges his nature and lowers it is ripe for attack and examination. Which is not to say that tragedy must preach revolution.

The Greeks could probe the very heavenly origin of their ways and return to confirm the rightness of laws. And Job[8] could face God in anger, demanding his right and end in submission. But for a moment everything is in suspension, nothing is accepted, and in this stretching and tearing apart of the cosmos, in the very action of so doing, the character gains "size," the tragic stature which is spuriously attached to the royal or the highborn in our minds. The commonest of men may take on that stature to the extent of his willingness to throw all he has into the contest, the battle to secure his rightful place in his world.

There is a misconception of tragedy with which I have been struck in review after review,[9] and in many conversations with writers and readers alike. It is the idea that tragedy is of necessity allied to pessimism. Even the dictionary says nothing more about the word than that it means a story with a sad or unhappy ending. This impression is so firmly fixed that I almost hesitate to claim that in truth tragedy implies more optimism in its author than does comedy, and that its final result ought to be the reinforcement of the onlooker's brightest opinions of the human animal.

---

[7] **immutable**—unchangeable.

[8] Job—in the Bible, an upright man whose faith in God survived the test of repeated calamities.

[9] review after review—of *Death of a Salesman*.

For, if it is true to say that in essence the tragic hero is intent upon claiming his whole due as a personality, and if this struggle must be total and without reservation, then it automatically demonstrates the indestructible will of man to achieve his humanity.

The possibility of victory must be there in tragedy. Where pathos rules, where **pathos**[10] is finally derived, a character has fought a battle he could not possibly have won. The pathetic is achieved when the protagonist is, by virtue of his witlessness, his insensitivity or the very air he gives off, incapable of grappling with a much superior force.

Pathos truly is the mode for the pessimist. But tragedy requires a nicer balance between what is possible and what is impossible. And it is curious, although edifying, that the plays we revere, century after century, are the tragedies. In them, and in them alone, lies the belief—optimistic if you will, in the perfectibility of man.

It is time, I think, that we who are without kings, took up this bright thread of our history and followed it to the only place it can possibly lead in our time—the heart and spirit of the average man.

[10] **pathos**—quality in life or art that arouses feelings of sympathy, pity, tenderness, or sorrow.

QUESTIONS TO CONSIDER

1. How does Miller conceive of the "tragic flaw"?

2. According to Miller, what fear unites traditional tragic heroes and ordinary people today?

3. How do the "purely psychiatric" and "purely sociological" views of life limit the possibility of creating modern tragedy?

4. Why does Miller believe that tragedy is more optimistic than comedy?

Black Experience in America

BY AUGUST WILSON

Since the 1980s, August Wilson (1945–) has been creating a cycle of plays dealing with African-American life in the 20th century. In the following interview with journalist Bill Moyers, he discusses the role of black culture in his work.

INTERVIEWER: Your plays are set in the past—Joe Turner's *Come and Gone* in 1911, Ma Rainey's *Black Bottom* in 1927, *Fences* in the 1950s. Do you ever consider writing about what's happening today?

WILSON: I suspect eventually I will get to that. Right now I enjoy the benefit of the historical perspective. You can look back to a character in 1936, for instance, and you can see him going down a particular path that you know did not work out for that character. Part of what I'm trying to do is to see some of the choices that we as blacks in America have made. Maybe we have made some incorrect choices. By writing about that, you can illuminate the choices.

INTERVIEWER: Give me an example of a choice that you think may have been the wrong one.

WILSON: I think we should have stayed in the South. We attempted to plant what in essence was an emerging culture, a culture that had grown out of our experience of 200 years as slaves in the South. The cities of the urban North have not been hospitable. If we had stayed in the South, we could have strengthened the culture. . . .

INTERVIEWER: One of your characters has said, "Everyone has to find his own song." How do these people find their song?

Wilson: They have it. They just have to realize that, and then they have to learn how to sing it. In that particular case, in *Joe Turner*, the song was the African identity. It was connecting yourself to that and understanding that this is who you are. Then you can go out in the world and sing your song as an African. . . .

INTERVIEWER: But if blacks keep looking for the African in them, if they keep returning spiritually or emotionally to their roots, can they ever come to terms with living in these two worlds? Aren't they always going to be held by the past in a way that is potentially destructive?

WILSON: It's not potentially destructive at all. To say that I am an African, and I can participate in this society as an African, is to say that I don't have to adopt European values, European aesthetics, and European ways of doing things in order to live in the world. We would not be here had we not learned to adapt to American culture. Blacks know more about whites in white culture and white life than whites know about blacks. We have to know because our survival depends on it. White people's survival does not depend on knowing blacks. . . .

INTERVIEWER: I was going to suggest that maybe the black middle class possesses [a] warrior spirit today in the sense that they're struggling in a white man's world to make it, to provide for their children, to keep that house, to pay that mortgage, to send those kids to school, to live responsibly. There's a struggle going on there in the black middle class.

WILSON: There probably is a struggle. But the real struggle, since an African first set foot on the continent, is the affirmation of the value of oneself. If in order to participate in American society and in order to accomplish some of the things which the black

middle class has accomplished, you have had to give up that self, then you are not affirming the value of the African being. You're saying that in order to do that, I must become like someone else.

I was in the bus station in St. Paul, and I saw six Japanese Americans sitting down having breakfast. I simply sat there and observed them. They chattered among themselves very politely, and they ate their breakfast, got up, paid the bill, and walked out. I sat there and considered, what would have been the difference if six black guys had come in there and sat down? What are the cultural differences? The first thing I discovered is that none of those Japanese guys played the jukebox. It never entered their minds to play the jukebox. The first thing when six black guys walk in there, somebody's going to go over to the jukebox. Somebody's going to come up and say, "Hey, Rodney, man, play this" and he's going to say, "No, man, play your own record. I ain't playin' what you want. I'm playin' my record, man. Put your own quarter in there." And he's going to make his selection.

The second thing I noticed, no one said anything to the waitress. Now six black guys are going to say, "Hey, mama, what's happenin'? What's your phone number? No, don't talk to him, he can't read. Give your phone number to me." The guy's going to get up to play another record, somebody's going to steal a piece of bacon off his plate, he's going to come back and say, "Man, who's been messin' with my food, I ain't playin' with you all, don't be messin' with my food." When the time comes to pay the bill, it's going to be "Hey, Joe, loan me a dollar, man." Right? So if you were a white person observing that, you would say, "They don't know how to act, they're too loud, they don't like one another, the guy wouldn't let him play the record, the guy stole food off his plate." But if you go to those six guys and say, "What's the situation here?" you'll find out they're the greatest of friends, and they're just having breakfast, the same way the Japanese guys had breakfast. But they do it a little differently. This is just who they are in the world.

INTERVIEWER: You've answered my question. I was going to ask you, don't you grow weary of thinking black, writing black, being asked questions about blacks?

WILSON: How could one grow weary of that? Whites don't get tired of thinking white or being who they are. I'm just who I am. You never transcend who you are. Black is not limiting. There's no idea in the world that is not contained by black life. I could write forever about the black experience in America.

QUESTIONS TO CONSIDER

1. What does Wilson see as a basic cultural need of African Americans?

2. What point does he make with his comparison of the Japanese Americans and African Americans?

Women Dramatists

BY MARSHA NORMAN

Among the most significant contemporary American dramatists is Marsha Norman (1947–), whose play 'night, Mother won the 1983 Pulitzer Prize. In the following interview, she discusses the role of women in contemporary theater.

INTERVIEWER: You just won a Susan Blackburn Award for *'night, Mother.* Do you think women writers need special encouragement?

NORMAN: There are a couple of things that I think. One, the appearance of significant women dramatists in significant numbers now is a real reflection of a change in women's attitudes towards themselves. It is a sudden understanding that they can be, and indeed are, the central characters in their own lives. That is a notion that's absolutely required for writing for the theater. It's not required for novels; you can indeed be an observer and write glorious novels, in which women may or may not be the central characters. But the notion of an *active* central character is required for the theater. Not until enough women in society realized that did the voices to express it arrive. What is perhaps responsible for so few of these plays being done—

and we'll exclude for the moment the fact that it takes a long time to develop the skills and the craft and takes a very particular background to produce a writer of staying power and quality—is the problem that the things we as women know best have not been perceived to be of critical value to society. The mother-daughter relationship is a perfect example of that. It is one of the world's great mysteries; it has confused and confounded men and women for centuries and centuries, and yet it has not been perceived to have critical impact on either the life of the family or the survival of the family. Whereas the man's ability to earn money, his success out in the world, his conflict with his father—those are all things that have been seen as directly influencing the survival of the family. Part of what we have begun to do, because of the increasing voice of women in the world, is redefine survival. What it means is the ability to carry on your life in such a way that it fulfills and satisfies you. With this new definition of survival, Mother looms large. What you hope for your life, how you define the various parameters[1] of what's possible for you, those are all things with which Mother is connected. She is the absolute source of self-respect and self-image and curiosity and energy. In fact, Mother is where "going on" comes from. Producing, Making Money, Making Your Way are all things that Dad has historically taken care of. But going on, that business of "Here we are; yet another day with yet another mess to clean up" is Mom.

INTERVIEWER: Maintenance?

NORMAN: As women, our historical role has been to clean up the mess. Whether it's the mess left by war or death or children or sickness. I think the violence you see in plays by women is a direct reflection of that historical role. We are not afraid to look under the bed, or to wash the sheets; we know that life is messy. We know that somebody has to clean it up, and that only if it is cleaned up can we hope to start over, and get better. Just because you clean up one mess, that doesn't mean there won't be another one. There is no end to mess, really, but you can't stop cleaning. This fearless "looking under the bed" is what you see in so many plays by women, and it's exciting. It says, "There is order to be brought from this chaos, and I will not stop until I have it." The lessons of all those years of domestic training—centuries, millennia of it—show up in the writing of today in a very powerful way.

INTERVIEWER: You seem to be saying that this idea of "cleaning up the mess" is giving the audience a new way to look at their own lives, to have courage, and feel that things aren't insurmountable. Do you have any comment on that in terms of the tragic turn[2] 'night, Mother took when compared with the more hopeful image of Arlie/Arlene's survival at the end of Getting Out?

NORMAN: Well, clearly you have your personal view of 'night, Mother. My sense of 'night, Mother is that it is, by my own definitions of these words, a play of nearly total triumph. Jessie is able to get what she feels she needs. That is not a despairing act. It may look despairing from the outside, but it has cost her everything she has. If Jessie says it's worth it, then it is.

INTERVIEWER: But suicide is not survival. That's what I'm questioning.

NORMAN: But see, by Jessie's definition of survival, it is. As Jessie says, "My life is all I really have that belongs to me, and I'm going to say what happens to it." . . . Jessie has taken an action on her own behalf that for her is the final test of all that she has been. That's how I see it. Now you don't have to see it that way; nor does anybody else have to see it that way.

INTERVIEWER: Better death with honor than a life of humiliation?

---

[1] parameters—defining factors.

[2] tragic turn—in Norman's two-character play 'night, Mother, a woman (Jessie) informs her mother of her intention to commit suicide later that evening. Despite the mother's attempt to argue her daughter out of this decision, she goes through with it at the end of the play.

NORMAN: Right. I think that the question the play asks is, "What does it take to survive? What does it take to save your life?" Now Jessie's answer is "It takes killing myself." Mama's answer is "It takes cocoa and marshmallows and doilies and the *TV Guide* and Agnes and the birds and trips to the grocery." Jessie feels, "No, I'm sorry. That's not enough."

INTERVIEWER: Do you think that art is genderless? Can you tell from an anonymous play whether the author is male or female?

NORMAN: Sometimes you know and sometimes you don't. My favorite saying is "All great art is **androgynous**."[3] But I don't know. I know that there are certain plays, *Requiem for a Heavyweight* or *Marty*,[4] for example, that come from a long life lived as a male. We all have secrets. There are things that you know, that you would have no way of knowing unless you had been there.

---

[3] **androgynous**—having both female and male characteristics.

[4] *Requiem for a Heavyweight* or *Marty*—television dramas by American playwrights Rod Serling (1924–1975) and Paddy Chayevsky (1923–1981), respectively.

QUESTIONS TO CONSIDER

1. Why does Norman feel that plays by women have not been widely produced until recent decades?

2. Why does she feel *'night, Mother* is "a play of nearly total triumph"?

On Stage

American Theater

In the 20th century, American dramatists absorbed modern theatrical styles and used them to create vigorously original dramas. American theater, which flourished in the 1940s and 1950s in the works of such playwrights as Tennessee Williams and Lorraine Hansberry, continues to be a vital force today.

▲

Actress Laurette Taylor is shown as Amanda Wingfield in the 1945
New York production of *The Glass Menagerie*.

◀ Laura Wingfield was played by Julie Haydon in the 1945 New York production of *The Glass Menagerie*.

In this 1986 Long Wharf Theatre production of *The Glass Menagerie*, Laura (Karen Allen) stays away from the table where Amanda (Joanne Woodward) and Tom (Treat Williams) are entertaining Jim (James Naughton), the Gentleman Caller.

▲

In Act One, Scene Two of a 1995 production of *A Raisin in the Sun* by Boston's Huntington Theatre Company, Mama (Esther Rolle) and Beneatha (B. W. Gonzalez) attempt to comfort Ruth (Marguerite Hannah), who is worried about the burden her pregnancy will be on the family.

▲
Mama (Claudia McNeil) and Walter (Sidney
Poitier) are at odds over how to spend the
insurance money in Act One, Scene Two of the
1959 New York production of *A Raisin in the Sun.*

In Act Two, Scene One, Walter bitterly confronts
George (Louis Gossett, Jr.) while an upset Ruth
(Ruby Dee) looks on. ▶

When Ntozake Shange's *for colored girls who have considered suicide/when the rainbow is enuf* won a Tony Award in 1976, it demonstrated that African-American themes had become mainstream. ▶

The plays of Sam Shepard, such as *True West* (1980), are marked by a combination of lyricism and violence. This 1982 off-Broadway production at Cherry Lane Theatre in New York featured John Malkovich (left) and Gary Sinise.

▲

Marsha Norman's 'night Mother, which dealt with the controversial theme of suicide, won the Pulitzer Prize in 1983. The original production, by the American Repertory Theatre in Cambridge, Massachusetts, featured Kathy Bates (left) as Jessica and Anne Pitoniak as Mama.

◀ *Zoot Suit* (1978), Luis Valdez's study of ethnic prejudice in Los Angeles during World War II, was the first play by a Mexican American to appear on Broadway.

Fences, one of August Wilson's dramas dealing with African-American life in the 20th century, won the Pulitzer Prize in 1985. ▶

The arrival on Broadway in 1993 of Tony Kushner's two-part *Angels in America,* a drama about the gay community and public policy in the age of AIDS, marked a turning point in the treatment of homosexual themes in American theater. ▶

Glossary of Drama and Theater Terms

act major division of a play.

antagonist principal character or force in opposition to the protagonist of a drama.

aside short speech or comment that is delivered by a character to the audience, but that is beyond the hearing of other characters who are present.

atmosphere See **mood**.

blank verse unrhymed verse in which each line has five accented syllables; the verse pattern in which Shakespeare wrote many of his plays.

cast of characters list of all the characters in a play; sometimes organized in order of importance, sometimes in order of appearance.

catharsis (from Greek, "purging") an emotional purification that, according to Aristotle's *Poetics,* is the effect of watching tragic drama. The purpose of viewing the terrible events presented in a tragedy is to arouse and dispel in the audience such emotions as pity and fear. See *Poetics.*

character person, animal, or other being that takes part in the action of a literary work. Events center on the lives of one or more characters, referred to as main characters. The other characters, called minor characters, interact with the main characters and help move the action along. Characters may be classified as either static or dynamic. **Static characters** tend to remain the same, unchanged by what they experience. In contrast, **dynamic characters** evolve as individuals, learning from their experiences and growing emotionally.

chorus in Greek drama, a group of actors who sing and dance their commentary on the dialogue and actions of the principal actors in the play.

climax the decisive point in a dramatic plot when the central conflict must be resolved in one way or another.

comedy dramatic work that is light and often humorous in tone, usually ending happily with a peaceful resolution of the main conflict. See **high** and **low comedy**, **romantic comedy**, and **satiric comedy**.

comedy of manners form of **satiric** or **high comedy** first popular in the 1600s which dealt with the vices and follies of the upper classes and was characterized by witty, and frequently bawdy, dialogue.

comic relief amusing episode in a serious or tragic drama that is introduced to relieve tension.

commedia dell'arte form of improvisational theater that originated in Italy in the 1500s, using stock characters and situations for which performers made up dialogue. See **stock character**.

conflict struggle between opposing forces that is the basis of a plot. An **external conflict** pits a character against fate, nature, society, or another character; an **internal conflict** is between opposing forces within a character.

dénouement See **resolution**.

▲
commedia dell'arte

dialogue conversation between two or more characters in a literary work. In drama, the story is told almost exclusively through dialogue.

downstage the stage area toward the audience.

drama type of literature that is primarily written to be performed for an audience.

dramatic unities characteristics of time, place, and action that defined Greek drama: a play was to present only one principal action occupying only one day and showing only what could be observed by a spectator sitting in one place.

dynamic character See **character**.

epic realism theater movement developed in Germany in the 1920s and '30s that rejected the emphasis on creating convincing theatrical illusion that was typical of **naturalism** and **realism**. It also rejected the emphasis on heightened aesthetic emotion typical of **symbolist drama** and **expressionism**. Instead, epic realism was frankly theatrical: for example, actors often addressed the audience and the staging sometimes called for the use of descriptive titles onstage, either carried by the actors on signs or projected on screens.

epilogue a concluding speech that follows the action of a play. See **naturalism**, **realism**, **symbolist drama**, and **expressionism**.

exposition the beginning part of a play, in which a dramatist explains the basic situation of the drama, identifies the setting, introduces the characters, establishes the mood and tone, and provides any important background information.

expressionism artistic movement that developed in Europe around the time of World War I. Influenced by the horrors of the war, expressionist theater sought to reveal the fragmented inner life of humanity through the presentations of fantasies, hallucinations, and nightmares.

external conflict See **conflict**.

falling action part of a plot that follows and shows the effects of the climax. As the falling action begins, the suspense is over, but the effects of the decision or action that caused the climax are not yet fully worked out.

farce See **low comedy**.

First Folio first substantially complete edition of Shakespeare's works, published in 1623.

◀ **Globe Theater**

foil character whose traits contrast with those of another character.

forestage in a proscenium theater, the part of the stage nearest the audience, usually projecting beyond the curtain.

fourth wall invisible "wall" through which the audience sees the box set of a realistic play.

Globe Theater eight-sided playhouse built in 1598 where most of Shakespeare's plays were performed.

high comedy comedy in which the humor arises from characterization, social satire, and wit. See **satiric comedy** and **comedy of manners**.

hubris (from Greek, "reckless pride") in some Greek tragedies, the tragic flaw that contributes to the main character's downfall.

internal conflict See **conflict**.

left in stage directions, the left side of the stage from the perspective of an actor facing the audience; from the audience's perspective, the right side of the stage.

low comedy comedy emphasizing absurd dialogue, bawdy jokes, visual gags, and physical humor. See **high comedy**.

masque type of lavish dramatic spectacle that was a feature of entertainments at the English court in the early 1600s. Masques were plays on pastoral and mythical themes that featured music, dance, large casts (many courtiers took part), beautiful scenery, extravagant costumes, and elaborate stagecraft.

◀ **Aristotle**

melodrama typical theatrical form of the 1800s, characterized by exaggerated sentiment, romantic plots, and elaborate staging.

monologue long speech spoken by a single character to himself or herself, or to the audience. See **soliloquy**.

mood emotional response created by a literary work. See **tone**.

morality play type of play popular in the 1400s and 1500s in which the characters are personifications of abstract qualities such as knowledge, beauty, and strength.

Moscow Art Theater influential independent theater company founded in 1898 by Konstantin Stanislavsky (1863–1938) and Vladimir Nemirovich-Danchenko (1859–1943). Rejecting the exaggerated vocal delivery and mannerisms of most 19th-century actors, Stanislavksy insisted that acting must be based on artistic "inner truth."

naturalism French literary movement of the 1870s, based on contemporary scientific theory and belief that existence was shaped by heredity and environment. Naturalist writers felt that plays should be rigorously detailed "case studies" or "slices of life," presenting their subjects with absolute fidelity and displaying no more artistic structure than life does. See **realism**.

Neoclassicism literature of the 1600s and 1700s that shows the influence of the Greek and Roman classics. For example, Neoclassical drama strictly adhered to the classical unities of time, place, and action. See **dramatic unities**.

orchestra central performance area of a Greek theater.

peripeteia (from Greek, "to change suddenly") in a dramatic plot, an unexpected turn of events or sudden reversal of fortune.

Pit in Shakespeare's Globe Theater, the open area in front of the stage which provided standing room for those who couldn't afford a seat in the surrounding galleries.

Poetics treatise on literature by Greek philosopher Aristotle (384–322 B.C.) that includes the first and most influential analysis of tragic drama. Approaching his subject in a scientific way, he defined the purpose and chief elements of tragedy. See **catharsis** and **dramatic unities**.

presentational style theater in which actors acknowledge the presence of the audience. See **representational style**.

prologue introduction to a play. A prologue may be in the form of a **monologue** by a character or a commentary by a **chorus**.

proscenium arch the frame around a **proscenium stage**.

proscenium stage performance space in which the audience views the action, as if through a picture frame. See **proscenium arch**.

protagonist main character in a literary work.

realism literary movement of the late 1800s that had its origin in naturalism and differed from it chiefly in how closely a dramatist attempted to reproduce the details of actual life. Like naturalist drama, realistic plays present problems of everyday life rendered in ordinary language, but are also carefully plotted and well-structured. See **naturalism**.

representational style theater in which actors are supposed to be living real lives that the audience is observing through an invisible "fourth wall." In representational theater, the actors do not acknowledge the presence of the audience. See **presentational style**.

resolution or **dénouement** final part of a plot, which follows—and often blends with—the falling action, completes the resolution of the conflict, and ties up loose ends.

right in stage directions, the right side of the stage from the perspective of an actor facing the audience; from the audience's perspective, the left side of the stage.

rising action in a plot, the events that lead to the climax by adding complications or expanding the conflict. Suspense usually builds during the rising action.

romantic comedy comedy in which the main characters are lovers, and the plot tends to follow the pattern of "boy finds girl, boy loses girl, boy finds girl again."

satiric comedy comedy that uses humor to ridicule foolish ideas or customs with the purpose of improving society. See **high comedy**.

scene subdivision of an act in a drama. Each scene usually establishes a separate time or place.

scrim or **transparency** backdrop curtain that becomes transparent when lighted from behind.

soliloquy monologue in which a character speaks his or her private thoughts aloud and appears to be unaware of the audience.

stage directions dramatist's instructions for performing a play. Usually set in italics, stage directions are located at the beginning of a play and throughout the text. Stage directions provide information about characters and setting of the play and suggest the use of costumes, scenery, props, lighting, and sound effects. Stage directions indicate the entrances and exits of characters (thus indicating who is on stage during a particular scene). Stage directions also indicate how characters act, move, speak, and react to other characters' words and actions.

static character See **character**.

stock character established character, such as braggart soldier, tricky servant, or ardent young lover, that is immediately recognized by an audience. See *commedia dell'arte*.

straight drama realistic play with serious subject matter but not a disastrous ending.

symbolist drama movement which developed in the 1890s, and in which the dramatic action, characters, setting, and language are all reflections of the playwright's inner life.

thrust stage a combination of the proscenium and the arena stages, with the audience sitting on two or three sides of the acting area.

tiring-house in Elizabethan theaters such as Shakespeare's Globe, the three-story structure that contained the various acting areas, as well as the performers'

dressing rooms. (*Tiring* is a shortened form of *attiring,* "dressing.") Forming the back of the different stages, the façade of the tiring house was the theater's permanent set.

tone writer's attitude, either stated or implied, to his or her subject matter. See **mood**.

tragedy form of drama in which the main character suffers disaster.

tragic hero main character of a Greek tragedy, defined by Aristotle in the *Poetics* as "a man who is not eminently good and just, yet whose misfortune is brought about not by vice and depravity, but by some error or frailty." See **hubris**.

transparency See **scrim**.

"university wits" students at English universities in the late 1500s who, after studying and imitating classical dramas, began writing their own plays for London theater companies. The most important was Christopher Marlowe (1564–1593), whose blank verse dramas, such as *Doctor Faustus,* were a great influence on Shakespeare.

upstage the stage area away from the audience.

well-made play 19th-century play that featured a formulaic, often melodramatic, study of middle-class domestic life in which some problem was neatly resolved in a conventionally moral ending.

wings the left and right sides of a stage immediately outside the acting area, usually unseen by the audience.

▲
Frontispiece of Marlowe's *Doctor Faustus*

Text

2 "Oedipus the King" by Sophocles, from *Three Theban Plays* by Sophocles, translated by Robert Fagles, copyright © 1982 by Robert Fagles. Used by permission of Viking Penguin, a division of Penguin Putnam Inc. **57** "The Medea," from *Euripides*, translated by Rex Warner. Reprinted by permission of The Bodley Head Limited as publisher. **100** "On Social Plays", copyright © 1955, 1978 by Arthur Miller; Copyright © 1978 by Viking Penguin Inc. from *The Theater Essays of Arthur Miller* by Arthur Miller, edited by Robert A. Martin. Used by permission of Viking Penguin, a division of Penguin Putnam Inc. **102** From *"Medea at Pescara"* from *The Eating of the Gods: An Interpretation of Greek Tragedy* by Jan Kott. Reprinted by permission of the author. **116** Notes to "Midsummer Night's Dream" from *The Complete Works of Shakespeare* 4th ed. by David Bevington. Copyright © 1992 by HarperCollins Publishers. Reprinted by permission of Addison-Wesley Educational Publishers, Inc. **189** Notes to "Othello" from *The Complete Works of Shakespeare* 4th ed. by David Bevington. Copyright 1992 by HarperCollins Publishers, Inc. Reprinted by permission of Addison-Wesley Educational Publishers, Inc. **301** *The Misanthrope Comedy in Five Acts*, copyright © 1955, 1954 and renewed 1983, 1982 by Richard Wilbur, reprinted by permission of Harcourt, Inc. CAUTION: Professionals and amateurs are hereby warned that this translation, being fully protected under the copyright laws of the United States of America, the British Commonwealth, including the Dominion of Canada, and all other countries which are signatories to the Universal Copyright Convention and the International Copyright Convention, is subject to royalty. All rights, including professional, amateur, motion picture, recitation, lecturing, public reading, radio broadcasting, and television, are strictly reserved. Particular emphasis is laid on the question of readings, permission for which must be secured from the author's agent in writing. Inquiries on professional rights (except for amateur rights) should be addressed to Mr. Gilbert Parker, William Morris Agency, 1350 Avenue of the Americas, New York, NY 10019; inquiries on translation rights should be addressed to Permissions Department, Harcourt, Inc., 6th Floor, Orlando, Florida 32887-6777. The amateur acting rights of *The Misanthrope* are controlled exclusively by Dramatists Play Service, Inc., 440 Park Ave. South, New York, NY 10016. No amateur performance of the play may be given without obtaining in advance the written permission of the Dramatists Play Service, Inc. and paying the requisite fee. **362** From *Shakespeare Alive!* by Joseph Papp and Elizabeth Kirkland, copyright © 1988 by New York Shakespeare Festival. Used by permission of Bantam Books, a division of Random House, Inc. **365** Short excerpt from the full translation of "The Rehearsal at Versailles" from *One-Act Comedies of Molière*, translated and with an Introduction by Albert Bermel. Reprinted by permission of the translator. **519** "Blood Wedding" by Federico Garcia Lorca, translation by James Graham-Lujan and Richard L. O'Connell, from *Three Tragedies*, copyright © 1947 by New Directions Publishing Corp. Reprinted by permission of New Directions Publishing Corp. **571** From "An Enemy of the People, 1882" from *Bernard Shaw, The Quintessence of Ibsenism* by George Bernard Shaw. Reprinted by permission of The Society of Authors, on behalf of the Bernard Shaw Estate. **573** From "Stanislavsky and the Bearer Bonds" from *Some Freaks* by David Mamet reprinted with the permission of The Wylie Agency, Inc. **575** From "The Poet and Sex" from *Lorca: The Poet and His People* by Arturo Barea, translated from the Spanish by Ilsa Barea. © Estate of Arturo Barea. Reprinted by permission of Uli Rusby Smith Literary Agency. **588** From *The Glass Menagerie* by Tennessee Williams. Copyright © 1945 by Tennessee Williams and Edwina D. Williams and renewed 1973 by Tennessee Williams. Reprinted by permission of Random House, Inc. **650** From *A Raisin In The Sun* by Lorraine Hansberry. Copyright © 1958 by Robert Nemiroff, as an unpublished work. Copyright © 1959, 1966, 1984 by Robert Nemiroff. Reprinted by permission of Random House, Inc. **651** From *Collected Poems* by Langston Hughes. Copyright © 1994 by the Estate of Langston Hughes. Reprinted by permission of Alfred A. Knopf, a division of Random House, Inc. **736** "Tragedy and the Common Man," copyright 1949, renewed © 1977 by Arthur Miller, from *The Theater Essays of Arthur Miller* by Arthur Miller, edited by Robert A. Martin. Used by permission of Viking Penguin, a division of Penguin Putnam Inc. **740** From *Bill Moyers: A World of Ideas* by Bill Moyers, copyright © 1989 by Public Affairs Television, Inc. Used by permission of Doubleday, a division of Random House, Inc. **743** From *Interviews With Contemporary Women Playwrights* by Kathleen Betsko and Rachel Koenig. Copyright © 1987 by Kathleen Betsko and Rachel Koenig. Reprinted by permission of HarperCollins Publishers, Inc., William Morrow.

Illustrations

Position of illustrations on a page is indicated by these abbreviations: (T) top, (C) center, (B) bottom, (L) left, (R) right.

viii–1 © The Granger Collection. **2** Scala/Art Resource, NY. **57** Culver Pictures. **105** British Museum, London, UK/Bridgeman Art Library. **106T** Eliot Elisofon/Timepix. **106B** Courtesy Library of Congress. **107T** Copyright 1907 by Underwood & Underwood. **107B, 108T** © The Granger Collection. **108B** Stock Montage, Inc. **109T, 109B** Scala/Art Resource, NY. **110, 111T** © The Granger Collection. **111B** T. Charles Erickson/Theatre Pix. **112** © The Granger Collection. **113T** Culver Pictures. **113B** Mark Kaufmann/Time Pix. **114–115** © The Granger Collection. **116** Culver Pictures. **189** © The Granger Collection. **301** Pushkin Museum, Moscow, Russia/ Bridgeman Art Library. **368** © The Granger Collection. **369T** Mansell Collection-Time Inc. **369B** Culver Pictures. **370** The Newberry Library. **371T** Culver Pictures. **371B** Frank Scherschel/LIFE/TimePix. **372R** © Chris Bennion/Theatre Pix. **372L, 372B** T. Charles Erickson/Theatre Pix. **373T, 373B** George Karger/Pix Inc. **374** Martha Swope/Timepix. **375** T. Charles Erickson/Theatre Pix.

376T, 376B © The Granger Collection. **377T, 377B** T. Charles Erickson/Theatre Pix. **380** Culver Pictures. **467** Mansell Collection/Time Inc. **519** © The Granger Collection. **577** T. Charles Erickson/Theatre Pix. **578** Martha Swope/Time Inc. **579T, 579B** Culver Pictures. **580T** © The Granger Collection. **580B, 581T, 581B** Culver Pictures. **582T, 582B** T. Charles Erickson/Theatre Pix. **583, 584, 585T, 585B** Martha Swope/Time Inc. **586, 587** Richard Feldman/Theatre Pix. **588, 650, 746** © The Granger Collection. **747T** Gordon Coster/Time-Life. **747B** T. Charles Erickson/Theatre Pix. **748** Richard Feldman/Theatre Pix. **749T, 749B** Gordon Parks/Time-Life. **750T** Chris Bennion/Theatre Pix. **750B** Martha Swope/Time Inc. **751** Richard Feldman/Theatre Pix. **752T** Courtesy Mark Taper Forum. **752B, 753** Chris Bennion/Theatre Pix. **754** © The Granger Collection. **755** British Library, London, UK/Bridgeman Art Library. **756** Kunsthistorisches Museum, Vienna, Austria/ Bridgeman Art Library. **757** © The Granger Collection.